CDMA Internetworking:
Deploying the Open A-Interface

Su-Lin Low and Ron Schneider

PH PTR

Prentice Hall PTR
Upper Saddle River, NJ 07458
www.prenhall.com

Library of Congress Cataloging-in-Publication Data

```
Low, Su-Lin.
     CDMA internetworking: deploying the Open A-Interface / Su-Lin Low
     and Ron Schneider.
       p.  cm.
     Includes bibliographical references and index.
     ISBN 0-13-088922-9
     1. Code division multiple access. 2. Internetworking
     (Telecommunication) I. Schneider, Ron. II. Title.
     TK5103.452.L69 2000
     621.3845--dc21                                        00-044135
```

Editorial/production supervision: *Nicholas Radhuber*
Cover designer: *Anthony Gemmellaro*
Cover illustration: *Tom Post*
Cover design director: *Jerry Votta*
Manufacturing manager: *Maura Goldstaub*
Marketing manager: *Bryan Gambrel*
Acquisitions editor: *Mary Franz*

© 2000 Prentice Hall PTR
Prentice-Hall, Inc.
Upper Saddle River, New Jersey 07458

Prentice Hall books are widely used by corporations and government agencies for training, marketing, and resale.
The publisher offers discounts on this book when ordered in bulk quantities.
For more information, contact Corporate Sales Department, Phone: 800-382-3419;
Fax: 201-236-7141; E-mail: corpsales@prenhall.com
Or write: Prentice Hall PTR, Corp. Sales Dept., One Lake Street, Upper Saddle River, NJ 07458.

Product names mentioned herein are the trademarks or registered trademarks of their respective owners.

Printed in the United States of America
10 9 8 7 6 5 4 3 2 1

ISBN 0-13-088922-9

Prentice-Hall International (UK) Limited, *London*
Prentice-Hall of Australia Pty. Limited, *Sydney*
Prentice-Hall Canada Inc., *Toronto*
Prentice-Hall Hispanoamericana, S.A., *Mexico*
Prentice-Hall of India Private Limited, *New Delhi*
Prentice-Hall of Japan, Inc., *Tokyo*
Pearson Education Asia, Pte. Ltd.
Editora Prentice-Hall do Brasil, Ltda., *Rio de Janeiro*

From Su-Lin: To Chock,
my parents, Ann and Pei Lin

From Ron: To Carolyn

Contents

List of Figures

List of Tables

Foreword

Since its public introduction by QUALCOMM in June 1988, *Code Division Multiple Access* (CDMA) has gained wide acceptance for cellular and personal communications and currently is the fastest-growing wireless technology. By reusing the entire frequency spectrum at every cell-site antenna, incorporating rapid power control of the radio signal to ensure high-quality reception at the lowest transmitter power, providing powerful error protection for all information bits, utilizing rake receivers to improve performance in the multipath fading encountered by radio signals, and instantaneously translating pauses in voice or data usage to or from a mobile to increased capacity for other users in the same direction, CDMA provides higher capacity, superior quality, and wider coverage per cell than competing TDMA technologies. Because of the advantages CDMA provides, it now appears that even non-CDMA operators and manufacturers will select CDMA technology for their next generation of service.

CDMA technology has been widely licensed by QUALCOMM with over 70 manufacturers including at least eleven manufacturers of infrastructure. These CDMA manufacturers are now upgrading to the first commercially available third-generation technology, 1x *Multi-Carrier* (MC), which provides a near doubling of voice capacity and mobile wireless Internet access at data rates over 300 Kbps. Work on CDMA *Direct Spread* (DS) as well as Multi-Carrier is moving ahead rapidly in standards groups and in engineering labs, and 1x *High Data Rate* (HDR)—a high speed, high capacity technology supporting 2.4 Mbps Internet access—is being trialed for early commercial introduction.

This book by Low and Schneider on the open A-Interface is thus very timely in that it supports the rapidly expanding engineering group engaged worldwide in third generation CDMA equipment design. Detailed knowledge of standard interfaces is crucial, because in the third generation ITU standard, both DS and MC modes are intended to work with both GSM MAP and

ANSI-41 (referred to as IS-41 in the book) mobile networks as well as the Internet. The ability to design, test, and interconnect equipment from many manufacturers and multiple generations is critical to timely and reliable network rollout. The experiences of Low and Schneider and their clear exposition should be of great benefit.

I am very excited to see how far CDMA technology has progressed since first thinking of its potential for mobile communications—initially in a mobile satellite context—during a drive from Los Angeles to San Diego with Klein Gilhousen less than fifteen years ago. It is even more exciting to see the rapid progress towards almost universal wireless voice and Internet access at low cost enabled by CDMA. Of course, the devil is in the details, and this book is a significant contribution towards understanding those details.

Irwin Mark Jacobs
Chairman & CEO
QUALCOMM

Preface

Wireless communications have been growing at a rate that has surpassed even the most optimistic industry observers. To take advantage of the tremendous growth opportunities in the wireless industry, network service providers have been fiercely competing to increase market share and build a customer base. This intense competition has resulted in reduced air time charges, expanded coverage, and more available supplementary services, all of which have further accelerated growth. Some industry professionals have predicted that the wireless phone will replace the standard landline phone within the next 5 years.

The expansion and popularity of the Internet, along with the addition of wireless data functionality to wireless networks, has also contributed greatly to the growth of the wireless industry. In fact, the anticipated consumer demand for high-bandwidth wireless data is commonly seen as the driving force behind current network upgrades and expansions. The number and types of companies aggressively investing in wireless communication illustrate the importance of wireless data. Nontraditional telecommunications companies, such as Cisco Systems, Intel, Microsoft, and 3Com, are investing heavily in wireless product development, and many have formed partnerships with wireless infrastructure manufacturers to help deliver wireless data services seamlessly to consumers.

Within the expanding wireless sector, the fastest growing wireless technology is *Code Division Multiple Access* (CDMA). This spread spectrum technique, developed by QUAL-COMM during the 1980's, provides increased network capacity and superior voice quality. The inherent advantages of CDMA have led to it being chosen worldwide as the third-generation technology for future wireless networks, which will provide consumers with advanced communication services and high-bandwidth data connections.

To meet the increasing demands of wireless consumers, network service providers are aggressively investing in wireless infrastructure equipment. Until recently, most infrastructure equipment used proprietary interfaces, and wireless service providers were often required to purchase complete networks from a single vendor. Specifically, both the *Base Station Controller* (BSC) and the *Mobile Switching Center* (MSC) were normally purchased from the same vendor or were developed jointly for a specific customer. This approach differed greatly from the land network models being used by large telecommunications companies, which emphasize standardized interfaces and network compatibility. Wireless service providers, such as Sprint PCS, soon began participating in the standardization of an "open" MSC–BSC interface that would provide them the flexibility to purchase compatible wireless equipment from various equipment vendors.

Purpose of this Book

It is our experience that engineers and software developers working on the development and testing of the open MSC–BSC interface are often overwhelmed by the enormous details associated with A-Interface messaging and procedures. Furthermore, the information required to understand the operation of the A-Interface fully is distributed over several published wireless standards, which can sometimes be difficult to read. Our goal in writing this book is to provide industry professionals with a single, comprehensive, and easy-to-read text that fully describes the operation of the open A-Interface. By focusing on core concepts, our intent is to provide a resource of invaluable information to CDMA wireless infrastructure engineers such as System Designers, Systems Engineers, Software Developers, Hardware Developers, Systems Integrators, and Systems Testers, who are directly working with the development and integration of the BSC with the MSC. We anticipate that Network Planners, Project Engineers, Program Managers, and Marketing Managers will also find the book a useful resource for understanding the details of MSC–BSC internetworking.

Approach

If we were simply to reword existing A-Interface and wireless standards, the book would be of little value to industry professionals. Therefore, we have included our own practical insights, based on our laboratory and field experiences, to help illustrate the important aspects of the open interface and to make the underlying concepts more tangible. We have also included an abundance of practical examples and illustrations to enhance the reader's understanding of the operation of the A-Interface. Based on our experiences in training other telecommunications engineers, we have found that providing practical examples is both an effective and an efficient teaching technique, and we have tried to utilize this approach throughout the book. Not only do we explain how the protocol is used, we explain how the A-Interface fits in an overall wireless network by integrating air-interface (IS-95) and network (IS-41) messaging into the A-Interface call flows.

How to Use This Book

The contents of this book can be divided into four areas:

- Introductory Material: Chapter 1
- Core Topics: Chapters 2–3
- Advanced Topics :   Chapters 4–9
- Forward-Looking Topics: Chapter 10

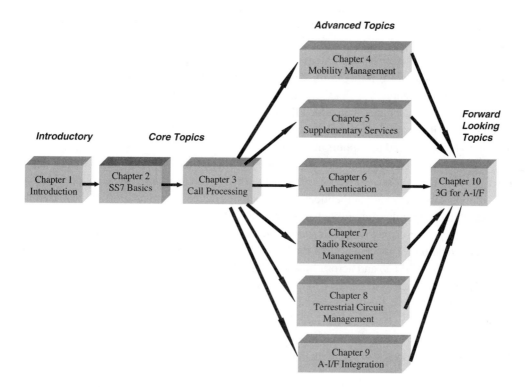

An introductory chapter presents the evolution of the A-Interface standardization process and describes how the A-Interface fits into the "big picture" of a CDMA wireless telecommunication network.

Chapter 2 provides an overview of *Signaling System 7* (SS7), which is used as the transport layer for A-Interface messaging. This chapter describes the fundamentals of SS7, including message structure, link alignment, and message routing. Because some readers may not be interested in this level of detail or may already have experience with SS7, this chapter may be skipped without loss of continuity.

Chapter 3 describes the basic Call Processing steps required of both the BSC and MSC to set up and tear down CDMA wireless calls. This important chapter covers Mobile Origination and Mobile Termination call setup, as well as call clearing scenarios initiated by the mobile station, the BSC, and the MSC. Call failure scenarios, such as timer expiration and unsuccessful resource allocation, are also covered. After completing this chapter, the reader will have the fundementals required to proceed to any of the advanced topics chapters.

Chapter 4 covers Mobility Management, which is the function in the BSC and MSC that manages the registration and mobile access status of subscriber mobiles. This includes management of mobile parameters, such as mobile location, mobile identity, and authentication status. Various mobile registration scenarios and interactions with the network are presented in this chapter.

Chapter 5 describes Supplementary Services, which consists of *Short Message Service* (SMS), *Message Waiting Indication* (MWI), Wireless Data, *Over-the-Air Service Provisioning* (OTASP), and call features such as Call Forwarding, Call Waiting and Three-Way Calling. This chapter covers the mechanism by which the supplementary service is delivered to the subscriber, together with illustrations on how the network entity, such as the SMS center and *Voice Mail System* (VMS), are used to support the feature.

Chapter 6 discusses Authentication, which is a technique used to ensure the security and privacy of wireless mobile subscribers in a network. This chapter contains scenarios illustrating how mobile subscribers are authenticated and includes detailed explanations on how the mobile station interacts with the *Authentication Center* (AC) through the BSC and MSC.

Chapter 7 describes Radio Resource Management, which consists of the radio resource channel allocation for voice and data traffic. In this chapter the management of handoffs within the BSC, between BSCs, and across MSCs is described.

Chapter 8 covers *Terrestrial Circuit Management* (TCM). This chapter describes the function contained in both the BSC and MSC that manages the terrestrial voice and data circuit resources.

Chapter 9 discusses the issues faced in integrating a BSC and an MSC. This chapter is included to provide engineers with insights into real-world implementation and testing considerations.

Chapter 10 gives an insight into the future development of the A-Interface standard, including an overview of third-generation systems.

An important part of understanding the overall A-Interface is being familiar with individual message-associated parameters. Therefore, both the call flow and associated message structures are presented for each function area described. This presentation method is consistent throughout the book and includes references to the CDGIOS A-Interface standard specification.

Acknowledgments

This book would not have been possible without the help and encouragement of many people. We would like to thank them for their efforts in improving the end results. However, before we do, we should mention that we have done our best to correct mistakes that the reviewers have pointed out. We alone are responsible for any remaining errors.

We would like to begin by giving special thanks to Sunil Patil of QUALCOMM, Ataur Shuman of Ericsson, Robin Crumpton of Nortel Networks, Walid Hamdy of QUALCOMM, and Erol Hepsaydir of Orange-Hutchison Telecoms Australia, who all spent many hours reviewing early drafts of this book. Their comments and insights undoubtedly improved the quality of this work.

We would also like to thank Ron Goodman of ERIM International and Mukesh Mittal, Fakhruddin Rashid, Dan Devine, Rick Rollans, Victor Pitones, Joe Pojunis, and Don Scheuer, all of Ericsson, for their valuable contributions.

Next, we would like to thank Mary Franz, Noreen Regina, and Nick Radhuber at Prentice Hall for their patience and guidance throughout the course of this project.

Finally, we are grateful to both Ericsson and QUALCOMM for providing us the opportunity to work in an exciting engineering environment on rewarding projects.

Introduction

As the number of wireless subscribers continues to grow at an astonishing rate, wireless service providers are aggressively expanding their networks to accommodate customer demand. To meet both network capacity requirements and new subscriber feature demands, *Code Division Multiple Access* (CDMA) technology has been chosen by a majority of North American, Asian, and Latin American service providers. In addition to providing superior voice quality and increased network capacity, CDMA also provides a clear migration path to *Third-Generation* (3G) technologies. Although first generation wireless networks were based on analog technology and second-generation systems (GSM, TDMA, CDMA) first incorporated digital techniques, third generation systems will be the first to combine high bandwidth data features, such as web browsing, with basic voice services. CDMA has been chosen as the sole worldwide standard to meet the high bandwidth demands of 3G systems.

Building or expanding a wireless network is highly capital-intensive, and the choice of an infrastructure vendor is critical. Because most current CDMA networks use a proprietary interface between the *Base Station Controller* (BSC) and the *Mobile Switching Center* (MSC), wireless service providers are forced to purchase both the MSC and BSC from the same infrastructure vendor. This type of network architecture often requires a service provider to rely on a single vendor for the initial network commissioning and future upgrades, which reduces competition for contract awards and increases risk. To mitigate risk and increase competition, the largest wireless service providers are now demanding an open interface, referred to as the *A-Interface*, between the BSC and the MSC. By standardizing this interface, wireless service providers will have the flexibility to purchase a BSC from one vendor and an MSC from another, therefore allowing them to reduce cost and more easily expand existing networks. A standardized MSC–BSC interface has the added advantage of providing a demarcation point between the BSC and MSC functional and operational responsibilities, thereby allowing network integrators and service providers to isolate and correct any network abnormalities by testing each entity separately.

To help meet the needs of the wireless industry, the *Telecommunications Industry Association* (TIA) developed an A-Interface standard known as *IS-634*. This standard contained ambiguities in the network implementation that prevented development of an open interface. As a result, the *CDMA Development Group* (CDG)—a nonprofit group consisting of nearly all the leading wireless service providers and infrastructure manufacturers—has taken a leading role in further standardizing the A-Interface to a truly open interface. This open interoperability standard developed by the CDMA development group is known as *CDGIOS*.

The objective of this chapter is to lay the foundation for understanding the open network A-Interface between the BSC and the MSC of a CDMA wireless telecommunication network. This chapter begins with a description of CDMA wireless network functions and is followed by an overview of the MSC–BSC interface, which describes how the A-Interface fits into an entire CDMA wireless network. A historic description of the A-Interface standard is also presented to provide the reader with insights into the evolution of the MSC–BSC interface toward open interoperability. Finally, the structure of the A-Interface specification document is explained to allow the reader to reference existing A-Interface standards easily.

1.1 CDMA Wireless Network Functions

The functions and features of a CDMA wireless network are often categorized into the following main functional areas:

- Call Processing
- Mobility Management
- Supplementary Services
- Radio Resource Management
- Terrestrial Facility Management

Call Processing refers to the steps required of both the BSC and MSC to set up and release wireless calls. Basic Call Processing functions include Mobile Origination and Mobile Termination call setup, as well as call clearing scenarios initiated by the mobile, the BSC, and the MSC. This functional area also includes call failure scenarios, such as timer expiration and unsuccessful resource allocation.

Mobility Management procedures are needed to manage the registration and access status of individual mobile subscribers. These procedures include management of mobile parameters such as mobile location, mobile identity, and authentication status in the *Visitor Location Register* (VLR), and *Home Location Register* (HLR). Through mobility management, wireless subscribers can roam seamlessly within a network and across networks deployed by other service providers. Mobility Management functions also include Authentication, which is a technique used to ensure the security and privacy of wireless mobile subscribers in a network.

Supplementary Services are wireless subscriber features that provide capabilities other than basic voice. *Short Message Service* (SMS), *Message Waiting Notification* (MWN), Wireless Data Services, *Over-the-Air Service Provisioning* (OTASP) and call features, such as Call Forwarding and Call Waiting, are all examples of supplementary services.

Radio Resource Management refers to allocating radio channels for both voice and data traffic. This function includes the management of handoffs within a BSC, between BSCs, and across MSCs.

Terrestrial Facility Management is the function contained in both the BSC and MSC that manages the terrestrial signaling links, routes, and voice circuit resources.

This book describes each of these functional areas by focusing on A-Interface messaging between the BSC and MSC. Interactions with the IS-95 air interface and the IS-41 network interface are also explained to provide more insight into the issues involved with implementing a complete CDMA wireless network.

1.2 Overview of the MSC–BSC Interface

A CDMA telecommunications network is made up of individual network components, each connected to at least one other network component, using a designated interface (see Figure 1-1). The network interfaces may carry signaling information, user data, or both. This section provides an overview of the interface connecting the BSC and MSC network components.

In CDMA networks, the BSC is the entity that controls the radio equipment used to communicate with mobile stations. In addition to interfacing with mobile stations over the air, the BSC also provides a means of connecting the mobiles to the *Public Switched Telephone Network* (PSTN) by interfacing with an MSC over the A-Interface. In addition to providing access to the PSTN, the MSC controls the mobility features associated with a mobile network.

Interoperability between multiple MSC and BSC vendors is possible only if both entities conform to a predefined protocol standard. The open A-Interface achieves interoperability between the BSC and MSC by specifying the following functional areas:

- Physical layer properties
- Transport layer properties and protocols
- Application layer message flows and parameter contents
- Functional operations
- Network operating procedures

Figure 1-1 shows how the MSC–BSC interface fits into a complete CDMA wireless network. The MSC–BSC interface is one of many wireless network interfaces denoted by a letter symbol, which have been standardized by the TIA of America to provide a generic reference to a network model [5]. Historically, infrastructure manufacturers have used proprietary protocols for many of the interfaces shown in Figure 1-1. CDMA equipment designers originally focused on providing complete network solutions to wireless service providers, and proprietary protocols were often seen as the best way to meet system requirements. However, as CDMA wireless networks evolve, many of those same manufacturers are now following the wireless industry trend toward standardized interfaces.

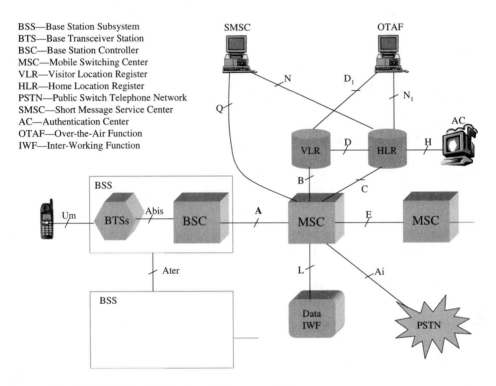

Figure 1-1   CDMA Network Interfaces between entities

The first and probably most important interface standardized for a CDMA network was the air interface. This interface, denoted by the letters *Um*, is the interface between a *Base Transceiver System* (BTS) and the mobile phone. The cellular standard (IS-95) and the Personal Communications standard (J-STD-8) specify, including the physical layer, how both the BTS and mobile should operate. By adhering to these standards, mobile phone and infrastructure equipment manufacturers have already achieved interoperability. CDMA phones manufactured by various companies seamlessly operate on infrastructure equipment designed and built by other, sometimes competing vendors.

Another important interface shown in Figure 1-1 is the interface between the MSC and BSC, which has been denoted by TIA as the A-Interface. This interface is crucial to the operation of a wireless network because of its role in the setup and release of wireless calls. The A-Interface is the subject of this book.

The aggregate of the BSC and the attached BTSs are collectively referred to as the *Base Station Subsystem* (BSS). The interface within the BSS that connects the BSC and a BTS is known as the *Abis-Interface*. This interface is used to exchange voice frames, call control messages, and BTS Operations and Maintenance (OA&M) information. Most existing CDMA networks use a propriety Abis interface, but there is an ongoing effort to standardize the BSC–BTS interface in 3G CDMA networks.

The interface used to connect two BSSs is designated the *Ater-Interface*. This interface is defined to facilitate the exchange of signaling information and user traffic between two BSCs, usually involving soft and softer handoffs. The Ater interface, which is discussed in more detail in the next section, is being further standardized in 3G systems.

To provide the full functionality required in a mobile network, the MSC also interfaces to several network entities other than the BSC. In North America, the IS-41 protocol standard is most often used for many of these external MSC interfaces. The HLR, a database where subscriber profile information is stored, typically communicates with the MSC using a version of IS-41. The VLR, which is a temporary database where active mobile subscriber information is stored for easy access, may either use IS-41 or a proprietary interface to communicate with the MSC. A proprietary MSC–VLR interface is sometimes used when the MSC and VLR are colocated or when the VLR software entity is running on the MSC platform.

Other common network entities that support mobile subscriber and network features include the Short Message Service Center (SMSC), Authentication Center (AC), and Over-the-Air Function (OTAF). These subsystems also use the IS-41 protocol standard to communicate with the MSC, VLR, and HLR.

The Ai interface provides the network with the capability to receive or terminate calls through the *Public Switched Telephone Network* (PSTN). Depending on the capabilities of both the MSC and the PSTN, the interface between the MSC and the PSTN may use one or more landline signaling protocols. *ISDN User Part* (ISUP), *Multi-Frequency R1* (MFR1) *Signaling* and *Multi-Frequency R2* (MFR2) *Signaling* are commonly used Ai interface protocols.

The L interface is used for communication between the Data Services Inter-Working Function (IWF) and the serving BSC/MSC. The IWF provides data capabilities to a CDMA network and is described in Section 5.5, "Circuit-Mode Data Services," on page 316.

The interfaces illustrated in Figure 1-1 play an important role in understanding the A-Interface protocol implementation. Where appropriate, the descriptions throughout the book reference the IS-95 and IS-41 to provide additional insights into how the A-Interface functions. There are other designated interfaces not shown in Figure 1-1 that may exist in a CDMA telecommunications network. However, because the interfaces are less common and do not affect the A-Interface, they have not been included. Table 1-1 summarizes the previously discussed CDMA network interfaces.

Table 1-1   CDMA Network Interfaces

I/F Name	Description	Ref Standard
Um	CDMA Air Interface	IS-95A[30], J-STD-8[31]
Abis	Proprietary, 3G standardardization in progress	
A	MSC–BSC open interface	IS-634, TSB-80[4], CDGIOS v2[2], IS-634A[3], CDGIOS v3[1], 3G-IOS v4, 3G-IOS v5
Ater	BSS–BSS open interface, may be proprietary for some vendors	IS-634A, CDGIOS v3, 3G-IOS v4, 3G-IOS v5
Ai	MSC–PSTN	MFR1—ITU Q.310-331 [45] MFR2—ITU Q.400-480 [45] ISUP—ANSI T1.113 [44]
B	MSC–VLR, typically proprietary and colocated	-
C,D,E,H, N,Q,N_1,D_1	Interfaces between network entities	IS-41C, IS-41D [32]
L	-IWF serving MSC–BSC interface, includes: -IWF to BSC via A-Interface (A5), using ISLP -IWF to PSTN via Ai-interface -IWF to MSC control interface	IS-658[43], IS-728 (ISLP) [42]

1.3 Open A-Interface Network Architecture

The original A-Interface architecture outlined in the IS-634, TSB-80, and CDGIOS version 2 standards consisted of a single A-Interface, which simply connected the MSC and BSC, and allowed signaling information and user traffic to be exchanged (see Figure 1-2).

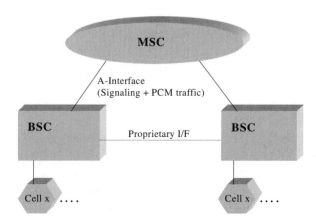

Figure 1-2   Original A-Interface architecture

In subsequent A-Interface standard developments, namely IS-634A and CDGIOS version 3, the architecture for the BSC–MSC interfaces is redefined to include additional open interface support. The original A-Interface is subdivided into two interfaces, one that carries signaling information (A1) and another that carries user traffic (A2). Two BSC–BSC interfaces (A3,A7) are newly specified to support BSC-to-BSC signaling. A BSC–IWF interface (A5) used to support circuit data is also specified (see Figure 1-3).

As mentioned previously, the original A-Interface defined in IS-634, TSB-80, and CDGIOS version 2 is now referred to in later standards as the *A1* and *A2 interfaces*. The A1-Interface is designated to carry signaling information, and the A2 connection is used for *Pulse Code Modulation* (PCM) user traffic, which may be voice or data. The A1 transport layer protocol is typically *Signaling System 7* (SS7). The A2 interface usually carries 64 kps/56 kbps PCM information. Throughout this book, references to the "A-Interface" refer to the aggregate of both the A1 and A2 interfaces.

The A5-Interface is a full duplex circuit data traffic byte stream connection between the MSC's IWF and the BSC's *Selection/Distribution Unit* (SDU). CDGIOS version 3 specifies that the IWF to be used for circuit data adaptation be located at the MSC.

The SDU is an entity within the BSC that is responsible for much of the CDMA functionality required for call processing and control. The SDU provides CDMA digital frame conversion and adaptation from PCM frames, delivers signaling (both layer 2 and layer 3) and traffic frames to the mobile, and performs power control. The SDU is also responsible for frames selection in the reversed link from multiple channel elements during voice calls and soft handoffs, and forward frame distribution to all channel elements in the forward link. The architecture shown in Figure 1-3, in which the SDU is located within the BSC, is referred to as *Architecture*

A in IS-634A. This is the architecture that is adopted in the IOS standard. A second type of architecture (not shown) is specified in IS-634A, whereby the SDU is located remotely from the BSCs [3].

The Ater interface is comprised of the newly designated A3 and A7 interfaces and are used for direct BSC-to-BSC communication. The A3 interface between two BSCs enables the SDU of the source BSC to communicate directly with the target BSC's radio traffic channel element, which is typically located at the BTS. This functionality allows a soft handoff to occur between the source BSC and the target BSC because the CDMA frame selection and distribution are done at a common SDU within the source BSC.

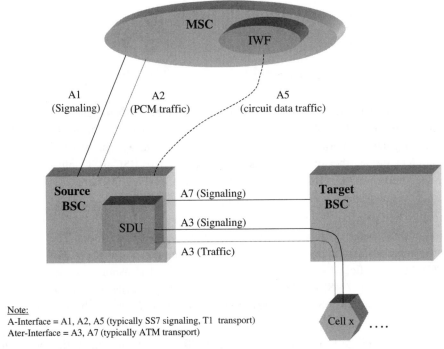

Figure 1-3   CDGIOS V3 A-Interface architecture

The A7 interface is used to exchange signaling information between two BSCs. This interface is used to exchange handoff messages during a direct BSC-to-BSC soft handoff.

The A3 interface is used for setting up the traffic connection between two BSCs during a direct inter-BSC soft handoff, providing both signaling and user traffic capabilities. The function of the A3 signaling interface is to set up and subsequently release A3 user traffic connections, which may consist of user traffic channels over ATM virtual circuits (see Section 1.5.2, "ATM as Transport Layer," on page 14). For example, an A3 Connect signaling message sent from the target BSC to the source BSC will trigger an A3 traffic interface connection to be established from the SDU at the source BSC to the radio channel element at the target BSC.

In summary, the combination of the A7 and A3 interfaces allows the execution of inter-BSC soft handoff. The source BSC first initiates the handoff request by signaling the target BSC using the A7-interface, and the target BSC then uses the A3 interfaces to establish an inter-BSC traffic connection. Table 1-2 summarizes the A-interfaces discussed above. The type of interface, connection entities, usage, and protocol layer standards are given. References to standards specifications are also provided.

Table 1-2 A-Interface and Ater-Interface Protocol Layer Implementation

I/F	Type	Enti-ties	Usage	Typical Implementation of Protocol Layers	Ref Standards
A1	Sig-naling	MSC–BSC	MSC–BSC functions	Application—CDGIOS Transport—SS7(MTP1,2,3) Physical—T1/ E1	CDGIOS v3 [1] T1.110–112 [9–11] T1.101–102,107 [6–8] G.701–704 [17–20]
A2	User Traffic	MSC–BSC	MSC-BSC dig-ital data	Physical—T1/ E1	T1.101–102,107 [6–8] G.701–704 [17–20]
A3	Sig-naling	SDU–BTS	Inter-BSS soft handoff	Application—CDGIOS Transport—TCP/IP Transport—ATM AAL5 Transport—ATM Physical—SONET	CDGIOS v3 [1] IETF RFC791,793,1483, 1577, 1883 [46–50] T1.635 [15], I.363.5 [26] T1.627 [14], I.361 [23] T1.646 [12], T1.105 [13], I.432 [16]
A3	User Traffic	SDU–BTS	Inter-BSS soft handoff	User frames—CDGIOS Transport—ATM AAL2 Transport—ATM Physical—SONET	CDGIOS v3 [1] I.363.2 [25] T1.627 [14], I.361 [23] T1.646 [12], T1.105 [13], I.432

Table 1-2   A-Interface and Ater-Interface Protocol Layer Implementation (Continued)

I/F	Type	Enti-ties	Usage	Typical Implementation of Protocol Layers	Ref Standards
A5	User Traffic	SDU–IWF	Circuit Data Services	User—Data Byte Stream Transport—ISLP Physical—T1/ E1	IS-707 [41] IS-658 [43], IS-728 [42] T1.101–102,107 [6–8] G.701–704 [17–20]
A7	Sig-naling	BSC–BSC	Inter-BSS soft handoff	Application—CDGIOS Transport—TCP/IP Transport—ATM AAL5 Transport—ATM Physical—SONET	CDGIOS v3 [1] IETF RFC791,793, 1483,1577,1883 [46–50] T1.635 [15], I.363.5 [26] T1.627 [14], I.361 [23] T1.646 [12], T1.105 [13], I.432

1.4 A-Interface Protocol Architecture

Figure 1-4 shows the protocol architecture used for A-Interface signaling traffic. The signaling interface between the MSC and BSC is made up of 3 main layers; the physical layer, the transport layer, and the mobile application layer.

The physical layer is the terrestrial transmission facility directly connecting the MSC and BSC. It includes physical and electrical characteristics, as well as channel, line coding, and framing specifications. The transport layer utilizes the physical layer to provide reliable datalink, network, and transport layer communication between the MSC and BSC. The transport layer provides services to the application layer, referred to as the *Mobile Application Part*, which is responsible for implementing the A-Interface messaging required to support the previously discussed five functional areas of a CDMA network (Call Processing, Supplementary Services, Mobility Management, Radio Resource Management, and Terrestrial Facilities Management).

The second interface shown in Figure 1-4 connects the mobile station with the BTS. The Um-Interface, sometimes called the *air interface*, utilizes the IS-95 protocol for underlying transport and physical layer transmissions between base stations and the mobile stations. As shown in Figure 1-4, the mobile application layer, implemented at the mobile station, consists of the Call Processing, Supplementary Services, and Mobility Management functions. Because the primary focus of this book is the A-Interface, specific Radio Resource Management functions related to the air interface are not presented here.

The following sections discuss the physical layer, transport layer, and application layer implementation of the A-Interface signaling protocol. Although the A-Interface specification does not impose any specific transport or physical layer implementation, digital T1–E1 interfaces and SS7 transport protocol are most commonly used.

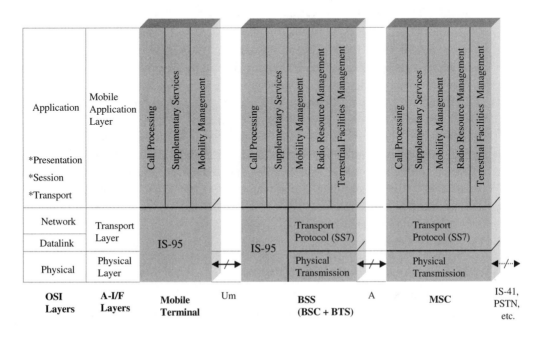

*These layers are not applicable in A-I/F

Figure 1-4   A-Interface protocol architecture

1.4.1   Physical Layer Implementation

The physical layer between the MSC and BSC is typically made up of terrestrial digital transmission links in the form of *Pulse Code Modulation* (PCM) channels of either 56 kbps or 64 kbps.

The A-Interface may be either T1 or E1, depending on the location of the network. Used throughout the United States and Canada, T1 digital transmission lines consists of 24 PCM channels that provide data rates of 1.544 Mbps (for more information regarding T1 specifications see references [6–8]). E1 digital transmissions lines consists of 32 PCM channels, providing data rates of 2.048 Mbps. E1 transmission is commonly used in European, Asian, and Latin American countries.

Recall that the A-Interface transports both signaling and user traffic between the MSC and BSC. Signaling traffic refers to the messaging, typically SS7, required to process calls and manage the network. An A-Interface signaling link occupies one PCM channel, or DS0, and utilizes the full 64 kbps. The signaling link may also be configured for 56 kbps; however, this is uncommon in today's networks because most modern switches support 64 kbps.

The second type of information sent across the A-Interface is user traffic, which refers to the actual voice or data frames. Once a call has been set up, the PCM channel selected to carry user traffic is used exclusively throughout the call. The T1/E1 trunks allocated for user traffic are usually configured as clear channels because the signaling DS0 is used for call setup and release.

1.4.2   SS7 as Transport Layer

Signaling System 7 (SS7) is the protocol most commonly used as the underlying transport layer for A-Interface application layer messaging between the MSC and BSC. The four SS7 layers utilized in the exchange of SS7 messages over the A-Interface are the *Message Transfer Part 1* (MTP1), MTP2, MTP3, and *Signaling Connection Control Part* (SCCP).

MTP1 is the physical layer used to connect the two nodes. MTP2 is the datalink layer used to improve the reliability of link transmissions. Error correction and retransmission schemes are some of the functions that the MTP2 layer employs to improve the reliability of transmissions. MTP3 is the network layer responsible for the routing of messages to the desired destination.

SCCP is the network and transport layer of SS7 that is used for encapsulating the A-Interface mobile application layer messages, also known as *Base Station Application Part* (BSAP) messages. These BSAP messages are sent across the link in the user data part of an SCCP message type. The A-Interface applications utilize the connection and connectionless services provided by the SCCP layer.

A more detailed description of SS7 is provided in Chapter 2, "Signaling System 7 Basics," on page 29. The SS7 specification for North American can be found in [9–11].

1.4.3   A-Interface Mobile Application Layer

Mobile application layer messages, also known as *BSAP messages*, are encapsulated in the SS7 SCCP transport layer messages before being transmitted over the MSC–BSC A-Interface. These BSAP messages are exchanged between the MSC and BSC to support CDMA network functions, such as Call Processing and Supplementary Services.

1.5   Ater-Interface Protocol Architecture

Figure 1-5 illustrates the protocol architecture used for Ater-Interface signaling traffic. As in the A-Interface protocol architecture, the signaling interface connecting two BSSs is made up of three main layers; the physical layer, the transport layer, and the mobile application layer. Although the CDGIOS standard does not impose a specific implementation, the Ater-Interface physical and transport layers typically use *Asynchronous Transfer Mode* (ATM) technology. An additional TCP/IP transport layer is included to provide reliable data transfer for the IOS application layer. The following sections discuss the physical layer, transport layer, and application layer implementation of the Ater-interface signaling protocol.

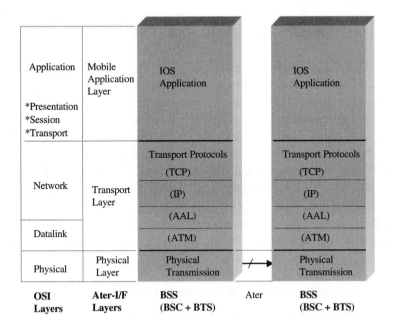

*These layers are not applicable in Ater-I/F

Figure 1-5 Ater-Interface protocol architecture

1.5.1   Physical Layer Implementation

As mentioned earlier, the physical layer between two different BSCs (A3 and A7) is typically implemented using ATM over *Synchronous Optical Network* (SONET) or *Synchronous Digital Hierarchy* (SDH). SONET is used in North America, and SDH is common in European and Asian countries. SONET is a fiber-based digital transmission facility that is typically implemented as an *Optical Carrier level 3* (OC-3), which supports data rates of up to 155.52 Mbps. The BSC-to-BSC interface may also use a coaxial T3 digital transmission that supports data rates up to 43.232 Mbps.

The ATM layer is used for both signaling and user traffic for the A3 and A7 interfaces. An ATM adaptation layer used for each interface type is discussed in Section 1.5.2, "ATM as Transport Layer," on page 14. The ATM physical layer with SONET is specified [12–13], and specifications for SDH can be found in [16–18].

1.5.2   ATM as Transport Layer

Asynchronous Transfer Mode (ATM) is used as the underlying transport layer for the A3 and A7 interfaces connecting two BSCs. As in the MSC–BSC interface, the A3 interface contains both signaling information and user traffic. The A7 interface contains only signaling information.

Both the A3 and A7 signaling interfaces, as shown in Figure 1-3, utilize *Transmission Control Protocol* (TCP) and *Internet Protocol* (IP) as an additional higher transport layer over ATM for reliable byte stream data transfer. The interface to the physical ATM layer is through an ATM Adaptation Layer known as *ATM Adaptation Layer 5* (AAL5) that provides fast, efficient packet-data services to the application layer. In CDGIOS version 3, only ATM *Permanent Virtual Circuits* (PVC) connections are required for the A3 and A7 signaling interfaces.

The TCP/IP protocol specification can be found in IETF RFC 791, 793, 1483, 1577, and 1883 [46–50]. The ATM Layer specifications can be found in [14] and [23], and the ATM AAL5 specifications can be found in [15] and [26].

Unlike the signaling interfaces, the A3 user traffic interface uses *ATM Adaptation Layer 2* (AAL2) circuit-oriented services for voice and data traffic (AAL2 specifications can be found in [25]).

1.5.3   Ater-Interface Mobile Application Layer

The Ater-Interface application layer consists of A3 and A7 IOS application messages that are encapsulated in the TCP/IP/ATM transport layer messages before being transmitted over the BSS–BSS interface. These application layer messages are exchanged between two BSSs to support CDMA inter-BSC soft handoffs.

1.6   BSAP Message and Parameter Structure

Application layer messages transferred between the MSC and BSC over the A-Interface are referred to as *Base Station Application Part* (BSAP) messages. BSAP messages are divided into two subcategories, *Base Station Management Application Part* (BSMAP) and *Direct Transfer Application Part* (DTAP), depending on whether the message is to be processed by the BSC.

BSMAP messages are used to exchange information between the BSC and MSC and are typically processed by both entities. An example of a BSMAP message is the Assignment Request message, which is sent by the MSC to request a terrestrial circuit from the BSC. The second type of BSAP messages, DTAP messages, are used for direct communication between the MSC and the mobile station. In the case of DTAP messages, the BSC acts only as a data pipeline, transferring the DTAP message to the mobile station without decoding its contents. SMS delivery is an example of a DTAP messaging.

BSAP messages are application layer messages that are encapsulated in the SCCP data portion of a SCCP message. Figure 1-6 shows the general format of both BSMAP and DTAP messages. The first octet in a BSAP message, the message discriminator octet, is used to indicate whether the message is a DTAP or BSMAP message. The BSAP application software running on both the BSC and MSC contains a message distribution function that uses this octet to distinguish between BSMAP and DTAP messages. How the remainder of the message is decoded depends on the message type indicated in the first octet.

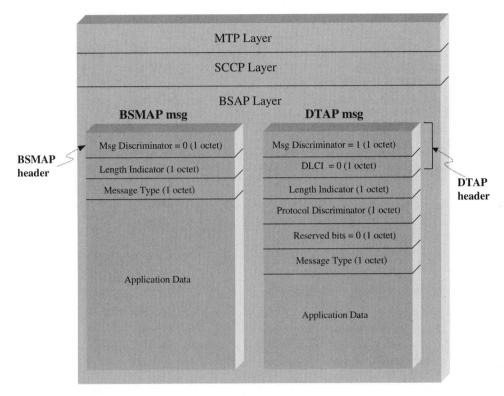

Figure 1-6 BSMAP and DTAP general message format

1.6.1 BSMAP Message

As shown in Figure 1-7, a message discriminator of 0 indicates to the BSAP distribution function that the message is a BSMAP message. Following the message discriminator octet is the length indicator, which specifies the length of the BSMAP message. This octet should not be confused with the SCCP length indicator that specifies the length of the overall SCCP message.

The next octet uniquely identifies the particular BSMAP message type. A complete list of BSMAP message types is given in Appendix Table A-1.

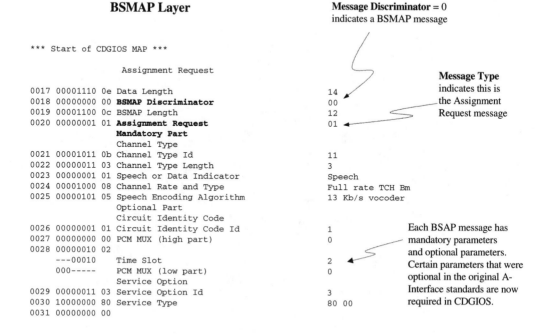

BSMAP Layer

```
*** Start of CDGIOS MAP ***

                Assignment Request
0017 00001110 0e Data Length
0018 00000000 00 BSMAP Discriminator
0019 00001100 0c BSMAP Length
0020 00000001 01 Assignment Request
                 Mandatory Part
                 Channel Type
0021 00001011 0b Channel Type Id
0022 00000011 03 Channel Type Length
0023 00000001 01 Speech or Data Indicator
0024 00001000 08 Channel Rate and Type
0025 00000101 05 Speech Encoding Algorithm
                 Optional Part
                 Circuit Identity Code
0026 00000001 01 Circuit Identity Code Id
0027 00000000 00 PCM MUX (high part)
0028 00000010 02
     ---00010    Time Slot
     000-----    PCM MUX (low part)
                 Service Option
0029 00000011 03 Service Option Id
0030 10000000 80 Service Type
0031 00000000 00
```

Message Discriminator = 0
indicates a BSMAP message

Message Type
indicates this is
the Assignment
Request message

14
00
12
01

11
3
Speech
Full rate TCH Bm
13 Kb/s vocoder

1
0

2
0

3
80 00

Each BSAP message has
mandatory parameters
and optional parameters.
Certain parameters that were
optional in the original A-
Interface standards are now
required in CDGIOS.

Figure 1-7 Example of a BSMAP message type

1.6.2 DTAP Message

A message discriminator of 1 indicates to the BSAP distribution function that the message is a DTAP message. Unlike BSMAP messages, DTAP messages contain a *Data Link Connection Identifier* (DLCI) parameter. This parameter is currently being used in *Global Systems for Mobile* (GSM) networks to indicate different *Signaling Access Point Identifiers* (SAPIs) on the radio interface. Each SAPI represents a different type of service connection. For example, a mobile can simultaneously be in a voice call with an SAPI = 0 and in a short message service transaction with an SAPI = 3. Because the DLCI parameter is not currently being used in IS95 CDMA systems, the DLCI parameter is set to 0.

The third octet specifies the length of the DTAP message and is followed by the Protocol Discriminator octet, which specifies the category of the message within DTAP functions. DTAP messages are categorized depending on their functions. Examples of DTAP categories are Call Processing, Mobility Management, and Facility Management. The protocol discriminator is followed by an octet of reserved bits, which are all set to 0, then the DTAP message type. A complete list of DTAP message types is given in Appendix Table A-2. Figure 1-8 shows an example DTAP message.

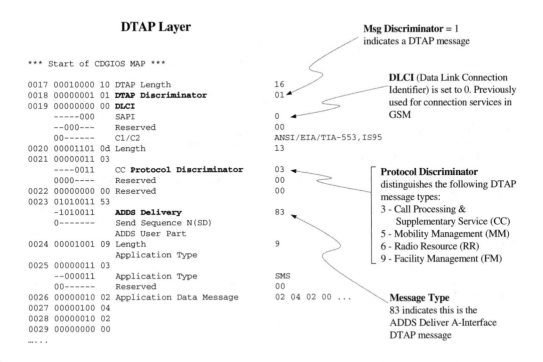

```
                            DTAP Layer                                          Msg Discriminator = 1
                                                                                indicates a DTAP message

*** Start of CDGIOS MAP ***
                                                                                DLCI (Data Link Connection
0017 00010000 10 DTAP Length                      16                            Identifier) is set to 0. Previously
0018 00000001 01 DTAP Discriminator               01                            used for connection services in
0019 00000000 00 DLCI                                                           GSM
        -----000    SAPI                          0
        --000---    Reserved                      00
        00------    C1/C2                          ANSI/EIA/TIA-553,IS95
0020 00001101 0d Length                           13
0021 00000011 03
        ----0011    CC Protocol Discriminator     03                           Protocol Discriminator
        0000----    Reserved                      00                           distinguishes the following DTAP
0022 00000000 00 Reserved                         00                           message types:
0023 01010011 53                                                               3 - Call Processing &
        -1010011    ADDS Delivery                 83                               Supplementary Service (CC)
        0-------    Send Sequence N(SD)                                        5 - Mobility Management (MM)
                    ADDS User Part                                             6 - Radio Resource (RR)
0024 00001001 09 Length                           9                            9 - Facility Management (FM)
                    Application Type
0025 00000011 03
        --000011    Application Type              SMS
        00------    Reserved                      00
0026 00000010 02 Application Data Message         02 04 02 00 ...              Message Type
0027 00000100 04                                                               83 indicates this is the
0028 00000010 02                                                               ADDS Deliver A-Interface
0029 00000000 00                                                               DTAP message
....
```

Figure 1-8   Example of a DTAP message type

1.6.3   A Note on Call Flow and Message Layout

The call flows presented throughout the book include both A-Interface and air interface (Um) messages. The A-Interface call flows are CDGIOS version 3 compliant and can be used as a guideline for future A-Interface standards. Where applicable, differences between current and future standards are discussed. The stages of the call flow are numbered sequentially, and A-Interface timers are included for completeness.

Following each call flow is a bitmap description of each message, including descriptions of the parameter *Information Elements* (IEs) that comprise the message. The table format used is similar to that found in earlier versions of CDGIOS and TSB-80 standards.

Table 1-3 illustrates the message table format used throughout the book. The table header includes the message name and the section in CDGIOS containing a description of the message.

Within the table, the first column, labeled *BitMap*, shows how the octets of each parameter IE are structured. The next column, *Param IE* indicates the name of the parameter. The column labeled *Range* specifies the values allowed by CDGIOS for the particular parameter. The *IOS Ref* column specifies the section in CDGIOS where the parameter can be found. The *Type* column indicates whether the parameter is mandatory, optional, required, or conditionally required. A brief explanation of each type is given as follows:

- M = Mandatory—parameter always included in the message
- O = Optional—parameter may be included in the message
- R = Required—parameter always included in CDGIOS, even though it was stated as optional in IS-634
- C = Conditionally Required—parameter included under stated conditions.

Table 1-3   Assignment Complete Message (CDGIOS 6.1.2.16)

BitMap	Param IE	#Oct	Range	Type	IOS Ref
0000 0000 (00H) LLLL LLLL	BSMAP header	2	Msg Discrim. = 0 (BSMAP) L = BSMAP msg length	M	6.2.2.1 6.2.2.3
0000 0010 (02H)	Message Type	1	Assignment Complete	M	6.2.2.4
0010 0011 (23H) nnnn nnnn nnnn nnnn	Channel Number	3	n = 0—set to 0 here.	M	6.2.2.6
0000 1010 (0AH) LLLL LLLL xiii iisa llll llll	Encryption Information	var-iable	L = 02H or 04H, x = 1 i = 00001—SME s = 1,0—status (1=active) a = 1,0—algo avail (1=avail) l = 00H—key length ……	O,C	6.2.2.12
0000 0011 (03H) ssss ssss ssss ssss	Service Option	3	e = 03H, s = 8000H—13K speech, 801FH—13K Markov ……	O,R	6.2.2.66

In the example presented in Table 1-3, the *Service Option* parameter IE has three octets, coded with the first octet as *03H*, followed by two octets specifying the service option, such as *8000H* for 13k voice. Note that *H* represents a hexadecimal number. This parameter IE is optional and is required in CDGIOS. It can be found under Section 6.2.2.66 of the A-Interface standard document.

1.6.4   BSAP Parameter Information Element (IE)

A-Interface messages are comprised of parameter IEs. These elements contain a unique identifier that distinguishes it from other IEs. Application layer software running on the MSC and BSC use the identifiers to decode incoming messages.

The IE identifiers are usually included in both BSMAP and DTAP messages; however, there are certain instances when the identifier is not required. When an IE is explicitly defined in the message structure, the identifier is omitted. For example, in a BSMAP message, the Header and Message Type IEs do not require identifiers. This is shown in the Assignment Complete message in Table 1-3.

Information element identifiers are also not required for mandatory DTAP messages elements. An example of this can be found in the Base Station Challenge Response Message, where the identifier is not included for the mandatory Authentication Response Parameter element [2].

The order of IEs must occur in the order specified in the standard. This is true of both mandatory parameters and, if present, optional parameters.

The format of parameter IEs contained in BSMAP and DTAP messages can be classified into four different types:

1. Type 1 IE:

   The format of type 1 IE is

   1eee xxxx,

   where *eee* is the element identifier and *xxxx* contains data. An example of a type 1 IE is the Location Update Type parameter (*1110 xxxx*).

2. Type 2 IE:

   Type 2 IEs contain no data. This type has format

   1010 eeee,

   where *eeee* is the element identifier. An example of this parameter type is the Voice Privacy Request IE (*1010 0001*).

3. Type 3 IE:

   Type 3 IEs have a fixed length and have at least one octet of data. The general format for this type is

   0eee eeee

   xxxx xxxx

   ....,

   where *0eee eeee* is the element identifier and *xxxx xxxx* contains the data. Notice that there is no length field because the parameter length is fixed. The Service Option element in the Assignment Complete message presented in Table 1-3 is an example of this parameter type. In this example, the IE is coded as *03H* followed by two octets representing the service option value. No length information is required.

4. Type 4 IE:

Type 4 IEs have the following format:

0eee eeee

LLLL LLLL

xxxx xxxx

xxxx xxxx

....

Because this type of information element is of variable length, the element identifier is followed by the length octet. The remainder of the element is data. The Encryption Information parameter, shown in Table 1-3, is an example of a type 4 IE.

Appendix Table A-1 contains a complete list of A-Interface BSMAP messages, including the Message Type ID and SCCP message type used for the transport layer. Also given in the appendix is the message protocol category (i.e., Call Processing, Mobility Management, Facilities Management, or Radio Resource Management) and references to the corresponding A-Interface standards document section. Appendix Table A-2 contains similar information for DTAP messages. Appendix C-1 on page 565 lists the parameter IE used in CDGIOS.

1.7   A-Interface Standard Evolution

As with most standards, the CDMA MSC–BSC A-Interface standard emerged over time and the objective of this section is to give an overview of that evolution. To understand how standards evolve, it is first necessary to become familiar with the standard bodies that govern the telecommunications industry.

1.7.1   Telecommunication Standards Organizations

As shown in Figure 1-9, the telecommunication industry has two main international organizations that are responsible for setting global standards and recommendations for telecommunication operations, namely, the *International Telecommunications Union* (ITU) and the *International Organization for Standardization* (ISO).

The ITU is a treaty organization of the United Nations that is responsible for recommending telecommunication standards for equipment and network operation internationally. The ITU is also responsible for spectrum frequency management and regulation.

The ISO is a voluntary, nongovernment organization whose responsibilities include developing standards in many areas, not only in the area of telecommunications. The ISO is comprised of various national standards bodies, one of which is the *American National Standards Institute* (ANSI). The ANSI standards body is responsible for accrediting U.S. national industry standard bodies in North America, such as the *Electronics Industry Alliance* (EIA) and the TIA. Whenever possible, ITU and ANSI work closely together to develop global telecommunication standards.

EIA is an industry standards body concerned with the development of industry standards in electronic components, consumer electronics, electronic information, and telecommunications. The TIA was formed by the Information and Telecommunications group within EIA and has since taken a lead role in developing North American telecommunications standards in radio, network access, and transmission technologies. The TIA, which is made up of individuals from telecommunication manufacturers, service providers, and the government, is an important developer and publisher of ANSI accredited standards.

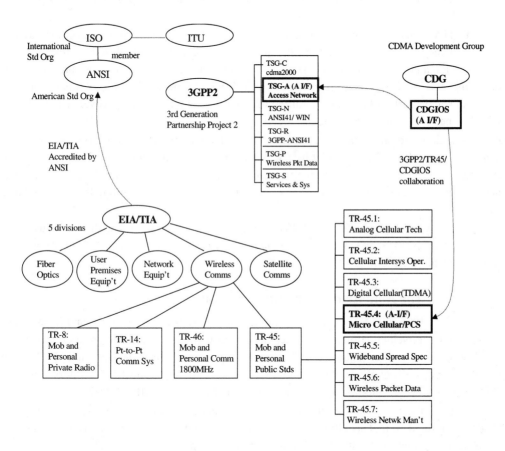

Figure 1-9   A-Interface Standards origin in the Standards organizations

The TIA's Standards and Technology Department is comprised of five main divisions that collectively contain over 70 standards development groups. The committees and subcommittees of the five divisions include Fiber Optics, User Premises Equipment, Network Equipment, Wireless Communications, and Satellite Communications. Each of the division comprises several working groups known as *TR* (Transmission) committees.

In particular, the Wireless Communications division consists of TR working committees that are responsible for setting standards in the wireless and telecommunications industry. The TR45 committee, named *Mobile and Personal Public Standard*, is where the main focus of the CDMA Telecommunications standardization effort lies. The TR45 committee is further divided up into working subgroups, such as radio technology and intersystem operations subcommittees. The MSC–BSC A-Interface standardization development occurs within the Micro Cellular/PCS TR45.4 working group. The TR45.4 group conducts regular meetings to discuss and develop the IS-634 standards. Figure 1-9 shows the organizational breakdown of TIA and its workgroups related to the A-Interface development.

In TIA, a standard is first published as an *Interim Standard* (IS). An interim standard has a limited three-year period whereby the standard is to be reaffirmed, modified, or rescinded. The reaffirmation and modification process ensures that the standard's specifications are still current, otherwise, the interim standard may be removed. If an interim standard represents an American National standard, it will also be submitted to ANSI for balloting and approval. The final result will then be an official ANSI standard document.

In addition to publishing interim standards, TIA also publishes *Telecommunications Systems Bulletins* (TSB). These bulletins are not formal standards, but instead contain technical information deemed valuable and timely to the industry. For example, TSB-80 is an A-Interface publication that addresses technical issues not specified within the initial IS-634 A-Interface standard.

As shown in Figure 1-9, the TR45.4 workgroup also collaborates with two industry consortiums, namely, the CDG and the *Third Generation Partnership Project 2* (3GPP2) group, on A-Interface development.

1.7.2 The A-Interface Standard Evolution

Prior to 1995, the A-Interface was traditionally a proprietary interface, and infrastructure manufacturer implementations varied, depending on their needs and system architecture. If a wireless service provider requested multiple vendor interoperability, the BSC and MSC vendors were required to develop an interface jointly. Because the MSC and BSC vendors were often fierce competitors, developing a joint MSC–BSC interface was a difficult task.

In 1995, the TIA published its first A-Interface standard, known as *IS-634*, with the goal of producing a standard that specifies both the protocol and network operations to enable interoperability between multiple MSC and BSC vendors. Although modified for CDMA, it is interesting to note that a significant portion of this initial CDMA A-Interface standard was adapted from the existing GSM A-Interface standard. Although this initial IS-634 standard was a commendable first attempt at MSC–BSC interoperability, ambiguities exist, due to the flexibility and options of implementation allowed by the standard. As a result, not all manufacturers implemented the A-Interface standard in the same manner, which led to the need for customization of the IS-634 protocol between BSC and MSC vendors.

Figure 1-10 shows an evolution of the A-Interface standard. The evolution started with the initial IS-634 standard. Following the initial publication, the TIA published an updated version of the A-Interface standard, called *TSB-80*; that addresses additional technical issues not covered by IS-634. However, the TSB-80 standard still lacks clarity in some areas and has resulted in some proprietary or customized implementations by vendors.

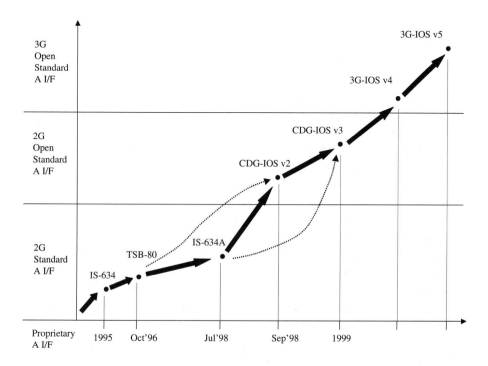

Figure 1-10   A-Interface Standard evolution

In 1998, the TIA developed revision A of the IS-634 standard, known as *IS-634A*. This standard has an option that allows vendors to implement an optimized call flow, eliminating redundant A-Interface signaling and message parameters. IS-634A also provides manufacturers the flexibility to implement two different A-Interface network architectures, depending on whether or not the SDU is colocated with the BSC. With the introduction of the IS-634A standard, the A-Interface standard has matured to a stage where manufacturers can implement new mobile services and features using IS-634A without significant difficulty. However some ambiguities still exist.

In 1998, the CDG, an independent industry consortium that is comprised of CDMA operators and manufacturers, developed an open A-Interface standard called *CDGIOS version 2.0.*

This standard, which originated from the Sprint IOS standard developed by Sprint PCS, includes optimized call flows, eliminates many ambiguities and unnecessary redundancies in the signaling protocol, and standardizes many of the optional message parameters. The CDGIOS version 2.0 standard is largely based on the TSB-80 standard; however, where possible, the standard also aligns with on going IS-634A agreements. CDGIOS version 2 became the first truly open A-Interface standard within the CDMA telecommunications industry, which allowed MSC and BSC vendors to operate without significant A-Interface protocol customization.

By this time, most industry partners, including both CDMA service providers and infrastructure manufacturers, have decided that the CDGIOS A-Interface standard is the most promising path to future A-Interface development. The TR45.4 workgroup efforts previously applied to IS-634B are now being channeled toward the development of the CDGIOS A-Interface standard. Both CDG and TR45.4 workgroups are contributing to the ongoing efforts.

CDGIOS version 3 is based on the IS-634A standard but has evolved from the open interface aspects of CDGIOS version 2. Specifically, the newly designated A3, A5, and A7 interfaces that are specified in IS-634A were introduced, but only one A-Interface network architecture model is specified (SDU colocated with the BSC). In addition, CDGIOS version 3 includes new services, such as EVRC, hard handoff improvements, and IS-95B support.

Meanwhile, the standardization effort for 3G mobile access networks heightened in 1999. The wireless industry began making additions to the A-Interface standard to facilitate 3G radio and access network technologies. An independent consortium of standard bodies, 3GPP2, was formed to address the ANSI/TIA/EIA-41 network evolution to 3G technologies. The 3GPP2 consists of many *Technical Specification Groups* (TSGs), as shown in Figure 1-9.

Specifically, TSG-A, named as *Access Network Interfaces* workgroup, has taken on the responsibility of developing the 3G A-Interface standard between the Radio Access Network (BSC) and the Core Network (MSC). The TIA TR45.4 committee, the CDGIOS workgroup, and the 3GPP2 TSG-A workgroup are jointly working toward a common goal to develop the 3G A-Interface standard. The 3G-IOS version 4 is the first 3G A-Interface standard, which includes 3G capabilities such as high-speed data, support for 3G cdma2000 phase I radio technologies, and enhanced subscriber services. 3G-IOS version 5 is also being developed for 3G cdma2000 phase 2 radio technology support.

Table 1-4 summarizes the different A-Interface standards that are being developed, noting the key features and differences.

Table 1-4   CDMA A-Interface Standards

Standard	Features	Published
IS-634	-first A-Interface standard published	1995
TSB-80	-based on IS-634 -addresses additional technical issues not covered in IS-634	Oct 1996
IS-634A	-new A-interfaces A3, A5, A7 -renamed original A-Interface to A1, A2 -new A-Interface network architecture A (SDU co-located with BSC) -new A-Interface network architecture B (SDU not co-located with BSC) -has options for optimized call flow	Jul 1998
CDGIOS V2.0	-optimized call flow and messaging -eliminated ambiguities in optional parameters and messaging -based on TSB-80, but aligned with IS-634A	Sep 1998
CDGIOS V3.1.1	-based on IS-634A, but evolved from CDGIOS V2.0 optimized call flow -new A-Interface network architecture A -new A-interfaces A3,A5, A7 -renamed original A-Interface to A1, A2 -EVRC support, hard handoff improvements, IS-95B support	1999
3G-IOS V4	-3G access network capabilities, e.g., high speed data, enhanced services -3G cdma2000 phase I	
3G-IOS V5	-3G cdma2000 phase II	

1.8 A-Interface Standard Specification Structure

Although there are several A-Interface standards, such as IS-634, TSB-80, CDGIOS v2, IS-634A, CDGIOS v3, they all follow a similar document structure. Figure 1-11 shows the layout of the CDGIOS open A-Interface standard specification document.

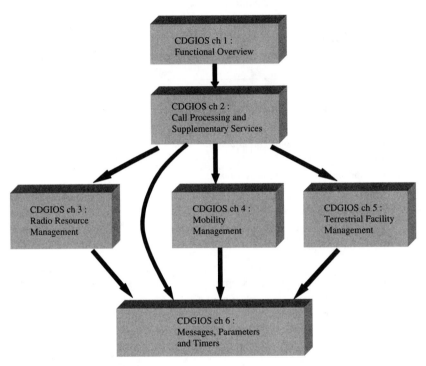

Figure 1-11 A-Interface Standard Specification structure

References

1. CDG-IOS version 3.1.1, *CDMA Development Group MSC to BS Interface Inter-Operability Specification*. June 1999.

2. CDG-IOS version 2.0, *CDMA Development Group MSC to BS Interface Inter-Operability Specification*. September 1998.

3. Telecommunications Industry Association, TIA/EIA/IS-634-A, *MSC-BS Interface (A-Interface) for Public 800 MHz*. July 1998.

4. Telecommunications Industry Association , TIA/EIA/TSB-80, *MSC-BS Interface (A-Interface) for Public 800 MHz*. October 1996.

5. Telecommunications Industry Association, PN-2716, *TR-45 Wireless Network Reference Model*, October 1997.

6. American National Standards Institute, ANSI T1.101, *Synchronization Interface Standards for Digital Networks*. February 1994.

7. American National Standards Institute, ANSI T1.102, *Digital Hierarchy—Electrical Interfaces*. December 1993.

8. American National Standards Institute, ANSI T1.107, *Digital Hierarchy—Formats Specifications*. July 1995.

9. American National Standards Institute, ANSI T1.110, *Signaling System No. 7 (SS7)—General Information*. June 1992.

10. American National Standards Institute, ANSI T1.111, *Signaling System No. 7 (SS7)—Message Transfer Part (MTP)*. June 1992.

11. American National Standards Institute, ANSI T1.112, *Signaling System No. 7 (SS7)—Signaling Connection Control Part (SCCP)*. October 1992.

12. American National Standards Institute, ANSI T1.646, *Broadband ISDN—Physical Layer Specification for User–Network Interfaces Including DS1/ATM*. May 1995.

13. American National Standards Institute, ANSI T1.105, *Synchronous Optical Network (SONET) Basic Description Including Multiplex Structure, Rates and Formats*. October 1995.

14. American National Standards Institute, ANSI T1.627, *Broadband ISDN—ATM Layer Functionality and Specification*. July 1993.

15. American National Standards Institute, ANSI T1.635, *Broadband ISDN—ATM Adaptation Layer Type 5 Common Part Functions and Specification*. January 1994.

16. International Telecommunications Union—Telecommunications Sector, ITU-T Recommendation I.432, *Broadband ISDN—User–Network Interface—Physical Layer Specification*. March 1993.

17. International Telecommunications Union— Telecommunications Sector, ITU-T Recommendation G.701, *Vocabulary of digital transmission and multiplexing, and pulse code modulation (PCM) terms*, 1993.

18. International Telecommunications Union—Telecommunications Sector, ITU-T Recommendation G.702, *General Aspects of Digital Transmission Systems—Terminal Equipment—Digital Hierarchy Bit Rates*. 1993.

19. International Telecommunications Union—Telecommunications Sector, ITU-T Recommendation G.703, *Physical/electrical characteristics of hierarchical digital interfaces*, 1998.

20. International Telecommunications Union—Telecommunications Sector, ITU-T Recommendation G.704, *Synchronous Frame Structure Used at 1544, 6312, 2048, 8488, and 44,736 kbps Hierarchical Levels*. October 1998.

21. International Telecommunications Union—Telecommunications Sector, ITU-T Recommendation Q.702, *Signalling data link*, 1988.

22. International Telecommunications Union—Telecommunications Sector, ITU-T Recommendation Q.511, *Exchange interfaces towards other exchanges*, 1988.

23. International Telecommunications Union—Telecommunications Sector, ITU-T Recommendation I.361, *Broadband ISDN–ATM Layer Specification*. November 1995.

24. International Telecommunications Union—Telecommunications Sector, ITU-T Recommendation I.363, *Broadband ISDN–ATM Adaptation Layer Specification*. March 1993.

25. International Telecommunications Union—Telecommunications Sector, ITU-T Recommendation I.363.2, *Broadband ISDN–ATM Adaptation Layer Type 2 Specification*. September 1997.

26. International Telecommunications Union—Telecommunications Sector, ITU-T Recommendation I.363.5, *Broadband ISDN– ATM Adaptation Layer Type 5 Specification*. August 1996.

27. International Telecommunications Union—Telecommunications Sector, ITU-T Recommendation Q.2110, *Broadband ISDN–ATM Adaptation Layer—Service Specific Connection Oriented Protocol (SSCOP)*. July 1994.

28. International Telecommunications Union—Telecommunications Sector, ITU-T Recommendation Q.2140, *Broadband ISDN–ATM Adaptation Layer—Service Specific Coordination Function for Signaling at the Network Node Interface (SSCF at NNI)*. February 1995.

29. International Telecommunications Union—Telecommunications Sector, ITU-T Recommendation Q.2931, *Broadband ISDN–Digital Subscriber Signaling No. 2 (DSS2) User–Network Interface Layer 3 Specification for Basic Call/Connection Control*. February 1995.

30. Telecommunications Industry Association, TIA/EIA/IS-95-A, *Mobile Station-Base Station Compatibility Standard for Dual-Mode Wideband Spread Spectrum Cellular Systems.* May 1995.

31. American National Standards Institute, ANSI J-STD-008, *Personal Station—Base Station Compatibility Requirements for 1.8 to 2.0 GHz Code Division Multiple Access (CDMA) Personal Communications Systems.* August 1995.

32. American National Standards Institute, ANSI TIA/EIA/IS-41-D, *Cellular Radio-Telecommunications Intersystem Operations.* December 1997.

33. Telecommunications Industry Association, TIA/EIA/IS-637, *Short Message Services for Wideband Spread Spectrum Cellular Systems.* December 1995.

34. Telecommunications Industry Association, TIA/EIA/IS-53-A, *Cellular Features Description.* April 1995.

35. Telecommunications Industry Association, TIA/EIA 664, *Cellular Features Description.* April 1995.

36. Telecommunications Industry Association, TIA/EIA/TSB-58, *Administration Parameter Value Assignments for TIA/EIA Wideband Spread Spectrum Standards.* April 1995.

37. Telecommunications Industry Association, TIA/EIA/IS-91, *Mobile Station – Base Station Compatibility Standard for 800MHz Analog Cellular.* October 1994.

38. Telecommunications Industry Association, TIA/EIA/IS-683-A, *Over-the-Air Service Provisioning of Mobile Stations in Spread Spectrum Systems.* June 1998.

39. Telecommunications Industry Association, TIA/EIA/IS-725, *IS-41-C Enhancements for OTASP, Over-the-Air Service Provisioning of Mobile Stations in Spread Spectrum Systems.* June 1997.

40. Telecommunications Industry Association, TIA/EIA/IS-99, *Data Service Option Standard for Wideband Spread Spectrum Digital Cellular System.* July 1995.

41. Telecommunications Industry Association, TIA/EIA/IS-707, *Data Service Options for Wideband Spread Spectrum Digital Cellular System.* February 1998.

42. Telecommunications Industry Association, TIA/EIA/IS-728, *Intersystem Link Protocol.* April 1997.

43. Telecommunications Industry Association, TIA/EIA/IS-658, *Data Services Interworking Function Interface for Wideband Spread Spectrum Systems.* 1997.

44. American National Standards Institute, ANSI T1.113, *Integrated Services Digital Network (ISDN) User Part.* 1992.

45. International Telecommunications Union - Telecommunications Sector, ITU-T Recommendation Q.310-331, Q.400-480, *Specifications of Signalling Systems R1 and R2.* 1985.

46. Internet Engineering Task Force, RFC 791, *Internet Protocol (IP).* 1981.

47. Internet Engineering Task Force, RFC 793, *Transmission Control Protocol (TCP).* 1981.

48. Internet Engineering Task Force, RFC 1483, *Multiprotocol encapsulation over ATM Adaptation Layer 5.* 1993.

49. Internet Engineering Task Force, RFC 1577, *Classical IP and ARP over ATM.* 1994.

50. Internet Engineering Task Force, RFC 1883, *Internet Protocol, Version 6 (Ipv6).* 1995.

51. Uyless Black, *ATM Resource Library (Volumes I, II, III),* December 1997, Upper Saddle River, NJ: Prentice Hall PTR.

Signaling System 7 Basics

Common *Channel Signaling* (CCS) was first introduced in the 1976 as a technique to improve the reliability and efficiency of call control in the public switching network [1]. The new signaling technique was designed to provide faster call setup times, utilize voice circuits more efficiently, and reduce fraudulent network usage. Prior to the introduction of CCS, the public switching network relied almost exclusively on *Channel Associated Signaling* (CAS) methods for call control. CAS systems, which are still in use today, transfer call control information over the same circuits used for voice or data using in-band signaling techniques.

Following the introduction of CCS, a specification for a second-generation CCS system was developed by CCITT and is now commonly known as *Signaling System No. 7* (SS7). The goal of the SS7 specification was to meet the needs of an all-digital, *Intelligent Network* (IN). SS7 has lived up to its early promises, today providing the signaling backbone for most of the world's telephone networks. In fact, because existing SS7 networks have proven to be flexible and reliable, they continue to expand both in size and functionality.

The successful use of SS7 in the public switching network made it a natural choice for exchanging messages between a *Base Station Controller* (BSC) and a *Mobile Switching Center* (MSC). Some of the important reasons why SS7 was chosen for the A-Interface are listed below:

1. SS7's popularity in the telecommunications industry. Most MSCs already support SS7 functionality and, therefore, have the hardware and much of the software required for an A-Interface. The availability of "off-the-shelf" SS7 hardware and software has also helped BSC vendors to speed up development of open system solutions. Because SS7 is

widely used throughout the world, a broad base of SS7 engineering expertise is available to both infrastructure equipment vendors and network service providers.

2. Reliability and robustness. Wireless subscribers increasingly expect the same reliability from their wireless network that they have become accustomed to from the existing land-line network.

3. Flexibility. Wireless features can continually be added without changing the basic signaling network structure

4. Fast call setup times that are comparable to landline networks. Setting up calls quickly is becoming increasingly important in the wireless industry.

Because SS7 is used for the A-Interface transport layer and the *Base Station Application Part* (BSAP) layer invokes features inherent in the protocol, knowledge of SS7 fundamentals is important. The objective of this chapter is to describe the key functions of SS7, primarily focusing on how SS7 is used by the MSC and BSC to exchange BSAP messages over the A-Interface. The chapter begins with a brief description of a customary SS7 network and is then followed by an explanation of the protocol's message structure and protocol layers. Although ANSI SS7 and ITU SS7 are very similar, this chapter discusses only ANSI SS7. Readers interested in ITU SS7 are encouraged to refer to the appropriate ITU standards [7].

2.1 The Signaling System 7 Network

A typical SS7 network consists of *Service Switching Points* (SSPs), *Signaling Transfer Points* (STPs), and *Service Control Points* (SCPs). These signaling points are interconnected using signaling links, as shown in an example network in Figure 2-1.

The three types of signaling points shown in Figure 2-1 provide all of the functions required of an SS7 network.

A *Service Switching Point* (SSP) is a signaling end point that originates and terminates SS7 messages. A voice call usually involves exchanging SS7 messages between a local and remote SSP.

A *Signaling Transfer Point* (STP) is a signaling node that relays or routes SS7 messages to another signaling node. An STP uses information contained in the routing portion of an SS7 messages to relay the message to an SSP, SCP, or another STP.

A *Service Control Point* (SCP) is a centralized database that contains information pertaining to an SSP. The information contained in this database can be queried by an SSP by sending the appropriate SS7 message across the network.

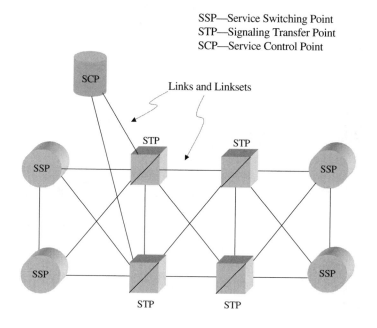

SSP—Service Switching Point
STP—Signaling Transfer Point
SCP—Service Control Point

Figure 2-1   An example SS7 network, consisting of SSP, STP, and SCP

Although the SS7 network used in the public switching network utilizes all three SS7 node types, the A-Interface configuration involves only point-to-point SSP connections. An example SS7 network architecture used for implementing an open A-Interface is shown in Figure 2-2. The architecture is a simplified version of a complete SS7 network because no STPs or SCPs are used. In fact, CDGIOS specifies that only a point-to-point connection is supported. In this example, two BSCs are connected to a single MSC, using a total of four SS7 signaling links. Although the number of signaling links used for each A-Interface is implementation-specific, multiple signaling links are typically configured between a BSC and MSC to improve reliability. Both the MSC and BSC are designated SSPs because they manage the setup and release of wireless calls through the exchange of SS7 messages with another SSP.

The BSC and MSC are physically and logically connected by signaling links. A signaling link connects one signaling point to another signaling point and is identified by a unique *Signaling Link Code* (SLC). Messages containing signaling information, known as *signal units*, are routed across the signaling links from the originating node to the destination node, using unique numerical node identifiers known as *point codes*. Message routing over a link set directly connecting two points is referred to as *Associated Mode* signaling.

A *Signaling Link Set* is a logical grouping of individual signaling links that is used for the transportation of signaling messages between two adjacent nodes. To avoid a single point of failure and to provide the ability to load-share across individual links, a signaling link set normally consists of two or more signaling links. In the example network shown in Figure 2-2, Link Set A comprises two signaling links.

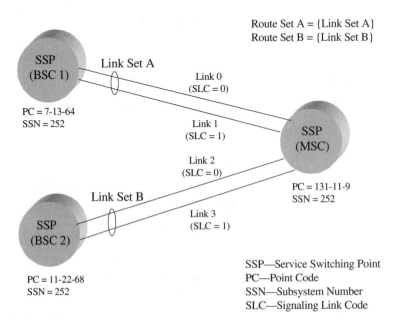

Figure 2-2   Example SS7 Network connecting one MSC and two BSCs

A *Combined Link Set* is usually a pair of signaling link sets that connect an SSP to a "mated" STP pair. In large SS7 networks, mated STP pairs are used for redundancy purposes to improve overall network reliability. The two STPs in a mated pair each have the same destinations and routes, and each can single-handedly accommodate message routing should the mated pair fail. Because the A-Interface architecture is typically point-to-point, no STP or combined link sets are present.

A *Route Set* is a logical grouping of individual routes that maybe used to reach a final destination node. Each route consists of a final Destination Point Code and a particular link set. From the MSC point of view, Figure 2-2 illustrates two route sets. Route Set A consists of a single route from the MSC to BSC 1, using Link Set A. The second Route Set shown in Figure 2-2, Route Set B, is between the MSC and BSC 2, and is comprised of Link Set B. Because there is normally only one route between the BSC and MSC, there is no need to specify route sets at the BSC.

2.2 Signaling System 7 Protocol Layers

As new requirements are being identified for today's telecommunication network, the system software and hardware responsible for implementing the new functionality becomes increasingly complex. To facilitate communication between hardware and software entities and to prevent modifications to one element from affecting other elements, the functions of the SS7 protocol are divided into defined layers. The protocol layers are shown in Figure 2-3.

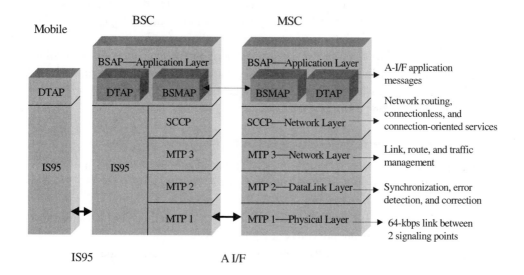

MTP—Message Transfer Part
SCCP—Signaling Connection Control Part
BSAP—Base Station Application Part
BSMAP—Base Station Management Application Part
DTAP—Direct Transfer Application Part

Figure 2-3 Signaling System 7 protocol layers

The *Message Transfer Part* (MTP) is composed of three distinct parts, namely, *Message Transfer Part 1* (MTP1), MTP2, and MTP3.

MTP1 is the SS7 physical layer that defines the physical, electrical, and functional characteristics of the *Signaling Data Link* (SDL). The ANSI SS7 MTP specification (ANSI T1.111 [5]) allows signaling rates of 56/64 kbps and 1.536 Mbps (ATM-based transmission). Although both the MSC and BSC usually allow the operator to specify the data rate, framing, and line coding desired, the most common physical layer implementation type used in North American systems is 64 kbps, *Extended Superframe Format* (ESF) frame format, and *Binary 8 Zero Substitution* (B8ZS) line coding. The 56 kbps rate applies to older framing types, such as *D4-framing*, where data bits are robbed for signaling, and is rarely used for the A-Interface.

MTP2 is the SS7 datalink layer that specifies the functions and procedures related to transferring signaling messages between two nodes. MTP2 is responsible for delimitation of signal units, error detection, error correction, and link failure detection.

MTP3 is the SS7 network layer that provides message routing between signaling points, routes traffic away from failed links, and controls traffic when congestion occurs. MTP3 also provides a method for periodically testing available links.

The *Signaling Connection Control Part* (SCCP), an MTP3 user, provides connectionless and connection-oriented services. The SCCP also provides network layer functions, such as enhanced routing methods. The SCCP uniquely identifies individual SCCP entities at the destination node, using a predetermined *Subsystem Number* (SSN).

The *Base Station Application Part* (BSAP) is the A-Interface application protocol used by both the MSC and BSC to support Call Processing, Radio Resource Management, and Mobility Management in a CDMA wireless network. Subsequent chapters of this book describe, in detail, how the BSAP application performs these functions.

2.3 Signaling System 7 Message Structure

Because one of the primary functions of MTP2 is signal unit delimitation, it is important to describe the three basic SS7 message structures first. The three types of SS7 messages are described below.

Fill-In Signal Units (FISUs) are used to monitor the signaling link and are transmitted continuously whenever there are no MSUs or LSSUs to be sent.

Link Status Signal Units (LSSUs) are used to indicate the status of the link to the remote end.

Message Signal Units (MSUs) are used to carry all the call control application and MTP3 network management information.

Although the message structures for all three message types are unique, several fields are common. Figure 2-4 illustrates the general SS7 message structure, and Table 2-1 describes the common fields.

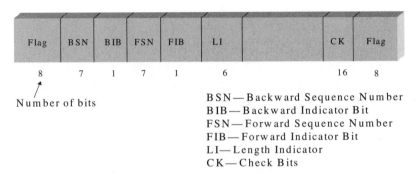

Figure 2-4 General Signaling System 7 message structure

Table 2-1   Common Fields in Signaling System 7 Message Structure

Bitmap	Parameter	#Oct	Range/ Description
0111 1110	Flag	1	This is an 8-bit pattern of *01111110* which allows easy detection of signal unit boundaries. The opening flag of a signal unit is normally the closing flag of the preceding signal unit.
b BBB BBBB	Backward Sequence Number and Indicator Bit	1	B = BSN—Backward Sequence Number Used to indicate to the remote end the sequence number of the message being acknowledged. b = BIB—Backward Indicator Bit Used for indicating a positive or negative acknowledgment to the remote end.
f FFF FFFF	Forward Sequence Number and Indicator Bit	1	F = FSN—Forward Sequence Number Used for indicating the sequence number of the message to the remote end. f = FIB—Forward Indicator Bit Used by the receiving end to indicate a positive or negative acknowledgment.
ss LL LLLL	Length Indicator	1	L = LI—Length Indicator, s = spare bits, set to 0 LI = 0 (FISU) LI = 1 or 2 (LSSU) LI > 2 (MSU)
cccc cccc cccc cccc	Check Bits	2	c = CK—Check Bits Used for error detection.

2.3.1   Fill-In Signal Unit

FISUs are the most basic type of SS7 message and are used by MTP2 to verify the integrity of a particular signaling link in the absence of other transmissions. The reliability of SS7 networks is improved by using FISUs to monitor the status of available signaling links continually. If a link fails, the failure is identified immediately, even if the link is not currently be used to transport user or link status information. Because FISUs do not contain any user or link status information, they are never retransmitted. To prevent retransmissions, FISU *Forward Sequence Numbers* (FSNs) are not incremented. As is described in Section 2.4.2, "Signal Unit Error Detection and Correction," on page 41, FISUs are also used to acknowledge received signal units, using the BSN field.

All FISUs are a fixed six octets in length and have the LI field set to zero. Figure 2-5 shows the message structure of an FISU and an example FISU message log.

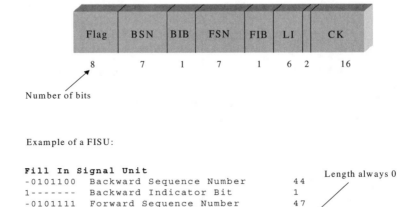

Figure 2-5   Fill-In Signal Unit message structure

2.3.2   Link Status Signal Unit

LSSUs are transmitted between two adjacent signaling points to indicate the status of the particular signaling link being used. LSSUs do not provide any information about other signaling links and, therefore, are not broadcast over the network. LSSUs are processed only within MTP2 and are not associated with any higher-level network management functions. However, MTP2 does relay signaling link status information to MTP3 for network management purposes.

Figure 2-6 shows the message structure of an LSSU, together with an example LSSU message log. Unlike the FISU, the LSSU contains link status information and, therefore, requires a nonzero length. The length indicator field for an LSSU is usually set to 1, specifying that the message contains a single octet indicating the status of the link. This octet is known as the *Status Field* (SF) octet.

The local link status is encoded in the three least significant bits of the *SF* octet of the LSSU message and can take on the following values:

- 000—*Out of Alignment* (SIO) is sent to indicate that the link has entered an initial alignment state and the local signaling point is ready to begin the alignment process. The alignment process will start upon receiving an SIO, SIN, or SIE from the remote signaling point.

- 001—*Normal Alignment* (SIN) is sent to indicate that link alignment has started, using the "Normal" alignment procedure. This link alignment process is used when the link being aligned is a redundant link.

- 010—*Emergency Alignment* (SIE) is sent to indicate that link alignment has started using the "Emergency" alignment procedure. This link alignment process is used when the link being aligned is the only available link between the two signaling points. An Emergency alignment requires a shorter proving period than does Normal alignment and is used to bring the link up quickly so that signaling traffic can be exchanged. The specific differences between the Normal and Emergency alignment procedures are described in Section 2.4.3, "Signaling Link Initial Alignment," on page 44.

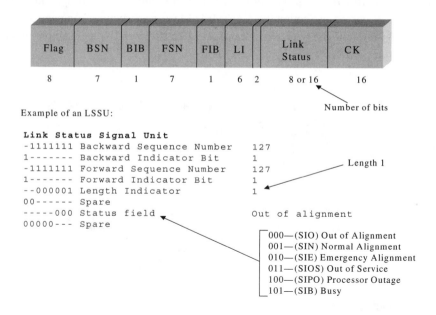

Figure 2-6 Link Status Signal Unit message structure

- 011—*Out of Service* (SIOS) is sent to indicate that the link is unable to transmit or receive MSUs. This link state occurs when excessive signal unit errors are detected or upon initial power-up. Upon a request from level 3 to initiate alignment, this state is exited, and LSSUs with SF set to SIO are sent to the adjacent node, indicating that the local alignment procedure has begun.

- 100—*Processor Outage* (SIPO) is sent to indicate that the local node is experiencing a processor outage and is unable to process messages received. Note that this is sent if the link is already aligned.

• 101—*Busy* (SIB) is sent to indicate that the local node is experiencing congestion at level 2. At this point, message acknowledgments are withheld at the local node. The remote end, upon receipt of the SIB, will inform level 3 of a congestion situation at the adjacent node, and MSU transmissions will be halted.

2.3.3 Message Signal Unit

A MSU contains application information or MTP3 network management information. All messages that are not FISU or LSSU are MSUs. In addition to the common fields previously discussed, the MSU has an 8-bit *Service Information Octet* (SIO) and a 56-bit routing label contained within a *Signaling Information Field* (SIF). The structure of the MSUs, including the SIO and SIF fields, is discussed in Section 2.5.1.1, "MSU Message Structure," on page 57.

Figure 2-7 shows the message structure of an MSU, followed by an example message log of an MSU message header.

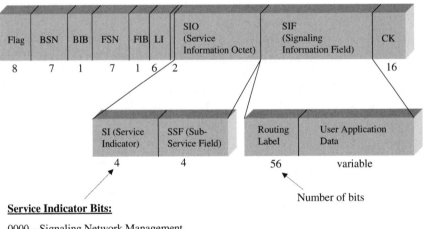

Service Indicator Bits:

0000—Signaling Network Management
0010—Signaling Network Testing & Maintenance
0011—Signaling Connection Control Part (SCCP) Message
0101—ISDN User Part

Figure 2-7 Message Signal Unit message structure

```
MTP Level 2 (MTP-L2)
 -0000111  Backward Sequence Number        7
 1-------  Backward Indicator Bit          1
 -0001000  Forward Sequence Number         8
 1-------  Forward Indicator Bit           1
 --100011  Length Indicator                35
 00------  Spare                           0
 ----0011  Service Indicator               SCCP
 --00----  Sub-Service: Priority           Spare/priority 0 (U.S.A. only)
 10------  Sub-Service: Network Ind        National message
 ***B3***  Destination Point Code          001-002-004
 ***B3***  Originating Point Code          001-001-001
 00010010  Signaling Link Selection        18
 ... (User Application Data)
```

Figure 2-8 Message Signal Unit message example

2.4 MTP2 Layer

The purpose of MTP2, together with the physical layer, is to provide the functionality and procedures needed to transfer signal units reliably between two directly connected signaling nodes over a single link. Messages that arrive at the MTP2 layer are processed for signal unit integrity before being passed to MTP3 for further processing. In addition to processing signal units, MTP2 provides link state and message congestion status to MTP3, which then performs signaling link management and traffic flow control. MTP2 link layer functions include:

1. Signal Unit Message Acceptance
2. Signal Unit Error Detection and Correction
3. Signaling Link Initial Alignment
4. Signaling Link Error Monitoring
5. Processor Outage Procedure
6. Signaling Link Flow Control (Congestion Control)

2.4.1   Signal Unit Message Acceptance

When a signal unit first arrives at the MTP2 datalink layer, the signal unit is processed and checked as to whether it is correctly formatted before being accepted by MTP2. The Signal Unit Message Acceptance function first verifies the integrity of the signal unit by processing the flag bits, FSN, FIB, BSN, BIB, LI, and CK bits, then passes it to the Signal Unit Error Detection and Correction function.

The Signal Unit Message Acceptance function includes:

• Signal Unit Alignment and Delimitation
• Bit Stuffing Removal
• Length Checking

Before one can fully understand how MTP2 Message Acceptance function works, it is first neccessary to understand how flags are used to deliminate signal units. A specific bit pattern, designated the *flag*, is attached to the signal unit before it is transmitted over the signaling link. The flag, which consists of the bit pattern *01111110*, is used to signify the start and end of a signal unit. Because this same bit pattern may also occur in the data portion of a message, steps must be taken to guarantee that the flag pattern is unique. Prior to attaching the flag, the transmitting node inserts a zero after every occurrence of five consecutive 1s in the signal unit. After removing the flag, the receiving node removes any zeros following five consecutive 1s.

Figure 2-9 illustrates the procedure used by layer 2 to validate received signal units. In Stage 1, the Signal Unit Alignment and Delimitation function first identifies the signal unit flag bit pattern *01111110*. A flag that is not immediately followed by another flag is identified as an opening flag, and the start of the signal unit is assumed. If, during the process of identifying an opening flag, more than six consecutive bits of 1 are encountered, the signal unit error rate monitor enters an "Octet-Counting" mode. However, the search continues for the next valid flag. To leave this "Octet-Counting" mode, a correctly checked MSU must be received and accepted.

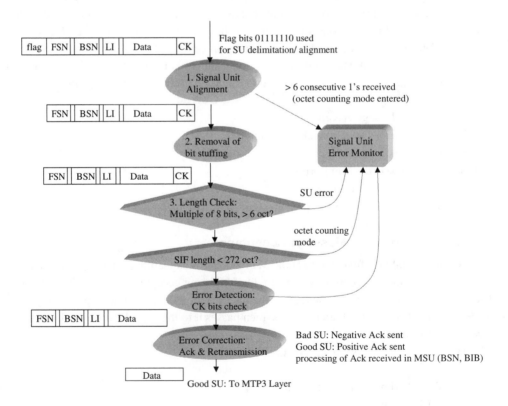

Figure 2-9   Signal Unit Message Acceptance

Stage 2 involves the removal of the previously "bit-stuffed" zeros once the signal unit's opening and closing flags have been identified and removed. Recall that prior to appending the flags, zeros were inserted by the transmitting node to ensure that the signal unit data does not contain the flag sequence.

Stage 3 of MTP2 Message Acceptance involves checking the length of the received signal unit. The error rate monitor is notified of an error if the length is not a multiple of 8 bits or is not greater than 6 octets. If the signal information field is greater than 272 octets, the Octet-Counting mode is entered. The LI bit is used to differentiate between an FISU, LSSU, or MSU, so that the signal units can be routed to the appropriate subsystems for further processing. Note that only LSSUs are processed within MTP2 layer, and all accepted MSUs are passed to MTP3. Because FISUs are only used to monitor the signaling link and to acknowledge other messages, they are never passed to MTP3.

The final step in the signal unit acceptance process involves the Signal Unit Error Detection and Correction function, which is discussed in detail in the next section. At the received node, the 16 CKs are computed independently, using the same error-detection function used at the transmit node. The computed CKs are compared with the received CKs and, if the CKs match, a positive acknowledgment is sent. Any discrepancies are interpreted as an error in transmission. If an error is detected, the Error Rate Monitor is notified, and a negative acknowledgment is sent to the remote end. Following an error, the Signal Unit Error Correction function is invoked.

2.4.2 Signal Unit Error Detection and Correction

The purpose of the Signal Unit Error Detection and Correction function is to ensure that signal unit errors are detected and corrected before they are accepted by MTP2 and passed to higher layers. Once transmission errors in the received MSUs are detected by the Signal Unit Error Detection function, the Signal Unit Error Correction function is triggered. FISUs and LSSUs do not undergo Error Correction, because these signal units do not contain user information.

To perform Signal Unit Error Detection, the transmitting node computes the CKs, using signal unit bits after the flag and before the 2 octet CKs. The receiving node performs the same computation and compares the result with the CKs received in the message. An inconsistency in the CKs is assumed to be caused by an error in transmission, and the signal unit is discarded. A negative acknowledgment is then sent to the remote end, and, Signal Unit Error Correction is performed. The signal unit error rate is monitored by MTP2, and layer 3 is notified if a predetermined threshold is exceeded.

Two methods of Signal Unit Error Correction are available. The Basic Method applies to signaling links using terrestrial transmissions, and the Preventive Cyclic Retransmission method applies to satellite-based transmissions. Because the vast majority of A-Interfaces utilize terrestrial resources, only the Basic Method is described here.

The Basic Method of Signal Unit Error Correction is a noncompelled, positive/negative acknowledgement, retransmission technique. Signal unit acknowledgement is done through the use forward and backward sequence numbers and forward and backward indicator bits (FSN, BSN, FIB, BIB [see Figure 2-4]). Retransmissions are requested by the receiving node through use of the forward and backward indicator bits FIB and BIB. The exchange of messages is non-compelled, meaning that the transmitting end may send messages before receiving acknowledgements for previously transmitted messages. This Error Correction method also ensures that MSUs are delivered in sequence, without duplications.

Each signaling node uniquely identifies a transmitted signal unit using an FSN. Because 7 bits are allocated for the FSN, 128 messages can be uniquely identified by layer 2. The FSN is incremented by 1 for each transmission. All transmitted messages are stored in a buffer at the transmitting end, known as the *retransmission buffer*, making them available for retransmission if needed. Messages remain in the retransmission buffer until they are positively acknowledged by the adjacent node. In the subsequent description, note that the *transmitter* refers to the original sender of the MSU, and *adjacent node* refers to the receiving end.

The BSN field is used by the adjacent node to indicate to the transmitter which message is being acknowledged. All message types, FISUs, LSSUs, and MSUs, may be used to acknowledge messages.

The BIB is a single status bit used by the adjacent node to indicate to the transmitter whether the acknowledgment is positive or negative. The FIB sent from the transmitter and the BIB sent from the receiver are used together to indicate a positive or negative acknowlegment.

The FIB is a single status bit that is sent along with the FSN field by the transmitting signaling point. This FIB value is a token, which, when received by the adjacent node, is returned by the adjacent node to inform the transmitting node whether the MSU was received correctly. To indicate a positive acknowledgment, the adjacent node puts the same FIB token value in the BIB and returns it to the transmitting node. At the transmitter, the node compares this received BIB to it's stored latest transmitted FIB. If the two are the same, the message corresponding to the received BSN is designated as having been positively acknowledged and is no longer available for retransmission. More than one MSU may be acknowledged if the received BSN is greater than the FSN, modulo 128, of previously transmitted but not yet acknowledged MSUs.

In the example in Figure 2-10, the first MSU sent by node A has an FSN=10 and a FIB=1, and is positively acknowledged by node B with an MSU having a BSN=10 and a BIB=1. When A receives this positive acknowledgment, it removes the MSU with FSN=10 from its retransmission buffer.

To indicate a negative acknowledgment, the adjacent node toggles the FIB token value received in the message that it wishes to acknowledge negatively, then sends the toggled token value in the BIB field to the transmitter. The BSN of this message is set to the value of the FSN corresponding to the last accepted signal unit at the adjacent node. The original transmitting node, upon receiving this message, compares the received BIB with its last transmitted FIB and determines that the acknowledgment is negative. The node then retransmits all available MSUs with FSNs greater than (modulo 128) the received BSN.

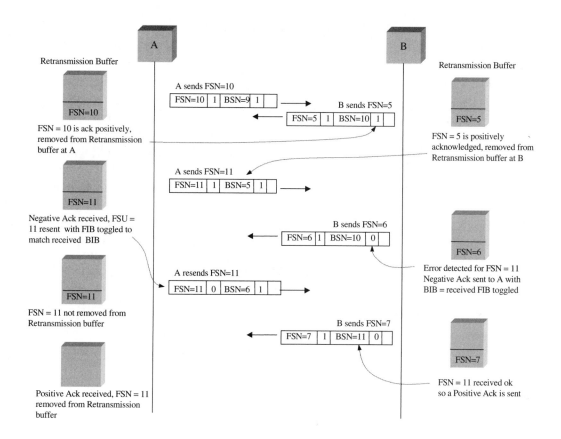

Figure 2-10   Signal Unit Error Detection and Correction

In the example in Figure 2-10, the second MSU sent by node A with FSN = 11 and FIB = 1 is corrupted during transmission. Node B returns an MSU with a BSN = 10 (the last accepted MSU) and a BIB = 0 (received FIB value toggled). When A receives this negative acknowledgment, it retransmits the MSU with FSN = 11, and sets the FIB = 0 to match the BIB that was received. This time, the MSU is accepted at node B, and a positive acknowledgment is returned to node A with BSN = 11 and BIB = 0 (matches received FIB).

In addition to CK errors, irregularities in the received FSN, BSN, or FIB may also trigger retransmissions.

Two conditions may result in a receiving node determining that a received signal unit contains an invalid FSN. In both cases, the received signal unit is simply discarded and a negative acknowledgment is sent. The first FSN error condition deals with FISUs. Because FSNs are not incremented for FISU transmissions, a FISU containing an FSN different from the last accepted signal is determined by the receiving node to be invalid. An MSU with an incorrect FSN may also trigger an error. If the FSN of a received MSU is not 1 more than the last accepted signal unit, the message is discarded and negatively acknowledged.

Errors found in the received FIB value will also cause the message to be discarded and a negative acknowledgment to be sent. If the FSN of a received MSU is one more than the last accepted signal unit but the FIB does not match the last transmitted BIB, an error is detected. Under normal nonerror transmissions, the FSN is incremented by 1, and the FIB should be set to the same token value as the received BIB from the remote end. However, unlike FSN errors, two of three received signal units with incorrect FIBs will result in the link being taken out of service. If this occurs, the receiving node notifies the remote end of its local link state by transmitting LSSUs with the link SF set to SIOS.

An incorrectly received BSN also results in the message being discarded and a negative acknowledgement being sent. Similar to the FIB error case, two of three received signal units with incorrect BSNs will result in the link being taken out of service. A received BSN that does not match any message in the local node's retransmission buffer is considered an error.

2.4.3   Signaling Link Initial Alignment

When a node first performs power-up initialization or during the recovery of a failed signaling link, the Signaling Link Initial Alignment procedure is used by MTP2 to bring a link into service. MTP3 sends a "start" indication to layer 2 to initiate the link alignment.

During the Signaling Link Alignment procedure, LSSUs are used to exchange link status information between 2 adjacent signaling points. The FSN and BSN fields of these LSSUs are normally set to 127, and the FIB and BIB bits are set to 1. The following status indications are used as part of the initial alignment procedure:

- *Out of Service* (SIOS): Sent when the local node is unable to process signal units.
- *Out of Alignment* (SIO): Sent when the local node has entered initial alignment but has not received an SIO, SIN, or SIE from the remote end.
- *Normal Alignment* (SIN): Sent to indicate that Normal Proving is being used to validate the alignment.
- *Emergency Alignment* (SIE): Sent to indicate Emergency Proving is being used to validate the alignment.

In the discussion of Signaling Link Initial Alignment procedure, the "Link State" is used to specify the actual state of the signaling link, and the "Initial Alignment State" is used to specify the state of the Initial Link Alignment process.

As shown in Figure 2-11, when a link is first powered up, LSSUs with link status indication SIOS are sent. At this point, the Link State is "Out of Service," and the Initial Alignment State is considered "Idle." SIOSs are continuously sent by layer 2 until a "Start" indication is received from MTP3.

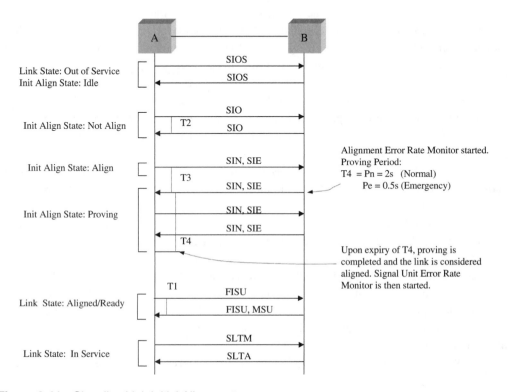

Figure 2-11 Signaling Link Initial Alignment

Once initial alignment has started, the Initial Alignment State transitions from Idle to the "Not-Aligned" state. Layer 2 begins sending LSSUs with status indication SIO, starts timer T2, and waits for an SIO, SIN, or SIE to be received from the remote end. When such LSSUs are received, the Initial Alignment State transitions to the "Align" state, and timer T2 is stopped.

At this point, the local terminal responds to the received SIO, SIN, or SIE with either an SIN or SIE, depending on the status of other signaling links between the two signaling points. The local terminal also starts timer T3. Upon receipt of an SIN or SIE from the remote end, the timer T3 is stopped, and the Initial Alignment State transitions to "Proving."

The Proving period is a duration whereby the integrity of the link is monitored before bringing the link into full service. The alignment procedure includes either a "Normal" or "Emergency" proving period, depending on the status of other signaling links between the two signaling points. MTP3 requests an Emergency Alignment if no other signaling links between the two signaling points are in service. Normal Alignment is requested when at least one other link is in service. The main difference between the two alignment types is the length of the proving period, which is specified by timer T4. The Emergency Alignment proving period is 0.5 seconds, and the Normal Alignment period is 2 seconds.

During the Proving period, the integrity of the link is monitored for errors. The Initial Alignment State transitions from "Aligned" to "Proving" after the Alignment Error Rate Monitor parameters are loaded and the proving period timer, T4, is started. LSSUs of SINs or SIEs are exchanged between the two adjacent nodes during this period.

Note that the link status indication SIN or SIE refers to the status of the links at the transmitting signaling point and is not changed based on the link status indication being received from the remote end. For example, if SIN is being sent by the local terminal and SIE is received from the remote end, the local node will continue to send SIN. However, an Emergency Proving period will be used at the local terminal.

If the number of link errors is below a predefined threshold at the end of the Proving period (when timer T4 expires), the link alignment is considered complete. The Link State then enters the "Aligned/Ready" state.

Once the link is aligned and in the "Aligned/Ready" Link State, FISUs are sent to the remote end, and the timer T1 is started to wait for a layer 2 acknowledgment. Upon receipt of a FISU or MSU from the remote end, the Link State at the local terminal enters the "In-Service" state, and the timer T1 is stopped. The link is now considered to be fully activated and can begin transmitting and receiving MSUs. Note that timer T1 is chosen so that four proving attempts can be performed. Once in the "In-Service" Link State, signaling link test messages, which are discussed in Section 2.5.9, "Signaling Link Test and Maintenance," on page 86, are exchanged between the two nodes to maintain link integrity.

In Section 2.7, "Bringing up a Signaling System 7 Link," on page 136, an example of a complete Signaling Link Alignment procedure, including bringing up the MTP2, MTP3, and SCCP layers, is described.

2.4.4   Signaling Link Error Monitoring

The Signaling Link Error Monitoring function is used for monitoring the error rates of a signaling link to ensure the integrity of the link and to notify MTP2 and MTP3 to take appropriate actions when the error thresholds are exceeded.

Two techniques are used by MTP2 to monitor signal link error rates, depending on the state of the link. The "Alignment Error Rate Monitor" method is used during the Signaling Link Initial Alignment process, which also includes link restoration. The second method, "Signal Unit Error Rate Monitor," is used for counting signal unit errors that are detected during the layer 2 Message Acceptance process. Immediately after a successful link alignment, the "Signal Unit Error Monitor" method is used to evaluate the quality of the link.

Alignment Error Rate Monitor (AERM)   During the Signaling Link Initial Alignment process, signal unit errors are simply counted for a specified time, known as the *Proving period*, as described in the previous section, "Signaling Link Initial Alignment," on page 44. This counter is set to zero whenever the Proving period is entered. If the number of detected errors exceeds the predetermined threshold before the Proving period expires, layer 3 is notified of the alignment failure. The Error Threshold and Proving period are set, based on the type of alignment requested, which can be "Normal" or "Emergency," as shown in Table 2-2.

In addition to the Proving period error monitoring, if an error is detected any time in the incoming bit stream, such as more than seven consecutive 1s being received, the Octet-Counting mode is entered. While in Octet-Counting mode, the AERM is incremented once for every N received octets until a correctly checked signal unit is detected.

Table 2-2   Alignment Error Rate Monitor

Alignment Type	Proving Period T4	Error Threshold
"Normal"	$T4_n = 2^{14}$ octets (2.0 seconds for 64 kbits/sec)	$T_{in} = 4$ bad signal units
"Emergency"	$T4_e = 2^{12}$ octets (0.5 seconds for 64 kbits/sec)	$T_{ie} = 1$ bad signal unit

Signal Unit Error Rate Monitor (SUERM)   In the SUERM, a "leaky-bucket" technique is used to monitor errors associated with an already-aligned signaling link. The error counter starts at zero when the link is first brought into service and is incremented every time a signal unit error is encountered. The following errors cause the error counter to be incremented:

- Signal unit is not a multiple of 8 bits
- Signal unit is not greater than 6 octets
- SIF is greater than 272 octets (Octet-Counting mode entered)
- CKs are incorrect

In the case when an Octet-Counting mode is entered, the error counter is incremented once for every N received octets until a correctly checking signal unit is detected. Recall that the Octet-Counting mode is entered when the SIF field is greater than 272 octets, or when there are more than six consecutive 1s during flag detection.

Unlike the AERM, the SUERM counter is decremented for every D consecutive error-free signal units received. If the error counter exceeds the predetermined threshold T, layer 3 is notified of a link failure. The error counter behavior is depicted in Figure 2-12.

The ANSI SS7 standard specifies the values of *T*, *D*, and *N* as follows:

- *T* = 64 signal units
- *D* = 256 signal units per signal unit error
- *N* = 16 octets

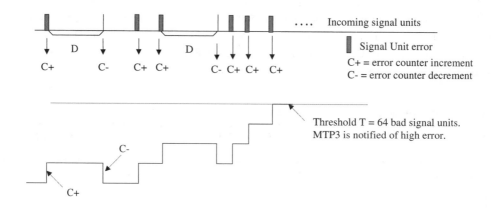

Figure 2-12   Signal Unit Error Rate Monitor

2.4.5   Processor Outage

A Processor Outage occurs when functional problems at levels greater than level 2 make a link unusable. For example, a processor error at the application layer may make it impossible to process messages at the higher layers, but layer 2 and 3 processing may be unaffected. MTP2 then performs the Processor Outage procedure to ensure that the adjacent node is informed, and normal operation can resume when the outage is cleared. Note that the detection of a Local Processor Outage is implementation-specific. Figure 2-13 shows the call flow for a Processor Outage condition.

Upon detecting a Local Processor Outage, layer 3 notifies layer 2 of the condition. Layer 2 subsequently transmits LSSUs with status indication SIPO to the remote signaling point and rejects incoming MSUs. During the Local Processor Outage, timers T5, T6, and T7 are suspended (see Section 2.4.7, "MTP2 Timers," on page 51).

At the remote signaling point, MTP2 notifies MTP3 of the Remote Processor Outage and begins transmitting FISUs. The FISUs are used to acknowledge message signal units that were previously accepted but not yet acknowledged.

The Local Processor Outage is cleared when layer 3 notifies layer 2 to resume normal operation or when layer 3 requests the layer 2 retransmission buffer to be cleared. If layer 3 informs layer 2 to resume normal operation, message signal units are accepted from the remote end, and message transmission restarts. The first such transmitted message acknowledges all messages previously accepted from the remote end before the Local Processor Outage condition occurred.

At the remote end, the Remote Processor Outage is cleared when a signal unit is correctly received by layer 2 or when layer 3 requests the MTP2 retransmission buffer to be cleared.

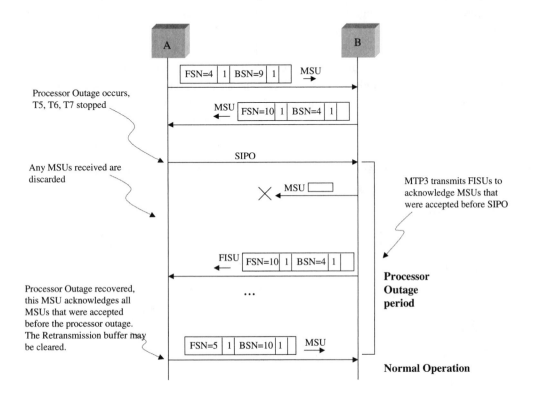

Figure 2-13 Processor Outage Procedure

2.4.6 MTP2 Flow Control (Congestion Control)

Congestion occurs when the receiving signaling point receives more MSUs than it can process and is, therefore, unable to accept incoming MSUs. At MTP2, the congested signaling point sends LSSUs with status indication Busy (SIB) and stops acknowledging MSUs. The mechanism for Congestion Detection and Abatement is a layer 2 implementation specific function. Layer 3 network management is notified when link congestion occurs and when it ceases. Figure 2-14 shows the call flow for a level 2 Flow Control when congestion occurs.

When congestion is detected at signaling point A, layer 2 withholds acknowledgment of MSUs and begins sending LSSUs with status indication SIB at T5 intervals. In order not to disrupt the message flow between the local congested node A and the remote node B, MSUs and

FISUs are sent from the congested end as usual but with BSN and BIB corresponding to the last acknowledged signal unit before congestion was detected.

Upon receipt of an LSSU with status indication SIB, the remote end, B, restarts the excessive delay of acknowledgment timer T7. This is because node A withholds acknowledgments to B during this congestion period and would cause the link to be taken out of service unnecessarily if T7 expires. The remote congestion timer T6 is started while waiting for the remote congestion condition to abate. Node B also reduces or stops sending MSUs to A.

When the conditions that triggered congestion control at the local node A cease, layer 2 continues the normal process of message acknowledgment. At the remote end B, the remote Congestion Abatement is indicated upon receiving an acknowledgment for an MSU in its retransmission buffer, and timer T6 is stopped. If, instead, congestion continues, expiry of timer T6 will cause the congested link to be taken out of service by the remote end.

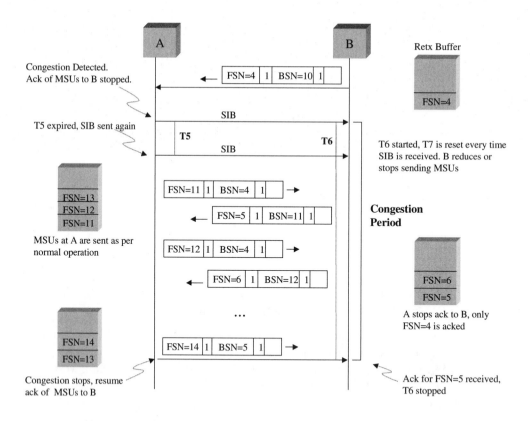

Figure 2-14   MTP2 Flow Control

2.4.7 MTP2 Timers

Table 2-3 summarizes ANSI MTP2 timers, the ranges specified in T1.111 [5], and the recommended values used in the industry. ANSI MTP2 timers include timers T1 to T8; however, T8 is used for high-speed 1.536-Mbps links and will not be discussed. Individual timer descriptions and call flows follow Table 2-3.

Table 2-3 MTP2 Timers

Timer	Range	Recomme- ded Values	Description
T1	12.9–16 s	13 s	Link State "Aligned/Ready" to "In-Service" timer (FISU → FISU, MSU)
T2	5–14 s	11.5 s	Init alignment state "Not-Aligned" timer (SIO → SIO, SIN, SIE)
T3	5–14 s	11.5 s	Init alignment state "Aligned" timer (SIN/SIE → SIN/SIE)
T4	Normal = 2.0 s Emergency = 0.5 s	P_n = 2.0 s P_e = 0.5 s	Proving period timer
T5	80–120 ms	100 ms	Retransmit SIB timer during congestion
T6	1–6 s	3 s	Remote congestion timer
T7	0.5–2 s	1 s	Excessive delay of acknowledgment timer
T8	100 ms	-	Interval timer for errored interval monitor Used for 1.536 Mbps link only

T1—Link State "Aligned/ Ready" Timer   This timer is started immediately after link alignment has been completed ("Aligned/Ready" link state) and is stopped upon receipt of an MSU or FISU, which transistions the link to the "In-Service" state. Timer T1 is used to indicate an error in the alignment process at the remote terminal or an error with the signaling link soon after alignment. If T1 expires, the link is taken out of service (Figure 2-15).

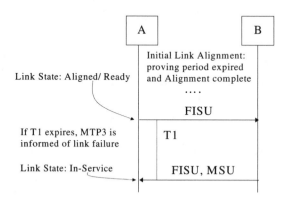

Figure 2-15   MTP2 Timer T1

T2—Initial Alignment State "Not-Aligned" Timer   This timer is used in the initial link alignment process. Timer T2 is started after layer 3 initiates link alignment, and SIOs are transmitted by the local node (the Initial Alignment state is in the "Not-Aligned" state). The timer is stopped upon receipt of an SIO, SIN, or SIE. If T2 expires, layer 3 is notified that alignment is not possible, and the alignment process is halted and restarted (Figure 2-16).

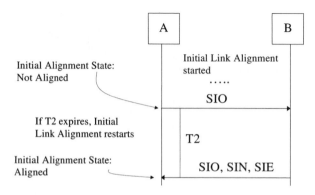

Figure 2-16   MTP2 Timer T2

T3—Initial Alignment State "Aligned" Timer This timer is used in the initial link alignment process and is started immediately after the local terminal begins sending SINs or SIEs (the Initial Alignment state is in the "Aligned" state). Timer T3 is stopped upon receipt of an SIN or SIE. If T3 expires, layer 3 is notified that alignment is not possible, and the alignment process is halted and restarted (Figure 2-17).

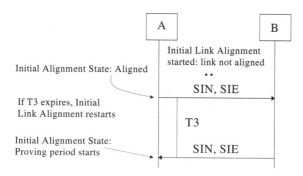

Figure 2-17 MTP2 Timer T3

T4—Initial Alignment State "Proving Period" Timer This timer is used in the initial link alignment process and is started when the Proving state in entered. While in the Proving state, signal unit errors are monitored by the AERM. If timer T4 expires before the AERM exceeds the error rate threshold, link alignment is complete. The value of T4 depends on the alignment requested by layer 3 and the physical layer data rates (56 kbps or 64 kbps). For a 64 kbps link, T4 is set to 2 seconds for Normal Alignment and 0.5 seconds for Emergency Alignment (Figure 2-18).

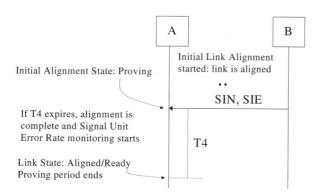

Figure 2-18 MTP2 Timer T4

T5—Retransmit SIB Timer During Congestion   This timer is used in layer 2 flow control. T5 timer is started when congestion at a signaling point is detected. Upon expiry of T5, LSSUs with status indication SIB are sent to the remote node, and T5 is restarted. Timer T5 remains active as long as congestion persists. Because the congested signaling point suspends message acknowledgments, SIBs are used to reset timer T7 (Excessive Delay of Acknowledgment timer) at the receiving end (Figure 2-19).

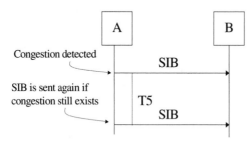

Figure 2-19   MTP2 Timer T5

T6—Remote Congestion Timer   This timer is used for layer 2 flow control. Timer T6 is started when congestion at a remote terminal is detected through the reciept of a SIB. This timer is stopped when either a positive or negative acknowledgment is received for a message in the retransmission buffer. MTP3 is notified of a link failure if timer T6 expires (Figure 2-20).

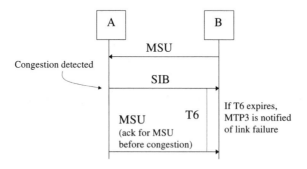

Figure 2-20   MTP2 Timer T6

T7—Excessive Delay of Acknowledgement Timer   Timer T7 is started whenever an MSU is sent and is stopped when a positive or negative acknowledgment is received. Upon T7 expiry, layer 3 is notified of a link failure (Figure 2-21).

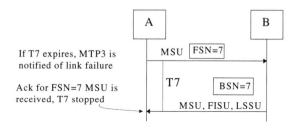

Figure 2-21   MTP2 Timer T7

2.5 MTP3 Layer

The function of the MTP3 layer is to provide the Network Management and Message Distribution functions required of a signaling point. Whereas MTP2 is responsible for individual links, MTP3 is responsible for the signaling network. As shown in Figure 2-22, the functions of MTP3 can be categorized into two main areas:

• Signaling Message Handling
• Signaling Network Management

MTP3 Signaling Message Handling functions are responsible for identifying messages destined for its own node and distributing messages to other entities. MTP3 Signaling Network Management functions provide MTP3 with the ability to maintain a signaling connection in the event of failures or network disruptions. For example, messages may be rerouted from a failed link to an alternate link to maintain an existing call connection. Signaling Network Management also includes the management of signaling link states.

2.5.1   Signaling Message Handling

The three primary functions of MTP3 Signaling Message Handling include:

• *Message Discrimination* of incoming messages, based on Routing Label
• *Message Distribution* of incoming messages, based on Service Indicator (SI) field
• *Message Routing* of outgoing messages

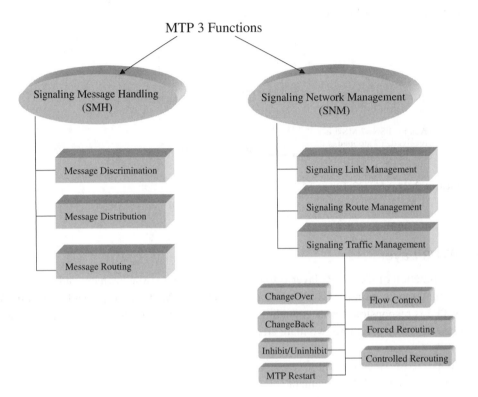

Figure 2-22   MTP3 functions

As incoming messages are received from MTP2, the layer 3 Message Discrimination function examines the Routing Label of the incoming message to determine whether it is destined for the local node. The Message Distribution function of MTP3 distributes the message to the appropriate level 3 entity, based on the information contained in the *Service Indicator* (SI) field. The *Destination Point Code* (DPC) and the Routing Table are used by the Message Routing function to determine the link and linkset to be used for transmission. MTP3 is also responsible for load sharing outgoing messages when more than one link is available.

To fully understand how MTP3 message discrimination, distribution, and routing works, it is first important to understand the structure of the *Message Signal Unit* (MSU).

2.5.1.1   MSU Message Structure

Figure 2-23 illustrates the structure of an MSU, focusing on the fields used by MTP3 for Message Handling. Although Figure 2-23 shows all MSU fields, recall that the flag, BSN, BIB, FSN, FIB, LI, and CK are removed by MTP2. Only the SIO and the SIF are used by layer 3. Table 2-4 summarizes these MSU common fields.

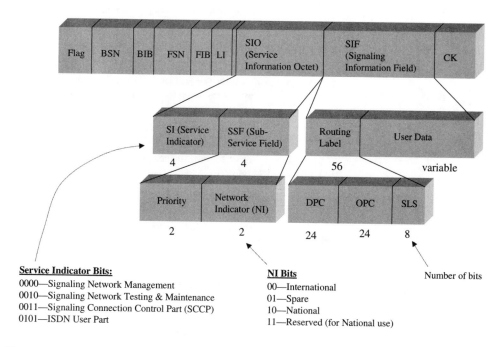

Figure 2-23   Message Signal Unit general message structure

The SIO consists of two parts, the *Sub-Service Field* (SSF) and the *Service Indicator* (SI). In the case of a signaling point processing both international and national SS7 messages, the two *Network Indicator* (NI) bits of the 4-bit SSF may be used to determine numbering schemes and possibly, the label structure. To specify an international message, NI bits of *00* or *01* are used. For National messages, NI bits of *10* or *11* is used. If the NI bits are set to National, the 2 spare bits can be used for indicating the Message Priority, with levels from 0 to 3.

The 4-bit SI portion of the SIO specifies how MTP3 should distribute the message. For example, if the SI bits are set to 0011, the MTP3 Message Distribution function will send the message to the SCCP layer for further processing. In the case of Signaling Network Management and Signaling Test and Maintenance messages, the messages are processed within MTP3 Signaling Network Management functions. The ISDN User Part indicator is not used for the A-Interface.

Table 2-4   Common Fields in an Message Signal Unit Message Structure

Bitmap	Parameter	#Oct	Range
nnpp SSSS	Service Information Octet (SIO)	1	n = NI—Network Indicator 00—International 01—Spare (for International use) 10—National 11—Reserved (for National use) Set to National for the A-Interface. p = priority—Set from 0 to 3, depending on message types. Applicable only if NI = national S = SI—Service Indicator (SI) This is used by MTP3 Message Distribution function for routing the messages to the appropriate subsystem for further processing. 0000—Signaling Network Management 0010—Signaling Network Testing & Maintenance 0011—Signaling Connection Control Part 0101—ISDN User Part
dddd dddd dddd dddd dddd dddd oooo oooo oooo oooo oooo oooo ssss ssss	Signaling Information Field (SIF)— Routing Label	7	d = DPC—Destination Point Code o = OPC—Origination Point Code In US National Network, the point codes are: Network Member—8 bits Network Cluster—8 bits Network ID—8 bits s = SLS—Signaling Link Selection This is used for load sharing purposes. An SLS value is chosen by the sender and is mapped to a physical link within a linkset.
DDDD DDDD DDDD DDDD	Signaling Information Field (SIF)— User Data	SIF = 8n, n ≥ 2 Min = 16 Max = 272	SIF—User Data User Data is dependent on the type of SI, which is described further in the following sections.

The SIF consists of the Routing Label and User Application Data. In a US National Network, the Routing Label is a 56-bit value that comprises the *Destination Point Code* (DPC), the

Origination Point Code (OPC), and the *Signaling Link Selection* (SLS). In ANSI SS7, the DPC and OPC are each coded as a 24-bit value comprising the Network Member, Network Cluster and Network ID. The point codes are used to identify a specific network node uniquely. The SLS is an 8-bit value used for load-sharing purposes when selecting an outgoing link.

The SIF User Data portion contains application-specific data, depending on the type of message. As is discussed in later sections, this information is coded with specific headers for MTP3 SNM messages, Signaling Test and Maintenance messages, and SCCP-type messages.

2.5.1.2   Message Discrimination and Distribution

The Message Discrimination Function is invoked for incoming messages handling. The Routing Label's DPC is checked to determine whether the receiving node is the final destination. If so, the message is sent to the Message Distribution function for further MTP3 processing. If the DPC does not match the receiving node and the signaling point has transfer capabilities, the message is sent to the MTP3 Message Routing function for transmission to the network.

Because the International and National SS7 message formats differ slightly, the NI bits in the SSF of the SIO are examined to determine the network type from which the message originated. In the case of a US National Network, the 2-bit priority field within the SSF is also processed. A high priority is assigned to MTP and SCCP messages that are critical to signaling network operations.

After the Message Discrimination function determines that the message is destined for the receiving node, the Message Distribution function is invoked. This function determines whether the message is to be passed to a layer 4 application, such as SCCP, or to another MTP3 function. As mentioned earlier, the distribution decision is based on the value of the 4-bit SI field contained in the SIO.

2.5.1.3   Message Routing and Load Sharing

Based on the DPC field contained in the Routing Label and a predefined MTP3 Routing Table, the MTP3 Message Routing function determines which Signaling Link Set (or Combined Link Set) the outgoing message is to be sent over. Also contained in the Routing Label is the SLS field, which is used to determine the link within the link set to be used for transmission.

The MTP3 Routing Table is a lookup table specifying outgoing Routes for every DPC to which this node is capable of routing messages. Each DPC entry has a set of available Routes, where each Route consists of a Link Set or Combined Link Set field. These route entries are usually configured by the network operator prior to bringing up the SS7 links. In general, SS7 allows more than one route to be configured for routing messages to a DPC. However, because the A-Interface network is specified to be a point-to-point connection, only one Link Set (route) is used for routing messages between the MSC and BSC.

An outgoing Link Set is usually selected based solely on the DPC and the predefined Routing Table, but there are several cases when information beyond the Routing Label is used, such as:

- Some Network Management messages require special handling. For example, Signaling Link Test messages must be routed over the link to which they refer.
- Signaling points handling both national and international messages may use the NI field to check the structure of the Routing Label point codes.
- Routing based on information in the SCCP layer may also be used. For example, although not used for the A-Interface, Global Title Translation may be used in SS7 networks that contain STPs.

After a Link Set is selected for an outgoing message, a load-sharing technique is used to chose a particular link within the Link Set. All signaling nodes load share messages that are at the same priority between links (or link sets) to the same destination. The objective of load sharing is to distribute outgoing signaling message traffic evenly over individual links within a single Link Set or a Combined Link Set. In the case of a Combined Link Set, load sharing across Link Sets is also performed.

Load sharing of messages between links within a Link Set or Combined Link Set is accomplished using the 8-bit SLS field contained in the Routing Label. The SLS value is provided by a user of the MTP, such as the SCCP or *ISDN User Part* (ISUP). Under normal routing conditions, layer 3 associates each SLS code with a Link Set and an individual Signaling Link. When a link or route fails, layer 3 reassigns the SLS codes to one of the remaining links or Link Sets.

Both 5-bit and 8-bit SLS codes are allowed, but the 8-bit code is preferred because of its ability to distribute traffic more evenly. Load sharing using a 5-bit SLS is identical to the 8-bit case, with the three most significant bits assumed to be zero.

In an SS7 network containing STPs, the SLS value that is transmitted in an MSU is further processed at a receiving STP node. If a received MSU is required to be transferred and the receiving signaling point has transfer capabilities (STP), the received SLS is again used to determine the next outgoing link for message transmission. Note that the SLS value at a signaling point is processed prior to transmission. One common load-sharing technique used to ensure that the SLS information used at subsequent signaling points is independent of information used at previous signaling points is the Bit Rotation technique. Bit Rotation involves rotating the five least significant bits of the SLS prior to transmitting the message (see T1.111 [5]). In a typical A-Interface point-to-point network, SLS Bit Rotation has no effect on message transmission because no STPs exist.

2.5.2 Signaling Network Management

Signaling Network Management (SNM) provides MTP3 with the ability to maintain or restore signaling services in the event of network disruptions. The three categories of SNM functions are:

1. Signaling Link Management
2. Signaling Route Management
3. Signaling Traffic Management

Signaling Link Management is used for the control of signaling link status through activating, deactivating, and restoring signaling links.

Signaling Route Management is used for the distribution of network status information throughout the network for routing purposes.

Signaling Traffic Management uses flow control and traffic diversion to control the signaling traffic flow over links between two adjacent nodes and over routes in an SS7 network.

2.5.2.1 Signaling Link Management

Signaling Link Management is the MTP3 SNM function that controls the status of the local signaling links and includes:

- Signaling Link Activation
- Signaling Link Restoration
- Signaling Link Deactivation
- Signaling Link Set Activation

Signaling Link Activation is the procedure of bringing a link into an "In-Service" Link State, using the Signaling Link Initial Alignment procedure, so that it can be used to carry user traffic. Signaling Link Activation may be performed explicitly by the operator to bring up an inactive link or may be invoked when an alternate link is to be brought into service after the original link goes out of service. Once the link is brought into service, the Signaling Link Test is started at periodic intervals to maintain the integrity of the link. This test involves the exchange of test messages known as *Signaling Link Test Message* (SLTM) and *Signaling Link Test Acknowledge* (SLTA) messages (see Section 2.5.9, "Signaling Link Test and Maintenance," on page 86). Once this test is successful, the link is considered to be "Available" and can continue to carry user traffic.

Signaling Link Restoration is the process of restoring a failed link after a failure condition is detected at the signaling link. Oscillation prevention procedures are implemented at MTP3 to prevent undesired oscillations between the "In-Service" and "Out of Service" states. These procedures involve the setting of oscillation timers that provide delays, preventing rapid link restoration when a failure occurs immediately after link alignment.

Signaling Link Deactivation is the process of bringing a link into an unavailable state. This occurs when a link is taken out of service explicitly by the operator, typically for maintenance purposes or because of the occurrence of a failure or block condition.

Signaling Link Set Activation is performed to bring a Link Set into service if the corresponding links are not yet in the "In-Service" state.

The above link management functions are used to manage the state of a signaling link. A signaling link is always considered by layer 3 to either be "Available" or "Unavailable." There are seven possible states of an Unavailable link, depending on the cause of unavailability. Possible causes of unavailability are Failed, Deactivated, Blocked, or Inhibited. More than one cause may be associated with an unavailable link. Figure 2-24 shows the seven different states associated with an Unavailable link, some of which are combinations of the unavailable causes. The link state transitions occur when specific trigger conditions are met.

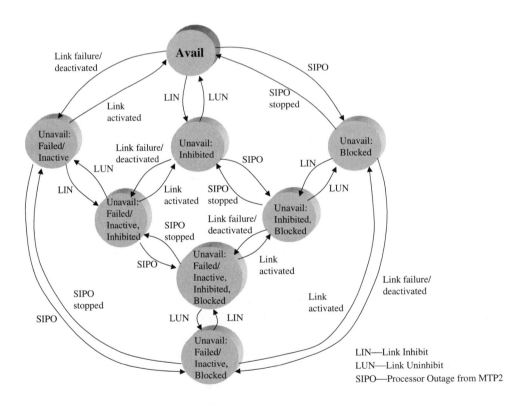

Figure 2-24 Signaling Link State transitions

A *Signaling Link Failure* transitions the state of a link to a "Failed" status. It typically occurs when a timer value expires during the course of Initial Link Alignment or when transmisson errors exceed an acceptable threshold (see Section 2.4.4, "Signaling Link Error Monitoring," on page 46). Recall that MTP2 is responsible for notifying layer 3 of a signaling link failure. Layer 3 also considers a link as Failed when it receives a Changeover request from a remote node. A failed signaling link is restored only after both connecting nodes complete the Initial Link Alignment process.

Signaling Link Deactivation transitions the state of a link to a "Deactivated" status. It occurs when a Signaling Link management or external management, such as operations and maintenance, explicitly deactivate the link. A deactivated Signaling Link is activated only after both ends complete the Initial Link Alignment process.

Signaling Link Blocking transitions the state of a link to a "Blocked" status. It occurs when layer 3 blocks a signaling link, due to a Processor Outage notification received from the remote end. A blocked link is unblocked when the processor outage at the remote end no longer exists.

Signaling Link Inhibiting transitions the state of a link to an "Inhibited" state. It occurs when a Signaling Link is locally or remotely inhibited by a management function. Layer 3 remotely inhibits a signaling link when a Link Inhibit request is received from a remote end. A link is designated *Locally Inhibited* only after the remote end acknowledges a previously transmitted Inhibit request. A link is Uninhibited when a Link Uninhibit request is received from the remote end or when an acknowledgment for a previously transmitted Uninhibit request is received. This topic is discussed further in Section 2.5.5, "Traffic Management: Inhibit/Uninhibit," on page 73.

2.5.2.2   Signaling Route Management

The Signaling Route Management function is used for ensuring a reliable transfer of messages between connecting signaling points. Information regarding the network status of Signaling Routes is communicated to other concerned nodes using Signaling Route Management messages. A Signaling Route is considered by MTP3 to be either Available, Restricted, Unavailable, Congested, or Uncongested.

Because the A-Interface network is a point-to-point network with only one route and one Link Set connecting the MSC and BSC, the Route Management functions are not typically used.

2.5.2.3   Signaling Traffic Management

The Signaling Traffic Management function is invoked when there is a need to redirect signaling traffic from a link or route to one or more other links or routes, due to failures, activations, or restorations of signaling links. In the case of a congested signaling point, the Signaling Traffic Management function may also be used to reduce traffic temporarily. The following procedures are used as part of Signaling Traffic Management:

- Changeover
- Changeback
- Management Inhibiting/Uninhibiting
- MTP Restart
- Signaling Traffic Flow Control
- Forced Rerouting
- Controlled Rerouting

The first two procedures listed, Changeover and Changeback, are used to divert signaling traffic from one signaling link to another if a link becomes unavailability due to a *Failed*, *Blocked*, or *Inhibited* condition. Signaling traffic is diverted back to the original link once it again becomes available.

The Management Inhibiting/Uninhibiting procedure is used when there is a need to inhibit or uninhibit the usage of a link, typically for maintenance purposes.

MTP Restart is used for controlling the availability of a link to a signaling point when it first comes into service. Although this procedure is not required for A-Interface implementation, it is briefly described in Section 2.5.6, "Traffic Management: MTP Restart," on page 81.

The Signaling Traffic Flow Control, Forced Rerouting, and Controlled Rerouting procedures are mostly associated with the control of traffic on routes between a local signaling point and the SS7 network. These procedures are typically used only when multiple routes (via STPs) to a destination node exist. In an A-Interface point-to-point network, there is little or no use for such functions, because only one route with one Link Set is used for connecting the MSC to the BSC. However, a brief description of these functions is given below and in Section 2.5.7, "Traffic Management: Flow Control," on page 85 and in Section 2.5.8, "Traffic Management: Forced/Controlled Rerouting," on page 85, for interested readers.

The Signaling Traffic Flow Control procedure is used for limiting traffic when congestion, overload, or network failure occurs for one or more routes to a destination. In a typical A-Interface network, only congestion control associated with a signaling point is applicable, which is mainly controlled by MTP2 Flow Control.

Forced and Controlled Rerouting procedures are used to divert traffic to an alternate route when an optimal route to a destination node is unavailable.

The use of each of these Traffic Management functions is described further in Sections 2.5.3 to 2.5.8.

2.5.3   Traffic Management: Changeover

The Changeover procedure is a Signaling Traffic Management function that is used to divert signaling traffic from a previously Available link whose state has changed to Unavailable. Depending on the network configuration, the diverted traffic may be sent to one or more Signaling Links within in the same Link Set or one or more different Link Sets. In an A-Interface point-to-point network that has only one Link Set, the traffic is diverted to an alternate signaling link within the same Link Set.

The Changeover procedure is initiated by Layer 3 when a Signaling Link fails, is inhibited, or is blocked. Once Changeover starts, transmission and acceptance of messages is halted on the unavailable link, LSSUs or FISUs are sent by layer 2 on that link, and an alternate Signaling Link is chosen.

A *Changeover Order* (COO) message is then sent on either link to the remote end point, and timer T2 is started while waiting for a *Changeover Acknowledge* (COA) from the remote end. Once the remote end responds with a COA message, timer T2 is stopped, and all traffic is diverted to the alternate link. An example of a Changeover and Changeback is discussed in Section 2.5.4.1, "Changeover/Changeback Example," on page 69.

Prior to signaling traffic being diverted to the alternate link, Buffer Updating of the retransmission buffer belonging to the unavailable link is accomplished by means of a handshake procedure. The procedure is based on the exchange of Changeover messages between the two end signaling points of the unavailable signaling link. The FSN of the last accepted MSU sent on the unavailable link is updated in the retransmission buffers at both end points. Once traffic is diverted to the alternate link, the MSUs that are pending acknowledgment on the unavailable link are then retransmitted to ensure in-sequence, reliable message delivery.

2.5.3.1   Time-Controlled Changeover

A Time-Controlled Changeover procedure is initiated when Changeover messages cannot be reliably exchanged or when the exchange is undesirable.

When a Time-Controlled Changeover occurs, timer T1 is started. Upon expiry of T1, the concerned signaling point starts sending traffic not yet transmitted over the unavailable signaling link on the alternate link. The purpose of the delay introduced by timer T1 is to help avoid or reduce missequencing of messages when Changeover occurs.

2.5.3.2   Changeover Message Structure

The format of the Changeover message is shown in Figure 2-25, and the SIF data fields are summarized in Table 2-5. The SI field of the SIO specifies an SNM message. The user data portion of the SIF contains heading codes H0 and H1, a Signaling Link Code, and the FSN of the last accepted MSU. Heading code H0 specifies the SNM message group, and heading code H1 identifies the Changeover message type, which includes the COO and COA. The SLC field identifies the SLC of the unavailable Signaling Link. The FSN field specifies the FSN of the last accepted message signal unit from the unavailable Signaling Link. The node receiving the Changeover message uses the transmitted FSN to update its retransmission buffer.

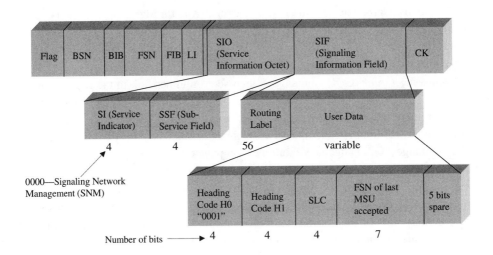

Figure 2-25   MTP3 Changeover message structure

Table 2-5   MTP3 Changeover Message Fields

Bitmap	Parameter	#Oct	Range
hhhh HHHH	Heading Code	1	H = Heading Code H0
			0001—Changeover/Changeback message
			0010—Emergency Changeover message
			0011—Transfer-controlled, Signaling-route-congestion-test
			0100—Transfer-prohibited/allowed/restricted message
			0101—Signaling-route-set-test message
			0110—Management inhibiting message
			0111—Traffic restart message
			1000—Signaling-data-link-connection message
			1010—MTP user flow control message
			h = Heading Code H1
			0001—Changeover Order signal (COO)
			0010—Changeover Ack signal (COA)
FFFF SSSS 0000 0FFF	Changeover SIF data	2	S = Signaling Link Code (SLC)
			Specifies the unavailable physical link.
			F = FSN of the last MSU Accepted

Figure 2-26 shows an example message log of a COO message. The heading code 0 is set to *0001*, signifying a Changeover/Changeback message type, and the heading code 1 of *0001* indicates a COO message. The FSN of the last accepted MSU is *100001,* or 33. The SLC of the unavailable link is 0.

```
-0101010  Backward Sequence Number      42
1-------  Backward Indicator Bit        1
-0101010  Forward Sequence Number       42
1-------  Forward Indicator Bit         1
--001011  Length Indicator              11
00------  Spare                         0
----0000  Service Indicator (SI)        Signaling network manage mess
--00----  Sub-Service: Priority         Spare/priority 0 (U.S.A. only)
10------  Sub-Service: Network Ind      National message
***B3***  Destination Point Code        001-001-001
***B3***  Originating Point Code        001-002-004
00000000  Signaling Link Code           0
Changeover Order
----0001  Heading code 0                1
0001----  Heading code 1                1
----0000  SLC                           0
0100001  FSN of last accepted MSU       33
```

Figure 2-26 MTP3 Changeover Order message example

Figure 2-27 shows an example message log of a COA message. As shown, the heading code 0 is *0001* signifying a Changeover/Changeback message type, and the heading code 1 of *0010* indicates a COA message. The FSN of the last accepted MSU in this direction is *100010,* or 34.

```
-0101010  Backward Sequence Number      42
1-------  Backward Indicator Bit        1
-0101010  Forward Sequence Number       42
1-------  Forward Indicator Bit         1
--001011  Length Indicator              11
00------  Spare                         0
----0000  Service Indicator (SI)        Signaling network manage mess
--00----  Sub-Service: Priority         Spare/priority 0 (U.S.A. only)
10------  Sub-Service: Network Ind      National message
***B3***  Destination Point Code        001-002-004
***B3***  Origination Point Code        001-001-001
00000000  Signaling Link Code           0
Changeover Ack
----0001  Heading code 0                1
0010----  Heading code 1                1
----0000  SLC                           0
0100010  FSN of last accepted MSU       34
```

Figure 2-27 MTP3 Changeover Acknowledge message example

2.5.4   Traffic Management: Changeback

The Changeback procedure is invoked to reverse the actions taken during the Changeover procedure. After the original signaling becomes available again, the Changeback procedure is used to divert traffic from the alternate Signaling Link back to the original Signaling Link. The alternate Signaling Link refers to the link that signaling traffic was diverted to during the Changeover procedure.

Changeback is initiated upon the restoration, unblocking, or uninhibiting of a previously unavailable signaling link. Changeback also may occur at the end of a MTP Restart procedure if multiple links are available at a signaling point.

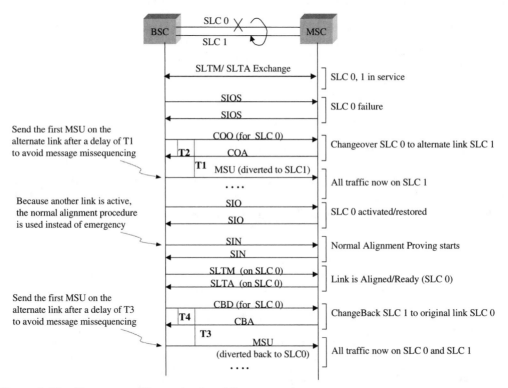

Figure 2-28   Changeover/Changeback call flow example

Upon initiation of the Changeback procedure, the concerned traffic on the alternate route is suspended, and new messages are stored in a Changeback buffer. A *Changeback Declaration* (CBD) message is sent to the remote end, and timer T4 is started while waiting for a *Changeback Acknowledge* (CBA) message. Upon receiving a CBA, timer T4 is stopped, and the diverted messages are then transmitted over the original signaling link.

As in the Time-Controlled Changeover procedure, a similar Time-Controlled Changeback procedure may be used at the end of a MTP Restart. The delay timer T3 is used to provide a waiting period before traffic is diverted to the available signaling link.

2.5.4.1   Changeover/Changeback Example

Figure 2-28 illustrates the call flow for Changeover and Changeback procedures and is followed by Figure 2-29, which shows the corresponding SS7 example message log. In this example, two signaling points (MSC and BSC) are connected, point to point, over a single link set that consists of two signaling links.

In the example call flow shown in Figure 2-28, SLC 0 becomes unavailable due to a link failure. LSSUs with link status indicator out of service (SIOS) are sent in both directions. Shortly after the failure, the BSC sends a COO to the MSC for SLC 0 and starts MTP3 timer T2. The MSC responds with a COA, which stops timer T2. In this example, a time-controlled changeover is used, where after a delay T1, all MSUs are sent over SLC 1.

When the conditions that caused the failure of SLC 0 subside, the link starts the initial alignment process. Because an alternative link is available, the link alignment process uses the normal proving period. Once the link alignment procedure completes, the BSC sends a *Signaling Link Test Message* (SLTM) over the restored link, SLC 0. The link becomes available only if this test is successful.

After receiving a *Signaling Link Test Acknowledgment* (SLTA), the BSC sends a CBD and starts timers T3 and T4. The MSC responds to the CBD with a CBA, which stops timer T4. Upon expiry of timer T3, which introduces a delay to prevent message missequencing, the BSC resumes sending MSUs over SLC 0.

```
+----------------+-----------------+------------------------------+-------
  From     Time                      OPC      DPC      MSG
+----------------+-----------------+------------------------------+-------
  1:C:4    22:37:31,367,720    1-2-4    1-1-1    T+M      SLTM
  1:D:4    22:37:31,377,906    1-1-1    1-2-4    T+M      SLTA
  1:D:3    22:38:00,225,721    1-1-1    1-2-4    SCCP     CR     BMAP   CL3I   CMSR
  1:C:3    22:38:00,245,280    1-2-4    1-1-1    SCCP     CC
  1:C:3    22:38:00,257,031    1-2-4    1-1-1    SCCP     DT1    BMAP   AREQ
  1:D:3    22:38:02,477,277    1-1-1    1-2-4    SCCP     DT1    BMAP   ACOM
  1:D:3    22:38:11,584,146    1-1-1    1-2-4    T+M      SLTM
  1:C:3    22:38:11,587,828    1-2-4    1-1-1    T+M      SLTA
  1:D:4    22:38:15,784,728    1-1-1    1-2-4    T+M      SLTM
  1:C:4    22:38:15,788,778    1-2-4    1-1-1    T+M      SLTA
  1:D:3    22:39:42,391,172    1-1-1    1-2-4    SCCP     IT
  1:D:3    22:40:14,915,237    1-1-1    1-2-4    SCCP     DT1    DTAP   FWI
  1:D:4    22:40:15,784,108    1-1-1    1-2-4    T+M      SLTM
  1:C:4    22:40:15,788,664    1-2-4    1-1-1    T+M      SLTA
  1:C:3    22:40:34,224,804                               MTP-L2   FISU
  1:C:3    22:40:34,227,560                               MTP-L2   LSSU-SIOS
  1:D:4    22:40:34,227,810    1-1-1    1-2-4    MTP3     COO
  1:C:4    22:40:34,360,920    1-2-4    1-1-1    MTP3     COA
  1:C:3    22:40:35,388,838                               MTP-L2   LSSU-SIO
```

1. Call setup ← on SLC 0

2. COO sent for SLC 0. MSU diverted to ← SLC 1

(Continued)

```
1:C:3   22:40:46,787,895                    MTP-L2  LSSU-SIO
1:C:3   22:40:46,790,522                    MTP-L2  LSSU-SIOS
1:C:3   22:40:48,390,239                    MTP-L2  LSSU-SIO
1:C:3   22:40:59,789,418                    MTP-L2  LSSU-SIO
1:C:3   22:40:59,792,177                    MTP-L2  LSSU-SIOS
1:D:4   22:41:15,783,796   1-1-1   1-2-4    T+M     SLTM
1:C:4   22:41:15,788,117   1-2-4   1-1-1    T+M     SLTA
1:C:3   22:41:25,792,593                    MTP-L2  LSSU-SIO
1:C:3   22:41:25,795,224                    MTP-L2  LSSU-SIOS
1:D:4   22:41:54,391,317   1-1-1   1-2-4    SCCP    IT
1:C:3   22:42:04,799,925                    MTP-L2  LSSU-SIOS
1:C:3   22:42:06,399,264                    MTP-L2  LSSU-SIO
1:D:4   22:42:24,552,060   1-1-1   1-2-4    SCCP    DT1   DTAP   FWI
1:C:3   22:43:09,807,677                    MTP-L2  LSSU-SIOS
1:C:3   22:43:11,407,146                    MTP-L2  LSSU-SIO
1:C:3   22:43:22,809,202                    MTP-L2  LSSU-SIOS
1:C:3   22:43:24,408,414                    MTP-L2  LSSU-SIO
1:D:3   22:43:28,933,103                    MTP-L2  FISU
1:D:3   22:43:28,935,099                    MTP-L2  LSSU-SIOS
1:D:3   22:43:28,935,974                    MTP-L2  LSSU-SIO
1:D:3   22:43:28,937,849                    MTP-L2  LSSU-SIE
1:C:3   22:43:28,938,289                    MTP-L2  LSSU-SIN
1:C:3   22:43:29,511,488   1-2-4   1-1-1    T+M     SLTM
1:D:3   22:43:29,518,179   1-1-1   1-2-4    T+M     SLTM
1:C:3   22:43:29,522,112   1-2-4   1-1-1    T+M     SLTA
1:D:3   22:43:29,522,804   1-1-1   1-2-4    T+M     SLTA
1:C:4   22:43:29,526,616   1-2-4   1-1-1    MTP3    CBD                3. SLC 0
1:D:4   22:43:29,535,936   1-1-1   1-2-4    MTP3    CBD         ◄───── resumed, CBD/
1:D:4   22:43:29,538,060   1-1-1   1-2-4    MTP3    CBA                CBA sent
1:C:4   22:43:29,539,367   1-2-4   1-1-1    MTP3    CBA
1:C:4   22:43:37,411,575   1-2-4   1-1-1    T+M     SLTM
1:D:4   22:43:37,421,136   1-1-1   1-2-4    T+M     SLTA
1:D:3   22:44:04,390,945   1-1-1   1-2-4    SCCP    IT                 4. Traffic back to
1:D:3   22:46:20,246,747   1-1-1   1-2-4    SCCP    DT1 DTAP FWI ◄───── SLC 0
1:D:3   22:46:29,483,130   1-1-1   1-2-4    T+M     SLTM
1:C:3   22:46:29,487,438   1-2-4   1-1-1    T+M     SLTA
```

Figure 2-29   Changeover/Changeback message log example

In the example message log shown in Figure 2-29, the BSC has point code 1-1-1, and the MSC has point code 1-2-4. The test equipment link pair designation C3/D3 corresponds to the first link with SLC0, and the link pair C4/D4 refers to the alternate link, SLC 1. At Stage 1, a call is set up on the C3/D3 link, and all MSUs are transmitted on this link.

At Stage 2, the C3/D3 link (SLC0) fails, and COO/COA messages are exchanged to divert traffic to the alternate link C4/D4, which is SLC 1. During the period when C3/D3 is unavailable, notice that the *Inactivity Test* (IT) message and the A-Interface *Flash With Information* (FWI) message are transmitted on the C4/D4 (SLC1) link.

At Stage 3, the C3/D3 link is activated and put in service again. CBD/CBA messages are exchanged, and traffic that originated from this link is now diverted back.

Stage 4 simply shows that, for this SCCP connection call, IT and FWI messages are now diverted back to the original C3/D3 link.

2.5.4.2 Changeback Message Structure

The format of the Changeback message is shown in Figure 2-30 and is followed by Table 2-6, which summarizes the individual fields in the Changeback message. The SI field of the SIO specifies an SNM message. The user data portion of the SIF contains heading codes H0, H1, and the SLC of the signaling link to which traffic will be diverted. Heading Code H0 specifies the SNM message group, and heading code H1 identifies the Changeback message type. The Changeback code is used to distinguish traffic being diverted from more than one alternate link to this SLC.

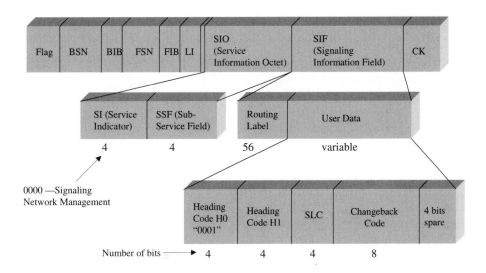

Figure 2-30 MTP3 Changeback message structure

Table 2-6   MTP3 Changeback Message Fields

Bitmap	Parameter	#Oct	Range
hhhh HHHH	Heading Code	1	H = Heading Code H0 = 0001—Changeover/Changeback h = Heading Code H1 0101—Changeback Declaration (CBD) 0110—Changeback Acknowledge (CBA)
CCCC SSSS 0000 CCCC	Change-back SIF data	2	S = Signaling Link Code (SLC) Specifies the unavailable physical link that has now become available. Traffic is to be diverted back to this link. C = Changeback Code This is used for distinguishing between multiple Changebacks to the same link when there are more than 2 links in the linkset. For those Changeback code CBDs that are not acknowledged, CBD is repeated.

Figure 2-31 shows an example message log of a CBD message. Heading code 0 is set to *0001*, signifying a Changeover/Changeback message type, and the heading code 1 of *0101* indicates a CBD message. The SLC of the original link is 0.

```
-0110101  Backward Sequence Number     53
1-------  Backward Indicator Bit       1
-0110100  Forward Sequence Number      52
1-------  Forward Indicator Bit        1
--001011  Length Indicator             11
00------  Spare                        0
----0000  Service Indicator            Signaling network manage mess
--00----  Sub-Service: Priority        Spare/priority 0 (U.S.A. only)
10------  Sub-Service: Network Ind     National message
***B3***  Destination Point Code       001-001-001
***B3***  Originating Point Code       001-002-004
00000000  Signaling Link Code          0
ChangeBack Declaration
----0001  Heading code 0               1
0101----  Heading code 1               5
----0000  SLC                          0
0001----  Changeback code              1
----0000  Changeback code              0
0000----  Spare                        0
```

Figure 2-31   MTP3 Changeback Declaration message example

Figure 2-32 shows an example message log of a COA message. The heading code 0 of *0001* signifies a Changeover/Changeback message type, and the heading code 1 of *0110* indicates a COA message.

```
-0110100  Backward Sequence Number      52
1-------  Backward Indicator Bit        1
-0110111  Forward Sequence Number       55
1-------  Forward Indicator Bit         1
--001011  Length Indicator              11
00------  Spare                         0
----0000  Service Indicator             Signaling network manage mess
--00----  Sub-Service: Priority         Spare/priority 0 (U.S.A. only)
10------  Sub-Service: Network Ind      National message
***B3***  Destination Point Code        001-002-004
***B3***  Originating Point Code        001-001-001
00000000  Signaling Link Code           0
ChangeBack Acknowledgement
----0001  Heading code 0                1
0110----  Heading code 1                6
----0000  SLC                           0
0001----  Changeback code               1
----0000  Changeback code               0
0000----  Spare                         0
```

Figure 2-32   MTP3 Changeback Acknowledge message example

2.5.5   Traffic Management: Inhibit/Uninhibit

Management Inhibiting may be performed when MTP management requests that a link be inhibited. The reasons for such a request is typically maintenance-related and prevents user traffic from being exchanged over a particular link. Inhibiting a link does not change its layer 2 status. A link previously in service stays in service and remains capable of transmitting and receiving maintenance and test messages.

A request for inhibiting a link will be denied if inhibiting the link will result in the signaling point being inaccessible. The request may also be denied if congestion is present.

The Link Inhibit process starts when a node transmits a *Link Inhibit* (LIN) message. Upon receiving an LIN message, the remote end responds with a *Link Inhibit Acknowledge* (LIA) message. MTP management may uninhibit a link by sending a *Link Uninhibit* (LUN) message to the remote end, which then responds with a *Link Uninhibit Acknowledge* (LUA) message.

During the period that a signaling link is inhibited, the signaling point that initiated the Link Inhibit periodically transmits *Link Local Inhibit* (LLI) test messages to the remote end. This is done to ensure that the inhibit status of the link on both ends match. *Link Remote Inhibit* (LRI) test messages are also periodically sent from the remote signal point.

2.5.5.1   Inhibit/Uninhibit Example

Figure 2-33 contains an example Link Inhibit and Uninhibit call flow. In the example shown, there are two signaling links, SLC0 and SLC1, connecting the BSC to the MSC. The link inhibiting procedure is initiated by the BSC when a request from MTP management to inhibit link SLC1 is received. After receiving the internal request, the BSC checks to see whether inhibiting the link will cause the destination signaling point to be inaccessible. If so, the link inhibit request is denied. If the link inhibit is allowed, an LIN message is sent to the MSC, and timer T14 is started.

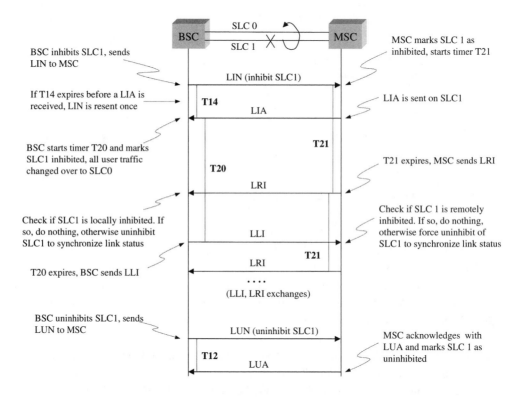

Figure 2-33   Inhibit/Uninhibit call flow example

Upon receiving the LIN message from the BSC, the MSC sends an LIA and marks the link as remotely inhibited. Timer T21 is started. The LIA is sent over the concerned link if it is being used for traffic. All subsequent user traffic is then diverted to the alternate link, SLC 0, using the time controlled Changeover procedure.

Upon receiving LIA, the BSC marks the link as locally inhibited, diverts traffic to SLC0 using the Time-Controlled Changeover procedure, and starts timer T20. If timer T14 expires before an LIA is received from the remote end, the procedure is restarted once more. When

Changeover has been completed, the link SLC1 is no longer available for carrying user traffic, but is still used for maintenance and test messages.

During the period when link SLC1 is inhibited, both BSC and MSC send inhibit maintenance test messages to ensure that both ends of the link agree on the status of the inhibited link. At the local terminal, which in this example is the BSC, an LLI test message is transmitted to the MSC upon expiry of timer T20. The MSC, upon receipt of LLI, checks whether SLC1 is inhibited remotely. If so, no further is taken; otherwise, a *Link Force Uninhibit* (LFU) message is sent to the BSC to synchronize the link states.

Similarly, the MSC sends an LRI test message to the BSC upon expiry of timer T21. Upon receipt of LRI, the BSC checks whether SLC1 is inhibited locally. If so, no further action is taken. Otherwise, the BSC sends an LUN to uninhibit the link.

The link inhibit test messages LLI and LRI are sent periodically at intervals T20 and T21, respectively, to maintain the consistency of the link states at both ends.

When MTP3 management at the BSC decides to uninhibit the link, it first determines whether a route to the remote end is available for sending an LUN message. If not, the concerned signaling link is labeled as *Failed* or *Processor Outage*, and MTP management is notified that the request is not possible. If a route does exist, such as SLC 0 in the example, the LUN message is sent, identifying the signaling link to be uninhibited, using the SLC field. Timer T12 is started at the BSC.

At the remote end, the MSC sends an LUA message and removes the Remote Inhibit status of the link. If the link status is not locally inhibited, blocked, or failed, the link is then put back into service using the Changeback procedure.

When the LUA is received at the BSC, the local link inhibit status is removed, Changeback to SLC1 is started, and timer T12 is stopped. If timer T12 expires, the procedure is tried one more time.

```
+----------------+----------+------------------------+--------------+
 From     Time              OPC      DPC     MSG
+----------------+----------+------------------------+--------------+
 1:D:3   22:13:11,587,088   1-1-1    1-2-4   T+M   SLTM
 1:C:3   22:13:11,591,519   1-2-4    1-1-1   T+M   SLTA
 1:D:4   22:13:20,418,545   1-1-1    1-2-4   SCCP  CR   BMA+  CL3I  CMSR
 1:C:4   22:13:20,438,230   1-2-4    1-1-1   SCCP  CC
 1:C:4   22:13:20,448,987   1-2-4    1-1-1   SCCP  DT1  BMA+  AREQ        ◄── 1. Call setup
 1:D:4   22:13:22,316,053   1-1-1    1-2-4   SCCP  DT1  BMA+  ACOM            on C4/D4
 1:D:4   22:13:29,487,406   1-1-1    1-2-4   T+M   SLTM
 1:C:4   22:13:29,491,469   1-2-4    1-1-1   T+M   SLTA
 1:D:4   22:13:55,377,063   1-1-1    1-2-4   SCCP  DT1  DTA+  FWI
 1:D:4   22:15:34,394,321   1-1-1    1-2-4   SCCP  IT
 1:C:3   22:15:57,212,491   1-2-4    1-1-1   T+M   SLTM
 1:D:3   22:15:57,221,308   1-1-1    1-2-4   T+M   SLTA
 1:D:3   22:16:08,105,795   1-1-1    1-2-4   MTP3  LIN         ◄────── 2. C4/D4 inhibited
 1:C:4   22:16:08,109,354   1-2-4    1-1-1   MTP3  LIA
 1:D:3   22:16:11,586,270   1-1-1    1-2-4   T+M   SLTM
 1:C:3   22:16:11,590,699   1-2-4    1-1-1   T+M   SLTA
```

(Continued)

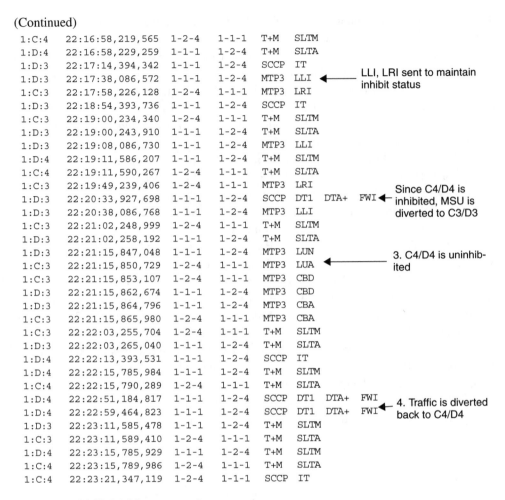

```
1:C:4    22:16:58,219,565    1-2-4    1-1-1    T+M    SLTM
1:D:4    22:16:58,229,259    1-1-1    1-2-4    T+M    SLTA
1:D:3    22:17:14,394,342    1-1-1    1-2-4    SCCP   IT
1:D:3    22:17:38,086,572    1-1-1    1-2-4    MTP3   LLI     ◄──────  LLI, LRI sent to maintain
1:C:3    22:17:58,226,128    1-2-4    1-1-1    MTP3   LRI              inhibit status
1:D:3    22:18:54,393,736    1-1-1    1-2-4    SCCP   IT
1:C:3    22:19:00,234,340    1-2-4    1-1-1    T+M    SLTM
1:D:3    22:19:00,243,910    1-1-1    1-2-4    T+M    SLTA
1:D:3    22:19:08,086,730    1-1-1    1-2-4    MTP3   LLI
1:D:4    22:19:11,586,207    1-1-1    1-2-4    T+M    SLTM
1:C:4    22:19:11,590,267    1-2-4    1-1-1    T+M    SLTA
1:C:3    22:19:49,239,406    1-2-4    1-1-1    MTP3   LRI                      Since C4/D4 is
1:D:3    22:20:33,927,698    1-1-1    1-2-4    SCCP   DT1    DTA+   FWI ◄──  inhibited, MSU is
1:D:3    22:20:38,086,768    1-1-1    1-2-4    MTP3   LLI                      diverted to C3/D3
1:C:3    22:21:02,248,999    1-2-4    1-1-1    T+M    SLTM
1:D:3    22:21:02,258,192    1-1-1    1-2-4    T+M    SLTA
1:D:3    22:21:15,847,048    1-1-1    1-2-4    MTP3   LUN                      3. C4/D4 is uninhib-
1:C:3    22:21:15,850,729    1-2-4    1-1-1    MTP3   LUA     ◄──────          ited
1:C:3    22:21:15,853,107    1-2-4    1-1-1    MTP3   CBD
1:D:3    22:21:15,862,674    1-1-1    1-2-4    MTP3   CBD
1:D:3    22:21:15,864,796    1-1-1    1-2-4    MTP3   CBA
1:C:3    22:21:15,865,980    1-2-4    1-1-1    MTP3   CBA
1:C:3    22:22:03,255,704    1-2-4    1-1-1    T+M    SLTM
1:D:3    22:22:03,265,040    1-1-1    1-2-4    T+M    SLTA
1:D:4    22:22:13,393,531    1-1-1    1-2-4    SCCP   IT
1:D:4    22:22:15,785,984    1-1-1    1-2-4    T+M    SLTM
1:C:4    22:22:15,790,289    1-2-4    1-1-1    T+M    SLTA
1:D:4    22:22:51,184,817    1-1-1    1-2-4    SCCP   DT1    DTA+   FWI ──  4. Traffic is diverted
1:D:4    22:22:59,464,823    1-1-1    1-2-4    SCCP   DT1    DTA+   FWI      back to C4/D4
1:D:3    22:23:11,585,478    1-1-1    1-2-4    T+M    SLTM
1:C:3    22:23:11,589,410    1-2-4    1-1-1    T+M    SLTA
1:D:4    22:23:15,785,929    1-1-1    1-2-4    T+M    SLTM
1:C:4    22:23:15,789,986    1-2-4    1-1-1    T+M    SLTA
1:C:4    22:23:21,347,119    1-2-4    1-1-1    SCCP   IT
```

Figure 2-34 Inhibit/Uninhibit message log example

In the example message log shown in Figure 2-34, the BSC has a point code of 1-1-1 and, the MSC has a point code of 1-2-4. The test equipment link pair designation C3/D3 corresponds to SLC 0, and the designation C4/D4 refers to SLC 1.

At Stage 1, a call is set up on the C4/D4 (SLC 1) link, and all associated MSUs are transmitted on this.

At Stage 2, the C4/D4 (SLC 1) link is locally inhibited by the BSC, following the exchange of LIN and LIA messages. Note that the MSC acknowledges the LIN with LIA transmitted on the inhibited link, SLC1. Subsequently, all user traffic, such as the Inactivity Test (SCCP-IT) and Flash With Information (FWI) messages, is diverted to SLC0 (C3/D3). During the period when SLC 1 is inhibited, link inhibit maintenance messages (LLI and LRI) are sent from the BSC and MSC, respectively, to maintain the consistency of the link inhibit states at both nodes.

At Stage 3, the C4/D4 (SLC 1) link is uninhibited by the BSC through the exchange of LUN and LUA messages. User traffic is changed back to SLC 1 with the exchange of CBD and CBA messages. Stage 4 shows that IT and FWI messages are returned to the original link.

2.5.5.2 Inhibit/Uninhibit Message Structure

The format of the Management Inhibit message is shown in Figure 2-35 and is followed by Table 2-7, which summarizes the fields within the SIF.

The Management Inhibit message type is an MTP3 SNM message and is identified using the 4 bits in the heading code H0, which is set to *0110*. The specific type of Management Inhibit message is further specified in the 4-bit H1 field. The link to be inhibited is identified by the 4-bit SLC field.

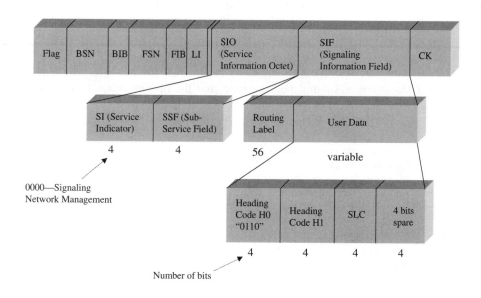

Figure 2-35   MTP3 Inhibit message structure

Table 2-7   MTP3 Inhibit Message Fields

Bitmap	Parameter	#Oct	Range
hhhh HHHH	Heading Code	1	H = Heading Code H0 = 0110—Management Inhibiting msgs h = Heading Code H1 0001—Link Inhibit (LIN) 0010—Link Uninhibit (LUN) 0011—Link Inhibit Ack (LIA) 0100—Link Uninhibit Ack (LUA) 0101—Link Inhibit Denied (LID) 0110—Link Force Uninhibit (LFU) 0111—Link Local Inhibit test (LLI) 1000—Link Remote Inhibit test (LRI)
0000 SSSS	Inhibit SIF data	1	S = Signaling Link Code (SLC) Specifies the physical link that is to be inhibited/uninhibited

Figure 2-36 shows an example LIN message. Notice that the heading code 0 is *0110*, which specifies a Management Inhibit message type, and the heading code 1 is set to *0001*, which specifies an LIN message. The SLC of the link to be inhibited is 1.

```
MTP Level 2 (MTP-L2)
 -0101011   Backward Sequence Number       43
 1-------   Backward Indicator Bit         1
 -0101011   Forward Sequence Number        43
 1-------   Forward Indicator Bit          1
 --001010   Length Indicator               10
 00------   Spare                          0
 ----0000   Service Indicator              Signaling network manage mess
 --11----   Sub-Service: Priority          priority 3 (U.S.A. only)
 10------   Sub-Service: Network Ind       National message
 ***B3***   Destination Point Code         001-002-004
 ***B3***   Originating Point Code         001-001-001
 00000001   Signaling Link Code            1
Link Inhibit
 ----0110   Heading code 0                 6
 0001----   Heading code 1                 1
 ----0001   SLC                            1
 0000----   Spare                          0
```

Figure 2-36   MTP3 Link Inhibit message example

Figure 2-37 shows an example LIA message. In this example, heading code 1 is set to *0011*, which specifies an LIA message. The SLC of the link that is being acknowledged as inhibited is 1.

```
MTP Level 2 (MTP-L2)
 -1001101  Backward Sequence Number      77
 1-------  Backward Indicator Bit        1
 -1001010  Forward Sequence Number       74
 1-------  Forward Indicator Bit         1
 --001010  Length Indicator              10
 00------  Spare                         0
 ----0000  Service Indicator             Signaling network manage mess
 --00----  Sub-Service: Priority         Spare/priority 0 (U.S.A. only)
 10------  Sub-Service: Network Ind       National message
 ***B3***  Destination Point Code        001-001-001
 ***B3***  Originating Point Code        001-002-004
 00000001  Signaling Link Code           1
Link Inhibit Ack
 ----0110  Heading code 0                6
 0011----  Heading code 1                3
 ----0001  SLC                           1
 0000----  Spare                         0
```

Figure 2-37 MTP3 Link Inhibit Acknowledge message example

Figure 2-38 shows an example LUN message. Heading code 1 is set to *0010*, indicating an LUN message. The SLC of the link to be uninhibited is 1.

```
MTP Level 2 (MTP-L2)
 -0111000  Backward Sequence Number      56
 1-------  Backward Indicator Bit        1
 -0111101  Forward Sequence Number       61
 1-------  Forward Indicator Bit         1
 --001010  Length Indicator              10
 00------  Spare                         0
 ----0000  Service Indicator             Signaling network manage mess
 --11----  Sub-Service: Priority         priority 3 (U.S.A. only)
 10------  Sub-Service: Network Ind       National message
 ***B3***  Destination Point Code        001-002-004
 ***B3***  Originating Point Code        001-001-001
 00000001  Signaling Link Code           1
Link Uninhibit
 ----0110  Heading code 0                6
 0010----  Heading code 1                2
 ----0001  SLC                           1
 0000----  Spare                         0
```

Figure 2-38 MTP3 Link Uninhibit message example

Figure 2-39 shows an example LUA message. Heading code 0 is set to *0110*, which specifies a Management Inhibit message type, and the heading code 1 of *0100* indicates an LUA message. The SLC of the link that is being acknowledged as uninhibited is 1.

```
MTP Level 2 (MTP-L2)
 -0111100  Backward Sequence Number        60
 1-------  Backward Indicator Bit          1
 -0111001  Forward Sequence Number         57
 1-------  Forward Indicator Bit           1
 --001010  Length Indicator                10
 00------  Spare                           0
 ----0000  Service Indicator               Signaling network manage mess
 --00----  Sub-Service: Priority           Spare/priority 0 (U.S.A. only)
 10------  Sub-Service: Network Ind         National message
 ***B3***  Destination Point Code          001-001-001
 ***B3***  Originating Point Code          001-002-004
 00000001  Signaling Link Code             1
Link Uninhibit Ack
 ----0110  Heading code 0                  6
 0100----  Heading code 1                  4
 ----0001  SLC                             1
 0000----  Spare                           0
```

Figure 2-39 MTP3 Link Uninhibit Acknowledge message example

Figure 2-40 shows an example LLI test message. Heading code 1 is set to *0111*, which specifies an LLI test message. The SLC of the link that is locally inhibited is 1.

```
MTP Level 2 (MTP-L2)
 -0101110  Backward Sequence Number        46
 1-------  Backward Indicator Bit          1
 -0110000  Forward Sequence Number         48
 1-------  Forward Indicator Bit           1
 --001010  Length Indicator                10
 00------  Spare                           0
 ----0000  Service Indicator               Signaling network manage mess
 --11----  Sub-Service: Priority           priority 3 (U.S.A. only)
 10------  Sub-Service: Network Ind         National message
 ***B3***  Destination Point Code          001-002-004
 ***B3***  Originating Point Code          001-001-001
 00000001  Signaling Link Code             1
Link Local Inhibit
 ----0110  Heading code 0                  6
 0111----  Heading code 1                  7
 ----0001  SLC                             1
 0000----  Spare                           0
```

Figure 2-40 MTP3 Link Locally Inhibit Test message example

Figure 2-41 shows an example of a LRI test message. The heading code 1 of *1000* specifies an LRI test message. The SLC of the link that is remotely inhibited is 1.

```
MTP Level 2 (MTP-L2)
 -0110000  Backward Sequence Number      48
 1-------  Backward Indicator Bit        1
 -0101111  Forward Sequence Number       47
 1-------  Forward Indicator Bit         1
 --001010  Length Indicator              10
 00------  Spare                         0
 ----0000  Service Indicator             Signaling network manage mess
 --00----  Sub-Service: Priority         Spare/priority 0 (U.S.A. only)
 10------  Sub-Service: Network Ind      National message
 ***B3***  Destination Point Code        001-001-001
 ***B3***  Originating Point Code        001-002-004
 00000001  Signaling Link Code           1
Link Remote Inhibit
 ----0110  Heading code 0                6
 1000----  Heading code 1                8
 ----0001  SLC                           1
 0000----  Spare                         0
```

Figure 2-41   MTP3 Link Remotely Inhibit Test message example

2.5.6   Traffic Management: MTP Restart

The MTP Restart procedure is presented here for completeness. However, a comprehensive understanding of MTP Restart is not essential to understanding SS7 and how it relates to the
A-Interface. The details of the MTP Restart procedures can be overwhelming to a first-time
reader.

The objective of the MTP Restart procedure is to bring into service sufficient signaling
links and routes to process the expected user traffic. During a restart, all MTP3 timers and
counters are reset, and the signaling link is resynchronized. The MTP Restart procedure is initiated when a signaling point first comes into service. When MTP Restart procedure has been
completed, the MTP3 layers at both signaling points are brought into service, and user MSU
exchange can begin. The *Traffic Restart Allowed* (TRA) and *Traffic Restart Waiting* (TRW)
SNM messages are both used in the MTP Restart process to indicate the status of the traffic
restart to remote nodes.

The MTP Restart procedure is not required for A-Interface implementation and may be
excluded to bring MTP3 layer into service as soon as possible. However, it is common for commercial MSCs and BSCs to include this functionality in their implementations.

If MTP Management determines that a full restart is required at a local node, it is important for the adjacent signaling nodes to be aware of the local node's unavailability before the
MTP Restart procedure begins. A guide timer T27, which is started when a signaling point
becomes unavailable, is used, along with the local processor outage (SIPO) status to ensure that
adjacent signaling points are aware of the local signaling point's unavailability. MTP restart

begins upon expiry of timer T27. The following subsections describe the procedures at both the local node that initiates the MTP Full Restart and the node adjacent to the restarting node.

2.5.6.1   Procedures at MTP Restart Node

Figure 2-42 shows an example of an MTP Restart procedure. The following description applies to the signaling point in which MTP restart is being initiated, which is node A in this example.

MTP Restart begins when a link comes into service at level 2 and the MTP Restart guide period T27 expires. The first step of MTP restart involves bringing up at least one link to level 3 in each link set, if available. Restarting node A starts timers T22 and T26 when the first link is in service at either level 2 or level 3 and begins processing TRW and TRA messages as soon as the first Signaling Link comes into service. Once the first signaling link in a Link Set becomes available at level 3, a TRW message is then transmitted, and message traffic is restarted at node A.

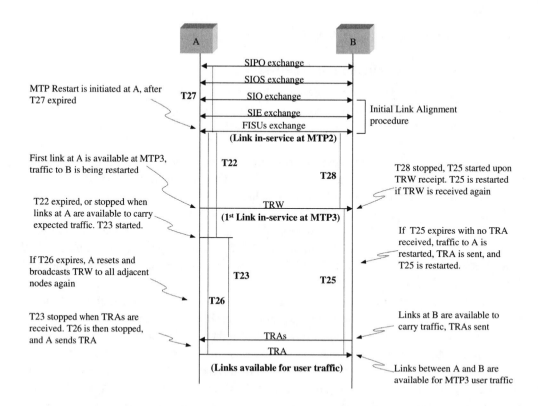

Figure 2-42 MTP Restart call flow example

When the MTP Management determines that an adequate number of links are in service and are available to handle the expected message traffic, timer T22 is stopped. Upon stopping T22 or when T22 expires, a new timer T23 is started to wait for TRA messages from node B.

The adjacent node B sends TRA when the first link to node A becomes available for traffic. Once TRAs have been received at node A for all available links or at the discretion of MTP management, Timer T23 is stopped. At this point, node A sends TRAs to all available signaling links to indicate the link's availability between nodes A and B, and stops timer T26.

The MTP Restart procedure is, thus, complete, and the links between A and B are now available for user MSU traffic.

Note that the purpose of timer T26 is to repeat the TRW, if applicable. Whenever T26 expires without sufficient TRAs receipt, the restarting signal point resends the TRW to all adjacent signaling points with available links and restarts timer T26.

Because the A-Interface nodes do not need transfer capability, the MTP restart procedure does not include the exchange of Transfer Prohibited or Transfer Restricted messages, and all timers associated with an STP.

2.5.6.2   Procedures at MTP Restart Adjacent Node

As shown in Figure 2-42, MTP Restart at adjacent node B begins when the first link to the previously inaccessible node A comes into service at level 2. When the link is in service, it takes into account any TRW or TRA messages received from the restarting signaling point—node A in this example. Timer T28 is started when this first link is in service at level 2 or 3, while waiting for a TRW from the MTP Restart node A.

Once a TRW is received from node A, T28 is stopped, and timer T25 is started to wait for a TRA from node A.

Meanwhile, when the first link at B becomes available at level 3 to carry traffic, it sends a TRA to the MTP Restart node A to indicate its link availability at B. The receipt of sufficient TRAs at node A will then trigger a sending of TRA from node A.

Upon receipt of a TRA from node A, timer T25 at node B is stopped. The links between node A and B are now available for carrying user MSU traffic and the MTP Restart is complete.

Timer T28 is to used to restart traffic at B if no TRW is received from node A before T28 expires and if a TRA is sent to A. If a TRA is received before T28 expires, T28 is stopped, and traffic is restarted.

The purposes of T25 is to restart traffic at node B if no TRA is received from node A before T25 expires. If timer T25 expires, a TRA is sent from node B, and T25 is restarted. If a TRW is received while T25 is running, T25 is restarted to wait for a TRA from node A.

2.5.6.3   Traffic Restart Message Structure

The format of the Traffic Restart message type is shown in Figure 2-43, followed by Table 2-8, which summarizes the fields within the SIF for this MTP3 message type.

The Traffic Restart message type is an MTP3 SNM message and is identified by setting the 4 bits of heading code H0 to *0111*. The specific type of Traffic Restart message is further specified in the 4-bit H1 field.

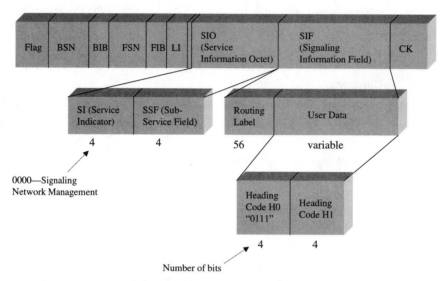

Figure 2-43 MTP3 Traffic Restart message structure

Table 2-8 MTP3 Traffic Restart Message Fields

Bitmap	Parameter	#Oct	Range
hhhh HHHH	Heading Code	1	H = Heading Code H0 = 0111—Traffic restart msgs h = Heading Code H1 0001—Traffic Restart Allowed (TRA) 0010—Traffic Restart Waiting (TRW)

Figure 2-44 shows an example of a TRA message. Heading code H0 is set to *0111*, which specifies a Traffic Restart message type and heading code 1 is set to *0001*, indicating that the message is a TRA message. No other fields are present in the SIF of this message. Upon exchanges of the TRA message at both BSC and MSC, the MTP Restart is completed, and MTP3 user traffic can begin.

```
MTP Level 2 (MTP-L2)
 -0000010  Backward Sequence Number        2
 1-------  Backward Indicator Bit          1
 -0000010  Forward Sequence Number         2
 1-------  Forward Indicator Bit           1
 --001001  Length Indicator                9
 00------  Spare                           0
 ----0000  Service Indicator               Signaling network manage mess
 --11----  Sub-Service: Priority           priority 3 (U.S.A. only)
 10------  Sub-Service: Network Ind        National message
 ***B3***  Destination Point Code          001-002-004
 ***B3***  Originating Point Code          001-001-001
 00000000  Signaling Link Code             0
Traffic Restart Allowed
 ----0111  Heading code 0                  7
 0001----  Heading code 1                  1
```

Figure 2-44   MTP3 Traffic Restart Allowed message example

2.5.7   Traffic Management: Flow Control

The purpose of Signaling Traffic Flow Control is to limit the amount of signaling traffic during a period of network failures or signaling point and signaling transfer point congestion.

For congestion control at a signaling point associated with a single Link Set to an adjacent node, the MTP level 2 Flow Control methods are applied at layer 2, as discussed in Section 2.4.6, "MTP2 Flow Control (Congestion Control)," on page 49. MTP3 is informed of the congestion status from level 2 through network management functions.

If MTP2 Flow Control is insufficient to control congestion, MTP3 may apply congestion control procedures as well. If such procedures are applied, they are implemented similar to MTP2 congestion control mechanisms, such as by discarding messages based on priority level and informing remote nodes about the congested situation.

Because the A-Interface network is point to point, congestion control schemes related to route availability will not be discussed here. Readers who are interested in the SS7 details relating to route management should refer to the ANSI SS7 standard T1.111 (MTP) [5].

2.5.8   Traffic Management: Forced/Controlled Rerouting

The purpose of Forced Rerouting is to restore the signaling capability between two signaling points in the event of a network failure. Because route failure is often due to a signaling point becoming inaccessible to an STP, Forced Rerouting diverts signaling messages to an alternate signaling route. Forced rerouting is initiated by the receipt of a *Transfer Prohibited* (TFP) message, indicating signal route unavailability. Once initiated, transmission of signaling traffic to the unavailable route is stopped, and the traffic is stored in a Forced Rerouting buffer. Once an alternate route has been identified, signaling traffic is restarted on the alternate route, beginning with the MSUs in the Forced Rerouting buffer.

The purpose of Controlled Rerouting is to restore the optimal signaling route between two signaling points. Controlled Rerouting is invoked when a previously unavailable route is restored. Signaling traffic is diverted back from the alternate route to the original route. Controlled Rerouting is initiated when a *Transfer Allowed* (TFA) or *Transfer Restricted* (TFR) message is received. A TFA message is sent by an STP to indicate to one or more adjacent signal points that traffic may be routed to it. A TFR is sent by an STP to inform one or more adjacent signal points not to send signal messages to it, if possible.

Because an A-Interface network is typically point to point, no STP or multiple routes are used when messages are exchanged between the BSC and MSC. The Force and Controlled Rerouting procedures are associated with the traffic management of multiple routes to a destination when network failures occur and, hence, are not relevant for the point-to-point A-Interface network. A brief overview of these functions will be given to introduce the reader to these Route Traffic Management procedures; further details can be found in the ANSI T1.111 (MTP) standard document [5].

2.5.9   Signaling Link Test and Maintenance

Whenever a signaling link is available, signaling link test messages are exchanged between the two end signaling points of a concerned link. The signaling link test procedure is also required when a link is first activated or restored.

The test procedure involves only two messages, the *Signaling Link Test Message* (SLTM) and the *Signaling Link Test Acknowledgment* (SLTA) message. The SLTM is sent by a node to test the integrity of a signaling link by putting a test pattern in the SLTM message. The link undergoing the test is also specified by the SLC in the SLTM message. The link is considered to be tested successfully if an SLTA message is received from the adjacent node having the same test pattern and the same SLC code. Each individual link is tested independently at both adjacent nodes with the SLTM/SLTA messages exchange.

2.5.9.1   Signaling Link Test Example

Figure 2-45 shows an example call flow for a signaling link test message exchange. Each signaling point has a supervisory timer for the SLTA messages and an interval timer for sending SLTM messages. Upon expiry of the SLTM interval timer, an SLTM is transmitted over the concerned link to the remote signaling point, and the SLTA supervisory timer is started.

Once the remote signaling point echoes the received pattern in an SLTA message and is received correctly at the transmitting node, the SLTA supervisory timer is stopped. If no acknowledgment is received before the SLTA supervisory timer expires, the SLTM is transmitted a second time. If no acknowledgment is received before the SLTA supervisory timer expires a second time, link management is notified of the link test failure, and the link is taken out of service.

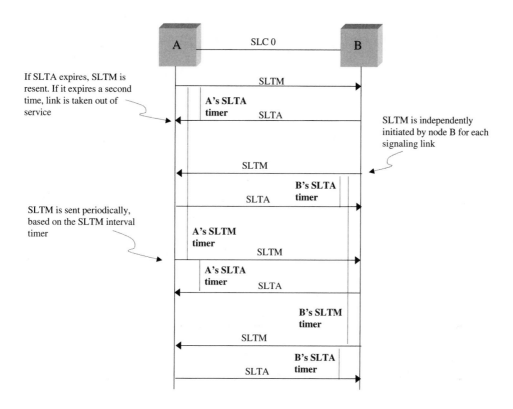

Figure 2-45   Signaling Link Test call flow example

2.5.9.2   Signaling Link Test Message Structure

The format of test messages is shown in Figure 2-46 and is followed by Table 2-9, which summarizes the SIF fields for SLTM and SLTA messages. The SI field of the SIO specifies a Signaling Network Testing and Maintenance message. The user data portion of the SIF contains heading codes H0 and H1, an SLC, an LI, and a test pattern. Heading code H0 specifies that the message is a test message, and heading code H1 identifies whether the message is an SLTM or SLTA message. The SLC field specifies the SLC of the link being tested, and the LI specifies the length of the test pattern field in octets. The originating signal point chooses this test pattern.

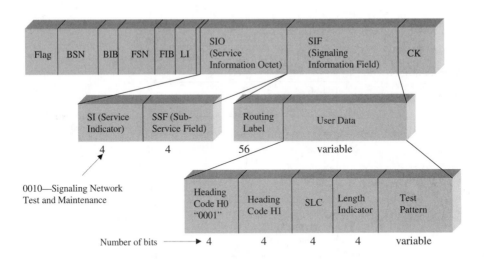

Figure 2-46 MTP3 Signaling Network Test and Maintenance message structure

Table 2-9 MTP3 Signaling Network Test and Maintenance Message Fields

Bitmap	Parameter	#Oct	Range
hhhh HHHH	Heading Code	1	H = Heading Code H0 = 0001—Test Messages h = Heading Code H1 0001—Signaling Link Test Msgs (SLTM) 0010—Signaling Link Test Ack (SLTA)
LLLL SSSS	SLC	1	S = Signaling Link Code (SLC), L = Length of Test Pattern Specifies the physical link being tested.
tttt tttt	Test Pattern	≤ 15	T = Test Pattern. Specifies the test pattern used in the link test.

Figure 2-47 shows an example SLTM message. Notice that the SI bit is set to *0010*, which implies an MTP3 Signaling Network Test and Maintenance message type. The heading code 0 is *0001*, indicating a test message type, and the heading code 1 is *0001*, which specifies an SLTM test message. The SLC of the link under test is 1 and the test pattern is *54 53 54*.

```
-1000110   Backward Sequence Number 70
1-------   Backward Indicator Bit           1
-1000101   Forward Sequence Number          69
1-------   Forward Indicator Bit            1
--001101   Length Indicator                 13
00------   Spare                            0
----0010   Service Indicator                Sig netwk test&maint spec msg
--00----   Sub-Service: Priority            Spare/priority 0 (U.S.A. only)
10------   Sub-Service: Network Ind         National message
***B3***   Destination Point Code           001-001-001
***B3***   Originating Point Code           001-002-004
00000001   Signaling Link Selection         1
Signaling Link Test Message
----0001   Heading code 0                   1
0001----   Heading code 1                   1
----0001   Signaling Link Code              1
0011----   Length Indicator                 3
***B3***   Test Pattern                     54 53 54
```

Figure 2-47   MTP3 Signaling Link Test message example

Figure 2-48 shows an example of an SLTA message that acknowledges the previously described SLTM message. The heading code 0 is *0001*, which specifies a test message type, and heading code 1 is set to *0010*, indicating that the message is an SLTA message. The SLC of the link being acknowledged is 1, and the test pattern echoed back is *54 53 54*. Upon receipt of this SLTA message, the originator of the SLTM message confirms a successful signaling link test, and the link remains in service.

```
-1000101   Backward Sequence Number         69
1-------   Backward Indicator Bit           1
-1000111   Forward Sequence Number          71
1-------   Forward Indicator Bit            1
--001101   Length Indicator                 13
00------   Spare                            0
----0010   Service Indicator                Sig netwk test & maint spec msg
--11----   Sub-Service: Priority            priority 3 (U.S.A. only)
10------   Sub-Service: Network Ind         National message
***B3***   Destination Point Code           001-002-004
***B3***   Originating Point Code           001-001-001
00000001   Signaling Link Selection         1
Signaling Link Test Ack
----0001   Heading code 0                   1
0010----   Heading code 1                   2
----0001   Signaling Link Code              1
0011----   Length Indicator                 3
***B3***   Test Pattern                     54 53 54
```

Figure 2-48   MTP3 Signaling Link Test Acknowledge message example

2.5.10 MTP3 Timers

Table 2-10 summarizes the timers used by the MTP3 layer and provides recommended industry values. For completeness, all MTP3 timers are summarized in the table. However, since an A-Interface network is typically point to point, without any STPs or multiple Routes and Link Sets, timers associated with STPs or multiple route management are not used. The following timers are typically used in the point-to-point A-Interface connection:

- Timers T1–T5 are associated with Changeover and Changeback procedures.
- Timers T12, T13, T14, T20, and T21 are associated with Link Inhibit and Uninhibit procedures.
- Timers T17, T19, T32, T33, and T34 are associated with the basic Signaling Link Activation and Restoration procedures.
- Timers T22, T23, T25–T29 are associated with the Traffic Restart procedure at a signaling point without transfer functions.

Recall that it is not mandatory for the A-Interface SS7 nodes to implement the Traffic Restart procedures.

Table 2-10   MTP3 Timers

Timer	Range	Recommended Values	Description	Comments
T1	0.5–1.2 s	0.8 s	Delay after Changeover in sending MSUs to avoid missequencing	Changeover Timer
T2	0.7–2.0 s	1.4 s	COO → COA Timer	Changeover Timer
T3	0.5–1.2 s	0.8 s	Delay after Changeback in sending MSUs to avoid missequencing	Changeback Timer
T4	0.5–1.2 s	0.8 s	CBD → CBA Timer	Changeback Timer
T5	0.5–1.2 s	0.8 s	CBA Timer on second attempt	Changeback Timer
T6	0.5–1.2 s	0.8 s	Delay on Controlled Rerouting	Not used in A-I/F
T7	1–2 s	1.5 s	Waiting for signaling data link connection acknowledgment	Not used in A-I/F

Table 2-10 MTP3 Timers (Continued)

Timer	Range	Recomme-ded Values	Description	Comments
T8	0.8–1.2 s	1 s	Transfer prohibited inhibit timer	Not used in A-I/F
T10	30–60 s	45 s	Waiting to repeat signaling route test msg	Not used in A-I/F
T11	30–90 s	60 s	Transfer Restricted timer	Not used in A-I/F
T12	0.8–1.5 s	1 s	LUN → LUA Timer	Uninhibit Timer
T13	0.8–1.5 s	1 s	LFU → LUN Timer	Uninhibit Timer
T14	2–3 s	2.5 s	LIN → LIA Timer	Inhibit Timer
T15	2–3 s	2.5 s	Waiting to repeat signaling route set congestion test	Not used in A-I/F
T16	1.4–2 s	1.7 s	Waiting for route set congestion status	Not used in A-I/F
T17	0.8–1.5 s	1 s	Delay between Initial Alignment Failure and Link Restart to avoid oscillation	Link Activation Timer
T18	2–20 s	11 s	Repeat TFR once by response method	Not used in A-I/F
T19	480–600 s	600 s	Failed link declaration timer	Link Activation Timer
T20	90–120 s	100 s	LLI repeat interval timer	Inhibit Timer
T21	90–120 s	100 s	LRI repeat interval timer	Inhibit Timer
T22	-	2 s	Waiting for available links to come into service	Traffic Restart Timer
T23	-	5 s	Waiting for TRA after T22 is stopped	Traffic Restart Timer

Table 2-10   MTP3 Timers (Continued)

Timer	Range	Recomme-ded Values	Description	Comments
T24	-	4 s	Timer at restarting node with transfer function, started after T23, waiting to broadcast all TRAs	Not used in A-I/F
T25	30–35 s	30 s	Waiting for TRA at remote traffic restart node after TRW is received	Remote Traffic Restart Timer
T26	12–15 s	14 s	TRW repeat Timer	Traffic Restart Timer
T27	2–5 s	3 s	Delay before a full restart	Traffic Restart Timer
T28	3–35 s	5 s	Waiting for TRW at remote traffic restart node after links in service at MTP2/3	Remote Traffic Restart Timer
T29	60–65 s	60 s	Timer started when TRA is sent due to unexpected receipt of TRA/TRW	Traffic Restart Timer
T30	30–35 s	32.5 s	Timer to limit TFP and TFR transmission due to unexpected receipt of TRA/TRW	Not used in A-I/F
T31	10–120 s	11 s	False link congestion detection timer	Not used in A-I/F
T32	5–120 s	90 s	Link oscillation timer—Procedure A	Link Restoration Timer
T33	60–600 s	330 s	Link oscillation Probation timer—Procedure B	Link Restoration Timer
T34	5–120 s	62.5 s	Link oscillation Suspension timer—Procedure B	Link Restoration Timer

T1—Delay after Changeover to send MSU This timer specifies the delay associated with a Time-Controlled Changeover procedure. A Time-Controlled Changeover is needed when it is not possible to exchange Changeover messages. Timer T1 is started when a Time-Controlled Changeover is initiated. The action taken by MTP3 during the interval of timer T1 depends on the conditions resulting in the Time-Controlled Changeover. The example below (Figure 2-49) illustrates how timer T1 is used in the case of remote processor outage to help avoid message missequencing.

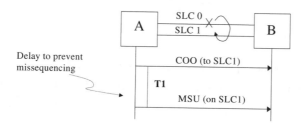

Figure 2-49 MTP3 Timer T1

T2—Waiting for COA Timer This timer is used during the Changeover procedure and is started while waiting for a COA after a COO has been sent. Upon expiry, traffic is started on the alternate link (Figure 2-50).

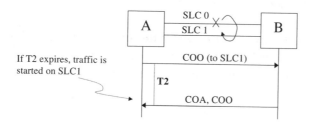

Figure 2-50 MTP3 Timer T2

T3—Delay after Changeback to Send MSU This delay timer, used for a Time-Controlled Changeback procedure, is started when a CBD is transmitted. The purpose of this timer is help prevent missequencing of signaling messages. Upon expiry, signal messages are transmitted over the newly available link (Figure 2-51).

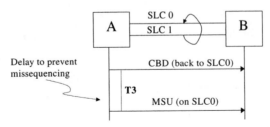

Figure 2-51   MTP3 Timer T3

T4—Waiting for CBA Timer   This timer is started when a CBD is sent and is stopped when a CBA is received. Upon expiry, a second CBD message is transmitted, and timer T5 is started (Figure 2-52).

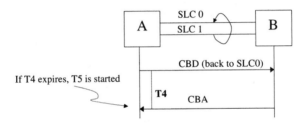

Figure 2-52   MTP3 Timer T4

T5—Waiting for CBA Timer on Second Attempt   This timer is started when timer T4 expires. If no CBA is received before timer T5 expires, maintenance functions are notified, and traffic is restarted on the newly available link (Figure 2-53).

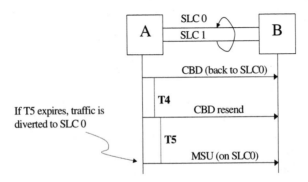

Figure 2-53   MTP3 Timer T5

T12—Waiting for LUA Timer This timer is started when an LUN message is sent and is stopped when a LUA is received. Upon expiry, a second LUN is transmitted. Upon second expiry, the Link Uninhibit process is terminated, and the link status remains unchanged (Figure 2-54).

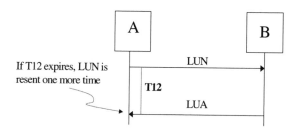

Figure 2-54 MTP3 Timer T12

T13—Waiting for Response to LFU Timer This timer is started when an LFU is sent to a remote signaling point to force an uninhibit on the link in order to synchronize the link states. Timer T13 is stopped upon receipt of an LUN message from the remote point. If timer T13 expires, a second LFU message is sent. Upon the second expiry, the uninhibit process is terminated (Figure 2-55).

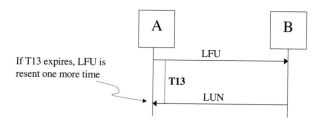

Figure 2-55 MTP3 Timer T13

T14—Waiting for LIA Timer This timer is started upon transmission of an LIN message and is stopped when an LIA is received. If timer T14 expires, a second link inhibit message is sent. Upon second expiry, the Link Inhibit process is terminated, and the link status remains unchanged (Figure 2-56).

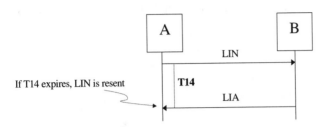

Figure 2-56 MTP3 Timer T14

T20,T21—LLI, LRI Repeat Timers   These timers are used as part of link maintenance after a link has been inhibited. The purpose of these timers is to help ensure that link status at both ends of an inhibited link is consistent. Timer T20 is started by the local signaling point when it receives an LIA in response to a previously sent LIN. Upon expiry of T20, an LLI test message is transmitted to the remote end, and T20 is restarted. If the link inhibit request is allowed at the remote signaling point, timer T21 is started by the remote end. Upon expiry of T21, an LRI test message is transmitted, and timer T21 is restarted (Figure 2-57).

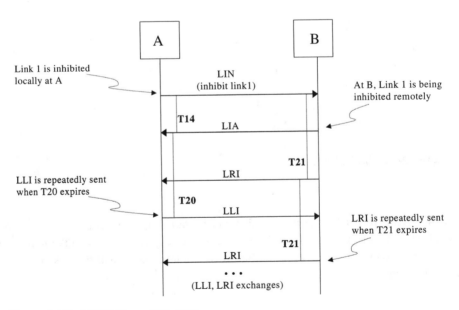

Figure 2-57 MTP3 Timer T20, T21

T17,T19—Link Activation Timers   Timer T17 specifies the delay between Initial Alignment Failure and link restart. The purpose of T17 is to provide a "guide period" to avoid oscillations when a link cannot be brought into service.

Timer T19 specifies the time that MTP3 waits for a signaling link to be brought into the active in-service state. Upon expiry, the Network Management function is notified of the inability to bring the signaling link into service and the link is declared "Failed" (Figure 2-58).

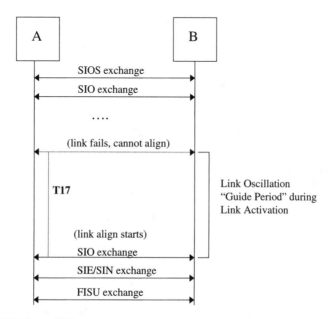

Figure 2-58   MTP3 Timer T17

T32 to T34—Link Restoration Timers   To prevent undesired oscillations between the "In-Service" and the "Out-of-Service" states during the restoration of a link, oscillation prevention procedures are implemented. If a failure occurs immediately after aligning a link, these oscillation timers provide guide periods that prevent rapid link restoration. Two such basic procedures are specified in the MTP3 standard: Procedure A and Procedure B.

Procedure A is used for ensuring that a link that fails during the restoration process does not immediately oscillate into link restoration again. Upon starting the link restoration process, the Link Oscillation Timer T32 is started. If the link fails before timer T32 expires, it is placed in a "Suspension" state until T32 expires. Any attempt to restore or activate a "Suspended" link is discarded. Once T32 expires, link restoration may resume (Figure 2-59).

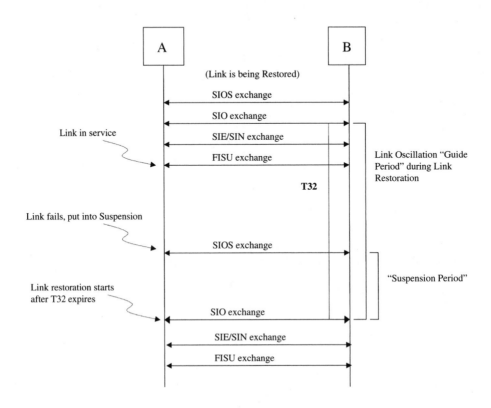

Figure 2-59   MTP3 Timer T32—Link Oscillation Prevention Procedure A

Procedure B is used for ensuring that, once a link is restored successfully, it is put on a Probation "guide period" to prevent immediate link restoration. After a link has been successfully restored to the in-service state, the Probation timer T33 is started. If the link fails before T33 expires, it is placed in a "Suspension" state for a period of T34. Suspension timer T34 is started once the link fails and enters the out-of-service state. During the "Suspended" state, any attempt to restore the link will be ignored (Figure 2-60).

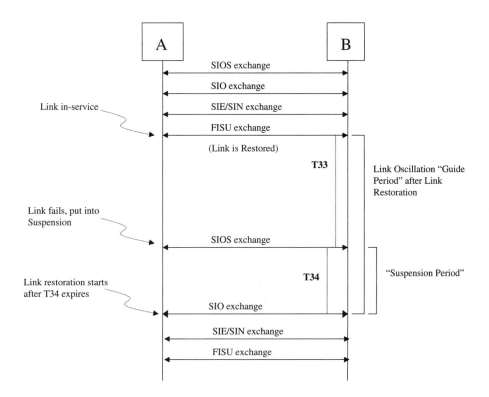

Figure 2-60 MTP3 Timers T33 and T34—Link Oscillation Prevention Procedure B

T22 to T28—Traffic Restart Timers These timers are associated with the MTP Traffic Restart procedure, which may be initiated when a signaling point is first brought into service.

Specifically, timers T22, T23, T26, and T27 are associated with the node that initiates the MTP Restart. Timers T25 and T28 are used by the adjacent node to the MTP Restart node.

T27 specifies a delay that is imposed between the sending of an SIPO and when a full link restart can begin. It serves as a guide period to ensure that adjacent nodes are aware of the unavailability of the node that is initiating the restart.

Timer T22 is started by the MTP Restart node when the first link comes into service at level 2 or 3 and is stopped when sufficient links at the local node come into service.

Timer T23 is started when T22 is stopped. The purpose of the timer is to wait for sufficient TRAs from available links to be received.

T26 is the timer used for repeating the Traffic Restart when insufficient TRAs are received and T26 has expired. In such a case, TRAs are sent to available links, and T26 is restarted.

T28 is the timer at the MTP3 Restart adjacent node that is started when the first link comes into service at level 2 or 3 while waiting for TRWs from the MTP Restart node. Upon expiry, if no TRW is received and if TRAs have already been sent, traffic is restarted at the remote node.

T25 is the timer at the MTP3 Restart adjacent node that is started or restarted whenever a TRW is received while waiting for TRA. If no TRA is received before T25 expires, traffic is restarted at the remote node.

For more details on the usage of the timers and their interactions in MTP Restart, refer to Section 2.5.6, "Traffic Management: MTP Restart," on page 81.

2.6 SCCP Layer

A fundamental feature of SS7 is the division of functionality into common message transfer parts and separate user parts. The SCCP provides additional network capabilities to the MTP, such as connection-oriented and connectionless services, with the purpose of reliably transferring signaling messages between user functions. Through the use of Primitives, the SCCP is both a user of MTP services and a provider of services to user applications (see Figure 2-3 on page 33). The *Transaction Capabilities Application Part* (TCAP) and *Base Station Application Part* (BSAP) are examples of user applications that utilize SCCP services. This book is filled with examples illustrating how BSAP applications, running on both the BSC and MSC, use the SCCP to exchange messages over the A-Interface.

The SCCP provides the ability to establish and control logical signaling connections, transfer data across established connections, and transfer signaling data units without logical connections. The SCCP also provides management functions, which control the availability of subsystems and broadcast status information to other nodes. Although not used in the point-to-point architecture of A-Interface, the SCCP has the capability to provide enhanced routing functions, many of which are used to provide advanced services in today's SS7 network.

2.6.1 SCCP Services

There are four classes of services provided to user applications by the SCCP. These services can be categorized into two functional areas:

1. Connectionless Services
   • Class 0: Basic Connectionless Class (used by the BSAP)
   • Class 1: Sequenced (MTP) Connectionless Class

2. Connection-Oriented Services
   • Class 2: Basic Connection-Oriented Class (used by the BSAP)
   • Class 3: Flow Control Connection-Oriented Class

Connectionless services are used when independent data units are to be sent between nodes (user applications) and no logical connection is set up for the delivery of these "packet" data units. Both Class 0 and Class 1 SCCP protocol types provide connectionless services (Figure 2-61).

Protocol Class 0 is a basic connectionless service that does not provide sequencing of data during data delivery. This class is usually used to deliver noncritical data when guarantee of delivery is minimal. With regard to the A-Interface, Class 0 services are used for messages not associated with an established call.

SCCP Management (SCMG) messages are also designated as Class 0. These messages are used for certain network management functions, such as bringing a subsystem into service, and are not used for basic call processing.

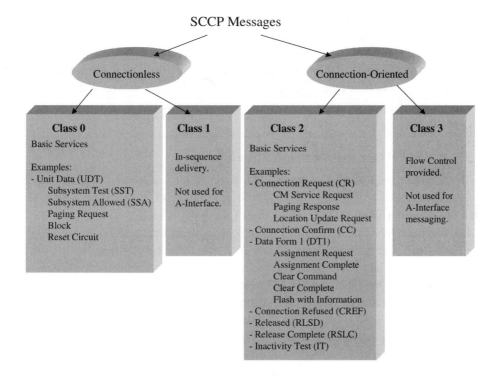

Figure 2-61   SCCP protocol classes

Protocol Class 1 service is an enhanced connectionless service that ensures that messages are delivered in sequence by controlling the SLS field that is transmitted. Currently, this class of service is not being used by BSAP applications to exchange messages across the A-Interface.

Connection-oriented services provide the ability to set up a dedicated logical signaling connection between two nodes for the purpose of in-sequence data delivery. Both Class 2 and Class 3 services provide connection-oriented functionality.

Protocol Class 2 service is used for basic connection-oriented services. This "circuit-switched" approach provides in-sequence data delivery by transmitting related messages over an established path, using the same SLS value. Each end node assigns a unique reference number, known as the *Source Local Reference* (SLR), to identify the SCCP connection. All A-Interface Call Processing procedures utilize Class 2 services. Specifically, the following Class 2 functions are used by BSAP applications in the setup and teardown of wireless calls.

- SCCP Connection Setup
- SCCP Connection Release
- SCCP Connection Data Transfer
- SCCP Connection Inactivity Control
- SCCP Connection Refusal

Protocol Class 3 service is an enhanced connection-oriented service that includes expedited data transfer using flow control techniques. Additional capabilities related to the detection of message loss and message sequence errors are also provided. This class of service is not currently being used by A-Interface applications.

2.6.2   SCCP General Message Structure

To understand the functions of the SCCP, it is important first to understand the basic structure of an SCCP message. Figure 2-62 illustrates the structure of an SCCP message and shows how the SCCP portion of an MSU is subdivided.

Recall that an MSU contains both a *Service Information Octet* (SIO) and *Signaling Information Field* (SIF). The SIO contains a *Service Indicator* (SI) field that specifies the user of the message and the SIF field contains user data. In an SCCP message, the 4-bit SI field is set to 0011, which identifies the MSU as an SCCP message.

The SIF also contains a Routing Label that specifies the origination point code, destination point code, and signaling link selection of the MSU. See Section 2.5.1.1, "MSU Message Structure," on page 57, for a detailed description of the Routing Label. The first octet of the SIF User Data field uniquely identifies the SCCP Message Type. This field is included for all SCCP messages, regardless of Class of service or function. Table 2-11 summarizes all SCCP Message Types and their corresponding 8-bit identifiers.

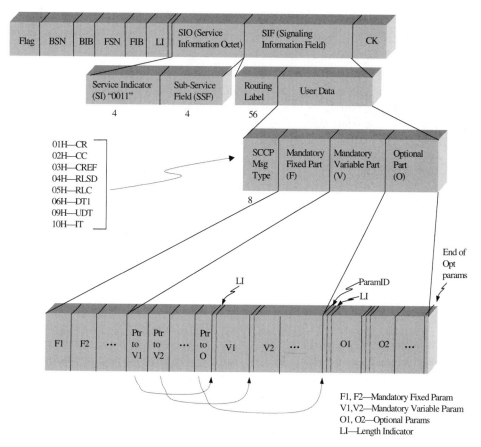

Figure 2-62 SCCP message structure

In addition to the SCCP Message Type field, each SCCP message is composed of up to three message parts. These message parts are designated *Mandatory Fixed, Mandatory Variable*, and *Optional*. The Mandatory Fixed field is required for all SCCP messages; however, depending on the message type, the Mandatory Variable and Option parts may or may not be included. Each message part contains one or more SCCP message parameters that provide message-specific information, such as *Source Local Reference* (SLR). Associated with each SCCP parameter group is a set of message coding schemes and rules:

Mandatory Fixed Part (F) The first field in the Mandatory Fixed Part is the 8-bit Message Type code. The order and length of parameters in this part are fixed, thus eliminating the need to include length and parameter identifiers (Parameter IDs). *Destination*

Local Reference (DLR) is an example of a parameter found in the Mandatory Fixed part of an SCCP Released message.

Mandatory Variable Part (V)   The Mandatory Variable message part contains required parameters that have variable lengths. An 8-bit length indicator is included to specify the length of each parameter.

The Mandatory Variable message part is divided into two sections, one containing a list of pointers and the other containing parameter information. The beginning of the Mandatory Variable message part contains a list of pointers, each one a single octet in length, which specify an offset from the pointer (inclusive) and the first octet (not inclusive) of that parameter. The pointer points to the length indicator containing the length, in octets, of the variable parameter. Following the length octet is the actual parameter information. Because the number of parameters (and pointers) in the Mandatory Variable part is fixed for a given message, no Parameter IDs are necessary. Although the order of the pointers is fixed for a particular SCCP message type, the order of the parameter information may differ because they are indexed individually.

If an SCCP message includes at least one optional parameter, an optional parameter pointer will follow the list of mandatory variable pointers. If the SCCP message allows optional parameters but none are included, an all-zero octet is used to indicate that no optional parameter information is present. If no optional parameters are allowed, the optional pointer is not present.

Optional Part (O)   As mentioned in the Mandatory Variable description, the last pointer contained in the Mandatory Variable part identifies the location of optional SCCP message parameters. Because optional parameters may or may not be included in a particular message, the Parameter ID must be included before each parameter value. For optional parameters of variable length, a 1-octet length indicator is also included after the Parameter ID. If multiple optional parameters are included in an SCCP message, they are sequentially positioned, each having a Parameter ID and, if required, a length indicator. A Parameter ID of all zero indicates the end of the Optional Part.

Table 2-11 presents the common SCCP message parameters used to compose an SCCP message. The table includes bitmaps, Parameter IDs, and octet lengths, and specifies in which message part (Mandatory Fixed [F], Mandatory Variable [V] , and Optional [O]) the parameter may be found. Brief descriptions of the individual parameters follow the table.

Table 2-11 Common Parameters in SCCP Message Structure

Bitmap	Param	ID	#Oct	Range	Type
tttt tttt	SCCP Message Type	-	1	SCCP Message Type 01H—Connection Request (CR) 02H—Connection Confirm (CC) 03H—Connection Refused (CREF) 04H—Released (RLSD) 05H—Release Complete (RLC) 06H—Data Form 1 (DT1) 09H—Unit Data (UDT) 10H—Inactivity Test (IT)	F
pppp pppp	Pointers	-	1	Pointers to V,O	V
LLLL LLLL	Length Indicator	-	1	Length of the parameter content	V,O
0000 0000	End of Optional Params	00H	1	End of Optional Params Indication	O
dddd dddd dddd dddd dddd dddd	Destination Local Reference (DLR)	01H	3	Reference number in the destination node that specifies this connection	F
ssss ssss ssss ssss ssss ssss	Source Local Reference (SLR)	02H	3	Reference number in the local node that specifies this connection	F

Table 2-11   Common Parameters in SCCP Message Structure (Continued)

Bitmap	Param	ID	#Oct	Range	Type
NRGG GGPS ssss ssss pppp pppp pppp pppp pppp pppp gggg gggg gggg gggg	Called Party Address Or Calling Party Address	03H 04H	≥ 1	First Octet = Address Indicator N = National Indicator 0—International, 1—National R = Routing Indicator 0—route by Global Title (GTT) 1—route by PC in routing label and SSN in Called Party Addr G = Global Title Indicator 0000—no GTT included 0001—GTT with translation type, number plan and encoding type 0010—GTT with translation type P = Point Code Indicator (1=included) S = SSN Indicator (1=included) Address Field includes: s = SSN (1 oct), p = point code (3 oct) g = Global Title	V,O
hhhh PPPP	Protocol Class	05H	1	P = Protocol Class 0,1—Connectionless 2,3—Connection h = msg handling If P = 2 or 3, h bits are spare = 0 If P = 0 or 1, h: 0000—discard msg on error 1000—return msg on error	F
0000 000S	Segment/Reas-sembling	06H	1	S = more data indication 0—no more data, 1—more data	F
ssss sss0 rrrr rrrM	Sequencing/Seg-menting	08H	2	This parameter is ignore for Class 2 s = send seq #, r = receive seq # M = 0—no more data, 1—more data	F
cccc cccc	Credit	09H	1	Used for Class 3 flow control	F,O

Table 2-11 Common Parameters in SCCP Message Structure (Continued)

Bitmap	Param	ID	#Oct	Range	Type
rrrr rrrr	Release Cause	0AH	1	Common SCCP release causes: 00H—end user originated (normal) 03H—SCCP user originated 08H—subsystem failure 0DH—rx inactivity timer expired	F
ffff ffff	Refusal Cause	0EH	1	Common SCCP refused causes: 00H—end user originated (normal) 03H—SCCP user originated 0AH—subsystem failure	F
dddd dddd	Data	0FH	> 1	Variable length	V,O
hhhh hhhh	SCCP Hop Counter	11H	1	Used if there is an SCCP relay point	O

The SCCP Message Type parameter is contained in the first octet of the User Data field and is used to identify individual SCCP messages.

Pointers are used to specify the offset, in octets, between the pointer and the Mandatory Variable or Optional parameter information.

The *Length Indicator* octet specifies the length, in octets, of the Mandatory Variable or Optional parameter information.

The *Destination Local Reference* (DLR) parameter contains a unique reference number that is used by the remote end to identify an SCCP connection. The *Source Local Reference* (SLR) is a reference number that is used for referencing an SCCP connection at a local node. The SLR value may be generated randomly when setting up an SCCP connection or it may be chosen from a predefined list of values. This numerical identifier is sent to the destination node during a connection request and a connection release to provide the destination node with the local connection information.

The Called/Calling Party Address parameter provides additional SCCP routing information, including the final DPC, OPC, *Subsystem Number* (SSN), and Global Title (see Section 2.6.6, "SCCP Connectionless Data Transfer," on page 126). Because A-Interface messaging is point to point, routing is done using point code and SSN only. The SSN is specified in CDGIOS to be 252.

The Protocol Class parameter is used for specifying whether the message is Class 0, Class 1, Class 2, or Class 3.

The Segmenting/Reassembling octet indicates whether the User Data has been segmented. When this parameter is set to 1, for example, in a *Data Form 1* (DT1) message, the receiving node collects and reassembles the segmented messages. This parameter is set to 0 in the final segmented message, indicating that it is the final segment. Although segmentation is rarely used for A-Interface messaging, it is allowed. A long SMS message is an example in which segmentation may be useful.

The Sequencing/Segmenting parameter is used exclusively for protocol Class 3 messaging and is ignored for Class 2 connections. This parameter is a Mandatory Fixed parameter in the SCCP *Inactivity Test* (IT) message, but is ignored by A-Interface applications.

The Credit parameter is used for flow control window size indication in Class 3 protocol flow control schemes. This parameter is not used for A-Interface messaging.

The Release Cause value is a mandatory fixed parameter in the SCCP Released (SCCP-RLSD) message and specifies the reason for releasing the SCCP connection.

The Refusal Cause value is a mandatory fixed parameter in the SCCP Connection Refused (SCCP-CREF) message and indicates the reason for refusing an SCCP connection. It is normally sent in response to an SCCP connection request.

The Data parameter is a variable parameter that contains higher-layer user application data. In A-Interface messages, all BSAP layer application data is included in this parameter.

The SCCP Hop Counter parameter is used for routing purposes only if there is an SCCP relay point. This parameter is not necessary in a point-to-point A-Interface network.

Note that the list of SCCP parameters presented in Table 2-11 is not inclusive. There are several SCCP parameters and message types intentionally excluded because they are not used by A-Interface BSAP applications. A complete list of all SCCP parameters and messages, along with detailed explanations, can be found in ANSI T1.112 [6].

2.6.3   SCCP Connection Setup and Release

Because a wireless network may have many simultaneous calls up at any given time, the BSAP applications running on both the BSC and MSC need a method of identifying A-Interface messages with a particular call and to ensure in-sequence delivery of those messages. Class 2 SCCP connection-oriented services are used for this task.

Class 2 connection-oriented services provide the capability to set up a logical SCCP connection, transfer data using the connection, and release connection resources. To perform these SCCP connection services, the following three parameters are used in Class 2 message exchange:

- *Source Local Reference* (SLR)
- *Destination Local Reference* (DLR)
- *Signaling Link Selection* (SLS)

When a node, usually the BSC, initiates a connection setup, it sends an *SCCP Connection Request* (SCCP-CR) message to the remote node that includes a unique local reference number, the SLR. This number is used by the remote node to reference the connection in subsequent messages. If the remote node decides to allow the connection, it responds to the connection request message with an *SCCP Connection Confirm* (SCCP-CC). Otherwise, an *SCCP Connection Refused* (SCCP-CREF) is returned (see Section 2.6.4, "SCCP Connection Refusal," on page 118).

Prior to sending an SCCP-CC message, the remote end also chooses a unique local reference number for the logical connection. At this point, each node has assigned its own unique identifier to the SCCP connection. The remote end includes its local identifier in the SLR parameter of the SCCP-CC message. Also included in the message is the DLR, which is set to the value received in the SLR field of the SCCP-CR message. Note that the DLR parameter in a Class 2 SCCP message specifies the logical connection reference used at the receiving node to identify the connection.

Both nodes are required to maintain both the local and remote references. Once a connection has been established, connection-oriented data transfer is possible using *SCCP Data Form 1* (SCCP-DT1) messages. The SCCP-DT1 message specifies the SCCP connection using the DLR.

The *Signaling Link Selection* (SLS) is the third SCCP parameter that plays an important role in providing connection-oriented services. The SLS is used to determine which outgoing signaling link will carry the SS7 message. To ensure in-sequence message delivery by choosing the same link, the SLS value for a specific connection remains fixed at each node. Note that the same signaling link may not be chosen by each node; however, each node will continue to use the same link for all subsequent connection messages.

When an SCCP connection is no longer needed, the initiating node sends an *SCCP Released* (SCCP-RLSD) message. The receiving node responds with an *SCCP Release Complete* (SCCP-RLC) to indicate that connection resources have been released.

2.6.3.1   SCCP Connection Setup and Release Example

Figure 2-63 shows how the BSC and MSC use an SCCP Class 2 connection to service a call. The purpose of the example is to illustrate SCCP connection-oriented functionality.

The example in Figure 2-63 begins with the BSC requesting an SCCP connection in response to a mobile origination attempt. Prior to sending the SCCP-CR message, the BSC sets the SLR for the requested connection to 713. The BSC will use 713 to reference the connection throughout the call. Upon sending the message, the BSC starts SCCP timer *Tconn_est*.

The MSC, after receiving the SCCP-CR, sets its own SLR to 2. Prior to notifying the BSC that it is allowing the connection, the MSC sets the DLR parameter to the value (713) received from the BSC in the SCCP-CR message. Both the SLR and DLR are packaged by the MSC into an SCCP-CC message that is sent to the BSC. Upon receipt of the SCCP-CC message, the BSC stops timer *Tconn_est*.

Once the SCCP connection has been established, subsequent data transfer may occur using SCCP-DT1 messages. Notice that the node originating the DT1 messages sets the DLR to the connection reference number used at the receiving end. For example, the third message in the call flow is a DT1 message being sent from the MSC to the BSC. The MSC sets the DLR parameter in this message to 713, which is the reference number that the BSC is using for the SCCP connection.

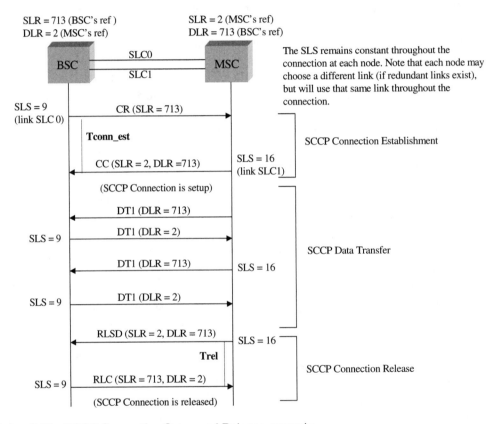

Figure 2-63   SCCP Connection Setup and Release example

After exchanging several DT1 messages, the MSC initiates the SCCP connection release by sending an SCCP-RLSD message. This message contains both the SLR and DLR parameters. The MSC starts timer *Trel*. The BSC responds with an SCCP-RLC message, indicating that the SCCP resource has been successfully released. Upon receiving the SCCP-RLC message, the MSC stops timer *Trel*.

Figure 2-64 illustrates how Class 2 SCCP connections provide in-sequence message delivery using a message summary example that is similar to information easily obtained using SS7 test equipment. In this Figure 2-64, *1:D:3* identifies the first signaling link (SLC 0), and *1:C:4* identifies the second signaling link (SLC 1). Notice that the BSC (1-1-1) uses an SLS of 9, which corresponds to the first link with SLC 0 (D:3), throughout the connection. This ensures that all messages from the BSC to the MSC (1-2-4) for this SCCP connection will arrive in sequence. The MSC uses an SLS of 16 for the duration of the call, which corresponds to the SLC 1. Recall that each node independently selects a signaling link for the SCCP connection, then stays with that link for the entire call. Descriptions of the individual messages, including message format tables and examples, follow Figure 2-64.

```
+----------------+-----------------+-----------------+---------------+
From    Time           OPC     DPC     SLS  SLR  DLR  MSG
+----------------+-----------------+-----------------+---------------+
1:D:3   22:13:20,418   1-1-1   1-2-4   9    713  -    CR   BSAP CMSR
1:C:4   22:13:20,438   1-2-4   1-1-1   16   2    713  CC
1:C:4   22:13:20,448   1-2-4   1-1-1   16   -    713  DT1  BSMAP   AREQ
1:D:3   22:13:22,316   1-1-1   1-2-4   9    -    2    DT1  BSMAP   ACOM
1:D:3   22:13:55,377   1-1-1   1-2-4   9    -    2    DT1  DTAP    FINF
1:D:3   22:24:20,264   1-1-1   1-2-4   9    -    2    DT1  BSMAP   CREQ
1:C:4   22:24:20,282   1-2-4   1-1-1   16   -    713  DT1  BSMAP   CLMD
1:D:3   22:24:20,643   1-1-1   1-2-4   9    -    2    DT1  BSMAP   CCOM
1:C:4   22:24:23,053   1-2-4   1-1-1   16   2    713  RLSD
1:D:3   22:24:23,065   1-1-1   1-2-4   9    713  2    RLC
```

Figure 2-64   SCCP Connection Setup/Teardown message log example

2.6.3.2   SCCP Connection Request Message Structure
Table 2-12 shows the message format of an SCCP-CR message. The first three parameters in the SCCP-CR message are contained in the Mandatory Fixed Part. These include the Message Type, SLR, and Protocol Class. The Called Party parameter, which contains additional routing information, is included in the Mandatory Variable Part. Because the A-Interface is a point-to-point connection, this parameter is set to include point code and SSN. The remaining parameters are optional and may or may not be present in the Optional Part.

Table 2-12   SCCP Connection Request Message Format

Bitmap	Parameter	#Oct	Range	Type
0000 0001 (01H)	SCCP Msg Type	1	Connection Request	F
ssss ssss ssss ssss ssss ssss	Source Local Reference	3	s = SLR number	F
0000 0010	Protocol Class	1	Class 2	F

Table 2-12   SCCP Connection Request Message Format (Continued)

Bitmap	Parameter	#Oct	Range	Type
LLLL LLLL NRGG GGPS ssss ssss pppp pppp pppp pppp pppp pppp	Called Party Address	≥ 3	L = length, N = 1—National R = 1—route by PC/SSN G = 0—no GTT P = 1—Point Code included S = 1—SSN included s = SSN, p = Point Code	V
	Credit	3	(not used in A-I/F)	O
	Calling Party Addr	≥ 3	(not used in A-I/F)	O
0000 1111 (0FH) LLLL LLLL dddd dddd	Data	3–130	L = length d = data	O
	SCCP Hop Counter	3	(not used in A-I/F)	O
0000 0000	End of Optional Params	1		O

Figure 2-65 shows an example of an SCCP-CR message being sent from a BSC to an MSC. The SCCP data begins with the SCCP Message Type octet, which is set to 1, identifying the message as a Connection Request. Following the Message Type are the SLR and Protocol Class parameters. The SLR is set to 713, and the Protocol Class is set to 2. Recall that the Message Type, SLR, and Protocol Class are all Mandatory Fixed parameters. The first portion of the Mandatory Variable Part comprises two pointers; the first points to the Called Party Address parameter at offset 2, and the second points to the start of the Optional Part, at offset 7. In this example, the Optional Part contains application layer data. Because the Data parameter is a variable-length parameter, the identifier is followed by an octet specifying the Data parameter's length. The last octet of this message is an octet of zeros, indicating the end of optional parameters.

```
MTP Level 2 (MTP-L2)
 -1000001  Backward Sequence Number        65
 1-------  Backward Indicator Bit          1
 -1000100  Forward Sequence Number         68
 1-------  Forward Indicator Bit           1
 --111111  Length Indicator                63
```

(Continued)

00------	Spare	0
----0011	Service Indicator	SCCP
--00----	Sub-Service: Priority	Spare/priority 0 (U.S.A. only)
10------	Sub-Service: Network Ind	National message
B3	Destination Point Code	1-2-4
B3	Originating Point Code	1-1-1

Connection Request

00001001	Signaling Link Selection	9
00000001	SCCP Message Type	1
B3	Source Local Reference	713
----0010	Protocol Class	Class 2
0000----	Spare	0
00000010	Pointer to parameter	2
00000111	Pointer to parameter	7

Called address parameter

00000101	Parameter Length	5
-------1	Subsystem No. Indicator	SSN present
------1-	Point Code Indicator	PC present
--0000--	Global Title Indicator	No global title included
-1------	Routing Indicator	Route on DPC + Subsystem No.
1-------	For national use	National address
11111100	Subsystem number	252
B3	Called Party SPC	1-2-4

Data parameter

00001111	Parameter name	Data
00110000	Parameter length	48
B48*	Data	00 2e 57 05 05 01 03...

End of optional parameters

00000000	Parameter name	End of Optional Params

Figure 2-65 SCCP Connection Request message example

2.6.3.3   SCCP Connection Confirm Message Structure

Table 2-13 shows the message format of an SCCP-CC. Unlike the Connection Request message, this message contains only Mandatory Fixed and Optional Parts. The first four message parameters, Message Type, DLR, SLR, and Protocol Class, are contained in the Mandatory Fixed part. The remaining parameters are optional and may or may not be present in the message. The Credit and Called Party Address fields are not usually included in the SCCP-CC message when used for A-Interface applications. The optional Data parameter may be used if the SCCP-CC message is "piggybacked" on an application layer message.

Figure 2-66 shows an example of an SCCP-CC message being sent from an MSC. The SCCP data begins with the SCCP Message Type octet, which is set to 2, identifying the message as a Connection Confirm. Following the Message Type are the DLR, SLR, and Protocol Class parameters. The DLR is set to 713, which is the value received in the previously described Connection Request message. The local MSC connection reference of 2 is contained in the SLR parameter. The Protocol Class is set to 2.

The Mandatory Variable Part of the Connection Confirm message has no parameter values and, therefore, is comprised of a single pointer that points to the Optional Part. Because this example Connection Confirmed message does not contain any optional parameters, the pointer octet is set to 0, indicating the end of the Optional Part.

Table 2-13   SCCP Connection Confirm Message Format

Bitmap	Parameter	#Oct	Range	Type
0000 0010 (02H)	SCCP Msg Type	1	Connection Confirm	F
dddd dddd dddd dddd dddd dddd	Destination Local Reference	3	d = DLR number	F
ssss ssss ssss ssss ssss ssss	Source Local Reference	3	s = SLR number	F
0000 0010	Protocol Class	1	Class 2	F
	Credit	3	(not used in A-I/F)	O
	Called Party Addr	≥ 4	(not used in A-I/F)	O
0000 1111 (0FH) LLLL LLLL dddd dddd	Data	3– 130	L = length d = data	O
0000 0000	End of Optional Params	1		O

```
MTP Level 2 (MTP-L2)
 -1000100  Backward Sequence Number     68
 1-------  Backward Indicator Bit       1
 -1000010  Forward Sequence Number      66
 1-------  Forward Indicator Bit        1
 --010001  Length Indicator             17
 00------  Spare                        0
 ----0011  Service Indicator            SCCP
 --00----  Sub-Service: Priority        Spare/priority 0 (U.S.A. only)
 10------  Sub-Service: Network Ind     National message
 ***B3***  Destination Point Code       1-1-1
```

(Continued)
```
***B3***    Originating Point Code        1-2-4
Connection Confirm
00010000    Signaling Link Selection      16
00000010    SCCP Message Type             2
***B3***    Destination Local Ref.        713
***B3***    Source Local Reference        2
----0010    Protocol Class                Class 2
0000----    Spare                         0
00000000    Pointer to parameter          0
```

Figure 2-66 SCCP Connection Confirm message example

2.6.3.4   SCCP Data Form 1 Message Structure

Table 2-14 shows the message format of SCCP-DT1 message. Because this message is used to transfer application data associated with a specific SCCP connection, the Data parameter is contained in the Mandatory Variable Part. The Mandatory Fixed DLR parameter, as mentioned previously, references the SCCP connection at the remote end.

Table 2-14 SCCP Data Form 1 Message Format

Bitmap	Parameter	#Oct	Range	Type
0000 0110 (06H)	SCCP Msg Type	1	Data Form 1	F
dddd dddd dddd dddd dddd dddd	Destination Local Reference	3	d = DLR number	F
0000 000S	Segmenting/ Reassembling	1	S = 0—no more data	F
LLLL LLLL dddd dddd …….	Data	2–256	L = length d = data	V

Figure 2-67 shows an example of an SCCP-DT1 message being sent from a BSC to an MSC. The SCCP data begins with the SCCP Message Type octet, which is set to 6, identifying the message as type DT1. Following the Message Type is the DLR, set to 2, and the Segmentation bit. The Segmentation bit is set to 0, indicating that no more data should be expected.

The Mandatory Variable Part of a DT1 message consists of a single pointer that points to the Mandatory Variable Data parameter. Because the Data parameter is of variable length, the length indicator follows. Note that, unlike the optional parameters described for the Connection Request message, no Parameter ID is necessary for this Mandatory Variable parameter.

```
MTP Level 2 (MTP-L2)
  -1000101  Backward Sequence Number      69
  1-------  Backward Indicator Bit        1
  -1001000  Forward Sequence Number       72
  1-------  Forward Indicator Bit         1
  --010101  Length Indicator              21
  00------  Spare                         0
  ----0011  Service Indicator             SCCP
  --00----  Sub-Service: Priority         Spare/priority 0 (U.S.A. only)
  10------  Sub-Service: Network Ind      National message
  ***B3***  Destination Point Code        1-2-4
  ***B3***  Originating Point Code        1-1-1
Data Form 1
  00001001  Signaling Link Selection      9
  00000110  SCCP Message Type             6
  ***B3***  Destination Local Ref.        2
  -------0  Segment/reass M indicator     No more data
  0000000-  Spare                         0
  00000001  Pointer to parameter          1
Data parameter
  00000110  Parameter length              6
  ***B6***  Data                          01 00 03 03 00 10
```

Figure 2-67   SCCP Data Form 1 message example

2.6.3.5   SCCP Released Message Structure

Table 2-15 shows the message format of an SCCP-RLSD message, which contains only Mandatory Fixed and Optional Parts. Because this message is used for tearing down an SCCP connection, the SLR and DLR parameters are sent to reference the connection to be torn down. The Mandatory Fixed Release Cause value indicates the reason why the SCCP connection is being released. An optional Data parameter also exists but is seldom used in A-Interface Implementation.

Table 2-15   SCCP Released Message Format

Bitmap	Parameter	#Oct	Range	Type
0000 0100 (04H)	SCCP Msg Type	1	Released	F
dddd dddd dddd dddd dddd dddd	Destination Local Reference	3	d = DLR number	F
ssss ssss ssss ssss ssss ssss	Source Local Reference	3	s = SLR number	F

Table 2-15   SCCP Released Message Format (Continued)

Bitmap	Parameter	#Oct	Range	Type
cccc cccc	Release Cause	1	Release cause reasons	F
0000 1111 (0FH) LLLL LLLL dddd dddd …….	Data	3–130	L = length d = data	O
0000 0000	End of Optional Params	1		O

Figure 2-68 shows an example of an SCCP-RLSD message being sent from an MSC to a BSC. The SCCP data begins with the SCCP Message Type octet, which is set to 4, identifying the message as type Released. Following the Message Type is the SLR, set to 2, and the DLR is set to 713. The SCCP release reason is specified as End User Originated, which is typical for a normal SCCP release.

Because, in this example, the SCCP-RLSD message does not contain any optional parameters, the pointer octet is set to 0, indicating the end of the Optional Part.

```
MTP Level 2 (MTP-L2)
 -1010101  Backward Sequence Number      85
 1-------  Backward Indicator Bit        1
 -1010100  Forward Sequence Number       84
 1-------  Forward Indicator Bit         1
 --010001  Length Indicator              17
 00------  Spare                         0
 ----0011  Service Indicator             SCCP
 --00----  Sub-Service: Priority         Spare/priority 0 (U.S.A. only)
 10------  Sub-Service: Network Ind      National message
 ***B3***  Destination Point Code        1-1-1
 ***B3***  Originating Point Code        1-2-4
 Released
 00010000  Signaling Link Selection      16
 00000100  SCCP Message Type             4
 ***B3***  Destination Local Ref.        713
 ***B3***  Source Local Reference        2
 00000000  Release Cause                 End user originated
 00000000  Pointer to parameter          0
```

Figure 2-68   SCCP Released message example

2.6.3.6   SCCP Release Complete Message Structure

Table 2-16 shows the message format of an SCCP-RLC message, which contains only Mandatory Fixed parameters. Because this message is used to acknowledge the release of an SCCP connection, the DLR and SLR parameters are sent to reference the released connection.

Table 2-16   SCCP Release Complete Message Format

Bitmap	Parameter	#Oct	Range	Type
0000 0101 (05H)	SCCP Msg Type	1	Release Complete	F
dddd dddd dddd dddd dddd dddd	Destination Local Reference	3	d = DLR number	F
ssss ssss ssss ssss ssss ssss	Source Local Reference	3	s = SLR number	F

Figure 2-69 shows an example of a SCCP-RLC message. The SCCP data begins at the SCCP Message Type, followed by the Mandatory Fixed DLR and SLR parameters.

```
MTP Level 2 (MTP-L2)
 -1000100  Backward Sequence Number      68
 1-------  Backward Indicator Bit        1
 -1001101  Forward Sequence Number       77
 1-------  Forward Indicator Bit         1
 --001111  Length Indicator              15
 00------  Spare                         0
 ----0011  Service Indicator             SCCP
 --10----  Sub-Service: Priority         priority 2 (U.S.A. only)
 10------  Sub-Service: Network Ind      National message
 ***B3***  Destination Point Code        1-2-4
 ***B3***  Originating Point Code        1-1-1
Release Complete
 00001001  Signaling Link Selection      9
 00000101  SCCP Message Type             5
 ***B3***  Destination Local Ref.        2
 ***B3***  Source Local Reference        713
```

Figure 2-69   SCCP Release Complete message example

2.6.4   SCCP Connection Refusal

When the node is unable or unwilling to grant a requested SCCP connection, it responds with an SCCP-CREF message. Although this message is used in many failure scenarios to reject an SCCP connection setup request, it is also utilized in successful short transactions. For example, during a successful mobile registration, the MSC responds to a Location Updating Request message with a Location Updating Accept message, which is contained in the Data parameter of an SCCP-CREF message. In such a scenario, the SCCP-CREF message contains sufficient information to complete the data transfer; therefore, no connection is necessary.

2.6.4.1   SCCP Connection Refusal Example

Figure 2-70 is an example message log showing Location Update and Location Update Accept messages being exchanged over an A-Interface. As mentioned earlier, these messages are used during the registration of a mobile station. A complete description of these two messages is provided in the Mobility Management chapter. The purpose of this example is to illustrate the message structure and content of the SCCP-CREF message.

The example starts with the BSC (1-1-1) sending a Location Updating message to the MSC (1-2-4) that contains mobile registration information. The message is sent as an SCCP-CR message. The MSC responds with a Location Updating Accept message, indicating that the registration was successful. The Location Update Accept message is sent as an SCCP-CREF message. Because the SCCP-CREF message contains all of the information required to complete the data exchange, no SCCP connection is set up. Also note that the MSC does not assign an SLR because it is refusing the connection.

```
+-----------------+---------+----------------------+---------------+
 From    Time          OPC       DPC      SLS  SLR  DLR  MSG
+-----------------+---------+----------------------+---------------+
 1:D:4  22:23:36,674  1-1-1    1-2-4    25   842  -    CR      BSMAP  LURQ
 1:C:4  22:23:36,695  1-2-4    1-1-1    5    -    842  CREF    DTAP   LUAC
```

Figure 2-70 SCCP Connection Refusal message log example

2.6.4.2   SCCP Connection Refused Message Structure

Table 2-17 shows the message format of an SCCP-CREF message. The first three parameters in the SCCP-CR message are contained in the Mandatory Fixed Part. These include the Message Type, DLR, and Refusal Cause. Unlike the SCCP-CR message, the Called Party parameter, which contains additional routing information, is included in the Optional Part. The only other optional parameter allowed is Data, which may be used for including application layer information.

Table 2-17 SCCP Connection Refused Message Format

Bitmap	Parameter	#Oct	Range	Type
0000 0011 (03H)	SCCP Msg Type	1	Connection Refused	F
dddd dddd dddd dddd dddd dddd	Destination Local Reference	3	d = DLR number	F

Table 2-17   SCCP Connection Refused Message Format (Continued)

Bitmap	Parameter	#Oct	Range	Type
cccc cccc	Refusal Cause	1	Refused cause reasons	F
0000 0011(03H) LLLL LLLL NRGG GGPS ssss ssss pppp pppp pppp pppp pppp pppp	Called Party Address	≥ 4	L = length, N = 1—National R = 1—route by PC/SSN G = 0—no GTT P = 1—PC included S = 1—SSN included s = SSN, p = Point Code	O
0000 1111 (0FH) LLLL LLLL dddd dddd	Data	3–130	L = length d = data	O
0000 0000	End of Optional Params	1		O

Figure 2-71 shows an example of an SCCP-CREF message. The SCCP data begins with the Message Type, which is set to 3, indicating a Connection Refusal message. The Mandatory Fixed DLR and Refusal Cause parameters follow the Message Type. In this example, the refusal reason is set to End User Originated, indicating that a normal refusal was invoked at the remote end.

The optional parameters Called Party Address and Data are included in the message. The Called Party Address provides additional routing information regarding the SSN (252). The Data field contains the Location Update Accept BSAP layer message.

```
MTP Level 2 (MTP-L2)
 -1010010  Backward Sequence Number        82
 1-------  Backward Indicator Bit          1
 -1001111  Forward Sequence Number         79
 1-------  Forward Indicator Bit           1
 --011110  Length Indicator                30
 00------  Spare                           0
 ----0011  Service Indicator               SCCP
 --00----  Sub-Service: Priority           Spare/priority 0 (U.S.A. only)
 10------  Sub-Service: Network Ind        National message
 ***B3***  Destination Point Code          1-1-1
 ***B3***  Originating Point Code          1-2-4
Connection Refused
 00000101  Signaling Link Selection        5
 00000011  SCCP Message Type               3
 ***B3***  Destination Local Ref.          842
```

(Continued)
```
00000000   Refusal Cause                      End user originated
00000001   Pointer to parameter               1
Called address parameter
00000011   Parameter name                     Called party address
00000101   Parameter Length                   5
-------1   Subsystem No. Indicator            SSN present
------1-   Point Code Indicator               PC present
--0000--   Global Title Indicator             No global title included
-1------   Routing Indicator                  Route on DPC + Subsystem No.
1-------   For national use                   National address
11111100   Subsystem number                   252
***B3***   Called Party SPC                   1-2-4
Data parameter
00001111   Parameter name                     Data
00000110   Parameter length                   6
***B6***   Data                               01 00 03 05 00 02
End of optional parameters
00000000   Parameter name                     End of Optional Params
```

Figure 2-71   SCCP Connection Refused message example

2.6.5   SCCP Connection Inactivity Control

When an SCCP connection is established, the SCCP Inactivity Control functions at both ends are invoked to perform inactivity tests that maintain the integrity of the connection. Specifically, the purposes of such inactivity tests are:

- To "keep alive" an SCCP connection by sending MSUs to the other end.
- To clean up stale SCCP connections on both ends.

Stale SCCP connections may occur if an SCCP-CC message is lost or if one end improperly terminates the data transfer, leaving the other node with an incorrect connection status. A link going out of service or resetting is an example of a scenario that may result in stale SCCP connections. Stale connections are finally released by SCCP Inactivity Control functions.

Inactivity Control is accomplished using the *Send Inactivity Timer* (*Tias*) and the *Receive Inactivity Timer* (*Tiar*). Both ends use these two SCCP timers to maintain established connections and to identify stale connections (Figure 2-72).

When an SCCP connection is established, each end starts timers *Tias* and *Tiar*. Upon expiry of *Tias*, the local node sends an *SCCP Inactivity Test* (SCCP-IT) message to the remote end.

Tiar is used to ensure that a connection gets torn down if the inactivity period exceeds the configured threshold. The timer is reset whenever a message (not only an IT message) is received. If there is no message received for a period exceeding *Tiar*, the timer expires, the connection is designated as being stale, and the local node initiates an SCCP release.

Notice that for Inactivity Control to function properly, the value of *Tiar* at the local node must be greater than that of *Tias* at the remote node. If this is not true, an established call will be released as soon as *Tiar* expires. The *Tiar* value is often set to a value at least twice that of the *Tias* value, allowing for at least one IT message loss before tearing down the connection.

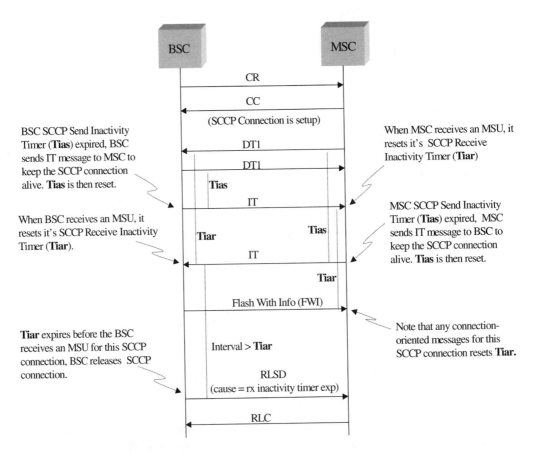

Figure 2-72   SCCP Inactivity Control call flow example

2.6.5.1   SCCP Inactivity Control Example

Figure 2-72 illustrates Inactivity Control message flow. After the SCCP connection has been established, the BSC sends an IT message whenever *Tias* expires. When the MSC receives the IT message, it resets *Tiar* because the successful receipt of a message indicates that the connection is still alive. Note that the *Flash With Information* (SCCP type DT1) message sent by the BSC also resets MSC timer *Tiar*.

Similarly, the MSC sends IT messages whenever its local *Tias* timer expires. Upon receipt of the IT message, the BSC resets its *Tiar* timer.

The call is this example is eventually torn down because the BSC did not receive any messages associated with the SCCP connection before *Tiar* expired. The BSC then initiates an abnormal SCCP release.

Figure 2-73 illustrates Inactivity Control using a message summary example that is similar to information easily obtained using SS7 test equipment. The log shows how IT messages are used to maintain an established SCCP connection. In this example, the BSC's point code is 1-1-1 and the MSC's point code is 1-2-4. BSC timers *Tias* and *Tiar* were set to 100 seconds and 11 min, respectively. These are not standard timer values but were chosen for this example to illustrate Inactivity Control functions better. MSC timers *Tias* and *Tiar* were set to 10 min and 20 min, respectively.

The SCCP connection is set up with the BSC's SLR of 713 and the MSC's SLR of 2. After the connection has been established, the BSC sends IT messages at intervals of 100 seconds, which is the value of *Tias* at the BSC. Note that after sending the FWI DT1 message, the BSC resets timer *Tias*.

The MSC sends an IT message after 10 min, which is the value of *Tias* at the MSC. Because *Tiar* at the BSC is set to 11 min, the receipt of this message keeps the SCCP connection alive, and the BSC resets *Tiar*.

However, due to an error condition at the MSC, the MSC does not send another IT message. At 22:34:25, the BSC's *Tiar* timer expires, and the BSC sends an SCCP-RLSD with a cause value of Receive Inactivity Timer Expired. The connection is eventually torn down, and all SCCP resources are released.

```
+----------------+---------+-------------------------+--------------+
  From    Time        OPC     DPC     SLS  SLR  DLR  MSG
+----------------+---------+-------------------------+--------------+
  1:D:4   22:13:20,418  1-1-1   1-2-4   9    713  -    CR  BSAP CMSR
  1:C:4   22:13:20,438  1-2-4   1-1-1   16   2    713  CC
  1:C:4   22:13:20,448  1-2-4   1-1-1   16   -    713  DT1  BSMAP   AREQ
  1:D:4   22:13:22,316  1-1-1   1-2-4   9    -    2    DT1  BSMAP   ACOM
  1:D:4   22:13:55,377  1-1-1   1-2-4   9    -    2    DT1  DTAP    FINF
  1:D:4   22:13:55,377  1-1-1   1-2-4   9    -    2    SCCP DT1    DTAP  FINF
  1:D:4   22:15:34,394  1-1-1   1-2-4   9    713  2    SCCP IT
  1:D:4   22:17:14,394  1-1-1   1-2-4   9    713  2    SCCP IT
  1:D:4   22:18:54,393  1-1-1   1-2-4   9    713  2    SCCP IT
  1:D:4   22:20:33,927  1-1-1   1-2-4   9    -    2    SCCP DT1    DTAP  FINF
  1:D:4   22:22:13,393  1-1-1   1-2-4   9    713  2    SCCP IT
  1:D:4   22:22:51,184  1-1-1   1-2-4   9    -    2    SCCP DT1    DTAP  FINF
  1:D:4   22:22:59,464  1-1-1   1-2-4   9    -    2    SCCP DT1    DTAP  FINF
  1:C:4   22:23:21,347  1-2-4   1-1-1   16   2    713  SCCP IT

  . . . . . . .

 (no MSU received from C:4 for > 11 mins, BSC initiate Abnormal SCCP Release)
  1:D:4   22:34:25,723  1-1-1   1-2-4   9    713  2    RLSD(Inact timer exp)
  1:C:4   22:34:25,994  1-2-4   1-1-1   16   2    713  RLC
  1:D:4   22:34:26,727  1-2-4   1-1-1   27   -    -    UDT  BSMAP   RSCirc
  1:C:4   22:34:26,920  1-1-1   1-2-4   8    -    -    UDT  BSMAP   RSCircAck
```

(Continued)
```
BSC                          MSC
Tias = 100 s                 Tias = 10 min
Tiar = 11 min                Tiar = 20 min
```

Figure 2-73   SCCP Inactivity Control message log example

2.6.5.2   SCCP Inactivity Test Message Structure

Table 2-18 shows the message format of an SCCP-IT message, which contains only Mandatory Fixed parameters. Because this message is used for maintaining an SCCP connection, the SLR and DLR parameters are sent to the remote end to identify the connection. The message also included the Protocol Class, which is set to 2 for A-Interface applications.

The Mandatory Fixed parameters Sequencing/Segmenting and Credit are not used for Class 2 connection. Both parameters are associated with flow control schemes and are simply ignored by A-Interface applications.

Table 2-18   SCCP Inactivity Test Message Format

Bitmap	Parameter	#Oct	Range	Type
0001 0000 (10H)	SCCP Msg Type	1	Inactivity Test	F
dddd dddd dddd dddd dddd dddd	Destination Local Reference	3	d = DLR number	F
ssss ssss ssss ssss ssss ssss	Source Local Reference	3	s = SLR number	F
0000 0010	Protocol Class	1	Class 2	F
ssss sss0 rrrr rrrM	Sequencing/Segmenting	2	(not used in A-I/F) s, r, M are ignored for A-I/F	F
cccc cccc	Credit	1	(not used in A-I/F)	F

Figure 2-74 shows an example of an IT message in a format similar to what would be seen on test equipment monitoring an A-Interface signaling link. The SCCP data begins with the SCCP Message Type, which is set to 16, indicating that the message is an IT message. The DLR, SLR, and Protocol Class follow the message type. Notice that the Sequencing/Segmenting and Credit parameters are included but set to 0, because they are not necessary for Class 2 services.

```
MTP Level 2 (MTP-L2)
 -1001000   Backward Sequence Number       72
 1-------   Backward Indicator Bit         1
 -1001100   Forward Sequence Number        76
 1-------   Forward Indicator Bit          1
 --010011   Length Indicator               19
 00------   Spare                          0
 ----0011   Service Indicator              SCCP
 --00----   Sub-Service: Priority          Spare/priority 0 (U.S.A. only)
 10------   Sub-Service: Network Ind       National message
 ***B3***   Destination Point Code         1-2-4
 ***B3***   Originating Point Code         1-1-1
Inactivity Test
 00001001   Signaling Link Selection       9
 00010000   SCCP Message Type              16
 ***B3***   Destination Local Ref.         2
 ***B3***   Source Local Reference         713
 ----0010   Protocol Class                 Class 2
 0000000-   Send Sequence Number           0
 -------0   More Data Indicator            No more data
 0000000-   Receive Sequence Number        0
 00000000   Credit                         0
```

Figure 2-74   SCCP Inactivity Test message example

Figure 2-75 shows an example of an SCCP-RLSD message that is sent when the *Tiar* Timer at a node expires. In this case, the Release Cause is set to Receive Inactivity Timer Expired to indicate that the SCCP release was initiated because of SCCP connection inactivity.

```
MTP Level 2 (MTP-L2)
 -1010101   Backward Sequence Number       85
 1-------   Backward Indicator Bit         1
 -1010100   Forward Sequence Number        84
 1-------   Forward Indicator Bit          1
 --010001   Length Indicator               17
 00------   Spare                          0
 ----0011   Service Indicator              SCCP
 --00----   Sub-Service: Priority          Spare/priority 0 (U.S.A. only)
 10------   Sub-Service: Network Ind       National message
 ***B3***   Destination Point Code         1-2-4
 ***B3***   Originating Point Code         1-1-1
Released
 00001001   Signaling Link Selection       9
 00000100   SCCP Message Type              4
 ***B3***   Destination Local Ref.         2
 ***B3***   Source Local Reference         713
 00001101   Release Cause                  13 - rx inactivitiy timer expire
 00000000   Pointer to parameter           0
```

Figure 2-75   SCCP Released with Inactivity Timer Expired Cause message example

2.6.6   SCCP Connectionless Data Transfer

There are instances when an SCCP connection is not required for data transfer between SCCP users. When data is to be delivered without setting up a connection, the SCCP Connectionless Data Transfer function is invoked. This function includes:

- Routing of message signal units using the Routing Label and SCCP Called Party Address
- Data information transfer using the *SCCP Unit Data* (SCCP-UDT) message

When routing UDT messages in an A-Interface point-to-point network, the SCCP Called Party Address field is set to the SSN of the adjacent node. CDGIOS specifies that an SSN of 252 be used to distinguish the A-Interface software entity at both the BSC and MSC. The UDT message is then delivered to the DPC specified in the Routing Label (or in the Called Party Address field, if present) and the SSN entity.

In a network with STPs, the routing of UDT messages can also be achieved using a Global Title in the Called Party Address field. If *Global Title Translation* (GTT) is specified, the string of digits in the Called Party Address field are translated to a point code and SSN using a GTT lookup table configured on the STP. The advantage of using an STP is that the originating node does not need to know the DPC and SSN of the message. By using the Global Title as a destination routing identity, the message can be forwarded to an intermediate STP that will then translate and route the message to the final DPC and SSN.

The Calling Party Address specifies the originator of this UDT message so that the receiving entity can reply to this message with the correct routing parameters, such as point code and SSN.

Note that because no connection is being set up, no SLR or DLR parameters are necessary. To ensure load sharing of UDT messages, the SLS value is chosen randomly each time a UDT message is sent.

```
+----------------+---------+--------------------------+---------------+
  From    Time            OPC      DPC      SLS  SSN  MSG
+----------------+---------+--------------------------+---------------+
  1:C:3   21:07:21,499   1-2-4    1-1-1    3    252  SCCP    UDT    BSMAP   RST
  1:D:3   21:07:21,649   1-1-1    1-2-4    18   252  SCCP    UDT    BSMAP   BLO
  1:C:3   21:07:21,666   1-2-4    1-1-1    5    252  SCCP    UDT    BSMAP   BLA
  1:D:3   21:07:21,702   1-1-1    1-2-4    3    252  SCCP    UDT    BSMAP   BLO
  1:D:3   21:07:21,707   1-1-1    1-2-4    19   252  SCCP    UDT    BSMAP   BLO
  1:D:3   21:07:21,712   1-1-1    1-2-4    4    252  SCCP    UDT    BSMAP   BLO
  1:D:3   21:07:21,717   1-1-1    1-2-4    20   252  SCCP    UDT    BSMAP   BLO
  1:D:3   21:07:21,722   1-1-1    1-2-4    5    252  SCCP    UDT    BSMAP   BLO
  1:D:3   21:07:21,727   1-1-1    1-2-4    21   252  SCCP    UDT    BSMAP   BLO
```

Figure 2-76   SCCP Connectionless Data Transfer message log example

2.6.6.1   Connectionless Data Transfer Example

Figure 2-76 illustrates Connectionless Data Transfer using a message summary example that is similar to information easily obtained using SS7 test equipment. The log shows UDT messages being exchanged between the MSC and BSC. In this example, the BSC's point code is 1-1-1 and the MSC's point code is 1-2-4.

The Subsystem value is set to 252, indicating that the message is destined for the A-Interface (BSAP) application running on the remote end. Because these messages are not associated with an SCCP connection, the SLS values for each UDT message is independent of each other.

2.6.6.2   Connectionless Unit Data Message Structure

Table 2-19 shows the message format of an SCCP-UDT message. All parameters in the UDT message are Mandatory. The first two parameters are contained in the Mandatory Fixed part and specify the Message Type and Protocol Class.

Because the main use of this message is to transfer data, the Called Party Address, Calling Party Address, and Data fields are mandatory and are used for message routing. The application data to be sent is packaged in the Data field. If the Calling Party Address information is not available, this mandatory parameter will contain only the length indicator followed, by the address indicator octet.

Table 2-19   SCCP Unit Data Message Format

Bitmap	Parameter	#Oct	Range	Type
0000 1001 (09H)	SCCP Msg Type	1	Unit Data	F
0000 0000	Protocol Class	1	Class 0	F
LLLL LLLL NRGG GGPS ssss ssss PPPP PPPP PPPP PPPP PPPP PPPP	Called Party Address	≥ 3	L = length, N = 1—National R = 1—route by PC/SSN G = 0— no GTT P = 1—PC included S = 1—SSN included s = SSN, p = point code	V
LLLL LLLL	Calling Party Address	≥ 2	(same as Called Party Address)	V
LLLL LLLL dddd dddd	Data	2– 252	L = length d = data	V

Figure 2-77 shows an example of a Unit Data message. The SCCP data begins at the SCCP Message Type, which is set to 9, indicating a UDT message. It is followed by the Mandatory Fixed Protocol Class parameter, which is set to 0.

The first part of the Mandatory Variable Part contains 3 pointers to the three Mandatory Variable parameters. The pointers to Called Party Address, Calling Party Address, and Data contain offsets of 3, 8, and 13, respectively. These parameters start with the length indicator, with no Parameter ID.

Both the Called and Calling Party addresses contain point code and SSN values and route based on these fields.

The UDT message does not contain a pointer to any Optional Part because no optional parameters are allowed in the message.

```
MTP Level 2 (MTP-L2)
 -0001000   Backward Sequence Number       8
 1-------   Backward Indicator Bit         1
 -0001110   Forward Sequence Number        14
 1-------   Forward Indicator Bit          1
 --100011   Length Indicator               35
 ----0011   Service Indicator              SCCP
 --00----   Sub-Service: Priority          Spare/priority 0 (U.S.A. only)
 10------   Sub-Service: Network Ind       National message
 ***B3***   Destination Point Code         1-2-4
 ***B3***   Originating Point Code         1-1-1
UDT (= Unitdata)
 00010101   Signaling Link Selection       21
 00001001   SCCP Message Type              9
 ----0000   Protocol Class                 Class 0
 0000----   Message Handling               Discard message on error
 00000011   Pointer to parameter           3
 00001000   Pointer to parameter           8
 00001101   Pointer to parameter           13
Called address parameter
 00000101   Parameter Length               5
 -------1   Subsystem No. Indicator        SSN present
 ------1-   Point Code Indicator           PC present
 --0000--   Global Title Indicator         No global title included
 -1------   Routing Indicator              Route on DPC + Subsystem No.
 1-------   For national use               National address
 11111100   Subsystem number               252
 ***B3***   Called Party SPC               1-2-4
Calling address parameter
 00000101   Parameter Length               5
 -------1   Subsystem No. Indicator        SSN present
 ------1-   Point Code Indicator           PC present
 --0000--   Global Title Indicator         No global title included
 -1------   Routing Indicator              Route on DPC + Subsystem No.
 1-------   For national use               National address
 11111100   Subsystem number               252
 ***B3***   Called Party SPC               1-1-1
```

(Continued)
```
Data parameter
00001001  Parameter length              9
***B9***  Data                         00 07 40 01 00 76 04 01 21
```

Figure 2-77 SCCP Unit Data message example

2.6.7 SCCP Subsystem States Management

Because a node may have several SCCP users running simultaneously, each entity is assigned a *Subsystem Number* (SSN). For example, an SSN of 7 specifies the VLR SCCP user function. CDGIOS states that 252 be used for the BSAP SCCP users. The SCCP subsystems running at a node each have a management function that maintains the status of its own subsystem and those with which it communicates. This management function includes updating subsystem status and accessibility through the exchange of the following messages:

• *Subsystem Status Test* (SST)—This is sent to solicit the status of the remote subsystem
• *Subsystem Allowed* (SSA)—This is sent in response to an SST to indicate that the specified subsystem is available
• *Subsystem Prohibited* (SSP)—This is sent to indicate that a subsystem is inaccessible, due to failures or other management reasons

These three messages are *SCCP Management* (SCMG) message types, which are connectionless UDT messages with specific SCMG headers.

2.6.7.1   Subsystem Status Test/Subsystem Allowed Example

When a previously inaccessible subsystem is brought into service, SST and SSA messages are exchanged to bring up the SCCP layer. This happens, for example, when the only available SS7 signaling link between 2 nodes first aligns. Figure 2-78 illustrates the call flow for such a scenario.

Once the only available SS7 link between the MSC and BSC aligns, the BSC and MSC both begin sending SST messages to the remote node, requesting the status of the A-Interface application (SSN of 252). If no response is received, the SST transmission is repeated at intervals specified by SCCP timer *Tstat_info*. Although at this point, MTP2 and MTP3 message exchange can occur, SCCP messages other than SCMG messages cannot yet be exchanged between the subsystems. Upon determining that it is able to process SCCP messages for the indicated SCCP subsystem, each node responds to the received SST messages with SSA messages, indicating that the entity is available for SCCP message traffic.

Note that the Called Party Subsystem number is set to 1, which specifies the SCCP Management subsystem. Section 2.7, "Bringing up a Signaling System 7 Link," on page 136, describes the link alignment process in detail, including message logs.

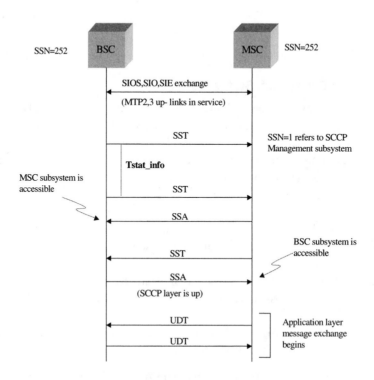

Figure 2-78   SCCP Subsystem Management call flow example

2.6.7.2   SCCP Management Message Structure

Table 2-20 shows the message format of SCMG messages. These messages are type UDT, as indicated in the SCCP Message Type parameter, and do not contain any optional parameters. The Called Party Address and Calling Party Address parameters are both set to SSN=1, denoting that the message is sent from the local SCCP Management function to a remote SCCP Management function.

These messages differ from previously described SCCP messages because Mandatory Variable Data parameter contains the actual SCMG message information. Following the Data parameter length, the SCMG Message Type parameter specifies whether the message is an SSA, SSP, or SST message. Next, the Affected SSN and Affected Point Code specify the remote subsystem under test. The Subsystem Multiplicity Indicator, which indicates the number of subsystems that are replicated, completes the message.

Table 2-20   SCCP Management Message Format

Bitmap	Parameter	#Oct	Range	Type
0000 1001 (09H)	SCCP Msg Type	1	Unit Data	F
0000 0000	Protocol Class	1	Class 0	F
LLLL LLLL aaaa aaaa	Called Party Address	≥ 3	L = length a = address data, SSN = 1	V
LLLL LLLL aaaa aaaa	Calling Party Address	≥ 3	L = length a = address data, SSN = 1	V
LLLL LLLL mmmm mmmm ssss ssss pppp pppp pppp pppp pppp pppp nnnn nnnn	Data	7	L = length of data m = SCMG Message Type 01H—Subsys Allowed (SSA) 02H—Subsys Prohibited (SSP) 03H—Subsys Status Test (SST) s = Affected SSN (subsys under test) p = Affected Point Code (point code of SSN under test) n = Subsys multiplicity indicator (Number of replicated subsys)	V

Figure 2-79 shows an example of an SST message. The message is SCCP type UDT, and both the Called and Calling Party parameters specify SSN 1, which is used to identify the SCCP management entity.

The SCMG Message data is contained in the Data portion of the UDT message. In this example, the SCMG Message Type is set to 3 to denote a SST message, and the subsystem to be tested is the BSAP A-Interface application that is identified by SSN 252.

```
MTP Level 2 (MTP-L2)
 -0000011  Backward Sequence Number      3
 1-------  Backward Indicator Bit        1
 -0000101  Forward Sequence Number       5
 1-------  Forward Indicator Bit         1
 --100000  Length Indicator             32
 00------  Spare                         0
```

(Continued)

```
--100000   Length Indicator              32
00------   Spare                         0
----0011   Service Indicator             SCCP
--10----   Sub-Service: Priority         priority 2 (U.S.A. only)
10------   Sub-Service: Network Ind      National message
***B3***   Destination Point Code        1-2-4
***B3***   Originating Point Code        1-1-1
Unitdata
00010001   Signaling Link Selection      17
00001001   SCCP Message Type             9
----0000   Protocol Class                Class 0
0000----   Message Handling              Discard message on error
00000011   Pointer to parameter          3
00001000   Pointer to parameter          8
00001101   Pointer to parameter          13
Called address parameter
00000101   Parameter Length              5
-------1   Subsystem No. Indicator       SSN present
------1-   Point Code Indicator          PC present
--0000--   Global Title Indicator        No global title included
-1------   Routing Indicator             Route on DPC + Subsystem No.
1-------   For national use              National address
00000001   Subsystem number              SCCP Management
***B3***   Called Party SPC              1-2-4
Calling address parameter
00000101   Parameter Length              5
-------1   Subsystem No. Indicator       SSN present
------1-   Point Code Indicator          PC present
--0000--   Global Title Indicator        No global title included
-1------   Routing Indicator             Route on DPC + Subsystem No.
1-------   For national use              National address
00000001   Subsystem number              SCCP Management
***B3***   Called Party SPC              1-1-1
Data parameter
00000110   Parameter length              6
***B6***   Data                          03 fc 04 02 01 01
Subsystem Status Test
00000011   Message Type                  3
11111100   Subsystem number              252
***B3***   Affected PC                   1-2-4
------01   SSN multiplicity Indicator    subsystem is solitary
000000--   Filler                        Spare
```

Figure 2-79 SCMG Subsystem Test message example

Because the SSA and SST messages are identical except for the Data parameter, Figure 2-80 shows only that one message parameter. In Figure 2-80, the SCMG Message is identified to be a SSA message and the SSN of 252 specifies that SCCP messages addressed to the remote A-Interface BSAP application will be accepted.

```
Subsystem Allowed
  00000001  Message Type                      1
  11111100  Subsystem number                  252
  ***B3***  Affected PC                       1-2-4
  ------01  SSN multiplicity ind              subsystem is solitary
  000000--  Filler                            Spare
```

Figure 2-80   SCMG Subsystem Allowed message example

2.6.8   SCCP Timers

Table 2-21 summarizes SCCP layer timers used in the SCCP layer, which are described in subsequent subsections.

Table 2-21   SCCP Timers

Timer	Range	Recommended Values	Description
Tconn_est	3–6 min	3 min	Connection Establishment Timer
Trel	10–20 s	15 s	Release Complete Timer
Trepeat_rel	10–20 s	15 s	Release Repeat waiting for Release Complete Timer
Tint	≤ 1 min	1 min	Interval waiting for Release Complete before releasing connection resources
Tfr	Tfr > Tiar	16 min	Freeze Timer, waiting to reuse local ref number
Tias	5–10 min	7 min	Send Inactivity Timer
Tiar	11–22 min	15 min	Receive Inactivity Timer
Tstat_info	-	30 s	Interval to repeat SST

Table 2-21   SCCP Timers (Continued)

Timer	Range	Recommended Values	Description
Tguard	-	15 s	Delay to resume normal operation after node recovers from failure
Tcoord_chg	-	30 s	Waiting for grant for subsys to go out of service (not used in A-I/F)
Tignore_SST	-	30 s	Delay for subsys between receiving grant to go out of service and actually going out of service (not used in A-I/F)
Trtg stat info	-	30 s	Delay between requests for subsystem routing status info (not used in A-I/F)
Treset	20–40 s	30 s	Waiting to receive a Reset Confirm (not used in A-I/F)

Tconn_est—**SCCP Connection Establishment Timer**   The node initiating an SCCP connection starts timer *Tconn_est* after sending an SCCP-CR message. The timer is stopped when either an SCCP-CC or SCCP-CREF message is received. Previously allocated SCCP resources are released upon expiry of *Tconn_est* (see Figure 2-63).

Trel—**SCCP Release Complete Timer**   The node initiating an SCCP release starts timer *Trel* after sending an SCCP-RLSD message. The timer is stopped upon receiving an SCCP-RLC from the remote end. See the next paragraph for a description of the procedure invoked upon expiry of this timer.

Trepeat_rel and *Tint*—**SCCP Release Timers**   Timers *Trepeat_rel* and *Tint* are used to control the frequency and duration of resending SCCP-RLSD messages after timer *Trel* expires. Upon expiry of timer *Trel*, a second SCCP-RLSD message is transmitted and timers *Trepeat_rel* and *Tint* are started. If Timer *Trepeat_rel* expires before an SCCP-RLC message is received, another SCCP-RLSD message is sent. The process is continued until timer *Tint* expires (see Figure 2-81).

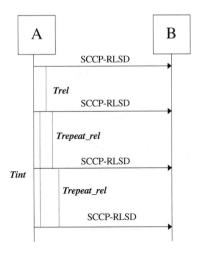

Figure 2-81 SCCP Timers *Trel*, *Trepeat_rel*, and *Tint*

***Tfr*—SCCP Freeze Timer** Timer *Tfr* is used to delay the reuse of local reference numbers when an SCCP connection is released. Timer *Tfr* is started after an SCCP connection has been released. Upon expiry, the previously assigned local reference number becomes available for a new SCCP connection. See Figure 2-82.

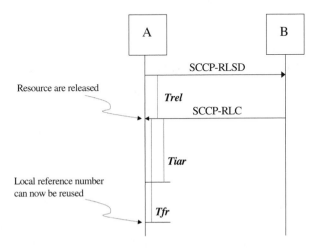

Figure 2-82 SCCP Timer *Tfr*

***Tias* and *Tiar*—Inactivity Control Timers**   Inactivity Control is accomplished, using the Send Inactivity Timer (*Tias*) and the Receive Inactivity Timer (*Tiar*). Both ends use these two SCCP timers to maintain established connections and to identify stale connections. A complete description is provided in Section 2.6.5, "SCCP Connection Inactivity Control," on page 121.

***Tstat_info*—Interval to Repeat SST Timer**   This timer is used to repeat the transmission of SST messages to a remote end if no SSA is received (see Figure 2-78).

***Tguard*—Delay to Resume Operation After Failure**   This timer is used to delay the normal operation after a node recovers from a failure condition. The purpose of this timer is to ensure that messages associated with an SCCP connection are not confused with reference numbers assigned before the failure condition occurred (see Figure 2-83).

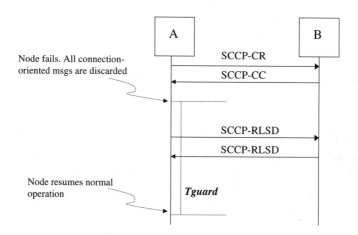

Figure 2-83   SCCP Timer *Tguard*

2.7 Bringing up a Signaling System 7 Link

Figure 2-84 illustrates the steps involved when bringing up the A-Interface when SS7 links are in the out-of-service state. The stages can be broken down into the following steps:

- Signaling Link Initial Alignment—brings SS7 links in service at MTP2
- MTP Traffic Restart—brings MTP3 layer in service for user traffic
- SST/SSA Exchange—brings SCCP layer subsystems in service
- Global Reset/Block Exchange—brings the BSAP layer in service for call processing

In Stage 1, the MTP2 Initial Link Alignment procedures are performed to bring the links in service at MTP2. This involves the exchange of SIOS, SIO, SIE, and FISUs to bring the link state to "Aligned/Ready." Once in the Aligned/Ready state, SLTMs and SLTAs are exchanged to maintain the integrity of the links.

In Stage 2, the MTP Restart procedure is invoked. Once TRAs are exchanged, the MTP3 layer is ready for user traffic. Note that this is not required in the A-Interface CDGIOS standard; it is, however often used in BSC and MSC systems.

In Stage 3, the SCCP management functions are invoked to solicit the status of the remote subsystems using SSTs. Once SSAs have been received at both ends, the SCCP layer is ready for SCCP user traffic exchange.

In Stage 4, SCCP message exchange at the application layer is performed to bring the terrestrial resources into service. Once this is done, the system is ready for Call Processing.

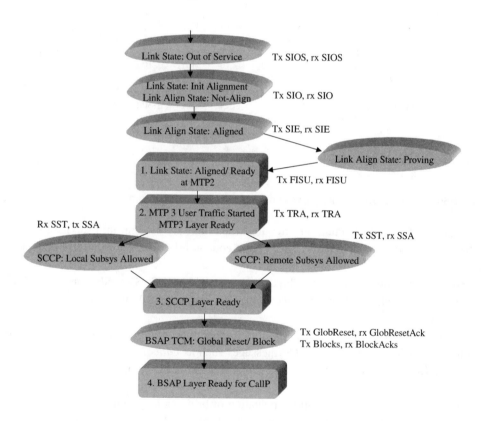

Figure 2-84   Steps in bringing up system with Signaling System 7 links

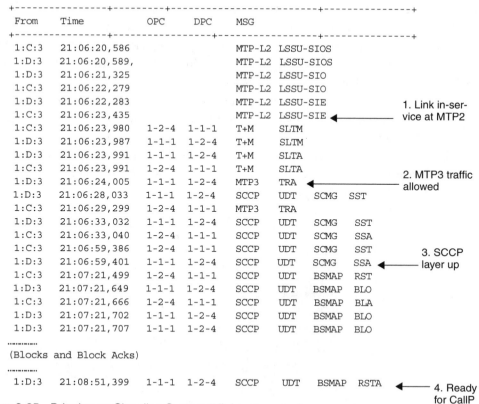

```
+-----------------+----------+-------------------------+--------------+
  From     Time             OPC    DPC    MSG
+-----------------+----------+-------------------------+--------------+
  1:C:3   21:06:20,586                    MTP-L2 LSSU-SIOS
  1:D:3   21:06:20,589,                   MTP-L2 LSSU-SIOS
  1:D:3   21:06:21,325                    MTP-L2 LSSU-SIO
  1:C:3   21:06:22,279                    MTP-L2 LSSU-SIO
  1:D:3   21:06:22,283                    MTP-L2 LSSU-SIE        1. Link in-ser-
  1:C:3   21:06:23,435                    MTP-L2 LSSU-SIE ◄───── vice at MTP2
  1:C:3   21:06:23,980    1-2-4  1-1-1    T+M    SLTM
  1:D:3   21:06:23,987    1-1-1  1-2-4    T+M    SLTM
  1:D:3   21:06:23,991    1-1-1  1-2-4    T+M    SLTA
  1:C:3   21:06:23,991    1-2-4  1-1-1    T+M    SLTA            2. MTP3 traffic
  1:D:3   21:06:24,005    1-1-1  1-2-4    MTP3   TRA    ◄─────── allowed
  1:D:3   21:06:28,033    1-1-1  1-2-4    SCCP   UDT  SCMG  SST
  1:C:3   21:06:29,299    1-2-4  1-1-1    MTP3   TRA
  1:D:3   21:06:33,032    1-1-1  1-2-4    SCCP   UDT  SCMG  SST
  1:C:3   21:06:33,040    1-2-4  1-1-1    SCCP   UDT  SCMG  SSA
  1:C:3   21:06:59,386    1-2-4  1-1-1    SCCP   UDT  SCMG  SST    3. SCCP
  1:D:3   21:06:59,401    1-1-1  1-2-4    SCCP   UDT  SCMG  SSA ◄─ layer up
  1:C:3   21:07:21,499    1-2-4  1-1-1    SCCP   UDT  BSMAP RST
  1:D:3   21:07:21,649    1-1-1  1-2-4    SCCP   UDT  BSMAP BLO
  1:C:3   21:07:21,666    1-2-4  1-1-1    SCCP   UDT  BSMAP BLA
  1:D:3   21:07:21,702    1-1-1  1-2-4    SCCP   UDT  BSMAP BLO
  1:D:3   21:07:21,707    1-1-1  1-2-4    SCCP   UDT  BSMAP BLO
............
(Blocks and Block Acks)
............
  1:D:3   21:08:51,399    1-1-1  1-2-4    SCCP   UDT  BSMAP RSTA ◄── 4. Ready
                                                                    for CallP
```

Figure 2-85   Bringing up Signaling System 7 links message log example

Figure 2-85 shows an actual message log when links are brought into service for the first time between an MSC and BSC. The BSC's point code is 1-1-1, and the MSC's point code is 1-2-4.

The first link undergoes initial link alignment with SIOS, SIO, SIE, and SLTM/SLTA exchanges. MTP3 traffic is then restarted with TRA exchanges. At this point, the MTP2 and MTP3 layers are in service.

The BSC and MSC then send SSTs to each other. Once both sides respond with SSAs to each other, the SCCP layer is up. SCCP messages such as *Global Reset* (RST), *Blocks* (BLO) and *Block Acknowledge* (BLA) can then be exchanged between the subsystems 252 at the BSC and MSC.

For a complete message log and explanation of bringing a system up from an out-of-service state to the application layer, including MTP2, MPT3, SCCP layers, Global Resets and Blocks, refer to Section 8.4.7, "Global Reset with Blocks Example Call Flow," on page 524.

References

1. American National Standards Institute, ANSI T1.101, *Synchronization Interface Standards for Digital Networks.* February 1994.
2. American National Standards Institute, ANSI T1.102, *Digital Hierarchy—Electrical Interfaces.* December 1993.
3. American National Standards Institute, ANSI T1.107, *Digital Hierarchy—Formats Specifications.* July 1995.
4. American National Standards Institute, ANSI T1.110, *Signaling System No. 7 (SS7)—General Information.* June 1992.
5. American National Standards Institute, ANSI T1.111, *Signaling System No. 7 (SS7)—Message Transfer Part (MTP).* June 1992.
6. American National Standards Institute, ANSI T1.112, *Signaling System No. 7 (SS7)—Signaling Connection Control Part (SCCP).* October 1992.
7. International Telecommunications Union—Telecommunications Sector, ITU-T Recommendation Q.700–849, *Specifications of Signaling System No. 7.*
8. T. Russel, *Signaling System #7*, New York: McGraw-Hill, 1995.
9. P.K. Bhatnagar, *Engineering Networks for Synchronization, CCS 7, and ISDN*, New Jersey: IEEE Press, 1997.

CHAPTER 3

Call Processing

*C*all Processing refers to the steps required of both the BSC and MSC to set up and tear down wireless calls. These steps include the allocation of terrestrial and radio resources, setting up the radio link, and connecting the mobile subscriber to the *Public Switch Telephone Network* (PSTN). Although the CDMA air interface has been standardized by the *Telecommunications Industry Association* (TIA) in TIA/EIA IS-95A, allowing various manufacturers' mobile phones to work seamlessly on different infrastructure equipment, the *Base Station Controller* (BSC) and *Mobile Switching Center* (MSC) interface has, until recently, been proprietary.

This chapter presents the call processing procedures and messaging specified by CDGIOS to achieve MSC and BSC interoperability between multiple vendors. This chapter builds on the general message format descriptions provided in Section 1.6, "BSAP Message and Parameter Structure," on page 14 by describing how A-Interface messages are used to set up and tear down wireless calls. Because the CDGIOS standard eliminated several redundant messages found in previous standards, namely, TSB-80, the message flows described in this chapter are sometimes referred to as *optimized* call flows. The following call processing scenarios are described:

- Mobile Origination Call Setup
- Mobile Termination Call Setup
- Mobile Initiated Call Clearing
- BSC Initiated Call Clearing
- MSC Initiated Call Clearing
- Abnormal SCCP Release

The special case of a mobile-to-mobile call can be thought of simply as a mobile origination followed by a mobile termination.

Along with detailed call flows, practical examples are included to illustrate important implementation issues. Although the primary focus of this chapter is A-Interface messaging, interdependencies between the air interface (IS-95) and the A-Interface are described to enhance the reader's understanding of CDMA call processing. The wireless network entities involved in basic call processing are shown in Figure 3-1.

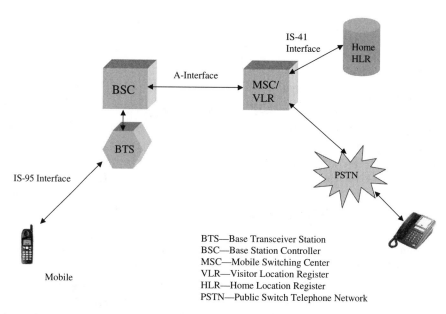

Figure 3-1   Call Processing elements in a CDMA Network

3.1 Mobile Origination

Most calls in a mobile network are mobile-originated. A successful mobile origination call setup begins with the mobile station sending an IS-95 Origination message to the BSC. The Origination message contains information, such as *International Mobile Subscriber Identifier* (IMSI) and *Electronic Serial Number* (ESN), that can be used to identify the mobile uniquely. Upon receiving an Origination message, the BSC packages the information into a *Connection Management* (CM) *Service Request* message, which is an *SCCP Connection Request* (SCCP-CR) message, and sends it across the A-Interface to the MSC. The MSC responds with an *SCCP Connection Confirm* (SCCP-CC) to complete the SCCP connection. After processing the received CM Service Request, the MSC sends an Assignment Request message to the BSC, requesting a terrestrial resource and specifying the service option to be used for the call. Once the BSC has successfully set up the radio link and allocated the corresponding terrestrial resource, it sends an Assignment Complete message to the MSC, indicating that the BSC has successfully set up the call. At this point, the call has been set up, and the MSC may send an in-band ring back tone to the mobile if appropriate. The call flow for a successful mobile origination is illustrated in Figure 3-2, followed by an individual description of each step.

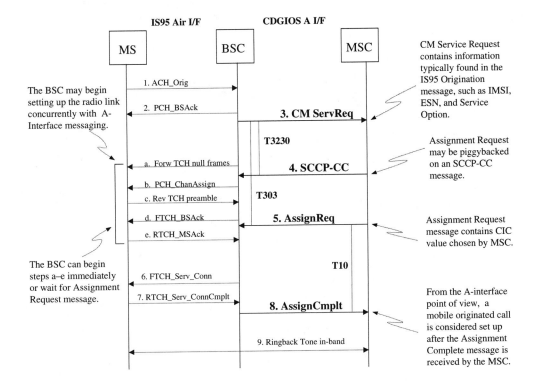

Figure 3-2 Mobile Origination call flow

3.1.1 **Mobile Origination Call Flow**

1. IS95_ACH_Orig (IS-95):

     A mobile origination call setup begins with the transmission of an IS-95 Origination Message over the Access Channel to the BSC. The Origination message contains both information needed to identify the mobile uniquely, such as IMSI and ESN, and information necessary to service the call, such as Called Party Digits and requested Service Option. Authentication values, used to protect further against wireless fraud, may also be present in the Origination message if the mobile is operating in an authentication-enabled network.

CDMA networks use the IMSI of a mobile station to identify it uniquely to the network. Depending on network configuration and service provider's requirements, IS-95 allows the mobile to use several techniques to identify itself during a mobile origination.

The IMSI length is set by the network service provider and is usually between 10 and 15 digits. The mobile is said to have an IMSI class of *0* if it has a 15-digit IMSI and a class of *1* if its IMSI contains less than 15 digits. IS-95 designates the IMSI_S parameter as the 10 least significant digits of the IMSI. The typical composition of a 15-digit IMSI is shown in Figure 3-3.

Figure 3-3 A 15-Digit IMSI format

The *Mobile Country Code* (MCC) specifies a county or region of operation, and IMSI_11_12 is usually set to the *Mobile Network Code* (MNC), which identifies the service provider's region. The network service provider programs the mobile's MCC and IMSI_11_12 with the values of its home network, and the BSC broadcasts its MCC and IMSI_11_12 parameters over the paging channel, using the IS-95 Extended System Parameters message.

As previously mentioned, there are several ways that a mobile station may use IMSI digits to identify itself to the BSC using the IS-95 Access Channel Origination message. If the mobile's MCC and IMSI_11_12 match those transmitted by the BSC in the paging channel IS-95 Extended Systems Parameter message, the mobile may choose to send only IMSI_S. In this case, the mobile sets IMSI_CLASS to *0* and IMSI_CLASS_0_TYPE to *00*, indicating that only IMSI_S digits will be included in the Access Channel message. IS-95 also allows the mobile to send IMSI_S and IMSI_11_12 or all three parameters, IMSI_S, IMSI_11_12, and MCC. If the mobile's MCC or IMSI_11_12 parameters do not match the values broadcast by the BSC, the mobile is required to send at least the minimum information needed to identify itself uniquely to the network.

2. IS95_PCH_BSAck (IS-95):

Upon receipt of an Access Channel Origination message, the BSC sends an IS-95 Base Station Acknowledgment Order message on the Paging Channel. Note that because the forward link has not yet been established, the IS-95 layer 2 acknowledgment for the Origination message is sent over the paging channel as an Order message.

3. CM Service Request (A-Interface):

Upon accepting the mobile's request for an origination, the BSC formats and sends a CM Service Request message to the MSC, prompting the MSC to begin setting up the call. Since the CM Service Request message is an SCCP-CR message, it also includes SCCP parameters required to establish an SCCP connection, namely, the BSC *Source Local Reference* (SLR) number.

Much of the information found in the origination message, including IMSI, ESN, and service option, is packaged into this DTAP message. The CM Service Request message may also contain a *Circuit Identity Code* (CIC) parameter that the BSC may include to specify a preferred terrestrial circuit to be used for the call.

The CM Service Request DTAP message is encapsulated in a BSMAP Complete Layer 3 Information message, which allows the MSC to process the message as a request for an SCCP connection. Upon sending the CM Service Request message, the BSC starts timers T3230 and T303.

4. SCCP Connection Confirm (A-Interface):

   If the MSC allows the requested SCCP connection, it sends the BSC an SCCP-CC message. This message contains both the connection reference number received from the BSC in the CM Service Request (denoted in this message as the *Destination Local Reference* [DLR]) and the local reference number generated at the MSC (denoted in this message as the SLR). The BSC stops timer T3230 upon receipt of the SCCP-CC message.

5. Assignment Request (A-Interface):

   After sending the SCCP-CC message, the MSC begins allocating the terrestrial resources required for the call. If required for the requested service option, the MSC allocates a *Pulse Code Modulation* (PCM) timeslot for the call, referred to as a CIC, on a trunk directly connecting the MSC and BSC. The MSC may honor the preferred CIC received in the CM Service Request or it may independently choose a terrestrial resource. The MSC sends the CIC information to the BSC in the Assignment Request message. Upon sending the Assignment Request message, the MSC starts timer T10. The BSC stops timer T303 after receiving the Assignment Request message.

   Although not shown in Figure 3-2, the MSC has the option of piggybacking the Assignment Request message on an SCCP-CC message. In this case, a separate SCCP-CC message is not needed.

   The choice of whether the BSC sets up the radio link before or after it receives the Assignment Request message is left to the BSC manufacturer. To reduce call setup time, the BSC may choose to begin setting up the radio link as soon as it receives the IS-95 Origination Message. The IS-95 messages exchanged between the BSC and mobile station while setting up the radio link are as follows:

   a. IS95_FTCH null frames:

      The BSC begins verifying the forward traffic channel by transmitting null traffic frames to the mobile.

   b. IS95_PCH_ChanAssign:

      The BSC instructs the mobile to go to the specified traffic channel.

c. IS95_RTCH preamble:

The mobile begins verifying the reverse traffic channel by transmitting preamble data.

d. IS95_FTCH_BSAck:

The BSC sends a Base Station Acknowledgment Order to the mobile to indicate acquisition of reverse traffic frames.

e. IS95_RTCH_MSAck:

Mobile responds with Mobile Station Acknowledgment Order.

6. IS95_FTCH_Serv_Conn (IS-95):

The BSC sends an IS-95 Service Connect message to the mobile on the forward traffic channel, which specifies the service configuration. This message is used to specify signaling and traffic frame rates.

7. IS95_RTCH_Serv_ConnCmplt (IS-95):

The mobile responds to the IS-95 Service Connect message with an IS-95 Service Connect Complete message.

8. Assignment Complete (A-Interface):

An Assignment Complete message is sent by the BSC once it has successfully allocated terrestrial resources and set up the radio link. The transmission of this message implies that the BSC has successfully set up the call. Included in this message is the service option parameter that specifies the final service option being used for the call. Upon receiving the Assignment Complete message, the MSC stops timer T10 and connects the mobile subscriber to the land party. The MSC may play an in-band tone, such as ringback or busy, to inform the mobile subscriber of the status of the call.

3.1.2   Mobile Origination Messages

This section describes the individual A-Interface messages exchanged between the MSC and BSC for a mobile-originated call. The focus of this section is the message structure and individual message parameters.

3.1.2.1   Complete Layer 3 Information

The Complete Layer 3 Information message, shown in Table 3-1, is a BSMAP message that contains a mandatory Layer 3 Information parameter used for encapsulating other messages, which are, typically, DTAP messages. Because this message is a BSMAP message that contains a DTAP message, it is sometimes a source of confusion. The Complete Layer 3 Information message is important to setting up a call because it provides the BSC with the ability to request an SCCP connection while including DTAP information in the message. The three DTAP messages usually encapsulated in the Complete Layer 3 Information message are CM Service Request, Paging Response, and Location Updating Request. The DTAP message is included in the Layer 3 *Information Element* (IE).

There are several methods of identifying cells within a wireless network. The two most common techniques are *Location Area Code* (LAC), which is a logical grouping of cells, and Cell ID, which is a unique numerical designation for individual cells. The Complete Layer 3 Information message contains a Cell Identifier IE that is used to indicate how the cell is being addressed. A cell discriminator of 1 specifies that both the LAC and Cell ID are included in the parameter, and a discriminator of 2 indicates that only Cell ID is being used. The cell identity may be used by the MSC to validate a cell for registrations, mobile originations, and mobile terminations. The MSC may use LAC to reduce the number of overhead pages. For example, while setting up a mobile-terminated call, the MSC may choose first to page the LAC that the mobile last registered from before paging all of the cells in a network.

- BSAP Message Type: BSMAP
- SCCP Message Type: SCCP-Connection Request (CR)
- Direction: BSC → MSC

Table 3-1   Complete Layer 3 Information Message (CDGIOS 6.1.2.1)

BitMap	Param IE	#Oct	Range	Type	IOS Ref
0000 0000 (00H) LLLL LLLL	BSMAP header	2	Msg Discrim. = 0 (BSMAP) L = BSMAP msg length	M	6.2.2.1 6.2.2.3
0101 0111 (57H)	Msg Type	1	Complete L3 Information	M	6.2.2.4
0000 0101 (05H) LLLL LLLL 0000 0001 (d=1) aaaa aaaa aaaa aaaa cccc cccc cccc ssss *OR* 0000 0010 (d=2) cccc cccc cccc ssss	Cell Identifier	5 or 7	L = length—03H or 05H d = cell discriminator 01H—LAC and Cellid 02H—Cellid a = Location Area Code c = cell id s = Sector Number, 0 for omni	M	6.2.2.20
0001 0111 (17H) LLLL LLLL dddd ddddd	Layer 3 Information	2	L = length, d = Layer 3 data, (CM Service Req, Paging Resp, Location Updating Req)	M	6.2.2.38

3.1.2.2   CM Service Request

The CM Service Request is a DTAP message contained in the Complete Layer 3 Information message. Table 3-2, which describes the CM Service Request message parameters, includes the Complete Layer 3 message header for completeness. Notice that because the CM Service Request message is a DTAP message, the parameter identifier is not included for mandatory parameters. Parameter identifiers are only included for optional parameters.

Because the CM Service Request is embedded in the Complete Layer 3 Information message, it starts with the parameter IE Protocol Discriminator instead of the generic DTAP header that is used for standalone DTAP messages. The Protocol Discriminator is set to *03H* to indicate that the message is a Call Processing message. The next octet is reserved and is followed by the Message Type IE, which is set to *24H* to indicate that the DTAP message is CM Service Request.

The first parameter in this message containing information about the requested mobile origination is the Classmark Information Type 2 IE. In the case of a Cellular (800-MHz) network, the information received by the BSC in the *Station Classmark* (SCM) Info field of the IS-95 Origination message is mapped into this IE. For PCS (1900-MHz) networks, the mapping is done using other Origination message parameters because no SCM field is specified in the Origination message described in J-STD-8. For example, in a PCS network, the CM Service Request parameters MOB_TERM and SLOTTED_MODE are mapped directly from J-STD-8 Origination message and the C=1 (CDMA) parameter is mapped from REQUEST_MODE field.

The Mobile Identity (IMSI) IE is a mandatory parameter used by the MSC to identify the originating mobile station. Depending on the IMSI type, this parameter contains between 10 and 15 digits. A 15-digit IMSI is required to support international roaming.

The Called Party BCD IE is a conditionally required parameter used by the MSC to identify the desired called party. If the DIGIT_MODE field received in the IS-95 Origination message is set to BCD, the BSC packages the called-party digits, number type, and number plan ID in this parameter. The Called Party BCD IE is conditionally required because some origination types, such as Markov, do not require a called-party string. This parameter (or the Called Party ASCII Number IE) is, however, required for voice and data calls where the MSC must route the call based on dialed digits.

The Mobile ESN IE is a required parameter that contains the *Electronic Serial Number* (ESN) of the originating mobile. The ESN is used by the MSC to validate the profile of the mobile subscriber stored in the *Home Location Register* (HLR).

To conserve power, a mobile station may operate in slotted mode. While in slotted mode, the mobile monitors only the paging channel during certain time intervals. The Slot Cycle Index IE specifies to the BSC and MSC the preferred slot cycle index by the mobile. Note that the maximum-allowed slot cycle index is determined by the BSC and is transmitted to the mobile in the IS-95 System Parameters message. IS-95 states that, although a mobile station may store a preferred slot cycle value greater than the maximum specified by the BSC, it must adhere to the maximum set in the network in which it is operating.

The required Service Option IE identifies the service option type being requested by the originating mobile. The MSC may choose to validate the requested service option type with the HLR and clear the call if the service option is not supported. Procedure to change the requested service option, known as *service option negotiation*, may also occur after the mobile is on the traffic channel.

There are several optional parameters in the CM Service Request message related to mobile authentication. Authentication, which is described in Chapter 6 on page 345, is a technique used in wireless networks to reduce fraud. The BSC requests mobile stations to include the standard Authentication data in Access Channel messages, such as an Origination, using the AUTH field of the IS-95 Access Parameters message. The CM Service Request AUTHR, RANDC, COUNT, and RAND parameters are sent only if authentication is enabled by the BSC. In addition to the standard authentication parameters, the Authentication Data IE is required when the requested service option is Asynchronous Data or Group 3 Fax. The Authentication Event IE is used to indicate authentication errors.

The optional Voice Privacy Request IE is sent whenever a mobile capable of *Voice Privacy* (VP) and *Signaling Message Encryption* (SME) requests voice privacy. If this parameter IE is present in the CM Service Request, the corresponding Assignment Request message received at the BSC also includes the Encryption Information IE, which contains the encryption keys necessary for performing voice privacy using a private long code mask. A complete description of VP is given in Section 6.7, "Signaling Message Encryption and Voice Privacy," on page 396.

The CM Service Request message also contains the required Radio Environment and Resources IE. The BSC uses this parameter to inform the MSC of resource allocation and availability, and the quality of the forward and reverse radio environments. If the BSC sets up the mobile station on the traffic channel before it receives the Assignment Request message from the MSC, the BSC sets the allocation field to "Resources are Allocated" and the availability field to "Resources are Available." If the mobile is already in the traffic channel before the Assignment Request message is received by the BSC, the BSC will inform the MSC that resources are allocated and available by setting the appropriate bits in this field.

The optional Called Party ASCII Number IE is sent whenever the mobile station sets the DIGIT_MODE field in the IS-95 Origination message to ASCII. Either the Called Party ASCII Number IE or the Called Party BCD Number IE is sent in the CM Service Request, but not both simultaneously.

The BSC may request the MSC to use a particular CIC for the pending origination by including the optional Circuit Identity Code IE. The MSC is not required to use the preferred CIC; however, doing so may improve overall network performance.

- BSAP Message Type: DTAP
- SCCP Message Type: SCCP-Connection Request (CR)
- Direction: BSC → MSC

Table 3-2   CM Service Request Message (CDGIOS 6.1.2.2)

BitMap	Param IE	#Oct	Range	Type	IOS Ref
0000 0000 (00H) LLLL LLLL	BSMAP header	2	Msg Discrim. = 0 (BSMAP) L = BSMAP msg length	M	6.2.2.1 6.2.2.3
0101 0111 (57H)	Msg Type	1	Complete L3 Information	M	6.2.2.4
0000 0101 (05H)	Cell Identifier	5 or 7	Same as element in Table 3-1, Complete L3 Information message.	M	6.2.2.20
0001 0111 (17H) LLLL LLLL	Layer 3 Info	2	L = length	M	6.2.2.38
rrrr 0011 (03H)	Protocol Discrim.	1	0011—Call Processing r = 0—reserved bits	M	6.2.2.39
0000 0000 (00H)	Reserved	1		M	6.2.2.40
0010 0100 (24H)	Msg Type	1	CM Service Request	M	6.2.2.4
1001 ssss (91H)	CM Serv	1	s = 0001—Mobile Orig Call	M	6.2.2.51
LLLL LLLL PPPr rppp rrrr rfff rCSE BDMr rrrr rrrr	Classmark Information Type 2	5	L = 04H, r = 0 – reserved P = MOB_P_REV, p = RF pwr class f = 000 (IS95)—freq capability C = 1—CDMA S = 1—slotted mode M = 1—capable of mob term Bits f, E, B and D are ignored by the MSC.	M	6.2.2.15
LLLL LLLL dddd ittt dddd dddd dddd dddd ..... [1111 dddd]	Mobile Identity (IMSI)	7–9	L = 06H–08H (10–15 digits) d = BCD digits, t =110—IMSI i = 0/1—even/odd indicator If even number of digits, last octet will have pattern 1111 in the upper 4 bits	M	6.2.2.16

Table 3-2 CM Service Request Message (CDGIOS 6.1.2.2) (Continued)

BitMap	Param IE	#Oct	Range	Type	IOS Ref
0101 1110 (5EH) LLLL LLLL 1ttt pppp nnnn nnnn nnnn nnnn ……..	Called Party BCD Number	2–19	L = 0–17 t = type of number (T1.607) 000—unknown 001— international 010—national p = number plan id (T1.607) 0000—unknown 0001—ISDN/telephony n= called party number	O,C	6.2.2.52
0000 1101 (0DH) LLLL LLLL 0000 ittt nnnn nnnn nnnn nnnn nnnn nnnn nnnn nnnn	Mobile Identity (ESN)	7	L = 05H i = 0—even t = 101—ESN n = ESN	O,R	6.2.2.16
0011 0101 (35H) rrrr riii	Slot Cycle Index	2	r = 0—reserved i = slot cycle index	O,C	6.2.2.17
0100 0010 (42H) LLLL LLLL rrrr tttt 0000 00nn nnnn nnnn nnnn nnnn	Authenti- cation Response Parameter (AUTHR)	6	L = 04H, r = 0—reserved tttt = 0001—AUTHR 0010—AUTHU 0100—AUTHBS n = 18-bit Auth result	O,C	6.2.2.46
0010 1000 (28H) rrrr rrrr	Auth Con- firmation Parameter (RANDC)	2	r = RANDC—first 8 bits of RAND This is sent only if received from mobile.	O,C	6.2.2.42
0100 0000 (40H) rrcc cccc	Auth Parameter COUNT	2	r = 0—reserved c = COUNT	O,C	6.2.2.47

Table 3-2 CM Service Request Message (CDGIOS 6.1.2.2) (Continued)

BitMap	Param IE	#Oct	Range	Type	IOS Ref
0100 0001 (41H) LLLL LLLL rrrr tttt nnnn nnnn nnnn nnnn nnnn nnnn nnnn nnnn	Auth Challenge Parameter (RAND)	7	L = 05H, r = 0—reserved tttt = 0001—RAND 0010—RANDU 0100—RANDSSD 1000—RANDBS n = RAND	O,C	6.2.2.45
0000 0011 (03H) ssss ssss ssss ssss	Service Option	3	s = 8000H—13K speech 0011H—13K high rate voice 0003H—EVRC 801FH—13K Markov 0009H—13K loopback 0004H—Async data rate set 1 0005H—G3 Fax rate set 1 000CH—Async Data rate set 2 000DH—G3 Fax rate set 2 0006H—SMS rate set 1 000EH—SMS rate set 2	O,R	6.2.2.66
1010 0001 (A1H)	VP Req	1	Voice Privacy Req	O,C	6.2.2.13
0001 1101 (1DH) 00ff rrAV	Radio Environment and Resources	2	A = Radio Resrc Allocated (0,1) V = Radio Resrc Available (0,1) f = forward radio environment r = reverse radio environment	O,R	6.2.2.82
0101 1011 (5BH) LLLL LLLL xttt pppp aaaa aaaa	Called Party ASCII Number	3–n	L = length, x = 1—extension bit t = type of number (T1.607) p = number plan id (T1.607) aaaa aaaa = ASCII Char (per octet)	O,C	6.2.2.105
0000 0001 (01H) mmmm mmmm mmmt tttt	Circuit Identity Code	3	m = spanid, t = timeslot on span Not required when servopt = Markov, loopback, SMS	O,C	6.2.2.22

Table 3-2   CM Service Request Message (CDGIOS 6.1.2.2) (Continued)

BitMap	Param IE	#Oct	Range	Type	IOS Ref
0100 1010 (4AH) LLLL LLLL vvvv vvvv	Authentication Event	3	L = 01H, v = 01H, 02H 01H—Auth requred, params not rx 02H—RAND/RANDC mismatch	O,C	6.2.2.114
0101 1001 (59H) llll llll dddd dddd dddd dddd dddd dddd	Authentication Data	5	L = 03H d = Auth Data	O,C	6.2.2.137

3.1.2.3   Assignment Request

The Assignment Request message is sent from the MSC to the BSC when terrestrial resources are available and the MSC is proceeding to set up the call. This message is usually sent as an *SCCP Data Form 1* (DT1) message, but it may also be piggybacked on an SCCP-CC message. Note that because the Assignment Request message is a BSMAP message type, both mandatory and optional parameters begin with the parameter identifier.

Following the BSMAP header and the Message Type IE is the Channel Type IE. The BSC ignores this parameter because the values are *Global Systems for Mobile* (GSM) A-Interface-specific and are of no significance to IS-95 CDMA systems. The Channel Type IE is simply hard-coded to the values shown in Table 3-3.

The next parameter in the Assignment Request message is the conditionally required Circuit Identity Code IE, which specifies the PCM circuit to be used for a call. The MSC has the option of honoring the preferred CIC received in the CM Service Request message or choosing its own. Upon receiving the Assignment Request message, the BSC allocates the CIC specified in this message. Although the standard provides no guidelines regarding logical span assignments, CIC codes used by both the MSC and BSC must match.

The optional Encryption Information IE is sent if VP is requested from the BSC in the CM Service Request and if the encryption keys are available from the Authentication Center. A complete description of VP can be found in Section 6.7, "Signaling Message Encryption and Voice Privacy," on page 396.

The required Service Option IE contains the same service option value requested in the CM Service Request message received from the BSC.

The Signal IE and the Calling Party IE are parameters that are used only when the Assignment Request refers to a mobile terminated call. These two parameters are used for indicating the alerting type and calling party information to the mobile.

The optional IS-95 Information Records parameter can be used to send IS-95 information records to the mobile station. Examples include Display, Calling Party Number, Signal, and

Message Waiting. This parameter should not carry redundant information included in other parameters, such as Signal and Calling Party ASCII Number.

- BSAP Message Type: BSMAP
- SCCP Message Type: SCCP-Connection Confirm (CC), or Data Form 1 (DT1)
- Direction: BSC ← MSC

Table 3-3   Assignment Request Message (CDGIOS 6.1.2.15)

BitMap	Param IE	#Oct	Range	Type	IOS Ref
0000 0000 (00H) LLLL LLLL	BSMAP header	2	Msg Discrim. = 0 (BSMAP) L = BSMAP msg length	M	6.2.2.1 6.2.2.3
0000 0001 (01H)	Msg Type	1	Assignment Request	M	6.2.2.4
0000 1011 (0BH) LLLL LLLL iiii iiii rrrr rrrr cccc cccc	Channel Type	5	L = 03H i = 01H—Speech r = 08H—Chan Rate = Full Rate c = 05H—13kbps vocoder	M	6.2.2.7
0000 0001 (01H) mmmm mmmm mmmt tttt	Circuit Identity Code	3	m = spanid, t = timeslot on span	O,C	6.2.2.22

Table 3-3 Assignment Request Message (CDGIOS 6.1.2.15) (Continued)

BitMap	Param IE	#Oct	Range	Type	IOS Ref
0000 1010 (0AH) LLLL LLLL xiii iisa llll llll kkkk kkkk kkkk kkkk kkkk kkkk kkkk kkkk kkkk kkkk kkkk kkkk kkkk kkkk kkkk kkkk *AND/ OR* xiii iisa llll llll uuuu uukk kkkk kkkk kkkk kkkk kkkk kkkk kkkk kkkk kkkk kkkk	Encryption Information	Var- iable	L = 08H, 0AH, or 12H x = 1 i = 00001—SME s = 1,0—status (1 = active) a = 1,0—algo avail (1 = avail) l = 08H—key length k = key value Present when Voice Privacy is requested and MSC has keys available at time message is sent. x = 1 i = 00100—private longcode s = 1,0—status a = 1,0—algo avail l = 06H—key length u = 0—unused bits k = key value	O,C	6.2.2.12
0000 0011 (03H) ssss ssss ssss ssss	Service Option	3	Same as element in Table 3-2, CM Service Request message.	O,R	6.2.2.66
0011 0100 (34H) SSSS SSSS rrrr rrPP	Signal (mob term calls only)	3	S = IS-95 Signal value 40H, 41H, 42H, 44H, 4FH, 81H, 82H, 83H, 84H, 85H, 86H, 87H, 88H, 89H, 8AH, 8BH P = pitch, r = 0—reserved	O,C	6.2.2.50

Table 3-3   Assignment Request Message (CDGIOS 6.1.2.15) (Continued)

BitMap	Param IE	#Oct	Range	Type	IOS Ref
0100 1011 (4BH) LLLL LLLL 0ttt nnnn 1pp0 00ss aaaa aaaa	Calling Party ASCII Number (mob term calls)	Var-iable	L = length t = type of number (T1.607) n = number plan id (T1.607) p = presentation id (T1.607) s = screening indicator (T1.607) a = Calling Party number	O,C	6.2.2.37
0001 0101 (15H) LLLL LLLL tttt tttt (1st record) llll llll cccc cccc ….. tttt tttt (2ndrecord) …..	IS-95 Infor-mation Records	Var-iable	L = length t = IS95 Info Record type l = Info Record length c = Info Record content	O,C	6.2.2.72

3.1.2.4   Assignment Complete

The Assignment Complete message is sent from the BSC to the MSC to indicate that the BSC has successfully set up the call. This message is sent only after the BSC receives an IS-95 Service Connect Complete message from the mobile. The Assignment Complete is a BSMAP message that is sent as an SCCP-DT1 message.

The first parameter, the Channel Number IE, is a mandatory parameter used to identify a logical channel number assigned to the equipment providing a traffic channel. Because this information is not normally used by the MSC, it is sometimes hard-coded to a value of 0 by the BSC.

The BSC includes the optional Encryption Information IE if the the parameter was included in the corresponding Assignment Request message. The transmission of this parameter by the BSC signifies the acceptance and execution of the requested encryption procedures. Note that no keys are included in this IE.

The Service Option IE is a required parameter that contains the same service option value received by the BSC in the Assignment Request message (Table 3-4).

- BSAP Message Type: BSMAP
- SCCP Message Type: SCCP-Data Form 1 (DT1)
- Direction: BSC → MSC

Table 3-4 Assignment Complete Message (CDGIOS 6.1.2.16)

BitMap	Param IE	#Oct	Range	Type	IOS Ref
0000 0000 (00H) LLLL LLLL	BSMAP header	2	Msg Discrim. = 0 (BSMAP) L = BSMAP msg length	M	6.2.2.1 6.2.2.3
0000 0010 (02H)	Msg Type	1	Assignment Complete	M	6.2.2.4
0010 0011 (23H) nnnn nnnn nnnn nnnn	Channel Number	3	n = 0—typcially set to 0 here.	M	6.2.2.6
0000 1010 (0AH) LLLL LLLL xiii iisa llll llll *AND/ OR* xiii iisa llll llll	Encryp- tion Infor- mation	Var- iable	L = 02H or 04H, x = 1 l = 00H—key length i = 00001—SME 00100—private LC s = 1,0—status (1 = active) a = 1,0—algo avail (1 = avail)	O,C	6.2.2.12
0000 0011 (03H) ssss ssss ssss ssss	Service Option	3	Same as element in Table 3-2, CM Service Request message.	O, R	6.2.2.66

3.1.3   Mobile Origination Example Call Flow

Figure 3-4 shows a practical example of a summary message call flow for a mobile-originated call. The purpose of Figure 3-4 is to present an overview of the messages exchanged between the BSC and MSC. Subsequent figures illustrate the complete message's content, including MTP and SCCP layers. The decoded message format is similar to what would be seen on test equipment monitoring the A-Interface signaling link.

The mobile origination example in Figure 3-4 starts with the transmission of a CM Service Request message from the BSC to the MSC. Because the CM Service Request is an SCCP-CR message, the MSC responds with an SCCP-CC. Notice that once the SCCP connection has been established, the MSC and BSC continue to use the same *Signaling Link Selection* (SLS), which maps the transmitted *Signaling System 7* (SS7) message to a specific *Signaling Link Code* (SLC). Each node independently chooses a signaling link for the SCCP connection and continues to use that link throughout the call. Although the MSC and BSC may each choose different links, SCCP connection-oriented messages for a particular call will be transported over the same signaling link relative to each node.

After confirming the SCCP connection, the MSC requests terrestrial resources by sending an Assignment Request. The BSC responds with an Assignment Complete, indicating that it has successfully set up the call. The remaining messages in Figure 3-4 are related to releasing the call and are discussed later (see Section 3.3, "Mobile-Initiated Call Clearing," on page 187).

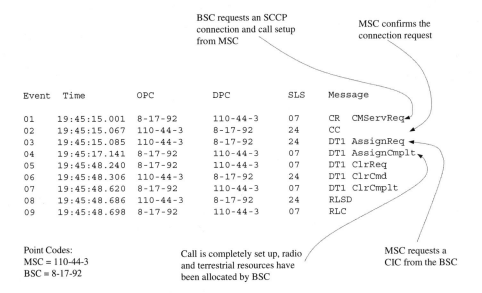

Figure 3-4 Mobile Origination Example call flow log

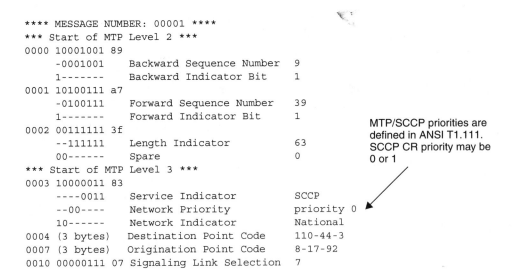

(Continued)

```
*** Start of SCCP ***                                    BSC local refer-
0011 00000001 01 Connection Request        01            ence number for this
0012 (3 bytes)    Source Local References  78695  ◄───── SCCP connection
0015 00000010 02 Protocol Class            2
0016 00000010 02 Mandatory Variable Ptr    0018
0017 00000111 07 Optional Ptr              0024
0018 00000101 05 Called Party Addr Length  5
0019 11000011 c3
     -------1     Subsys Num Indicator      Included
     ------1-     Point Code Indicator      Included
     --0000--     Global Title indicator    No GTT included
     -1------     Routing indicator         DPC/SSN
     1-------     Reserved for National use          Subsystem number, spec-
0020 11111100 fc Subsystem Number          252  ◄───── ified in IOS to be 252
0021 (3 bytes)    Signaling Point Code      110-44-3
0024 00001111 0f Data PNC                  15
*** Start of CDGIOS MAP ***
                  Complete Layer 3 Information
0025 00110001 31 Data Length               49
0026 00000000 00 BSMAP Discriminator       00
0027 00101111 2f BSMAP Length              47
0028 01010111 57 Complete Layer 3 Info     87
0029 00000101 05 Cell Identifier           5
0030 00000011 03 Length                    3
0031 00000010 02 Cell Identifier Discrim   CI only
0032 00000001 01 CI Value                  01 22
0033 00100010 22
0034 00010111 17 Layer 3 Information       23
0035 00100111 27 Length                    39
0036 00000011 03 Protocol Discriminator    Call Processing
0037 00000000 00 Reserved
0038 00100100 24 CC Message Selection      CM Service Request
0039 10010001 91
     ----0001     CM Service Type           MobOrig Call
     1001----     Element Identifier        09
                  Classmark Info Type 2
0040 00000100 04 Length                    4
0041 00100000 20
     -----000     RF Power Capability       Class 1, veh and portable
     ---00---     Reserved                  0
     001-----     MOB_P_REV                 1
0042 00000000 00
     -----000     Frequency Capability      band number 0
     00000---     Reserved                  0
0043 01110010 72
     -------0     Reserved                  0
     ------1-     Mobile Term               capable of rcving call
     -----0--     DTX                       DTX is incapable
     ----0---     Bandwidth                 Mobile limited to 20 MHz Band
     ---1----     Extended Protocol (EP)    Full reverse control channel
     --1-----     Slotted paging            allowed
```

(Continued)

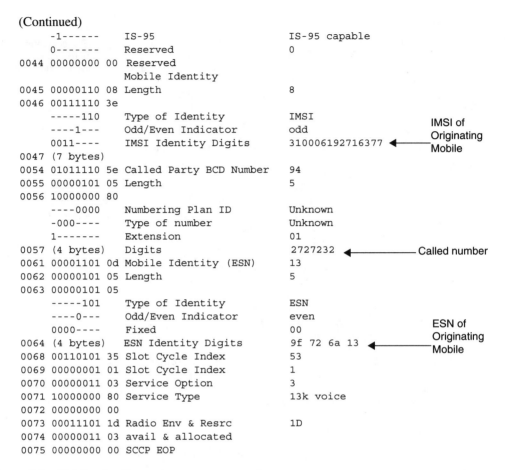

```
          -1------    IS-95                   IS-95 capable
          0-------    Reserved                0
     0044 00000000 00 Reserved
                      Mobile Identity
     0045 00000110 08 Length                  8
     0046 00111110 3e
          -----110    Type of Identity        IMSI
          ----1---    Odd/Even Indicator       odd
          0011----    IMSI Identity Digits    310006192716377
     0047 (7 bytes)
     0054 01011110 5e Called Party BCD Number 94
     0055 00000101 05 Length                  5
     0056 10000000 80
          ----0000    Numbering Plan ID       Unknown
          -000----    Type of number          Unknown
          1-------    Extension               01
     0057 (4 bytes)   Digits                  2727232
     0061 00001101 0d Mobile Identity (ESN)   13
     0062 00000101 05 Length                  5
     0063 00000101 05
          -----101    Type of Identity        ESN
          ----0---    Odd/Even Indicator      even
          0000----    Fixed                   00
     0064 (4 bytes)   ESN Identity Digits     9f 72 6a 13
     0068 00110101 35 Slot Cycle Index        53
     0069 00000001 01 Slot Cycle Index        1
     0070 00000011 03 Service Option          3
     0071 10000000 80 Service Type            13k voice
     0072 00000000 00
     0073 00011101 1d Radio Env & Resrc       1D
     0074 00000011 03 avail & allocated
     0075 00000000 00 SCCP EOP
```

IMSI of Originating Mobile

Called number

ESN of Originating Mobile

Figure 3-5 CM Service Request message example

Figure 3-5, above, shows an example of a decoded CM Service Request message that is similar to what may be seen on test equipment monitoring the A-Interface during a mobile-originated call. All layers of the message are included to help illustrate SS7, SCCP, and Application layer functionality.

The decoded message starts with MTP2, which contains the forward and backward sequence numbers, forward and backward indicator bits, and the overall message length. Recall that forward and backward sequence numbers and indicator bits are used by MTP2 to acknowledge received messages. The next layer shown in the example is MTP3, which contains information about the message type and provides routing information. Because all A-Interface messages are users of the SCCP layer, the MTP3 Service Indicator bits are set to SCCP. The *Origination Point Code* (OPC) and *Destination Point Code* (DPC) indicate that the message was sent from the BSC (8-17-92) to the MSC (110-44-3).

Because the CM Service Request is the first message sent by the BSC during a mobile origination, the BSC uses this message to request an SCCP connection from the MSC. In the decoded example of Figure 3-5, the SCCP layer indicates that the message is an SCCP-CR message type. The SCCP layer of the message specifies that message routing should be done using point code and *Subsystem Number* (SSN). The SCCP layer also contains an SLR (78695), which is a unique numerical identifier that the BSC uses to reference the SCCP connection. This identifier allows the BSC to distinguish between many simultaneous SCCP connections.

Following the SCCP layer is the CDGIOS application layer. The application layer of the message identifies the message type as BSMAP and the specific message as Complete Layer 3 information. In this example, the cell discriminator specifies that only Cell ID is included. Following the Cell ID parameter is the encapsulated CM Service Request message, which contains information sent from the mobile subscriber during the origination. The Class Mark Information IE indicates that the mobile has a power class of 1 and is CDMA (IS-95) capable. The next IE, the Mobile Identity IE, specifies the IMSI of the originating mobile. Several optional parameters are also included in this example message, such as Called Party BCD Number, Mobile Identity (ESN), Slot Cycle Index, and Service Option.

```
**** MESSAGE NUMBER: 00002 ****
*** Start of MTP Level 2 ***
0000 10100111 a7
     -0100111    Backward Sequence Number   39
     1-------    Backward Indicator Bit     1
0001 10001010 8a
     -0001010    Forward Sequence Number    10
     1-------    Forward Indicator Bit      1
0002 00010001 11
     --010001    Length Indicator           17
     00------    Spare                      0
*** Start of MTP Level 3 ***
0003 10010011 93
     ----0011    Service Indicator          SCCP          Priority of SCCP
     --01----    Network Priority           priority 1 ◄── connection confirm is 1
     10------    Network Indicator          National
0004 (3 bytes)   Destination Point Code     8-17-92
0007 (3 bytes)   Origination Point Code     110-44-3
0010 00011000 18 Signaling Link Selection   24
*** Start of SCCP ***
0011 00000010 02 Connection Confirm         02
0012 (3 Bytes)   Dest Local References      78695
0015 (3 Bytes)   Source Local References    15432236
0018 00000010 02
                                                          Connection-
     ----0010    Protocol Class             Class 2 ◄──────── oriented
     0000----    Spare                      00
0019 00000000 00 Optional Pointer           Points to Nothing
```

Figure 3-6 SCCP Connection Confirm message example

The SCCP-CC message shown in Figure 3-6, above, is a relatively simple message used by the MSC to indicate that the SCCP connection requested by the BSC in the CM Service request is being allowed. The SCCP-CC message contains both the SLR (15432236) and the DLR (78695), a feature that is often useful when troubleshooting. Notice that the DLR is set to the value that the MSC received in the SLR field of the CM Service Request message. The SLR in this message is the locally generated MSC reference for the SCCP connection. Once the SCCP connection has been established, the SLR and DLR can be used to determine which SCCP messages belong to a particular call.

```
**** MESSAGE NUMBER: 00003 ****
*** Start of MTP Level 2 ***
0000 10100111 a7
     -0100111    Backward Sequence Number   39
     1-------    Backward Indicator Bit     1
0001 10001011 8b
     -0001011    Forward Sequence Number    11
     1-------    Forward Indicator Bit      1
0002 00011101 1d
     --011101    Length Indicator           29
     00------    Spare                      0
*** Start of MTP Level 3 ***
0003 10000011 83
     ----0011    Service Indicator          SCCP
     --00----    Network Priority           priority 0
     10------    Network Indicator          National
0004 (3 bytes)   Destination Point Code     8-17-92
0007 (3 bytes)   Origination Point Code     110-44-3
0010 00011000 18 Signaling Link Selection   24
*** Start of SCCP ***
0011 00000110 06 Data Form 1                06
0012 (3 bytes)   Dest Local References      78695
0015 00000000 00 Segment/Reassembling       0
0016 00000001 01 Variable Pointer           01
*** Start of CDGIOS MAP ***
                 Assignment Request
0017 00001110 0e Data Length                14
0018 00000000 00 BSMAP Discriminator        00
0019 00001100 0c BSMAP Length               12
0020 00000001 01 Assignment Request         01
0021 00001011 0b Channel Type               11
0022 00000011 03 Length                     3
0023 00000001 01 Speech or Data Indicator   Speech
0024 00001000 08 Channel Rate and Type      Full rate TCH Chan Bm
0025 00000101 05 Speech Encoding Algorithm  13 Kb/s
0026 00000001 01 Circuit Identity Code      1
0027 00000000 00 PCM MUX (high part)        0
0028 00000010 37
     ---00111    Time Slot                  7
     011-----    PCM MUX (low part)         3
```

DataForm 1 priority can be 0 or 1, it should match what was used in the SCCP connection request.

MSC chooses a CIC from a list of available resources.

(Continued)

```
0029 00000011 03 Service Option          3                     13K voice,
0030 10000000 80 Service Type            13k voice    ◄──────  should match CM
0031 00000000 00                                               Service Request
```

Figure 3-7   Assignment Request message example

An example Assignment Request message is shown in Figure 3-7, above. The Assignment Request message is sent from the MSC to the BSC when terrestrial resources are available and the MSC is proceeding to set up the call. In this example, the MSC is requesting that CIC 103 be used for voice. The service option requested in the CM Service Request message received from the BSC is echoed in the Service Option parameter of this message. The DLR included by the MSC in the SCCP layer of the message is set to 78695, which is the reference number that the BSC has assigned to the SCCP connection. The Channel Type information is included in the message but is not used by the BSC. Notice that the Assignment Request message is an SCCP type DT1, which is used to exchange information between the MSC and BSC after an SCCP connection has been established.

```
**** MESSAGE NUMBER: 00004 ****
*** Start of MTP Level 2 ***
0000 10001100 8c
     -0001100      Backward Sequence Number   12
     1-------      Backward Indicator Bit     1
0001 10101001 a9
     -0101001      Forward Sequence Number    41
     1-------      Forward Indicator Bit      1
0002 00011000 18
     --011000      Length Indicator           24
     00------      Spare                      0
*** Start of MTP Level 3 ***
0003 10000011 83
     ----0011      Service Indicator          SCCP
     --00----      Network Priority           priority 0
     10------      Network Indicator          National
0004 (3 bytes)     Destination Point Code     110-44-3
0007 (3 bytes)     Origination Point Code     8-17-92
0010 00000111 07 Signaling Link Selection     7
*** Start of SCCP ***
0011 00000110 06 Data Form 1                  06
0012 (3 bytes)     Dest Local References      15432236
0015 00000000 00 Segment/Reassembling         0
0016 00000001 01 Variable Pointer             01
*** Start of CDGIOS MAP ***
                   Assignment Complete
0017 00001001 09 Data Length                  9
0018 00000000 00 BSMAP Discriminator          00
0019 00000111 07 BSMAP Length                 7
0020 00000010 02 Assignment Complete          02
```

(Continued)

```
0021 00100011 23 Channel Number          35
0022 00000000 00 Value                    00 00
0023 00000000 00
0024 00000011 03 Service Option           13k voice  ◄── Service option 13k voice,
0025 10000000 80                                           should match
0026 00000000 00                                           Assignment Request
                                                           message
```

Figure 3-8 Assignment Complete message example

The Assignment Complete message is sent by the BSC to the MSC to indicate that the BSC has successfully set up the call. The example message shown in Figure 3-8, above, contains a Channel Number ID, not typically used by the MSC, and the Service Option, which should match what was received in the corresponding Assignment Request message. The DLR refers to the SCCP connection reference number used by the MSC. Like the Assignment Request message, the Assignment Complete is an SCCP-DT1 message type.

3.2 Mobile Termination

A successful mobile termination call setup begins with the MSC receiving an incoming call for a previously registered mobile subscriber. The MSC responds to the incoming request by sending a Paging Request message, over the A-Interface, to the BSC from which the mobile last registered.

Upon receiving the Paging Request message, the BSC sends an IS-95 General Page message to notify the mobile station of the call. Whether the BSC pages the mobile station using all cells or just a group of cells (LAC) is BSC implementation-specific. If the IMSI received in the IS-95 General Page message matches the identity of the mobile station's stored IMSI, the mobile responds with an IS-95 Page Response message over the Access Channel. The IS-95 Page Response message contains information similar to the IS-95 Origination message, such as IMSI, ESN, and Service Option.

Upon receiving the IS-95 Page Response, the BSC formats and sends a Paging Response message over the A-Interface to the MSC. The Page Response message is an SCCP-CR message, and the MSC, upon allowing the connection, replies with an SCCP-CC.

After processing the received Paging Response, the MSC sends an Assignment Request message to the BSC, requesting a *Circuit Identity Code* (CIC) and specifying the service option to be used. Once the BSC has successfully set up the radio link and allocated the corresponding terrestrial resource (CIC), it sends an Assignment Complete. At this point, the call has been set up and the MSC is waiting for the Connect message, indicating that the mobile subscriber has answered the call. The call flow for a successful mobile-terminated call is illustrated in Figure 3-9, and is followed by detailed descriptions of each step.

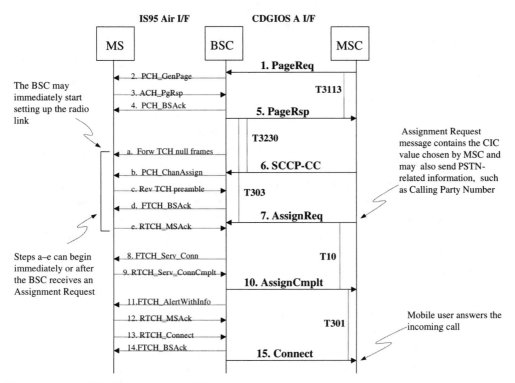

Figure 3-9 Mobile Termination call flow

3.2.1 Mobile Termination Call Flow

1. Paging Request (A-Interface):

   After receiving an incoming call for a previously registered mobile subscriber, the MSC sends a Paging Request across the A-Interface to inform the BSC of the pending call. The MSC has the option of sending the Paging Request message to all BSCs or to only the BSC from which the mobile station last registered. Upon sending the Page Request, the MSC starts timer T3113.

2. IS95_PCH_GenPage (IS-95):

   In response to receiving an A-Interface Paging Request message from the MSC, the BSC pages the requested mobile station using an IS-95 General Page message over the paging channel. IS-95 allows the BSC to page a mobile, using one of several options, depending on the mobile station's IMSI class type and parameters previously broadcast by the BSC in the IS-95 Extended System Parameters message. Two key parameters contained in the

Extended Systems Parameter message are the *Mobile Country Code* (MCC) and IMSI_11_12. The MCC is used to specify a county or region of operation, and IMSI_11_12 is usually set to the *Mobile Network Code* (MNC), which identifies the service provider's region. A mobile is said to have an IMSI class of *0* if it has a 15-digit IMSI, and an IMSI class of *1* if it has less than 15 digits in the IMSI. IS-95 designates the IMSI_S parameter as the 10 least significant digits of the IMSI. See Figure 3-3 in Section 3.1.1 on page 143.

The BSC can address a mobile station using one of several paging options, known as *paging class* and *subclass*, depending on whether a mobile station's MCC and IMSI_11_12 match what was broadcast by the BSC in the Extended Systems Parameter message. For example, to page a home mobile subscriber, the BSC may send an IS-95 General Page message to an IMSI Class 0 mobile with a paging option of PAGE_CLASS=*00* and PAGE_SUBCLASS=*00*, indicating that only IMSI_S is included in the message. IMSI_S is sufficient information to identify the mobile uniquely because it is a home mobile subscriber. For the case of a roaming mobile outside its home network, the BSC may page with PAGE_CLASS=*00* and PAGE_SUBCLASS=*01*, indicating that both IMSI_S and IMSI_11_12 (MNC) are included in the IS-95 General Page message. Both IMSI_S and MNC are required to identify a roaming subscriber uniquely.

3. IS95_ACH_PgRsp (IS-95):

Upon receiving an IS-95 General Page message that matches the identity (IMSI) of a mobile station, the mobile responds with an IS-95 Page Response over the access channel. The IS-95 Page Response message contains information similar to that found in the IS-95 Origination message, such as, IMSI, ESN, and Service Option.

Similar to both the IS-95 General Page and Origination messages, the access channel Page Response message also has several options of identifying the mobile to the BSC. For example, if the mobile's MCC and IMSI_11_12 match those transmitted by the BSC in the paging channel IS-95 Extended System Parameters message, the mobile, if it chooses, may send only IMSI_S. In this case, the mobile sets IMSI_CLASS to *0* and IMSI_CLASS_0_TYPE to *00*, indicating that only IMSI_S digits will be included in the access channel message. IS-95 also allows the mobile to send IMSI_S and IMSI_11_12 or all three parameters, IMSI_S, IMSI_11_12, and MCC. In the case where the mobile's MCC or IMSI_11_12 parameters do not match the broadcast values, the mobile is required to send at least the minimum information needed to identify the mobile uniquely.

4. IS95_PCH_BSAck (IS-95):

Upon receipt of an Access Channel Page Response message, the BSC sends an IS-95 Base Station Acknowledgment Order message on the Paging Channel. Note that because the forward link has not yet been established, the IS-95 layer 2 acknowledgment for the Page Response message is sent over the paging channel as an Order message.

5. Paging Response (A-Interface):

Upon receiving an IS-95 Page Response from the requested mobile station, the BSC formats and sends a Paging Response message to the MSC, prompting the MSC to begin setting up the call. Because the Page Response message is an SCCP-CR message, it also includes SCCP parameters required to establish an SCCP connection, such as the BSC's *Source Local Reference* (SLR) number. Much of the information found in the IS-95 Page Response message, including IMSI, ESN, and Service Option, is packaged into this DTAP message. Note that the Paging Response DTAP message is encapsulated in a BSMAP Complete Layer 3 Information message, which allows the MSC to process the message as a request for an SCCP connection. Upon receiving the Page Response message, the MSC stops timer T3113. The BSC starts timers T3230 and T303.

6. SCCP-CC (A-Interface):

If the MSC allows the requested SCCP connection, it sends the BSC an SCCP-CC message. This message will contain both the connection reference number received from the BSC in the Paging Response message (denoted the *Destination Local Reference* [DLR]) and the local reference number generated at the MSC (denoted the SLR). The BSC stops Timer T3230 upon receipt of the SCCP-CC message.

7. Assignment Request (A-Interface):

After sending the SCCP-CC message, the MSC begins allocating the terrestrial resources required for the call. If required, the MSC allocates a PCM time slot for voice, referred to as a CIC, on a trunk directly connecting the MSC and BSC. The MSC may honor the preferred CIC received in the Paging Response or it may independently choose a terrestrial resource. The MSC sends the CIC information to the BSC in the Assignment Request message. Upon sending the Assignment Request message, the MSC starts timer T10. The BSC stops timer T303 after receiving the Assignment Request message.

For mobile-terminated calls, the MSC may also include the Signal IE and Calling Party Number IE in the Assignment Request message, which will then be packaged by the BSC into an IS-95 Alert With Information message. The Signal IE specifies the alerting tone to be used by the mobile to alert the user, and the Calling Party Number IE specifies how the Calling Party information is to be displayed on the mobile unit. The signal and calling party information can also be sent to the BSC, using the optional IS-95 Information Records IE.

Although not shown in Figure 3-9, the MSC has the option of piggybacking the Assignment Request message on an SCCP-CC message. In this case, a separate SCCP-CC message is not sent to the BSC.

The choice of whether the BSC sets up the radio link before or after it receives the Assignment Request message is left to the manufacturer. To reduce call setup time, the BSC may chose to start setting up the radio link upon receiving the IS-95 Page Response message instead of waiting for an Assignment Request message. The IS-95 messages exchanged between the BSC and mobile station while setting up the radio link are as follows:

   a. IS95_FTCH null frames:

   The BSC begins verifying the forward traffic channel by transmitting null traffic frames to the mobile.

   b. IS95_PCH_ChanAssign:

   BSC instructs the mobile to go to the specified traffic channel.

   c. IS95_RTCH preamble:

   The mobile begins verifying the reverse traffic channel by transmitting preamble data.

   d. IS95_FTCH_BSAck:

   BSC sends a Base Station Acknowledgment Order to the mobile to indicate acquisition of reverse traffic frames.

   e. IS95_RTCH_MSAck:

   Mobile responds with Mobile Station Acknowledgment Order.

8. IS95_FTCH_Serv_Conn (IS-95):

   The BSC sends an IS-95 Service Connect message to the mobile on the forward traffic channel, specifying the service configuration. Both signaling and traffic frame rates are specified in this message.

9. IS95_RTCH_Serv_ConnCmplt (IS-95):

   The mobile responds to the IS-95 Service Connect message with an IS-95 Service Connect Complete message.

10. Assignment Complete (A-Interface):

   An Assignment Complete message is sent from the BSC once it has successfully allocated terrestrial resources and set up the radio link. The transmission of this message implies that the BSC has successfully set up the call. Included in this message is the Service Option parameter, which specifies the final service option being used for the call. Upon receiving the Assignment Complete message, the MSC stops timer T10 and starts connect timer T301.

11. IS95_FTCH_AlertWithInfo (IS-95):

   The BSC sends an IS-95 Alert With Information message to alert the mobile user of the incoming call. Any Signal IE, Calling Party IE, or other IS-95 Information Records information sent by the MSC in the Assignment Request is included in this message. If no signaling information is included in the Alert with Information message, the mobile will use its default alerting option. This message is sent on the Forward Traffic Channel.

12. IS95_RTCH_MSAck (IS-95):

The mobile responds to the Alert with Information message with a Mobile Station Acknowledgment Order on the Reverse Traffic Channel.

13. IS95_RTCH_Connect (IS-95):

When the mobile user answers the call, the mobile station sends an IS-95 Connect Order to the BSC on the Reverse Traffic Channel.

14. IS95_FTCH_BSAck (IS-95):

The BSC acknowledges the Connect Order by sending a forward traffic channel Base Station Acknowledgment Order to the mobile.

15. Connect (A-Interface):

Upon receiving an IS-95 Connect Order, the BSC sends a Connect message to the MSC over the A-Interface. The land party and mobile subscriber are now connected. The MSC stops the connect timer, T301.

3.2.2   Mobile Termination Messages

This section describes the individual A-Interface messages exchanged between the MSC and BSC for a mobile-terminated call. The focus of this section is the message structure and individual message parameters.

3.2.2.1   Paging Request

The first message sent over the A-Interface for a mobile-terminated call is the Paging Request message. This message is formatted and sent by the MSC and includes the information required to identify the terminating mobile station uniquely. The Paging Request message is a class 0 connectionless SCCP Unit Data (UDT) message. Note that because this is a BSMAP message, all parameters have their parameter identifiers included in the message.

The Mobile Identity parameter is a mandatory message parameter that contains the IMSI of the terminating mobile station. The IMSI may contain between 10 and 15 digits (Table 3-5), depending on the IMSI class (see Section 3.2.1, "Mobile Termination Call Flow," on page 165).

Because an MSC may page multiple mobile stations simultaneously, the Paging Request message has an optional Tag IE that may be used by the MSC to identify and track pages sent to a specific mobile station. If a Tag value is included by the MSC in the Paging Request message, the BSC will include the same Tag value in the corresponding Page Response message.

The optional Cell Identifier List IE contains a list of Cell Identifiers, where each Cell Identifier specifies the cell(s) to page. Cell Discriminator type 5, which specifies paging by *Location Area Code* (LAC), is usually the preferred method of paging. However, both MSC and BSC vendors are allowed the flexibility to implement other paging algorithms. The Cell Identifier List IE is included when there are multiple cells within a BSC and the MSC wishes to page several cells using one Paging Request message. Each Cell Identifier List has the flexibility of being addressed by LAC or Cell ID only. When the Cell Identifier List IE is absent, the BSC will flood-page all cells in the network.

The optional Slot Cycle Index IE is included in the Paging Request message when the mobile is operating in slotted mode. When a mobile first registers, its preferred Slot Cycle Index is sent in the Location Updating Request, and the value is stored by the *Visitor Location Register* (VLR). The BSC uses the stored Slot Cycle Index value to page the mobile station. If this parameter is not present, the mobile station is assumed to be operating in nonslotted mode. The maximum allowable Slot Cycle Index that a mobile used for monitoring the paging channel is set by the BSC, and is broadcast over the paging channel in the IS-95 System Parameters message.

The required Service Option IE is sent by the MSC to indicate the type of service option being requested by the land party, such as voice or data. Before sending the Paging Request, the MSC may validate the requested service option type by querying the subscriber's HLR profile. Note that Service Option negotiation can also occur after the mobile is on the Traffic Channel.

- BSAP Message Type: BSMAP
- SCCP Message Type: SCCP-Unit Data (UDT)
- Direction: BSC ← MSC

Table 3-5   Paging Request Message (CDGIOS 6.1.2.3)

BitMap	Param IE	#Oct	Range	Type	IOS Ref
0000 0000 (00H) LLLL LLLL	BSMAP header	2	Msg Discrim. = 0 (BSMAP) L = BSMAP msg length	M	6.2.2.1 6.2.2.3
0101 0010 (52H)	Msg Type	1	Paging Request	M	6.2.2.4
0000 1101 (0D) LLLL LLLL dddd ittt dddd dddd .... [1111 dddd]	Mobile Identity (IMSI)	8–10	L = 06H–08H (10–15 digits) d = 00H–09H i = 0/1—even/odd indicator t = 110—IMSI	M	6.2.2.16
0011 0011 (33H) tttt tttt tttt tttt tttt tttt tttt tttt	Tag	5	t = 00000000H–FFFFFFFFH	O,C	6.2.2.62

Table 3-5 Paging Request Message (CDGIOS 6.1.2.3) (Continued)

BitMap	Param IE	#Oct	Range	Type	IOS Ref
0001 1010 (1AH) LLLL LLLL dddd dddd (d=5) aaaa aaaa aaaa aaaa OR LLLL LLLL dddd dddd (d=2) cccc cccc cccc ssss	Cell Identifier List	5	L = length, d = cell discriminator 05H—LAC 02H—Cellid a = Location Area Code c = cell id s = Sector Number, 0 for omni When this element is omitted, all cells contained in the BS are included in the page.	O,C	6.2.2.21
0011 0101 (35H) ssss siii	Slot Cycle Index	2	s = 0—spare i = slot cycle index	O,C	6.2.2.17
0000 0011 (03H) ssss ssss ssss ssss	Service Option	3	Same as element in Table 3-2, CM Service Request message.	O,R	6.2.2.66

3.2.2.2   Complete Layer 3 Information

During a mobile-terminated call setup, the Complete Layer 3 BSMAP message is used to encapsulate the DTAP Paging Response message. For further details regarding this message, refer to Section 3.1.2.1, "Complete Layer 3 Information," on page 146.

3.2.2.3   Paging Response

The Paging Response message, like the CM Service Request, is a DTAP message that is encapsulated in the Complete Layer 3 BSMAP message. Table 3-6, which describes the Page Response message parameters, includes the Complete Layer 3 message header for completeness.

Because the Paging Response is embedded in the Complete Layer 3 Information message, it starts with the parameter IE Protocol Discriminator instead of the generic DTAP header that is used for standalone DTAP messages. The Protocol Discriminator is set to 03H to indicate that the message is a Call Processing message. The next octet is reserved and is followed by the Message Type IE, which is set to 27H to indicate that the DTAP message is a Paging Response message.

The Classmark Information Type 2 IE contains information about the mobile station received by the BSC in the IS-95 Page Response message. In the case of Cellular (800-MHz) networks, the information received by the BSC in the *Station Classmark* (SCM) Info field is mapped into this IE. For *Personal Communications System* (PCS) (1900-MHz) networks, the mapping is done from other Page Response parameters because no SCM field is specified in J-STD-8. For example, in a PCS network, the Paging Response parameters MOB_TERM and SLOTTED_MODE are mapped directly from J-STD-8 Page Response message, and the C=1 (CDMA) parameter is mapped from REQUEST_MODE field.

The IMSI of a mobile uniquely identifies it to the network. The Mobile Identity (IMSI) IE is a mandatory parameter used by the MSC to identify the terminating mobile station. Depending on the IMSI type, this parameter contains between 10 and 15 digits. The mobile is said to have an IMSI class of *0* if it has a 15-digit IMSI and a class of *1* if its IMSI contains less than 15 digits. A 15-digit IMSI is required to support international roaming.

The optional Tag IE, if present, should match what was received by the MSC in the corresponding Paging Request message. This parameter allows the MSC to correlate Paging Request messages with Paging Response messages.

The Mobile ESN IE is a required parameter that contains the *Electronic Serial Number* (ESN) of the terminating mobile. The ESN is used by the MSC to validate the profile of the mobile subscriber stored in the *Home Location Register* (HLR).

To conserve power, a mobile station may operate in slotted mode. While in slotted mode, the mobile monitors the paging channel only during certain time intervals. The Slot Cycle Index IE specifies to the BSC and MSC the slot cycle being used by the mobile. Note that the maximum allowed Slot Cycle Index is determined by the BSC and is transmitted to the mobile in the IS-95 System Parameters message. Even though the mobile station may store a slot cycle value greater than the maximum specified by the BSC, it must adhere to the maximum set in the network in which it is operating.

The required parameter Service Option IE identifies the service option type being requested. The MSC may choose to validate the requested service option type with the HLR and clear the call if the service option is not supported. Service option negotiation can also occur once the mobile is in the traffic channel state.

There are several optional parameters in the Paging Response message related to mobile authentication. The BSC requests mobile stations to include the standard authentication data in Access Channel messages, such as a Page Response message, using the AUTH field of the IS-95 Access Parameters message. The Paging Response parameters AUTHR, RANDC, COUNT, and RAND are sent only if authentication is enabled at the BSC. The Authentication Event IE is used to indicate authentication errors. Chapter 6 on page 345 provides a complete description of authentication procedures and parameters.

The optional Voice Privacy Request IE is sent whenever a mobile capable of *Voice Privacy* (VP) and *Signaling Message Encryption* (SME) requests voice privacy. If this parameter IE is present in the Paging Response, the corresponding Assignment Request message received at the BSC will include the Encryption Information IE, containing the encryption keys necessary for performing VP using a private longcode mask. A complete description of VP is given in Section 6.7, "Signaling Message Encryption and Voice Privacy," on page 396.

The BSC may request the MSC to use a particular CIC for the pending origination by including the optional Circuit Identity Code IE. The MSC is not required to use the preferred CIC; however, doing so may improve overall network performance.

The Paging Response message also contains the required Radio Environment and Resources IE. The BSC includes this parameter to inform the MSC of resource allocations and the quality, as measured by the BSC, of the forward and reverse radio environments. If the mobile is already in the traffic channel before the Assignment Request message is received by the BSC, the BSC will inform the MSC that resources are allocated and available by setting the appropriate bits in this field.

- BSAP Message Type: DTAP
- SCCP Message Type: SCCP-Connection Request (CR)
- Direction: BSC $\rightarrow$ MSC

Table 3-6   Paging Response Message (CDGIOS 6.1.2.4)

BitMap	Param IE	#Oct	Range	Type	IOS Ref
0000 0000 (00H) LLLL LLLL	BSMAP header	2	Msg Discrim. = 0 (BSMAP) L = BSMAP msg length	M	6.2.2.1 6.2.2.3
0101 0111 (57H)	Msg Type	1	Complete L3 Information	M	6.2.2.4
0000 0101 (05H)	Cell Identifier	5 or 7	Same as element in Table 3-1, Complete L3 Info message.	M	6.2.2.20
0001 0111 (17H) LLLL LLLL	Layer 3 Info	2	L = length	M	6.2.2.38
rrrr 0011 (03H)	Protocol Discrim.	1	0011—Call Processing r = 0—reserved bits	M	6.2.2.39
0000 0000 (00H)	Reserved	1		M	6.2.2.40
0010 0111 (27H)	Msg Type	1	Paging Response	M	6.2.2.4
LLLL LLLL	Classmark Info Type 2	5	Same as element in Table 3-2, CM Service Request message.	M	6.2.2.15

Table 3-6   Paging Response Message (CDGIOS 6.1.2.4) (Continued)

BitMap	Param IE	#Oct	Range	Type	IOS Ref
LLLL LLLL	Mobile Identity (IMSI)	7–9	Same as element in Table 3-2, CM Service Request message.	M	6.2.2.16
0011 0011 (33H) tttt tttt tttt tttt tttt tttt tttt tttt	Tag	5	t = 00000000H–FFFFFFFFH	O,C	6.2.2.62
0000 1101 (0DH)	Mobile Identity (ESN)	7	Same as element in Table 3-2, CM Service Request message.	O,R	6.2.2.16
0011 0101 (35H) rrrr riii	Slot Cycle Index	2	r = 0—reserved i = slot cycle index	O,C	6.2.2.17
0100 0010 (42H)	Auth Response (AUTHR)	6	Same as element in Table 3-2, CM Service Request message.	O,C	6.2.2.46
0010 1000 (28H) rrrr rrrr	Auth Confirm (RANDC)	2	Same as element in Table 3-2, CM Service Request message.	O,C	6.2.2.42
0100 0000 (40H) rrcc cccc	Auth Param COUNT	2	Same as element in Table 3-2, CM Service Request message.	O,C	6.2.2.47
0100 0001 (41H)	Auth Chal- lenge (RAND)	7	Same as element in Table 3-2, CM Service Request message.	O,C	6.2.2.45
0000 0011 (03H)	Service Option	3	Same as element in Table 3-2, CM Service Request message.	O,R	6.2.2.66
1010 0001 (A1H)	VP Req	1	Voice Privacy Req	O,C	6.2.2.13
0000 0001 (01H) mmmm mmmm mmmt tttt	Circuit Iden- tity Code	3	m = spanid, t = timeslot	O,C	6.2.2.22

Table 3-6   Paging Response Message (CDGIOS 6.1.2.4) (Continued)

BitMap	Param IE	#Oct	Range	Type	IOS Ref
0100 1010 (4AH)	Authentication Event	3	Same as element in Table 3-2, CM Service Request message.	O,C	6.2.2.114
0001 1101 (1DH) 00ff rrAV	Radio Environment and Resources	2	Same as element in Table 3-2, CM Service Request message.	O,R	6.2.2.82

3.2.2.4   Assignment Request

The Assignment Request message is sent from the MSC to the BSC when terrestrial resources are available and the MSC is proceeding to set up the call. This message is usually sent as an SCCP-DT1 message, but it may also be piggybacked on an SCCP-CC message. Note that, because the Assignment Request message is a BSMAP message type, all the parameters, both mandatory and optional, have the parameter IE included.

Following the BSMAP header and the Message Type IE is the Channel Type IE, which has no impact on call processing. The BSC ignores this parameter because the values are GSM A-Interface-specific and are of no significance to IS-95 CDMA systems.

The next parameter in the Assignment Request message is the conditionally required Circuit Identity Code IE, which specifies the PCM circuit to be used for a call. The MSC has the option of honoring the preferred CIC received in the CM Service Request message or choosing one of its own. Upon receiving the Assignment Request message, the BSC allocates the CIC specified in this message. Although the standard provides no guidelines regarding logical span assignments, CIC codes used by both the MSC and BSC must match.

The optional Encryption Information IE is sent if Voice Privacy IE is requested from the BSC in the Paging Response and if the encryption keys are available from the Authentication Center. A complete description of VP can be found in Section 6.7, "Signaling Message Encryption and Voice Privacy," on page 396.

The required Service Option IE contains the same service option value requested in the Paging Response message received from the BSC.

The Signal IE and the Calling Party IE are parameters included only when the Assignment Request refers to a mobile-terminated call and are used for indicating the alerting type and calling party information to the mobile, respectively.

The Calling Party ASCII Number IE specifies the presentation and screening options to the mobile. Display of the calling number information by the mobile is dependent on the presentation and screening bits. Based on the mobile subscriber calling number presentation and restriction fields in the HLR, the MSC can choose to display the Calling Party Number or not. The network can also screen the Calling Party Number if requested by the calling party. The presentation indicator bits can take on the following values as:

- 00—Presentation allowed
- 01—Presentation restricted
- 10—Number not available, due to inter-working

The screening indicator bits can take on the following values:

- 00—User-provided, not screened
- 01—User-provided, verified, and paused
- 10—User-provided, verified, and failed
- 11—Network-provided

The optional IS-95 Information Records parameter can be used to send IS-95 Information Records to the mobile station. Examples include Display, Calling Party Number, Signal, and Message Waiting. This parameter should not carry redundant information included in other parameters, such as Signal and Calling Party ASCII Number.

See Table 3-3 on page 154, under the Mobile Origination section, for the complete format of the Assignment Request message.

3.2.2.5   Assignment Complete

The Assignment Complete message is sent from the BSC to the MSC to indicate that the BSC has successfully set up the call. This message is sent only after the BSC receives an IS-95 Service Connect Complete message from the mobile. The Assignment Complete message, a BSMAP message, is sent as an SCCP-DT1 message.

The first parameter, the Channel Number IE, is a mandatory parameter used to identify a logical channel number assigned to the equipment providing a traffic channel. Because this information is not normally used by the MSC, it is sometimes hard-coded to a value of 0 by the BSC.

The optional Encryption Information IE is included in the Assignment Complete message by the BSC if the same IE was sent by the MSC in the Assignment Request message. The transmission of this parameter by the BSC signifies the acceptance and execution of the requested encryption procedures. Note that no keys are included in this IE.

The Service Option IE is a required parameter that contains the same service option value received by the BSC in the Assignment Request message.

See Table 3-4 on page 157, under the Mobile Origination section, for the complete format of the Assignment Complete message.

3.2.2.6   Connect

The Connect message is sent from the BSC to the MSC to indicate that the mobile subscriber has answered the call. The Connect message can be used by the MSC to start the billing process. The Connect message contains only header and message type information (Table 3-7).

- BSAP Message Type: DTAP
- SCCP Message Type: SCCP-Data Form 1 (DT1)
- Direction: BSC → MSC

Table 3-7   Connect Message (CDGIOS 6.1.2.10)

BitMap	Param IE	#Oct	Range	Type	IOS Ref
0000 0001 (01H) ccrr rsss LLLL LLLL	DTAP header	3	Msg Discrim. = 1 (DTAP) DLCI = "ccrr rsss" = 0 L = DTAP msg length	M	6.2.2.1 6.2.2.2 6.2.2.3
rrrr 0011 (03H)	Protocol Dis-criminator	1	0011—Call Processing r = 0—reserved	M	6.2.2.39
0000 0000 (00H)	Reserved Bits	1		M	6.2.2.40
0000 0111 (07H)	Msg Type	1	Connect	M	6.2.2.4

3.2.3   Mobile Termination Example Call Flow

Figure 3-10 shows a practical example of a summary message call flow for a mobile-terminated call. The purpose of Figure 3-10 is to present an overview of the messages exchanged between the BSC and MSC. Subsequent figures illustrate the complete message's content, including MTP and SCCP layers. The decoded message format is similar to what would be seen on test equipment monitoring the A-Interface signaling link.

The mobile termination example in Figure 3-10 starts with the MSC sending a Paging Request to the BSC. The BSC, after receiving a response from the requested mobile, sends a Paging Response message to the MSC, indicating that the mobile responded. Because the Page Response is an SCCP-CR message, the MSC then responds with an SCCP-CC. Notice that once the SCCP connection has been established, the MSC and BSC continue to use the same SLS, which maps the transmitted SS7 messages to a specific signaling link code. Each node independently chooses a signaling link for the SCCP connection and continues to use that link throughout the call. Although the MSC and BSC may each choose different links, SCCP connection oriented messages for a particular call will be transported over the same signaling link from a node.

After confirming the SCCP connection, the MSC request terrestrial resources by sending an Assignment Request. The BSC responds with an Assignment Complete, indicating that it has successfully set up the call. Finally, the Connect message is sent from the BSC to the MSC when the mobile user answers the alerting mobile station. The remaining messages in Figure 3-10 are related to releasing the call and are discussed later, in the mobile-initiated call clearing section.

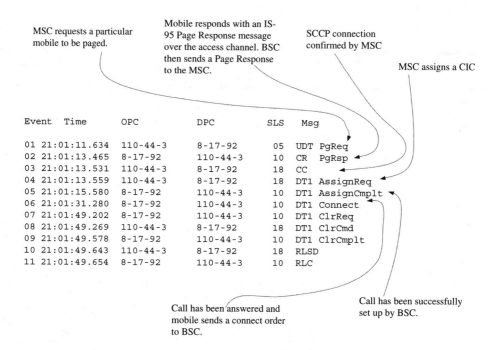

Figure 3-10   Mobile Termination Example call flow log

```
**** MESSAGE NUMBER: 00001 ****
*** Start of MTP Level 2 ***
0000 11000111 c7
     -1000111    Backward Sequence Number    71
     1-------    Backward Indicator Bit       1
0001 10101110 ae
     -0101110    Forward Sequence Number     46
     1-------    Forward Indicator Bit        1
0002 00110000 30
     --110000    Length Indicator            48
     00------    Spare                        0
*** Start of MTP Level 3 ***
0003 10000011 83
     ----0011    Service Indicator           SCCP
     --00----    Network Priority            priority 0
     10------    Network Indicator           National Network
0004 (3 bytes)   Destination Point Code      8-17-92
0007 (3 bytes)   Origination Point Code      110-44-3
0010 00000101 05 Signaling Link Selection    5
```

(Continued)

```
*** Start of SCCP ***
0011 00001001 09 Unitdata                        09                      Connectionless
0012 00000000 00                                                         message
     ----0000    Protocol Class             Class 0
     0000----    Message Handling           no special options
0013 00000011 03 Called Party Address       Offset 0016
0014 00000101 05 Calling Party Address      Offset 0019
0015 00001010 0a Data Portion Pointer       Offset 0025
0016 00000010 02 Called Party Addr Length   2
0017 11000001 c1
     -------1    Subsys Number Indicator    Included
     ------0-    Point Code Indicator       Excluded
     --0000--    Global Title indicator     No GTT included
     -1------    Routing indicator          route by DPC/SSN
     1-------    Reserved for National use  National use
0018 11111100 fc Subsystem Number           252
0019 00000101 05 Calling Party Addr Length  5
0020 11000011 c3
     -------1    Subsys Number Indicator    Included
     ------1-    Point Code Indicator       Included
     --0000--    Global Title indicator     No GTT included
     -1------    Routing indicator          route by DPC/SSN
     1-------    Reserved for National use  National use
0021 11111100 fc Subsystem Number           252
0022 (3 bytes)   Signaling Point Code       110-44-3
*** Start of CDGIOS MAP ***
                 Paging Request
0025 00011100 1c Data Length                28
0026 00000000 00 BSMAP Discriminator        00
0027 00011010 1a BSMAP Length               26
0028 01010010 52 Paging Request             82
0029 00001101 0d Mobile Identity (IMSI)     13
0030 00001000 08 Length                     8
0031 00111110 3e
     -----110    Type of Identity           110 - IMSI          Page by IMSI
     ----1---    Odd/Even Indicator         odd
     0011----    IMSI Identity Digits       310006197889514
0032 (7 bytes)
0039 00110011 33 Tag                        51                  Tag is used by MSC to
0040 (4 bytes)   Tag Value                  72 02 00 05         uniquely identify the
0041 00011010 1a Cell Identifier List       1A                  paging request sent to
0042 00000011 03 Length                     3                   the BSC
0043 00000101 05 Cell Discriminator         LAC
0044 00000111 07                            1822
0045 00011110 1e                                                Included only if
0046 00110101 35 Slot Cycle Index           53                  mobile is operat-
0047 00000001 01 value                      1                   ing in slotted
0048 00000011 03 Service Option             3                   mode
0049 (2 bytes)   Service Type               13K Speech
```

Figure 3-11 Paging Request message example

Figure 3-11, shows an example of a decoded Paging Request message that is similar to what may be seen on test equipment monitoring the A-Interface during a mobile-terminated call. All layers of the message are included to help illustrate SS7, SCCP, and Application layer functionality.

The decoded message starts with MTP2, which contains the forward and backward sequence numbers, forward and backward indicator bits, and the overall message length. Recall that forward and backward sequence numbers and indicator bits are used by MTP2 to acknowledge received messages. The next layer shown in the example is MTP3, which contains information about the message type and provides routing information. Because all A-Interface messages are users of the SCCP layer, the MTP3 Service Indicator bits are set to SCCP. The OPC and DPC indicate that the message was sent from the MSC (110-44-3) to the BSC (8-17-92).

The example Paging Request message shown in Figure 3-11 illustrates the format of an SCCP-UDT message. Because the Paging Request message is a Class 0 connectionless message, which does not require an SCCP connection, the SCCP layer does not contain an SLR number. In the case of a mobile-terminated call, the SCCP connection is not initiated until after the BSC has received a Page Response from the mobile station. Notice that the subsystem number being addressed to is 252, which is the A-Interface subsystem in CDGIOS.

The example Paging Request message contains the mandatory Mobile Identity IE and optional Tag, Cell Identifier List, Slot Cycle Index, and Service Option parameters. The Mobile Identity indicates that the page is for a mobile whose IMSI is 310006197889514. The MSC has assigned a Tag value of 72020005 to the example Paging Request and may use the Tag value to correlate the message with received Paging Responses.

```
**** MESSAGE NUMBER: 00002 ****
*** Start of MTP Level 2 ***
0000 10101110 ae
     -0101110    Backward Sequence Number    46
     1-------    Backward Indicator Bit      1
0001 11001000 c8
     -1001000    Forward Sequence Number     72
     1-------    Forward Indicator Bit       1
0002 00111111 3f
     --111111    Length Indicator            63
     00------    Spare                       0
*** Start of MTP Level 3 ***
0003 10000011 83
     ----0011    Service Indicator           SCCP
     --00----    Network Priority            priority 0
     10------    Network Indicator           National Network
0004 (3 bytes)  Destination Point Code       110-44-3        SCCP connection is
0007 (3 bytes)  Origination Point Code       8-17-92    ◄─── requested by the BSC
0010 00001010 0a Signaling Link Selection    10
*** Start of SCCP ***
0011 00000001 01 Connection Request          01
```

(Continued)

```
0012 (3 bytes)     Source Local References    78696    ◄────────BSC's local refer-
0015 00000010 02                                                ence of this SCCP
     ----0010      Protocol Class             Class 2          connection
     0000----      Spare                      00
0016 00000010 02 Mandatory Variable Ptr       Offset 0018
0017 00000111 07 Optional Pointer             Offset 0024
0018 00000101 05 Called Party Addr Length     5
0019 11000011 c3
     -------1      Subsys Number Indicator     Included
     ------1-      Point Code Indicator        Included
     --0000--      Global Title indicator      No GTT included
     -1------      Routing indicator           route by DPC/SSN
     1-------      Reserved for National       National use
0020 11111100 fc Subsystem Number             252
0021 (3 bytes)   Signaling Point Code         110-44-3
0024 00001111 0f Data PNC                     15
*** Start of CDGIOS MAP ***
                 Complete Layer 3 Information
0025 00101110 2e Data Length                  46
0026 00000000 00 BSMAP Discriminator          00
0027 00101100 2c BSMAP Length                 44
0028 01010111 57 Complete Layer 3 Info        87
0029 00000101 05 Cell Identifier              5
0030 00000011 03 Length                       3
0031 00000010 02 Cell Identifier Discrim      CI only
0032 00010001 11 CI Value                     11 43
0033 01000011 43
0034 00010111 17 Layer 3 Information          23
0035 00100100 24 Length                       36
0036 00000011 03 Protocol Discriminator       Call Processing
0037 00000000 00 Reserved                     00
0038 00100111 27 CC Message Selection         Paging Response
                 Classmark Info Type 2
0039 00000100 04 Length                       4
0040 00100000 20
     -----000      RF Power Capability         Class 1, vehicle and portable
     ---00---      Reserved                    0
     001-----      MOB_P_REV                   1
0041 00000000 00
     -----000      Frequency Capability        band number 0
     00000---      Reserved                    00
0042 01110010 72
     -------0      Reserved                    0
     ------1-      Mobile Term                 capable of rcving call
     -----0--      DTX                         DTX is incapable
     ----0---      Bandwidth                   Mobile limited to 20 MHz Band
     ---1----      Extended Protocol (EP)      Full reverse control channel
     --1-----      Slotted                     Slotted paging request allowed
     -1------      IS-95                       IS-95 capable
     0-------      Reserved                    0
0043 00000000 00 Reserved                     0
```

(Continued)

```
                    Mobile Identity
0044 00001000 08 Length                     8
0045 00111110 3e
     -----110     Type of Identity          110 - IMSI
     ----1---     Odd/Even Indicator         odd
     0011----     IMSI Identity Digits       310006197889514
0046 (7 bytes)
0053 00110011 33 Tag                        51
0054 (4 bytes)   Tag Value                  72 02 00 05  ◄──  Must match the
0058 00001101 0d Mobile Identity (ESN)      13                Tag identifier sup-
0059 00000101 05 Length                     5                 plied by MSC in
0060 00000101 05                                              the Paging
     -----101     Type of Identity          101 - ESN         Request message
     ----0---     Odd/Even Indicator         even
     0000----     Fixed                      00
0061 (4 bytes)   ESN Identity Digits        9f 1c 47 a3
0065 00110101 35 Slot Cycle Index           53
0066 00000001 01
     -----001     Slot Cycle Index          1
     00000---     Spare                      00
0067 00000011 03 Service Option             3
0068 10000000 80 Service Type               13K voice
0069 00000000 00
0070 00011101 1d Radio Env & Resrc          1D
0071 00000011 03                            avail & allocated
0072 00000000 00 SCCP EOP
```

Figure 3-12   Paging Response message example

A decoded example of a Paging Response message is given in Figure 3-12, above. The BSC uses this message to transfer information about the mobile station to the MSC and to request an SCCP connection for the call. As seen in the example, the Paging Request message is an SCCP-CR message type, and the SCCP layer of the message specifies that message routing should be done using point code and subsystem number. The SCCP layer also contains an SLR (78696), which is a unique numerical identifier that the BSC uses to reference the SCCP connection. This identifier allows the BSC to distinguish between many simultaneous SCCP connections.

Following the SCCP layer is the CDGIOS application layer. The application layer of the message identifies the message type as BSMAP and the specific message as Complete Layer 3 information. In this example, the cell discriminator specifies that only Cell ID is included. Following the Cell ID parameter is the encapsulated Paging Response message, which contains information sent from the mobile station in the IS-95 Page Response. The Class Mark Information IE indicates that the mobile has a power class of 1 and is CDMA (IS-95)-capable. The next IE, the mandatory Mobile Identity IE, specifies the IMSI of the mobile. Following the IMSI is the Tag value that was included in the Paging Request message received from the MSC. Also included in the example message are Mobile Identity (ESN), Slot Cycle Index, and Service Option.

```
**** MESSAGE NUMBER: 00003 ****
*** Start of MTP Level 2 ***
0000 11001000 c8
     -1001000    Backward Sequence Number   72
     1-------    Backward Indicator Bit     1
0001 10101111 af
     -0101111    Forward Sequence Number    47
     1-------    Forward Indicator Bit      1
0002 00010001 11
     --010001    Length Indicator           17
     00------    Spare                      0
*** Start of MTP Level 3 ***
0003 10010011 93
     ----0011    Service Indicator          SCCP
     --01----    Network Priority           priority 1
     10------    Network Indicator          National Network
0004 (3 bytes)   Destination Point Code     8-17-92
0007 (3 bytes)   Origination Point Code     110-44-3
0010 00010010 12 Signaling Link Selection   18
*** Start of SCCP ***
0011 00000010 02 Connection Confirm         02
0012 (3 bytes)   Dest Local References      78696
0015 (3 bytes)   Source Local References    15432238
0018 00000010 02 Protocol Class             Class 2
0019 00000000 00 Optional Pointer
```

Connection Confirm priority is 1

BSC's local reference of SCCP connection

MSC's local reference of this SCCP connection

Figure 3-13 SCCP Connection Confirm message example

The SCCP-CC message shown in Figure 3-13, above, is a simple but important message used by the MSC to indicate that the SCCP connection requested in the CM Service request is being allowed. The SCCP-CC message contains both the SLR (15432238) and DLR (78696), a feature that is often useful when troubleshooting. Notice that the DLR is set to the value that the MSC received in the SLR field of the Paging Response message. The SLR in this message is the locally generated MSC reference for the SCCP connection. Once the SCCP connection has been established, the SLR and DLR can be used to determine which SCCP messages belong to a particular call.

```
**** MESSAGE NUMBER: 00004 ****
*** Start of MTP Level 2 ***
0000 11001000 c8
     -1001000    Backward Sequence Number   72
     1-------    Backward Indicator Bit     1
0001 10110000 b0
     -0110000    Forward Sequence Number    48
     1-------    Forward Indicator Bit      1
0002 00101110 2e
```

(Continued)
```
      --101110     Length Indicator          46
      00------     Spare                     0
*** Start of MTP Level 3 ***
0003 10000011 83
      ----0011     Service Indicator         SCCP
      --00----     Network Priority          priority 0
      10------     Network Indicator         National Network
0004 (3 bytes)     Destination Point Code    8-17-92
0007 (3 bytes)     Origination Point Code    110-44-3
0010 00010010 12   Signaling Link Selection  18
*** Start of SCCP ***
0011 00000110 06   Data Form 1               06
0012 (3 bytes)     Dest Local References     78696
0015 00000000 00   Segment/Reassembling      0
0016 00000001 01   Variable Pointer          01
*** Start of CDGIOS MAP ***
                   Assignment Request
0017 00011111 1f   Data Length               31
0018 00000000 00   BSMAP Discriminator       00
0019 00011101 1d   BSMAP Length              29
0020 00000001 01   Assignment Request        01
0021 00001011 0b   Channel Type              11
0022 00000011 03   Length                    3
0023 00000001 01   Speech or Data Indicator  Speech
0024 00001000 08   Channel Rate and Type     Full rate TCH Bm
0025 00000101 05   Speech Encoding Algorithm 13 Kb/s
0026 00000001 01   Circuit Identity Code Id  1
0027 00000000 00   PCM MUX (high part)       0
0028 00000010 02
      ---00010     Time Slot                 2
      000-----     PCM MUX (low part)        0
0029 00000011 03   Service Option            3
0030 10000000 80   Service Type              13k speech
0031 00000000 00
0032 00110100 34   Signal                    52
0033 10000001 81   Signal Value              Long
0034 00000000 00   Alert Pitch               Medium
0035 01001011 4b   Calling Party ASCII       75
0036 00001100 0c   Length                    12
0037 00100001 21
      ----0001     Numbering Plan ID         ISDN/Tele(E.164/E.163)
      -010----     Type of Number            National
      0-------     Extension                 Included
0038 10000011 83
      ------11     Screening Indicator
      ---000--     Spare                     00
      -00-----     Presentation Indicator
      1-------     Extension                 01
0039(10 bytes)     ASCII String              6192716377
```

MSC chooses a CIC from a list of available resources

Only sent for mobile terminated calls. Identifies how the mobile should be alerted

Only sent for mobile terminated calls.

Figure 3-14 Assignment Request message example

An example Assignment Request message is shown in Figure 3-14, above. Assignment
Request messages are SCCP type DT1, which are used to exchange information between the
MSC and BSC after an SCCP connection has been established. The DLR included by the MSC
in the SCCP layer of the message is set to 78696, which is the reference number that the BSC
has assigned to the SCCP connection for this call.

This Assignment Request message is sent from the MSC to the BSC when terrestrial
resources are available and the MSC is proceeding to set up the call. In this example, the MSC
requests that CIC 2 be used by the BSC for voice traffic. In the case of mobile-terminated calls,
the Assignment Request message may contain information used by the mobile station to alert
the mobile user. The example message in Figure 3-14 instructs the mobile to use the long signaling, medium pitch, and to present the calling party digits (caller ID). The Channel Type information is included in the message but is not used by the BSC.

```
**** MESSAGE NUMBER: 00005 ****
*** Start of MTP Level 2 ***
0000 10110001 b1
     -0110001    Backward Sequence Number   49
     1-------    Backward Indicator Bit     1
0001 11001010 ca
     -1001010    Forward Sequence Number    74
     1-------    Forward Indicator Bit      1
0002 00011000 18
     --011000    Length Indicator           24
     00------    Spare                      0
*** Start of MTP Level 3 ***
0003 10000011 83
     ----0011    Service Indicator          SCCP
     --00----    Network Priority           priority 0
     10------    Network Indicator          National
0004 (3 bytes)   Destination Point Code     110-44-3
0007 (3 bytes)   Origination Point Code     8-17-92
0010 00001010 0a Signaling Link Selection   10
*** Start of SCCP ***
0011 00000110 06 Data Form 1                06
0012 (3 bytes)   Dest Local References      15432238
0015 00000000 00 Segment/Reassembling       0
0016 00000001 01 Variable Pointer           01
*** Start of CDGIOS MAP ***
                 Assignment Complete
0017 00001001 09 Data Length                9
0018 00000000 00 BSMAP Discriminator        00
0019 00000111 07 BSMAP Length               7
0020 00000010 02 Assignment Complete        02
0021 00100011 23 Channel Number             35
0022 (2 bytes)   Value                      00 00
0024 00000011 03 Service Option             13k Speech
0025 (2 bytes)
```

Figure 3-15   Assignment Complete message example

The Assignment Complete message is sent from the BSC to the MSC to indicate that the BSC has successfully set up the call. The example message shown in Figure 3-15, above, contains a Channel Number ID, not typically used by the MSC, and the Service Option, which should match what was received in the Assignment Request message. The DLR refers to the SCCP connection reference number used by the MSC. Like the Assignment Request message, the Assignment Complete is an SCCP-DT1 message type.

```
**** MESSAGE NUMBER: 00006 ****
*** Start of MTP Level 2 ***
0000 10110001 b1
     -0110001    Backward Sequence Number   49
     1-------    Backward Indicator Bit     1
0001 11001011 cb
     -1001011    Forward Sequence Number    75
     1-------    Forward Indicator Bit      1
0002 00010101 15
     --010101    Length Indicator           21
     00------    Spare                      0
*** Start of MTP Level 3 ***
0003 10000011 83
     ----0011    Service Indicator          SCCP
     --00----    Network Priority           priority 0
     10------    Network Indicator          National
0004 (3 bytes)   Destination Point Code     110-44-3
0007 (3 bytes)   Origination Point Code     8-17-92
0010 00001010 0a Signaling Link Selection   10
*** Start of SCCP ***
0011 00000110 06 Data Form 1                06
0012 (3 bytes)   Dest Local References      15432238
0015 00000000 00 Segment/Reassembling       0
0016 00000001 01 Variable Pointer           01
*** Start of CDGIOS CC ***
                 Connect
0017 00000110 06 DTAP Length                6
0018 00000001 01 Discriminator              01
0019 00000000 00 DLCI
     -----000    SAPI                       0
     --000---    Reserved                   00
     00------    C1/C2                      ANSI/EIA/TIA-553,IS95
0020 00000011 03 Length                     3
0021 00000011 03 CC Protocol Discrim        03
0022 00000000 00 Reserved                   00
0023 00000111 07 Connect                    07
```

Figure 3-16   Connect message example

An example Connect message is shown in Figure 3-16, above. The BSC uses the Connect message to notify the MSC that the call has been answered. The Connect message does not contain any information about the call except the DLR of the SCCP connection.

3.3 Mobile-Initiated Call Clearing

A successful mobile-initiated call clearing begins when the mobile subscriber ends an existing call by pressing the end button or by powering down the mobile station. The mobile station sends an IS-95 Release Order to the BSC to indicate the end of the call.

Upon receiving an IS-95 Release Order from the mobile station, the BSC sends the MSC a Clear Request message, requesting that the call be torn down. The MSC responds to the Clear Request with a Clear Command. The BSC sends an IS-95 Forward Traffic Channel Release Order to the mobile station and a Clear Complete to the MSC. Finally, the SCCP connection is released on both ends using the *SCCP Released* (SCCP-RLSD) and *SCCP Release Complete* (SCCP-RLC) messages. The call flow is illustrated in Figure 3-17 and is followed by a more detailed description of each step.

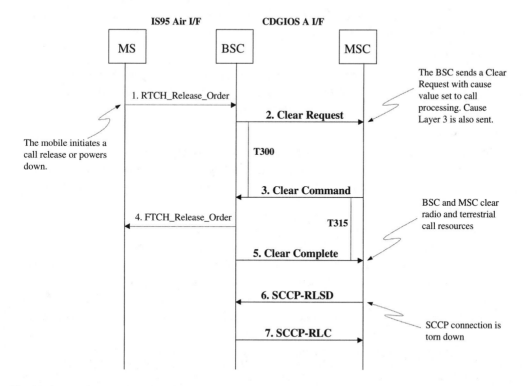

Figure 3-17   Mobile-Initiated Call Clearing call flow

3.3.1   Mobile-Initiated Call Clearing Call Flow

1. IS95_RTCH_Release (IS-95):

   When a mobile subscriber ends a call, either by pressing the "END" button or by powering down the mobile, an IS-95 Reverse Traffic Channel Release Order is sent by the mobile station to the BSC. The Release Order message indicates whether the release was normal or with power down indication.

2. Clear Request (A-Interface):

   Upon receiving an IS-95 Release Order, the BSC sends a Clear Request to the MSC with a cause value of call processing and a layer 3 cause value of normal termination. The layer 3 cause value allows the BSC to send the reason for the mobile station release to the MSC. After sending the Clear Request message, the BSC starts timer T300 and waits for a Clear Command from the MSC.

3. Clear Command (A-Interface):

   The MSC, upon receipt of the Clear Request message, transmits a Clear Command to the BSC and starts clearing its terrestrial resources. During this time, the BSC continues clearing the radio and terrestrial resources previously allocated for the call. The MSC starts timer T315 and waits for a Clear Complete message from the BSC. Upon receipt of the Clear Command message, the BSC stops timer T300.

4. IS95_FTCH_ Release (IS-95):

   After receiving a Clear Command and releasing terrestrial resources, the BSC sends an IS-95 Release Order to the mobile. The mobile and BSC both release traffic channel radio resources.

5. Clear Complete (A-Interface):

   After successfully deallocating all radio and terrestrial resources, the BSC sends a Clear Complete message to the MSC, indicating that it has cleared all resources previously allocated for the call. The MSC stops timer T315 upon receipt of the Clear Complete message.

6. SCCP-RLSD (A-Interface):

   Once the BSC acknowledges that it has cleared all resources by sending a Clear Complete message, the MSC informs the BSC that the SCCP connection for the call is being released by sending an SCCP-RLSD message. The message indicates to the BSC that it should release the specified SCCP connection. To identify the SCCP connection, both DLR and SLR reference numbers are included in the message. The DLR refers to the BSC's local reference number, and the SLR refers to the MSC's local reference number. The release reason for the SCCP-RLSD message is also included in the message and is typically set to "end user originated," indicating a normal SCCP user termination.

7. SCCP-RLC (A-Interface):

The BSC, upon receipt of the SCCP-RLSD message, releases the SCCP resources previously allocated for the call and sends an SCCP-RLC message to the MSC, indicating that the SCCP connection has been successfully torn down. At this stage, all radio, terrestrial, and SCCP resources at both the MSC and BSC have been released.

3.3.2 Mobile-Initiated Call Clearing Messages

This section describes the individual A-Interface messages exchanged between the MSC and BSC for a mobile-initiated call clearing. The focus of this section is the message structure and individual message parameters.

3.3.2.1 Clear Request

The Clear Request message shown in Table 3-8 is a BSMAP message sent by the BSC to request the MSC to clear a call. Because the Clear Request message refers to an existing call and therefore, an existing SCCP connection, the message is coded as an SCCP-DT1 message. Although the implementation of each cause value is vendor-specific, the values can be broadly classified into categories specified in the standard.

The mandatory Cause IE value indicates the category of call release reasons to the MSC. In a mobile-initiated call clearing scenario, this Cause parameter is typically set to "call processing," and the optional Cause Layer 3 IE is then used to provide more details about the call release reason.

Although the Cause Layer 3 IE is optional, the parameter is generally sent for mobile-initiated call clearing scenarios because including this parameter provides the MSC with additional information about the reason for clearing the call. The cause values are implementation-specific because the standard does not provide any hard rules relating to their usage.

- BSAP Message Type: BSMAP
- SCCP Message Type: SCCP-Data Form 1 (DT1)
- Direction: BSC → MSC

Table 3-8 Clear Request Message (CDGIOS 6.1.2.20)

BitMap	Param IE	#Oct	Range	Type	IOS Ref
0000 0000 (00H) LLLL LLLL	BSMAP header	2	Msg Discrim.= 0 (BSMAP) L = BSMAP msg length	M	6.2.2.1 6.2.2.3
0010 0010 (22H)	Msg Type	1	Clear Request	M	6.2.2.4

Table 3-8   Clear Request Message (CDGIOS 6.1.2.20) (Continued)

BitMap	Param IE	#Oct	Range	Type	IOS Ref
0000 0100 (04H) LLLL LLLL 0ccc cccc	Cause	3	L = 01H, c = Cause values 00—radio interface msg failure 01—radio interface failure 07—OAM&P intervention 09—call processing 0D—timer expired 20—equipment failure 60—protocol error	M	6.2.2.19
0000 1000 (08H) LLLL LLLL xccr llll xvvv vvvv	Cause Layer 3	4	L = 02H, x = 1, r = 0—spare cc = Coding std, 00—ITU llll = location bits, 0100—pub netwk serving remote user v = cause layer3 0010000—normal clearing 0011111—normal unspecified Present when CauseIE = *callp*	O,C	6.2.2.55

3.3.2.2   Clear Command

The Clear Command message shown in Table 3-9 is a BSMAP message sent by the MSC to clear a specific call. Because the Clear Command message refers to an existing call, the message is coded as an SCCP-DT1 message. The MSC sends a Clear Command message to the BSC to indicate that it has started releasing resources related to a specific call and to instruct the BSC to do the same. Similar to the Clear Request message, the assignment of cause values is vendor-specific.

The mandatory Cause IE value specifies the category of the call release reason to the BSC. In mobile-initiated and BSC-initiated call clearing scenarios, this value is typically set to the same Cause IE value sent by the BSC in the Clear Request message.

The optional Cause Layer 3 IE provides additional information about the reason for releasing a call. This parameter is generally included in the Clear Command message for MSC initiated call clearing scenarios only where the Cause IE is set to call processing. It is usually not present for mobile- and BSC-initiated call clearing scenarios.

- BSAP Message Type: BSMAP
- SCCP Message Type: SCCP-Data Form 1 (DT1)
- Direction: BSC ← MSC

Table 3-9 Clear Command Message (CDGIOS 6.1.2.21)

BitMap	Param IE	#Oct	Range	Type	IOS Ref
0000 0000 (00H) LLLL LLLL	BSMAP header	2	Msg Discrim. = 0 (BSMAP) L = BSMAP msg length	M	6.2.2.1 6.2.2.3
0010 0000 (20H)	Msg Type	1	Clear Command	M	6.2.2.4
0000 0100 (04H) LLLL LLLL 0ccc cccc	Cause	3	L = 01H, c = cause value 07—OAM&P intervention 09—call processing 0A—reversion to old channel 0B—handoff successful 20—equipment failure 60—protocol error 78—do not notify MS	M	6.2.2.19
0000 1000 (08H) LLLL LLLL xccr llll xvvv vvvv	Cause Layer 3	4	L = 02H, x = 1, r = 0—spare cc = Coding std, 00—ITU llll = 0100—location bits v = cause L3 0010000—normal clearing 0011111—normal unspecified 0010001—user busy 0010011—user alerting no ans Present for MSC-initiated call clearing and when Cause IE is set to "call processing"	O,C	6.2.2.55

3.3.2.3 Clear Complete

The Clear Complete message is a BSMAP message sent as an SCCP-DT1 message type. The BSC sends a Clear Complete message to the MSC to indicate that it has successfully cleared both radio and terrestrial resources related to a specific call. The Clear Complete message contains only one optional parameter, the optional Power Down Indicator, which is used to indicate to the MSC that the mobile user terminated the call by powering off the mobile station (Table 3-10).

- BSAP Message Type: BSMAP
- SCCP Message Type: SCCP-Data Form 1 (DT1)
- Direction: BSC → MSC

Table 3-10   Clear Complete Message (CDGIOS 6.1.2.22)

BitMap	Param IE	#Oct	Range	Type	IOS Ref
0000 0000 (00H) LLLL LLLL	BSMAP header	2	Msg Discrim. = 0 (BSMAP) L = BSMAP msg length	M	6.2.2.1 6.2.2.3
0010 0001 (21H)	Msg Type	1	Clear Complete	M	6.2.2.4
1010 0010	Power Down Indicator	1		O,C	6.2.2.60

3.3.3   Mobile-Initiated Call Clearing Example Call Flow

Figure 3-18 shows a practical example of a summary message call flow for a mobile-initiated call clearing scenario. Subsequent figures illustrate the complete message's content, including MTP and SCCP layers. The decoded message format is similar to what would be seen on test equipment monitoring the A-Interface signaling link.

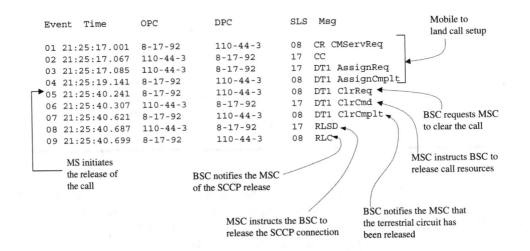

Figure 3-18   Mobile-Initiated Call Clearing example call flow log

The summary example in Figure 3-18 starts with the successful completion of a mobile-originated call. After the call has been up for nearly 20 seconds, the mobile user ends the call, prompting the mobile station to initiate call clearing. The BSC responds to the mobile's request by sending a Clear Request message to the MSC, then the MSC responds to the Clear Request with a Clear Command. After clearing its resources, the BSC sends a Clear Complete to the MSC and SCCP resources are then cleared on both nodes through the exchange of SCCP Released and Release Complete messages.

```
**** MESSAGE NUMBER: 00005 ****
*** Start of MTP Level 3 ***
0003 10000011 83
        ----0011    Service Indicator       SCCP
        --00----    Network Priority        priority 0
        10------    Network Indicator       National
0004 (3 bytes)  Destination Point Code  110-44-3
0007 (3 bytes)  Origination Point Code  8-17-92
0010 00001000 08 Signaling Link Selection  8
*** Start of SCCP ***
0011 00000110 06 Data Form 1             06
0012 (3 bytes)  Dest Local References    15432240
0015 00000000 00 Segment/Reassembling    0
0016 00000001 01 Variable Pointer        01
*** Start of CDGIOS MAP ***
                    Clear Request
0017 00001010 0a Data Length             10
0018 00000000 00 BSMAP Discriminator     00
0019 00001000 08 BSMAP Length            8
0020 00100010 22 Clear Request           34
0021 00000100 04 Cause                   4
0022 00000001 01 Length                  1
0023 00001001 09
        -0001001    Cause Value             Call Proc
0024 00001000 08 Cause Layer 3           8
0025 00000010 02 Length                  2
0026 10000100 84
        ----0100    Location                Public Netwk
        ---0----    Reserved
        -00-----    Coding Standard         Q.931
        1-------    Extension               01
0027 10010000 90
        -0010000    Cause Value             Normal Clearing
        1-------    Extension               01
```

> For mobile-initiated call clearing, the BSC will include only a Cause Layer 3 value if the Cause value is call processing.

Figure 3-19 Clear Request message example

Figure 3-19, above, illustrates the message structure and content of a Clear Request message. In this example, the BSC (8-17-92) requests the call associated with DLR 15432240 be cleared by the MSC (110-44-3). The mandatory Cause IE is set to *call processing*, and the Cause Layer 3 IE is set to *normal clearing*.

```
**** MESSAGE NUMBER: 00006 ****
*** Start of MTP Level 3 ***
0003 10000011 83
        ----0011    Service Indicator          SCCP
        --00----    Network Priority           priority 0
        10------    Network Indicator          National
0004 (3 bytes)     Destination Point Code     8-17-92
0007 (3 bytes)     Origination Point Code     110-44-3
0010 00010001 11 Signaling Link Selection     17
*** Start of SCCP ***
0011 00000110 06 Data Form 1                   06
0012 (3 bytes)     Dest Local References       78704
0015 00000000 00 Segment/Reassembling          0
0016 00000001 01 Variable Pointer              01
*** Start of CDGIOS MAP ***
                    Clear Command
0017 00000110 06 Data Length                    6
0018 00000000 00 BSMAP Discriminator           00
0019 00000100 04 BSMAP Length                   4
0020 00100000 20 Clear Command                 32
0021 00000100 04 Cause                          4
0022 00000001 01 Length                         1
0023 00001001 09
        -0001001    Cause Value           Call Processing
        0-------    Extension             Excluded
```

The Cause Layer 3 IE is included only when MSC initiates call clearing with the Cause IE set to call processing.

Figure 3-20   Clear Command message example

Figure 3-20, above, shows the message structure and content of a Clear Command message sent from the MSC (110-44-3) to the BSC (8-17-92). The DLR value in this example refers to the BSC's SCCP connection reference for this call. The mandatory Cause IE is set to *call processing*, and the optional Cause Layer 3 IE is not present.

```
**** MESSAGE NUMBER: 00007 ****
*** Start of MTP Level 3 ***
0003 10000011 83
        ----0011    Service Indicator          SCCP
        --00----    Network Priority           priority 0
        10------    Network Indicator          National
0004 (3 bytes)     Destination Point Code     110-44-3
0007 (3 bytes)     Origination Point Code     8-17-92
0010 00001000 08 Signaling Link Selection      8
*** Start of SCCP ***
0011 00000110 06 Data Form 1                   06
0012 (3 bytes)     Dest Local References       15432240
0015 00000000 00 Segment/Reassembling          0
0016 00000001 01 Variable Pointer              01
*** Start of CDGIOS MAP ***
                    Clear Complete
0017 00000011 03 Data Length                    3
0018 00000000 00 BSMAP Discriminator           00
```

Message will include the optional IE *Power Down Indicator* if the MS ends the call by powering down.

(Continued)
```
0019 00000001 01 BSMAP Length             1
0020 00100001 21 Clear Complete           33
```

Figure 3-21   Clear Complete message example

Figure 3-21, above, shows the message structure and content of a Clear Complete message sent from the BSC to the MSC. The DLR value in the example refers to the MSC's SCCP connection reference for this call. Because the mobile subscriber pressed the "END" button on the mobile station, terminating the call, the optional Power Down Indicator IE was not included in the message.

```
**** MESSAGE NUMBER: 00008 ****
*** Start of MTP Level 3 ***
0003 10100011 a3
     ----0011    Service Indicator       SCCP                  ◄── SCCP release
     --10----    Network Priority        priority 2                has the highest
     10------    Network Indicator       National                  MTP 3 priority
0004 (3 bytes)   Destination Point Code  8-17-92
0007 (3 bytes)   Origination Point Code  110-44-3
0010 00010001 11 Signaling Link Selection 17
*** Start of SCCP ***
0011 00000100 04 Released                04
0012 (3 bytes)   Dest Local References   78704
0015 (3 bytes)   Source Local References 15432240
0018 00000011 03 Release Cause           SCCP user originated
0019 00000000 00 Optional Pointer        Points to Nothing
```

Figure 3-22   SCCP Released message example

Figure 3-22, above, contains an example of an SCCP-RLSD message. The two important fields in the SCCP-RLSD message are the SLR and DLR, which specify the SCCP connection to be released. Recall that all existing calls have an SCCP connection associated with them. The SCCP-RLSD message does not contain any application layer information.

```
**** MESSAGE NUMBER: 00009 ****
0003 10100011 a3
     ----0011    Service Indicator       SCCP
     --10----    Network Priority        priority 2
     10------    Network Indicator       National
0004 (3 bytes)   Destination Point Code  110-44-3
0007 (3 bytes)   Origination Point Code  8-17-92
0010 00001000 08 Signaling Link Selection 8
*** Start of SCCP ***
0011 00000101 05 Release Complete        5
0012 (3 bytes)   Dest Local References   15432240
0015 (3 bytes)   Source Local References 78704
```

Figure 3-23   SCCP Release Complete message example

Figure 3-23, contains an example of an SCCP-RLC message. Like the SCCP-RLSD message, the two important fields in the SCCP-RLC message are the SLR and DLR, which specify the SCCP connection to be released. The SCCP-RLC message does not contain any application layer information.

3.4 BSC-Initiated Call Clearing

Under certain adversarial conditions, an established call to a mobile station may be lost. Two examples of such conditions are loss of radio signal and internal BSC failure. The BSC responds to a lost call by initiating call clearing.

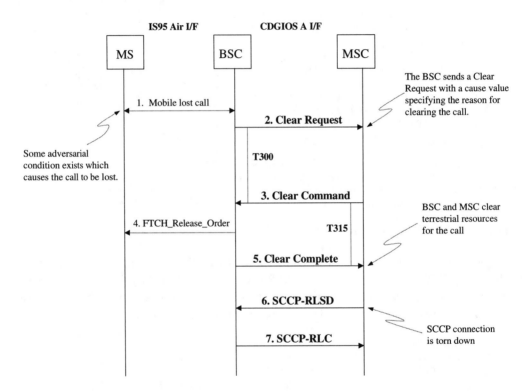

Figure 3-24   BSC-Initiated Call Clearing call flow

The call flow for BSC-initiated call clearing (Figure 3-24) is nearly identical to mobile-initiated call clearing. The main difference is that the BSC triggers the call clearing procedure instead of being directed by the mobile to clear the call. Upon determining that the call has dropped, the BSC sends a Clear Request to the MSC, requesting that the call be cleared. The MSC responds to the Clear Request with a Clear Command, instructing the BSC to clear resources associated with the dropped call. After clearing resources, the BSC then sends a Clear

Complete to the MSC, indicating that the resources previously allocated to the call have be released. Finally, the SCCP connection is released on both ends through the exchange of SCCP Released and Release Complete messages. The BSC-initiated call clearing message flow is illustrated in Figure 3-24. A more detailed description of each individual step follows.

3.4.1 BSC-Initiated Call Clearing Call Flow

1. (Mobile Lost Call):

   There are several reasons why a call may be lost at the BSC, such as radio interface failure, radio interface message failure, operations and maintenance intervention, equipment failure, and protocol error.

2. Clear Request (A-Interface):

   Upon determining that a call has been lost, the BSC sends a Clear Request to the MSC with a Cause IE value specifying the reason for the call release. For example, if the RF signal to a mobile were lost, the BSC would send a Clear Request with the Cause IE set to radio interface failure. Unlike a mobile-initiated clearing, no Cause Layer 3 IE is included in the Clear Request message when the BSC initiates call clearing. The Cause Layer 3 IE is not required because the reason for the call clearing is provided to the MSC in the Cause IE. The BSC starts timer T300.

3. Clear Command (A-Interface):

   The MSC, upon receipt of the Clear Request message, transmits a Clear Command to the BSC and starts clearing its terrestrial resources. During this time, the BSC continues clearing the radio and terrestrial resources previously allocated for the call. The MSC starts timer T315 and waits for a Clear Complete message from the BSC. Upon receipt of the Clear Command message, the BSC stops timer T300.

4. IS95_FTCH_ Release (IS-95):

   The BSC sends an IS-95 Release Order to the mobile station to initiate a proper release of the call. The mobile and BSC terminate traffic channel radio resources.

5. Clear Complete (A-Interface):

   After successfully deallocating all radio and terrestrial resources, the BSC sends a Clear Complete message to the MSC, indicating that it has cleared all resources previously allocated for the call. The MSC stops timer T315 upon receipt of the Clear Complete message.

6. SCCP-RLSD (A-Interface):

   Once the BSC acknowledges that it has cleared all resources, the MSC informs the BSC that the SCCP connection for the call is being released by sending an SCCP Released message, which indicates to the BSC that it should release the specified SCCP connection. To identify the SCCP connection, both DLR and SLR reference numbers are included in the message. The DLR refers to the BSC's local reference number, and the SLR refers to the MSC's local reference. The release reason for the SCCP-RLSD is also included in the message and is typically set to "end user originated," indicating a normal SCCP user termination.

7. SCCP-RLC (A-Interface):

The BSC, upon receipt of the SCCP-RLSD message, releases the SCCP resources previously allocated for the call. After releasing the SCCP resource, the BSC sends an SCCP-RLC message to the MSC, indicating that the SCCP connection has been successfully torn down. At this stage, all radio, terrestrial, and SCCP resources, both at the MSC and BSC, have been released.

3.4.2   BSC-Initiated Call Clearing Messages

The following are the detail descriptions of the A-Interface messages that are used in the BSC-initiated call clearing procedure. The message formats are the same as those presented in the mobile-initiated call clearing section (see Section 3.3.2, "Mobile-Initiated Call Clearing Messages," on page 189) and, therefore, are not repeated here.

3.4.2.1   Clear Request

The Clear Request message is a BSMAP message sent by the BSC to request the MSC clearing of a specific call. Because the Clear Request message refers to an existing call, and therefore, an existing SCCP connection, the message is coded as an SCCP-DT1 message.

The mandatory Cause IE value indicates the category of call release reasons to the MSC. Two examples of Cause IE values used for BSC call clearing include radio interface failure and equipment failure. The choice of Cause values is left to vendor implementation. One example implementation is to categorize all BSC timer expires as radio interface message failures. Table 3-8 on page 189 contains a complete list of possible Cause values.

In the case of BSC-initiated call clearing, the optional Cause Layer 3 IE is typically not included. Recall that for mobile-initiated call clearing, the Cause Layer 3 IE is used to expand further upon the Cause IE value, which is usually set to call processing.

3.4.2.2   Clear Command

The Clear Command message is a BSMAP message sent by the MSC to clear a specific call. Because the Clear Command message refers to an existing call and, therefore, an existing SCCP connection, the message is coded as an SCCP-DT1 message. The MSC sends a Clear Command message to the BSC to indicate that it has started releasing resources related to a specific call and to instruct the BSC to do the same. Similar to the Clear Request message, the assignment of cause values is vendor-specific.

The mandatory Cause IE value specifies the category of the call release reason to the BSC. In mobile-initiated and BSC-initiated call clearing scenarios, this value is typically set to the same Cause IE value sent by the BSC in the Clear Request message.

The optional Cause Layer 3 IE provides additional information about the reason for releasing a call. This parameter is generally included in the Clear Command message for MSC-initiated call clearing scenarios only where the Cause IE is set to call processing. It is usually not present for mobile- and BSC-initiated call clearing scenarios.

3.4.2.3   Clear Complete

The Clear Complete message is a BSMAP message sent as an SCCP-DT1 message type. The BSC sends a Clear Complete message to the MSC to indicate that it has successfully cleared both radio and terrestrial resources related to a specific call. The optional Power Down indicator IE is not used for BSC-initiated call clearing.

3.4.3   BSC-Initiated Call Clearing Example Call Flow

Figure 3-25 shows a summary message call flow for a BSC-initiated call clearing scenario. Subsequent figures illustrate the complete message's content, including MTP and SCCP layers. The decoded message format is similar to what would be seen on test equipment monitoring the A-Interface signaling link.

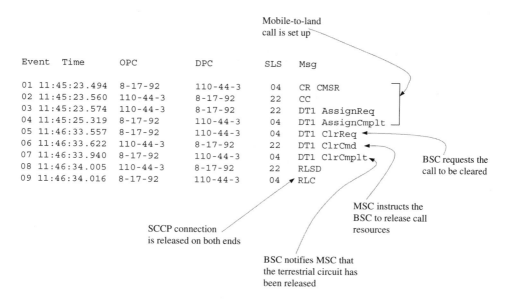

Figure 3-25   BSC-Initiated Call Clearing example call flow log

The summary example in Figure 3-25 starts with the successful completion of a mobile-originated call. After the call has been up for nearly 9 seconds, the BSC initiates call clearing by sending a Clear Request message to the MSC. The MSC responds to the Clear Request with a Clear Command. After clearing its resources, the BSC sends a Clear Complete to the MSC. SCCP resources are then cleared on both sides through the exchange of SCCP Released and Release Complete messages.

```
**** MESSAGE NUMBER: 00005 ****
*** Start of MTP Level 3 ***
0003 10000011 83
        ----0011    Service Indicator          SCCP
        --00----    Network Priority           priority 0
        10------    Network Indicator          National
0004 (3 bytes)   Destination Point Code        110-44-3
0007 (3 bytes)   Origination Point Code        8-17-92
0010 00000100 04 Signaling Link Selection      04
*** Start of SCCP ***
0011 00000110 06 Data Form 1                    06
0012 (3 bytes)   Dest Local References          15432240
0015 00000000 00 Segment/Reassembling           0
0016 00000001 01 Variable Pointer               01
*** Start of CDGIOS MAP ***
                 Clear Request
0017 00000110 06 Data Length                    6
0018 00000000 00 BSMAP Discriminator            00
0019 00000100 04 BSMAP Length                   4
0020 00100010 22 Clear Request                  34      Cause for the BSC initi-
0021 00000100 04 Cause                          4   ◄── ated clear request. Note
0022 00000001 01 Length                         1       that Cause Layer 3 is
0023 00000001 01                                        not included.
        -0000001    Cause Value               Radio Interface Failure
        0-------    Extension                 Excluded
```

Figure 3-26 Clear Request message example

Figure 3-26, above, illustrates the message structure and content of a Clear Request message. In this example, the BSC (8-17-92) requests the call associated with DLR 15432240 to be cleared by the MSC (110-44-3), due to loss of RF power. The mandatory Cause IE is set to *radio interface failure*, and the optional Cause Layer 3 IE is not included in the message.

```
**** MESSAGE NUMBER: 00006 ****
*** Start of MTP Level 3 ***
0003 10000011 83
        ----0011    Service Indicator          SCCP
        --00----    Network Priority           priority 0
        10------    Network Indicator          National
0004 (3 bytes)   Destination Point Code        8-17-92
0007 (3 bytes)   Origination Point Code        110-44-3
0010 00010110 16 Signaling Link Selection      22
*** Start of SCCP ***
0011 00000110 06 Data Form 1                    06
0012 (3 bytes)   Dest Local References          78704
0015 00000000 00 Segment/Reassembling           0
0016 00000001 01 Variable Pointer               01
*** Start of CDGIOS MAP ***
                 Clear Command
0017 00000110 06 Data Length                    6
0018 00000000 00 BSMAP Discriminator            00
```

(Continued)

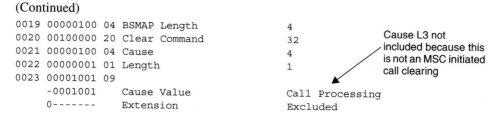

```
0019 00000100 04 BSMAP Length              4
0020 00100000 20 Clear Command             32             Cause L3 not
0021 00000100 04 Cause                     4              included because this
0022 00000001 01 Length                    1              is not an MSC initiated
0023 00001001 09                                          call clearing
     -0001001       Cause Value            Call Processing
     0-------       Extension              Excluded
```

Figure 3-27   Clear Command message example

Figure 3-27 shows the message structure and content of a Clear Command message sent from the MSC (110-44-3) to the BSC (8-17-92). The DLR value in this example refers to the BSC's SCCP connection reference for this call The mandatory Cause IE is set to *call processing,* and the optional Cause Layer 3 IE is not present.

```
**** MESSAGE NUMBER: 00007 ****
*** Start of MTP Level 3 ***
0003 10000011 83
     ----0011       Service Indicator       SCCP
     --00----       Network Priority        priority 0
     10------       Network Indicator       National
0004 (3 bytes)      Destination Point Code  110-44-3
0007 (3 bytes)      Origination Point Code  8-17-92
0010 00000100 04 Signaling Link Selection   04
*** Start of SCCP ***
0011 00000110 06 Data Form 1                06
0012 (3 bytes)      Dest Local References   15432240
0015 00000000 00 Segment/Reassembling       0
0016 00000001 01 Variable Pointer           01
*** Start of CDGIOS MAP ***
                    Clear Complete
0017 00000011 03 Data Length                3
0018 00000000 00 BSMAP Discriminator        00
0019 00000001 01 BSMAP Length               1
0020 00100001 21 Clear Complete             33
```

Figure 3-28   Clear Complete message example

Figure 3-28, above, shows the message structure and content of a Clear Complete message sent from the BSC to the MSC. The DLR value in the example refers to the MSC's SCCP connection reference for this call. The optional Power Down Indicator IE is not included because the clearing was BSC-initiated.

```
**** MESSAGE NUMBER: 00008 ****
*** Start of MTP Level 3 ***
0003 10100011 a3
     ----0011       Service Indicator       SCCP
     --10----       Network Priority        priority 2
```

(Continued)

```
       10------     Network Indicator         National
0004 (3 bytes)     Destination Point Code     8-17-92
0007 (3 bytes)     Origination Point Code     110-44-3
0010 00010110 16 Signaling Link Selection     22
*** Start of SCCP ***
0011 00000100 04 Released                     04
0012 (3 bytes)    Dest Local References       78704  -
0015 (3 bytes)    Source Local References     15432240
0018 00000011 03 Release Cause               SCCP user originated
0019 00000000 00 Optional Pointer            Points to Nothing
```

Figure 3-29 SCCP Released message example

Figure 3-29, above, contains an example of an SCCP-RLSD message. The two important fields in the SCCP-RLSD message are the SLR and DLR, which specify the SCCP connection to be released. Recall that all existing calls have an SCCP connection associated with them. The SCCP-RLSD message does not contain any application layer information.

```
**** MESSAGE NUMBER: 00009 ****
*** Start of MTP Level 3 ***
0003 10100011 a3
       ----0011    Service Indicator          SCCP
       --10----    Network Priority           priority 2
       10------    Network Indicator          National
0004 (3 bytes)     Destination Point Code     110-44-3
0007 (3 bytes)     Origination Point Code     8-17-92
0010 00000100 04 Signaling Link Selection     04
*** Start of SCCP ***
0011 00000101 05 Release Complete            5
0012 (3 bytes)    Dest Local References       15432240
0015 (3 bytes)    Source Local References     78704  -
```

Figure 3-30 SCCP Release Complete message example

Figure 3-30, above, contains an example of an SCCP-RLC message. Like the SCCP-RLSD message, the two important fields in the SCCP-RLC message are the SLR and DLR, which specify the SCCP connection to be released. The SCCP-RLC message does not contain any application layer information.

3.5 MSC-Initiated Call Clearing

The MSC, similar to the BSC and mobile station, also has the ability to clear an established call. MSC call clearing usually occurs in response to a land subscriber ending a call. However, the MSC may also call clear because the land subscriber is busy, unavailable, or due to an internal error.

Figure 3-31 shows the message flow for an MSC-initiated call clearing. The message flow is similar to mobile and BSC call clearing, with the main difference being that the Clear Request message is not sent from the BSC. After deciding to clear the call, the MSC sends a Clear Command to the BSC, instructing the BSC to clear resources. The BSC responds with a Clear Complete, indicating that it has successfully cleared previously allocated resources. The MSC then sends an SCCP-RLSD message, and the BSC follows with an SCCP-RLC.

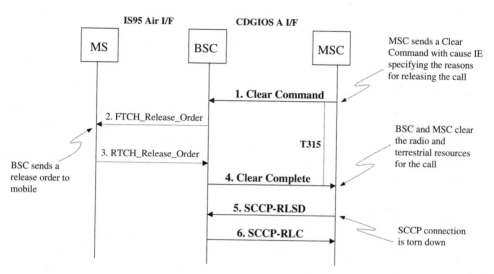

Figure 3-31   MSC-Initiated Call Clearing call flow

3.5.1   MSC-Initiated Call Clearing Call Flow

1. Clear Command (A-Interface):

   The MSC, upon detection of a call release or normal land party termination, sends a Clear Command to the BSC and initiates clearing of its own terrestrial resources. After receiving the Clear Command, the BSC begins releasing call resources. The MSC starts timer T315.

2. IS95_FTCH_ Release (IS-95):

   The BSC sends an IS-95 Release Order to the mobile to initiate a proper release of the call. The mobile and BSC terminate traffic channel radio resources.

3. IS95_RTCH_ Release (IS-95):

   The mobile sends an IS-95 Release Order to the BSC over the reverse traffic channel to acknowledge the BSC's Release Order.

4. Clear Complete (A-Interface):

   After successfully releasing previously allocated radio and terrestrial resources, the BSC sends a Clear Complete message to the MSC. The MSC may then include the previously unavailable resources in its list of available resources. The MSC stops timer T315 upon receipt of the Clear Complete message.

5. SCCP-RLSD (A-Interface):

Once the BSC acknowledges that it has cleared all resources, the MSC informs the BSC that the SCCP connection for the call is being released by sending an SCCP-RLSD message. The message indicates to the BSC that it should release the specified SCCP connection. To identify the SCCP connection, both DLR and SLR reference numbers are included in the message. The DLR refers to the BSC's local reference number and the SLR refers to the MSC's local reference. The release reason for the SCCP-RLSD is also included in the message and is typically set to "end user originated," indicating a normal SCCP user termination.

6. SCCP-RLC (A-Interface):

The BSC, upon receipt of the SCCP-RLSD message, releases the SCCP resources previously allocated for the call. After releasing the SCCP resource, the BSC sends an SCCP-RLC message to the MSC, indicating that the SCCP connection has been successfully torn down. At this stage, all radio, terrestrial, and SCCP resources, both at the MSC and BSC, have been released.

3.5.2 MSC-Initiated Call Clearing Messages

The following are the detail descriptions of the A-Interface messages that are used in the MSC-initiated call clearing procedure. Because the message formats are the same as those presented in the mobile-initiated call clearing section (see Section 3.3.2, "Mobile-Initiated Call Clearing Messages," on page 189), they are not repeated here.

3.5.2.1   Clear Command

The Clear Command message is a BSMAP message sent by the MSC to clear a specific call. Because the Clear Command message, refers to an existing call and, therefore, an existing SCCP connection, the message is coded as an SCCP-DT1 message. The MSC sends a Clear Command message to the BSC to indicate that it has started releasing resources related to a specific call and to instruct the BSC to do the same.

The mandatory Cause IE value specifies the category of the call release reason to the BSC. In the event that a land party terminates a call normally, a Cause IE value of "call processing" is sent in the Clear Command message, and additional information about the release reason is included in the Cause Layer 3 IE. The MSC may also be required to release a call due to non-call reasons not related to call processing. An example of these is handoff successful. In this case, the Cause IE would be set to *handoff successful*, and no Cause Layer 3 information is included. No Cause Layer 3 IE information is necessary if call clearing is due to direct BSC–MSC operations.

The optional Cause Layer 3 IE provides additional information about the reason for releasing a call. This parameter is generally included in the Clear Command message for MSC initiated call clearing scenarios only where the Cause IE is set to call processing. Including this parameter provides a means for the MSC to communicate the reason for call clearing to the

BSC. Possible Cause Layer 3 IE settings include normal release, user busy, user alerting no answer, and normal unspecified. The coding of the Cause Layer 3 IE also includes a 4-bit location field, which identifies the location of the originator for this cause value. For example, 0100 indicates public network serving remote user. The Cause Layer 3 IE contains a 2-bit coding standard field that can be used specify that the cause values have been coded as per ITU recommendation Q.931 [10].

3.5.2.2   Clear Complete

The Clear Complete message is a BSMAP message sent as an SCCP-DT1 message type. The BSC sends a Clear Complete message to the MSC to indicate that it has successfully cleared both radio and terrestrial resources related to a specific call. The optional Power Down indicator IE is not used for MSC-initiated call clearing.

3.5.3   BSC–MSC Call Clear Collision

It is possible that both the MSC and BSC attempt to clear the same call at the same time. In this scenario, the BSC sends a Clear Request message while the MSC is in the process of sending a Clear Command (Figure 3-32). In such a situation, the MSC ignores the Clear Request message received from the BSC and continues to wait for the Clear Complete message. The MSC stops timer T315 when it receives a Clear Complete message.

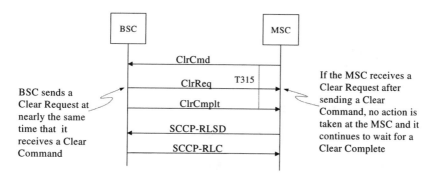

Figure 3-32   BSC–MSC Call Clear Collision call flow

3.5.4   MSC-Initiated Call Clearing Example Call Flow

Figure 3-33 shows a summary message call flow for an MSC-initiated call clearing scenario. Subsequent figures illustrate the complete message's content, including MTP and SCCP layers. The decoded message format is similar to what would be seen on test equipment monitoring the A-Interface signaling link.

The summary example in Figure 3-33 starts with the successful completion of a mobile-originated call. After the call has been up for nearly 45 seconds, the MSC initiates call clearing by sending a Clear Command to the BSC. After clearing its resources, the BSC sends a Clear

Complete to the MSC. SCCP resources are then cleared on both sides, through the exchange of SCCP-RLSD and SCCP-RLC messages.

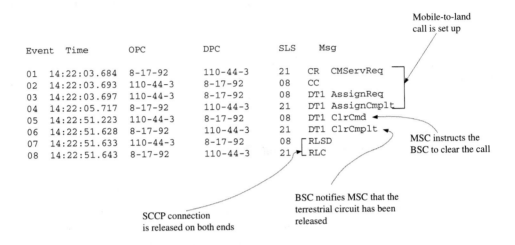

Figure 3-33   MSC-Initiated Call Clearing example call flow log

```
**** MESSAGE NUMBER: 00005 ****
*** Start of MTP Level 3 ***
0003 10000011 83
      ----0011    Service Indicator          SCCP
      --00----    Network Priority           priority 0
      10------    Network Indicator          National
0004 (3 bytes)    Destination Point Code     8-17-92
0007 (3 bytes)    Origination Point Code     110-44-3
0010 00001000 08 Signaling Link Selection    8
*** Start of SCCP ***
0011 00000110 06 Data Form 1                 06
0012 (3 bytes)    Dest Local References      78704
0015 00000000 00 Segment/Reassembling        0
0016 00000001 01 Variable Pointer            01
*** Start of CDGIOS MAP ***
                  Clear Command
0017 00001010 0a Data Length                 10
0018 00000000 00 BSMAP Discriminator         00
0019 00001000 08 BSMAP Length                8
0020 00100000 20 Clear Command               32
0021 00000100 04 Cause                       4
0022 00000001 01 Length                      1
```

(Continued)

```
0023 00001001 09
     -0001001    Cause Value            Call Ctrl       Cause Layer 3 is
     0-------    Extension              Excluded        included when MSC
0024 00001000 08 Cause Layer 3         8               initiates call clearing
0025 00000010 02 Length                2               and cause is call con-
0026 10000100 84                                       trol.
     ----0100    Location               Public Network
     ---0----    Reserved               00              Reason for clearing
     -00-----    Coding Standard        Q.931           the call. BSC may
     1-------    Extension              01              use for performance
0027 10010000 90                                       statistics.
     -0010000    Cause Value            Normal Clearing
     1-------    Extension              01
```

Figure 3-34   Clear Command message example

Figure 3-34, above, shows the message structure and content of a Clear Command message sent from the MSC (110-44-3) to the BSC (8-17-92). The mandatory Cause IE is set to call processing, and the optional Cause Layer 3 IE is set to normal clearing.

```
**** MESSAGE NUMBER: 00006 ****
*** Start of MTP Level 3 ***
0003 10000011 83
     ----0011    Service Indicator       SCCP
     --00----    Network Priority        priority 0
     10------    Network Indicator       National
0004 (3 bytes)   Destination Point Code  110-44-3
0007 (3 bytes)   Origination Point Code  8-17-92
0010 00010101 15 Signaling Link Selection 21
*** Start of SCCP ***
0011 00000110 06 Data Form 1             06
0012 (3 bytes)   Dest Local References   15432240
0015 00000000 00 Segment/Reassembling    0
0016 00000001 01 Variable Pointer        01
*** Start of CDGIOS MAP ***
                 Clear Complete
0017 00000011 03 Data Length             3
0018 00000000 00 BSMAP Discriminator     00
0019 00000001 01 BSMAP Length            1
0020 00100001 21 Clear Complete          33
```

Figure 3-35   Clear Complete message example

Figure 3-35, above, shows the message structure and content of a Clear Complete message sent from the BSC to the MSC. The DLR value in the example refers to the MSC's SCCP connection reference for this call. The optional Power Down Indicator IE is not included because the clearing was MSC-initiated.

```
**** MESSAGE NUMBER: 00007 ****
*** Start of MTP Level 3 ***
0003 10000011 83
     ----0011    Service Indicator           SCCP
     --10----    Network Priority            priority 2
     10------    Network Indicator           National
0004 (3 bytes)   Destination Point Code      8-17-92
0007 (3 bytes)   Origination Point Code      110-44-3
0010 00001000 08 Signaling Link Selection    8
*** Start of SCCP ***
0011 00000100 04 Released                    04
0012 (3 bytes)   Dest Local References       78704
0015 (3 bytes)   Source Local References     15432240
0018 00000000 00 Release Cause               end user originated
0019 00000000 00 Optional Pointer            Points to Nothing
```

Figure 3-36 SCCP Released message example

Figure 3-36, above, contains an example of an SCCP-RLSD message. The two important fields in the SCCP-RLSD message are the SLR and DLR, which specify the SCCP connection to be released. The SCCP-RLSD message does not contain any application layer information.

```
**** MESSAGE NUMBER: 00008 ****
*** Start of MTP Level 3 ***
0003 10100011 a3
     ----0011    Service Indicator           SCCP
     --10----    Network Priority            priority 2
     10------    Network Indicator           National Network
0004 (3 bytes)   Destination Point Code      110-44-3
0007 (3 bytes)   Origination Point Code      8-17-92
0010 00010101 15 Signaling Link Selection    21
*** Start of SCCP ***
0011 00000101 05 Release Complete            5
0012 (3 bytes)   Dest Local References       15432240
0015 (3 bytes)   Source Local References     78704
```

Figure 3-37 SCCP Release Complete message example

Figure 3-37, above, contains an example of an SCCP-RLC message. Like the SCCP-RLSD message, the two important fields in the SCCP-RLC message are the SLR and DLR, which specify the SCCP connection to be released. The SCCP-RLC message does not contain any application layer information.

3.6 BSC-Initiated Abnormal SCCP Release

Under certain adverse conditions, the BSC may need to clear an SCCP connection without first exchanging BSMAP Clear Command and Clear Complete messages with the MSC. It does this by initiating an Abnormal SCCP Release. For example, a BSC-initiated Abnormal SCCP Release occurs when the SCCP Receive Inactivity Timer (*Tiar*) expires at the BSC. In this case, the expired inactivity timer indicates to the BSC that the existing SCCP connection is stale, prompting the BSC to clear the resource.

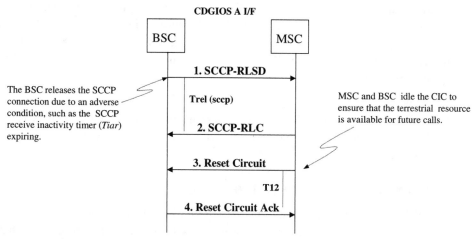

Figure 3-38 BSC-Initiated Abnormal SCCP Release call flow

A BSC initiated Abnormal SCCP Release begins with the BSC sending an SCCP-RLSD message to the MSC. The MSC responds with an SCCP-RLC message, followed by a BSMAP Reset Circuit. The Reset Circuit, which is discussed in Section 8.3, "Reset Circuits," on page 510, is used to reset the state of the CIC associated with the call being cleared. After resetting the CIC, the BSC responds with a Reset Circuit Acknowledge message. Figure 3-38, above, illustrates the message flow for a BSC-initiated Abnormal SCCP Release.

3.6.1 BSC-Initiated Abnormal SCCP-RLSD Call Flow

1. SCCP Released:

   The primary difference between an SCCP Released message used in a BSC-initiated Abnormal SCCP Release and that used in a normal call clearing scenario is the release reason. For the case of an abnormal release, the release reason contained in the SCCP Released message will not contain "end user originated." Instead, the release reason will specify the error condition resulting in the abnormal release, such as SCCP receive inactivity timer expiry. See Table 2-11, "Common Parameters in SCCP Message Structure," on page 105 for a complete list of possible SCCP release reasons. The BSC starts SCCP timer *Trel*.

2. SCCP Release Complete:

   The MSC, upon receipt of the SCCP Released message, releases the SCCP resources associated with the DLR of the received message. After the MSC has completed releasing the

SCCP resources, it sends an SCCP Release Complete message to the BSC. The BSC stops SCCP timer *Trel* in response to receiving this message.

3. Reset Circuit:

The MSC idles the terrestrial resource (CIC) associated with the released SCCP connection and sends a Reset Circuit message to the BSC, instructing the BSC to do the same. A complete description of the Reset Circuit message is given in Section 8.3.4, "Reset Circuit Messages," on page 512. The MSC starts timer T12 to wait for a Reset Circuit Acknowledgment message.

4. Reset Circuit Acknowledge:

The BSC, upon receipt of the Reset Circuit message, idles terrestrial resources (CIC) specified in the received message and responds with a Reset Circuit Acknowledge message. The MSC stops timer T12.

3.7 MSC-Initiated Abnormal SCCP Release

The MSC may also initiate an Abnormal SCCP Release. The message flow is very similar to the BSC-initiated abnormal SCCP release scenario, with the only difference being that the MSC initiates the release, and the BSC sends the Reset Circuit message. Figure 3-39 shows the message flow for an MSC-initiated abnormal SCCP release.

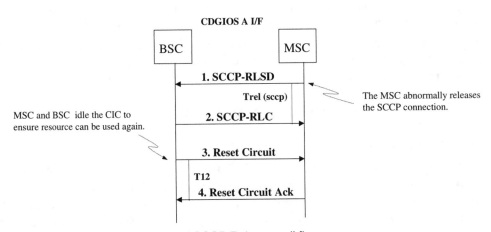

Figure 3-39   MSC-Initiated Abnormal SCCP Release call flow

3.8 Call Failure Scenarios

Previously, the call flows presented in this chapter described only successful scenarios. Because even the best-designed networks fail a small percentage of calls, a discussion of Call Processing would not be complete without describing A-Interface failure scenarios.

The successful setup and clearing of calls is dependent on both the MSC and BSC being compliant with the A-Interface standard. Protocol compliance implies that both ends agree on call flow procedures, message structure, message parameters, and execution of the call flow within specified timer ranges. CDGIOS also specifies messages and procedures to ensure that both the MSC and BSC handle failure scenarios appropriately.

Although there are numerous reasons why a call setup or clearing may fail, the most common failures are due to timer expiry and resource unavailability. Table 3-11 provides a description of application layer timers used for basic call processing, along with recommended values and allowable ranges. Even though CDGIOS provides default timer values, it is important that both the MSC and BSC vendors agree on actual values before integration.

The call failure descriptions presented in this section are categorized into mobile origination, mobile termination, mobile-initiated call clearing, BSC-initiated call clearing, MSC-initiated call clearing, and abnormal SCCP release scenarios.

Table 3-11   A-Interface Call Processing Timers

Timers	Recomme- nded (secs)	Range (secs)	Trigger Entity	Description
T10	5	0–99	MSC	AssignReq → AssignCmplt Timer
T12	60	0–255	Both	Reset Circuit → Reset Circuit Ack Timer
T20	5	0–99	BSC	AssignFailure → ClrCmd Timer
T300	5	0–99	BSC	ClrReq → ClrCmd Timer
T301	30	0–60	MSC	AssignCmplt → Connect Timer
T303	12	0–99	BSC	CMServReq/ PageRsp → AssignReq Timer
T315	5	0–99	MSC	CMServReq/ PageRsp → AssignReq Timer
T3113	(see description)	0–99	MSC	PageRequest Retry Timer. Recommended: T3113 = 4.72 + (1.28 x 2 $^{\text{slot cycle index}}$)
T3230	5	0–99	BSC	CMServReq/ PageRsp → SCCP-CC Timer

3.8.1 Mobile Origination Call Failures

Figure 3-40 provides an illustrative summary of possible failure events that would prevent the successful setup of a mobile-originated call. Each failure point is briefly described in the diagram, and the corresponding CDGIOS section is referenced. The objective of Figure 3-40 is to provide an overview of mobile origination failure scenarios. The details and message flow of each failure case are described in the following sections.

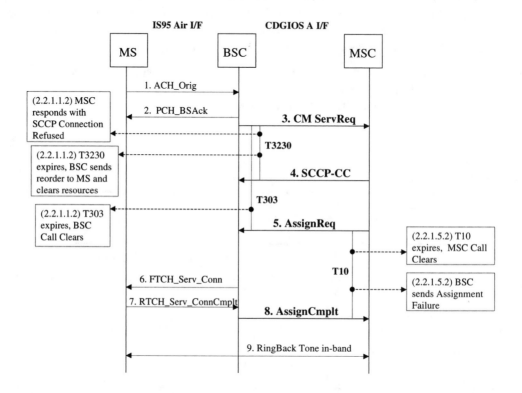

Figure 3-40 Mobile Origination call failure points

SCCP-CREF Received at BSC Conditions may exist when the MSC chooses to refuse a BSC-requested SCCP connection for a mobile-originated call. For example, the MSC may deny the originating mobile service because it is an unregistered mobile or identified by the MSC as a clone. In this case, the MSC simply responds to the BSC SCCP connection request with an SCCP Connection Refused, ending the origination attempt and instructing the BSC to clear associated call resources. The call flow is shown in Figure 3-41.

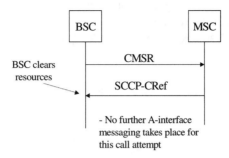

Figure 3-41   Mobile Origination call failure: SCCP-CREF received at BSC

BSC T3230 Timer Expiry   After sending an SCCP-CR message, such as a CM Service Request, the BSC waits for an SCCP-CC or SCCP-CREF response from the MSC. Timer T3230 is used to specify the maximum time interval that the BSC will wait for a response (Figure 3-42). If timer T3230 expires before a response is received at the BSC, the BSC sends an IS-95 Reorder Order message to the mobile station over the paging channel (if the mobile is not in traffic channel yet), then clears resources associated with the failed call attempt. Upon receiving the Reorder Order, the mobile station plays a reorder tone to inform the mobile user of the failed call.

If the mobile is already being set up on a traffic channel, the Reorder indication may be sent over the forward traffic channel, using the IS-95 Alert With Information message.

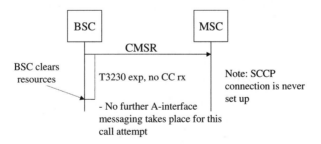

Figure 3-42   Mobile Origination call failure: BSC T3230 Timer Expiry

BSC T303 Timer Expiry   In the process of a successful call setup, the BSC expects to receive an Assignment Request message from the MSC shortly after receiving an SCCP-CC. There are several conditions, such as unavailable terrestrial resources, which may prevent the

MSC from sending an Assignment Request message to the BSC. The amount of time that the BSC will wait for an Assignment Request message is specified by timer T303. Upon expiry of T303, the BSC initiates call clearing by sending a Clear Request message to the MSC, indicating the reason for the Clear Request by setting the Cause IE to timer expired. Figure 3-43 shows the complete call flow for timer T303 expiry. Note that BSC timer T303 needs to be set to a value greater than that of timer T3230.

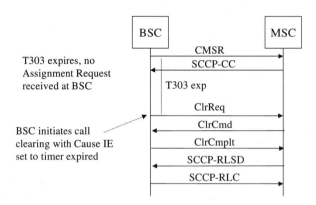

Figure 3-43 Mobile Origination call failure: BSC T303 Timer Expiry

MSC T10 Timer Expiry   MSC timer T10 specifies the amount of time that the MSC will wait for an Assignment Complete message from the BSC. One reason the BSC may not send an Assignment Complete message is that it was unable to set up the radio channel. Upon expiry of timer T10, the MSC initiates call clearing by sending a Clear Command message with a cause value indicating MSC timer expiry. Figure 3-44 illustrates the message flow for timer T10 expiry.

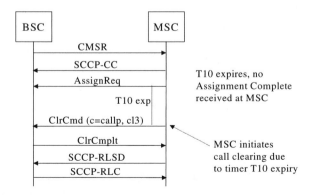

Figure 3-44 Mobile Origination call failure: MSC T10 Timer Expiry

Mobile Origination Assignment Failure   In the event that the BSC is unable to set up the terrestrial or the radio resource after the Assignment Request is received from the MSC, it may respond with an Assignment Failure message, indicating the reason for the failure. For example, if the MSC requested an invalid CIC in the Assignment Request message, the BSC would respond with an Assignment Failure message, specifying that the requested terrestrial resource is unavailable.

After sending an Assignment Failure message, the BSC starts timer T20 and waits for a Clear Command from the MSC. The MSC, in response to receiving an Assignment Failure message, may first send a Progress message to the BSC, instructing the mobile to play a progress tone to the mobile user while the call is being torn down. The Progress message contains a Signal IE parameter used to specify the tone to be played, usually an abbreviated reorder or reorder tone. The BSC extracts the Signal IE value from the Progress message and packages it into an IS-95 Flash With Information message, which it sends to the mobile station on forward traffic channel. The MSC then initiates call clearing by sending the BSC a Clear Command. The BSC, upon receiving this message, stops timer T20. Figure 3-45 shows the complete message flow.

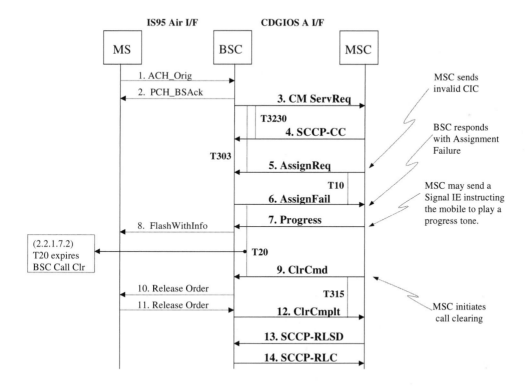

Figure 3-45   Mobile Origination call failure: Assignment Failure

The message format of the Assignment Failure message is shown in Table 3-12. The Assignment Failure message is a simple BSMAP message with a mandatory Cause IE used to specify the reason for the failure. One common assignment failure scenario, often encountered during initial equipment installation and verification, occurs when the terrestrial resource (CIC) requested by the MSC does not correspond to resources available at the BSC. This error is usually due to a CIC list configuration error at either the MSC or BSC. Recall that in the Assignment Request message, CIC values are comprised of an 11-bit PCM identifier (high and low) and a 5-bit time slot field. The PCM identifier can be thought of as a logical span ID, which must match the logical span assignment at the BSC. If these logical assignments do not match, an Assignment Failure message will be sent by the BSC, specifying that the requested resources are unavailable.

Table 3-12   Assignment Failure Message (CDGIOS 6.1.2.17)

BitMap	Param IE	#Oct	Range	Type	IOS Ref
0000 0000 (00H) LLLL LLLL	BSMAP header	2	Msg Discrim. = 0 (BSMAP) L = BSMAP msg length	M	6.2.2.1 6.2.2.3
0000 0011 (03H)	Msg Type	1	Assignment Failure	M	6.2.2.4
0000 0100 (04H) LLLL LLLL xccc cccc	Cause	3	L = 01H, x = 0—extension bit c = cause value 00H—radio i/f msg fail 01H—radio i/f fail 07H—OAM&P intervention 20H—Equipment failure 21H—No radio resource 22H—Req. terrestrial rsrc unavail 25H—BS not equipped 26H—mobile not equipped 30H—transcoding/rate adapt unavail 50H—Terrestrial cic already alloc 60H—Protocol error	M	6.2.2.19

Table 3-13 shows the format of the Progress message. The Progress message is a DTAP message with two optional parameters. The message may contain either the Signal IE or the IS-95 Information Records IE, but not both. The MSC may use one of the optional parameters to specify the progress tone to be played by the mobile station.

Table 3-13 Progress Message (CDGIOS 6.1.2.12)

BitMap	Param IE	#Oct	Range	Type	IOS Ref
0000 0001 (01H) ccrr rsss LLLL LLLL	DTAP header	3	Msg Discrim. =1 (DTAP) DLCI = "ccrr rsss" = 0 L = DTAP msg length	M	6.2.2.1 6.2.2.2 6.2.2.3
rrrr 0011 (03H)	Protocol Discriminator	1	0011—Call Processing r = 0—reserved	M	6.2.2.39
0000 0000 (00H)	Reserved Bits	1		M	6.2.2.40
0000 0011 (03H)	Msg Type	1	Progress	M	6.2.2.4
0011 0100 (34H) SSSS SSSS rrrr rrPP	Signal	3	S = signal 63H—abbrev intercept 65H—abbrev reorder 02H—intercept 03H—reorder P = pitch, r = 0—reserved	O,C	6.2.2.50
0001 0101 (15H) LLLL LLLL tttt tttt (1st record) llll llll cccc cccc cccc cccc ….. tttt tttt (2nd record) llll llll …..	IS-95 Information Records	variable	L = length t = IS-95 Info Record type l = Info Record length c = Info Record content	O,C	6.2.2.72

Assignment Failure—BSC T20 Timer Expiry The BSC starts timer T20 after sending an Assignment Failure message to the MSC. Timer T20 specifies the amount of time that the BSC waits for a Clear Command. Upon expiry of T20, the BSC initiates call clearing by sending a Clear Request message to the MSC. Figure 3-46 illustrates the call flow.

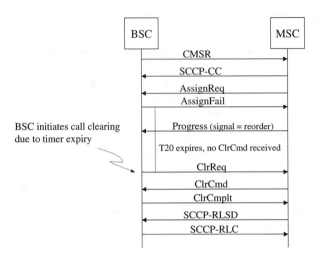

Figure 3-46 Mobile Origination call failure: BSC T20 Timer Expiry

Assignment Failure—MSC Assignment Request Retry Depending on the cause value supplied to the MSC in the Assignment Failure message, the MSC may retry the resource assignment by sending a second Assignment Request message with a different CIC value. If the new CIC is available, the BSC will set up the call based on the new terrestrial circuit, then will send an Assignment Complete message to the MSC, indicating that the second assignment was successful. Figure 3-47 shows retry message flow. It should be noted that assignment retry is implementation-specific, and CDGIOS specifies it as an option only to increase call set up success rates.

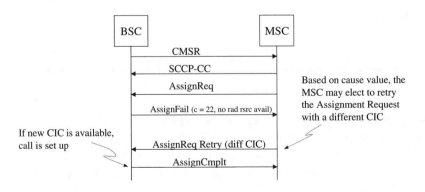

Figure 3-47 Mobile Origination call failure: MSC Assignment Retry

MSC Unsupported Service Option   Figure 3-48 shows the call flow for unsupported service options. This failure case may occur if the mobile station requests a service option not supported or recognized by the MSC. The MSC responds to an unsupported service option request by initiating call clearing.

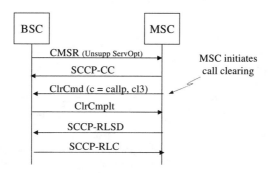

Figure 3-48   Mobile Origination call failure: Unsupported service option at MSC

CIC Required but Not Sent   A protocol error occurs when the BSC requires a CIC assignment to set up a call and the MSC does not include the CIC IE in the Assignment Request message. When the BSC receives the Assignment Request with the missing CIC, it initiates call clearing by sending a Clear Request message to the MSC with the Cause IE set to protocol error. Figure 3-49 shows the message flow resulting from a protocol error.

Recall that certain service options, such as Markov calls and service options for short messaging (6 and 14), do not require terrestrial resources and can be successfully set up by the BSC without an assigned CIC.

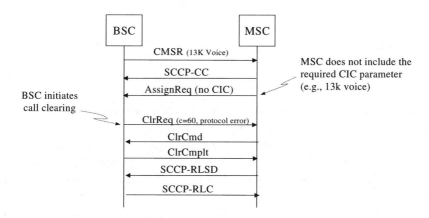

Figure 3-49   Mobile Origination call failure: CIC required but not sent

3.8.2   Mobile Termination Call Failures

Figure 3-50 provides an overview of failures that may occur during the setup of mobile-terminated calls. Each failure point is identified and briefly described in Figure 3-50, along with a reference to the corresponding CDGIOS section. Detailed message flows and descriptions for each failure scenario follow the summary diagram.

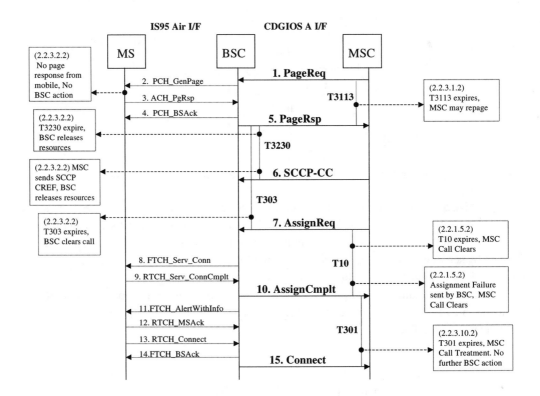

Figure 3-50   Mobile Termination call failure points

MSC T3113 Timer Expiry   If the MSC does not receive a Paging Response message from the BSC in response to a previously transmitted Paging Request, it may repage the mobile or cease the call attempt. Timer T3113 species how long that the MSC will wait for a Page Response before either failing the call or repaging the mobile. Figure 3-51 shows the message flow for the case in which the MSC repages. The decision of whether to repage or simply to drop the call attempt is left to the MSC vendor.

If the MSC implementation does not repage in response to T3113 expiring, the BSC takes no further action, and the MSC applies a call treatment tone to the land subscriber. For the case of an MSC implementing repaging, the MSC will send a second Paging Request to the BSC and restart timer T3113. Upon the second expiry of T3113, no more repage attempts will be made.

In a network consisting of multiple BSCs connected to a single MSC, the MSC may first send a Paging Request message to the BSC with which the mobile last registered. If no Page Response is received before T3113 expires, the MSC may choose to page other select BSC(s) or all BSCs. The MSC may also choose a paging scheme that involves flood-paging of all BSCs for both the first and subsequent Page Request. CDGIOS allows the MSC and BSC vendors to choose the paging technique best suited for their networks.

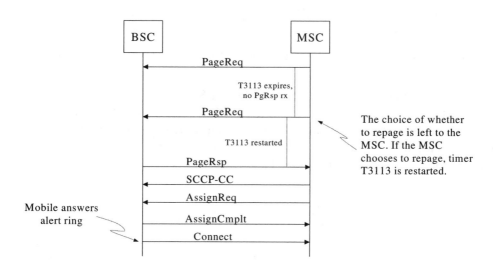

Figure 3-51   Mobile Termination call failure: MSC T3113 Timer Expiry

SCCP Connection Refused Received at BSC   Conditions may exist at the MSC that cause it to refuse the BSC-requested SCCP connection requested in the Paging Response message. For example, the MSC may deny the terminating mobile service because it failed the authentication process. In this case, the MSC simply responds to the BSC SCCP connection request with an SCCP Connection Refused, ending the terminating call attempt and instructing the BSC to clear associated call resources. The call flow is shown in Figure 3-52.

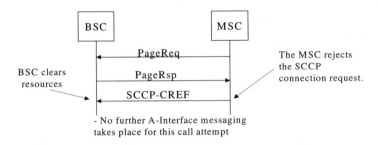

Figure 3-52 Mobile Termination call failure: SCCP-CREF received at BSC

BSC T3230 Timer Expiry After sending an SCCP-CR message, such as a Paging Response, the BSC waits for an SCCP-CC or SCCP-CREF response from the MSC. Timer T3230 is used to specify the maximum time interval that the BSC will wait for a response. If timer T3230 expires before a response is received at the BSC, the BSC simply clears the call, freeing any previously allocated resources. Figure 3-53 illustrates the message flow.

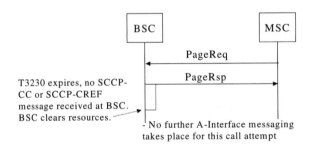

Figure 3-53 Mobile Termination call failure: BSC T3230 Timer Expiry

BSC T303 Timer Expiry See the description under mobile origination call failures in the section, "BSC T303 Timer Expiry," on page 213.

MSC T10 Timer Expiry See the description under mobile origination call failures in the section, "MSC T10 Timer Expiry," on page 214.

Mobile Termination Assignment Failure The mobile-terminated assignment failure scenario message flow shown in Figure 3-54 is similar to the mobile-origination case described earlier in this chapter in the section, "Mobile Origination Assignment Failure," on page 215. In the event that the BSC is unable to set up the terrestrial or the radio resource after the Assignment Request is received from the MSC, it may respond with an Assignment Failure message, indicating the reason for the failure.

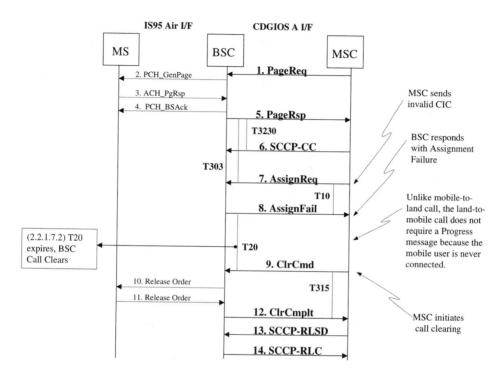

Figure 3-54 Mobile Termination call failure: Assignment Failure

For example, if the MSC requested an invalid CIC in the Assignment Request message, the BSC would respond with an Assignment Failure message, specifying that the requested terrestrial resource is unavailable. After sending an Assignment Failure message, the BSC starts timer T20 and waits for a Clear Command from the MSC. Upon receiving the Assignment Failure message, the MSC then initiates call clearing by sending the BSC a Clear command. The BSC, upon receiving this message, stops timer T20.

Assignment Failure—BSC T20 Timer Expiry The BSC starts timer T20 after sending an Assignment Failure message to the MSC. Timer T20 specifies the amount of time that the BSC waits for a Clear Command. Upon expiry of T20, the BSC initiates call clearing by sending a Clear Request message to the MSC. Figure 3-55 illustrates the call flow.

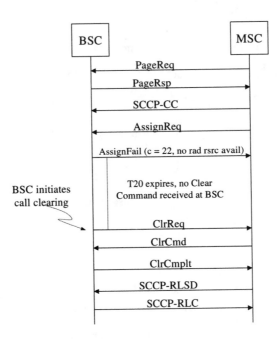

Figure 3-55 Mobile Termination call failure: BSC T20 Timer Expiry

MSC T301 Timer Expiry The final step in completing a mobile-terminated call requires the mobile subscriber to answer the alerting mobile. Timer T301 defines how long the MSC waits for the BSC to send a Connect message. Upon expiry of T301, the MSC may play a treatment to the land party, such as an announcement, or it may forward the call to another number, as specified in the mobile subscriber's profile. Subsequent actions, mainly how the call is cleared, are not specified in CDGIOS and are left to vendor implementation. Figure 3-56 shows the message flow for T301 expiry.

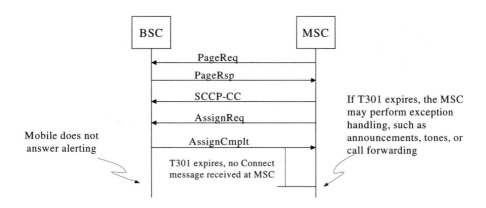

Figure 3-56   Mobile Termination call failure: MSC T301 Timer Expiry

3.8.3   Mobile and BSC-Initiated Call Clearing Failures

Figure 3-57 summarizes the failure conditions associated with mobile-initiated and BSC-initiated call clearing. Each point of failure is briefly described in the diagram, along with a reference to the corresponding CDGIOS section. As with mobile origination and termination failure scenarios, the failures primarily focus on timer expiry. Following the summary figure, descriptions of individual failure conditions are provided. Because the message flows for mobile-initiated and BSC-initiated call clearing are nearly identical, both are covered simultaneously.

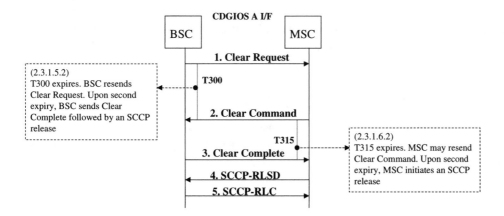

Figure 3-57   Mobile-Initiated and BSC-Initiated Call Clearing failure points

BSC T300 Timer Expiry   After sending a Clear Request, the BSC starts timer T300 and waits for a Clear Complete from the MSC. If timer T300 expires before the BSC receives a Clear Command from the MSC, the BSC may send a second Clear Request or release call resources. CDGIOS allows the BSC vendor to choose whether to send a second Clear Request. If the BSC does retry and T300 expires a second time, the BSC must tear down the SCCP connection and release resources. The message flow for T300 expiry is shown in Figure 3-58.

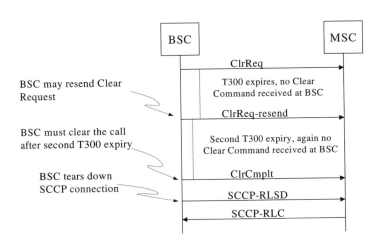

Figure 3-58   Mobile- and BSC-Initiated Call Clearing failure:BSC T300 Timer Expiry

MSC T315 Timer Expiry   Timer T315 defines the amount of time that the MSC will wait for the BSC to respond to a Clear Command with a Clear Complete before either resending the Clear Command or clearing the call. CDGIOS allows the MSC vendor to decide whether the MSC resends the Clear Command after the first T315 expiry. If timer T315 expires a second time, the MSC must clear call resources, including the SCCP connection. Figure 3-59 shows the message flow for timer T315 expiry.

3.8.4   MSC-Initiated Call Clearing Failures

The only MSC-initiated call failure scenario is T315 expiry. Because this failure condition is identical to T315 expiring during a BSC-initiated call clearing, see the description provided in the previous section, "MSC T315 Timer Expiry," on page 226.

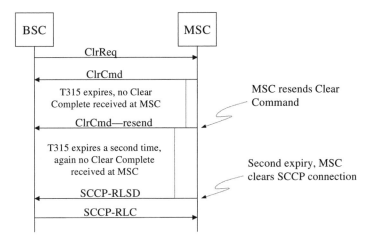

Figure 3-59   Mobile- and BSC-Initiated Call Clearing failure:MSC T315 Timer Expiry

References

1. CDG-IOS version 3.1.1, *CDMA Development Group MSC to BS Interface Inter-Operability Specification*. June 1999.

2. CDG-IOS version 2.0, *CDMA Development Group MSC to BS Interface Inter-Operability Specification*. September 1998.

3. Telecommunications Industry Association, TIA/EIA/IS-634-A, *MSC-BS Interface (A-Interface) for Public 800 MHz*. July 1998.

4. Telecommunications Industry Association , TIA/EIA/TSB-80, *MSC-BS Interface (A-Interface) for Public 800 MHz*. October 1996.

5. Telecommunications Industry Association, TIA/EIA/IS-95-A, *Mobile Station-Base Station Compatibility Standard for Dual-Mode Wideband Spread Spectrum Cellular Systems*. May 1995.

6. American National Standards Institute, ANSI J-STD-008, *Personal Station—Base Station Compatibility Requirements for 1.8 to 2.0 GHz Code Devision Multiple Access (CDMA) Personal Communications Systems*. August 1995.

7. American National Standards Institute, ANSI TIA/EIA/IS-41-D, *Cellular Radio-Telecommunications Intersystem Operations*. December, 1997.

8. Mouly, Michel, and M.B Pautet, *The GSM System for Mobile Communications*, Michel Mouly and Marie Bernadette Pautet, 1992.

9. American National Standards Institute, ANSI T1.607, *Digital Subscriber Signaling System Number 1 (DSS 1) – Layer 3 Signaling Specification for Circuit-Switched Bearer Services*. February 1996.

10. International Telecommunications Union—Telecommunications Sector, ITU-T Recommendation Q.931, *ISDN User–Network Interface Layer 3 Specification for Basic Call Control*. May 1998.

Mobility Management

W hen a mobile subscriber signs up for service with a wireless network service provider, a unique subscriber profile is created in the *Home Location Register* (HLR) database. The information contained in the subscriber profile determines how and when a mobile subscriber can access the mobile network. Each profile includes information such as subscribed supplementary services, *Electronic Serial Number* (ESN), authentication data, roaming restrictions, dialing plans, carrier access code, and other network access parameters.

Mobility Management refers to the functions at both the *Base Station Controller* (BSC) and *Mobile Switching Center* (MSC) that manage mobile station registrations and network access status. The most common registration type is Power-Up registration, but Timer-Based and Zone (location)-based mobile registrations are also popular. Upon registering with a network, a mobile station provides information to the BSC regarding its location, identity, registration type, and, if applicable, authentication parameters. The BSC transfers the registration information over the A-Interface to the MSC, which registers the mobile subscriber in the *Visitor Location Register* (VLR) database after verifying the mobile subscriber's access status from the HLR profile.

4.1 Mobility Management Overview

This section gives an overview of Mobility Management, focusing on the process of mobile registrations. Authentication and encryption procedures are also briefly discussed here; however, a complete description of authentication and encryption procedures is provided in Chapter 6, "Authentication," on page 345.

The purpose of mobile registrations is to report current mobile parameter settings and the mobile station's location to the serving system. The serving network uses the received information, along with the subscriber profile data stored in the home system's HLR, to allow or refuse the mobile station network access.

Once triggered, the mobile sends a registration access message on the radio link, which the BSC then formats and sends to the MSC over the A-Interface. Upon receiving the registration information, the MSC updates the VLR and HLR, usually over an IS-41 interface.

4.1.1   IS-95 Mobile Registration

In IS-95 CDMA systems, mobile registrations occur under various scenarios. Table 4-1 summarizes the registration types specified in IS-95, although not all registration types are currently supported over the A-Interface. For example, the ability to allow the MSC to order a registration is not currently supported.

The method used by the mobile to trigger a registration is specified by parameters sent by the BSC over the IS-95 air interface. The BSC is normally responsible for registration system parameter setting. However, the MSC may also specify registration parameters using the A-Interface Set Control Channel Parameter message, such as with the RAND authentication broadcast parameter (See Chapter 6, "Authentication," on page 345).

The IS-95 System Parameters message is broadcast by the base station over the paging channel and contains message fields that specify the registration type to be used by mobile stations accessing the network. The fields are indicated in column 3 in Table 4-1, under the *IS-95 Sys Param msg field* column heading. If, for example, the POWER_UP_REG field bit is set to 1, mobile stations shall register every time they power up by sending an IS-95 Registration message. The IS-95 Registration message contains a REG_TYPE field that indicates the type of registration being performed. Column 2 in Table 4-1 specifies the IS-95 Registration Type field.

Table 4-1   IS-95 Mobile Registration Types

Registra-tion Type	IS-95 REG_TYPE	IS-95 Sys Param msg field	Description
Power-Up	1	POWER_UP_ REG	During a power-up registration, the mobile sends an IS-95 Registration message after entering the Idle mode.
Power-Down	3	POWER_DOWN_ REG	During a power-down registration, the mobile sends an IS-95 Registration message to the base station before powering off.

Table 4-1   IS-95 Mobile Registration Types (Continued)

Registra-tion Type	IS-95 REG_TYPE	IS-95 Sys Param msg field	Description
Timer-Based	0	REG_ PRD	If REG_PRD is non-zero, timer-based registration is invoked. If non-zero, mobiles register at a timer interval specified by: $2 \wedge [REG\_PRD/4] \times 0.08$ seconds.
Distance-Based	6	REG_ DIST, BASE_ LAT, BASE_LONG	If REG_DIST is non-zero, distance-based registration is turned on. Mobiles register after moving a specified distance from the last-registered base station. The distance is given by: Distance = sqrt$[(\Delta lat)^2 + (\Delta long)^2]/16$, where Δlat = {BASE_LAT- BASE_LAT_REG} and $\Delta long$ = {BASE_LONG-BASE_LONG_REG} $\times \cos(\pi/180 \times BASE\_LAT\_REG/14400)$.
Zone-Based	2	REG_ ZONE, TOTAL_ZONES, ZONE_ TIMER	If the zone that the mobile moves into is not in the stored list of visited zones, registration will occur. The REG_ZONE field identifies the zone of the base station and is added to the stored list after registration occurs. A maximum number of zones retained by the mobiles is specified by the BSC, using the TOTAL_ZONES parameter. A zone is maintained until ZONE_TIMER expires. The registration type is disabled if TOTAL_ZONES = 0.
Parameter-change	4	PARAMETER_ REG	This registration type occurs if there are changes in: Preferred slot cycle index (SLOT_CYCLE_INDEX), Slotted mode indicator (SLOTTED_MODE), Call termination indicators (MOB_TERM_HOME, MOB_TERM_FOR_SID, MOB_TERM_FOR_NID), Band and Power classes, Rates, and Operating modes. Parameter-change Registration also occurs when the base station's SID/NID does not match any entries in mobile's SID_NID_LIST.

Table 4-1   IS-95 Mobile Registration Types (Continued)

Registra- tion Type	IS-95 REG_TYPE	IS-95 Sys Param msg field	Description
Ordered	5	-	The base station can order the mobile to register through an IS-95 Registration Request Order message on the Paging Channel. Currently, the A-Interface standard does not support this type of registration. Vendors can choose to implement this feature at the BSC.
Implicit	-	-	When a mobile accesses the network via an IS-95 Origination message or IS-95 Page Response message, the received mobile parameters are used by the MSC to perform an implicit registration.
Traffic Channel	-	-	The base station can notify a mobile that it is registered by sending an IS-95 Mobile Station Registered message if registration parameters were obtained after the mobile has been assigned a traffic channel. Currently, the A-Interface standard does not support this type of registration.

4.1.2   Location Update Procedure

Mobile registration is also referred to as *Location Updating* in open A-Interface standards. The purpose of the Location Update procedure specified in CDGIOS is to register the location and stored parameters of a mobile subscriber so that a decision can be made by the network to allow or deny the mobile access to the network. Figure 4-1 illustrates the Location Update process. Upon initiating a registration, the mobile station sends registration information over the air to the BSC, which then forwards the received parameters to the MSC across the A-Interface, using a Location Updating Request message. Upon receiving a Location Updating Request message from the BSC, the MSC/VLR sends an IS-41 Registration Notification (IS41_REGNOT) message to the home HLR over an IS-41 interface. The HLR then queries its subscriber database using the received mobile *International Mobile Subscriber Identifier* (IMSI) and ESN parameters to check the access status of this mobile subscriber.

If the mobile is marked as a fraudulent or a delinquent subscriber, it is denied access. The denial of access is communicated to the MSC/VLR by an "access denied" indication in the IS41_regnot return message sent from the HLR. The MSC notifies the BSC of a failed registration attempt by sending it a Location Updating Reject message. The BSC then sends an IS-95 Registration Reject Order to the mobile.

If the mobile access is accepted, the HLR returns an access accepted indication by sending a list of subscriber profile parameters to the MSC/VLR, including calling features subscription status, such as Call Forwarding number, Call Waiting, and Three-Way Calling. This information is sent from the HLR to MSC/VLR in the IS41_regnot return result. Upon receiving the IS41_regnot return result, the MSC sends a Location Updating Accept message to the BSC, prompting the BSC to send an IS-95 Registration Accept Order message to the mobile. In the example shown in Figure 4-1, mobile A (858-770-6375) is in the coverage area of its home system and registers in the network via the home BSC and home MSC/VLR.

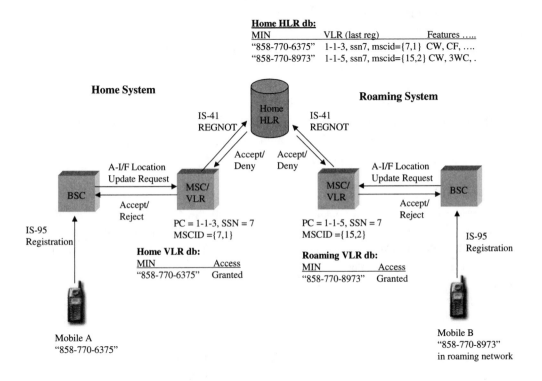

Figure 4-1   Mobile Network Registration process

Because it is typically quicker to query the VLR than the HLR, the VLR database is used as a temporary database to validate mobiles during origination and termination attempts. If a registration was successful, the mobile's entry in the VLR database is marked as active. The subscriber parameters are stored temporarily in the VLR until the VLR's mobile active timer expires or until the mobile deregisters by powering down or moving to a new network.

Service providers often have roaming agreements that allow subscribers from a foreign system to access a local network. Although additional IS-41 network messaging is required, a similar procedure is used to register roaming mobiles attempting to access a foreign network. At the mobile station's home HLR database, the identification of the MSC/VLR that the mobile last registers with is stored in the subscriber profile. This MSC/VLR identification is typically in the form of the VLR's point code, *Subsystem Number* (SSN), and MSC_ID. The MSC_ID, which consists of the Market ID (or *System Identity* [SID]) and the Switch Number of the serving system, is used to identify the serving node uniquely. Because many wireless networks operated by many different service providers may be connected together, this information is critical for roaming call delivery. In the example shown in Figure 4-1, mobile B (858-770-8973) is registered in a roaming network (i.e., the serving VLR does not belong to the home system). When a call is to be terminated to this mobile, the home HLR database is queried to determine the last-registered VLR of the mobile. In this example, the VLR is the Roaming System's VLR with point code 1-1-5, and MSCID = {15,2}. The home system can then use this information to deliver the incoming call to the foreign network successfully. For more details on roaming operation, refer to the IS-41 standard [7].

4.1.3   Authentication and Privacy

Because preventing fraud is a major concern of wireless service providers, authentication and privacy are an important part of the mobility management. Both topics are discussed in detail in Chapter 6, "Authentication," on page 345.

4.2 Location Update

The purpose of a Location Update procedure specified in CDGIOS is to register the location and stored parameters of a mobile subscriber so that a decision can be made by the network to allow or deny the mobile access to the network. The Location Update process results in either a successful registration (accepted) or an unsuccessful registration (rejected). The call flows and associated messages are presented in this section.

4.2.1   Location Update Accept Call Flow

Figure 4-2 illustrates the call flow for the successful Location Update of a mobile. The types of registrations required by the network are first broadcast over the paging channel by the BSC, using the IS-95 System Parameters message, which may include registration-specific parameters, such as the timer-based registration period. The mobile initiates the registration process when the registration procedure is triggered.

Upon receipt of the IS-95 Registration message, the BSC sends a Location Updating Request message to the MSC. This message includes all associated mobile location, authentication, and identity parameters. The MSC then queries the subscriber profile stored in the HLR database, usually using an IS-41 interface, and transfers the mobile registration parameters received from the BSC. The HLR returns the subscriber profile and access status to the MSC. If the registration is successful, the subscriber profile is updated in the VLR, and the mobile is allowed network access. Otherwise, the mobile is denied network services. The details of the individual stages are provided following Figure 4-2.

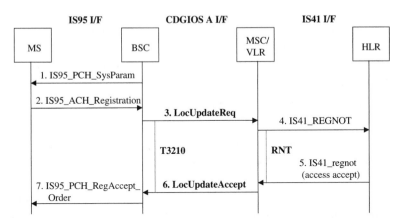

Figure 4-2   Location Update Accept call flow

1. IS95_PCH_SysParams (IS-95):

   The base station broadcasts global system parameters over the paging channel using the IS-95 System Parameters message. Registration parameters, such as the registration type to be used by the mobile, are included in this message.

2. IS95_ACH_Registration (IS-95):

   The mobile initiates the registration process by sending an IS-95 Registration message to the BSC over the access channel. This registration message includes mobile parameters such as IMSI, ESN, protocol software revision, Slot Cycle Index, mobile termination indicator, and authentication parameters, if authentication is enabled by the network.

3. LocUpdateReq (A-Interface):

   Upon receipt of the IS-95 Registration message, the BSC sends the MSC a Location Updating Request message that contains the mobile's registration information. This message is sent as an *SCCP Connection Request* (SCCP-CR) message. The BSC starts timer T3210 to wait for a Location Updating Accept or Reject message.

4. IS41_REGNOT (IS-41):

   The MSC/VLR sends an IS41_REGNOT message to the HLR to register the mobile. Upon receiving the IS41_REGNOT message, the HLR queries its subscriber database to check the mobile subscriber's profile. At this point, the serving system's VLR point code, SSN, and MSC_ID are updated in the HLR database as the last-registered system.

   If authentication is enabled, additional IS-41 messaging occurs (see Section 6.2.1, "Global Challenge—Location Update Call Flow," on page 354).

The MSC starts the *Registration Notification Timer* (RNT), which has a default value of 12s [7].

5. IS41_regnot (IS-41):

The HLR responds to the IS41_REGNOT message with an IS41_regnot return result message. This message contains information regarding the mobile subscriber's profile and is used to update the VLR database. If the registration was successful, the mobile is updated in the VLR database as active with access granted.

The MSC stops timer RNT upon receipt of the IS41_regnot return result from the HLR.

6. LocUpdateAccept (A-Interface):

The MSC sends the Location Updating Accept message to the BSC, which CDGIOS specifies to be sent as an *SCCP Connection Refused* (SCCP-CREF) message. The BSC stops timer T3210 upon receipt of the Location Updating Accept or Reject message.

If T3210 expires before the receipt of a Location Updating Accept or Reject message, the BSC may resend the Location Updating Request message, up to a vendor-specific number of times.

7. IS95_PCH_RegAcceptOrder (IS-95):

The IS-95 Registration Accept Order message is sent by the BSC to the mobile over the paging channel.

4.2.2   Location Update Reject Call Flow

During the process of performing a Location Update, the HLR may indicate to the MSC/VLR that the mobile is being denied network access. In this case, the MSC sends a Location Updating Reject message to the BSC, which subsequently sends an IS-95 Registration Reject Order to the mobile station. The reasons for access denial is network-dependent, but may occur because the mobile is determined to be delinquent or is a fraud mobile. Access may also be denied if roaming agreements are not in place between the serving network provider and the home network provider.

Figure 4-3 shows the call flow for an unsuccessful Location Update of a mobile, followed by descriptions of the individual stages.

Since Stages 1–4 are similar to Stages 1–4 in the previous section, Section 4.2.1, "Location Update Accept Call Flow," on page 234, they are not repeated here.

5. IS41_regnot (IS-41):

The HLR returns the IS41_regnot return result message to the MSC/VLR that indicates that the registration was unsuccessful. The message also includes the reason for denying network access. The mobile is updated in the VLR database as active with access denied. The MSC stops timer RNT upon receipt of the IS41_regnot return result from the HLR.

6. LocUpdateReject (A-Interface):

Upon receiving an IS41_regnot return result message from the HLR indicating that the registration was unsuccessful, the MSC sends a Location Updating Reject message to the BSC. This A-Interface message includes the rejection cause mapped from the IS-41 access denied reason, such as "Illegal mobile" or "roaming not allowed." In CDGIOS, the Location Updating Reject message is sent as an SCCP-CREF message.

The BSC stops timer T3210 upon receipt of the Location Updating Reject message. If T3210 expires before the receipt of a Location Updating Accept or Reject message, the BSC may resend the Location Updating Request message. The maximum number of times that the BSC resends the Location Updating Request message is vendor-specific.

7. IS95_PCH_RegRejectOrder (IS-95):

The IS-95 Registration Reject Order message is sent by the BSC to the mobile over the paging channel.

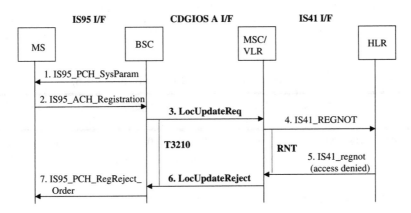

Figure 4-3 Location Update Reject call flow

4.2.3 Location Update Messages

The following sections contain detailed descriptions of the A-Interface messages used in the Location Update procedures (Table 4-2).

4.2.3.1 Location Updating Request

The Location Updating Request message is a DTAP message that is encapsulated in a Complete Layer 3 BSMAP message. The message format includes the Complete Layer 3 message header, which is described in detail in Section 3.1.2.1, "Complete Layer 3 Information," on page 146.

The Mobile Identity IMSI IE, Classmark Information Type 2 IE, Mobile Identity ESN IE, and Slot Cycle Index IE are described in detail in Section 3.1.2.2, "CM Service Request," on page 148 and, therefore, are not repeated here.

The authentication parameters AUTHR, RANDC, COUNT, RAND, and Authentication Event are used only for authentication purposes and are sent when authentication is turned on. More details can be found in Section 6.2.2.1, "Location Updating Request," on page 357.

The optional Location Area Identification IE is used to indicate a group of cells defined using a *Location Area Code* (LAC) and is typically used if the MSC pages mobiles by LAC. However, because the Cell Identifier IE also provides Cell ID and LAC information, this field is optional.

The Registration Type IE specifies the type of IS-95 registration that was triggered at the mobile. This value is mapped directly from the REG_TYPE parameter in the IS-95 Registration message.

- BSAP Message Type: DTAP, encapsulated in Complete L3 BSMAP
- SCCP Message Type: SCCP-Connection Request (CR)
- Direction: BSC → MSC

Table 4-2   Location Updating Request Message (CDGIOS 6.1.4.8)

BitMap	Param IE	#Oct	Range	Type	IOS Ref
0000 0000 (00H) LLLL LLLL	BSMAP header	2	Msg Discrim. = 0 (BSMAP) L = BSMAP msg length	M	6.2.2.1 6.2.2.3
0101 0111 (57H)	Message Type	1	Complete L3 Information	M	6.2.2.4
0000 0101 (05H)	Cell Identifier	5 or 7	Same as element in Table 3-2, CM Service Request	M	6.2.2.20
0001 0111 (17H) LLLL LLLL	Layer 3 Information	2	L = length	M	6.2.2.38
rrrr 0101 (05H)	Protocol Discriminator	1	0101—Mobility Mangement r = 0—reserved bits	M	6.2.2.39
0000 0000 (00H)	Reserved Bits	1	-	M	6.2.2.40
0000 1000 (08H)	Message Type	1	Location Updating Request	M	6.2.2.4

Table 4-2   Location Updating Request Message (CDGIOS 6.1.4.8) (Continued)

BitMap	Param IE	#Oct	Range	Type	IOS Ref
LLLL LLLL	Mobile Identity (IMSI)	7–9	Same as element in Table 3-2, CM Service Request	M	6.2.2.16
0001 0011 (13H) cccc cccc nnnn cccc nnnn nnnn llll llll llll llll	Location Area Identification	6	c = MCC n = MNC l = Location Area Code	O,C	6.2.2.43
0001 0010 (12H)	Classmark Info Type 2	6	Same as element in Table 3-2, CM Service Request	O,R	6.2.2.15
0001 1111 (1FH) tttt tttt	Registration Type	2	t = IS-95 REG_TYPE 0,1,2,3,4,6	O,R	6.2.2.61
0000 1101 (0DH)	Mobile Identity (ESN)	7	Same as element in Table 3-2, CM Service Request	O,R	6.2.2.16
0011 0101 (35H) rrrr riii	Slot Cycle Index	2	Same as element in Table 3-2, CM Service Request	O,C	6.2.2.17
0100 0010 (42H) LLLL LLLL rrrr tttt 0000 00nn nnnn nnnn nnnn nnnn	Authentication Response Parameter (AUTHR)	6	L = 04H r = 0—reserved tttt = 0001—AUTHR n = 18-bit Auth result	O,C	6.2.2.46
0010 1000 (28H) rrrr rrrr	Authentication Confirmation Parameter (RANDC)	2	r = RANDC—first 8 bits of RAND. This element is required when authentication is enabled in the system and the value is received from the MS.	O,C	6.2.2.42
0100 0000 (40H) rrcc cccc	Authentication Parameter COUNT	2	r = 0, c = COUNT	O,C	6.2.2.47

Table 4-2   Location Updating Request Message (CDGIOS 6.1.4.8) (Continued)

BitMap	Param IE	#Oct	Range	Type	IOS Ref
0100 0001 (41H) LLLL LLLL rrrr tttt nnnn nnnn nnnn nnnn nnnn nnnn nnnn nnnn	Authentica- tion Chal- lenge Parameter (RAND)	7	L = 05H r = 0—reserved tttt = 0001—RAND n = RAND	O,C	6.2.2.45
0100 1010 (4AH) LLLL LLLL vvvv vvvv	Authentica- tion Event	3	L = 01H, v = 01H, 02H 01H—Auth required, params not received from MS 02H—Auth required, RAND/ RANDC mismatch	O,C	6.2.2.114

4.2.3.2   Location Updating Accept

This message is sent from the MSC as an SCCP-CREF message to indicate to the BSC that the Location Updating Request has been accepted and that the mobile is successfully registered at the VLR.

If the optional Location Area Identification IE is included in this message, it is set to the same value previously sent by the BSC in the Location Updating Request message (Table 4-3).

- BSAP Message Type: DTAP
- SCCP Message Type: SCCP-Connection Refused (CREF)
- Direction: BSC ← MSC

Table 4-3   Location Updating Accept Message (CDGIOS 6.1.4.9)

BitMap	Param IE	#Oct	Range	Type	IOS Ref
0000 0001 (01H) ccrr rsss LLLL LLLL	DTAP header	3	Msg Discrim. = 0 (DTAP) s = 0—SAPI c = 0, r = 0—reserved bits DLCI = "ccrr rsss" = 0 L = DTAP msg length	M	6.2.2.1 6.2.2.2 6.2.2.3
rrrr 0101 (05H)	Protocol Dis- criminator	1	0101—Mobility Management r = 0—reserved bits	M	6.2.2.39

Table 4-3 Location Updating Accept Message (CDGIOS 6.1.4.9) (Continued)

BitMap	Param IE	#Oct	Range	Type	IOS Ref
0000 0000 (00H)	Reserved Bits	1		M	6.2.2.40
0000 0010 (02H)	Message Type	1	Location Updating Accept	M	6.2.2.4
0001 0011 (13H) cccc cccc nnnn cccc nnnn nnnn llll llll llll llll	Location Area Identification	6	c = MCC n = MNC l = Location Area Code	O,C	6.2.2.43

4.2.3.3   Location Updating Reject

This message is sent by the MSC to indicate to the BSC that the Location Updating Request has been rejected and that the mobile registration has failed.

The mandatory Reject Cause IE specifies the reason the registration was rejected. Possible cause values include "Unknown IMSI," "Roaming not allowed," "Network Failure," "Congestion," and "Illegal mobile" (Table 4-4).

- BSAP Message Type: DTAP
- SCCP Message Type: SCCP-Connection Refused (CREF)
- Direction: BSC ← MSC

Table 4-4 Location Updating Reject Message (CDGIOS 6.1.4.10)

BitMap	Param IE	#Oct	Range	Type	IOS Ref
0000 0001 (01H) ccrr rsss LLLL LLLL	DTAP header	3	Msg Discrim.= 0 (DTAP) DLCI = "ccrr rsss" = 0 L = DTAP msg length	M	6.2.2.1 6.2.2.2 6.2.2.3
rrrr 0101 (05H)	Protocol Discriminator	1	0101—Mobility Management r = 0—reserved bits	M	6.2.2.39
0000 0000 (00H)	Reserved Bits	1		M	6.2.2.40

Table 4-4   Location Updating Reject Message (CDGIOS 6.1.4.10) (Continued)

BitMap	Param IE	#Oct	Range	Type	IOS Ref
0000 0100 (04H)	Message Type	1	Location Updating Reject	M	6.2.2.4
cccc cccc	Reject Cause	1	c = reject cause 03H—Illegal mobile 0BH—Roaming not allowed 51H—Network failure 56H—Congestion	M	6.2.2.44

4.2.4   Location Update Accept Example Call Flow

Figure 4-4 shows a practical example of a summary message call flow for a successful mobile location update. The purpose of Figure 4-4 is to present an overview of the messages exchanged between the BSC and MSC. Subsequent figures illustrate the complete message's content, including MTP and SCCP layers. The decoded message format is similar to what would be seen on test equipment monitoring the A-Interface signaling link. In this example, the BSC's point code is 1-1-1, and the MSC's point code is 1-2-4.

```
Event   Time            OPC     DPC     SLS     Messages
1       21:05:55,485    1-1-1   1-2-4   15      SCCP-CR    LocUpdateReq
2       21:05:55,508    1-2-4   1-1-1   7       SCCP-CREF  LocUpdateAccept
```

Figure 4-4   Location Update Accept example call flow

The example call flow in Figure 4-4 starts with the BSC sending a Location Updating Request message to the MSC, which is sent as an SCCP-CR message. The MSC, upon querying the HLR and determining that the mobile subscriber registration was successful, returns a Location Updating Accept message.

```
1:D:3:-:64  21:05:55,485,025  1-1-1  1-2-4  SCCP  CR  BMA+  CL3I  LURQ  DTA+
----0011    Service Indicator             SCCP
--00----    Sub-Service: Priority         Spare/priority 0 (U.S.A. only)
10------    Sub-Service: Network Ind      National message
***B3***    Destination Point Code        1-2-4
***B3***    Originating Point Code        1-1-1
ANSI SCCP T1.112-1988 for US-41  (SCCP)   CR (= Connection Request)
00010000    Signaling Link Selection      16
00000001    SCCP Message Type             1
***B3***    Source Local Reference        17984
----0010    Protocol Class                Class 2
0000----    Spare                         0
00000010    Pointer to parameter          2
00000111    Pointer to parameter          7
```

(Continued)
```
Called address parameter
00000101  Parameter Length              5
-------1  Subsystem No. Indicator       SSN present
------1-  Point Code Indicator          PC present
--0000--  Global Title Indicator        No global title included
-1------  Routing Indicator             Route on DPC + Subsystem No.
1-------  For national use              National address
11111100  Subsystem number             252
***B3***  Called Party SPC              1-2-4
Data parameter
00001111  Parameter name                Data
00101001  Parameter length              41
**B37***  Data                          00 23 57 05 03 02 ....
End of optional parameters
00000000  Parameter name                End of Optional Params
CDGIOS MSC-BSC (BSSMAP) (BMA+)  CL3I (= Complete Layer 3 Information)
Complete Layer 3 Information
-------0  Discrimination bit D          BSSMAP
0000000-  Filler                        0
00100111  Message Length                39
01010111  Message Type                  87
00000101  IE Name                       Cell Identifier
00000101  IE Length                     5
00000001  Cell ID discriminator         LAC & CI used
***B2***  LAC                           298
***B2***  CI                            17
00010111  IE Name                       Layer 3 Information
00011101  IE Length                     29
**B27***  L3 Message Contents           05 00 08 06 36 30 ...
CDGIOS MSC-BSC (DTAP) LURQ (= Location Updating ReQuest)
Location Updating ReQuest
----0101  Protocol Discriminator        Mobility Management msg
0000----  reserved                      0
00000000  reserved                      0
-0001000  Message Type                  8
0-------  Send Sequence Number          0
Mobile IDentity
00001000  IE Length                     8
-----110  Type of Identity              IMSI
----1---  Odd/Even Indicator            odd
**b44***  Identity digits               310008582480020
00010010  IE Name                       Classmark Information Type 2
00000100  IE Length                     4
-----000  RF power capability           Class 1, vehicle and portable
00000---  reserved                      0
-----000  Frequency capability          Band number 0
----1---  SM capability                 Present
-000----  Spare                         0
0-------  reserved                      0
-------0  ANSI/EIA/TI A-553             Capability is unknown
------1-  Mobile Term                   IS-95 cap receiv incom calls
```

(Continued)

```
-----0--   DTX                          Not the mob is capable of DTX
----0---   Bandwidth                    Limited to the 20MHz band
---1----   Extended Protocol            Capable
--1-----   Slotted                      Slotted paging request mode
-1------   IS-95                        Mobile is capable
0-------   IS-91                        Capability is unknown
-------0   IS-54                        Capability is unknown
0000000-   Spare                        0
00011111   IE Name                      Registration Type
00000000   Location Registration Type   Timer-based
00001101   IE Name                      Mobile Identity
00000101   IE Length                    5
-----101   Type of Identity             ESN
00000---   Filler                       0
***B4***   ESN                          325295873
00110101   IE Name                      Slot Cycle Index
-----010   Slot Cycle Index             2
00000---   Spare                        0
```

Figure 4-5   Location Updating Request message example

Figure 4-5, above, shows an example of a decoded Location Updating Request message that is similar to what may be seen on test equipment monitoring the A-Interface during a mobile registration. The Registration Type for this example is Timer-Based, and the mobile is operating in slotted mode and has a preferred Slot Cycle Index of 2. The mobile is located in Cell ID 17.

Note that in this example message, no authentication parameters are included. Section 6.2.3, "Global Challenge—Location Update Example," on page 358 presents a Location Updating Request message example with authentication parameters.

```
1:C:3:-:64   21:05:55,508,628  1-2-4  1-1-1  SCCP  CREF  DTA+  LUAC
----0011   Service Indicator          SCCP
--00----   Sub-Service: Priority      Spare/priority 0 (U.S.A. only)
10------   Sub-Service: Network Ind   National message
***B3***   Destination Point Code     1-1-1
***B3***   Originating Point Code     1-2-4
ANSI SCCP T1.112-1988 for US-41  (SCCP)  CREF (= Connection Refused)
00011101   Signaling Link Selection   29
00000011   SCCP Message Type          3
***B3***   Destination Local Ref.     17984
00000000   Refusal Cause              End user originated
00000001   Pointer to parameter       1
Called address parameter
00000011   Parameter name             Called party address
00000101   Parameter Length           5
-------1   Subsystem No. Indicator    SSN present
------1-   Point Code Indicator       PC present
--0000--   Global Title Indicator     No global title included
-1------   Routing Indicator          Route on DPC + Subsystem No.
```

(Continued)

```
1-------   For national use             National address
11111100   Subsystem number             252
***B3***   Called Party SPC             1-2-4
Data parameter
00001111   Parameter name               Data
00000110   Parameter length             6
***B6***   Data                         01 00 03 05 00 02
End of optional parameters
00000000   Parameter name               End of Optional Params
CDGIOS MSC-BSC(DTAP) (DTA+)   LUAC (= Location Updating ACcept)
Location Updating ACcept
-------1   Discrimination bit D         DTAP
0000000-   Filler                       0
-----000   SAPI                         0
--000---   Spare                        0
00------   Radio channel id             ANSI-553,IS-91,IS-54,IS-95
00000011   Message Length               3
----0101   Protocol Discriminator       Mobility Management msg
0000----   reserved                     0
00000000   reserved                     0
-0000010   Message Type                 2
0-------   Send Sequence Number         0
```

Figure 4-6   Location Updating Accept message example

Figure 4-6, above, shows an example of a decoded Location Updating Accept message. Even though this message is sent as an SCCP-CREF message, it is used to indicate that Location Updating Request has been accepted. No IMSI or mobile identity is needed because the SCCP-CREF message includes the DLR of 17984, which can be used to correlate the message to the previously received SCCP-CR (Location Updating Request) message's SLR of 17984. No other BSAP parameters are included.

References

1. CDG-IOS version 3.1.1, *CDMA Development Group MSC to BS Interface Inter-Operability Specification*. June 1999.
2. CDG-IOS version 2.0, *CDMA Development Group MSC to BS Interface Inter-Operability Specification*. September 1998.
3. Telecommunications Industry Association, TIA/EIA/IS-634-A, *MSC-BS Interface (A-Interface) for Public 800 MHz*. July 1998.
4. Telecommunications Industry Association , TIA/EIA/TSB-80, *MSC-BS Interface (A-Interface) for Public 800 MHz*. October 1996.
5. Telecommunications Industry Association, TIA/EIA/IS-95-A, *Mobile Station-Base Station Compatibility Standard for Dual-Mode Wideband Spread Spectrum Cellular Systems*. May 1995.
6. American National Standards Institute, ANSI J-STD-008, *Personal Station – Base Station Compatibility Requirements for 1.8 to 2.0 GHz Code Devision Multiple Access (CDMA) Personal Communications Systems*. August

1995.

7.   American National Standards Institute, ANSI TIA/EIA/IS-41-D, *Cellular Radio-Telecommunications Intersystem Operations*. December 1997.

CHAPTER 5

Supplementary Services

Early wireless networks were designed with the fundamental goal of providing users with reliable voice service. Customers using the introductory networks were new to wireless technology and were satisfied with simply being able to make and receive voice calls. Now, however, wireless phones are commonplace, and wireless users are demanding more and increasingly sophisticated supplementary network services that extend beyond basic voice.

Today's CDMA networks are being designed to meet customer demands in supplementary services and advanced wireless features. This chapter describes these supplementary services and focuses on how the open A-Interface accommodates the additional messaging required to support these features. The following supplementary services are covered in this chapter:

- *Short Message Services* (SMS) delivery
- *Message Waiting Indicator* (MWI) delivery
- Common cellular features specified in TIA/EIA 664
- Features Activation/Deactivation/Registration
- Call Waiting
- Three-Way Calling
- Call Forwarding
- *Over-the-Air Service Provisioning* (OTASP)
- Data Services

Figure 5-1 illustrates a modular network architecture in which the application services are implemented as external network entities. These network applications usually interface directly with the *Mobile Switching Center* (MSC) and communicate indirectly with the mobile station to offer various features. The MSC normally provides switching and signaling functionality, and the *Base Station Controller* (BSC) is responsible for setting up radio resources. The combination of the MSC and the BSC acts primarily as a pipeline between the mobile station and the supplementary service application. The messages and call flow procedures specified in CDGIOS are used mainly to transfer supplementary service application data between a mobile station and the service providing network entity.

Figure 5-1 provides an overview of how the land network (IS-41), A-Interface (CDGIOS), and air interface (IS-95) are all used to deliver supplementary services. The diagram includes some common messages used over the various interfaces.

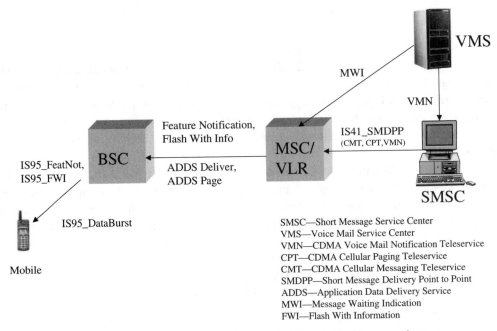

Figure 5-1   Short Messages Services and Message Waiting Indication overview

5.1 Short Message Services

Short Message Services are supplementary network services that allow short messages to be sent to and from a mobile station. For example, SMS allows a mobile station to act as a pager capable of receiving or delivering alphanumeric text. SMS is also commonly used to deliver voice mail notifications.

SMS delivery refers to an SMS message being delivered either from a remote SMS application to a mobile station or from a mobile station to a remote SMS application. In both cases, the delivery may occur when the mobile is idle or in traffic. The term *traffic* is used instead of conversation because a mobile may be in a nonvoice call, such as fax or data.

During mobile-originated SMS delivery, the mobile station generates an SMS message through an SMS application running on the mobile station. This application communicates, via the BSC and MSC, with the remote SMS application running on a *Short Message Service Center* (SMSC). The final destination of the message may be a land party or another mobile station.

In the case of a mobile-terminated SMS delivery, the SMSC is the originator. Although the SMSC is considered the originator of the message, the content of the SMS message may be from another network entity, such as an email server or a voice mail device. In addition to individual mobile-terminated SMS deliveries, third-generation CDMA networks may provide a third SMS delivery method, known as *SMS broadcast*. This technique, described in 3G-IOS v4, provides the capability to send mobile-terminated SMS messages to a group of mobile stations within a BSC service area.

As mentioned earlier, the delivery of an SMS message may occur when the mobile station is either idle or in a call. If the mobile is idle, the paging channel is used to deliver the SMS message and no A-Interface SCCP connection is necessary. If the mobile is in a call at the time the SMS message is to be delivered, the traffic channel is used to deliver the message over the air, and the existing *Signaling Connection Control Part* (SCCP) connection assigned to the call is used for A-Interface messaging. If an SMS delivery to an idle mobile involves a message that is too long to be delivered over the paging channel, the mobile may be brought into the traffic state to allow the message to be sent over the traffic channel.

The descriptions of various SMS delivery scenarios presented in this section focus on A-Interface messaging. Message flows, message descriptions, and examples are provided for the following scenarios:

• Mobile-terminated SMS while in traffic
• Mobile-originated SMS while in traffic
• Mobile-terminated SMS in idle mode
• Mobile-originated SMS in idle mode
• Optimized mobile-terminated SMS in idle mode
• SMS Delivery in traffic channel using Service Option 6/14

A comprehensive description of the SMS protocol can be found in the Appendix Section 5.A, "Short Message Service Protocol Overview," on page 325. Although a complete understanding of the SMS protocol used by SMS applications is not necessary to understand how SMS messages are delivered over the A-Interface, the information presented in Appendix Section 5.A may add to the reader's overall understanding of wireless networks. Appendix Section 5.A covers the protocol architecture, SMS transport and teleservice layer message structures, and how SMS applications reliably exchange messages.

5.1.1   Mobile-Terminated Short Message Service in Traffic

When the MSC receives a request from the SMSC to deliver an SMS message to a mobile station, it first checks the state of the mobile. If the mobile is currently in a call, the MSC packages the received SMS information into an *Application Data Delivery Service* (ADDS) message that is sent to the BSC over the A-Interface. The ADDS Deliver message is used to encapsulate the SMS Point-to-Point Transport Layer message, which was generated at the MSC or received by the MSC from another network entity. The BSC, upon receipt of the ADDS Deliver message, removes the message header information in the ADDS message and packages the content of the ADDS User Part into an IS-95 Data Burst message. The IS-95 Data Burst message is then sent to the mobile on the forward traffic channel.

If the ADDS Deliver message sent from the MSC to the BSC includes a Tag value, an acknowledgment must be sent back to the MSC. In this case, the BSC sends the MSC an ADDS Deliver Acknowledge message after receiving the layer 2 acknowledgment from the mobile station. The ADDS Deliver Acknowledge message sent from the BSC includes the same Tag value previously received from the MSC in the ADDS Deliver message.

An SMS application may also request a transport layer acknowledgement from the SMS application running on the mobile station. The transport layer acknowledgment indicates that not only has the message been delivered to the mobile (layer 2 acknowledgment), but also that the SMS application running on the mobile station was successful in decoding the message contents. If the originating SMS application requires a transport layer acknowledgment from the mobile station and the SMS application running on the mobile station was successful in decoding the message, the mobile station then sends a transport layer acknowledgment using an IS-95 Data Burst message on the reverse traffic channel. The BSC, upon receipt of this message, packages the acknowledgment in an ADDS Deliver message, which it sends to the MSC. The MSC then sends an acknowledgment to the SMSC.

The message flow for delivery of an SMS message to a mobile station in traffic is shown in Figure 5-2 and is followed by descriptions of the individual steps.

1. (Mobile in a Call) :

   The mobile is in a call on the traffic channel.

2. IS41_SMSREQ (IS-41):

   The SMSC initiates delivery of a mobile terminated SMS message by sending an IS-41 SMS Request message to the mobile's *Home Location Register* (HLR), requesting the SMS address to be used to deliver the SMS message. This IS-41 message includes the identity of the mobile station.

3. IS41_smsreq (IS-41):

   In response to the received IS41_SMSREQ message, the HLR sends an IS41_smsreq return result to the SMSC, specifying the address to be used for the SMS delivery. The address is usually the point code of the *Visitor Location Register* (VLR)/MSC with which the mobile last registered. Other addressing schemes are also allowed and are described in the IS-41 standard [7].

4. IS41_SMDPP (IS-41):

After receiving the SMS address in the IS41_smsreq return result, the SMSC sends an IS-41 Delivery Point-to-Point (IS41_SMDPP) message, which encapsulates the SMS transport layer message in the SMS Bearer Data field, to the specified SMS address. After sending the IS41_SMDPP message, the SMSC starts timer SMT (Short Message Delivery Timer), which has a default value of 45 seconds [7]. If the SMSC requires a Transport Layer acknowledgment, the Bearer Reply Option field in the SMS Point-to-Point Transport Layer message is included. This message also includes the identity of the mobile station.

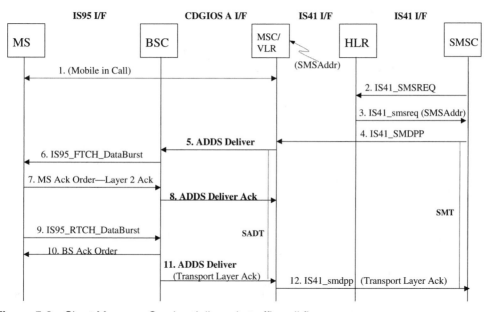

Figure 5-2 Short Message Service delivery in traffic call flow

5. ADDS Deliver (A-Interface):

When the MSC receives an IS41_SMDPP message, it removes the IS-41 header information and repackages the SMS Point-to-Point Transport Layer part in an A-Interface ADDS Deliver message. The ADDS Deliver message is then sent to the BSC. Upon sending the ADDS Deliver message, the MSC starts the SADT (Short Message Air Delivery Timer) timer. The default SADT timer value is 18 seconds.

If the MSC requests a layer 2 acknowledgment from the mobile, it includes a Tag value in the ADDS Deliver message. The Tag *Information Element* (IE) may be used by the MSC to determine which ADDS Deliver message is being acknowledged.

6. IS95_FTCH_DataBurst (IS-95):

The BSC removes the ADDS Deliver header information and repackages the SMS Point-to-Point Transport Layer part in an IS-95 Data Burst message that is sent to the mobile over the forward traffic channel.

7. MS_Ack_Order—Layer2 Ack (IS-95):

If the MSC includes the Tag IE in the ADDS Deliver message, the BSC will request a layer 2 acknowledgement from the mobile in the IS-95 Data Burst message. The mobile acknowledges the received message by sending the BSC an IS-95 Mobile Station Acknowledgment Order on the reverse traffic channel.

If the BSC requests and does not receive a layer 2 acknowledgment (Mobile Station Acknowledge Order), it may retransmit the IS-95 Data Burst message. The number of retransmissions is vendor implementation-specific.

8. ADDS Deliver Ack (A-Interface):

Upon receipt of the layer 2 acknowledgment from the mobile, the BSC sends an ADDS Deliver Acknowledgment message to the MSC to acknowledge the delivery of the SMS message to the mobile. The Tag IE included in this message is set to the same value that was previously received by the BSC in the corresponding ADDS Deliver message.

9. IS95_RTCH_DataBurst (IS-95):

If an SMS Transport Layer acknowledgment is requested by the SMS application running on the SMSC, the mobile's SMS application will generate an SMS Acknowledge Transport Layer message and package it in an IS-95 Data Burst message, which is sent to the BSC, using the reverse traffic channel.

10. BS_Ack_Order (IS-95):

The BSC responds to the reverse traffic channel IS-95 Data Burst message with a Base Station Acknowledgment Order message on the forward traffic channel.

11. ADDS Deliver (Transport Layer Ack) (A-Interface):

Upon receipt of the IS-95 Data Burst message, the BSC repackages the SMS Acknowledge Transport Layer message into an ADDS Deliver message and sends the message to the MSC. Note that the BSC does not process the Transport Layer message; it simply passes the information to the MSC. The MSC stops timer SADT.

12. IS41_smdpp (Transport Layer Ack) (IS-41) :

Upon receiving the ADDS Deliver message containing the Transport Layer Acknowledgement, the MSC repackages the information in an IS41_smdpp message and sends it to the SMSC. The IS41_smdpp return result message is a response to the IS41_SMDPP message received from the SMSC during the initial SMS delivery request.

5.1.2 Mobile-Originated Short Message Service in Traffic

The SMS application running on a mobile station may also have the capability to originate SMS messages. Figure 5-3 illustrates the call flow for mobile-originated SMS while in traffic. If the mobile user wishes to send an SMS while in a call, the mobile station sends the BSC an IS-95 Data Burst message encapsulating the SMS data. The BSC responds with an IS-95 Base Station Acknowledgment Order message on the forward traffic channel and sends an ADDS Deliver that contains the SMS message to the MSC.

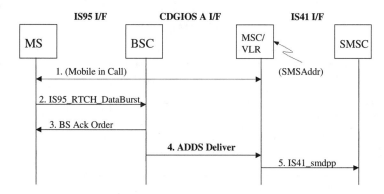

Figure 5-3 Mobile Origination of Short Message Service while in traffic

5.1.3 Short Message Service in Traffic Messages

The only two A-Interface messages used for delivery of SMS messages while a mobile is in a call are the ADDS Deliver and ADDS Deliver Acknowledgment message. The message structure and parameter settings are discussed for each message in the following sections.

5.1.3.1 ADDS Deliver

The ADDS Deliver message is a *Direct Transfer Application Part* (DTAP) message that is sent by the MSC to the BSC whenever an SMS message is to be delivered to a mobile already in a call. The ADDS Deliver message (Table 5-1) is also used by the BSC to send SMS information to the MSC when the mobile station originates an SMS message or when the mobile station sends a Transport Layer Acknowledgment.

The ADDS User Part IE contains the SMS Transport Layer message that originates from the SMS bearer service end point. In the case of a mobile-terminated SMS message, the SMS Transport Layer message typically originates from the SMSC.

The Tag IE is used by the MSC to solicit a layer 2 acknowledgment from the mobile station for a particular SMS delivery. When the Tag IE is included, the BSC responds to the ADDS Deliver message with an ADDS Deliver Acknowledge message, indicating the receipt of a layer 2 acknowledgment from the mobile. The Tag IE may also used by the MSC to determine which ADDS Deliver message is being acknowledged.

- BSAP Message Type: DTAP
- SCCP Message Type: SCCP-Data Form 1 (DT1)
- Direction: BSC ↔ MSC

Table 5-1   ADDS Deliver Message (CDGIOS 6.1.7.3)

BitMap	Param IE	#Oct	Range	Type	IOS Ref
0000 0001 (01H) ccrr rsss LLLL LLLL	DTAP header	3	Msg Discrim. = 1 (DTAP) DLCI = "ccrr rsss" = 0 L = DTAP msg length	M	6.2.2.1 6.2.2.2 6.2.2.3
rrrr 0011 (03H)	Protocol Discriminator	1	0011—Call Processing r = 0—reserved	M	6.2.2.39
0000 0000 (00H)	Reserved Bits	1		M	6.2.2.40
0101 0011 (53H)	Msg Type	1	ADDS Deliver	M	6.2.2.4
LLLL LLLL rrbb bbbb aaaa aaaa	ADDS User Part	> 2	L = User Part length, r = 0 b = 03H—SMS, 04H—OTASP a = Application data (ref IS-637)	M	6.2.2.67
0011 0011 (33H) tttt tttt tttt tttt tttt tttt tttt tttt	Tag	5	t = 00000000H–FFFFFFFFH	O,C	6.2.2.62

5.1.3.2   ADDS Deliver Acknowledgment

The ADDS Deliver Acknowledge message is a DTAP message sent from the BSC to the MSC upon receipt of a layer 2 acknowledgment from the mobile station. The BSC requests a layer 2 acknowledgment from the mobile if the MSC previously included the Tag IE in the ADDS Deliver message (Table 5-2). The Tag value included in the ADDS Deliver Acknowledgment is set to the same value previously received in the corresponding ADDS Deliver message.

The Cause IE here is used to specify the reason for a layer 2 acknowledgment failure.

- BSAP Message Type: DTAP
- SCCP Message Type: SCCP-Data Form 1 (DT1)
- Direction: BSC → MSC

Table 5-2   ADDS Deliver Ack Message (CDGIOS 6.1.7.5)

BitMap	Param IE	#Oct	Range	Type	IOS Ref
0000 0001 (01H) ccrr rsss LLLL LLLL	DTAP header	3	Msg Discrim. = 1 (DTAP) DLCI = "ccrr rsss" = 0 L = DTAP msg length	M	6.2.2.1 6.2.2.2 6.2.2.3
rrrr 0011 (03H)	Protocol Discriminator	1	0011—Call Processing r = 0—reserved	M	6.2.2.39
0000 0000 (00H)	Reserved Bits	1		M	6.2.2.40
0101 0100 (54H)	Msg Type	1	ADDS Deliver Ack	M	6.2.2.4
0011 0011 (33H)	Tag	5	Same as element in Table 5-1, ADDS Deliver msg.	O,C	6.2.2.62
0000 0100 (04H) LLLL LLLL 0ccc cccc	Cause	3	L = 01H c = 70H—Reject indication from mobile	O,C	6.2.2.19

5.1.4   Mobile-Terminated SMS in Traffic Example

Figure 5-4 shows a summary of the A-Interface message used to deliver an SMS message to a mobile currently in a voice call. The purpose of Figure 5-4 is to present an overview of the messages exchanged between the BSC and MSC. Subsequent figures illustrate the complete message's content, including *Message Transfer Part 3* (MTP3) and SCCP message layers. The decoded message formats presented are similar to what would be seen on test equipment monitoring the A-Interface signaling link. The BSC's point code is 8-17-92 and the MSC's point code is 110-44-3.

The example shown in Figure 5-4 begins with a mobile-to-mobile call. The MSC and BSC successfully setup the mobile-to-mobile call through the exchange of A-Interface messages described in Section 3.1.2, "Mobile Origination Messages," on page 146, and Section 3.2.2, "Mobile Termination Messages," on page 169. The Connect message, event 10 in the example, indicates that the second mobile user answered the incoming call. The SMS message delivery to the mobile (m1) begins after the mobile is in a voice call. An ADDS Deliver message containing the SMS message and a Tag IE is sent from the MSC to the BSC, prompting the BSC to send the SMS message in an IS-95 Data Burst message to the mobile (m1). Because the Tag IE was included by the MSC in the ADDS Deliver message, the BSC requests a layer 2 acknowledgment from the mobile. Upon receiving the acknowledgment, the BSC sends the MSC an ADDS Deliver Acknowledgment that contains the same Tag value previously received from the MSC.

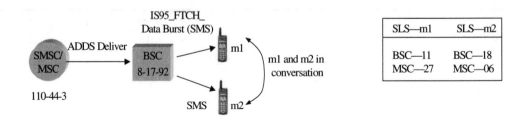

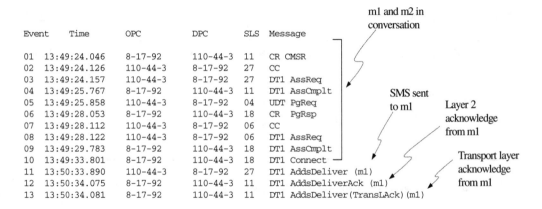

Figure 5-4   Short Message Service in traffic example call flow

In the example shown in Figure 5-4, the SMS application running on the SMSC requests a Transport Layer Acknowledgment from the SMS application running on the mobile station. Immediately following the layer 2 acknowledgment, the mobile station sends the BSC an SMS Transport Layer Acknowledgment that the BSC encapsulates within an ADDS Deliver message, which is then sent to the MSC.

Note that the ADDS Deliver and ADDS Deliver Acknowledge are sent using SLS 27 (MSC) and SLS 11 (BSC), which correspond to the signaling links associated with the mobile's SCCP connection.

```
**** MESSAGE NUMBER: 00011 ****
*** Start of MTP Level 3 ***
0003 10000011 83
      ----0011    Service Indicator        SCCP
      --00----    Network Priority         priority 0
```

(Continued)

```
         10------      Network Indicator        National          SMS from MSC
0004 (3 bytes)    Destination Point Code     8-17-92      ◄──────── to BSC
0007 (3 bytes)    Origination Point Code     110-44-3
0010 00011011 1b Signaling Link Selection    27
*** Start of SCCP ***
0011 00000110 06 Data Form 1                 06
0012 (3 bytes)    Dest Local References      78695
0015 00000000 00 Segment/Reassembling        0
0016 00000001 01 Variable Pointer            01
*** Start of CDG IOS MAP ***
                  SMS Delivery
0017 00101100 2c DTAP Length                 44
0018 00000001 01 DTAP Discriminator          01
0019 00000000 00 DLCI
     -----000      SAPI                       0
     --000---      Reserved
     00------      C1/C2                      ANSI/EIA/TIA-553,IS54,IS95
0020 00101001 29 Length                      41
0021 00000011 03 CC Protocol Discrim         03
0022 00000000 00 Reserved
0023 01010011 53 ADDS Delivery               83
                  ADDS User Part
0024 00100000 20 Length                      32
0025 00000011 03
     --000011      Application Type           SMS
     00------      Reserved                   00
0026 00000000 00 Application Data Message    00 00 02 10 ...
0027 00000000 00
0028 00000010 02
0029 00010000 10
0030 00000010 02
0031 00000010 02                                                SMS Point-to-Point Trans-
0032 00000111 07 ◄──────────────────────────────────────────── port Layer message as
0033 00000010 02                                                defined in IS-637
0034 10000000 80
0035 01001000 48
0036 11010001 d1
0037 01011001 59
0038 11100010 e2
0039 01000000 40
0040 00000110 06
0041 00000001 01
0042 00000000 00
0043 00001000 08
0044 00001100 0c
0045 00000001 01
0046 00000111 07
0047 00000000 00
0048 00101011 2b
0049 01000011 43
0050 00101011 2b
```

(Continued)
```
0051 01100011 63
0052 01100011 63
0053 01111000 78
0054 00001000 08
0055 00000001 01
0056 00000000 00
0057 00110011 33 Tag                        51
0058 (4 bytes)    Value                      f3 42 01 07
```

ADDS Deliver Ack
should include this
tag value

Figure 5-5 ADDS Deliver message example

Figure 5-5 shows the decoded ADDS Deliver message summarized in Figure 5-4. The decoded message is similar to what may be seen on test equipment monitoring the A-Interface during an SMS message delivery to a mobile in traffic.

The SLS value of 27 and the DLR value of *78695* indicate that this SCCP-DT1 message is sent from the MSC to the BSC using the SCCP connection previously established for mobile m1. Note that the ADDS Deliver message is a DTAP message with protocol type set to Call Processing.

In the ADDS User Part, the application type is set to SMS, signifying that the user data embedded in the user part is related to SMS operation. The ADDS User Part in this example contains the SMS Transport Layer message to be delivered to the mobile station. The SMS Transport Layer message format is specified in IS-637 and described in Appendix Section 5.A, "Short Message Service Protocol Overview," on page 325. Note that the first octet in the Application Data Message of the ADDS User Part has a value of zero, which indicates that the data corresponds to an SMS Point-to-Point Transport Layer message.

A Tag IE with a value of *f3 42 01 07* is included in the example ADDS Deliver message (Figure 5-5) to solicit a layer 2 acknowledgment from the mobile station.

```
**** MESSAGE NUMBER: 00012 ****
*** Start of MTP Level 3 ***
0003 10000011 83
     ----0011    Service Indicator        SCCP
     --00----    Network Priority         priority 0
     10------    Network Indicator        National
0004 (3 bytes)   Destination Point Code   110-44-3
0007 (3 bytes)   Origination Point Code   8-17-92
0010 00001011 0b Signaling Link Selection 11
*** Start of SCCP ***
0011 00000110 06 Data Form 1              06
0012 (3 bytes)   Dest Local References    15432236
0015 00000000 00 Segment/Reassembling     0
0016 00000001 01 Variable Pointer         01
*** Start of CDG IOS MAP ***
                 ADDS Delivery Ack
0017 00001011 0b DTAP Length              11
0018 00000001 01 DTAP Discriminator       01
```

(Continued)
```
0019 00000000 00 DLCI
0020 00001000 08 Length                      8
0021 00000011 03 CC Protocol Discrim        03
0022 00000000 00 Reserved
0023 01010100 54 ADDS Delivery Ack          84
0024 00110011 33 Tag                        51
0025 (4 bytes)   Value                      f3 42 01 07 ◄──────
```

This tag value was received in the corresponding ADDS Deliver from the MSC

Figure 5-6   ADDS Deliver Acknowledge message example

Figure 5-6 shows the decoded ADDS Deliver Acknowledge message summarized in Figure 5-4. This message is formatted and sent by the BSC upon receipt of the layer 2 acknowledgment from the mobile station. Note that the SLS value of 11 and DLR value of 15432236 signifies the transfer of this message from the BSC to the MSC, using the SCCP connection established for the call (mobile m1).

The same Tag value (f3 42 01 07) previously received in the corresponding ADDS Deliver message is echoed in this message. The MSC may use this Tag value to identify which ADDS Deliver message is being acknowledged.

```
**** MESSAGE NUMBER: 00013 ****
*** Start of MTP Level 3 ***
0003 10000011 83
     ----0011    Service Indicator           SCCP
     --00----    Network Priority            priority 0
     10------    Network Indicator           National
0004 (3 bytes)   Destination Point Code      110-44-3
0007 (3 bytes)   Origination Point Code      8-17-92
0010 00001011 0b Signaling Link Selection    11
*** Start of SCCP ***
0011 00000110 06 Data Form 1                 06
0012 (3 bytes)   Dest Local References       15432236
0015 00000000 00 Segment/Reassembling        0
0016 00000001 01 Variable Pointer            01
*** Start of CDG IOS MAP ***
                 SMS Delivery
0017 00010101 15 DTAP Length                 21
0018 00000001 01 DTAP Discriminator          01
0019 00000000 00 DLCI
0020 00010010 12 Length                      18
0021 00000011 03 CC Protocol Discrim         03
0022 00000000 00 Reserved
0023 01010011 53 ADDS Delivery               83
                 **ADDS User Part**
0024 00001110 0e Length                      14
0025 00000011 03 Application Type            SMS
0026 00000010 02 **Application Data Message** 02 04 07 02 ...
0027 00000100 04
0028 00000111 07
0029 00000010 02
```

(Continued)

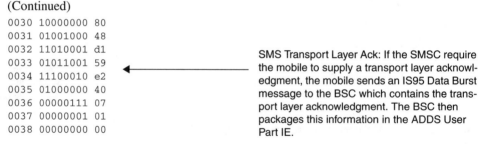

```
0030 10000000 80
0031 01001000 48
0032 11010001 d1
0033 01011001 59
0034 11100010 e2
0035 01000000 40
0036 00000111 07
0037 00000001 01
0038 00000000 00
```

SMS Transport Layer Ack: If the SMSC require
the mobile to supply a transport layer acknowledgment, the mobile sends an IS95 Data Burst
message to the BSC which contains the transport layer acknowledgment. The BSC then
packages this information in the ADDS User
Part IE.

Figure 5-7   ADDS Deliver (as a Transport Layer Ack) message example

Figure 5-7 shows the decoded ADDS Deliver message summarized in Figure 5-4 (event 13). Unlike the example ADDS Deliver message previously described in Figure 5-5, this message is sent from the BSC to the MSC and contains the Transport Layer Acknowledgment requested by the SMS application running on the SMSC. The first octet in the Application Data Message of the ADDS User Part IE has a value of 2, which implies that the data is an SMS Acknowledge Transport Layer message.

5.1.5   Mobile-Terminated Short Message Service in Idle Mode

The procedure for terminating an SMS message to an idle mobile is similar to terminating a message to a mobile in a call. When the MSC first receives a request from the SMSC to deliver an SMS message to a mobile station, it first checks the state of the mobile. If the mobile is not in a call, the MSC packages the received SMS information into an ADDS Page message and sends the message to the BSC over the A-Interface. Like the ADDS Deliver message, the ADDS Page message is used to encapsulate the SMS Point-to-Point Transport Layer message to be sent to the mobile. The BSC, upon receipt of the ADDS Page message, removes the message header information and packages the content of the ADDS User Part parameter into an IS-95 Data Burst message that it then sends to the mobile station on the paging channel.

The MSC requests a layer 2 acknowledgment from the mobile station by including the optional Tag IE in the ADDS Page message. After receiving the ADDS Page message from the MSC, the BSC packages the SMS Point-to-Point Transport Layer message in an IS-95 Data Burst message that is sent over the paging channel to the mobile. After receiving a layer 2 acknowledgment from the mobile, the BSC sends an ADDS Page Acknowledgment to the MSC, which includes the same Tag value previously received in the corresponding ADDS Page message.

An SMS application may request a Transport Layer Acknowledgement from the SMS application running on the mobile station. The Transport Layer Acknowledgment indicates that not only has the message been delivered to the mobile (layer 2 acknowledgment), but also that the SMS application was successful in decoding the message contents. If the originating SMS application requires a Transport Layer Acknowledgment for the message, the mobile station indicates that it successfully received and decoded the SMS message by sending a transport layer acknowledgment using an IS-95 Data Burst message on the access channel. Upon receipt of this access channel message, the BSC packages the SMS message in an ADDS Transfer message that is sent to the MSC. The MSC then sends an acknowledgment to the SMSC.

The message flow for delivery of an SMS message to a mobile station in idle mode is shown in Figure 5-8 and is followed by descriptions of the individual steps.

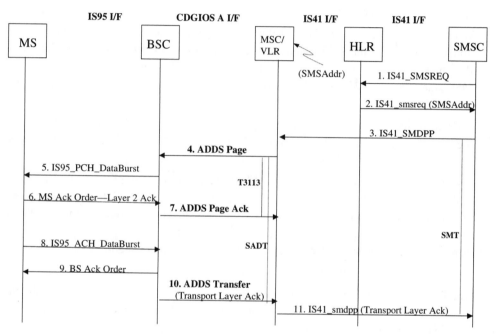

Figure 5-8   Short Message Service in idle mode call flow

1. IS41_SMSREQ (IS-41):

   The SMSC initiates delivery of a mobile-terminated SMS message by sending an IS-41 SMS Request message to the mobile's home HLR, requesting the SMS address to be used to deliver the SMS message. This message includes the identity of the mobile station.

2. IS41_smsreq (IS-41):

   In response to the received IS41_SMSREQ message, the HLR sends an IS41_smsreq return result to the SMSC, specifying the address to be used for the SMS delivery. The address is usually the point code of the VLR/MSC from which the mobile last registered. Other addressing schemes are also allowed and are described in the IS-41 standard [7].

3. IS41_SMDPP (IS-41):

   After receiving the SMS address in the IS41_smsreq return result, the SMSC sends an IS-41 Delivery Point-to-Point (IS41_SMDPP) message, which encapsulates the SMS Transport Layer message in the SMS Bearer Data field, to the specified SMS address. After sending the IS41_SMDPP message, the SMSC starts timer *Short Message Delivery Timer* (SMT), which has a default value of 45 seconds [7]. If the SMSC requires a Transport Layer Acknowledgment, the Bearer Reply Option field in the SMS Point-to-Point Transport Layer message is included. This message also includes the identity of the mobile station.

4. ADDS Page (A-Interface):

When the MSC receives an IS41_SMDPP message, it removes the IS41 header information and repackages the SMS Point-to-Point Transport Layer part in an A-Interface ADDS Page message, which is then sent to the BSC. Upon sending the ADDS Page message, the MSC starts the *Short Message Air Delivery Timer* (SADT) timer. The default SADT timer value is 18 seconds.

If the MSC requires a layer 2 acknowledgment from the mobile, it includes a Tag value in the ADDS Page message. The Tag IE may be used by the MSC to determine which ADDS Page message is being acknowledged.

The decision as to whether to send the ADDS Page message to all the BSCs or the BSC with which the mobile last registered is left up to the MSC vendor. If the MSC requests a layer 2 acknowledgment, it starts timer T3113 immediately after sending the ADDS Page message to the BSC. Upon T3113 expiry, the MSC may retransmit the ADDS Page message to one or more BSCs, depending on MSC vendor implementation.

5. IS95_PCH_DataBurst (IS-95):

The BSC removes the ADDS Page message header information and repackages the SMS Point-to-Point Transport Layer part in an IS-95 Data Burst message that is sent to the mobile over the paging channel.

The maximum length of an SMS message that can be transmitted over the paging channel depends on the BSC configuration. It is, therefore, possible for MSC to request delivery of an SMS message over the paging channel that exceeds the maximum allowed by the BSC. If the MSC includes the Tag IE in such a request, the BSC should send an ADDS Page Acknowledgment to the MSC, indicating a failure by setting the Cause IE to ADDS message too long for delivery.

6. MS_Ack_Order—Layer2 Ack (IS-95):

If the MSC includes the Tag IE in the ADDS Page message, the BSC will request a layer 2 acknowledgement from the mobile in the IS-95 Data Burst message. The mobile acknowledges the received message by sending the BSC a Mobile Station Acknowledgment Order on the access channel.

7. ADDS Page Ack (A-Interface):

Upon receipt of the layer 2 acknowledgment from the mobile, the BSC sends an ADDS Page Acknowledgment to the MSC to confirm the delivery of the SMS message to the mobile. The Tag IE included in this message is set to the same value that was received by the BSC in the corresponding ADDS Page message. The MSC stops timer T3113.

If the BSC is unable to send the SMS message to the mobile due to equipment failure or if the message is too long to fit into the paging channel, the BSC returns the ADDS Page Acknowledgment to the MSC with the appropriate cause values. The MSC stops timer T3113.

If the MSC does not receive an ADDS Page Acknowledgment before T3113 expires, the MSC may retransmit the ADDS Page message a second time and restart timer T3113.

8. IS95_ACH_DataBurst (IS-95):

If an SMS Transport Layer Acknowledgment is requested by the SMS application running on the SMSC, the mobile's SMS application will generate an SMS Acknowledge Transport Layer message and package it in an IS-95 Data Burst message, which is sent to the BSC using the access channel.

9. BS_Ack_Order (IS-95):

The BSC responds to the mobile with an IS-95 Base Station Acknowledgment Order message to confirm receipt of the IS-95 Data Burst message on the access channel.

10. ADDS Transfer (Transport Layer Ack) (A-Interface):

The BSC, upon receipt of the IS-95 Data Burst message, repackages the SMS Acknowledge Transport Layer message into an ADDS Transfer message and sends the message to the MSC. Note that the BSC does not process the Transport Layer message, it simply passes the information to the MSC. The MSC stops timer SADT.

11. IS41_smdpp (Transport Layer Ack) (IS-41):

Upon receiving the ADDS Transfer message containing the Transport Layer Acknowledgement, the MSC repackages the information in an IS41_smdpp message and sends it to the SMSC. The IS41_smdpp return result message is a response to the IS41_SMDPP message received from the SMSC during the initial SMS delivery request.

5.1.6 Mobile-Originated Short Message Service in Idle Mode

The SMS application running on a mobile station may also have the capability of originating SMS messages. If the mobile user wishes to send an SMS while in idle mode, the mobile station sends the BSC an IS-95 Data Burst message encapsulating the SMS data over the access channel. The BSC responds with an IS-95 Base Station Acknowledgment Order message on the paging channel. The BSC then sends an ADDS Transfer message that contains the SMS Point-to-Point Transport Layer message to the MSC. The message flow for a mobile-originated point-to-point SMS message is illustrated in Figure 5-9.

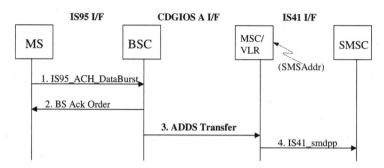

Figure 5-9 Mobile Origination of Short Message Service while mobile is idle

5.1.7 Optimized Mobile-Terminated SMS in Idle Mode

The idea of optimized SMS delivery to an idle mobile is based on the MSC knowing the location of a mobile station and the notion that a Paging Request message is usually shorter than an ADDS Page message.

Because a mobile's location may have changed since last registering, the first step to optimized SMS delivery to an idle mobile involves determining the mobile station's current location. The MSC sends a Paging Request message to the BSC with the service option set to SMS (6 for SMS rate set 1, or 14 for SMS rate set 2). The BSC, depending on vendor implementation, then pages available mobile stations, using all network cells or a subset of cells. After receiving a response from the mobile station, the BSC sends the MSC a Paging Response message over the A-Interface. This message includes a Cell Identifier IE that specifies the location (cell and/or *Location Area Code* [LAC]) of the mobile. At this point, the MSC may choose, depending on the length of the SMS message, to deliver the SMS message over the paging channel or to set up a call and deliver the message over the traffic channel (see Section 5.1.10, "Mobile-Terminated SMS with Service Option 6/14," on page 276). If the MSC determines that the message is small enough to send over the paging channel, the MSC sends the BSC an *SCCP-Connection Refused* (SCCP-CREF) message in response to the previously received Paging Response message.

The MSC next sends an ADDS Page message to the BSC that includes the SMS Point-to-Point Transport Layer part. The ADDS Page message may also contain the optional Cell Identifier List IE, which indicates the cells and location areas that the BSC should use to deliver the message. By using the location received in the Paging Response message, the MSC can optimize the delivery of SMS messages by addressing only relevant cells or location areas. The subsequent messages, namely, the ADDS Page Acknowledgment and ADDS Transfer, are used for layer 2 and Transport Layer acknowledgments. The complete call flow for optimized SMS deliver to an idle mobile is shown in Figure 5-10.

Steps 1–3 are identical to those described for SMS delivery to an idle mobile station (see Section 5.1.5, "Mobile-Terminated Short Message Service in Idle Mode," on page 260).

4. Paging Request (ServOpt 6/14) (A-Interface):

The MSC sends a Paging Request message to the BSC that specifies either Service Option 6 (SMS rate set 1, 9.6kbs) or Service option 14 (SMS rate set 2, 14.4kbps). The MSC starts timer T3113.

5. IS95_PCH_GenPage (IS-95):

The BSC sends the IS-95 General Page over the paging channel to page the mobile.

6. IS95_ACH_PgRsp (IS-95):

The mobile responds with an IS-95 Page Response over the access channel.

7. BS_Ack_Order (IS-95):

The BSC acknowledges the receipt of the Page Response message.

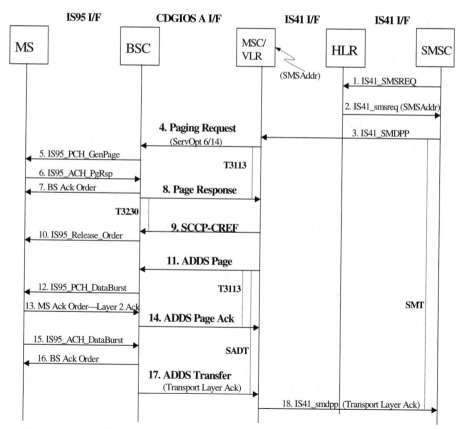

Figure 5-10 Optimized Short Message Service in idle mode call flow

8. Page Response (A-Interface):

The BSC sends the Paging Response message to the MSC with the service option set to SMS. Included in this message is the location (Cell ID or LAC) of the mobile station. The BSC starts timer T3230. The MSC stops timer T3113 upon receipt of the Page Response message.

9. SCCP-CREF (A-Interface):

If the MSC decides that the SMS message should be sent over the paging channel, it sends an SCCP-CREF to release the SCCP connection. At this point, the MSC has knowledge of the cell location of the mobile and can direct the ADDS Page message to the relevant cell location. The BSC stops timer T3230 upon receipt of the SCCP-CREF message.

10. IS95_Release_Order (IS-95):

The BSC sends an IS-95 Release Order to the mobile to release any traffic channel setup.

Stages 11–18 are the same as Stages 4–11 in Section 5.1.5, "Mobile-Terminated Short Message Service in Idle Mode," on page 260.

5.1.8   Short Message Service in Idle Mode Messages

The following sections contain detailed descriptions of the A-Interface messages used in the delivery of SMS to an idle mobile station.

5.1.8.1   ADDS Page

The ADDS Page message is a *Base Station Management Application Part* (BSMAP) message that is sent from the MSC to the BSC whenever an SMS message is to be delivered to an idle mobile. This message is a connectionless *SCCP-Unit Data* (SCCP-UDT) message. The message structure and parameters are shown in Table 5-3.

The Mobile Identity *International Mobile Subscriber Identifier* (IMSI) IE is mandatory and is used by the BSC to identify the mobile station to which the SMS message is delivered.

The ADDS User Part IE contains the SMS Transport Layer message that originated from the SMS bearer service end point. In the case of a mobile-terminated SMS message, the SMS Transport Layer message typically originates from the SMSC.

The Tag IE is used by the MSC to solicit a layer 2 acknowledgment from the mobile, in response to the SMS delivery. When the Tag IE is included, the BSC responds to the ADDS Page message with an ADDS Page Acknowledge message, indicating the receipt of a layer 2 acknowledgment from the mobile. The Tag IE may also be used by the MSC to determine which ADDS Page message is being acknowledged.

The optional Cell Identifier List IE specifies the cells or LACs that the BSC should use to deliver the message. This message parameter may include a location area or a list of cell identifiers, or a combination of both. When this parameter is not included, the BSC flood-pages all of the cells controlled by the BSC.

The optional Slot Cycle Index IE is included whenever slotted paging is being used. When a mobile station registers, the VLR stores the slot cycle being used by the mobile, and the stored value is included in this message to allow the BSC to send the SMS message at a time when the mobile is listening for paging channel messages.

- BSAP Msg Type: BSMAP msg
- SCCP Msg Type: SCCP-UnitData (UDT)
- Direction: BSC ← MSC

Table 5-3   ADDS Page Message (CDGIOS 6.1.7.1)

BitMap	Param IE	#Oct	Range	Type	IOS Ref
0000 0000 (00H) LLLL LLLL	BSMAP header	2	Msg Discrim. = 0 (BSMAP) L = BSMAP msg length	M	6.2.2.1 6.2.2.3
0110 0101 (65H)	Msg Type	1	ADDS Page	M	6.2.2.4
0000 1101 (0DH) LLLL LLLL dddd ittt dddd dddd .... [1111 dddd]	Mobile Identity (IMSI)	8–10	L = 06H–08H (10–15 digits) i = 0/1—even/odd indicator t = 110—IMSI d = IMSI digits	M	6.2.2.16
0011 1101 (3DH) LLLL LLLL rrbb bbbb aaaa aaaa	ADDS User Part	> 2	L = User Part length r = 00 b = 03H for SMS a = Application data (IS-637)	M	6.2.2.67
0011 0011 (33H)	Tag	5	Same as element in Table 5-1, ADDS Deliver msg.	O,C	6.2.2.62
0001 1010 (1AH)	Cell Identifier List	Variable	Same as element in Table 3-5, Paging Request msg.	O,C	6.2.2.21
0011 0101 (35H) rrrr riii	Slot Cycle Index	2	r = 0—reserved i = Slot Cycle Index	O,C	6.2.2.17

5.1.8.2   ADDS Page Acknowledgment

The ADDS Page Acknowledgment message (Table 5-4) is a BSMAP message sent from the BSC to the MSC upon receipt of a layer 2 acknowledgment from the mobile station. The

BSC requests a layer 2 acknowledgment from the mobile if the MSC previously included the Tag IE in the corresponding ADDS Page message.

The mandatory Mobile Identity IMSI and *Electronic Serial Number* (ESN) IEs are both sent in the ADDS Page Acknowledgment message. Note that because the ADDS Page and ADDS Page Acknowledgment messages are connectionless SCCP-UDT messages, no connection references are available to identify the mobile. Instead, the IMSI and ESN values are used to identify uniquely which mobile the message is intended for.

The Tag value included in the ADDS Page Acknowledgment is set to the same value previously received in the ADDS Page message.

The Cause IE in this message is used to specify the reason for a layer 2 acknowledgment failure.

The Cell Identifier IE is a required parameter used to indicate to the MSC the location of the mobile that responded to the previously transmitted ADDS Page message.

- BSAP Message Type: BSMAP
- SCCP Message Type: SCCP-Unit Data (UDT)
- Direction: BSC → MSC

Table 5-4   ADDS Page Acknowledgment Message (CDGIOS 6.1.7.4)

BitMap	Param IE	#Oct	Range	Type	IOS Ref
0000 0000 (00H) LLLL LLLL	BSMAP header	2	Msg Discrim. = 0 (BSMAP) L = BSMAP msg length	M	6.2.2.1 6.2.2.3
0110 0110 (66H)	Msg Type	1	ADDS Page Ack	M	6.2.2.4
0000 1101 (0DH)	Mobile Identity (IMSI)	8–10	Same as element in Table 5-3, ADDS Page message.	M	6.2.2.16
0011 0011 (33H)	Tag	5	Same as element in Table 5-1, ADDS Deliver msg.	O,C	6.2.2.62
0000 1101 (0DH)	Mobile Identity (ESN)	7	Same as element in Table 3-2, CM Service Request msg.	O,R	6.2.2.16

Table 5-4   ADDS Page Acknowledgment Message (CDGIOS 6.1.7.4) (Continued)

BitMap	Param IE	#Oct	Range	Type	IOS Ref
0000 0100 (04H) LLLL LLLL 0ccc cccc	Cause	3	L = 01H, c = 71H, 20H 20H—equipment failure 71H—ADDS Msg too long	O,C	6.2.2.19
0000 0101 (05H)	Cell Identifier	5 or 7	Same as element in Table 3-1, Complete L3 Information msg.	O,R	6.2.2.20

5.1.8.3   ADDS Transfer

This BSMAP message is sent from the BSC to the MSC whenever an idle mobile station originates an SMS message, encapsulating the SMS Point-to-Point Transport Layer information. The ADDS Transfer message is also used for encapsulating an SMS Acknowledge Transport Layer message when a Transport Layer Acknowledgment is requested of the SMS application running on the mobile station (Table 5-5).

The mandatory Mobile Identity IMSI and ESN IEs are used for identifying the mobile from which the SMS message originated.

The mandatory ADDS User Part IE contains either an SMS Point-to-Point or SMS Acknowledge Transport Layer message, depending on whether the ADDS Transfer was initiated by a mobile-originated SMS delivery or in response to a previously received ADDS Page message requesting a Transport Layer Acknowledgment.

The optional authentication parameters AUTHR, RANDC, COUNT, and RAND are included only when authentication is enabled. A detailed discussion of authentication procedures is presented in Section 6.1, "Authentication Overview," on page 346.

The Cell Identifier IE is a required parameter used to indicate to the MSC the location of the mobile station.

- BSAP Message Type: BSMAP
- SCCP Message Type: SCCP-Unit Data (UDT)
- Direction: BSC → MSC

Table 5-5   ADDS Transfer Message (CDGIOS 6.1.7.2)

BitMap	Param IE	#Oct	Range	Type	IOS Ref
0000 0000 (00H) LLLL LLLL	BSMAP header	2	Msg Discrim. = 0 (BSMAP) L = BSMAP msg length	M	6.2.2.1 6.2.2.3
0110 0111 (67H)	Msg Type	1	ADDS Transfer	M	6.2.2.4
0000 1101 (0DH)	Mobile Identity (IMSI)	8–10	Same as element in Table 5-3, ADDS Page message.	M	6.2.2.16
0011 1101 (3DH)	ADDS User Part	> 2	Same as element in Table 5-3, ADDS Page message.	M	6.2.2.67
0000 1101 (0DH)	Mobile Identity (ESN)	7	Same as element in Table 3-2, CM Service Request msg.	O,R	6.2.2.16
0100 0010 (42H)	Auth Response Parameter (AUTHR)	6	Same as element in Table 3-2, CM Service Request msg.	O,C	6.2.2.46
0010 1000 (28H)	Auth Confirmation Parameter (RANDC)	2	Same as element in Table 3-2, CM Service Request msg.	O,C	6.2.2.42
0100 0000 (40H)	Auth Parameter COUNT	2	Same as element in Table 3-2, CM Service Request msg.	O,C	6.2.2.47
0100 0001 (41H)	Auth Challenge Parameter (RAND)	7	Same as element in Table 3-2, CM Service Request msg.	O,C	6.2.2.45
0100 1010 (4AH)	Authentication Event	3	Same as element in Table 3-2, CM Service Request msg.	O,C	6.2.2.114
0000 0101 (05H)	Cell Identifier	5 or 7	Same as element in Table 3-1, Complete L3 Info msg.	O,R	6.2.2.20

5.1.9   Optimized Mobile-Terminated SMS in Idle Mode Example

Figure 5-11 shows a practical example of a summary message call flow for an optimized SMS delivery in an idle mobile station. The purpose of Figure 5-11 is to present an overview of the messages exchanged between the BSC and MSC. Subsequent figures illustrate the complete content of the messages, presented in a decoded message format similar to what would be seen on test equipment monitoring the A-Interface signaling link.

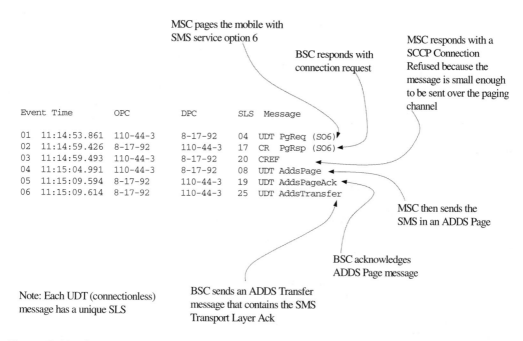

Figure 5-11   Optimized Short Message Service in idle mode example call flow

In the example shown in Figure 5-11, the MSC first requests the BSC to page the desired mobile station with SMS Service Option 6. After the mobile responds with an IS-95 Page Response, the BSC sends a Paging Response to the MSC over the A-Interface that includes the location of the mobile station. Because, in this example, the SMS message is determined by the MSC to be short enough to be sent on the paging channel, the MSC releases the SCCP connection by sending an SCCP-CREF message to the BSC. The MSC follows the SCCP-CREF message with an ADDS Page message, prompting the BSC to send the SMS message to the mobile station, using the paging channel. The BSC requests a layer 2 acknowledgment from the mobile station because the Tag IE was included in the ADDS Page message received from the MSC. Upon receipt of the layer 2 acknowledgment from the mobile, the BSC sends an ADDS Page Acknowledge message. In addition to the layer 2 acknowledgment, the mobile station also sends an IS-95 Data Burst message on the access channel that contains the requested Transport Layer

Acknowledgment. The BSC packages the acknowledgment and sends it to the MSC in an ADDS Transfer message.

As shown in Figure 5-11, the ADDS Page, ADDS Page Acknowledge, and ADDS Transfer messages are all connectionless SCCP-UDT messages that use different SLS values. In these examples, the BSC's point code is 8-17-92, and the MSC's point code is 110-44-3.

```
**** MESSAGE NUMBER: 00004 ****
*** Start of MTP Level 3 ***
0003 10000011 83
     ----0011    Service Indicator         SCCP
     --00----    Network Priority          priority 0
     10------    Network Indicator         National
0004 (3 bytes)   Destination Point Code    8-17-92
0007 (3 bytes)   Origination Point Code    110-44-3
0010 00001000 08 Signaling Link Selection  8
*** Start of SCCP ***
0011 00001001 09 Unitdata 09
0012 00000000 00 Protocol Class            Class 0
0013 00000011 03 Called Party Address      Offset 0016
0014 00000101 05 Calling Party Address     Offset 0019
0015 00001010 0a Data Portion Pointer      Offset 0025
0016 00000010 02 Called Party Addr Length  2
0017 11000001 c1
     -------1    Subsys Number Indicator   Included
     ------0-    Point Code Indicator      Excluded
     --0000--    Global Title indicator    No GTT included
     -1------    Routing indicator         route by DPC/SSN
     1-------    Reserved for National use
0018 11111100 fc Subsystem Number          252
0019 00000101 05 Calling Party Addr Length 5
0020 11000011 c3
     -------1    Subsys Number Indicator   Included
     ------1-    Point Code Indicator      Included
     --0000--    Global Title indicator    No GTT included
     -1------    Routing indicator         route by DPC/SSN
     1-------    Reserved for National use
0021 11111100 fc Subsystem Number          252
0022 (3 bytes)   Signaling Point Code      110-44-3
*** Start of CDGIOS MAP ***
                 SMS Page
0025 00111001 39 Data Length               57
0026 00000000 00 BSMAP Discriminator       00
0027 00110111 37 BSMAP Length              55
0028 01100101 65 ADDS Page                 101
0029 00001101 0d Mobile Identity           13
0030 00001000 08 Length                    8
0031 00111110 3e
     -----110    Type of Identity          IMSI
     ----1---    Odd/Even Indicator        odd
     0011----    IMSI Identity Digits      310006197889514
0032 (7 bytes)
```

(Continued)

```
0039 00111101 3d ADDS User Part          61
0040 00100000 20 Length                  32
0041 00000011 03 Application Type        SMS
0042 00000000 00 Application Data        00 00 02 10 ...
0043 00000000 00
........
0071 00110011 33 Tag                     51                    Tag value to be
0072 (4 bytes)    Tag Value              53 40 00 08  ◄──── included by the BSC
0076 00011010 1a Cell Identifier List    26                    in the ADDS Page
0077 00000011 03 Length                  3                     Ack after it receives
0078 00000010 02 Cell Identifier Discrim CI Only              a layer 2 Ack from
0079 (2 bytes)    CI Value               11 43                 the mobile
0081 00110101 35 Slot Cycle Index        53
0082 00000010 02 Value                   2
```

Figure 5-12 ADDS Page message example

Figure 5-12 shows the decoded ADDS Page. The decoded message is similar to what may be seen on test equipment monitoring the A-Interface during an SMS message delivery to an idle mobile.

Unlike the previously described ADDS Deliver message, the ADDS Page message is a connectionless SCCP-UDT message and does not require an SCCP connection. Because no SCCP connection reference is available, the Mobile Identity IMSI is included in this message to identify the terminating mobile.

The ADDS User Part IE in this example contains the SMS Point-to-Point Transport Layer message to be delivered to the idle mobile station. The SMS Transport Layer message format is specified in IS-637 and described in Appendix Section 5.A, "Short Message Service Protocol Overview," on page 325. Note that the first octet in the Application Data Message of the ADDS User Part has a value of zero, which indicates that the data corresponds to an SMS Point-to-Point Transport Layer message.

A Tag IE with a value of *53 40 00 08* is included in the example ADDS Page message to solicit a layer 2 acknowledgment from the mobile station.

The ADDS Page also may contain information about how the MSC should page the mobile. In this example, both the mobile station's location and Slot Cycle Index are specified in the Cell Identifier List and Slot Cycle Index IEs.

```
**** MESSAGE NUMBER: 00005 ****
*** Start of MTP Level 3 ***
0003 10000011 83
     ----0011    Service Indicator        SCCP
     --00----    Network Priority         priority 0
     10------    Network Indicator        National
0004 (3 bytes)   Destination Point Code   110-44-3
0007 (3 bytes)   Origination Point Code   8-17-92
0010 00010011 13 Signaling Link Selection 19
*** Start of SCCP ***
```

(Continued)
```
0011 00001001 09 Unitdata                           09
0012 00000000 00 Protocol Class                     Class 0
0013 00000011 03 Called Party Address               Offset 0016
0014 00001000 08 Calling Party Address              Offset 0022
0015 00001101 0d Data Portion Pointer               Offset 0028
0016 00000101 05 Called Party Addr Length           5
0017 11000011 c3 Called Party Addr Ind
0018 11111100 fc Subsystem Number                   252
0019 (3 bytes)    Signaling Point Code              110-44-3
0022 00000101 05 Calling Party Addr Length          5
0023 11000011 c3 Calling Party Addr Ind
0024 11111100 fc Subsystem Number                   252
0025 (3 bytes)    Signaling Point Code              8-17-92
*** Start of CDGIOS MAP ***
                  SMS Page Ack
0028 00011110 1e Data Length                        30
0029 00000000 00 BSMAP Discriminator                00
0030 00011100 1c BSMAP Length                       28
0031 01100110 66 SMS Page Ack                       102
0032 00001101 0d Mobile Identity                    13
0033 00001000 08 Length                             8
0034 00111110 3e
     -----110     Type of Identity                  IMSI
     ----1---     Odd/Even Indicator                odd
     0011----     IMSI Identity Digits              310006197889514
0035 (7 bytes)
0042 00110011 33 Tag                                51
0043 (4 bytes)    Tag Value                         53 40 00 08  ◄──── Tag matches ADDS
0047 00001101 0d Mobile Identity (ESN)              13                 Page sent by MSC
0048 00000101 05 Length                             5
0049 00000101 05
     -----101     Type of Identity                  ESN
     ----0---     Odd/Even Indicator                even
     0000----     Fixed                             00
0050 (4 bytes)    ESN Identity Digits               9f 1c 47 a3
0054 00000101 05 Cell Identifier                    05
0055 00000011 03 Length
0056 00000010 02 Cell Discriminator                 Cell ID only
0057 00010001 11 Cell ID                            1143H
0058 01000011 43
```

Figure 5-13   ADDS Page Acknowledgment message example

Figure 5-13 shows the decoded ADDS Page Acknowledgment message. This message is formatted and sent by the BSC upon receipt of the layer 2 acknowledgment from the mobile.

Because this message is a connectionless SCCP-UDT Message, the mandatory Mobility Identity IMSI and required ESN IEs are required.

The same Tag value (53 40 00 08) previously received in the ADDS Page message is echoed in this message.

The ADDS Page Acknowledgment message also contains the Cell Identifier IE, which provides the MSC with information about the mobile station's location.

```
**** MESSAGE NUMBER: 00006 ****
*** Start of MTP Level 3 ***
0003 10000011 83
     ----0011    Service Indicator        SCCP
     --00----    Network Priority         priority 0
     10------    Network Indicator        National
0004 (3 bytes)   Destination Point Code   110-44-3
0007 (3 bytes)   Origination Point Code   8-17-92
0010 00011001 19 Signaling Link Selection 25
*** Start of SCCP ***
0011 00001001 09 Unitdata                 09
0012 00000000 00 Protocol Class           Class 0
0013 00000011 03 Called Party Address     Offset 0016
0014 00001000 08 Calling Party Address    Offset 0022
0015 00001101 0d Data Portion Pointer     Offset 0028
0016 00000101 05 Called Party Addr Length 5
0017 11000011 c3 Called Party Addr Ind
0018 11111100 fc Subsystem Number         252
0019 (3 bytes)   Signaling Point Code     110-44-3
0022 00000101 05 Calling Party Addr Length 5
0023 11000011 c3 Calling Party Addr Ind
0024 11111100 fc Subsystem Number         252
0025 (3 bytes)   Signaling Point Code     8-17-92
*** Start of CDGIOS MAP ***
                 ADDS Transfer
0028 00101001 29 Data Length              41
0029 00000000 00 BSMAP Discriminator      00
0030 00100111 27 BSMAP Length             39
0031 01100111 67 ADDS Transfer            103
0032 00001101 0d Mobile Identity          13
0033 00001000 08 Length                   8
0034 00111110 3e
     -----110    Type of Identity         IMSI
     ----1---    Odd/Even Indicator       odd
     0011----    IMSI Identity Digits     310006197889514
0035 (7 bytes)
0042 00111101 3d ADDS User Part           61
0043 00001110 0e Length                   14
0044 00000011 03 Application Type         SMS
0045 00000010 02 Application Data         02 04 07 02 ...
0046 00000100 04
0047 00000111 07
0048 00000010 02
0049 10000000 80
0050 01001000 48
0051 11010001 d1
0052 01011001 59
0053 11100010 e2
0054 01000000 40
```

(Continued)

```
0055 00000111 07
0056 00000001 01
0057 00000000 00
0058 00001101 0d Mobile Identity (ESN)      13
0059 00000101 05 Length                     5
0060 00000101 05
     -----101     Type of Identity          ESN
     ----0---     Odd/Even Indicator        even
     0000----     Fixed                     00
0061 (4 bytes)    ESN Identity Digits       9f 1c 47 a3
0065 00000101 05 Cell Identifier            05
0066 00000011 03 Length
0067 00000010 02 Cell Discriminator         Cell ID only
0068 00010001 11
0069 01000011 43
```

Figure 5-14   ADDS Transfer (as a Transport Layer Ack) message example

Figure 5-14 shows the decoded ADDS Transfer message. This message is sent from the BSC to the MSC and contains the Transport Layer Acknowledgment requested by the SMS application running on the SMSC. The first octet in the Application Data Message of the ADDS User Part IE has a value of 2, which implies that the data is an SMS Acknowledge Transport Layer message.

The ADDS Transfer message also contains the mandatory Mobile Identity IMSI IE and the required ESN and Cell Identifier IEs. Note that, in this example, none of the optional Authentication parameters are included.

5.1.10 Mobile-Terminated SMS with Service Option 6/14

Limitations regarding the maximum length of an SMS message that can be delivered over the paging channel make it sometimes necessary to bring a mobile station into the traffic state before delivering the message over the traffic channel. Service Options 6 (SMS rate set 1, 9.6 kbps) and 14 (SMS rate set 2, 14.4 kbps) are both used for this purpose. The complete call flow for a Service Option 6/14 call is shown in Figure 5-15. Because the majority of steps in the call flow are very similar to previously discussed scenarios, the discussion in this section focuses only on the unique aspects of a Service Option 6/14 call.

The SMS delivery starts with the MSC sending a Paging Request message to the BSC with the Service Option IE set to 6 or 14. After receiving a response from the mobile station, the BSC sends the MSC a Paging Response message over the A-Interface. At this point, the MSC may choose, depending on the length of the SMS message, to deliver the SMS message over the paging channel (discussed in Section 5.1.5, "Mobile-Terminated Short Message Service in Idle Mode," on page 260) or to set up a call and deliver the message over the traffic channel. If the MSC chooses to deliver the SMS message over the traffic channel, it sends an *SCCP-Connection Confirm* (SCCP-CC) message to the BSC, followed by an Assignment Request. Note that no

Circuit Identity Code (CIC) is necessary in the Assignment Request because the SMS delivery occurs using traffic channel signaling frames, and no voice frames are exchanged. The BSC replies with an Assignment Complete after successfully setting up the call. The mobile, triggered by the request Service Option of 6 or 14, automatically sends an IS-95 Service Connect message to the BSC, which prompts the BSC to send a Connect message across the A-Interface. At this point the mobile is in the traffic state and the pending SMS message can be delivered to the mobile using the ADDS Deliver message. The MSC initiates clearing the call after successful delivery of the SMS message.

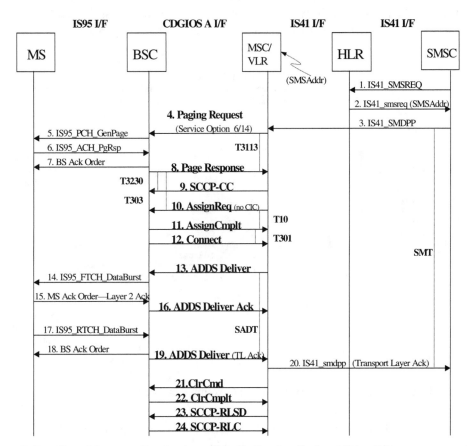

Figure 5-15 Short Message Service in traffic with Service Option 6/14 call flow

5.1.11 Mobile-Terminated SMS with Service Option 6 Example

Figure 5-16 shows an example summary message call flow for a mobile-terminated SMS delivery using Service Option 6. In this example, the BSC's point code is 8-17-92, and the MSC's point code is 110-44-3.

The Service Option 6 SMS delivery example begins when the MSC is requested to send an SMS message to an idle mobile that it determines is too long for the paging channel. The MSC then initiates a call setup with Service Option 6 so that the SMS message can be delivered using the traffic channel.

There are three distinct stages in the call flow example shown in Figure 5-16. First, the mobile is put into the traffic channel using a normal mobile-terminated call setup procedure. The main difference from a voice call setup is that the Service Option IE in the Paging Request, Paging Response, Assignment Request, and Assignment Complete is set to 6. Secondly, the Assignment Request message contains no CIC value because only traffic channel signaling information is used to send the message. Thirdly, the value of the Signal IE in the Assignment Request message is set to "Alerting Off" because no mobile user intervention is required.

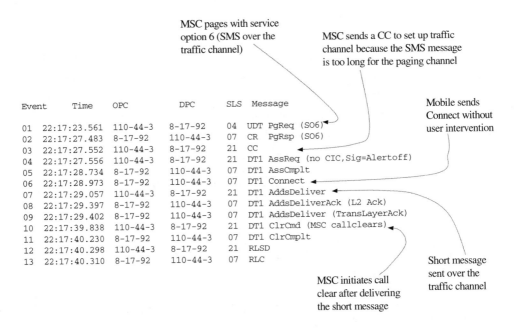

Figure 5-16   SMS in traffic with Service Option 6 example call flow

Once the call is set up, the MSC sends an ADDS Deliver message to the BSC, which is no different than a normal SMS delivery to a mobile in a call. After delivering the SMS message successfully, the MSC initiates call clearing.

Because the ADDS Deliver and ADDS Deliver Acknowledge messages are similar to those as presented in the example in Section 5.1.4, "Mobile-Terminated SMS in Traffic Example," on page 255, the only decoded message shown for this example is the Assignment Request.

Figure 5-17 illustrates a typical Assignment Request message used in a Service Option 6 or 14 call setup. Unlike a normal voice call setup, the example message contains no CIC value, and the Signal IE value is set to "Alerting Off" to prevent ringing at the mobile station.

```
**** MESSAGE NUMBER: 00004 ****
*** Start of CDGIOS MAP ***
                       Assignment Request
0017 00001110 0e Data Length                   14
0018 00000000 00 BSMAP Discriminator           00
0019 00001100 0c BSMAP Length                  12
0020 00000001 01 Assignment Request            01
0021 00001011 0b Channel Type                  11
0022 00000011 03 Length                        3
0023 00000001 01 Speech or Data Indicator      Speech
0024 00001000 08 Channel Rate and Type         Full rate TCH Channel Bm
0025 00000101 05 Speech Encoding Algorithm     13 Kb/s vocoder
0026 00000011 03 Service Option                3
0027 (2 bytes)   Service Type                  6 - SMS Rate Set1
0029 00110100 34 Signal                        52
0030 01001111 4f Signal Value                  Alerting Off
0031 00000000 00 Alert Pitch                   Medium pitch
```

Figure 5-17   Assignment Request (for Service Option 6) message example

5.1.12 ADDS Messages Error Handling

When a mobile rejects an ADDS Page or ADDS Deliver message, it sends an IS-95 Reject Order to the BSC. This may occur, for example, if a mobile does not support SMS and it receives an IS-95 Data Burst message that contains an SMS message. Upon receiving the IS-95 Reject Order, the BSC sends a rejection message over the A-Interface to the MSC to inform the MSC of the failed delivery.

Figure 5-18 shows the call flow for handling an ADDS Page/Deliver when the mobile rejects the IS-95 Data Burst message. Stages 1 through 3 pertain to the previously discussed IS-41 SMS Delivery Point-to-Point messages being delivered to the MSC from the SMSC.

4. ADDS Page/ADDS Deliver (A-Interface):

The MSC sends the SMS message to the BSC, using either an ADDS Page or ADDS Deliver message, depending on whether the mobile is in a call.

5. IS95_DataBurst (IS-95):

The BSC sends the mobile the SMS message using an IS-95 Data Burst message.

6. IS95_Reject_Order (IS-95):

The mobile station rejects the IS-95 Data Burst message and sends the BSC an IS-95 Reject Order message.

The IS-95 Reject Order message contains a *Rejection Order Qualification Code* (ORDQ) field that is used to indicate the reason the mobile rejected the message. For example, if the mobile station does not support SMS, the ORDQ field of the Reject Order will be set to 6, specifying that the rejected message requires a capability not supported by the mobile station.

7. Rejection Message (A-Interface):

The BSC, upon receipt of the IS-95 Reject Order message, sends an A-Interface Rejection message to the MSC that includes the cause value parameters received from the mobile station in the IS-95 Reject Order message.

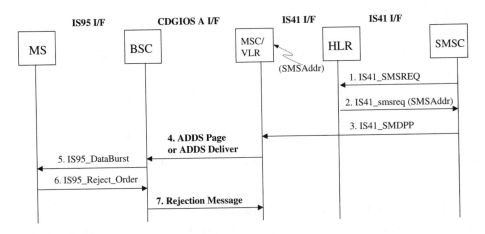

Figure 5-18 ADDS Messages Error Handling call flow

Because the ADDS Page and ADDS Deliver messages are used not only for SMS, the call flow shown in Figure 5-18 applies to the general rejection error case. *Over-the-Air Service Provisioning* (OTASP) is an example of another feature that also uses the ADDS Deliver message and may result in a Rejection message.

The A-Interface Rejection message may be coded as a BSMAP or DTAP message, depending on whether the mobile station is in a call. Table 5-6 shows the BSMAP format used for the Rejection message when a mobile is idle. The message is sent as a connectionless SCCP-UDT message and contains the mobile station's IMSI and ESN, which are required to identify the mobile. The Rejection message also contains an IS-95 Cause IE that contains the same cause value provided to the BSC in the IS-95 Reject Order message sent by the mobile station.

- BSAP Message Type: BSMAP
- SCCP Message Type: SCCP-Unit Data (UDT)
- Direction: BSC → MSC

Table 5-6 Rejection BSMAP Message (CDGIOS 6.1.8.1)

BitMap	Param IE	#Oct	Range	Type	IOS Ref
0000 0000 (00H) LLLL LLLL	BSMAP header	2	Msg Discrim. = 0 (BSMAP) L = BSMAP msg length	M	6.2.2.1 6.2.2.3
0101 0110 (56H)	Msg Type	1	Rejection	M	6.2.2.4
0000 1101 (0DH)	Mobile Identity (IMSI)	8–10	Same as element in Table 5-3, ADDS Page message.	O,R	6.2.2.16
0000 1101 (0DH)	Mobile Identity (ESN)	7	Same as element in Table 3-2, CM Service Request msg.	O,R	6.2.2.16
0110 0010 (62H) LLLL LLLL cccc cccc	IS-95 Cause Value	3	L = 01H, c = IS-95 Reject Order Qualification Code (ORDQ) 01H—unspecified 02H—msg not accepted in state 03H—msg struct not accepted 04H—msg field not valid range 05H—msg type or order code not understood 06H—capability not supp by MS 07H—msg cannot be handled by current MS config	O,R	6.2.2.110

When an IS-95 Reject Order is received from a mobile currently in a call, the BSC sends a DTAP Rejection message to the MSC. The message format for the *SCCP-Data Form 1* (SCCP-DT1) message is show in Table 5-7. Because this message refers to an existing SCCP connection, the mobile's IMSI and ESN are not required. The DTAP Rejection message simply contains the IS-95 Cause Value IE, which contains the same cause value provided to the BSC in the IS-95 Reject Order message sent by the mobile station.

- BSAP Message Type: DTAP
- SCCP Message Type: SCCP-Data Form 1 (DT1)
- Direction: BSC → MSC

Table 5-7   Rejection DTAP Message (CDGIOS 6.1.8.1)

BitMap	Param IE	#Oct	Range	Type	IOS Ref
0000 0001 (01H) ccrr rsss LLLL LLLL	DTAP header	3	Msg Discrim. = 1 (DTAP) DLCI = "ccrr rsss" = 0 L = DTAP msg length	M	6.2.2.1 6.2.2.2 6.2.2.3
rrrr 0011 (03H)	Protocol Discriminator	1	0011—Call Processing r = 0—reserved	M	6.2.2.39
0000 0000 (00H)	Reserved Bits	1		M	6.2.2.40
0101 0110 (56H)	Msg Type	1	Rejection	M	6.2.2.4
0110 0010 (62H) LLLL LLLL cccc cccc	IS95 Cause Value	3	L = 01H, c = IS-95 Reject Order Qualification Code (ORDQ) 01H—unspecified 02H—msg not accepted in state 03H—msg struct not accepted 04H—msg field not valid range 05H—msg type or order code not understood 06H—capability not supp by MS 07H—msg cannot be handled by current MS config	O,R	6.2.2.110

5.2 Message Waiting Indication

Depending on network configuration, see Figure 5-1, a CDMA wireless network may notify mobile subscribers of voice mail through the use of SMS messages or *Message Waiting Indication* (MWI). If the *Voice Mail Service* (VMS) entity uses the SMSC to notify mobile subscribers of pending voice mail, a *Voice Mail Notification* (VMN) Teleservice SMS message is sent to the mobile from the SMSC. In this case, after a message has been recorded for a mobile subscriber, the VMS center notifies the SMSC of the message. The SMSC then formats and sends an SMS message to the MSC, which then delivers the notification to the mobile's SMS application.

A second method of message waiting notification, referred to as MWI, utilizes a non-standardized direct interface between the VMS and the MSC. The number of messages waiting for a mobile subscriber is sent from the VMS entity to the MSC, which then requests the BSC to notify the mobile station of the pending voice mail messages over the A-Interface. Depending on whether a mobile station is in a call, the MSC requests the BSC to notify the mobile station by sending either a Feature Notification or a *Flash With Information* (FWI) A-Interface message.

5.2.1   MWI Delivery in Idle Mode Call Flow

When a voice mail is received for a mobile subscriber at the VMS, a VMN is sent to the MSC, indicating the number of pending voice mail messages for the subscriber. If the mobile is idle, the MSC packages this information in an A-Interface Feature Notification message and sends it to the BSC. Upon receipt of the Feature Notification message, the BSC generates an IS-95 Feature Notification message and sends it to the mobile using the paging channel. If a layer 2 acknowledgment is required, the mobile station responds with a Mobile Station Acknowledgment Order on the access channel. The BSC then sends a Feature Notification Acknowledgment message to the MSC, indicating the successful delivery of the MWI.

Figure 5-19 illustrates the call flow for a MWI delivery to an idle mobile, followed by descriptions of the individual steps.

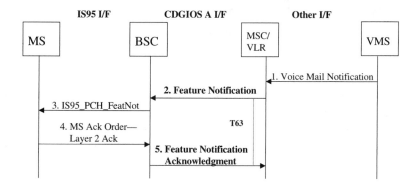

Figure 5-19   Message Waiting Indication in idle mode call flow

1. Voice Mail Notification (VMS–MSC Interface):

   The VMS sends a VMN to the MSC. The VMN specifies the mobile station and the number of unread messages. It may also contain the calling party number of the person who left the voice mail message.

2. Feature Notification (A-Interface):

   The MSC sends a Feature Notification message to the BSC that encapsulates the VMN feature parameters received from the VMS. Because the mobile is idle and no SCCP connection exists, the Mobile Identity (IMSI) IE and Cell Identifier List IE are required by the BSC to identify and page the desired mobile station.

If the MSC requires a layer 2 acknowledgment from the mobile station, it includes the Tag IE in the Feature Notification message sent to the BSC. The MSC starts timer T63. Upon expiry of T63, the MSC may resend the Feature Notification message.

3. IS95_PCH_FeatNot (IS-95):

The BSC packages the information received from the MSC and sends an IS-95 Feature Notification message to the mobile on the paging channel. This message contains information such as the number of messages waiting and how the mobile subscriber should be alerted.

4. MS Ack Order—Layer2 Ack (IS-95):

The mobile station acknowledges the IS-95 Feature Notification by sending an Mobile Station Acknowledgment Order on the access channel. This is required if the Tag IE is included in the A-Interface Feature Notification message sent by the MSC.

5. Feature Notification Acknowledgment (A-Interface):

The BSC, upon receipt of the layer 2 acknowledgment, sends a Feature Notification Acknowledgment message to the MSC. The Tag value included in this message is the same value that was received from the MSC in the Feature Notification message.

5.2.2 MWI in Idle Mode Messages

The following sections contain detailed descriptions of the A-Interface messages used for MWI to an idle mobile station.

5.2.2.1 Feature Notification

The Feature Notification message is a BSMAP message that may be sent from the MSC to the BSC whenever the VMS sends a voice mail MWI message to the MSC. The message contains information about the identity of the mobile and how the mobile should be paged, and specifies how the mobile station should alert the user. This message is a connectionless SCCP-UDT message.

The Mobile Identity IMSI IE is mandatory and is used by the BSC to identify the mobile to which the SMS message is to be delivered.

The Tag IE is used by the MSC to solicit a layer 2 acknowledgment from the mobile in response to the message notification. When the Tag IE is included, the BSC responds to the Feature Notification message with a Feature Notification Acknowledge message, indicating the receipt of a layer 2 acknowledgment from the mobile. The Tag IE may also be used by the MSC to reference which Feature Notification message is being acknowledged.

The optional Cell Identifier List IE specifies the cells or location area that the BSC should use to deliver the message. This message parameter may include a location area or a list of cell identifiers, or a combination of both. When this IE is not included, the BSC will flood-page all of the cells controlled by the BSC.

The optional Slot Cycle Index IE is included whenever slotted paging is being used. When a mobile station registers, the VLR stores the slot cycle being used by the mobile, and the MSC includes this parameter to allow the BSC to send the IS-95 Feature Notification message at a time when the mobile is listening for paging channel messages.

The optional Signal IE specifies the alerting type that the mobile station should use for the Feature Notification.

The optional MWI IE specifies the number of messages waiting at the VMS for the mobile subscriber.

The optional Calling Party ASCII Number IE may be used to indicate the callback number of the person who deposited the message at the VMS.

Note that the use of the Signal IE, MWI IE, and Calling Party ASCII Number IE are all vendor implementation-specific.

The optional IS-95 Information Records parameter can be used to send IS-95 information records to the mobile station. Examples include Display, Called Party Number, Calling Party Number, Signal, and Message Waiting. This parameter should not carry redundant information included in other parameters, such as Signal and Calling Party ASCII Number.

- BSAP Message Type: BSMAP
- SCCP Message Type: SCCP-Unit Data (UDT)
- Direction: BSC ← MSC

Table 5-8   Feature Notification Message (CDGIOS 6.1.3.9)

BitMap	Param IE	#Oct	Range	Type	IOS Ref
0000 0000 (00H) LLLL LLLL	BSMAP header	2	Msg Discrim. = 0 (BSMAP) L = BSMAP msg length	M	6.2.2.1 6.2.2.3
0110 0000 (60H)	Msg Type	1	Feature Notification	M	6.2.2.4
0000 1101 (0DH)	Mobile Identity (IMSI)	8–10	Same as element in Table 5-3, ADDS Page message.	M	6.2.2.16
0011 0011 (33H)	Tag	5	Same as element in Table 5-1, ADDS Deliver msg.	O,C	6.2.2.62
0001 1010 (1AH)	Cell Identifier List	Variable	Same as element in Table 3-5, Paging Request msg.	O,C	6.2.2.21
0011 0101 (35H) rrrr riii	Slot Cycle Index	2	r = 0—reserved i = Slot Cycle Index	O,C	6.2.2.17

Table 5-8   Feature Notification Message (CDGIOS 6.1.3.9) (Continued)

BitMap	Param IE	#Oct	Range	Type	IOS Ref
0011 0100 (34H) SSSS SSSS rrrr rrPP	Signal	3	S = IS-95 Signal value P = pitch, r = 0—reserved	O,C	6.2.2.50
0011 1000 (38H) wwww wwww	Message Waiting Indication	2	w = 00H–FFH Number of msgs at VMS	O,C	6.2.2.48
0100 1011 (4BH)	Calling Party ASCII Number	Variable	Same as element in Table 3-3, Assignment Request msg.	O,C	6.2.2.37
0001 0101 (15H)	IS-95 Info Records	Variable	Same as element in Table 3-3, Assignment Request msg.	O,C	6.2.2.72

5.2.2.2   Feature Notification Acknowledgment

This message is sent by the BSC to indicate that it has received a layer 2 acknowledgment from the mobile station.

Because the Feature Notification Acknowledgment message is a SCCP connectionless UDT message, the mandatory IMSI IE is necessary to identify the mobile station sending the layer 2 acknowledgment.

The Tag IE contains the same Tag value included in the corresponding Feature Notification message received from the MSC.

- BSAP Message Type: BSMAP
- SCCP Message Type: SCCP-Unit Data (UDT)
- Direction: BSC → MSC

Table 5-9   Feature Notification Ack Message (CDGIOS 6.1.3.10)

BitMap	Param IE	#Oct	Range	Type	IOS Ref
0000 0000 (00H) LLLL LLLL	BSMAP header	2	Msg Discrim. = 0 (BSMAP) L = BSMAP msg length	M	6.2.2.1 6.2.2.3
0110 0001 (61H)	Msg Type	1	Feature Notification Ack	M	6.2.2.4

Table 5-9 Feature Notification Ack Message (CDGIOS 6.1.3.10) (Continued)

BitMap	Param IE	#Oct	Range	Type	IOS Ref
0000 1101 (0DH)	Mobile Identity (IMSI)	8–10	Same as element in Table 5-3, ADDS Page message.	M	6.2.2.16
0011 0011 (33H)	Tag	5	Same as element in Table 5-1, ADDS Deliver msg.	O,C	6.2.2.62

5.2.3   MWI Delivery in Idle Mode Example Call Flow

Figure 5-20 shows a summary message call flow for an MWI delivery to an idle mobile. Subsequent figures illustrate the complete message content, including MTP and SCCP layers. The summary and decoded message formats are similar to what would be seen on test equipment monitoring the A-Interface signaling link. In this example, the BSC's point code is 8-17-92, and the MSC's point code is 110-44-3.

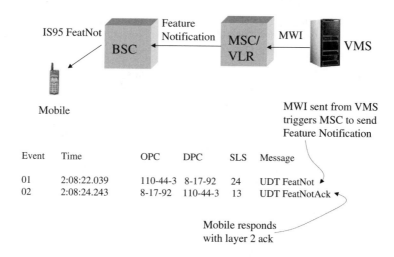

Figure 5-20   Message Waiting Indication in idle mode example call flow

The message waiting notification begins when the VMS indicates to the MSC that a voice mail message is pending for a particular mobile subscriber. Upon determining that the mobile is idle, the MSC sends a connectionless SCCP-UDT Feature Notification message to the BSC. Included in this message is the Tag IE used by the MSC to request a layer 2 acknowledgment from the mobile. About 2 seconds later, the BSC receives a layer 2 acknowledgment from the mobile on the access channel and sends a Feature Notification Acknowledgment message to the

MSC. This message includes the mobile identity IMSI and the Tag value that was received by the BSC earlier in the Feature Notification message.

Figure 5-21 shows the decoded Feature Notification message. The message is a BSMAP message sent as connectionless SCCP-UDT message.

The mandatory IMSI field uniquely identifies *310006197889514* as the desired mobile station, and the Slot Cycle Index of *1* is used by the BSC to send the message during the correct paging time slot.

The MWI shows that seven messages are pending for this subscriber. The Tag value of *88 a2 00 08* is used for requesting a layer 2 acknowledgment from the mobile and correlate the response received.

```
**** MESSAGE NUMBER: 00001 ****
*** Start of MTP Level 3 ***
0003 10000011 83
     ----0011    Service Indicator        SCCP
     --00----    Network Priority         priority 0
     10------    Network Indicator        National
0004 (3 bytes)   Destination Point Code   8-17-92
0007 (3 bytes)   Origination Point Code   110-44-3
0010 00011000 18 Signaling Link Selection 24
*** Start of SCCP ***
0011 00001001 09 Unitdata                 09
0012 00000000 00
     ----0000    Protocol Class           Class 0
     0000----    Message Handling         no special options
0013 00000011 03 Called Party Address     Offset 0016
0014 00000101 05 Calling Party Address    Offset 0019
0015 00001010 0a Data Portion Pointer     Offset 0025
0016 00000010 02 Called Party Addr Length 2
0017 11000001 c1 Called Party Addr Ind
0018 11111100 fc Subsystem Number         252
0019 00000101 05 Calling Party Addr Length 5
0020 11000011 c3 Calling Party Addr Ind
0021 11111100 fc Subsystem Number         252
0022 (3 bytes)   Signaling Point Code     110-44-3
*** Start of CDGIOS MAP ***
                 Feature Notification
0025 00011011 1b Data Length              27
0026 00000000 00 BSMAP Discriminator      00
0027 00011001 19 BSMAP Length             25
0028 01100000 60 Feature Notification     96
0029 00001101 0d Mobile Identity          13
0030 00001000 08 Length                   8
0031 00111110 3e
     -----110    Type of Identity         IMSI
     ----1---    Odd/Even Indicator       odd
     0011----    IMSI Identity Digits     310006197889514
0032 (7 bytes)
0039 00110011 33 Tag                      51
0040 (4 bytes)   Tag Value                88 a2 00 08
```

(Continued)
```
0044 00011010 1a Cell Identifier List    26
0045 00000011 03 Length                   3
0046 00000010 02 Cell Identifier Discrim  CI Only
0047 00010001 11 CI Value                 11 43
0048 01000011 43
0049 00110101 35 Slot Cycle Index         53
0050 00000001 01 Value                    1
0051 00111000 38 Message Waiting Ind      56
0052 00000111 07 Number of Messages       7
```

Figure 5-21   Feature Notification message example

Figure 5-22 shows the decoded Feature Notification Acknowledge. Like the Feature Notification message, this message is a BSMAP message sent as a connectionless SCCP-UDT message.

The mandatory Mobile Identity (IMSI) parameter contains the digits *310006197889514*, which uniquely identifies the acknowledging mobile. The Tag IE of *88 a2 00 08* is the same value received from the MSC in the Feature Notification message.

```
**** MESSAGE NUMBER: 00002 ****
*** Start of MTP Level 3 ***
0003 10000011 83
     ----0011     Service Indicator         SCCP
     --00----     Network Priority          priority 0
     10------     Network Indicator         National
0004 (3 bytes)    Destination Point Code    110-44-3
0007 (3 bytes)    Origination Point Code    8-17-92
0010 00001101 0d Signaling Link Selection   13
*** Start of SCCP ***
0011 00001001 09 Unitdata                   09
0012 00000000 00
     ----0000     Protocol Class            Class 0
     0000----     Message Handling          no special options
0013 00000011 03 Called Party Address       Offset 0016
0014 00001000 08 Calling Party Address      Offset 0022
0015 00001101 0d Data Portion Pointer       Offset 0028
0016 00000101 05 Called Party Addr Length   5
0017 11000011 c3 Called Party Addr Ind
0018 11111100 fc Subsystem Number           252
0021 (3 bytes)   Signaling Point Code       110-44-3
0022 00000101 05 Calling Party Addr Length  5
0023 11000011 c3 Calling Party Addr Ind
0024 11111100 fc Subsystem Number           252
0025 (3 bytes)   Signaling Point Code       8-17-92
*** Start of CDGIOS MAP ***
                 Feature Notification Ack
0028 00010010 12 Data Length                18
0029 00000000 00 BSMAP Discriminator        00
0030 00010000 10 BSMAP Length               16
```

(Continued)
```
0031 01100001 61 Feature Notification Ack   97
0032 00001101 0d Mobile Identity            13
0033 00001000 08 Length                      8
0034 00111110 3e
     -----110     Type of Identity          IMSI
     ----1---     Odd/Even Indicator        odd
     0011----     IMSI Identity Digits      310006197889514
0035 (7 bytes)
0042 00110011 33 Tag                        51
0043 (4 bytes)   Tag Value                  88 a2 00 08
```

Figure 5-22   Feature Notification Acknowledge message example

5.2.4   MWI Delivery in Traffic Channel Call Flow

The procedure for delivering VMN to a mobile in a call is similar to that of an idle mobile. The main difference is that the Flash With Information message is used instead of the Feature Notification message. Figure 5-23 shows the call flow for a MWI delivery to a mobile on a traffic channel followed by a description of each step.

When a voice mail is received for a mobile subscriber at the VMS, a VMN is sent from the VMS to the MSC, specifying the number of pending messages. If the mobile is in a call, the MSC packages the message notification information in a DTAP Flash With Information message and sends it to the BSC, using the existing SCCP connection.

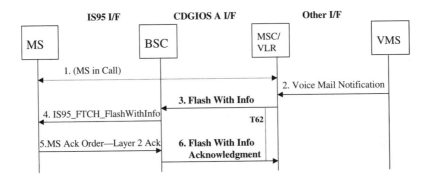

Figure 5-23   Message Waiting Indication in traffic call flow

Upon receipt of the Flash With Information message, the BSC formats an IS-95 Flash With Information message containing the message waiting information and sends it to the mobile station on the forward traffic channel. The MSC requests a layer 2 acknowledgment from the mobile station by including the Tag IE in the A-Interface Flash With Information message.

Upon receipt of the IS-95 Flash With Information message, the mobile station sends a layer 2 acknowledgment to the BSC. The BSC then sends a Flash With Information Acknowledge message to the MSC to indicate the successful delivery of the MWI to the mobile.

1. (Mobile Station in Call):

   The mobile is in a call on the traffic channel.

2. Voice Mail Notification (VMS–MSC Interface):

   The VMS sends a VMN to the MSC, specifying the mobile station and the number of unread messages. The VMS may also indicate the calling party number of the person who left the voice mail message.

3. Flash With Information (A-Interface):

   The MSC sends a Flash With Information message to the BSC that encapsulates the VMN feature parameters received from the VMS. Because the mobile is already in a call, the existing SCCP connection is used when sending this SCCP-DT1 message.

   If the MSC requires a layer 2 acknowledgment from the mobile station, it includes the Tag IE in the Feature Notification message sent to the BSC. The MSC starts timer T62. Upon expiry of T62, the MSC may resend the Flash With Information message.

4. IS95_FTCH_FlashWithInfo (IS-95):

   The message waiting information received from the MSC in the A-Interface Flash with Information message is packaged by the BSC and sent to the mobile station, using an IS-95 Flash With Information message. This message contains information such as the number of messages waiting and how the mobile subscriber should be alerted.

5. MS Ack Order- Layer2 Ack (IS-95):

   The mobile station acknowledges the IS-95 Flash With Information message by sending an Mobile Station Acknowledgment Order on the reverse traffic channel.

6. Flash With Information Acknowledgment (A-Interface):

   The BSC, upon receipt of the layer 2 acknowledgment, sends a Flash With Information Acknowledgment message to the MSC. The Tag value included in this message is the same value that was received from the MSC in the Flash With Information message.

5.2.5 Message Waiting Indication Delivery During Call Setup

A voice mail message notification may occur during the process of a call being set up. If the MSC is in the process of setting up a call, CDGIOS specifies that it should queue Flash With Information messages until the mobile has acquired the traffic channel. However, it is possible that a race condition occurs in which a VMN is received by the MSC at nearly the same time that a mobile station sends an IS-95 Origination message.

Figure 5-24 illustrates the message flow when, just prior to the BSC receiving a mobile origination attempt, the MSC is triggered to send a MWI to the same mobile station. Because the mobile may not yet have acquired the traffic channel, the MSC sends the BSC a Feature Notification message over the A-Interface, requesting that the notification be sent over the paging channel. Soon after the BSC receives the Feature Notification message, the mobile acquires the traffic channel. Because the mobile is on the traffic channel at this point, no paging channel IS-95 Feature Notification is sent out by the BSC or, if it is sent out, the mobile may not have received it during the mobile's transition to the traffic channel state. The MSC, upon receipt of the Assignment Complete message from the BSC, resends the MWI message as a Flash With Information message (Stages 9–12). The mobile responds with layer 2 acknowledgment, indicating the receipt of the MWI.

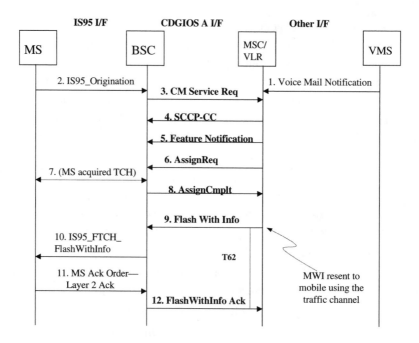

Figure 5-24   Message Waiting Indication during call setup call flow

5.2.6   Message Waiting Indication in Traffic Channel Messages

The following sections contain detail descriptions of the A-Interface messages that are used in MWI delivery to a mobile in traffic channel.

5.2.6.1   Flash With Information

The Flash With Information message is a general purpose message used by both the BSC and MSC to support several cellular network features. For example, in addition to MWI, the Flash With Information message is also used by the BSC to notify the MSC that a mobile subscriber wishes to activate a remote feature, such as Three-Way Calling. Table 5-10 presents the structure of a Flash With Information message.

The first optional parameter in the Flash With Information message is the Called Party BCD Number. This information element is included when the mobile subscriber invokes a cellular feature such as Call Waiting or Three-Way Calling. During feature activation, the BSC places the string dialed by the mobile in the Called Party BCD IE and sends the message to the MSC. The MSC is then responsible for invoking the requested feature.

The optional Signal IE specifies the alerting type that the mobile station should use for the feature notification.

The optional Message Waiting Indication IE specifies the number of messages waiting at the VMS for the mobile subscriber.

The optional Calling Party ASCII Number IE may be used to indicate the callback number of the person who deposited the message at the VMS.

Note that the use of the Signal IE, Message Waiting Indication IE, and Calling Party ASCII Number IE are all vendor implementation-specific.

The Tag IE is used by the MSC to solicit a layer 2 acknowledgment from the mobile in response to the message notification. When the Tag IE is included, the BSC responds to the Flash With Information message with a Flash With Information Acknowledge message, indicating the receipt of a layer 2 acknowledgment from the mobile. The Tag IE may also be used by the MSC to reference the Flash With Information message being acknowledged.

The optional IS-95 Information Records parameter can be used to send IS-95 information records to the mobile station. Examples include Display, Called Party Number, Calling Party Number, Signal, and Message Waiting. This parameter should not carry redundant information included in other parameters in this message, such as Signal and Calling Party ASCII Number.

- BSAP Message Type: DTAP
- SCCP Message Type: SCCP-Data Form 1 (DT1)
- Direction: BSC ↔ MSC

Table 5-10   Flash With Information Message (CDGIOS 6.1.3.7)

BitMap	Param IE	#Oct	Range	Type	IOS Ref
0000 0001 (01H) ccrr rsss LLLL LLLL	DTAP header	3	Msg Discrim. = 1 (DTAP) DLCI = "ccrr rsss" = 0 L = DTAP msg length	M	6.2.2.1 6.2.2.2 6.2.2.3
rrrr 0011 (03H)	Protocol Discriminator	1	0011—Call Processing r = 0—reserved	M	6.2.2.39

Table 5-10   Flash With Information Message (CDGIOS 6.1.3.7) (Continued)

BitMap	Param IE	#Oct	Range	Type	IOS Ref
0000 0000 (00H)	Reserved Bits	1		M	6.2.2.40
0001 0000 (10H)	Msg Type	1	Flash With Information	M	6.2.2.4
0101 1110 (5EH)	Called Party BCD Number	2–19	Same as element in Table 3-2, CM Service Request msg.	O,C	6.2.2.52
0011 0100 (34H) SSSS SSSS rrrr rrPP	Signal	3	S = IS-95 Signal value P = pitch, r = 0—reserved	O,C	6.2.2.50
0011 1000 (38H) wwww wwww	Message Wait-ing Indication	2	w = 00H–FFH Number of msgs at VMS	O,C	6.2.2.48
0100 1011 (4BH)	Calling Party ASCII Number	Var-iable	Same as element in Table 3-3, Assignment Request msg.	O,C	6.2.2.37
0011 0011 (33H)	Tag	5	Same as element in Table 5-1, ADDS Deliver msg.	O,C	6.2.2.62
0001 0101 (15H)	IS-95 Info Records	Var-iable	Same as element in Table 3-3, Assignment Request msg.	O,C	6.2.2.72

5.2.6.2   Flash With Information Acknowledgment

This message is sent by the BSC to indicate that it has received a layer 2 acknowledgment from the mobile station. The Tag IE in this message contains the same Tag value included in the corresponding Flash With Information message received from the MSC.

Unlike the Feature Notification messages for MWI delivery to an idle mobile, there is no need for mobile identity parameters such as IMSI, because an established SCCP connection already exists.

- BSAP Message Type: DTAP
- SCCP Message Type: SCCP-Data Form 1 (DT1)
- Direction: BSC ↔ MSC

Table 5-11   Flash With Information Ack Message (CDGIOS 6.1.3.8)

BitMap	Param IE	#Oct	Range	Type	IOS Ref
0000 0001 (01H) ccrr rsss LLLL LLLL	DTAP header	3	Msg Discrim. = 1 (DTAP) DLCI = "ccrr rsss" = 0 L = DTAP msg length	M	6.2.2.1 6.2.2.2 6.2.2.3
rrrr 0011 (03H)	Protocol Discriminator	1	0011—Call Processing r = 0—reserved	M	6.2.2.39
0000 0000 (00H)	Reserved Bits	1		M	6.2.2.40
0101 0000 (50H)	Msg Type	1	Flash With Information Ack	M	6.2.2.4
0011 0011 (33H)	Tag	5	Same as element in Table 5-1, ADDS Deliver msg.	O,C	6.2.2.62

5.2.7   MWI Delivery in Traffic Example Call Flow

Figure 5-25 shows a summary message call flow for an MWI delivery to a mobile already in a call. Subsequent figures illustrate the complete message content, including MTP and SCCP layers. In this example, the BSC's point code is 8-17-92, and the MSC's point code is 110-44-3.

The message waiting notification begins when the VMS indicates to the MSC that a voice mail message is pending for a particular mobile subscriber. The MSC, upon determining that the mobile is in a call, sends a connection-oriented SCCP-DT1 Flash With Information Message to the BSC, using the previously established SCCP connection. Included in this message is the Tag IE, which is used by the MSC to request a layer 2 acknowledgment from the mobile station. Less than 1 second later, the BSC receives a layer 2 acknowledgment from the mobile on the reverse traffic channel and sends a Flash With Information Acknowledgment message to the MSC, indicating that the MWI delivery was successful.

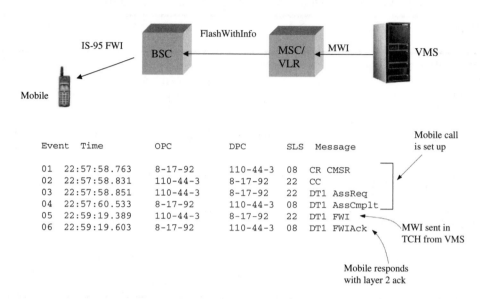

Figure 5-25 Message Waiting Indication in traffic example call flow

Figure 5-26 shows the decoded DTAP Flash With Information message. Note that this message is sent as an SCCP-DT1 message using the existing SCCP connection. The *Destination Local Reference* (DLR) of the BSC is 78695.

The MWI shows that five messages are pending for this subscriber. The Tag value of *77 04 00 0e* is used for requesting a layer 2 acknowledgment from the mobile and correlating the response received.

```
          **** MESSAGE NUMBER: 00005 ****
*** Start of MTP Level 3 ***
0003 10000011 83
     ----0011    Service Indicator          SCCP
     --00----    Network Priority           priority 0
     10------    Network Indicator          National
0004 (3 bytes)   Destination Point Code     8-17-92
0007 (3 bytes)   Origination Point Code     110-44-3
0010 00010110 16 Signaling Link Selection   22
*** Start of SCCP ***
0011 00000110 06 Data Form 1                06
0012 (3 bytes)   Dest Local References      78695
0015 00000000 00 Segment/Reassembling       0
0016 00000001 01 Variable Pointer           01
*** Start of CDG IOS MAP ***
```

(Continued)
```
                        Flash With Information
0017 00001101 0d DTAP Length                  13
0018 00000001 01 DTAP Discriminator           01
0019 00000000 00 DLCI
0020 00001010 0a Length                       10
0021 00000011 03 SS Protocol Discriminator 03
0022 00000000 00 Reserved
0023 00010000 10 Flash With Information       16
0024 00111000 38 Message Waiting Indicator 56
0025 00000101 05 Number of Messages          5
0026 00110011 33 Tag                          51
0027 (4 bytes)   Value                        77 04 00 0e
```

Figure 5-26   Flash With Information message example

Figure 5-27 shows the decoded Flash With Information Acknowledge message. Like the Flash With Information, this message is a DTAP message sent as a connection-oriented SCCP-DT1 message. The DLR of the MSC is *15432238*.

The Tag IE of *77 04 00 0e* is the same value received from the MSC in the Flash With Information message received earlier.

```
**** MESSAGE NUMBER: 00006 ****
*** Start of MTP Level 3 ***
0003 10000011 83
     ----0011    Service Indicator          SCCP
     --00----    Network Priority           priority 0
     10------    Network Indicator          National
0004 (3 bytes)   Destination Point Code     110-44-3
0007 (3 bytes)   Origination Point Code     8-17-92
0010 00001000 08 Signaling Link Selection   8
*** Start of SCCP ***
0011 00000110 06 Data Form 1                06
0012 (3 bytes)   Dest Local References      15432238
0015 00000000 00 Segment/Reassembling       0
0016 00000001 01 Variable Pointer           01
*** Start of CDG IOS MAP ***
                    Flash with Information Ack
0017 00001011 0b DTAP Length                11
0018 00000001 01 DTAP Discriminator         01
0019 00000000 00 DLCI
0020 00001000 08 Length                     8
0021 00000011 03 SS Protocol Discriminator 03
0022 00000000 00 Reserved
0023 01010000 50 Flash with Info Ack        80
0024 00110011 33 Tag                        51
0025 (4 bytes)   Value                      77 04 00 0e
```

Figure 5-27   Flash With Information Acknowledge message example

5.3 Cellular Call Features

The TIA/EIA/664 [12] standard specifies how cellular call services features should operate in wireless networks. The objective of TIA/EIA/664 is to describe cellular services and features in such a manner that mobile subscribers can expect consistent services and procedures regardless of the system they are using. For example, how a user invokes Call Forwarding or Three-Way Calling should not vary, depending on the MSC or BSC equipment manufacturer. Popular features described in the standard include Call Forwarding, *Calling Number ID Presentation* (CNIP), *Calling Number ID Restriction* (CNIR), Call Barring, Call Waiting, and Three-Way Conference Calling. The TIA/EIA/664 standard describes how these cellular features interact with each other and, in the case of multiple features being invoked, specifies which feature has priority. The procedures for remotely activating and deactivating these features using "*" feature codes are also described in the standard. The TIA/EIA/664 standard replaces the previously used interim IS-53 [9] standard.

The MSC and mobile station are primarily responsible for triggering and executing call features. The BSC mainly acts as an information pipe, transferring the necessary feature data or user action. In fact, some of the cellular features described in TIA/EIA/664 are MSC-centric and do not require any A-Interface messaging. How the MSC, for example, implements Call Forwarding and Call Barring is not described in this text because these features have no impact on the A-Interface. Because mobile subscribers need the ability to turn these features on and off, the messaging required for remote activation, deactivation, and registration is presented in this section. Specifically, this section focuses on how the A-Interface supports the following cellular subscriber features:

- Remote Feature Activation/Deactivation/Registration
- Call Waiting (with CNIP)
- Three-Way Conference Calling
- DTMF Transmissions
- CNIP/CNIR Feature
- Distinctive Ringing

The A-Interface supports TIA/EIA/664 supplementary services mainly through the use of the general purpose Flash With Information and the Feature Notification messages.

The Flash With Information is a DTAP message that is used by both the BSC and MSC to exchange call feature information when a mobile is engaged in a call. For example, the BSC uses this message to notify the MSC that a mobile subscriber pressed the "send" button to invoke a cellular feature during a call. The same message can also be sent from the MSC to the BSC to alert a mobile subscriber of a call feature, such as Call Waiting. The Flash With Information message may include required call feature information such as Display, Calling Party Number (if Caller ID feature is enabled), and Signal by including the optional IS-95 Information Records parameter.

The second commonly used message, the Feature Notification message, is used whenever call feature information needs to be sent to an idle mobile station. Instead of sending the mobile cellular feature information over the traffic channel, as is done with the Flash With Information Message, the Feature Notification message is sent over the paging channel. The content of the Feature Notification message is very similar to that of the Flash With Information message.

5.3.1   Remote Feature Registration/Activation/Deactivation

Because the cellular feature needs of an individual mobile subscriber may change, wireless networks must be flexible enough to allow a mobile subscriber to modify his or her feature profile. This is accomplished through remote feature Registration, Activation, and Deactivation, using predefined feature code strings. For example, a mobile subscriber may decide to turn on *Call Forwarding No Answer* (CFNA) by entering the string "*92" and pressing the send button. In the same network, a subscriber would deactivate CFNA by entering the string "*920" and pressing the send button.

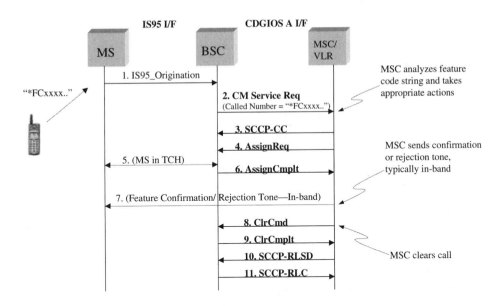

Figure 5-28   Idle Mode Feature Remote Activation/Deactivation/Registration

If a mobile subscriber is authorized for a particular feature, he or she may need to register the feature first. In the example of Call Forwarding, the mobile subscriber needs to specify the forward-to number during the feature registration process by entering the string "*FCxxxxxxx," where the x's represent the desired forward-to number and *FC* represents the feature code string. Once registered, the subscriber then activates or deactivates a given feature, using the appropriate feature code. Not all cellular features require registration, activation, and deactivation. CNIP is an example of a cellular feature that does not require registration, activation, or deactivation.

The call flow for the remote activation, deactivation, and registration of a call feature from an idle mobile is shown in Figure 5-28. The only difference between the three functions is the feature code string contained in the Called Party parameter of the CM Service Request message. The remote activation, deactivation, or registration begins as a normal mobile origination (stages 1–6). Both the IS-95 Origination and the A-Interface CM Service Request messages contain the dialed feature code in the called party field. The MSC analyzes the feature code string and, if required, takes the appropriate actions. A confirmation or rejection tone, usually in-band, is then played by the MSC to the mobile to indicate the success or failure of the feature action (stage 7). The MSC then initiates call clearing (stages 8–11).

The message flow for the remote activation, deactivation, and registration of a call feature by a mobile already in a call is show in Figure 5-29. In this case, the general-purpose Flash With Information message is used to convey the feature code string (stages 1–3). After analyzing the called party number, the MSC sends an in-band confirmation or rejection tone to the mobile, indicating the success or failure of the feature action (stage 4).

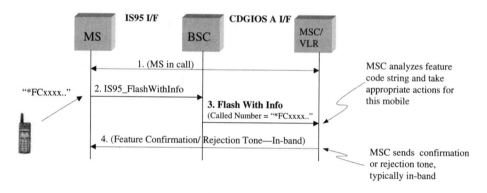

Figure 5-29   Traffic Mode Feature Remote Activation/Deactivation/Registration

5.3.2   Call Waiting (with CNIP) Feature

The Call Waiting feature provides notification of an incoming call when a mobile subscriber is already in a call. Upon receiving the incoming call, the MSC alerts the mobile subscriber and, if required, sends the Calling Party Identification information. If he or she desires, the mobile user can then connect to the incoming call by sending a flash signal to the MSC. The mobile subscriber sends a flash signal by pressing the send key without digits. After receiving the flash signal, the MSC then performs the necessary call control connection. The mobile can then toggle between the two calls by subsequent flash indications. Throughout the call, the BSC–MSC interface uses the same SCCP connection, and all call control is performed by the MSC.

The message flow for Call Waiting is shown in Figure 5-30, followed by the individual call flow stages.

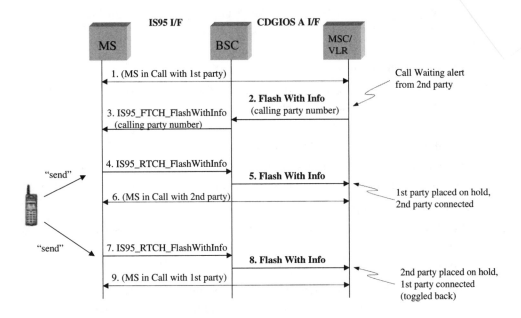

Figure 5-30 Call Waiting Feature call flow

1. (MS in call with first Party) :

   The mobile station is in a two-way call. Both the MSC and BSC have already established an SCCP connection for the call.

2. Flash With Information (MSC to BSC) (A-Interface):

   The MSC receives an incoming call for the busy mobile. The MSC first queries the VLR to determine the state of the requested mobile station. After determining that the mobile is busy, the MSC queries the HLR to check whether the Call Waiting feature is authorized and activated. If the feature is both authorized and activated, the MSC invokes the Call Waiting feature by sending a Flash With Information message across the A-Interface to alert the mobile of the incoming call. If CNIP is enabled and authorized for the indicated mobile subscriber, the MSC will also include the Calling Party Number IE in the Flash With Information message. The Call Waiting tone is typically applied in-band by the MSC. In this example, if CNIP was not enabled, there would be no need for the Flash With Information message; the MSC would simply notify the mobile subscriber of the incoming call by playing an in-band tone.

3. IS95_FTCH_FlashWithInfo (Calling Party number) (IS-95):

The BSC repackages the information contained in the A-Interface Flash With Information message received from the MSC and sends an IS-95 Flash With Information message to the mobile station using the forward traffic channel. This message includes the Calling Party Number of the incoming call. The mobile subscriber is then alerted of the incoming call.

4. IS95_RTCH_FlashWithInfo (IS-95):

The mobile user decides to acknowledge the incoming call by pressing the send button. In response, the mobile station sends the BSC an IS-95 Flash With Information message, indicating the user flash action.

5. Flash With Information (BSC to MSC) (A-Interface):

The BSC, upon receipt of the IS-95 Flash With Information message, translates the message into the A-Interface Flash With Information message that is then sent to the MSC.

6. (MS in call with second party) :

The MSC connects the mobile subscriber to the second party and places the original party on hold.

7. IS95_RTCH_FlashWithInfo (IS-95):

The mobile subscriber decides to reconnect to the original party by flashing a second time. An IS-95 Flash With Information message is then sent from the mobile station to the BSC.

8. Flash With Information (BSC to MSC) (A-Interface):

The BSC responds to the received IS95 Flash With Information message by sending an A-Interface Flash With Information message to the MSC, indicating that the mobile subscriber wishes to toggle back to the first party.

9. (MS in call with first party) :

The MSC places the mobile in call back with the first party and places the second party on hold.

5.3.3 Three-Way Calling Feature

The Three-Way Calling feature allows a mobile subscriber who is already engaged in a two-way call to add in a third caller, so that all parties may communicate directly. After the initial two-way call has been established, the controlling mobile initiates a three-way call by flashing (pressing the send button with no digits) to the MSC. The MSC then places the noncontrolling party of the original two-way call on hold and waits for the mobile station to send the called party string for the second leg of the three-way call. After receiving the called party string, the MSC sets up the second leg of the three-way call between controlling mobile user and the second party. The controlling mobile completes the three-way call by flashing one more time, which triggers the MSC to connect all three parties. Note that both call control and switching are performed by the MSC, and the BSC simply transfers information. Figure 5-31 shows the call flow for Three-Way Calling.

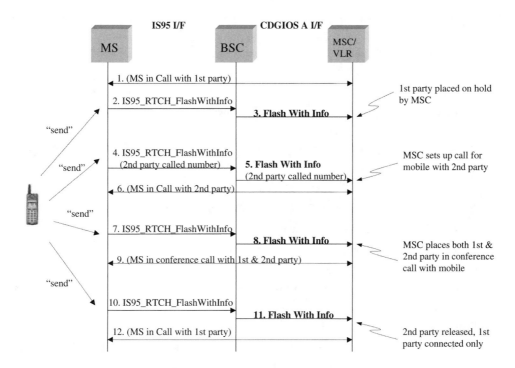

Figure 5-31 Three-Way Calling Feature call flow

1. (MS in call with first Party) :

The mobile is in a two-way call with either a land or mobile subscriber.

2. IS95_RTCH_FlashWithInfo (IS-95):

The controlling mobile user initiates a three-way call by flashing. The mobile station sends an IS-95 Flash With Information message on the reverse traffic channel to the BSC.

3. Flash With Information (A-Interface):

The BSC sends the A-Interface Flash With Information message to the MSC, indicating that the first party be put on hold.

4. IS95_RTCH_FlashWithInfo (second party Called Number) (IS-95):

The mobile user dials the number of the second party, which is then sent to the BSC in an IS-95 Flash With Information message, using the reverse traffic channel.

5. Flash With Information (second party Called Number) (A-Interface):

   The BSC repackages the called party number and sends a Flash With Information message over the A-Interface to the MSC. The Called Party Number IE of the Flash With Information message contains the dialed digit information.

   It should be noted that stages 2 and 3 can be omitted. To initiate a three-way call, the mobile user can also simply dial the second party without first flashing. In this case, the MSC simultaneously puts the first party on hold and connects the mobile to the second party.

6. (MS in call with second party):

   Upon the second party answering, the MSC connects the two parties.

7. IS95_RTCH_FlashWithInfo (IS-95):

   The mobile sends another IS-95 Flash With Information message to establish the conference call with both parties.

8. Flash With Information (A-Interface):

   The BSC sends the A-Interface Flash With Information message to the MSC.

9. (MS in call with first and second party):

   The MSC places the mobile in a conference call with both parties.

10. IS95_RTCH_FlashWithInfo (IS-95):

    When the mobile decides to release the second party, it sends an IS-95 Flash With Information message to release the call.

11. Flash With Information (A-Interface):

    The BSC sends the A-Interface Flash With Information message to the MSC, indicating that the second party should be released.

12. (MS in call with first party):

    Upon receipt of another Flash With Information message, the MSC releases the second party from the call. The mobile remains connected to the first party.

5.3.4   Dual Tone Multi-Frequency Transmission Feature

Dual Tone Multi-Frequency (DTMF) is a common signaling technique used in the United States to indicate to the remote end which digits on a push button pad were selected by the local telephone user. In DTMF, each button on the telephone key pad is represented by a tone that is made up of two frequencies. When a digit is pressed, the local phone transmits the appropriate tone to the network. Upon receiving the special tone, the remote end determines which particular digit (including * and #) was selected by decoding the tone. This technique, also know as *touch tone dialing*, is also used in many telecommunication applications for menu selection and password entry. Voice Mail Systems commonly use this signaling technique.

IS-95 allows the mobile station to send DTMF tones in-band using voice frames, or out-of-band using the IS-95 Send Burst DTMF message. In cases when the mobile sends DTMF digits through an IS-95 Send Burst DTMF message, the BSC is required to translate the DTMF information from this message and generate the in-band DTMF tone to the MSC. Figure 5-32 shows the call flow for DTMF generation scenarios.

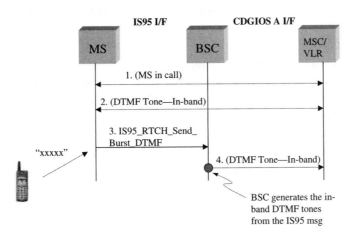

Figure 5-32 Dual Tone Multi-Frequency Generation call flow

1. (MS in call):

The mobile is in conversation.

2. (DTMF tone—in-band):

In-band DTMF tones may be sent to and from the mobile station. In this case, no A-Interface or IS-95 signaling is required.

3. IS95_RTCH_Send_Burst_DTMF (IS-95):

The mobile station may also use out-of-band signaling to specify DTMF digits. In this case, an IS-95 Send Burst DTMF message is sent on the reverse traffic channel from the mobile station to the BSC, which includes the DTMF digits and tone generation information such as the pulse "On" and "Off" intervals.

4. (DTMF tone—in-band) (A-Interface):

The BSC, upon receipt of the IS-95 Send Burst DTMF message, generates the DTMF tones from the information in the IS-95 message and injects these tones in the PCM stream to the MSC.

5.3.5   CNIP/CNIR Feature Support

As with other cellular call features, authorizations for CNIP and CNIR are specified in the subscriber's home HLR profile. If enabled, CNIP and CNIR information is specified in the Calling Party ASCII Number IE. Depending on the call scenario, this IE may be included in the

Assignment Request or Flash With Information A-Interface messages. The two scenarios are described as follows:

- Mobile-Terminated Call Setup:

  The Calling Party ASCII Number IE is sent in the Assignment Request message.

- Call Waiting alert during an established call:

  In the case of Call Waiting, the Calling Party Number IE is sent in a Flash With Information message to the mobile, together with the Call Waiting alert tone. The Call Waiting tone is specified using the Signal IE in the Flash With Information message or is played in-band by the MSC (see Section 5.3.2, "Call Waiting (with CNIP) Feature," on page 300).

5.3.6   Distinctive Ringing Feature Support

Both IS-95 and CDGIOS contain provisions for specifying distinctive ringing patterns to the mobile station. The MSC does this by sending a special alerting type value in the Signal IE or IS-95 Information Records IE (Signal) in the following two messages:

- Assignment Request message:

  This Signal IE or IS-95 Information Records IE in this message is sent during a mobile-terminated call setup to enable distinctive ringing pattern in the mobile.

- Alert With Information message :

  At any time during the mobile terminated call setup, the MSC may send this message with the IS-95 Information Records IE set to the desired Signal alerting type.

5.3.7   Features with No Impact on A-Interface

Many cellular call features are MSC centric and have no special A-Interface messaging. The following list contains some of the common MSC-centric features typically implemented in today's wireless networks.

- Call Barring
- Voice Answering
- Call Forwarding
- Call Forwarding Unconditional (CFU)
- Call Forwarding Busy (CFB)
- Call Forwarding No Answer (CFNA)
- Emergency Services
- Operator Assistance
- Hotlining

- Carrier Access Dialing
- Automatic Roaming
- Autonomous Registration
- Call Delivery
- Location Services

Most of these features are supported through normal A-Interface call setup messaging. For example, in Carrier Access Dialing or Emergency Services, the special dialed digits are contained in the Called Party Number IE of the CM Service Request, the same as with any other mobile-originated call.

For Location Services, such as Lawful Intercept and E911, the location of the mobile station is provided through the Cell Identifier parameter during certain call scenarios.

5.4 Over-the-Air Service Provisioning

Over-the-Air Service Provisioning (OTASP) is a feature that provides wireless service providers the ability to provision mobile phones remotely using the air interface. This feature allows network service providers to sell mobile phones through retail outlets that do not have on-site capability to program wireless phones with specific network parameters. OTASP also allows network providers to modify mobile operation parameters directly from the network. OTASP includes the following features:

- Download of the *Number Assignment Module* (NAM) operational parameters.

  The NAM is a set of *Mobile Identification Number* (MIN) and IMSI-related parameters that are stored in the mobile station's memory and used for mobile identification.

- A-Key creation through electronic key exchanges.
- Download of *System Selection for Preferred Roaming* (SSPR).

  SSPR allows a mobile to access a list of preferred service providers' networks, which may include roaming agreements with these service providers. *System ID* (SID), *Network ID* (NID), Band Class, and CDMA frequencies are all used to identify the preferred roaming systems.

- Download of *Service Programming Lock* (SPL) parameters to prevent fraudulent access of OTASP parameters.

  The SPL feature uses a secret *Service Programming Code* (SPC) assigned to a mobile station to prevent an unauthorized network entity from provisioning the mobile. In addition to the SPC, a NAM Lock parameter may also be used to prevent unauthorized access of NAM parameters during network-initiated OTASP sessions.

Figure 5-33 shows the network entities and interfaces utilized in the transfer of OTASP application data in a CDMA wireless network.

The *Over-the-Air Function* (OTAF) network entity interfaces directly with the Customer Service Center and has IS-41 interfaces connecting it with the MSC and HLR/*Authentication Center* (AC). In some network architectures, the OTAF may be located together with the HLR or SMS center.

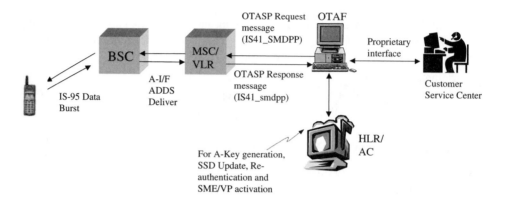

Figure 5-33   Over-the-Air Service Provisioning over CDMA network architecture

5.4.1   OTASP Protocol Stack

Several network protocols are used for OTASP. The IS-41 protocol is utilized to transfer OTASP application messages between the OTAF entity and the MSC. Each OTASP application message is encapsulated in an IS-41 SMS Message Delivery Point-to-Point (IS41_SMDPP) message. OTASP application data is exchanged between the MSC and BSC using A-Interface ADDS Deliver messages, and IS-95 Data Burst messages are used to exchange OTASP information between the BSC and the mobile station. Figure 5-34 illustrates the network entities, protocols, and interfaces involved in OTASP.

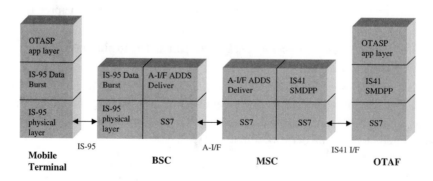

Figure 5-34   OTASP application data over CDMA system transport protocol

5.4.2   OTASP Procedure and Call Flow

The OTASP procedure consists of the following stages:

1. OTASP Call Setup:

   Initial mobile provisioning using OTASP begins with the setup of a voice call to the Customer Service Center. Subscriber billing information, such as a credit card number or mailing address, may be obtained before the Customer Service center starts the OTASP procedure.

2. OTASP Data Exchange (Upload):

   The Customer Service Center may request, through the OTAF entity, that the mobile station upload configuration parameters, such as mobile directory number, IMSI, SID, mobile protocol and software versions, and any preferred roaming list, if available. The purpose of this OTASP stage is to ensure that the service provisioning can be performed from the OTAF and to collect any preexisting configured parameters from the mobile.

3. A-Key Generation:

   If the mobile is authentication capable and authentication is required in the network, the A-Key Generation procedure may be executed to establish a common secure A-Key between the mobile and the AC. This is done through key exchanges and cryptographic algorithms between the mobile and AC. The A-Key is used as a secure input during the mobile authentication process.

4. SSD Update:

   After the A-Key has been successfully generated, the *Shared Secret Data* (SSD) update procedure is then performed. The purpose of SSD update is to synchronize the SSD value stored in both the mobile station and the authentication center. Like the A-Key, the SSD value is used during the mobile authentication process.

5. OTASP Reauthentication, SME and VP activation:

   To protect sensitive subscriber information during the OTASP data transfer, the OTAF can turn on *Signaling Message Encryption* (SME) and *Voice Privacy* (VP) for mobiles supporting these features. Before SME and VP can be activated, the mobile is authenticated using a Reauthentication procedure similar to normal authentication.

6. OTASP Data Exchange (Download):

   This OTASP stage involves downloading the mobile station with the desired network operating parameters. If SME and VP are being used, they are first turned on before the OTAF begins downloading mobile provisioning parameters, such as directory number, IMSI, SID, NID, MCC, and preferred roaming list.

7. OTASP Call Clearing:

   After OTASP data is exchanged successfully, the MSC initiates clearing the call. Service can now begin for the mobile station.

Note that the A-Key generation, SSD Update, and Reauthentication procedures are optional and are executed only if authentication is turned on at the network and the mobile station is capable of authentication. If authentication is being used, the optional SME and VP procedures may or may not be invoked during OTASP.

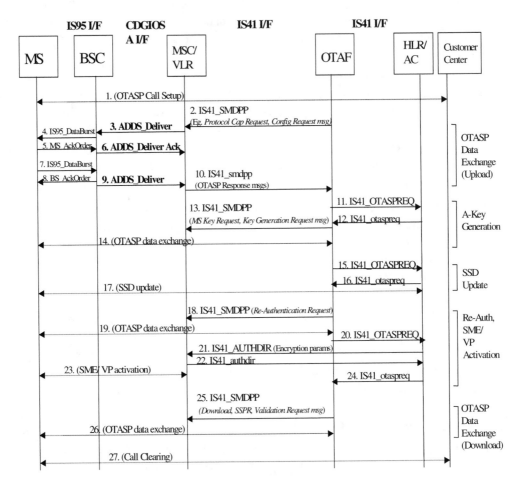

Figure 5-35   OTASP call flow and stages

5.4.2.1   OTASP Call Setup

The OTASP Call Setup stage is shown as Stage 1 in Figure 5-35. OTASP may be initiated either by the mobile user or the network. In user-initiated OTASP, the new subscriber must first activate the mobile by entering an activation code. The activation code consists of a designated feature code (*FC) and a two-digit system selection code that specifies the CDMA frequency band and block used by the desired service provider. For example, a system selection code of *03* indicates to the mobile that a 1.8-GHz, B Block system is to be acquired. After acquiring the system, the mobile station initiates a call setup with a voice service option and the MSC routes the call, based on the feature code, to the Customer Service Center. An operator at the Customer Service Center collects billing information and other relevant account data before invoking the OTASP feature to provision the phone remotely.

Network-initiated OTASP, which provides network service providers a means to modify NAM indicators and parameters, requires that the mobile station be idle and monitoring the desired CDMA Paging Channel. The network initiates an OTASP call by sending an IS-95 General Page message to the mobile, requesting Service Option 18 (multiplex option 1, rate set 1) or Service Option 19 (multiplex option 2, rate set 2). The multiplex option specifies the signaling traffic types used for the CDMA traffic frames.

Note that the OTASP procedure can be executed only while the mobile is in the CDMA conversation state and the mobile's ESN is used throughout the OTASP procedure to identify the mobile station.

5.4.2.2   OTASP Data Exchange (Upload)

Stages 2–10 of Figure 5-35 show an example of an OTASP data exchange during parameter upload from the mobile. Recall that parameters may be requested by the OTAF to be uploaded from the mobile to ensure proper service programming. The stages in the call flow are as follows:

2. IS41_SMDPP (IS-41):

   The OTAF encapsulates the OTASP application data message in an IS-41 SMDPP message. During this stage, the OTASP message sent by the OTAF are Request messages that require mobile responses. These Request/Response messages include:

   • Configuration Request/Response messages

   This Request message is used to request mobile NAM configuration parameters, such as directory number, IMSI, SID, NID, MCC, and mobile protocol revision.

   • Protocol Capability Request/Response messages

   This Request message is used to request the mobile's software revision for OTASP features, such as NAM Download and A-Key exchange.

   • SSPR Configuration Request/Response message

   This Request message is used to request the mobile's preferred roaming list, if one exists.

Stages 3–9 are similar to an SMS message delivery to a mobile station, except that in this case, the application data is an OTASP message instead of an SMS message.

10. IS41_smdpp (IS-41):

The MSC, upon receipt of an OTASP response message from the BSC/mobile, packages the OTASP message in an IS41_smdpp message and sends it to the OTAF for further processing.

5.4.2.3   A-Key Generation

If authentication is enabled by the network and if the mobile supports authentication, the mobile A-Key may be generated during the OTASP session. Stages 11–14 of Figure 5-35 show the A-Key generation procedure. The steps are described below:

11. IS41_OTASPREQ (IS-41):

The OTAF initiates the A-Key generation by sending an IS41_OTASPREQ message to the AC.

12. IS41_otaspreq (IS-41):

The AC acknowledges the IS41_OTASPREQ message.

13. IS41_SMDPP (IS-41):

The OTAF encapsulates each of the following OTASP application data messages in an IS41_SMDPP message, used for generating the A-Key:

• MS Key Request message
• Key Generation Request message

For further details on the computation of the A-Key during OTASP, refer to IS-683A [13].

Stage 14 is the OTASP data exchange for the A-Key generation, which is similar to stages 3–10 described previously in Section 5.4.2.2, "OTASP Data Exchange (Upload)," on page 311. Stages 13 and 14 are repeated for each OTASP application data message exchange.

5.4.2.4   SSD Update

Following the successful generation of the A-Key, the OTAF will send an IS41_OTASPREQ message to the AC to initiate an SSD update. Recall that the SSD update is used to synchronize the SSD stored in both the mobile and the AC. The SSD update procedure is shown in Stages 15–17 of Figure 5-35.

15. IS41_OTASPREQ (IS-41):

The OTAF requests an SSD update action to be taken by the AC.

16. IS41_otaspreq (IS-41):

The AC acknowledges the IS41_OTASPREQ message.

Stage 17 refers to the SSD update procedure between the AC and the mobile station, and is described in greater detail in Section 6.6, "Shared Secret Data Update," on page 383.

5.4.2.5 OTASP Reauthentication, SME, and VP Activation

To provide secure OTASP programming sessions and to protect sensitive mobile subscriber information, SME and VP encryption procedures can be activated prior to the download of OTASP data messages.

Following successful A-Key generation and SSD Update, the OTAF performs Reauthentication procedures to authenticate the mobile before activating SME and VP encryption. Stages 18–19 in Figure 5-35 shows the Reauthentication procedure, whereby a global challenge authentication is performed (see Section 6.1, "Authentication Overview," on page 346).

18. IS41_SMDPP (IS-41) (Reauthentication Request):

The OTAF generates a random value, designated *RAND*, to be used as input to the authentication process and forwards the data to the MSC.

19. (OTASP Data Exchange):

The steps in the OTASP Data Exchange are similar to stages 3–10. Upon receipt of the OTASP Reauthentication Request message, the mobile station responds with a Reauthentication Response message that contains the authentication results.

20. IS41_OTASPREQ (IS-41):

The authentication result is forwarded by the OTAF to the AC, which performs the authentication operation.

21. IS41_AUTHDIR (IS-41)(Encryption Parameters):

Upon successful authentication, the AC activates SME and VP by sending the encryption keys for SME and VP to the MSC.

22. IS41_authdir (IS-41):

The MSC acknowledges the IS41_AUTHDIR message.

23. (SME/VP Activation):

SME and VP are activated using procedures described in Section 6.7, "Signaling Message Encryption and Voice Privacy," on page 396.

24. IS41_otaspreq (IS-41):

The AC responds to the OTASPREQ sent earlier by the OTAF.

5.4.2.6 OTASP Data Exchange (Download)

Stages 25–26 of Figure 5-35 illustrate the OTASP Data download procedure, which involves downloading network parameters to the mobile station. If authentication is enabled, the download of these sensitive mobile parameters is done after SME/VP is activated. The OTASP Data Exchange call flow is similar to Stages 2–10, described previously in Section 5.4.2.2, "OTASP Data Exchange (Upload)," on page 311 for OTASP Data upload.

The service provisioning parameters are carried within the OTASP Request messages. The mobile responds to each request, indicating the status of the download. The following OTASP application messages are used to download parameters to the mobile station.

• Download Request messages:

This message is used to download NAM configuration parameters, such as directory number, IMSI, SID, NID, and MCC.

• SSPR Download Request message:

This message is used to download the preferred roaming list to a mobile.

• Validation Request message:

This may be used to change the SPC code or NAM Lock information.

At the end of the download session, the OTAF sends a Commit Request message to instruct the mobile station to store the OTASP parameters permanently.

5.4.2.7   Call Clearing

OTASP calls are cleared, using the same steps as any other MSC-initiated call clearing.

5.4.3   OTASP Application Data Messages

Table 5-12 summarizes the various OTASP application data messages used to support the transfer and control of OTASP data exchanges between the network OTASP function (OTAF) and the mobile station. A brief functional description and standards reference is provided for each message. Note that an OTASP Request message refers to the network-mobile direction and that an OTASP Response message is from the mobile station to the network.

Table 5-12   OTASP Application Data Messages

OTASP Message	Function	OTASP Msg ID	Ref to IS-683A	Description
Download Request/ Response	NAM + mobile params download	01H	4.5.1.2/ 3.5.1.2	Download of the mobile params, including Mobile Directory Number, NAM parameters such as IMSI/MIN, ACCOLC, mobile termination indicators (MOB_TERM_HOME, MOB_TERM_FOR_NID/SID), SID/NID pairs.
Configuration Request/ Response	NAM + mobile params upload	00H	4.5.1.1/ 3.5.1.1	Upload of any mobile parameters, including Mobile Directory Number, NAM parameters such as SLOTTED_MODE, MOB_P_REV, IMSI/MIN, ACCOLC, mobile termination indicators (MOB_TERM_HOME, MOB_TERM_FOR_NID/SID), SID/NID pairs, MAX_SID_NID, etc.

Table 5-12   OTASP Application Data Messages (Continued)

OTASP Message	Function	OTASP Msg ID	Ref to IS-683A	Description
Protocol Capability Request/ Response	Mobile software version upload	06H	4.5.1.7/ 3.5.1.7	Upload of mobile feature software version, including NAM download, Key exchange, SSPR, SPL, OTAPA, feature protocol version.
SSPR Download Request/ Response	Preferred Roam List download	08H	4.5.1.9/ 3.5.1.9	Download of Preferred Roaming List information to the mobile station
SSPR Configuration Request/ Response	Preferred Roam List upload	07H	4.5.1.8/ 3.5.1.8	Upload of any Preferred Roaming List information from the mobile station.
Validation Request/ Response	SPL params download	09H	4.5.1.10/ 3.5.1.10	Download of SPL parameters E.g. SPC and NAM_LOCK.
OTAPA Request/ Response	OTAPA process control	0AH	4.5.1.11/ 3.5.1.11	Network-initiated OTASP request to stop/ start.
Commit Request/ Response	OTAPA process control	05H	4.5.1.6/ 3.5.1.6	Indication to commit to the OTASP parameters.
MS Key Request/ Response	A-Key creation	02H	4.5.1.3/ 3.5.1.3	Used for requesting A-key generation at both the mobile and AC. A-key generation parameters PARAM_P and PARAM_G are sent to the mobile.

Table 5-12   OTASP Application Data Messages (Continued)

OTASP Message	Function	OTASP Msg ID	Ref to IS-683A	Description
Key Generation Request/ Response	A-Key creation	03H	4.5.1.4/ 3.5.1.4	Used for A-key generation, after MS Key Request. A-key generation parameters BS_RESULT and MS_RESULT are exchanged.
Re-Authenticate Request/ Response	Re-Auth procedure	04H	4.5.1.5/ 3.5.1.5	Used to authenticate the mobile station. If successful, SME/VP encryption operation may be activated.

5.5 Circuit-Mode Data Services

Mobile phone users are increasingly relying on data capable wireless networks to meet both their personal and business needs. Data features have become so popular that an individual strolling through any modern airport will undoubtedly encounter mobile users accessing data through their phones.

This section provides an overview of how circuit-mode data services are implemented in a wireless network and specifically addresses how the A-Interface is used to provide these services. A second type of data services, known as *packet data*, is discussed in the next section, Section 5.6, "Packet Data Services," on page 321.

In a wireless network, circuit-mode data refers to Asynchronous Data and Fax services that are provided through a dedicated circuit dial-up connection to a remote host via the *Public Switched Telephone Network* (PSTN). The mobile station, BSC, and the *Inter-Working Function* (IWF) together provide the functionality usually associated with a standard wireline modem.

Although this section describes the network architecture, data protocol stack, and service operations associated with circuit data services, a complete description of circuit-mode data services can be found in IS-99 [15] and IS-707 [16].

5.5.1   Network Architecture

Figure 5-36 illustrates the network entities and interfaces used for implementing circuit-mode data services. The data or fax application resides on *Terminal Equipment 2* (TE2), usually a laptop computer, which is directly connected to the mobile station using a data cable supplied by the mobile phone manufacturer. Most of today's CDMA mobile stations utilize an RS-232 serial interface to connect the mobile station to terminal equipment. The data-capable mobile station is known as a *Mobile Termination 2* (MT2) device, and the interface connecting the MT2 and the TE2 is referred to as the *Rm-Interface*.

As with voice calls, the mobile station interfaces to the BSC through the Um-Interface, utilizing IS95 traffic frames. The A5-Interface connects the BSC to the IWF, usually via the MSC. The A5 connection provides full duplex octet stream data transfer between the BSC and IWF.

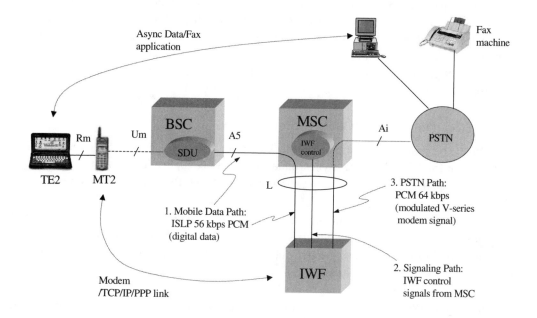

Figure 5-36   Circuit-Mode Data network architecture

CDGIOS specifies that the IWF be located, or anchored, at the MSC. This approach separates the BSC's *Selection/Distribution Unit* (SDU) and the IWF, preventing data loss resulting from PSTN disconnects during intersystem handoffs between BSCs. With this architecture, once a circuit-data call is set up, the IWF remains "anchored" at the originating MSC, even if inter-BSC handoffs take place.

Figure 5-36 also shows the interfaces associated with an IWF that is anchored at the MSC. The primary function of an IWF is to act as a data signal converter between the fixed network (PSTN) and the mobility network (MSC/BSC), providing circuit-mode data access for mobile users in the mobility network. The IWF is typically implemented as a V-series modem pool, responsible for signal adaptation and modulation/demodulation between PSTN-based or ISDN-based application data and the serving MSC/BSC. Whenever circuit data is requested, the mobile station sends modem commands to the IWF, which then configures a modem in the modem pool for the specified data service type. The combination of the mobile station, SDU, and IWF emulates a standard telephone modem used for dial-up connections to the PSTN.

The interface connecting the IWF and the MSC/BSC, referred to as the *L-Interface*, consists of three parts, the Signaling Path, the Mobile Data Path, and the PSTN Path. The Signaling Path carries control signal data between the IWF and the MSC, allowing the MSC to control the IWF. The Mobile Data Path is used to transfer to the IWF, the data present on the A5-Interface. CDGIOS specifies the use of the *Intersystem Link Protocol* (ISLP), described in the next section and in IS-728, for the A5-Interface. The PSTN path carries the modulated modem signals to and from the PSTN.

5.5.2   Mobile Circuit Data Protocol Stack

Figure 5-37 illustrates the protocol stack used for circuit-mode data services applications, as defined in IS-707.4 [16]. The asynchronous data and fax applications communicate with the remote host application layer, using the wireless network and PSTN as transport, network, link and relay layers.

The relay layer from the mobile data terminal to the mobile station consists of a simple serial RS-232 interface. From the mobile station to the BSC, *Radio Link Protocol* (RLP) frames are transmitted to the BSC, using IS-95 traffic frames. The RLP protocol layer provides the required increased radio transmission reliability necessary for data transmissions, primarily through retransmission schemes.

From the BSC to the IWF, the ISLP protocol is used as a relay layer for the A5 octet stream connection. Because the IS-95 over-the-air data rates differ from the terrestrial PCM rates used at the IWF, the BSC's SDU must rate-adapt the RLP frames into ISLP frames, which are then to be transmitted over the 56 kbps or 64 kbps terrestrial PCM connection. The primary function of the ISLP protocol at the BSC is to adapt the lower-speed RLP frames (13 kbps or less) into the terrestrial PCM stream. At the IWF, the ISLP adapts the TCP/IP/PPP frames from terrestrial PCM stream (see IS-728 on ISLP protocol [18]).

As it receives ISLP frames from the BSC/MSC, the IWF converts, then modulates the digital data, using a modem in the modem pool. The modulated data is sent out to the PSTN PCM 64 kbps stream. In the reverse direction, the IWF accepts incoming modulated modem signals from the PSTN PCM 64 kbps stream, converts the modulated signals to ISLP frames, and then sends the PCM data to the MSC. The MSC transfers the PCM data to the BSC, using an A-Interface terrestrial circuit. At the BSC, the ISLP frames are decoded and packaged into RLP frames, which are then transmitted to the mobile station, using the IS-95 air interface.

Note that, between the mobile station and the IWF, there exists a TCP/IP/*Point-to-Point Protocol* (PPP) transport, network, and link layer to ensure reliable data delivery between the two entities. An additional modem application interface layer also exists between the mobile station and the IWF, above the transport layer. The purpose of this application interface layer is to exchange modem control commands used by the IWF to configure the modem. As mentioned earlier, the mobile station and IWF together emulate a standard telephone modem.

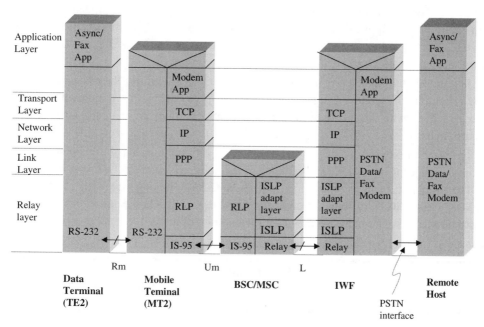

Figure 5-37 Protocol stack for mobile Circuit-Mode data services

5.5.3 Circuit Data Service Operation

The call procedures for mobile-originated and -terminated data call data are very similar to those described for voice calls in Section 3.1, "Mobile Origination," on page 142, and Section 3.2, "Mobile Termination," on page 164. The only difference is that the service option field is that of the requested data service option.

A data-capable wireless network needs a method of distinguishing incoming data calls from incoming voice calls. This is typically done by provisioning data services at the HLR for a subscriber in the form of multiple *Directory Numbers* (DNs). Each DN is associated with a separate service option, such as data or fax. Descriptions of the various data service options can be found in IS-707 [16]. Table 5-13 summarizes the different circuit-mode data service options supported in CDGIOS.

During a mobile-originated circuit data call, the dialed string from the data terminal ATD command is placed in an IS-95 Origination message, which the BSC sends to the MSC/IWF in the Called Party ASCII IE or Called Party BCD IE of the CM Service Request. Upon receiving a request for a data service option, the BSC initiates the A5 ISLP connection, and the MSC sets up the L-Interface to the IWF. Once the L-Interface to the IWF is established, the PPP layer between the mobile station and the IWF is initiated. The PPP *Internet Protocol Control Protocol* (IPCP) (ref. RFC 1332 [33]) is used to set up a temporary IP address for the mobile.

The network and transport layers (TCP/IP) are then established between the mobile station and the IWF. The mobile application interface can then begin sending the modem configuration command to peer application interface at the IWF. The IWF/MSC collects the dialed digits and establishes the dial-up connection from the mobile to the PSTN, as is done with a standard landline modem connection.

In a mobile-terminated circuit data call, the MSC first identifies the call as a data or fax call by examining the incoming digits. Next, the BSC pages the mobile station with the service option associated with the incoming DN. Subsequent operations are then similar to a mobile-originated data call.

In regard to mobility management, all types of soft and hard handoffs are supported for data calls, except for Inter-MSC Inter-BSC hard handoffs, which are not yet specified in CDG-IOS. The supported handoff types include Intra-BSC Soft Handoff, Inter-BSC Soft Handoff, Intra-MSC Intra-BSC Hard Handoff, and Intra-MSC Inter-BSC Hard Handoff. Once a data call is in progress, the IWF remains anchored for the duration of the call.

Table 5-13   Circuit-Mode Data Service Options

Service Option	Service Option Number	Ref Standards Document
Async Data, Rate Set 1	4	TIA/EIA/IS-99
Async Data, Rate Set 1 default, rev 1	4100	TIA/EIA/IS-707.4
Async Data, Rate Set 2	12	TIA/EIA/IS-707.4
Fax, Rate Set 1	5	TIA/EIA/IS-99
Fax, Rate Set 1 default, rev 1	4101	TIA/EIA/IS-707.4
Fax, Rate Set 2	13	TIA/EIA/IS-707.4

5.5.4   Digital and Analog Fax Services

The use of fax services in a wireless CDMA network comprises two different types, Digital PC Fax and Analog Fax. Both categories of services employ digital fax technology for encoding/decoding the fax image, known as *Group 3 Fax*. The *International Telecommunications Union* (ITU) standard T.4 [21] specifies the Group 3 digital image encoding. Group 1 and Group 2 Fax services employ analog image encoding and are rarely used in modern fax equipment.

For Digital PC Fax, a *Data Terminal Equipment* (DTE), normally a laptop or PC running fax application software, is connected via an RS-232 to a CDMA mobile (see Figure 5-36 on page 317). The DTE's fax software is responsible for the encoding/decoding the fax images using the T.4 standard. The *Data Circuit-Terminating Equipment* (DCE), which comprises the CDMA mobile and the IWF fax modem, is responsible for the digital-to-analog modem interface to the PSTN and fax protocol communication and negotiation with the remote fax machine using the ITU T.30 standard [22]. A fax modem with such responsibilities in a DTE-DCE fax setup is known as a *Class 2.0 fax modem* (see EIA/TIA 592 [24]). In a Class 1 fax modem, the modem has minimal responsibilities except for V-series modem functions. Conversely, in a Class 3 fax modem, the modem has expanded responsibilities, including T.4 image encoding.

In Analog Fax, a conventional Group 3 fax machine is connected via an RJ-11 analog interface to a subscriber unit with digital CDMA wireless capabilities, such as a *Wireless Local Loop* (WLL) phone. The fax machine communicates with the WLL unit, using the T.30 fax session, and the WLL unit converts the analog signals to digital data to be sent to the IWF. From the BSC's IWF point of view, the WLL is simply a DTE as before. The Class 2.0 fax modem at the IWF then converts the digital signal to analog PSTN interface, and sets up the second T.30 fax session with the remote fax machine.

5.6 Packet Data Services

Aside from circuit-mode data services, many CDMA networks also provide the capability for mobile packet data calls to external packet data networks. Although packet data has not yet been standardized in CDGIOS version 3, several infrastructure vendors have already implemented packet data functionality by connecting the BSC directly to a packet data network, bypassing the A-Interface. Third-generation wireless standards attempt to standardize how packet data is implemented and are briefly discussed in Section 10.1, "3G Packet Data Architecture," on page 544.

This section gives an overview of a typical packet data services implementation used in many current CDMA network. Additional information regarding packet data services can be found in IS-707 [16].

5.6.1 Packet Data Network Architecture

The packet data network architecture includes interfaces to an *Inter-Working Function* (IWF) that provides a gateway to the packet data network. This IWF serves as a terminating point for the packet data connection from the Internet/intranet network and provides a direct *Point-to-Point Protocol* (PPP) link layer connection to the mobile station application.

An overview of the CDMA network architecture that supports packet data services is shown in Figure 5-38. The mobile data application typically resides in a *Terminal Equipment 2* (TE2), which is a data terminal device physically connected to a mobile station. The mobile station is known as a *Mobile Termination 2* (MT2) device, which has an interface such as RS-232 that can be linked to the TE2. This interface is referred to as the *Rm-Interface* and is specified in

IS-707.5A [17].

On the infrastructure side, the BSC provides the Um air interface link to the mobile station and the associated radio resources for the packet data call. The MSC is involved only in the packet data call setup and does not participate in the packet data transfer.

Beyond the BSC, a packet data IWF provides the necessary functions to support packet data services for the mobile terminal. It establishes a reliable link layer to the mobile station using common link layer protocols such as *Point-to-Point Protocol* (PPP) and provides the router gateway to the *Packet Data Network* (PDN), which can be either the Internet or private data networks. The L-Interface connects the BSC/MSC to the IWF function.

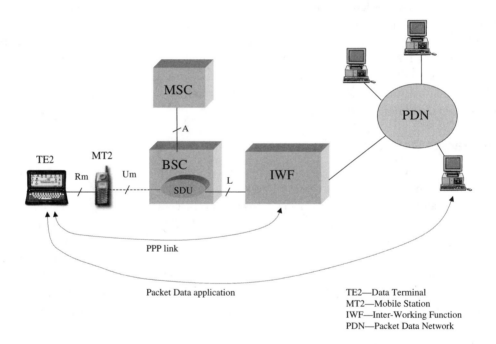

Figure 5-38   A-Interface network architecture with Packet Data support

5.6.2   Packet Data Protocol Stack

Figure 5-39 shows an overview of the protocol stack in a mobile packet data application between a mobile data terminal and a remote host. The protocol stack is divided mainly into the relay layer, link layer, network layer, and application layer. The application layer includes the transport layer and other higher-layer protocols.

The relay layer is mainly responsible for the transmission of user data across the various interfaces connecting the entities in the wireless and packet data network. The interface between the mobile data terminal and the mobile station is typically RS-232 but can be any type of interface. As with voice, the Um-Interface between the mobile station and the BSC uses CDMA air interface technology to transfer packet data. Because the loss of data bits in a packet data call has a much more adverse affect than a voice call, additional steps must be taken to improve the transmission reliability. To provide a better datalink layer transmission on the air interface, a *Radio Link Protocol* (RLP) is used to encapsulate link layer packet data and format the information into CDMA radio channel frames. RLP also uses retransmission schemes to reduce error rates (see IS-707.2 [16]). From the serving BSC/MSC to the IWF and, finally, to the remote host on the packet data network, any relay layer technology can be used.

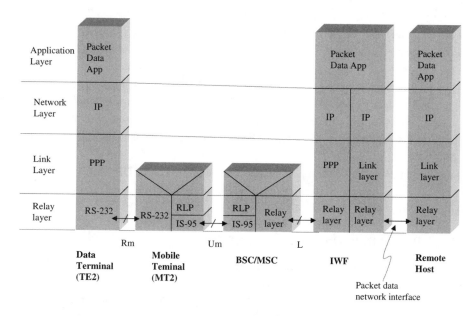

Figure 5-39   Protocol stack for mobile Packet Data services using Relay Layer Rm

The link layer is responsible for establishing a reliable, low-error link connection between the mobile data terminal and the remote host packet data application. Between the mobile data application and the IWF at the infrastructure, a PPP link layer is commonly used to provide a method for transporting the IP data packets over a serial connection (see IETF RFC 1661 [35]). Any link layer protocol, such as ethernet, X.25, frame relay, ATM, and token ring may be used from the IWF gateway to the remote host over the packet data network.

Note that the PPP connection from the IWF is terminated at different points on the mobile side, depending on which of the two different protocol options are chosen on the Rm-Interface (see IS-707.5 [16]). The two Rm protocol options are:

• Relay Layer Rm
• Network Layer Rm

In the Relay Layer Rm option, the data terminal (TE2) implements the link layer protocol, such as PPP, as well as the network and higher-layer protocols. Thus, the PPP link layer is established between the mobile data terminal and the IWF. Figure 5-39 shows this Relay Layer Rm option.

In the Network Layer Rm option, the mobile station (MT2) implements the packet data PPP link layer and network layers. It is, therefore, responsible for the packet data PPP link termination from the IWF and performs packet data network layer functions. The network layer between the MT2 and the TE2 is, thus, independent from the network layer between the MT2 and the IWF, and can be implemented using separate protocols.

At the packet data Network Layer, the *Internet Protocol* (IP) is a commonly used network protocol for packet data applications (see IETF RFC 791 [31]). IP packets that encapsulate higher layer packet data protocols are transferred between the mobile data application and the remote packet data host, using the reliable link layers and relay layers. *Cellular Digital Packet Data* (CDPD) is also another type of network layer application that is supported for packet data application.

At the packet data Application Layer, protocols such as TCP, UDP, Mobile IP, and higher-layer protocols are exchanged between the mobile data terminal and the remote host over the packet data network.

5.6.3   Packet Data Operation

A packet data call is initiated by the mobile station's data application when it first sets up a connection with the BSC. The selection of a packet data service type can be accomplished using the AT command protocol between the data terminal and the mobile station or directly, using the user interface on the mobile. The mobile station establishes the radio channel with the BSC and performs a packet data call setup similar to a mobile-originated voice call but uses the packet data service option supported by the both the BSC and MSC. No dialed string is necessary because no call connection is made to the PSTN, and no CIC is allocated between the BSC and MSC because the packet data call is routed directly to the IWF.

Once the packet data service option is set up and the radio channel is allocated, RLP synchronization between the mobile station and the BSC begins. After RLP synchronization, PPP frames are then exchanged between the mobile station and the IWF to establish the PPP link. In a Simple IP implementation, a dynamic IP address is assigned by the IWF. For Mobile IP service, the mobile requests for its own IP address to be used for mobile IP data delivery from its home system. An overview of Mobile IP can be found in *Mobile IP, The Internet Unplugged* by James D. Solomon [37]. After the IWF establishes the PPP link with the mobile, packet data delivery can then occur between the mobile data application and the packet data network.

The PPP link, when established, may be in the Active or Dormant state. When the packet data transfer is in progress, the PPP link state is Active, and radio resources have been allocated. The PPP link state may transition from active to dormant mode when the mobile releases the call or after the absence of data exchange for a specified period of time. Radio resources are released during the transition from active to dormant mode. When in the Dormant state, the status of the PPP link, including the IP address assigned, the mobile's IMSI and other session information are stored at the IWF. Later, when there are packets to be transferred to the mobile station, this PPP link is reactivated without the need to reinitialize the link layer and higher layers. This approach reduces call setup times and better utilizes radio resources when packet data inactivity occurs at the mobile data terminal application.

The Dormant mode feature of packet data services also allows a form of mobile-terminated packet data delivery from the network side. When the mobile's PPP link is in the Dormant state, packets destined for the mobile may arrive from an external router to the IWF, which can then be delivered to the mobile because the mobile's IP address is "visible" from the network. The BSC then establishes radio resources, using the mobile-terminated call setup procedure, and reactivates the PPP link. This is known as *Network-Initiated Dormant Mode Reactivation*. A similar process occurs during mobile-initiated dormant mode reactivation.

5.A Short Message Service Protocol Overview

To understand fully how SMS services are delivered in a CDMA network, it is helpful first to understand the SMS application layer functions. This section explains the SMS protocol architecture, the SMS transport and teleservice layer message structures, and how the SMS application reliably delivers SMS messages to the remote SMS application.

Note that this section is included for information purposes to introduce the reader to the SMS application and protocol architecture. For SMS delivery operations related to the A-Interface, refer to Section 5.1, "Short Message Services," on page 248.

5.A.1 Short Message Service Protocol Architecture

The SMS protocol consists of four distinct layers, the Link Layer, the SMS Relay Layer, the SMS Transport Layer, and the SMS Teleservice Layer. Figure 5-40 shows how the protocol layers are arranged within each subsystem in a CDMA network.

The mobile station and SMS Message Center are referred to as *SMS Bearer Service End Points*, and each contains an SMS application that provides SMS Teleservice Layer functions. There are three CDMA Teleservice types available in CDMA networks, *Cellular Paging Teleservice* (CPT), *Cellular Messaging Teleservice* (CMT), and *Voice Mail Notification* (VMN). The Teleservice Layer translates the type of teleservice that is being used into an SMS Teleservice Layer message. Each teleservice type consists of different options to format the SMS message. CPT and CMT are commonly used for text or paging services, and VMN may be used for notification of voice mail when a voice mail entity is attached to an SMSC.

The Transport Layer at the SMS application end points encapsulates the Teleservice Layer message in its Bearer Data parameter in an SMS Transport Layer message. The Transport Layer, together with the underlying Relay Layer, are collectively called the *bearer service*. The Transport Layer functions as an interface between the Teleservice Layer and the Relay Layer. The Relay layer interfaces directly with the Link Layer, which is used to carry the actual traffic.

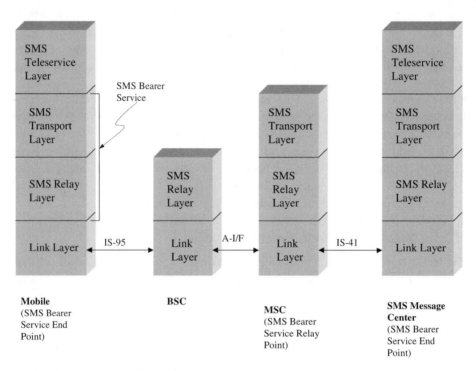

Figure 5-40   Short Message Service protocol layers

As shown in Figure 5-40, the MSC in the CDMA network functions as an SMS bearer service relay point, which carries the SMS Transport Layer to ensure the reliable end-to-end delivery of the SMS messages by incorporating acknowledgment schemes when required. The transport layer can process SMS transport layer messages, reformat headers, and relay confirmations and acknowledgment of SMS deliveries. These relay points do not have the Teleservice layer application. The BSC in the CDMA network is simply providing a data pipe to relay the SMS transport layer messages to the mobile.

The Relay layer provides the necessary interface between the Transport Layer and the underlying Link Layer. It also provides any error indication from the Link Layer delivery to the Transport Layer. The Relay layer uses the IS-41 protocol from the SMSC to the MSC, the A-Interface protocol from the MSC to the BSC, and the IS-95 air interface from the BSC to the mobile station.

5.A.2 Short Message Service Reliable Delivery Procedure

The delivery of SMS messages between the SMSC and the mobile may employ acknowledgment schemes at the relay, transport, and teleservice layers to provide a form of reliable delivery service to the SMS relay and bearer end points.

To deliver an SMS message from the SMS message center to a mobile station, the SMS message center first encapsulates the SMS Transport Layer message in an IS-41 message type, for example an *IS-41 SMS Delivery Point-to-Point* (IS41_SMDPP) message. The MSC then strips off the IS-41 headers, packages the SMS Transport Layer message into the A-Interface ADDS Deliver message or ADDS Page message, and forwards it to the BSC. The BSC strips off the A-Interface headers and repackages the SMS Transport Layer message into an IS-95 Data Burst message to be sent to the mobile, either on the paging channel or on the traffic channel.

To solicit a Relay Layer (layer 2) acknowledgment from the mobile, the MSC includes a Tag IE in the ADDS Page/Deliver message sent to the BSC. When the mobile sends a layer 2 acknowledgment over an IS-95 link to the the BSC, the BSC relays the layer 2 acknowledgment to the MSC by sending either an ADDS Deliver Ack message or an ADDS Page Ack message. If no layer 2 (Relay Layer) acknowledgment has been received at the MSC, the Transport Layer is informed.

In addition to the Relay Layer acknowledgment, the SMS application at the originating bearer end point may also request an SMS Transport Layer acknowledgment by including the *Bearer Reply Option* parameter in the SMS Point-to-Point Transport Layer message. The receiving transport layer at the end point should then send an SMS Acknowledge Transport Layer message to the originating transport layer. Upon receipt of the Transport Layer acknowledgment, the originating Transport Layer correlates the SMS Acknowledgement message with the SMS Point-to-Point message that it sent out earlier by using the REPLY_SEQ parameter, which indicates the sequence number of the message. If an error occurs in the process, the transport layer message includes the Cause Codes parameter, with the SMS_CauseCode value set to one of the values defined in the SMS_CauseCode table in IS-41 [7]. In the case of an error, the Teleservice Layer informs that errors were received and that the message cannot be delivered.

At the Teleservice Layer, an end-user acknowledgment may also be requested by including the *Reply Option* parameter in the SMS Deliver Teleservice Layer message. The acknowledgment can be in the form of "user acknowledgment" teleservice message type, whereby the user explicitly replies to the mobile-terminated SMS Deliver message. For a mobile-originated SMS to another mobile, this acknowledgment can be in the form of a "delivery acknowledgment" teleservice message type that the Teleservice Layer at the SMS center sends to an originating SMS mobile when a Transport Layer acknowledgment is received from the destination mobile (see Section 5.A.4, "The SMS Teleservice Layer Message," on page 334 for the format of these messages).

5.A.3 The Short Message Service Transport Layer Message

The SMS Transport Layer message is used for transferring SMS application layer messages, from one SMS application to another. It consists of a *Bearer Data* field that encapsulates the SMS Teleservice Layer message. There are three main types of SMS Transport Layer messages and each is identified by a unique SMS_MSG_TYPE parameter at the start of the SMS Transport Layer message:

- 00H—SMS Point-to-Point Transport Layer message
- 01H—SMS Broadcast Transport Layer message
- 02H—SMS Acknowledge Transport Layer message

The following subsections describe the message structure for the three main SMS Transport Layer message types. Note that the references in these subsections refer to the IS-637 standard document and not the IOS document, as in other sections.

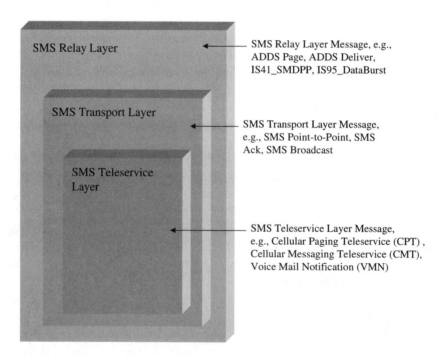

Figure 5-41 Short Message Service message encapsulated in different protocol layers

5.A.3.1 SMS Point-to-Point Transport Layer Message

This message is sent when the SMS application submits an SMS message to be sent to the remote end SMS application. It is packaged in the IS41_SMDPP message and in the ADDS User Part data in the A-Interface ADDS Deliver or ADDS Page message. It is then finally sent as the content of the IS-95 Data Burst messages. Figure 5-41 shows how an SMS message is encapsulated in the various protocol layers.

Table 5-14 shows the format for an SMS Point-to-Point Transport Layer message. The SMS_MSG_TYPE indicates the type of SMS Transport Layer message, which, in this case, is an SMS Point-to-Point Transport Layer message.

The Teleservice Identifier indicates the type of teleservice that is being sent in the bearer data, including *CDMA Cellular Paging Teleservice* (CPT), *CDMA Cellular Messaging Teleservice* (CMT) and *CDMA Voice Mail Notification* (VMN).

The Originating Address parameter is the SMS Originator address, which is typically the SMS address of the SMS center that is specified in the IS-41 SMS Delivery Point-to-Point message. This is mandatory for mobile-terminated SMS message, but is not sent in mobile-origination messages. If a Transport Layer acknowledgment is requested, the SMS Transport Layer at the mobile station will send an SMS Acknowledge Transport Layer message back to the SMSC with the Destination Address set to this Originating Address of the SMSC.

The Originating Subaddress parameter is any subaddress field that may be needed to identify the originating SMSC.

The Destination Address parameter is mandatory for mobile-originated SMS messages, and is not present for mobile-terminated SMS messages. This parameter indicates the address of the destination SMS application.

The Bearer Reply Option, when present, is used for requesting a Transport Layer Acknowledgment at the SMS Transport Layer of the mobile station. The SMS sequence number is also given here to indicate which SMS sequence number to reference when sending back the SMS Acknowledge message.

The Bearer Data parameter is a variable length field that comprises the SMS Teleservice Layer message. Depending on the teleservice type, this message is coded up with different headers and options. For the details of the teleservice messages, see Section 5.A.4, "The SMS Teleservice Layer Message," on page 334.

Figure 5-42 shows an example of an SMS Transport Layer message, which was packaged into the ADDS User Part of the A-Interface ADDS Deliver message.

Table 5-14   SMS Point-to-Point Transport Layer Message (IS-637, 3.4.2.1)

BitMap	Parameter	#Oct	Range	Type	IS-637 Ref
0000 0000 (00H)	SMS_MSG _TYPE	1	00H—SMS Point-to-Point	M	3.4
0000 0000 (00H) LLLL LLLL tttt tttt tttt tttt	Teleservice Identifier	4	L = 02H, t = sms teleservice 4097—CPT 4098—CMT 4099—VMN	M	3.4.3.1
0000 0010 (02H) LLLL LLLL aaaa aaaa	Originating Address	Var-iable	L = param length a = addr of SMS originator This is set to the Orig Addr of the SMSC as specified in the IS41 SMDPP msg. Note: absent for mob orig msg	M	3.4.3.3
0000 0011 (03H) LLLL LLLL aaaa aaaa	Originating Subaddress	Var-iable	L = param length a = subaddr of SMS originator	O	3.4.3.4
0000 0100 (04H) LLLL LLLL aaaa aaaa	Destination Address	Var-iable	L = param length a = addr of SMS destination Note: absent for mob term msg	M	3.4.3.3
0000 0101 (05H) LLLL LLLL aaaa aaaa	Destination Subaddress	Var-iable	L = param length a = subaddr of SMS destination	O	3.4.3.4
0000 0110 (06H) LLLL LLLL ssss ss00	Bearer Reply Option	3	L = 01H—param length s = REPLY_SEQ number of the SMS which ack is requested	O	3.4.3.5
0000 1000 (08H) LLLL LLLL dddd dddd	Bearer Data	Var-iable	L = param length, d = bearer data as defined in the Teleser-vice Message layer	O	3.4.3.7

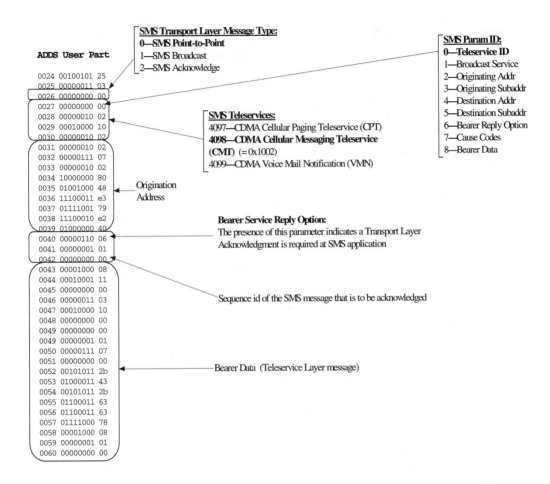

Figure 5-42   Example of an SMS Point-to-Point Transport Layer message

5.A.3.2   SMS Broadcast Transport Layer Message

The SMS Broadcast message may be sent from an SMSC to all mobile SMS applications within a MSC or BSC. The SMS_MSG_TYPE and Bearer Data are as described in the previous section.

The Broadcast Service Category is used for identifying the type of service supported by the SMS message.

Table 5-15   SMS Broadcast Transport Layer Message (IS-637, 3.4.2.2)

BitMap	Parameter	#Oct	Range	Type	IS-637 Ref
0000 0001 (01H)	SMS_MSG _TYPE	1	01H—SMS Broadcast	M	3.4
0000 0001 (01H) LLLL LLLL cccc cccc cccc cccc	Broadcast Service Category	4	L = 02H—length c = broadcast service category	M	3.4.3.2
0000 1000 (08H) LLLL LLLL dddd dddd	Bearer Data	Variable	L = param length d = bearer data as defined in the Teleservice Message layer	O	3.4.3.7

5.A.3.3   SMS Acknowledge Transport Layer Message

The SMS Acknowledge Transport Layer message is sent if the SMS Point-to-Point Transport Layer message that is received earlier contained the *Bearer Reply Option* parameter. This message provides the requested Transport Layer Acknowledgment.

The SMS_MSG_TYPE indicates the type of SMS Transport Layer message, which, in this case, is an SMS Acknowledge Transport Layer message.

The Destination Address parameter is mandatory for mobile-originated messages and is not present for mobile-terminated messages. This paramter indicates the address of the destination SMS application.

The Cause Code parameter, if there are no errors, includes only the sequence number of the SMS message being acknowledged. If a transport layer delivery problem occurs, the appropriate cause value is also included. The cause values are as defined in the SMS_CauseCode Table in IS-41 [7].

Figure 5-43 shows an example of an SMS Acknowledge Transport Layer message, which was packaged into the ADDS User Part of the A-Interface ADDS Deliver message.

Table 5-16   SMS Acknowledge Transport Layer Message (IS-637, 3.4.2.3)

BitMap	Parameter	#Oct	Range	Type	IS-637 Ref
0000 0010 (02H)	SMS_MSG_TYPE	1	02H—SMS Acknowledge	M	3.4
0000 0100 (04H) LLLL LLLL aaaa aaaa	Destination Address	Var-iable	L = param length a = addr of SMS destination For an SMS delivery to a mob, This is set to the Orig Addr of the received SMS Pt-to-Pt msg. Note: absent for mob term msg	M	3.4.3.3
0000 0101 (05H) LLLL LLLL aaaa aaaa	Destination Subaddress	Var-iable	L = param length a = subaddr of SMS destination	O	3.4.3.4
0000 0111 (07H) LLLL LLLL rrrr rree cccc cccc	Cause Codes	3 or 4	L = 01H, 02H—param length e = error class 00—no error 10—temporary error 11—permanent error r = reply sequence number of the SMS msg to be acked. c = error cause identifier. (will not be included if no err) As defined in the SMS_ CauseCode Table in IS-41	M	3.4.3.6

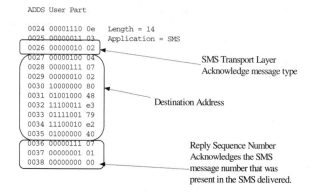

ADDS User Part

```
0024 00001110 0e    Length = 14
0025 00000011 03    Application = SMS
0026 00000010 02
0027 00000100 04
0028 00000111 07
0029 00000010 02
0030 10000000 80
0031 01001000 48
0032 11100011 e3
0033 01111001 79
0034 11100010 e2
0035 01000000 40
0036 00000111 07
0037 00000001 01
0038 00000000 00
```

SMS Transport Layer
Acknowledge message type

Destination Address

Reply Sequence Number
Acknowledges the SMS
message number that was
present in the SMS delivered.

SMS Transport Layer Ack:
The SMSC (or other device) may require the Mobile Station to supply a Transport Layer acknowledge. To accomplish this, the mobile sends an IS95 RevTCH Data Burst message to the BSC that contains the Transport Layer acknowledgements. The BSC then packages this information in the ADDS User Part IE of the ADDS Deliver message.

Figure 5-43   Example of an SMS Acknowledge Transport layer message

5.A.4   The SMS Teleservice Layer Message

The SMS teleservice is the SMS application running at the bearer service end points, such as the mobile station and SMS message center. There are three main CDMA Teleservice types, each with a unique Teleservice ID:

- 4097—*CDMA Cellular Paging Teleservice* (CPT)
- 4098—*CDMA Cellular Messaging Teleservice* (CMT)
- 4099—*CDMA Voice Mail Notification* (VMN)

CPT and CMT are commonly used for SMS services, and VMN is used for voice mail notification when the VMS is connected to an SMSC.

For each teleservice, there are different teleservice message types that are supported; each is identified by a unique MESSAGE_TYPE ID at the teleservice layer:

- 0001—SMS Deliver (mobterm)—CPT, CMT, VMN
- 0010—SMS Submit (moborig)—CPT, CMT
- 0011—SMS Cancel (moborig)—CMT
- 0101—SMS User Ack (both)—CMT
- 0100—SMS Deliver Ack (mobterm)—CPT, CMT

This section focuses on the SMS Deliver message type because it is one of the most commonly used SMS teleservice message types.

SMS Submit messages are sent when a mobile originates an SMS message; SMS Cancellation is sent when the mobile cancels the SMS message.

SMS User Acknowledgment is sent by a mobile when a user acknowledges a previously received SMS Deliver message that had the Reply Option field set to user acknowledgment requested.

SMS Delivery Acknowledgment is sent to a mobile, which originates an SMS message when the final destination mobile receives the SMS Deliver message and returns a Transport Layer SMS Acknowledgment message. The original SMS Deliver message uses the Reply Option field to request for a delivery acknowledgment.

The Teleservice layer translates the type of teleservice that is being used into a Teleservice layer message and passes this Teleservice message to the Transport Layer, which will then package the message into the bearer data field of the Transport Layer message. The Teleservice ID present in the SMS Point-to-Point Transport Layer message indicates the type of teleservice that is sent in its Bearer Data field. Note that the Broadcast Messaging Teleservice does not have a Teleservice ID in the SMS Broadcast Transport Layer message.

5.A.4.1   SMS Deliver CPT Teleservice Layer Message

The CPT Teleservice is described in Section 6.2 of IS-53A [9]. For point-to-point SMS message delivery, the SMS Deliver message is used to send the CPT Teleservice message.

The Message Identifier parameter specifies which type of Teleservice Layer message is being sent. A message identifier of *0001* indicates an SMS Deliver Teleservice Layer message (Table 5-17).

The User Data field contains the CPT Teleservice message that was submitted and was to be delivered to the end-user SMS application.

The Message Center Time Stamp parameter, when included, indicates the time that the message is sent from the SMS center.

The Priority Indicator parameter indicates the priority of the message in four different levels.

The Privacy Indicator parameter specifies the level of privacy of the message being sent, in four different levels.

The Reply Option parameter specifies whether acknowledgment at the Teleservice Layer is requested. If the Reply Option is set to "user acknowledgment," the user at the destination mobile is notified that an explicit acknowledgment is requested. When the user acknowledges the SMS Deliver message, an SMS User Acknowledgment Teleservice Layer message is sent. If the Reply Option is set to "delivery acknowledgment," usually for a mobile-originated SMS, the SMS center will send an SMS Delivery Acknowledgment Teleservice Layer message to the originating mobile when the SMSC receives a Transport Layer acknowledgment from the destination mobile.

The Number of Messages parameter indicates the number of messages stored at the SMSC.

The Call Back Number parameter indicates the number to be dialed in reply to a received SMS message. Usually, CPT paging services or VMN voice mail services make use of this parameter.

Table 5-17   SMS Deliver Teleservice Layer Message for CPT (IS-637, 4.3.3)

BitMap	Parameter	#Oct	Range	Type	IS-637 Ref
0000 0000 (00H) LLLL LLLL tttt iiii iiii iiii iiii 0000	Message Identifier	1	L = 03H—subparam length t = 0001—SMS Deliver i = message identifier To identify the SMS message being delivered or submitted.	M	4.5.1
0000 0001 (01H) LLLL LLLL dddd dddd ……	User Data	Variable	L = subparam length d = user data	O	4.5.2
0000 0011 (03H) LLLL LLLL yyyy yyyy mmmm mmmm dddd dddd hhhh hhhh nnnn nnnn ssss ssss	Message Center Time Stamp	8	L = 06H—subparam length y = 0–99—year m = 1–12—month d = day of the month h = 0–23—hour n = 0–59—minutes s = 0–59—seconds	O	4.5.4
0000 1000 (08H) LLLL LLLL pp00 0000	Priority Indicator	3	L = 01H—subparam length p = priority 00—normal 01—interactive 10—urgent 11—emergency	O	4.5.9
0000 1001 (09H) LLLL LLLL pp00 0000	Privacy Indicator	3	L = 01H—subparam length p = privacy 00—not restricted 01—restricted 10—confidential 11—secret	O	4.5.10

Table 5-17 SMS Deliver Teleservice Layer Message for CPT (IS-637, 4.3.3) (Continued)

BitMap	Parameter	#Oct	Range	Type	IS-637 Ref
0000 1010 (0AH) LLLL LLLL ud00 0000	Reply Option	3	L = 01H—subparam length d = Delivery ack request u = positive user ack req	O	4.5.11
0000 1011 (0BH) LLLL LLLL cccc cccc	Number of Messages	3	L = 01H—subparam length c = message count	O	4.5.12
0000 1110 (0EH) LLLL LLLL aaaa aaaa ….	Call Back Number	Variable	L = subparam length a = callback number	O	4.5.15

5.A.4.2 SMS Deliver CMT Teleservice Layer Message

The CMT Teleservice is described in Section 6.3 of IS-53A [9]. For point-to-point SMS message delivery, the SMS Deliver message is used to send the CMT Teleservice message.

The Message Identifier parameter specifies which type of Teleservice Layer message is being sent. A message identifier of *0001* indicates an SMS Deliver Teleservice Layer message (Table 5-18).

The User Data, Message Center Time Stamp, Priority Indicator, Privacy Indicator, Reply Option, Number of Messages, and Call Back Number parameters are discussed in the previous section for CPT.

The Validity Period-Absolute is an indication from an originating SMS Teleservice to the SMS center, which specifies the message expiration time after which the message should be removed from the SMSC if no acknowledgment has been received from the destination mobile.

The Validity Period-Relative has the same meaning as the above, except that the time period is measured from when the message is received by the SMSC.

The Language Indicator parameter indicates the language of the SMS message sent. In the case when this is different from the mobile's preferred language, the message may be discarded.

Table 5-18 SMS Deliver Teleservice Layer Message for CMT (IS-637, 4.3.4)

BitMap	Parameter	#Oct	Range	Type	IS-637 Ref
0000 0000 (00H) LLLL LLLL tttt iiii iiii iiii iiii 0000	Message Identifier	1	L = 03H—subparam length t = 0001—SMS Deliver i = message identifier To identify the SMS message being delivered or submitted.	M	4.5.1
0000 0001 (01H) …..	User Data	Variable	Same as parameter in Table 5-17, SMS Deliver msg for CPT.	O	4.5.2
0000 0011 (03H) …..	Message Center Time Stamp	8	Same as parameter in Table 5-17, SMS Deliver msg for CPT.	O	4.5.4
0000 0100 (04H) LLLL LLLL yyyy yyyy mmmm mmmm dddd dddd hhhh hhhh nnnn nnnn ssss ssss	Validity Period - Absolute	8	L = 06H—subparam length y = 0–99—year m = 1–12—month d = day of the month h = 0–23—hour n = 0–59—minutes s = 0–59—seconds	O	4.5.5
0000 0101 (05H) LLLL LLLL pppp pppp	Validity Period - Relative	3	L = 01H—subparam length p = relative validity period	O	4.5.6
0000 1000 (08H) …..	Priority Indicator	3	Same as parameter in Table 5-17, SMS Deliver msg for CPT.	O	4.5.9
0000 1001 (09H) ….	Privacy Indicator	3	Same as parameter in Table 5-17, SMS Deliver msg for CPT.	O	4.5.10
0000 1010 (0AH) ……..	Reply Option	3	Same as parameter in Table 5-17, SMS Deliver msg for CPT.	O	4.5.11

Table 5-18 SMS Deliver Teleservice Layer Message for CMT (IS-637, 4.3.4)
(Continued)

BitMap	Parameter	#Oct	Range	Type	IS-637 Ref
0000 1011 (0BH)	Number of Messages	3	Same as parameter in Table 5-17, SMS Deliver msg for CPT.	O	4.5.12
0000 1100 (0CH) LLLL LLLL	Alert on Message Delivery	2	L = 00H—subparam length Alert is requested	O	4.5.13
0000 1101 (0DH) LLLL LLLL llll llll	Language Indicator	3	L = 01H—subparam length l = language 00H—unknown 01H—English 02H—French 03H—Spanish	O	4.5.14
0000 1110 (0EH)	Call Back Number	Variable	Same as parameter in Table 5-17, SMS Deliver msg for CPT.	O	4.5.15

Figure 5-44 shows an example of an SMS Deliver CMT Teleservice Layer message, which was packaged into the bearer data portion of an SMS Point-to-Point Transport Layer message. The Transport Layer message was then encapsulated within an A-Interface ADDS Deliver message.

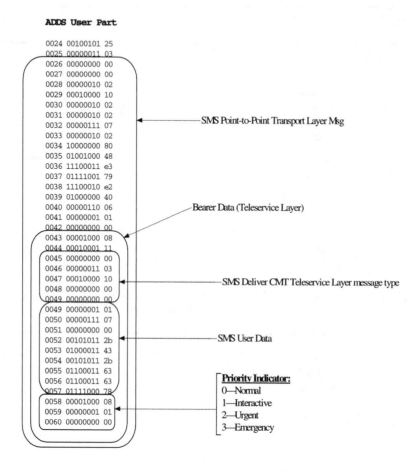

ADDS User Part

Figure 5-44 Example of an SMS Deliver CMT Teleservice Layer message

5.A.4.3   SMS Deliver VMN Teleservice Layer Message

The VMN teleservice is described in IS-91 [11]. For point-to-point SMS message delivery, the SMS Deliver message is used to send the VMN Teleservice message.

The parameters in this message are similar to the ones describe for CPT and CMT, except that in a VMN message, the Number of Messages parameter is mandatory. This indicates the number of messages that are stored in the VMS (Table 5-19).

Table 5-19   SMS Deliver Teleservice Layer Message for VMN (IS-637, 4.3.5)

BitMap	Parameter	#Oct	Range	Type	IS-637 Ref
0000 0000 (00H) LLLL LLLL tttt iiii iiii iiii iiii 0000	Message Identifier	1	L = 03H—subparam length t = 0001—SMS Deliver i = message identifier To identify the SMS message being delivered or submitted.	M	4.5.1
0000 0001 (01H) …..	User Data	Variable	Same as parameter in Table 5-17, SMS Deliver msg for CPT.	O	4.5.2
0000 0011 (03H) …..	Message Center Time Stamp	8	Same as parameter in Table 5-17, SMS Deliver msg for CPT.	O	4.5.4
0000 1000 (08H) …..	Priority Indicator	3	Same as parameter in Table 5-17, SMS Deliver msg for CPT.	O	4.5.9
0000 1001 (09H) ….	Privacy Indicator	3	Same as parameter in Table 5-17, SMS Deliver msg for CPT.	O	4.5.10
0000 1011 (0BH) ……..	Number of Messages	3	Same as parameter in Table 5-17, SMS Deliver msg for CPT.	O	4.5.12
0000 1100 (0CH) LLLL LLLL	Alert on Message Delivery	2	L = 00H—subparam length Alert is requested, implementation specific.	O	4.5.13
0000 1110 (0EH) …..	Call Back Number	Variable	Same as parameter in Table 5-17, SMS Deliver msg for CPT.	O	4.5.15

References

1. CDG-IOS version 3.1.1, *CDMA Development Group MSC to BS Interface Inter-Operability Specification.* June 1999.

2. CDG-IOS version 2.0, *CDMA Development Group MSC to BS Interface Inter-Operability Specification.* September 1998.

3. Telecommunications Industry Association, TIA/EIA/IS-634-A, *MSC-BS Interface (A-Interface) for Public 800 MHz.* July 1998.

4. Telecommunications Industry Association , TIA/EIA/TSB-80, *MSC-BS Interface (A-Interface) for Public 800 MHz.* October 1996.

5. Telecommunications Industry Association, TIA/EIA/IS-95-A, *Mobile Station-Base Station Compatibility Standard for Dual-Mode Wideband Spread Spectrum Cellular Systems.* May 1995.

6. American National Standards Institute, ANSI J-STD-008, *Personal Station – Base Station Compatibility Requirements for 1.8 to 2.0 GHz Code Devision Multiple Access (CDMA) Personal Communications Systems.* August 1995.

7. American National Standards Institute, ANSI TIA/EIA/IS-41-D, *Cellular Radio-Telecommunications Intersystem Operations.* December 1997.

8. Telecommunications Industry Association, TIA/EIA/IS-637, *Short Message Services for Wideband Spread Spectrum Cellular Systems.* December 1995.

9. Telecommunications Industry Association, TIA/EIA/IS-53-A, *Cellular Features Description.* April 1995.

10. Telecommunications Industry Association, TIA/EIA/TSB-58, *Administration Parameter Value Assignments for TIA/EIA Wideband Spread Spectrum Standards.* April 1995.

11. Telecommunications Industry Association, TIA/EIA/IS-91, *Mobile Station—Base Station Compatibility Standard for 800MHz Analog Cellular.* October 1994.

12. Telecommunications Industry Association, TIA/EIA 664, *Cellular Features Description.* April 1995.

13. Telecommunications Industry Association, TIA/EIA/IS-683-A, *Over-the-Air Service Provisioning of Mobile Stations in Spread Spectrum Systems.* June 1998.

14. Telecommunications Industry Association, TIA/EIA/IS-725, *IS-41-C Enhancements for OTASP, Over-the-Air Service Provisioning of Mobile Stations in Spread Spectrum Systems.* June 1997.

15. Telecommunications Industry Association, TIA/EIA/IS-99, *Data Service Option Standard for Wideband Spread Spectrum Digital Cellular System.* July 1995.

16. Telecommunications Industry Association, TIA/EIA/IS-707, *Data Service Options for Wideband Spread Spectrum Digital Cellular System.* February 1998.

17. Telecommunications Industry Association, TIA/EIA/IS-707A, *Data Service Options for Wideband Spread Spectrum Digital Cellular System.* March 1999.

18. Telecommunications Industry Association, TIA/EIA/IS-728, *Intersystem Link Protocol.* April 1997.

19. Telecommunications Industry Association, TIA/EIA/IS-658, *Data Services Interworking Function Interface for Wideband Spread Spectrum Systems.* 1997.

20. Telecommunications Industry Association, TIA/EIA/IS-737, *Intersystem Operations Support for Data Services.* 1997.

21. Internation Telecommunications Union, ITU-T Recommendation T.4, *Standardization of Group 3 Facsimile Terminals for Document Transmission.* July 1996.

22. Internation Telecommunications Union, ITU-T Recommendation T.30, *Procedures for Document Facsimile Transmission in the General Switched Telephone Network.* July 1996.

23. Telecommunications Industry Association, EIA/TIA-232-E, *Interface Between DTE and DCE Employing Serial Binary Data Interchange.* 1991.

24. Telecommunications Industry Association, EIA/TIA-592, *Asynchronous Facsimile DCE Control Standard—Ser-*

vice Class 2.0. 1993.

25. Telecommunications Industry Association, EIA/TIA-602, *Serial Asynchronous Automatic Dialing and Control*.1992.

26. Telecommunications Industry Association, EIA/TIA-605, *Facsimile DCE-DTE Packet Protocol Standard*. 1992.

27. Telecommunications Industry Association, EIA/TIA-615, *Extensions to Serial Asynchronous Automatic Dialing and Control*. 1993.

28. Telecommunications Industry Association, ANSI/TIA/EIA-617, *Enband DCE Control for Asynchronous DTE–DCE Interfaces*. 1996.

29. Telecommunications Industry Association, TIA/EIA/IS-131, *Data Transmission Systems and Equipment- Extensions to Serial Asynchronous Dialing and Control*. 1993.

30. Telecommunications Industry Association, TIA/EIA/IS-134, *Amendments to TIA-592 to support T.30*. 1993.

31. Internet Engineering Task Force, RFC 791, *Internet Protocol (IP)*. 1981.

32. Internet Engineering Task Force, RFC 793, *Transmission Control Protocol (TCP)*. 1981.

33. Internet Engineering Task Force, RFC 1332, *The PPP Internet Protocol Control Protocol (IPCP)*. 1992.

34. Internet Engineering Task Force, RFC 1570, *PPP LCP Extensions*. 1994.

35. Internet Engineering Task Force, RFC 1661, *The Point-to-Point Protocol (PPP)*. 1994.

36. Internet Engineering Task Force, RFC 1662, *PPP in HDLC Framing*.1994.

37. James D. Solomon, *Mobile IP: The Internet Unplugged*, New York:Prentice Hall, 1998.

CHAPTER 6

Authentication

$\mathbf{T}$he overwhelming growth in the number of wireless subscribers has also resulted in increased network fraud. Telecommunication fraud costs the industry a reported $12 billion a year [1], and as much as $500 million of that may be directly related to wireless fraud. The most common form of wireless fraud is referred to as *counterfeiting* or *cloning*. Cloning occurs when a valid customer's mobile identity is duplicated in another mobile, which is then used for unauthorized access to network services. The charges incurred by the clone mobile are billed to the valid customer's account, which results in lost operator revenue. To combat wireless fraud, many service providers have deployed Authentication-enabled networks that rely on the exchange of secret codes based on a complex algorithm between mobile stations and the *Mobile Switching Center* (MSC) to validate a mobile.

CDMA networks inherently provide security and identification procedures to help identify and reduce fraudulent network use. As discussed in Section 3.1.1, "Mobile Origination Call Flow," on page 143, an *International Mobile Subscriber Identifier* (IMSI) and an *Electronic Serial Number* (ESN) are used to identify mobile stations uniquely in a CDMA network. The IMSI is set by the network service provider and usually consists of between 10 and 15 digits. The factory-set ESN consists of at least 32 bits and is stored in inaccessible memory in the mobile station. CDMA mobile stations are designed so that any attempt to modify the ESN circuitry will result in an unusable phone. The MSC's decision to allow or refuse a mobile in non-Authentication-enabled networks is normally based on the received IMSI and ESN. If the two values received match a subscriber profile stored in the *Home Location Register* (HLR), the mobile is granted access to the network. This simple procedure does a good job keeping "honest" people honest but is susceptible to more sophisticated fraud techniques. To thwart these advanced fraudulent methods, CDMA networks provide an additional mobile station validation procedure known as *Authentication*.

The authentication process validates a mobile station for network access by using an authentication algorithm common to both the mobile station and the network *Authentication Center* (AC). A mobile is either authorized or denied use of the network, based on the outcome of the authentication process. The algorithm used in IS-95 CDMA networks by both the AC and the mobile station is known as the *CAVE algorithm*. This algorithm is independently executed at both the mobile station and the AC using the same set of inputs, such as stored secret, a transmitted random number, and mobile parameters, such as IMSI and ESN. When programming a mobile for use in an Authentication-enabled network, the network service provider downloads a unique secret authentication parameter known as the *A-Key*. Only the individual mobile station and the AC know the A-Key, and it is never transmitted over the air. A mobile is successfully authenticated when the CAVE algorithm outputs at both the mobile station and AC match; otherwise, the mobile is considered a fraud and is refused network services.

There are several operational scenarios during which the authentication process may be invoked. In an Authentication-enabled network, the authentication process usually occurs during mobile registrations, mobile originations, and mobile terminations. The authentication process may, however, be explicitly invoked at any time by the AC.

In addition to authentication, the mobile subscriber can also request privacy services from the network through the use of encryption keys. If privacy services are requested, encryption algorithms are used to encrypt both the IS-95 signaling messages and voice frames that are transmitted over the air.

The following section describes the overall concept of the authentication processes. Subsequent sections further discuss the individual call flows and messages used during various authentication and privacy scenarios.

6.1 Authentication Overview

Figure 6-1 illustrates the steps involved in authenticating a mobile station. If network authentication is enabled, a random number (RAND) is generated by either the *Base Station Controller* (BSC) or MSC and is made known to both the mobile stations and the AC. The BSC notifies the mobile stations that they should include authentication parameters in access channel messages by setting the AUTH field in the IS-95 Access Parameters paging channel message. Also included in the IS-95 Access Parameters message is a RAND field that is used to transfer the BSC- or MSC-generated random number to the mobile station.

In addition to RAND, three other input parameters are also applied to the CAVE algorithms at both the mobile stations and the AC to compute authentication "signatures." Specifically, these three additional CAVE algorithm inputs include a locally stored *Shared Secret Data* (SSD) parameter, the mobile's ESN, and the mobile station's IMSI (certain authentication scenarios require the use of the dialed digits instead of the mobile station's IMSI). The SSD parameter is derived locally from the stored A-Key. The mobile station's A-Key, SSD, ESN, and IMSI digits are all prestored at the AC in a secure database.

Based on the four authentication inputs, both the mobile station and AC calculate individual authentication results, and a comparison is done at either the mobile station or the AC. The comparison is typically done at the AC, however, the Base Station Challenge scenario requires the comparison to be done at the mobile station. If the authentication signatures are to be compared at the AC, the mobile station sends its authentication result to the BSC over the air using the IS-95 interface. The BSC then formats the authentication information in an A-Interface message that is sent to the MSC. If an external AC is being used, the MSC transfers the authentication information using an IS-41 or a proprietary interface. Some MSCs contain an internal AC and, therefore, do not require an external interface. A similar transfer of messages occurs in the opposite direction if the comparison is instead done at the mobile station.

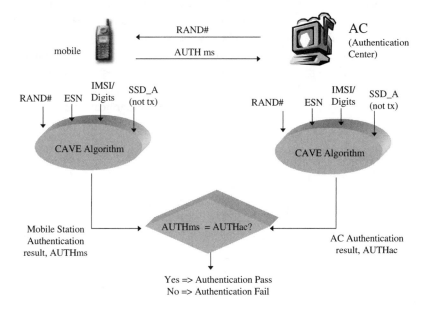

Figure 6-1 Authentication Process overview

When the authentication results match, the "authenticated" mobile station is provided services by the network. If the authentication process fails, the network may deny services to the mobile station or the AC may request an SSD Update to ensure that both the mobile station and the AC are using the most up-to-date information. If an SSD Update is performed, the AC follows with a Unique Challenge to retry the authentication procedure using the updated parameters. An SSD Update commonly occurs when a mobile station first originates a call in an Authentication-enabled network. Initially, the mobile's SSD will be zero, and an authentication signature mismatch will occur. The AC then performs an SSD Update to synchronize values and subsequently validate service.

The three authentication procedures specified in CDGIOS are *Global Challenge*, *Unique Challenge*, and *SSD Update*.

The Global Challenge process uses a common random number (RAND) that is periodically updated and transmitted to mobiles stations over the paging channel. All mobiles accessing a particular cell use the same RAND value as an input to the authentication process. Global Challenge usually occurs when mobile stations register or during call origination and termination attempts. In the case of Global Challenge, the mobile station sends its CAVE algorithm result to the AC, which then compares the received value with its computed result.

Unique Challenge is a procedure used by the AC to request that authentication be performed on a particular mobile station. Unlike Global Challenge, the Unique Challenge process involves the use of a unique random number (RANDU) generated specifically at the AC for an individual mobile station. Unique Challenge may occur any time the AC or network operator desires and is not restricted to mobile registrations or access attempts. The CAVE algorithm result is sent from the mobile station to the AC for comparison.

SSD Update is a procedure whereby the AC requests a mobile station to update its stored SSD value and may be invoked either when the authentication process fails or when the AC or network operator specifies.

The following list summarizes the relationship between authentication procedures and network operating scenarios.

1. Global Challenge
 • Location Update
 • Mobile Origination Call Setup
 • Mobile Termination Call Setup

2. Unique Challenge
 • Paging Channel
 • Traffic Channel

3. SSD Update in Traffic Channel
 • A Base Station Challenge
 • An optional Unique Challenge

6.1.1   Authentication Parameters

Global Challenge, Unique Challenge, and SSD Update procedures each use a subset of the available authentication parameters that are summarized in Table 6-1. The purpose of this section is to describe the individual parameters.

The RAND parameter is a 32-bit random number that is broadcast over the paging channel in the IS-95 Access Parameters message and is used as a CAVE algorithm input during Global Challenges. Whether this parameter is generated by the MSC or BSC depends on vendor implementation and network design considerations.

The Authentication Confirmation Parameter (RANDC) is simply the 8 most significant bits of the broadcast RAND value. The network compares the received RANDC parameter with the most significant 8 bits of the RAND value previously transmitted.

RANDU is a 24-bit random number that is generated by either the AC or the MSC and is used during Unique Challenges.

The RANDSSD parameter is a 56-bit random number generated by the HLR/AC and is used during the SSD Update procedure.

RANDBS is a 32-bit random number generated by the mobile station that is used as an input to the CAVE algorithm during a Base Station Challenge.

The mobile station A-Key is a unique secret 64-bit key that is programmed by the network service provider. The secret A-Key is also is stored in a secured AC database. This key is never transmitted across any network interfaces and is known only to the mobile station and the AC.

The SSD parameter is generated using RANDSSD, ESN, and A-Key inputs and provides a second layer of security during the authentication process. The SSD parameter, like the A-Key, is never transmitted across any network interfaces.

SSD_A is the 64 most significant bits of the SSD parameter and is used as an input to the CAVE algorithm.

SSD_B is the 64 least significant bits of the SSD parameter and is used for *Voice Privacy* (VP) and *Signaling Message Encryption* (SME).

The mobile station's ESN is a unique identifier set by the mobile station manufacturer.

The IMSI_S1 parameter is 24-bit value that is derived from the IMSI_S digits and a mapping scheme that converts the 7 least significant IMSI_S digits into a 24-bit value.

Figure 6-2 illustrates the relationship between IMSI_S, IMSI_S1 and IMSI_S2. Recall that IMSI_S is the 10 least significant digits of the mobile station's IMSI. The least significant 7 bits of IMSI_S are referred to as IMSI_S1 and the 3 most significant bits of IMSI_S are denoted IMSI_S2. Because the mobile station respectively stores IMSI_S1 and IMSI_S2 as 24- and 10-bit binary numbers, IMSI_S1, and IMSI_S2 are further broken down into 3-digit and 1-digit groupings. Mapping functions are used to convert these decimal groupings into binary representations. The result is a 24-bit binary representation for IMSI_S1 and a 10-bit binary representation for IMSI_S2. The two mapping functions used for the conversion are specified below and are followed by an example. Mapping 1 is used to convert a 3-digit decimal number $(D_1 D_2 D_3)$ to a 10-digit binary representation. Mapping 2 simply converts a decimal digit (D_1) to its *Binary Coded Decimal* (BCD) representation.

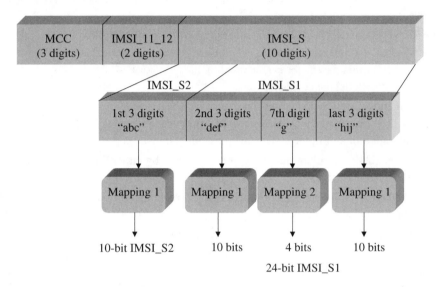

Figure 6-2   24-bit IMSI_S1 and 10-bit IMSI_S2 digits for Authentication inputs

• Mapping 1:

$$100*D_1 + 10*D_2 + D_3 - 111 \tag{6.1}$$

• Mapping 2:

$$D_1 \rightarrow BCD \tag{6.2}$$

Example:

Mobile Station's **IMSI** = 210089429354613

• **IMSI_S** = 9429354613

• **IMSI_S2** = 942 (abc)

   Using Mapping 1: abc = 942 = 9*100 + 4*10 + 2 –111 = 11 0011 1111

• 10-bit **IMSI_S2** = 11 0011 1111

• **IMSI_S1** = 9354613 (defghij)

   Using Mapping 1: def = 9*100 + 3*10 + 5 – 111 = 11 0011 1000

   Using Mapping 2: g = 4 = 0100

   Using Mapping 1: hij = 6*100 + 1*10* 3 – 111 = 01 1111 0110

• 24-bit **IMSI_S1** = 1100 1110 0001 0001 1111 0110

The Global Authentication DIGITS parameter contains the last 6 digits of the dialed digits string entered by the mobile user during an origination. If less than 6 digits are dialed, the most significant bits of IMSI_S1 are used to replace the absent digits. The DIGITS parameter is used only as an input to the CAVE algorithm during mobile originations.

The COUNT parameter provides an added level of security to help identify clone mobile stations. Both the mobile station and the AC independently store and update the COUNT parameter. COUNT is updated when the mobile sets up a call or when the IS-95 Parameter Update Order is sent to the mobile on the forward traffic channel. Note that the latter is performed by a procedure known as Parameter Update in IS-634A; however, this procedure is not required in CDGIOS. When the received COUNT value does not match the value stored at the AC, the mobile station may be declared a clone and denied network services.

The AUTHR parameter contains the result of the CAVE algorithm during the Global Challenge process. Both the mobile station and the AC compute this parameter, and the two results are compared at the AC. If the authentication signatures match, the mobile station is "authenticated."

The AUTHU parameter contains the CAVE algorithm result computed during a Unique Challenge. Both the mobile station and the AC compute this parameter, and the values are compared at the AC.

The AUTHBS parameter contains the CAVE Algorithm result computed during a Base Station Challenge. Unlike Global and Unique Challenges, the AUTHBS value computed by the AC is sent to the mobile station, which then compares the result with its own computed value.

Table 6-1 Authentication Parameters

Parameter	#Bits	Description
RAND	32	Random number broadcast in the paging channel IS-95 Access Parameters message that is chosen by either the BSC or MSC. Used as an input to the CAVE algorithm during Global Challenge.
RANDC	8	8 most significant bits of RAND, sent by the mobile station.
RANDU	24	Random number generated by the AC or MSC. Used as an input to the CAVE algorithm during Unique Challenge.
RANDSSD	56	Random number generated by the HLR or AC. Used as an input to the SSD Update procedure.
RANDBS	32	Random number generated by the mobile during Base Station Challenge. Used as an input to the CAVE algorithm.

Table 6-1   Authentication Parameters (Continued)

Parameter	#Bits	Description
A-Key	64	Service provider programmed secret key used for generating the SSD.
SSD	128	Shared Secret Data, a second-level security key derived from the A-Key.
SSD_A	64	Most significant 64 bits of SSD. Used as an input to the CAVE algorithm.
SSD_B	64	Least significant 64 bits of SSD. Used for VP and SME.
ESN	32	Unique Electronic Serial Number assigned to the mobile station by the manufacturers. Used as an input to the CAVE Algorithm.
IMSI_S1	24	The least significant 7 digits of IMSI_S mapped to a 24-bit binary representation. IMSI_S is the least significant 10 digits of the mobile station's IMSI. Used as an input to the CAVE algorithm.
IMSI_S2	10	The 3 most significant digits of IMSI_S mapped to a 10-bit binary representation. Used as an input to the CAVE Algorithm for Unique Challenges. Note that only the 8 least significant of the binary representation are used as input to the CAVE Algorithm.
DIGITS	24	The last 6 digits of the dialed string entered by the subscriber during an origination. Used as an input to the CAVE Algorithm during mobile originations.
COUNT	6	Counter that relects the number of mobile call attempts. Used to help identify clone mobile stations.
AUTHR	18	Authentication result of CAVE Algorithm during Global Challenge.
AUTHU	18	Authentication results of CAVE Algorithm during Unique Challenge.
AUTHBS	18	Authentication results of CAVE Algorithm during Base Station Challenge.

6.1.2   Summary of Authentication Parameters

Table 6-2 summarizes which authentication parameters are used during Global Challenge, Unique Challenge, Base Station Challenge, and SSD Update. Global Challenge is further broken down into the three main operational scenarios—mobile registration, mobile origination, and mobile termination. Note that the output for the SSD Update procedure is the SSD parameter and not the CAVE authentication signature.

Table 6-2 Summary of Authentication Input and Output Parameters

Procedure	Rand# Input	SSD input	ESN	Auth_Data	Result
Registration	RAND	SSD_A	ESN	IMSI_S1	AUTHR
Mobile Origination	RAND	SSD_A	ESN	Dialed digits	AUTHR
Mobile Termination	RAND	SSD_A	ESN	IMSI_S1	AUTHR
Unique Challenge	RANDU + 8 bits of IMSI_S2	SSD_A	ESN	IMSI_S1	AUTHU
Base Station Challenge	RANDBS	SSD_A	ESN	IMSI_S1	AUTHBS
SSD Update	RANDSSD	A-Key	ESN	-	SSD

6.2 Global Challenge—Location Update

In an Authentication-enabled network, Global Challenge Authentication is performed when an Authentication-capable mobile station registers or performs a location update. This section describes the call flow and messages associated with a Global Challenge during a mobile station registration.

The Global Challenge authentication process utilizes a random number (RAND), which is broadcast by the BSC to mobile stations over the paging channel. The broadcast RAND value, along with the locally stored SSD_A, ESN, and IMSI_S1 parameters are input to the CAVE algorithm at both the mobile station and the AC, resulting in an authentication signature. The AC compares the CAVE algorithm result received from the mobile station with its own computed value (see Figure 6-1). If the values match, the mobile station is allowed to use network services.

Figure 6-3 shows the high-level message flow associated with mobile registration when Authentication is enabled. During registration, the mobile station computes an authentication result AUTHR using the RAND parameter broadcast to it over the paging channel. The RANDC, ESN, IMSI, AUTHR, and COUNT parameters are passed from the mobile station to the BSC using the IS-95 Registration message. The BSC then places the received information in an A-Interface Location Updating Request message that is sent to the MSC. The MSC passes the relevant authentication information to the AC, which checks whether the received AUTHR matches its locally computed AUTHR value. The AC also checks the COUNT value it receives with its stored COUNT value. If either AUTHR or COUNT do not match, the mobile may be declared a clone, and service may be denied.

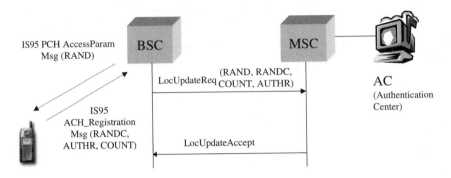

Figure 6-3 Global Challenge—Location Update

6.2.1 Global Challenge—Location Update Call Flow

Figure 6-4 illustrates the complete message flow for a mobile registration in an Authenticated-enabled network. Descriptions of individual messages follow the call flow diagram. The descriptions assume that both the network and mobile are Authentication-enabled.

1. Set Ctrl Ch Params (RAND) (A-Interface):

   The random number (RAND) used in Global Challenge can be generated either at the BSC or MSC. If the RAND parameter is generated at the MSC, it is transferred to the BSC using the A-Interface Set Control Channel Parameters message. The MSC starts timer T101 to wait for an acknowledgment.

2. IS95_PCH_AccssParams (RAND) (IS-95):

   The BSC sends an IS-95 Access Parameters message over the paging channel with the *AUTH* field set to 1 and the RAND field set to the current RAND value. To discourage fraudulent attempts, the RAND value may be periodically updated and transmitted to mobile stations.

3. Set Ctrl Ch Params Ack (A-Interface):

   After the BSC updates the paging channel messages with the overhead information received from the MSC, it sends a Set Control Channel Parameter Acknowledgment message to the MSC. If timer T101 expires before receipt of the acknowledgment, the MSC may choose to resend the Set Control Channel Parameter message one more time.

4. IS95_ACH_Registration (RANDC, AUTHR, COUNT) (IS-95):

   The mobile station registers by sending an IS-95 Registration message over the access channel. The *AUTH_MODE* field of the IS-95 Registration message is set to *01,* and the corresponding authentication parameters RANDC, AUTHR, and COUNT are included.

5. LocUpdateReq (RANDC, RAND, COUNT, AUTHR) (A-Interface):

The BSC, upon receipt of the IS-95 Registration message, sends a Location Updating Request to the MSC that contains the mobile's registration parameters. The BSC starts timer T3210 to wait for either a Location Updating Accept or Reject message.

Note that if authentication is enabled at the BSC and authentication parameters RANDC, AUTHR, and COUNT are not received from the mobile, the optional Authentication Event IE is set to *1* and is included in this message.

The BSC correlates the RANDC value received from the mobile with the RAND value that the BSC previously sent over the paging channel. If there is a mismatch between RANDC and RAND, the BSC sets the Authentication Event to *2*, which notifies the MSC of the mismatch. The MSC or AC may then take further action to resolve the mismatch.

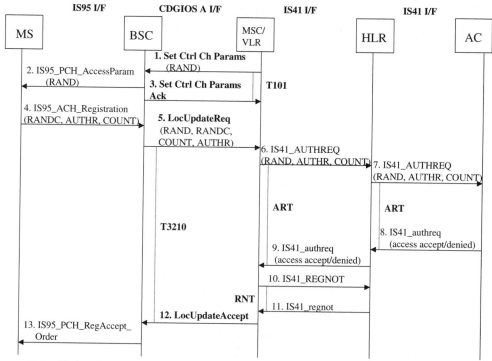

Figure 6-4   Global Challenge in Location Update call flow

6. IS41_AUTHREQ (RAND, AUTHR, COUNT) (IS-41):

Upon receipt of the Location Updating Request, the MSC verifies the received authentication parameters. The MSC then sends the HLR an IS41_AUTHREQ message that includes RAND, AUTHR, and COUNT.

The MSC starts timer ART (*Authentication Request Timer*), which has a default value of 6 seconds, while waiting for an IS41_authreq return result or return error [8].

7. IS41_AUTHREQ (RAND, AUTHR, COUNT) (IS-41):

The HLR passes on the IS41_AUTHREQ message to the AC and starts timer ART.

8. IS41_authreq (access accept/denied) (IS-41):

Upon receipt of the IS41_AUTHREQ message, the AC computes the authentication signature using the CAVE algorithm and compares the result with the value computed by the mobile station. It also compares the COUNT value received with its locally stored value. If both AUTHR and COUNT match, the mobile station is considered to be authenticated, and the AC sends the HLR an IS41_authreq return result, indicating the success of the authentication process.

If the authentication comparison fails, the AC includes the Deny Access parameter in the IS41_authreq message that it sends to the HLR. Upon receiving the IS41_authreq message, the MSC sends a Location Updating Reject message to the BSC with a cause reason of Illegal MS, indicating that the mobile failed the authentication process. The BSC subsequently sends an IS-95 Registration Reject Order message to the mobile station on the paging channel.

The HLR stops timer ART upon receipt of the IS41_authreq message from the AC.

9. IS41_authreq (access accept/denied) (IS-41):

The IS41_authreq message is passed from the HLR to the MSC. The MSC stops timer ART upon receipt of the IS41_authreq return result or return error message from the HLR.

10. IS41_REGNOT (IS-41):

If the IS41_authreq message received by the MSC indicates that the authentication was successful, the MSC/VLR sends an IS41_REGNOT message to the HLR to register the mobile. The MSC starts timer RNT (*Registration Notification Timer*), which has a default value of 12 seconds [8].

11. IS41_regnot (IS-41):

The HLR sends an IS41_regnot message to the MSC that indicates whether or not the registration was successful. Upon receipt of this message, the MSC stops timer RNT.

12. LocUpdateAccept (A-Interface):

After receiving an indication from the HLR that the registration was successful, the MSC sends a Location Updating Accept to the BSC. Otherwise, the MSC sends a Location Updating Reject message with the appropriate cause value. The BSC stops timer T3210 upon receipt of either the Location Updating Accept or Reject messages.

13. IS95_PCH_RegAcceptOrder (IS-95):

The BSC notifies the mobile station of the successful registration by sending an IS-95 Registration Accept Order message over the paging channel.

6.2.2 Global Challenge—Location Update Messages

The following sections describe the A-Interface messages used in the Global Challenge procedure during mobile registrations. As mentioned earlier in this chapter, the Set Control Channel Parameters and Set Control Channel Parameters Acknowledgment messages may be used for transferring the RAND from the MSC to the BSC. The Set Control Parameters and Set Control Parameters Acknowledgment messages are described in Section 7.1.3, "Set Control Channel Parameters Messages," on page 412, and are not repeated here.

6.2.2.1 Location Updating Request

Because the Location Updating Request message is described in Section 4.2.3.1, "Location Updating Request," on page 237, this section focuses only on the authentication parameters contained in the Location Updating Request that are used during the Global Challenge procedure. Table 6-3 summarizes the authentication-related parameters contained in the Location Updating message. The parameters listed in Table 6-3 are common to all Global Challenges scenarios and are also present in CM Service Request and Paging Response messages.

The IMSI and ESN IE are used as authentication inputs to the CAVE algorithm during mobile registration. Specifically, the inputs to the CAVE algorithm include IMSI_S1, which is derived from the IMSI IE.

The AUTHR IE is the 18-bit authentication result. In the Location Updating Request message, AUTHR refers to the value computed by the mobile station using RAND, SSD_A, ESN, and IMSI_S1 as inputs to the CAVE algorithm.

The RANDC IE is the most significant 8 bits of the 32-bit RAND value broadcast by the BSC using the paging channel IS-95 Access Parameters message.

The COUNT IE is incremented each time the mobile sets up a call or when the AC decides to update its value using administrative procedures.

The RAND IE is the 32-bit random number generated by the BSC or MSC and is broadcast to mobile stations over the paging channel.

The BSC uses the Authentication Event IE to indicate any abnormal or failure conditions during the authentication process. For example, an authentication event of value *1* signifies that the required authentication parameters were not received from the mobile station. An Authentication Event parameter value of *2* indicates mismatch between RAND and RANDC.

Table 6-3   Authentication Parameters in LocUpdReq (CDGIOS 6.1.4.8)

BitMap	Param IE	#Oct	Range	Type	IOS Ref
LLLL LLLL	Mobile Identity (IMSI)	7–9	Same as the element in Table 4.2, Location Updating Request	M	6.2.2.16
0000 1101 (0DH)	Mobile Identity (ESN)	7	Same as the element in Table 4.2, Location Updating Request	O,R	6.2.2.16

Table 6-3   Authentication Parameters in LocUpdReq (CDGIOS 6.1.4.8) (Continued)

BitMap	Param IE	#Oct	Range	Type	IOS Ref
0100 0010 (42H)	Auth Response Parameter (AUTHR)	6	Same as the element in Table 4.2, Location Updating Request	O,C	6.2.2.46
0010 1000 (28H)	Auth Confirmation Parameter (RANDC)	2	Same as the element in Table 4.2, Location Updating Request	O,C	6.2.2.42
0100 0000 (40H)	Auth Parameter COUNT	2	Same as the element in Table 4.2, Location Updating Request	O,C	6.2.2.47
0100 0001 (41H)	Auth Challenge Parameter (RAND)	7	Same as the element in Table 4.2, Location Updating Request	O,C	6.2.2.45
0100 1010 (4AH)	Authentication Event	3	Same as the element in Table 4.2, Location Updating Request	O,C	6.2.2.114

6.2.3   Global Challenge—Location Update Example

Figure 6-5 contains an example message that illustrates Global Challenge-related parameters present in a Location Updating Request message. The decoded message format is similar to what would be seen on test equipment monitoring the A-Interface signaling link during a mobile station registration.

```
*** Start of CDGIOS MAP ***
                 Complete Layer 3 Information
0025 00111000 38 Data Length              56
0026 00000000 00 BSMAP Discriminator      00
0027 00110110 36 BSMAP Length             54
0028 01010111 57 Complete Layer 3 Info    87
0029 00000101 05 Cell Identifier          5
0030 00000011 03 Length                   3
0031 00000010 02 Cell Identifier Discrim  CI Only
0032 00010001 11 CI Value                 11 43
0033 01000011 43
0034 00010111 17 Layer 3 Information      23
0035 00101110 2e Length                   46
0036 00000101 05 Protocol Discrim         Mobility Management
0037 00000000 00 Reserved                 00
0038 00001000 08 Location Updating Request 8
0039 00001000 08 Mobile Identity Length   8
```

(Continued)

```
0040 00111110 3e
     -----110      Type of Identity          110 - IMSI
     0011----      IMSI Identity Digits       310006197889514
0041 (7 bytes)
0048 00010010 12 Classmark Info Type 2        18
0049 00000100 04 Length                       4
0050 (4 bytes)    Classmark Info Type 2        00 00 73 00
0054 00011111 1f Registration Type            31
0055 00000001 01 Registration Type            Power Up
0056 00001101 0d Mobile Identity ESN          13
0057 00000101 05 Length                       5
0058 00000101 05
     -----101      Type of Identity           101 - ESN
0059 (4 bytes)    ESN Identity Digits          9f 1c 47 a3
0063 00110101 35 Slot Cycle Index             53
0064 00000001 01 Value                        1
0065 01000010 42 Authentication Response      66
0066 00000100 04 Length                       4
0067 00000001 01 Type                         AUTHR
0068 (3 bytes)    AUTHR Value                  11 c3 39      Authentication
0071 00101000 28 Auth Confirmation            40            Parameters are
0072 01110011 73 Value                        49            included if
0073 01000000 40 Auth COUNT                   64   ◄─────── Authentication is
0074 00000111 07 Count                        7             enabled at the
0075 01000001 41 Authentication Challenge     65            BSC/MSC
0076 00000101 05 Length                       5
0077 00000001 01 Param                        RAND
0078 (4 bytes)    RAND Value                  73 7c 15 4d
```

Figure 6-5 Location Updating Request with Authentication message example

The RAND value included in the example message (73 7c 15 4d) was previously broadcast by the BSC over the paging channel and is the value used by the mobile station to compute AUTHR. The authentication result, AUTHR (11 c3 39), is the authentication signature computed by the mobile station using the CAVE algorithm.

6.3 Global Challenge—Mobile Origination

In an Authentication-enabled network, Global Challenge is also performed when a user originates a call with an Authentication-capable mobile. This section describes the call flow and messages associated with a Global Challenge during a mobile station origination attempt.

The Global Challenge procedure invoked during a mobile origination uses RAND, SSD_A, ESN and dialed digits as inputs to the CAVE algorithm. This input parameter set is similar to the set used in mobile registration Global Challenge, with the only difference being that the last 6 digits of the dialed number are used instead of IMSI_S1. If less than 6 digits are dialed, the most significant bits of IMSI_S1 are used to fill in the missing digits. Figure 6-6 illustrates the high-level call flow for a mobile origination in an Authentication-enabled network.

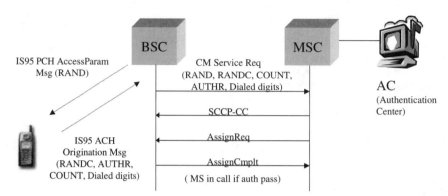

Figure 6-6 Global Challenge—Mobile Origination

During a mobile origination, the mobile station computes an authentication result (AUTHR) using the RAND parameter previously broadcast by the BSC over the paging channel. The RANDC, ESN, Dialed digits, AUTHR, and COUNT authentication parameters are sent from the mobile station to the BSC in an IS-95 Origination message. The BSC then transfers the authentication information to the MSC by including the authentication parameters in a CM Service Request message. Upon receiving the CM Service Request message, the MSC transfers the authentication-specific data to the AC. Next, the AC compares the received AUTHR value to its locally computed value. If the results match, the mobile is authenticated. The AC also verifies the COUNT it received by comparing it with its locally stored value of COUNT. If the COUNT values do not match, the mobile may be declared a clone, and network service may be denied.

After the mobile has been successfully authenticated, the MSC sends an Assignment Request, and the BSC replies with an Assignment Complete.

6.3.1   Global Challenge—Mobile Origination Call Flow

Figure 6-7 illustrates the complete message flow for a mobile origination in an Authenticated-enabled network. Descriptions of individual messages follow the call flow diagram. The descriptions assume that both the network and mobile are Authentication-enabled.

Note that, based on the authentication result, the MSC/HLR decides whether to accept or deny services to the mobile station. If services are allowed, the MSC sends an Assignment Request to the BSC to set up the call. Otherwise, the MSC may choose to clear the call.

1. Set Ctrl Ch Params (RAND) (A-Interface):

   The random number (RAND) used in Global Challenge can be generated either at the BSC or MSC. If the RAND parameter is generated at the MSC, it is transferred to the BSC using the A-Interface Set Control Channel Parameters message. The Set Control Channel

Parameters message is used to transfer downlink information from the MSC to the BSC. The MSC starts timer T101 to wait for an acknowledgment.

2. IS95_PCH_AccssParams (RAND) (IS-95):

The BSC sends an IS-95 Access Parameters message over the paging channel with the AUTH field set to 1 and the RAND field set to the current RAND value. To discourage fraudulent attempts, the RAND value may be periodically updated and transmitted to mobile stations.

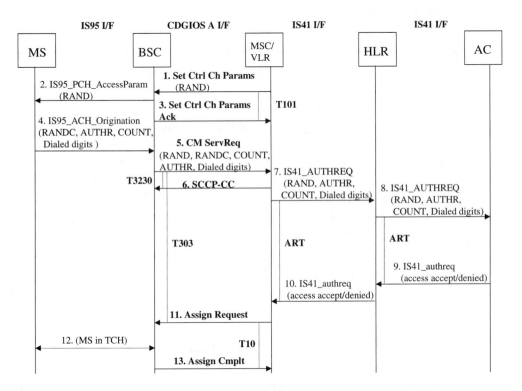

Figure 6-7 Global Challenge in Mobile Origination call flow

3. Set Ctrl Ch Params Ack (A-Interface):

After the BSC updates the paging channel messages with the overhead information received from the MSC, it sends a Set Control Channel Parameter Acknowledgment message to the MSC. If timer T101 expires before receipt of the acknowledgment, the MSC may choose to resend the Set Control Channel Parameter message one more time.

4. IS95_ACH_Origination (RANDC, AUTHR, COUNT, Dialed digits) (IS-95):

   Upon an origination attempt by the mobile user, the mobile station sends an IS-95 Origination message over the access channel. The AUTH_MODE field contained in the IS-95 Origination message is set to *01*, indicating that authentication parameters RANDC, AUTHR, COUNT, and Dialed Digits have been included in the message.

   The mobile stores the value of the previously received RAND parameter and sends the BSC only the 8 most significant bits of RAND, which is referred to as RANDC. The AUTHR parameter is the result of the CAVE algorithm that the mobile computes using the current stored value of RAND, ESN, SSD_A, and the Dialed digits.

5. CM Service Request (RANDC, RAND, COUNT, AUTHR, Dialed digits) (A-Interface):

   The BSC, upon receipt of the mobile's IS-95 Origination message, sends a CM Service Request message to the MSC that contains the received origination parameters. The BSC starts timer T3230 to wait for a *SCCP Connection Confirm* (SCCP-CC) and timer T303 to wait for an Assignment Request message.

   Note that if authentication is enabled at the BSC and authentication parameters RANDC, AUTHR and COUNT are not received from the mobile, the optional Authentication Event IE is set to *1* and is included in this message, notifying the MSC that the required authentication parameters were not received.

   The BSC correlates the RANDC value received from the mobile with the RAND value that the BSC previously sent over the paging. If there is a mismatch between RANDC and RAND, the BSC sets the Authentication Event parameter to *2*, which notifies the MSC of the mismatch.

   The optional Authentication Data IE, which contains the last 6 dialed digits used for authentication, may also be included by the BSC. Although optional for other calls, this parameter is required when the requested service option is asynchronous data and fax.

6. SCCP-CC (A-Interface):

   The MSC sends an SCCP-CC message to the BSC to complete the establishment of the SCCP connection. The BSC stops timer T3230 upon the receipt of SCCP-CC.

7. IS41_AUTHREQ (RAND, AUTHR, COUNT, Dialed digits) (IS-41):

   After verifying that the authentication parameters have been received and that the RANDC parameter matches the most significant 8 bits of RAND, the MSC sends an IS-41 Authentication Request message to the HLR. This message contains the authentication information previously received in the CM Service Request.

   In the case of mobile origination Global Challenge, the IS41_AUTHREQ message includes the Dialed Digits parameter, and the System Access Type value is set to Call Origination. The MSC starts timer ART (*Authentication Request Timer*), which defaults to 6 seconds, while waiting for an IS41_authreq return result or return error [8].

8. IS41_AUTHREQ (RAND, AUTHR, COUNT, Dialed digits) (IS-41):

   The HLR passes the IS41_AUTHREQ message to the AC and starts timer ART.

9. IS41_authreq (access accept/denied) (IS-41):

   Upon receipt of the IS41 AUTHREQ message, the AC computes the authentication signature using the CAVE algorithm and compares the result with the value computed by the mobile station. It also compares the COUNT value received with its locally stored value. If both AUTHR and COUNT match, the mobile station is considered to be authenticated, and the AC sends the HLR an IS41_authreq return result, indicating the success of the authentication process.

   If the authentication comparison fails, the AC includes the Deny Access parameter in the IS41_authreq message that it sends to the HLR. The MSC will then deny service access to the mobile and initiate call clearing.

   If *Signaling Message Encryption* (SME) and *Voice Privacy* (VP) are enabled for the mobile station, the AC will also include encryption information in the IS41_authreq message (see Section 6.7, "Signaling Message Encryption and Voice Privacy," on page 396).

10. IS41_authreq (access accept/ denied) (IS-41):

    The IS41_authreq message is passed from the HLR to the MSC. The MSC stops timer ART upon receipt of the IS41_authreq return result or return error message from the HLR.

11. Assign Request (A-Interface):

    Upon receiving an indication that the authentication process was successful, the MSC continues setting up of the call. The MSC sends an Assignment Request to the BSC and allocates any required terrestrial circuit resource. The BSC stops timer T303 upon receipt of the Assignment Request message. The MSC then starts timer T10 while waiting the corresponding Assignment Complete message from the BSC.

12. (MS in Traffic Channel) :

    The BSC continues setting up of the radio link and terrestrial resources.

13. Assign Cmplt (A-Interface):

    After completing the setup of the radio link and terrestrial resource, the BSC sends an Assignment Complete message to the MSC to indicate a successful call setup. The MSC stops timer T10 upon receipt of the Assignment Complete message.

6.3.2   Global Challenge—Mobile Origination Messages

The following are the detail descriptions of the A-Interface messages that are used in the Global Challenge procedure during a mobile origination.

6.3.2.1   CM Service Request

Because the CM Service Request message is described in detail in Section 3.1.2.2, "CM Service Request," on page 148, only the message parameters associated with Global Challenge authentication are discussed here. Table 6-4 summarizes the parameters used in the Global Challenge procedure during a mobile origination. Many of the parameters listed in Table 6-4 are common to all Global Challenge scenarios and are also included in Location Updating Request and Paging Response messages. The authentication parameters included in the CM Service Request message that are absent in the Location Updating Request and Paging Response messages are the Called Party Number, Called Party ASCII Number, and Authentication Data parameters.

Depending on what is received in the IS-95 Origination message from the mobile station, the CM Service Request message contains either the Called Party BCD Number IE or the Called Party ASCII IE. The mobile station uses the DIGIT_MODE field in the IS-95 Origination message to indicate whether the Called Party Number included in the message is BCD or ASCII. The last 6 digits of the dialed string contained in either parameter are used as an input to the CAVE algorithm. If the dialed string contains less than 6 digits, IMSI_S1 is used to fill in the missing digits.

The ESN IE is also used as an authentication input to the CAVE algorithm during a mobile origination.

The AUTHR IE contains the 18-bit authentication result for Global Challenges. For a mobile-originated call, AUTHR is computed at the mobile station using RAND, SSD_A, ESN, and Dialed digits as input authentication parameters to the CAVE algorithm

The RANDC IE is the most significant 8 bits of the 32-bit RAND value broadcast by the BSC using the paging channel IS-95 Access Parameters message.

The COUNT IE is incremented each time the mobile sets up a call or when the AC decides to update the value using administrative procedures.

The RAND IE is the 32-bit random number generated by the BSC or MSC and is broadcast to mobile stations over the paging channel.

The BSC uses the Authentication Event IE to indicate any abnormal or failure conditions during the authentication process. For example, an authentication event of value *1* signifies that required authentication parameters were not received from the mobile station. An Authentication Event parameter value of *2* indicates mismatch between RAND and RANDC.

The optional Authentication Data IE contains a 24-bit number derived from the last 6 digits of the Called Party string. This IE is required when the service option type is Asynchronous Data or Fax and is optional for other service option types.

Table 6-4   Authentication Parameters in CMServReq (CDGIOS 6.1.2.2)

BitMap	Param IE	#Oct	Range	Type	IOS Ref
0101 1110 (5EH)	Called Party BCD Number	2–19	Same as the element in Table 3-2, CM Service Request	O,C	6.2.2.52
0000 1101 (0DH)	Mobile Identity (ESN)	7	Same as the element in Table 3-2, CM Service Request	O,R	6.2.2.16
0100 0010 (42H)	Auth Response Parameter (AUTHR)	6	Same as the element in Table 3-2, CM Service Request	O,C	6.2.2.46
0010 1000 (28H)	Auth Confirmation Parameter (RANDC)	2	Same as the element in Table 3-2, CM Service Request	O,C	6.2.2.42
0100 0000 (40H)	Auth Parameter COUNT	2	Same as the element in Table 3-2, CM Service Request	O,C	6.2.2.47
0100 0001 (41H)	Auth Challenge Parameter (RAND)	7	Same as the element in Table 3-2, CM Service Request	O,C	6.2.2.45
0101 1011 (5BH)	Called Party ASCII Number	3-n	Same as the element in Table 3-2, CM Service Request	O,C	6.2.2.105
0100 1010 (4AH)	Authentication Event	3	Same as the element in Table 3-2, CM Service Request	O,C	6.2.2.114
0101 1001 (59H)	Authentication Data	5	Same as the element in Table 3-2, CM Service Request	O,C	6.2.2.137

6.3.3   Global Challenge—Mobile Origination Example

Figure 6-8 shows an example of a CM Service Request message that contains authentication parameters used for Global Challenge during a mobile origination. The decoded message format is similar to what would be seen on test equipment monitoring the A-Interface signaling link.

In the example message shown, the Called Party BCD IE contains the string (2727232) dialed by the mobile user. The authentication result AUTHR (80 c7 52) contained in this message is compared by the Authentication Center to its own locally computed result. If the two match, the Global Challenge is successful, and the MSC continues the call setup by sending an Assignment Request message to the BSC.

```
*** Start of CDGIOS MAP ***
                    Complete Layer 3 Information
0025 01000010 42 Data Length                66
0026 00000000 00 BSMAP Discriminator        00
0027 01000000 40 BSMAP Length               64
0028 01010111 57 Complete Layer 3 Info      87
0029 00000101 05 Cell Identifier            5
0030 00000011 03 Length                     3
0031 00000010 02 Cell Identifier Discrim    CI only
0032 (2 bytes)    CI Value                  11 43
0034 00010111 17 Layer 3 Information        23
0035 00111000 38 Length                     56
0036 00000011 03 Protocol Discriminator     Call Processing
0037 00000000 00 Reserved                   00
0038 00100100 24 CC Message Selection       CM Service Request
0039 10001001 91 Service Type               Mobile Origination
0040 00000100 04 ClassM Info Type2 Length   4
0041 (4 bytes)    Classmark Info Type 2     00 00 73 00
0045 00001000 08 Mobile Identity Length     8
0046 00111110 3e
     -----110     Type of Identity          IMSI
     0011----     IMSI Identity Digits      310006197889514
0047 (7 bytes)
0054 01011110 5e Called Party BCD Number    94
0055 00000101 05 Length                     5
0056 10000000 80
     ----0000     Numbering Plan ID         unknown
     -000----     Type of number            unknown
0057 (4 bytes)    Digits (Dialed)           2727232
0061 00001101 0d Mobile Identity (ESN)      13
0062 00000101 05 Length                     5
0063 00000101 05 Type of Identity           ESN
0064 (4 bytes)    ESN Identity Digits       9f 1c 47 a3
0068 00110101 35 Slot Cycle Index           53
0069 00000001 01 Value                      1
0070 01000010 42 Auth. Response Param       66
0071 00000100 04 Length                     4
0072 00000001 01 Type                       AUTHR
0073 (3 bytes)    AUTHR Value               80 c7 52
0076 00101000 28 Auth. Confirmation         40
0077 11101010 ea Value                      234
0078 01000000 40 Auth. Param. COUNT         64
0079 00000000 00 Count                      0
0080 01000001 41 Authentication Challenge   65
0081 00000101 05 Length                     5
```

Authentication Parameters are included if Authentication is enabled at the BSC/MSC

(Continued)

```
0082 00000001 01 Param                    RAND
0083 (4 bytes)  ·RAND Value              ea 27 f3 b8
0087 00000011 03 Service Option           3
0088 10000000 80 Service Type             13k speech
0089 00000000 00
0090 00011101 1d Radio Env & Resrc        1D
0091 00000011 03                          avail & allocated
```

Figure 6-8 CM Service Request with Authentication message example

6.4 Global Challenge—Mobile Termination

In an Authentication-enabled network, Global Challenge Authentication is also performed when an incoming call is terminated to an Authentication-capable mobile station. This section describes the call flow and messages associated with a Global Challenge during a mobile-terminated call. The Global Challenge procedure for a mobile-terminated call utilizes the same four CAVE algorithm inputs as Registration. RAND, SSD_A, ESN, and IMSI_S1 are used to compute the authentication result (AUTHR). Figure 6-9 illustrates the high-level call flow for a mobile termination in an Authentication-enabled network.

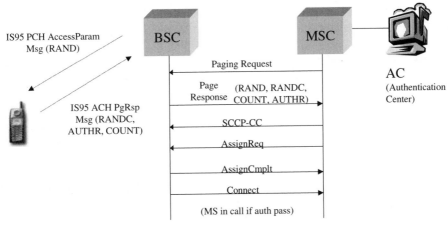

Figure 6-9 Global Challenge—Mobile Termination

During a mobile termination, the mobile station computes an authentication result (AUTHR) using the RAND parameter previously broadcast by the BSC over the paging channel. The RANDC, ESN, IMSI, AUTHR, and COUNT parameters are passed from the mobile station to the BSC using the IS-95 Page Response message and are then sent to the MSC in the Paging Response message. These parameters are finally transferred to the AC. Upon receiving the authentication parameters from the MSC/HLR, the AC performs the CAVE Algorithm computation with the same inputs used by the mobile station and compares the result with the received

AUTHR value. The mobile station is authenticated if the values match. The AC also checks the COUNT value received with its locally stored value of COUNT. A mismatch in COUNT values could indicate that the mobile station is a clone and network services may be denied.

6.4.1   Global Challenge—Mobile Termination Call Flow

Figure 6-10 illustrates the complete message flow for a mobile-terminated call in an Authentication-enabled network. Descriptions of individual messages follow the call flow diagram. The descriptions assume that both the network and mobile are Authentication-enabled.

Note that, based on the authentication result, the MSC/HLR decides whether to accept or deny services to the mobile station. If services are allowed, the MSC sends an Assignment Request to the BSC to set up the call. Otherwise, the MSC may choose to clear the call.

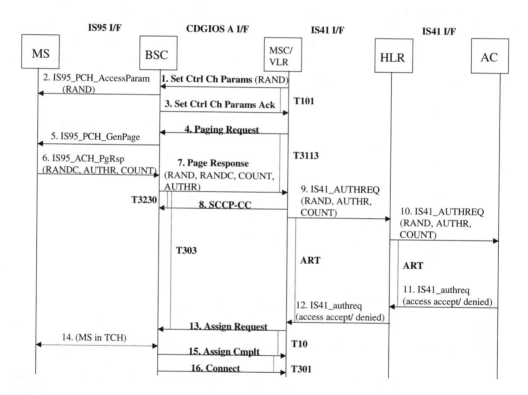

Figure 6-10   Global Challenge in Mobile Termination call flow

1. Set Ctrl Ch Params (RAND) (A-Interface):

The random number (RAND) used in Global Challenge can be generated at either the BSC or MSC. If the RAND parameter is generated at the MSC, it is transferred to the BSC using the A-Interface Set Control Channel Parameters message. The MSC starts timer T101 to wait for an acknowledgment.

2. IS95_PCH_AccssParams (RAND) (IS-95):

The BSC sends an IS-95 Access Parameters message over the paging channel with the AUTH field set to *1* and the RAND field set to the current RAND value. To discourage fraudulent attempts, the RAND value may be periodically updated and transmitted to mobile stations.

3. Set Ctrl Ch Params Ack (A-Interface):

After the BSC updates the paging channel messages with the overhead information received from the MSC, it sends a Set Control Channel Parameter Acknowledgment message to the MSC. If timer T101 expires before receipt of the acknowledgment, the MSC may choose to resend the Set Control Channel Parameter message one more time.

4. Paging Request (A-Interface):

During mobile termination, the MSC initiates paging of a mobile station by sending a Paging Request message to the BSC. Upon sending the Paging Request message, the MSC starts timer T3113 to wait for a Paging Response.

5. IS95_PCH_Genpage (IS-95):

The BSC pages the mobile station by sending an IS-95 General Page message.

6. IS95_ACH_PgRsp (RANDC, AUTHR, COUNT) (IS-95):

The mobile responds to the IS-95 General Page message by sending an IS-95 Page Response message over the access channel. The AUTH_MODE field of the IS-95 Page Response message is set to *01* and the corresponding authentication parameters RANDC, AUTHR, and COUNT are included.

The mobile stores the value of the previously received RAND parameter and sends the BSC only the 8 most significant bits of RAND, referred to as RANDC. The AUTHR parameter sent by the mobile station is the result of the CAVE algorithm that the mobile computes using the current stored value of RAND, ESN, SSD_A, and the IMSI_S1.

7. Paging Response (RANDC, RAND, COUNT, AUTHR) (A-Interface):

The BSC, upon receipt of the mobile's IS-95 Page Response message, sends an A-Interface Paging Response message to the MSC. The MSC stops timer T3113 upon receipt of the Paging Response. The BSC starts timer T3230 to wait for an SCCP-CC and starts timer T303 to wait for an Assignment Request message.

Note that if authentication is enabled at the BSC and authentication parameters RANDC, AUTHR, and COUNT are not received from the mobile, the optional Authentication Event IE is set to *1* and is included in this message, notifying the MSC that the required authentication parameters were not received.

The BSC correlates the RANDC value received from the mobile with the RAND value that the BSC previously sent over the paging channel. If there is a mismatch between

RANDC and RAND, the BSC sets the Authentication Event parameter to *2*, which notifies the MSC of the mismatch.

Stages 8–15 are similar to stages 6–13 in Section 6.3.1, "Global Challenge—Mobile Origination Call Flow," on page 360 and will not be repeated here.

6.4.2   Global Challenge—Mobile Termination Messages

The following sections describe the A-Interface messages that are used for Global Challenge during a mobile termination.

6.4.2.1   Paging Response

Because the Paging Response message is described in Section 3.2.2.3, "Paging Response," on page 171, only the message parameters associated with Global Challenge authentication are discussed here. Table 6-5 summarizes the parameters used in the Global Challenge procedure during a mobile termination.

The ESN IE is one of the four authentication inputs to the CAVE algorithm during a mobile termination Global Challenge.

The AUTHR IE contains the 18-bit authentication result computed by the mobile station. For a mobile-terminated call, AUTHR is computed using RAND, SSD_A, ESN, and IMSI_S1 as input authentication parameters to the CAVE algorithm.

The RANDC IE contains the most significant 8 bits of the 32-bit RAND value previously broadcast by the BSC using the paging channel IS-95 Access Parameters message.

The COUNT IE is incremented each time the mobile sets up a call or when the AC decides to update the value using administrative procedures.

The RAND IE is the 32-bit random number generated by the BSC or MSC and is broadcast to mobile stations over the paging channel.

The BSC uses the Authentication Event IE to indicate any abnormal or failure conditions during the authentication process. For example, an Authentication Event of value *1* signifies that required authentication parameters were not received from the mobile station. An Authentication Event parameter value of *2* indicates mismatch between RAND and RANDC.

Table 6-5   Authentication Parameters in PageResp (CDGIOS 6.1.2.4)

BitMap	Param IE	#Oct	Range	Type	IOS Ref
LLLL LLLL	Mobile Identity (IMSI)	7–9	Same as the element in Table 3-6, Paging Response	M	6.2.2.16
0000 1101 (0DH)	Mobile Identity (ESN)	7	Same as the element in Table 3-6, Paging Response	O,R	6.2.2.16

Table 6-5   Authentication Parameters in PageResp (CDGIOS 6.1.2.4) (Continued)

BitMap	Param IE	#Oct	Range	Type	IOS Ref
0100 0010 (42H)	Auth Response Parameter (AUTHR)	6	Same as the element in Table 3-6, Paging Response	O,C	6.2.2.46
0010 1000 (28H)	Auth Confirmation Parameter (RANDC)	2	Same as the element in Table 3-6, Paging Response	O,C	6.2.2.42
0100 0000 (40H)	Auth Parameter COUNT	2	Same as the element in Table 3-6, Paging Response	O,C	6.2.2.47
0100 0001 (41H)	Auth Challenge Parameter (RAND)	7	Same as the element in Table 3-6, Paging Response	O,C	6.2.2.45
0100 1010 (4AH)	Authentication Event	3	Same as the element in Table 3-6, Paging Response	O,C	6.2.2.114

6.4.3   Global Challenge—Mobile Termination Example

Figure 6-11 shows an example of a Paging Response message that contains authentication parameters used for Global Challenge during a mobile termination. The decoded message format is similar to what would be seen on test equipment monitoring the A-Interface signaling link.

In this example message, RANDC (c8) matches the most significant 8 bits of RAND (c8 17 45 de). The authentication result AUTHR (13 9f 85) contained in this message is subsequently compared by the AC with its own locally computed result. If the two match, the Global Challenge is successful, and the MSC continues the call setup by sending an Assignment Request message to the BSC.

```
*** Start of CDGIOS MAP ***
                Complete Layer 3 Information
0025 00111111 3f Data Length             63
0026 00000000 00 BSMAP Discriminator      00
0027 00111101 3d BSMAP Length             61
0028 01010111 57 Complete Layer 3 Info    87
0029 00000101 05 Cell Identifier           5
0030 00000011 03 Length                    3
0031 00000010 02 Cell Identifier Discrim  CI only
0032 00010001 11 CI Value                 11 43
0033 01000011 43
0034 00010111 17 Layer 3 Information      23
```

(Continued)

```
0035 00110101 35 Length                         53
0036 00000011 03 Protocol Discriminator         Call Processing
0037 00000000 00 Reserved                        00
0038 00100111 27 CC Message Selection            Paging Response
0039 00000100 04 ClassM Info Type2 Length        4
0040 (4 bytes)    ClassM Info Type2 value        00 00 73 00
0044 00001000 08 Mobile Identity Length          8
0045 00111110 3e
     -----110    Type of Identity                IMSI
     0011----    IMSI Identity Digits            310006197889514
0046 (7 bytes)
0053 00110011 33 Tag Id                          51
0054 (4 bytes)    Tag Value                      42 15 00 77
0058 00001101 0d Mobile Identity (ESN)           13
0059 00000101 05 Length                          5
0060 00000101 05 Type of Identity                ESN
0061 (4 bytes)    ESN Identity Digits            9f 1c 47 a3
0065 00110101 35 Slot Cycle Index                53
0066 00000001 01 Value                           1
0067 01000010 42 Auth. Response Param            66
0068 00000100 04 Length                          4
0069 00000001 01 Type                            AUTHR
0070 (3 bytes)    AUTHR Value                    13 9f 85
0073 00101000 28 Auth. Confirmation              40
0074 11001000 c8 Value                           200
0075 01000000 40 Auth. Param. COUNT              64
0076 00000000 00 Count                           0
0077 01000001 41 Auth. Challenge                 65
0078 00000101 05 Length                          5
0079 00000001 01 Param                           RAND
0080 (4 bytes)    RAND Value                     c8 17 45 de
0084 00000011 03 Service Option                  3
0085 10000000 80 Service Type                    13K Speech
0086 00000000 00
0087 00011101 1d Radio Env & Resrc               1D
0088 00000011 03                                 avail & allocated
```

Authentication Parameters are included if Authentication is enabled at the BSC/MSC

Figure 6-11   Paging Response with Authentication message example

6.5 Unique Challenge

Unique Challenge is a procedure used by the AC to request that authentication be performed on an individual mobile station. Unlike Global Challenge, the Unique Challenge process involves the use of a unique random number (RANDU) generated specifically at the AC for a particular mobile station. Unique Challenge may occur any time the AC or network operator desires and is not restricted to mobile registrations or access attempts. The SSD Update process also uses Unique Challenge authentication. Depending on the state of the mobile station, Unique Challenges may occur over the paging channel or traffic channel.

During a Unique Challenge, the inputs into the CAVE Algorithm are RANDU (combined with the 8 least significant bits of IMSI_S2), SSD_A, ESN, and IMSI_S1. RANDU is generated by the AC and transferred to the mobile station using the A-Interface Authentication Request and IS-95 Authentication Challenge messages. Upon receiving the IS-95 Authentication Challenge message, the mobile station computes the authentication result AUTHU and sends it to the BSC in an IS-95 Authentication Challenge Response message. AUTHU is then passed from the BSC to the MSC using the A-Interface Authentication Response message. The MSC then compares AUTHU values. A high-level summary message call flow is provided in Figure 6-12.

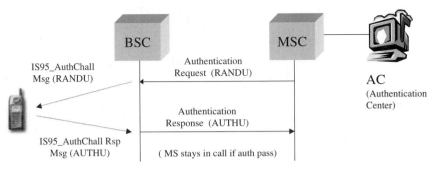

Figure 6-12   Unique Challenge

6.5.1   Unique Challenge Call Flow

In some networks, the SSD information used in the Unique Challenge process is shared between the MSC/VLR and the AC to reduce IS-41 message traffic. The MSC/VLR in a shared SSD network stores individual mobile station SSDs and is able to compute AUTHU and perform the comparison without assistance from the AC. The detailed Unique Challenge call flow presented in Figure 6-13 applies to networks where the SSD information is not shared between the AC and the serving MSC/VLR. Please refer to the IS-41 standard for further information regarding the IS-41 messaging when SSD is shared [8].

The AC triggers a Unique Challenge by sending an IS41_AUTHDIR message is to the HLR/MSC. Included in this message is information such as the authentication random number (RANDU) and the corresponding Unique Challenge authentication result (AUTHU). Upon receiving this IS41_AUTHDIR message, the MSC sends an A-Interface Authentication Request message to the BSC that includes RANDU. The BSC then forwards RANDU to the mobile station in an IS-95 Authentication Challenge message. After receiving the Unique Challenge request, the mobile station calculates the unique challenge result AUTHU and sends the value to the BSC. The BSC forwards AUTHU received from the mobile station to the MSC, which performs the AUTHU comparison and reports the result to the AC. If authentication fails, the MSC may deny service or initiate an SSD Update.

As mentioned earlier, a Unique Challenge can occur when the mobile is idle or in traffic. The only difference regarding the A-Interface is the message type used for the Authentication Request and Response messages. BSMAP message types are used if the mobile is idle, and DTAP message types are used if the mobile is in traffic.

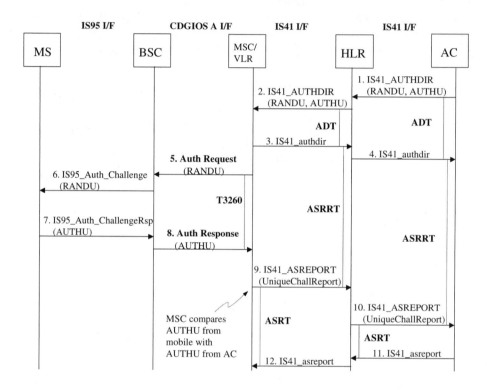

Figure 6-13   Unique Challenge call flow, Shared Secret Data not shared

1. IS41_AUTHDIR (RANDU, AUTHU) (IS-41):

The AC initiates a Unique Challenge by sending an authentication directive IS41_AUTHDIR message to the HLR. Included in this message is an AC generated random number (RANDU) and the authentication signature (AUTHU). Recall that AUTHU is computed using RANDU (combined with IMSI_S2), IMSI_S1, SSD_A, and ESN as inputs to the CAVE Algorithm. The AC starts timer ADT (*Authentication Directive Timer*), which has default value of 6 seconds [8].

The IS41_AUTHDIR message is a general-purpose authentication directive that may be used by the AC to invoke a Unique Challenge, update the mobile's SSD, or update the mobile's COUNT parameter.

2. IS41_AUTHDIR (RANDU, AUTHU) (IS-41):

The HLR simply passes on the IS41_AUTHDIR message to the MSC and starts timer ADT, which has a default value of 6 seconds [8].

3. IS41_authdir (IS-41):

The MSC returns an empty IS41_authdir return result to the HLR to indicate that the IS41_AUTHDIR message has been accepted. The HLR stops timer ADT upon receipt of IS41_authdir message and starts timer ASRRT (*Authentication Status Report Response Timer*). The ASRRT timer is started whenever an authentication operation that requires an authentication status report is initiated. The default ASRRT timer value is 6 seconds [8].

4. IS41_authdir (IS-41):

After receiving an IS41_authdir from the MSC, the HLR sends an empty IS41_authdir to the AC. The AC then stops timer ADT and starts timer ASRRT, while waiting for the Authentication Status Report from the MSC. The default ASRRT value is 24 seconds [8].

5. Auth Request (RANDU) (A-Interface):

Meanwhile, the MSC invokes the Unique Challenge by sending the BSC an Authentication Request message that contains RANDU. If the mobile station is idle, this message is sent as a BSMAP message using the connectionless *SCCP-Unit Data* (SCCP-UDT) message type. If the mobile is in traffic, this message is sent as a DTAP message type using the connection-oriented *SCCP-Data Form 1* (SCCP-DT1) message type. The MSC starts timer T3260 while waiting for an Authentication Response message.

6. IS95_Auth_Challenge (RANDU) (IS-95):

The BSC sends the Unique Challenge parameter RANDU to the mobile station in an IS-95 Authentication Challenge message on either the paging or the forward traffic channel.

7. IS95_Auth_ChallengeRsp (AUTHU) (IS-95):

Upon receiving RANDU in the IS-95 Authentication Challenge message, the mobile station computes the Unique Challenge authentication result (AUTHU) using the CAVE algorithm. The mobile station sends AUTHU to the BSC in an IS-95 Authentication Challenge Response message. If the mobile station is idle, this message is sent to the BSC on the access channel; otherwise, it is sent over the reverse traffic channel.

8. Auth Response (AUTHU) (A-Interface):

Upon receipt of the IS-95 Authentication Challenge Response message from the mobile station, the BSC sends the AUTHU result to the MSC using the Authentication Response message. The Authentication Response message is sent as either a BSMAP or DTAP message, depending on the state of the mobile. If the mobile station is in a call and an SCCP connection has already been established, this message is sent as DTAP message. Otherwise, the BSMAP message type is used.

The MSC stops timer T3260 upon receipt of the Authentication Response message. If T3260 expires before any Authentication Response is received from the BSC, the MSC may choose to retry the Authentication Request or it may deny access and initiate call clearing. CDGIOS also allows the MSC to invoke other failure procedures chosen by the MSC vendor or network service provider.

If the mobile station does not respond to the Unique Challenge, the BSC will send this message to the MSC with a Cause Layer 3 value indicating the reason for the failure.

9. IS41_ASREPORT (UniqueChallReport) (IS-41):

The MSC compares the value of AUTHU received from the mobile station with the AUTHU value received earlier by the AC. The result of the comparison is sent to the HLR in an IS41_ASREPORT message. The Unique Challenge Report parameter of the IS41_ASREPORT message contains the result of the AUTHU comparison. The MSC starts timer ASRT (*Authentication Status Report Timer*), which has a default value of 6 seconds [8], while waiting for an acknowledgment from the AC. The HLR stops timer ASRRT upon receipt of the IS41_ASREPORT message.

10. IS41_ASREPORT (UniqueChallReport) (IS-41):

The HLR passes on the IS41_ASREPORT to the AC and starts timer ASRT. The AC stops timer ASRRT upon receipt of the IS41_ASREPORT message.

11. IS41_asreport (IS-41):

The AC returns an IS41_asreport return result to the HLR to indicate receipt of the IS41_ASREPORT message. The HLR stops timer ASRT.

12. IS41_asreport (IS-41):

The HLR sends an IS41_asreport return result to the MSC to indicate the AC's receipt of the IS41_ASREPORT message. The MSC stops timer ASRT.

6.5.2   Unique Challenge in Idle Mode Messages

The following text describes the A-Interface messages used in the Unique Challenge process. If a Unique Challenge is requested for an idle mobile, the Authentication Request and Response messages are sent as BSMAP messages (Table 6-6) using the SCCP-UDT message type. The Authentication Request and Response messages are sent as DTAP messages using the SCCP-DT1 message type if the mobile station is already in traffic.

6.5.2.1   Authentication Request BSMAP message

The Authentication Request message is used by the MSC to invoke a Unique Challenge for a particular mobile station. The message contains the RANDU value received by the MSC in the AC's authentication directive.

The mandatory 24-bit RANDU IE is one of four inputs to the CAVE Algorithm used by the mobile station to compute the authentication signature AUTHU.

The IMSI, Tag, Cell Identifier List, and Slot Cycle Index parameters are all associated with sending messages over the paging channel. These parameters are not needed if the mobile station is in traffic.

The IMSI IE uniquely identifies the mobile station for which the Unique Challenge is being requested.

The Tag IE allows the MSC to correlate the transmitted Authentication Request message with the received Authentication Response from the BSC.

The Cell Identifier List IE specifies the list of cells or *Location Area Code* (LAC) to be used to for the over-the-air transmission.

The Slot Cycle Index IE specifies the last registered Slot Cycle Index of the mobile station and is used by the BSC to send the paging message using the correct paging slot.

- BSAP Message Type: BSMAP
- SCCP Message Type: SCCP-Unit Data (UDT)
- Direction: BSC ← MSC

Table 6-6 Authentication Request BSMAP Message (CDGIOS 6.1.4.1)

BitMap	Param IE	#Oct	Range	Type	IOS Ref
0000 0000 (00H) LLLL LLLL	BSMAP header	2	Msg Discrim. = 0 (BSMAP) L = BSMAP msg length	M	6.2.2.1 6.2.2.3
0100 0101 (45H)	Msg Type	1	Authentication Req Msg	M	6.2.2.4
0100 0001 (41H) LLLL LLLL rrrr tttt nnnn nnnn nnnn nnnn nnnn nnnn	Authentica-tion Challenge Parameter (RANDU)	6	L = 04H r = 0—reserved tttt = 0010 n = 24bit RANDU	M	6.2.2.45
0000 1101 (0D)	Mobile Iden-tity (IMSI)	8–10	Same as the element in Table 3-2, CM Service Request	O,R	6.2.2.16
0011 0011 (33H)	Tag	5	Same as the element in Table 3-5, Paging Request	O,C	6.2.2.62
0001 1010 (1AH)	Cell Identifier List	Var-iable	Same as the element in Table 3-5, Paging Request	O,C	6.2.2.21
0011 0101 (35H) rrrr riii	Slot Cycle Index	2	r = 0—reserved i = 000–111	O,C	6.2.2.17

6.5.2.2   Authentication Response BSMAP message

This message is sent from the BSC in response to the Authentication Request message and contains the mobile station-computed Unique Challenge authentication result AUTHU (Table 6-7).

The mandatory AUTHU IE contains the 18-bit AUTHU authentication result computed by the mobile station and received by the BSC in the IS-95 Authentication Challenge Response message.

The IMSI and ESN IE uniquely identify the mobile responding to the unique challenge.

The Tag IE is included if the corresponding Authentication Request message contained the Tag IE.

- BSAP Message Type: BSMAP
- SCCP Message Type: SCCP-Unit Data (UDT)
- Direction: BSC → MSC

Table 6-7   Authentication Response BSMAP Message (CDGIOS 6.1.4.2)

BitMap	Param IE	#Oct	Range	Type	IOS Ref
0000 0000 (00H) LLLL LLLL	BSMAP header	2	Msg Discrim. = 0 (BSMAP) L = BSMAP msg length	M	6.2.2.1 6.2.2.3
0100 0110 (46H)	Msg Type	1	Authentication Response Msg	M	6.2.2.4
0100 0010 (42H) LLLL LLLL rrrr tttt 0000 00nn nnnn nnnn nnnn nnnn	Authentication Response Parameter (AUTHU)	6	e = 42H L = 04H—param length r = 0—reserved tttt = 0010 n = 18bit AUTHU result	M	6.2.2.46
0000 1101 (0D)	Mobile Identity (IMSI)	8–10	Same as the element in Table 3-2, CM Service Request	O,R	6.2.2.16
0011 0011 (33H)	Tag	5	Same as the element in Table 3-5, Paging Request	O,C	6.2.2.62
0000 1101 (0DH)	Mobile Identity (ESN)	7	Same as the element in Table 3-2, CM Service Request	O,R	6.2.2.16

6.5.3   Unique Challenge in Traffic Channel Messages

The following sections describe the Unique Challenge A-Interface messages used when a mobile station is already in a call. If a mobile station is in a call, location and mobile identification information is not needed in the DTAP Authentication Request and Response messages. The mobile is simply identified by the existing SCCP connection previously established for the call.

6.5.3.1   Authentication Request DTAP message

The Authentication Request message is used by the MSC to invoke a Unique Challenge for a particular mobile station. The message contains the RANDU value received by the MSC in the AC's authentication directive (Table 6-8).

The mandatory 24-bit RANDU IE is one of four inputs to the CAVE algorithm used by the mobile station to compute the authentication signature AUTHU.

- BSAP Message Type: DTAP
- SCCP Message Type: SCCP-Data Form1 (DT1)
- Direction: BSC ← MSC

Table 6-8   Authentication Request DTAP Message (CDGIOS 6.1.4.1)

BitMap	Param IE	#Oct	Range	Type	IOS Ref
0000 0001 (01H) ccrr rsss LLLL LLLL	DTAP header	3	Msg Discrim. = 1 (DTAP) DLCI = "ccrr rsss" = 0 L = DTAP msg length	M	6.2.2.1 6.2.2.2 6.2.2.3
rrrr 0101 (05H)	Protocol Discriminator	1	0101—Mobility Management r = 0—reserved bits	M	6.2.2.39
0000 0000 (00H)	Reserved Bits	1		M	6.2.2.40
0100 0101 (45H)	Msg Type	1	Authentication Req Msg	M	6.2.2.4
LLLL LLLL rrrr tttt nnnn nnnn nnnn nnnn nnnn nnnn	Authentication Challenge Parameter (RANDU)	5	L = 04H, r = 0—reserved tttt = 0010 n = 24-bit RANDU	M	6.2.2.45

6.5.3.2   Authentication Response DTAP message

This message is sent from the BSC in response to the Authentication Request message and contains the mobile station-computed Unique Challenge authentication result AUTHU (Table 6-9).

The mandatory AUTHU IE contains the 18-bit AUTHU authentication result computed by the mobile station and received by the BSC in the IS-95 Authentication Challenge Response message.

- BSAP Message Type: DTAP
- SCCP Message Type: SCCP-Data Form1 (DT1)
- Direction: BSC → MSC

Table 6-9   Authentication Response DTAP Message (CDGIOS 6.1.4.2)

BitMap	Param IE	#Oct	Range	Type	IOS Ref
0000 0001 (01H) ccrr rsss LLLL LLLL	DTAP header	3	Msg Discrim. = 1 (DTAP) DLCI = "ccrr rsss" = 0 L = DTAP msg length	M	6.2.2.1 6.2.2.2 6.2.2.3
rrrr 0101 (05H)	Protocol Discriminator	1	0101—Mobility Management r = 0—reserved bits	M	6.2.2.39
0000 0000 (00H)	Reserved Bits	1		M	6.2.2.40
0100 0110 (46H)	Msg Type	1	Authentication Response Msg	M	6.2.2.4
LLLL LLLL rrrr tttt 0000 00nn nnnn nnnn nnnn nnnn	Authentication Response Parameter (AUTHU)	5	L = 04H—param length r = 0—reserved tttt = 0010 n = 18-bit AUTHU result	M	6.2.2.46

6.5.4   Unique Challenge Example Call Flow

Figure 6-14 contains a summary message call flow for the Unique Challenge procedure. In the example shown, the mobile station is already in a voice call when the Unique Challenge is initiated. The purpose of Figure 6-14 is to present an overview of the messages exchanged between the BSC and MSC, and subsequent figures illustrate the complete message's content, including MTP3 and SCCP layers. The decoded message format is similar to what would be seen on test equipment monitoring the A-Interface signaling link. The BSC's point code is 8-17-92, and the MSC's point code is 110-44-3.

```
Event      Time         OPC          DPC          SLS  Message        Mobile call is set up.

 01  11:25:13.592    8-17-92      110-44-3      15  CR   CMSR    ┐
 02  11:25:13.661    110-44-3     8-17-92       29  CC           │
 03  11:25:13.705    110-44-3     8-17-92       29  DT1  AssReq   │
 04  11:25:15.449    8-17-92      110-44-3      15  DT1  AssCmplt ┘
 05  11:28:16.051    110-44-3     8-17-92       29  DT1  AuthReq(UniqC)
 06  11:28:16.271    8-17-92      110-44-3      15  DT1  AuthRsp(UniqC)
```

The mobile responds to the
Unique Challenge with AUTHU

AC sends a Unique
Challenge to the mobile
over the traffic channel

Figure 6-14   Unique Challenge in traffic channel example call flow

The first four A-Interface messages shown in Figure 6-14 are exchanged between the MSC and BSC as part of a normal mobile-originated call setup. Approximately three minutes after the call has been set up, the AC initiates a Unique Challenge by triggering the MSC to send the BSC an Authentication Request message over the A-Interface. The mobile responds to the Unique Challenge with an authentication result that the BSC relays to the MSC in the Authentication Response message. Because the mobile station is already in a call when the Unique Challenge occurs, both the Authentication Request and Response messages are sent as SCCP-DT1 messages.

```
**** MESSAGE NUMBER: 0005 ****
*** Start of MTP Level 3 ***
0003 10000011 83
     ----0011    Service Indicator          SCCP
     --00----    Network Priority           priority 0
     10------    Network Indicator          National
0004 (3 Bytes)   Destination Point Code     8-17-92
0007 (3 Bytes)   Origination Point Code     110-44-3
0010 00011101 1d Signaling Link Selection   29
*** Start of SCCP ***
0011 00000110 06 Data Form 1                06
0012 (3 Bytes)   Dest Local References      78696
0015 00000000 00 Segment/Reassembling       0
0016 00000001 01 Variable Pointer           01
*** Start of CDGIOS MM ***
                 Authentication Request
0017 00001011 0b DTAP Length                11
0018 00000001 01 Discriminator              01
0019 00000000 00 DLCI
```

(Continued)
```
0020 00001000 08 Length                      8
0021 00000101 05 MM Protocol Discrim          5
0022 00000000 00 Reserved
0023 01000101 45 Authentication Request       69
0024 00000100 04 Length                       4
0025 00000010 02 Authentication Challenge     RANDU
0026 01010100 54 RANDU Value                  54 37 e9
0027 00110111 37
0028 11101001 e9
```

RANDU value is input to the CAVE algorithm during a Unique Challenge

Figure 6-15 Authentication Request (Unique Challenge) DTAP message example

Figure 6-15 shows the decoded example Authentication Request message summarized in Figure 6-14. The Authentication Request message contains the RANDU value used in a Unique Challenge to compute the authentication signature. Because the mobile station is already in a call, this message is coded as a DTAP message, and no specific cell identity or mobile identity information is required.

```
**** MESSAGE NUMBER: 0006 ****
*** Start of MTP Level 3 ***
0003 10000011 83
     ----0011    Service Indicator        SCCP
     --00----    Network Priority         priority 0
     10------    Network Indicator        National
0004 (3 Bytes)   Destination Point Code   110-44-3
0007 (3 Bytes)   Origination Point Code   8-17-92
0010 00001111 0f Signaling Link Selection 15
*** Start of SCCP ***
0011 00000110 06 Data Form 1              6
0012 (3 Bytes)   Dest Local References    15432238
0015 00000000 00 Segment/Reassembling     0
0016 00000001 01 Variable Pointer         01
*** Start of CDGIOS MM ***
                 Authentication Response
0017 00001011 0b DTAP Length              11
0018 00000001 01 Discriminator            01
0019 00000000 00 DLCI
0020 00001000 08 Length                   8
0021 00000101 05 MM Protocol Discrim      05
0022 00000000 00 Reserved
0023 01000110 46 Authentication Response  70
0024 00000100 04 Length                   4
0025 00000010 02 Type                     AUTHU
0026 01100111 67 AUTHU Value              67 04 d1
0027 00000100 04
0028 11010001 d1
```

Mobile-computed result of CAVE algorithm.

Figure 6-16 Authentication Response (Unique Challenge) DTAP message example

Figure 6-16 shows the decoded example Authentication Request message summarized in Figure 6-14. Only the mobile-computed authentication result (AUTHU) is included in the example message.

6.6 Shared Secret Data Update

The SSD Update procedure is used in CDMA networks as a second level of security in the authentication process. The procedure provides a means to synchronize locally stored mobile station and AC SSD information. Using the previously programmed A-Key and a standardized SSD Generation algorithm, both the mobile station and the AC have the capability to update their locally stored SSD values. Recall that A-Keys are individually assigned to each mobile station and are stored in a secure AC database. Neither A-Key nor SSD information is ever broadcast over the air.

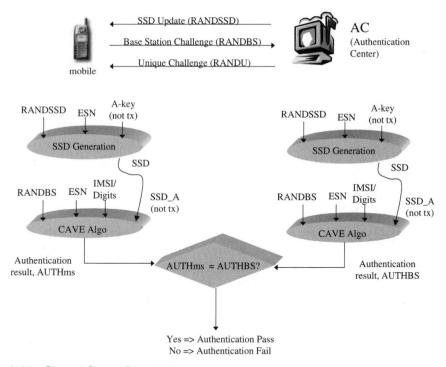

Figure 6-17   Shared Secret Data Update process

In an Authentication-enabled network, an SSD Update may be performed periodically by network management or when the AC determines that a Global or Unique Challenge has failed. An SSD Update commonly occurs when a mobile station registers in a network for the first time. In the case of an initial mobile station registration, its SSD is often zero, which results in an authentication failure. The authentication failure triggers the AC to perform an SSD Update to synchronize SSD information.

Figure 6-17 provides an overview of the SSD Update procedure. The SSD Generation algorithm that is used by both the mobile station and AC requires ESN, RANDSSD, and A-Key as inputs. RANDSSD is a random number generated by the AC specifically for the SSD update. The RANDSSD parameter is sent over the air to the mobile station, which then uses the received random number to update its stored SSD value. After updating the SSD, the mobile station initiates a Base Station Challenge to verify the accuracy of the new SSD value. The mobile station starts the Base Station Challenge procedure by sending the BSC a random number (RANDBS) that is used by the AC to compute the authentication result, AUTHBS. The authentication value (AUTHBS) computed by the AC is transferred to the BSC, which then sends the result to the mobile station. The mobile station compares the AUTHBS value received from the BSC with its locally computed AUTHBS value. If the two match, the mobile notifies the network that the SSD Update was successful. Otherwise, the network is informed that the update failed.

After the SSD Update and Base Station Challenge procedures have been completed, a Unique Challenge may be triggered by the MSC to validate the mobile station further before granting service. Note that in CDGIOS, SSD Update is invoked only when the mobile is already in the traffic state.

6.6.1   Shared Secret Data Update Call Flow

Figure 6-18 illustrates the SSD Update call flow, which begins when the AC sends an IS41_AUTHDIR message to the HLR/MSC. The IS41_AUTHDIR message contains the RANDSSD parameters used by the SSD Generation algorithm and the RANDU and AUTHU parameters that may be used later by the MSC during the optional Unique Challenge. The MSC forwards the RANDSSD in an SSD Update Request message to the BSC, which then instructs the mobile station to perform an SSD Update.

After updating its SSD data, the mobile station initiates a Base Station Challenge to confirm the SSD changes. The RANDBS value associated with Base Station Challenge is relayed to the AC, which computes the authentication result, AUTHBS. IS-41 messaging is used to relay the authentication result to the MSC, which then sends the value to the BSC using a Base Station Challenge Response message. Upon receiving the AUTHBS value from the BSC, the mobile station compares the two AUTHBS values and reports the result to the BSC. The BSC sends the SSD Update result to the MSC using the SSD Update Response message. At this point, the MSC may initiate a Unique Challenge. If so, the MSC sends the BSC an Authentication Request message to the BSC that includes the RANDU value previously received from the AC. Upon receiving the Unique Challenge authentication signature (AUTHU) in the Authentication Response message from the BSC, the MSC notifies the HLR/AC of the SSD Update result by including the SSD Update Report parameter in the IS41_ASREPORT message.

Recall that in CDGIOS, SSD Updates are performed only when the mobile is in traffic and the associated A-Interface messages are sent as DTAP message types that utilize the existing

SCCP connections. Also, if SSD information is shared, the MSC/VLR will have the capability to authenticate the mobile and initiate Unique Challenges directly. For more details on IS-41 call flows when SSD is shared, refer to IS-41 standards [8].

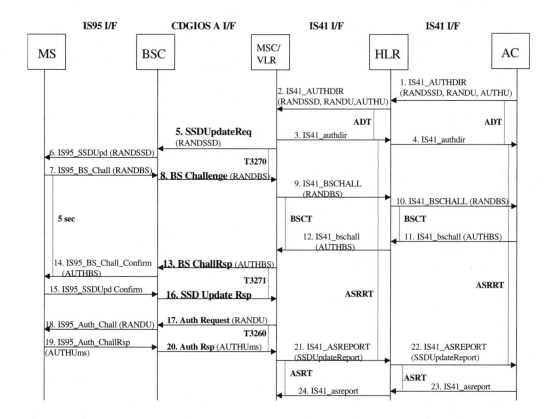

Figure 6-18 Shared Secret Data Update call flow, Shared Secret Data not shared

1. IS41_AUTHDIR (RANDSSD, RANDU, AUTHU) (IS-41):

The AC initiates an SSD Update by sending an authentication directive IS41_AUTHDIR message to the HLR. Included in this message are RANDSSD, RANDU, and AUTHU. RANDSSD is eventually passed to the mobile station and is used along with the ESN and A-Key to compute the new SSD. RANDU and AUTHU may be used later for a Unique Challenge after the Base Station Challenge has been performed. Upon sending this message, the AC starts the *Authentication Directive Timer* (ADT). The default ADT value is 6 seconds [8].

The IS41_AUTHDIR message is a general-purpose authentication directive that can be used by the AC to either invoke a unique challenge or update the mobile station's SSD.

2. IS41_AUTHDIR (RANDSSD, RANDU, AUTHU) (IS-41):

The HLR simply passes on the IS41_AUTHDIR message to the MSC and starts timer ADT.

3. IS41_authdir (IS-41):

The MSC returns an empty IS41_authdir return result to the HLR to indicate that the IS41_AUTHDIR message has been accepted. The HLR stops timer ADT upon receipt of IS41_authdir message and starts the *Authentication Status Report Response Timer* (ASRRT). The default ASRRT value is 24 seconds. ASRRT is started whenever an authentication operation that requires an authentication status report is initiated [8].

4. IS41_authdir (IS-41):

The HLR passes on the empty IS41_authdir return result to the AC. The AC stops timer ADT upon receipt of IS41_authdir message and starts the *Authentication Status Report Response Timer* (ASRRT) while waiting for the Authentication Status Report from the MSC.

5. SSDUpdateReq (RANDSSD) (A-Interface):

The MSC sends an SSD Update Request message to the BSC to invoke a mobile station SSD Update. The RANDSSD parameter that originated from the AC is included in this message and is eventually used by the mobile station to updates its SSD. The MSC starts timer T3270.

6. IS95_SSDUp (RANDSSD) (IS-95):

The BSC sends the received RANDSSD parameter to the mobile station using the IS-95 SSD Update message.

7. IS95_BS_Chall (RANDBS) (IS-95):

Upon receiving RANDSSD, the mobile station computes a new SSD value using the SSD Generation algorithm and input parameters RANDSSD, ESN, and A-Key. After updating its SSD, the mobile station then attempts to confirm the new SSD value by performing a Base Station Challenge. The mobile station generates a 32-bit random number (RANDBS) and computes the Base Station Challenge authentication result (AUTHBS) using authentication inputs RANDBS, ESN, IMSI_S1, and the new SSD_A value. RANDBS is sent to the BSC using the IS-95 Base Station Challenge Order. The mobile starts a 5 seconds timer to wait for an IS-95 Base Station Challenge Confirmation Order message.

8. BS Challenge (RANDBS) (A-Interface):

Upon receipt of the IS-95 Base Station Challenge Order message from the mobile station, the BSC sends the MSC a Base Station Challenge message that contains the RANDBS value.

The MSC stops timer T3270 upon receipt of the Base Station Challenge message. If T3270 expires before the Base Station Challenge message is received from the BSC, the MSC may choose to retry the SSD Update Request once more or it may deny access immediately. Upon second expiry, the MSC sends an IS41_ASREPORT message to the HLR/AC that contains an SSD Update Report field, indicating that the SSD Update failed.

9. IS41_BSCHALL (RANDBS) (IS-41):

The MSC sends the Base Station Challenge parameter RANDBS to the HLR using the IS41_BSCHALL message. The MSC starts timer *Base Station Challenge Timer* (BSCT). The default BSCT timer value is 3 seconds [8].

10. IS41_BSCHALL (RANDBS) (IS-41):

The HLR passes on the base station challenge parameter RANDBS to the AC and starts timer BSCT.

11. IS41_bschall (AUTHBS) (IS-41):

Upon receipt of the Base Station Challenge, the AC computes the Base Station Challenge authentication result (AUTHBS) using IMSI_S1, ESN, the updated SSD_A, and the RANDBS value received from the mobile station. The AC then sends the computed AUTHBS value to the HLR using the IS41_bschall return result message. The HLR stops timer BSCT.

12. IS41_bschall (AUTHBS) (IS-41):

The HLR forwards AUTHBS to the MSC and stops timer BSCT.

13. BS ChallRsp (AUTHBS) (A-Interface):

The MSC sends the AUTHBS value computed by the AC to the BSC using the Base Station Challenge Response message. The MSC starts timer T3271 while waiting for an SSD Update Response.

14. IS95_BS_Chall_Confirm (AUTHBS) (IS-95):

The BSC sends an IS-95 Base Station Challenge Confirmation Order that contains AUTHBS. If this message is not received within 5 seconds after the IS-95 Base Station Challenge Order was sent, the mobile station abandons the Base Station Challenge.

15. IS95_SSDUpd_Confirm (IS-95):

The mobile station compares the AUTHBS received from the AC with its locally calculated AUTHBS. If the two match, the mobile station notifies the BSC of the successful SSD Update by sending an IS-95 SSD Update Confirmation Order.

However, if the AUTHBS signatures do not match, the mobile station sends an IS-95 SSD Update Rejection Order to the BSC. The BSC then notifies the MSC of the failed SSD Update by sending an A-Interface SSD Update Response message with the Cause Layer 3 value set to "SSD Update Rejected." The MSC indicates the failure to the HLR/AC using the IS41_ASREPORT message.

16. SSD Update Rsp (A-Interface):

The BSC sends the SSD Update Response message to the MSC after receiving an IS-95 SSD Update Confirmation Order or an IS-95 SSD Update Rejection Order message from the mobile station.

The MSC stops timer T3271 upon receipt of the SSD Update Response message. If T3271 expires before a SSD Update Response message is received, the MSC notifies the HLR/AC that the SSD Update procedure failed using the IS41_ASREPORT message.

The final stages (17–24) of the call flow shown in Figure 6-18 relate to the Unique Challenge and subsequent status report (see Section 6.5.1, "Unique Challenge Call Flow," on page 373). The status of the SSD Update procedure is contained in the SSD Update Report field of the IS41_ASREPORT message.

6.6.2   Shared Secret Data Update Messages

The following sections contain detail descriptions of the A-Interface DTAP messages that are used during the SSD Update procedure. Note that SSD Update for an idle mobile station is not required for CDGIOS.

6.6.2.1   Shared Secret Data Update Request

This message is sent from the MSC to the BSC to request that the SSD of a specified mobile station be updated.

The RANDSSD IE contains the 56-bit random number generated by the AC and is used by the mobile station to compute a new SSD (Table 6-10).

- BSAP Message Type: DTAP
- SCCP Message Type: SCCP-Data Form 1 (DT1)
- Direction: BSC ← MSC

Table 6-10   SSD Update Request DTAP Message (CDGIOS 6.1.4.4)

BitMap	Param IE	#Oct	Range	Type	IOS Ref
0000 0001 (01H) ccrr rsss LLLL LLLL	DTAP header	3	Msg Discrim. = 1 (DTAP) DLCI = "ccrr rsss" = 0 L = DTAP msg length	M	6.2.2.1 6.2.2.2 6.2.2.3
rrrr 0101 (05H)	Protocol Discriminator	1	0101—Mobility Management r = 0—reserved bits	M	6.2.2.39
0000 0000 (00H)	Reserved Bits	1		M	6.2.2.40

Table 6-10 SSD Update Request DTAP Message (CDGIOS 6.1.4.4) (Continued)

BitMap	Param IE	#Oct	Range	Type	IOS Ref
0100 0111 (47H)	Msg Type	1	SSD Update Msg	M	6.2.2.4
LLLL LLLL rrrr tttt nnnn nnnn nnnn nnnn nnnn nnnn nnnn nnnn nnnn nnnn nnnn nnnn nnnn nnnn	Authentication Challenge Parameter (RANDSSD)	9	L = 08H r = 0—reserved tttt = 0100 n = 56-bit RANDSSD	M	6.2.2.45

6.6.2.2   Base Station Challenge

The Base Station Challenge message is sent by the BSC to the MSC to initiate verification of the newly computed SSD.

The RANDBS IE contains a 32-bit random number generated by the mobile station and is used by the Authentication Center to compute AUTHBS (Table 6-11).

- BSAP Message Type: DTAP
- SCCP Message Type: SCCP-Data Form 1 (DT1)
- Direction: BSC → MSC

Table 6-11 Base Station Challenge DTAP Message (CDGIOS 6.1.4.5)

BitMap	Param IE	#Oct	Range	Type	IOS Ref
0000 0001 (01H) ccrr rsss LLLL LLLL	DTAP header	3	Msg Discrim. = 1 (DTAP) DLCI = "ccrr rsss" = 0 L = DTAP msg length	M	6.2.2.1 6.2.2.2 6.2.2.3
rrrr 0101 (05H)	Protocol Discriminator	1	0101—Mobility Management r = 0—reserved bits	M	6.2.2.39
0000 0000 (00H)	Reserved Bits	1		M	6.2.2.40

Table 6-11   Base Station Challenge DTAP Message (CDGIOS 6.1.4.5) (Continued)

BitMap	Param IE	#Oct	Range	Type	IOS Ref
0100 1000 (48H)	Msg Type	1	BS Challenge Msg	M	6.2.2.4
LLLL LLLL rrrr tttt nnnn nnnn nnnn nnnn nnnn nnnn nnnn nnnn	Authentication Challenge Parameter (RANDBS)	6	L = 05H r = 0—reserved tttt = 1000 n = 32-bit RANDBS	M	6.2.2.45

6.6.2.3   Base Station Challenge Response

This message is sent by the MSC to the BSC after the AC responds to a Base Station Challenge during the SSD Update process.

The AUTHBS IE contains an 18-bit authentication result that the AC computed using inputs RANDBS, ESN, IMSI_S1, and the new SSD (Table 6-12).

- BSAP Message Type: DTAP
- SCCP Message Type: SCCP-Data Form 1 (DT1)
- Direction: BSC ← MSC

Table 6-12   Base Station Challenge Response DTAP Message (CDGIOS 6.1.4.6)

BitMap	Param IE	#Oct	Range	Type	IOS Ref
0000 0001 (01H) ccrr rsss LLLL LLLL	DTAP header	3	Msg Discrim. = 1 (DTAP) DLCI = "ccrr rsss" = 0 L = DTAP msg length	M	6.2.2.1 6.2.2.2 6.2.2.3
rrrr 0101 (05H)	Protocol Discriminator	1	0101—Mobility Management r = 0—reserved bits	M	6.2.2.39
0000 0000 (00H)	Reserved Bits	1		M	6.2.2.40

Table 6-12   Base Station Challenge Response DTAP Message (CDGIOS 6.1.4.6) (Continued)

BitMap	Param IE	#Oct	Range	Type	IOS Ref
0100 1001 (49H)	Msg Type	1	BS Challenge Response Msg	M	6.2.2.4
LLLL LLLL rrrr tttt 0000 00nn nnnn nnnn nnnn nnnn	Authentication Challenge Parameter (AUTHBS)	5	L = 04H r = 0—reserved tttt = 0100 n = 18-bit AUTHBS	M	6.2.2.46

6.6.2.4   Shared Secret Data Update Response

This message is sent from the BSC to the MSC after the Base Station Challenge result is received from the mobile.

The optional Cause Layer 3 IE is included if the mobile indicates an SSD Update failure. An SSD Update Response message that does not contain the Cause Layer 3 IE implies a successful SSD Update (Table 6-13).

- BSAP Message Type: DTAP
- SCCP Message Type: SCCP-Data Form 1 (DT1)
- Direction: BSC → MSC

Table 6-13   SSD Update Response DTAP Message (CDGIOS 6.1.4.7)

BitMap	Param IE	#Oct	Range	Type	IOS Ref
0000 0001 (01H) ccrr rsss LLLL LLLL	DTAP header	3	Msg Discrim. = 1 (DTAP) DLCI = "ccrr rsss" = 0 L = DTAP msg length	M	6.2.2.1 6.2.2.2 6.2.2.3
rrrr 0101 (05H)	Protocol Discriminator	1	0101—Mobility Management r = 0—reserved bits	M	6.2.2.39
0000 0000 (00H)	Reserved Bits	1		M	6.2.2.40

Table 6-13   SSD Update Response DTAP Message (CDGIOS 6.1.4.7) (Continued)

BitMap	Param IE	#Oct	Range	Type	IOS Ref
0100 1010 (4AH)	Msg Type	1	SSD Update Response Msg	M	6.2.2.4
0000 1000 (08H) LLLL LLLL xccr llll xvvv vvvv	Cause Layer 3	4	L = 02H, x = 1, r = 0—reserved cc = 00—Coding std (ITU) llll = 0100—location bits = pub netwk serving remote user v = cause layer3 0FH—Procedure failed 3BH—SSD Update reject	O,C	6.2.2.55

6.6.3   SSD Update with Unique Challenge Example Call Flow

Figure 6-19 contains a summary message call flow for an SSD Update followed by a Unique Challenge. The purpose of Figure 6-19 is to present an overview of the messages exchanged between the BSC and MSC. Subsequent figures illustrate the complete messages content, including MTP and SCCP layers. The decoded message format is similar to what would be seen on test equipment monitoring the A-Interface signaling link. The BSC's point code in this example is 8-17-92, and the MSC's point code is 110-44-3.

The example message flow begins with the mobile station originating a call in an Authentication-enabled network. During the origination, the Global Challenge fails, possibly because of an SSD mismatch, and the AC initiates the SSD Update procedure. When the AC triggers the SSD Update, the MSC sends the BSC an SSD Update Request message that contains the RANDSSD parameter, which is then sent to the mobile station. Within 0.2 seconds, the mobile responds with a Base Station Challenge, which the BSC then relays to the MSC/AC/network. The AC responds to the Base Station Challenge and the mobile determines that the SSD Update was successful.

Immediately following the SSD Update success, the MSC issues a Unique Challenge to the mobile, which is also successful.

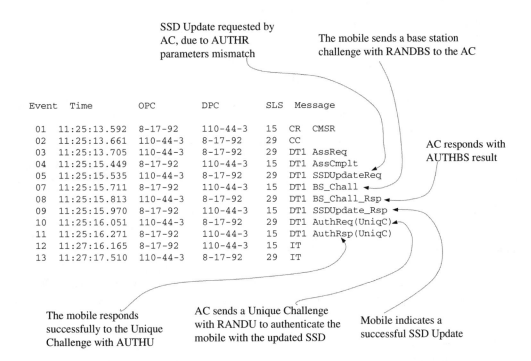

SSD Update requested by
AC, due to AUTHR
parameters mismatch

The mobile sends a base station
challenge with RANDBS to the AC

Event	Time	OPC	DPC	SLS	Message
01	11:25:13.592	8-17-92	110-44-3	15	CR CMSR
02	11:25:13.661	110-44-3	8-17-92	29	CC
03	11:25:13.705	110-44-3	8-17-92	29	DT1 AssReq
04	11:25:15.449	8-17-92	110-44-3	15	DT1 AssCmplt
05	11:25:15.535	110-44-3	8-17-92	29	DT1 SSDUpdateReq
07	11:25:15.711	8-17-92	110-44-3	15	DT1 BS_Chall
08	11:25:15.813	110-44-3	8-17-92	29	DT1 BS_Chall_Rsp
09	11:25:15.970	8-17-92	110-44-3	15	DT1 SSDUpdate_Rsp
10	11:25:16.051	110-44-3	8-17-92	29	DT1 AuthReq(UniqC)
11	11:25:16.271	8-17-92	110-44-3	15	DT1 AuthRsp(UniqC)
12	11:27:16.165	8-17-92	110-44-3	15	IT
13	11:27:17.510	110-44-3	8-17-92	29	IT

AC responds with
AUTHBS result

The mobile responds
successfully to the Unique
Challenge with AUTHU

AC sends a Unique Challenge
with RANDU to authenticate the
mobile with the updated SSD

Mobile indicates a
successful SSD Update

Figure 6-19   Shared Secret Data Update with Unique Challenge example call flow

Figure 6-20 shows an example of a decoded SSD Update Request message that is similar
to what may be seen on test equipment monitoring the A-Interface during an SSD Update of a
mobile in traffic. Only the SSD input parameter RANDSSD, which is an input to the mobile station's SSD Generation algorithm, is included.

```
**** MESSAGE NUMBER: 00005 ****
*** Start of MTP Level 3 ***
0003 10000011 83
     ----0011     Service Indicator         SCCP
     --00----     Network Priority          priority 0
     10------     Network Indicator         National
0004 (3 Bytes)    Destination Point Code    8-17-92
0007 (3 Bytes)    Origination Point Code    110-44-3
0010 00011101 1d Signaling Link Selection   29
*** Start of SCCP ***
0011 00000110 06 Data Form 1                6
0012 (3 Bytes)    Dest Local References     78696
0015 00000000 00 Segment/Reassembling       0
0016 00000001 01 Variable Pointer           01
```

(Continued)
```
*** Start of CDGIOS MM ***
                        SSD Update Request
0017 00001111 0f DTAP Length              15
0018 00000001 01 Discriminator            DTAP
0019 00000000 00 DLCI
0020 00001100 0c Length                   12
0021 00000101 05 MM Protocol Discrim      5
0022 00000000 00 Reserved
0023 01000111 47 SSD Update Request       71
0024 00001000 08 Auth Challenge Length    8
0025 00000100 04 Auth Challenge Param     RANDSSD
0026 10100111 a7 RANDSSD Value            a7 49 5a c8 ...
0027 01001001 49                               ◄──────── Input to SSD gener-
0028 01011010 5a                                         ation algorithm
0029 11001000 c8
0030 10101000 a8
0031 01001100 4c
0032 01110100 74
```

Figure 6-20 Shared Secret Data Update Request message example

Figure 6-21 shows an example of a decoded Base Station Challenge message. Only the authentication input parameter RANDBS, which is used as an input to the AC's CAVE Algorithm, is contained in the message.

```
**** MESSAGE NUMBER: 00007 ****
*** Start of MTP Level 3 ***
0003 10000011 83
     ----0011     Service Indicator        SCCP
     --00----     Network Priority         priority 0
     10------     Network Indicator        National
0004 (3 Bytes)    Destination Point Code   110-44-3
0007 (3 Bytes)    Origination Point Code   8-17-92
0010 00001111 0f Signaling Link Selection  15
*** Start of SCCP ***
0011 00000110 06 Data Form 1               6
0012 (3 Bytes)    Dest Local References    15432238
0015 00000000 00 Segment/Reassembling      0
0016 00000001 01 Variable Pointer          01
*** Start of CDGIOS MM ***
                 Base Station Challenge
0017 00001100 0c DTAP Length               12
0018 00000001 01 Discriminator             01
0019 00000000 00 DLCI
0020 00001001 09 Length                    9
0021 00000101 05 MM Protocol Discrim       5
0022 00000000 00 Reserved
0023 01001000 48 Base Station Challenge    72
0024 00000101 05 Auth Challenge Length     5        Input to CAVE algo for
0025 00001000 08 Auth Challenge Param      RANDBS ◄── BS challenge
```

(Continued)
```
0026 11010001 d1 RANDBS Value            d1 17 79 e5
0027 00010111 17
0028 01111001 79
0029 11100101 e5
```

Figure 6-21 Base Station Challenge message example

Figure 6-22 shows an example of a decoded Base Station Challenge Response message. Only the Base Station Challenge authentication result parameter AUTHBS is included at the application layer.

```
**** MESSAGE NUMBER: 00008 ****
*** Start of MTP Level 3 ***
0003 10000011 83
     ----0011    Service Indicator          SCCP
     --00----    Network Priority           priority 0
     10------    Network Indicator          National
0004 (3 Bytes)   Destination Point Code     8-17-92
0007 (3 Bytes)   Origination Point Code     110-44-3
0010 00011101 1d Signaling Link Selection   29
*** Start of SCCP ***
0011 00000110 06 Data Form 1                6
0012 (3 Bytes)   Dest Local References      78696
0015 00000000 00 Segment/Reassembling       0
0016 00000001 01 Variable Pointer           01
*** Start of CDGIOS MM ***
                 Base Station Challenge Response
0017 00001011 0b DTAP Length                11
0018 00000001 01 Discriminator              01
0019 00000000 00 DLCI
0020 00001000 08 Length                     8
0021 00000101 05 MM Protocol Discrim        05
0022 00000000 00 Reserved
0023 01001001 49 BS Challenge Response      73
0024 00000100 04 Auth Response Param Length 4
0025 00000100 04 Type                       AUTHBS      Result of CAVE algo-
0026 00000111 07 AUTHBS Value               07 f1 8e ◄──  rithm for BS challenge
0027 11110001 f1
0028 10001110 8e
```

Figure 6-22 Base Station Challenge Response message example

Figure 6-23 shows an example of a decoded SSD Update Response message. No specific parameters are present at the application layer because the message simply indicates a successful SSD Update.

```
**** MESSAGE NUMBER: 00009 ****
*** Start of MTP Level 3 ***
0003 10000011 83
        ----0011    Service Indicator          SCCP
        --00----    Network Priority           priority 0
        10------    Network Indicator          National
0004 (3 Bytes)    Destination Point Code       110-44-3
0007 (3 Bytes)    Origination Point Code       8-17-92
0010 00001111 0f Signaling Link Selection      15
*** Start of SCCP ***
0011 00000110 06 Data Form 1                    6
0012 (3 Bytes)    Dest Local References         15432238
0015 00000000 00 Segment/Reassembling           0
0016 00000001 01 Variable Pointer               01
*** Start of CDGIOS MM ***
                    SSD Update Response
0017 00000110 06 DTAP Length                     6
0018 00000001 01 Discriminator                  DTAP
0019 00000000 00 DLCI
0020 00000011 03 Length                          3
0021 00000101 05 MM Protocol Discrim             5
0022 00000000 00 Reserved
0023 01001010 4a SSD Update Response            74
```

Figure 6-23   Shared Secret Data Update Response message example

6.7 Signaling Message Encryption and Voice Privacy

Signaling Message Encryption (SME) and *Voice Privacy* (VP) are optional techniques that may be used in CDMA networks to increase the security of signaling and voice traffic frames exchanged between the BSC and mobile stations. VP may be initiated by either the mobile station during call setup or by the BSC if the mobile station is already in a call. The network is responsible for activating SME. VP and SME both require authentication to be enabled in the network, and both techniques use the 64 least significant bits of the SSD, known as SSD_B, as input.

SME is an optional technique that CDMA networks sometime use to protect sensitive subscriber information contained in signaling frames transmitted over-the-air. If SME is requested by the network, signaling frames are encrypted using an algorithm know to both the network and the mobile station. The encryption algorithm used in CDMA system is the *Cellular Message Encryption Algorithm* (CMEA). CMEA is described in "Common Cryptographic Algorithms," which is governed under the *US International Traffic and Arms Regulations* (ITAR) and the Export Administration Regulations. TIA acts as the facilitator for providing such information.

SME is individually controlled by the BSC for each call. During call setup, the BSC may request SME by setting the ENCRYPT_MODE field in IS-95 Channel Assignment message to 1. The BSC may also use the IS-95 Extended Handoff Direction message or the IS-95 Message Encryption Mode Order to request signaling message encryption from a particular mobile station. The CMEA encryption key information is transferred to the BSC from the MSC during the call setup process and is used by the BSC to encrypt some IS-95 signaling messages. It should be noted that not all IS-95 traffic channel signaling messages are encrypted [7].

The VP encryption technique uses a *Private Long Code* (PLC) mask for PN spreading in the reverse traffic channel and for data scrambling in the forward traffic channel. The mobile station requests VP by setting the *Privacy Mode* (PM) field in the IS-95 Origination message or the IS-95 Page Response message to 1. If a mobile station is already in a call, either the BSC or mobile station may use the IS-95 Long Code Transition Request Order message to transition from the public to the PLC mask. The BSC may also invoke the transition by sending the IS-95 Extended Handoff Direction message with the PRIVATE_LCM bit set.

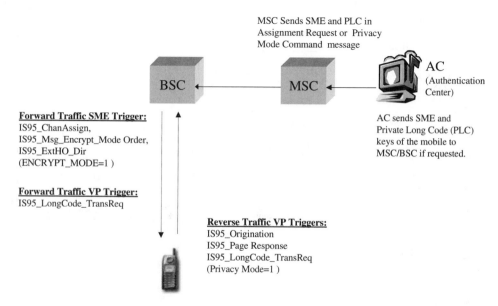

Figure 6-24   Signaling Message Encryption and Voice Privacy overview

Figure 6-24 contains an overview of the entities and general messages involved in the support of SME and VP. The AC holds the encryption keys for SME and the PLC mask used for VP. When SME or VP services are requested, the encryption keys are sent by the AC to the MSC, which then passes the information to the BSC in the form of an Assignment Request or Privacy Mode Command message. If the request for VP is received during a call setup, the Assignment Request message contains the encryption information. The Privacy Mode Command message is used by the MSC if the mobile station is already in an established call. Upon receiving the SME and VP encryption information from the MSC, the BSC uses the data to encrypt the traffic signaling and voice frames before transmission of the IS-95 message over the air.

6.7.1   SME and VP Request in Call Setup Call Flow

Figure 6-25 shows the call flow for the activation of SME and VP during a mobile origination. Only a mobile origination call flow is presented because SME and VP for a mobile-terminated call is similar. During a mobile-terminated call, the mobile station's request for VP services is contained in the Paging Response message instead of the CM Service Request message. Descriptions of the individual steps shown in Figure 6-25 follow the diagram.

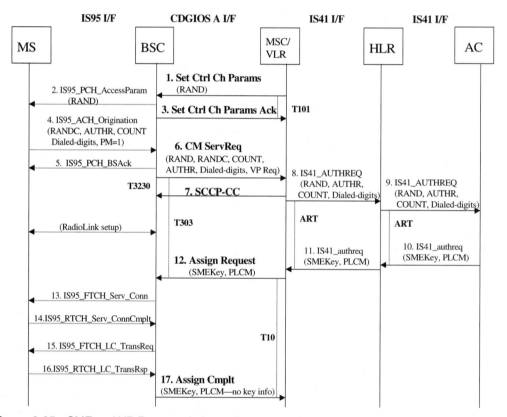

Figure 6-25   SME and VP Request during call setup call flow

When a call is set up in an Authentication-enabled network, the mobile station may request VP services by including the optional Voice Privacy Request IE in either the CM Service Request or Paging Response messages. Upon receiving a valid request for VP, the network approves the request and sends the required encryption information to the BSC. Specifically, the Assignment Request message sent from the MSC to the BSC includes the Encryption Information IE, which contains the PLC mask and SME Key needed by the mobile station. Recall that Global Challenge parameters must be received and authentication turned on in order for SME and VP to be activated in the network. If the Encryption Information IE is included in the Assignment Request message, it is also included in the Assignment Complete message, without the encryption key information.

1. Set Ctrl Ch Params (RAND) (A-Interface):

   The MSC sends a Set Control Channel Parameter message to the BSC, including any parameter that the MSC wants to broadcast over the paging channel to the mobile. As mentioned previously, CDGIOS indicates that this message be sent only by the MSC to change the RAND authentication parameter when both the MSC and BSC support MSC-generated RAND. Note that if RAND is generated at the BSC, the MSC is not required to send this message.

   The MSC may also include an optional Tag value that may later be used by the MSC to identify the acknowledgment received from the BSC. The same Tag value included in the Set Control Channel Parameter message is included by the BSC in the Set Control Channel Parameter Acknowledge message.

   The MSC starts timer T101 to wait for an acknowledgment.

2. IS95_PCH_AccssParams (RAND) (IS-95):

   The BSC packages the RAND value received from the MSC into an IS-95 Access Parameters message that is sent over the paging channel to mobile stations using the network. The IS-95 Access Parameters message is a broadcast message used by the BSC to define parameters used by the mobile stations when transmitting to the BSC over the access channel.

3. Set Ctrl Ch Params Ack (A-Interface):

   After the BSC updates the paging channel messages with the overhead information received from the MSC, it sends a Set Control Channel Parameter Acknowledgment message to the MSC. If a Tag value was included in the corresponding Set Control Channel Parameter message received from the MSC, the same Tag value is included by the BSC in this message.

   The MSC stops timer T101 upon receipt of the Set Control Channel Parameter Acknowledge message. If T101 expires before receipt of the acknowledgment, the MSC may choose to resend the Set Control Channel Parameter message one more time.

4. IS95_ACH_Origination (RANDC, AUTHR, COUNT, Dialed digits, PM = 1) (IS-95):

   The call flow associated with a mobile originated call begins with the mobile station sending an IS-95 Origination message over the access channel. If the authentication is enabled in the network and the mobile station supports authentication, the AUTH_MODE field of the IS-95 Origination message is set to 1, and authentication parameters RANDC, AUTHR, COUNT, and Dialed digits are included in the message. The mobile station requests VP services by setting the PM field to 1.

5. IS95_PCH_BSAck (IS-95):

The Base Station acknowledges the receipt of the IS-95 Origination message.

6. CM Service Request (RANDC, RAND, COUNT, AUTHR, Dialed digits, VP Req) (A-Interface):

Upon receipt of the IS-95 Origination message, the BSC sends a CM Service Request to the MSC that contains parameters received in the IS-95 Origination message. The BSC starts timer T3230 to wait for an SCCP-CC message and timer T303 to wait for an Assignment Request message. The Voice Privacy Request IE is included in this message to indicate to the MSC that VP operation is being requested from the mobile station.

7. SCCP-CC (A-Interface):

The MSC sends the SCCP-CC message to the BSC after establishing the SCCP connection. The BSC stops timer T3230 upon the receipt of SCCP-CC.

8. IS41_AUTHREQ (RAND, AUTHR, COUNT, Dialed-digits) (IS-41):

Upon receipt of the CM Service Request, the MSC verifies that the authentication parameters are received and that the RANDC parameter matches the first 8 bits of RAND. The MSC then requests that the received authentication signature be verified by sending an IS-41 Authentication Request message to the HLR. The IS-41 Authentication Request message contains authentication parameters RAND, AUTHR, COUNT, and Dialed digits received from the BSC. The MSC starts the *Authentication Request Timer* (ART), which has a default value of 6 seconds, while waiting for an IS41_authreq return result or return error.

9. IS41_AUTHREQ (RAND, AUTHR, COUNT, Dialed digits) (IS-41):

The HLR passes on the IS-41 Authentication Request message to the AC and starts the ART.

10. IS41_authreq (SMEKey, PLCM) (IS-41):

The AC, upon receipt of the IS41_AUTHREQ message, verifies the authentication signature received from the mobile station. If the Global Challenge is successful, the AC sends the SME Key and PLC mask encryption information to the HLR in an IS41_authreq message.

If the authentication fails, the AC includes the *Deny Access* parameter in the IS41_authreq message sent to the HLR. The MSC then denies network services to the mobile station and initiates call clearing.

The HLR stops timer ART upon receipt of the IS41_authreq return result message from the AC.

11. IS41_authreq (SMEKey, PLCM) (IS-41):

The IS41_authreq message containing the encryption keys is passed from the HLR to the MSC. The MSC stops timer ART upon receipt of the IS41_authreq return result or return error message.

12. Assign Request (SMEKey, PLCM) (A-Interface):

After receiving notification that the authentication process was successful, the MSC continues with the call setup by sending an Assignment Request message to the BSC. The encryption information SME Key and CDMA Private Long Code Mask Key are both included in this message. The BSC stops timer T303 upon receipt of the Assignment Request message. The MSC starts timer T10 while waiting for the Assignment Complete message from the BSC.

13. IS95_FTCH_Serv_Conn (IS-95):

The BSC sends an IS-95 Service Connect message to set the service option and service configuration of the mobile station.

14. IS95_RTCH_Serv_ConnCmplt (IS-95):

The mobile station responds with an IS-95 Service Connect Complete message.

15. IS95_FTCH_LC_TransReq (IS-95):

The BSC then initiates VP by sending the IS-95 Long Code Transition Request Order on the forward traffic channel to the mobile station.

16. IS95_RTCH_LC_TransRsp (IS-95):

The mobile executes the voice privacy encryption procedures and responds with the IS-95 Long Code Transition Response Order on the reverse traffic channel.

17. Assign Cmplt (SMEKey, PLCM—no key info) (A-Interface):

After completing the setup of the radio link and terrestrial resources, the BSC sends an Assignment Complete message to the MSC to indicate a successful call setup. The Encryption Information IE contains the SME Key and PLC mask fields, including status, but no keys are included. The Encryption Information IE is included only if it was received in the Assignment Request message. The MSC stops timer T10 upon receipt of the Assignment Complete message.

6.7.2 SME and VP Request in Traffic Channel Call Flow

SME and VP can also be invoked after a mobile station is already in a call. The Privacy Mode Command is used by the MSC to invoke both SME and VP.

This scenario typically occurs when the encryption information is not available at the MSC at the time the Assignment Request message is sent to the BSC. If the encryption information is received by the MSC after the Assignment Request message has been sent to the BSC, the MSC waits for the Assignment Complete message before sending the encryption information in a Privacy Mode Command. The choice of whether to send the encryption information in the Assignment Request or the Privacy Mode Command during call setup is left to the MSC manufacturer.

Figure 6-26 illustrates the call flow for activation of SME and VP after a mobile station is already in traffic. The mobile origination portion of the call flow is similar to that presented in Figure 6-25, except that no SME Key or PLC mask information is sent in either the Assignment Request and Assignment Complete messages. Instead, the encryption information is contained in the Privacy Mode Command, which is used to trigger the VP and SME operations. Only the additional call flow stages not present in Figure 6-25 are discussed below:

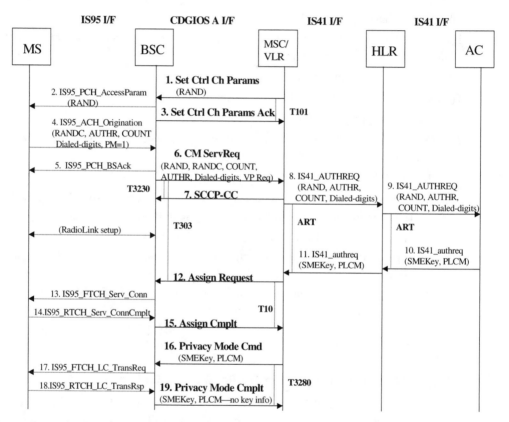

Figure 6-26   SME and VP Request in Traffic Channel call flow

16. Privacy Mode Cmd (SMEKey, PLCM) (A-Interface):

   The MSC sends the encryption information SME Key and PLC mask to the BSC in a Privacy Mode Command message, requesting the BSC to provide VP and SME services. The MSC starts timer T3280 to wait for a Privacy Mode Complete message from the BSC.

17. IS95_FTCH_LC_TransReq (IS-95):

   The BSC initiates VP by sending an IS-95 Long Code Transition Request Order to the mobile station on the forward traffic channel.

18. IS95_RTCH_LC_TransRsp (IS-95):

The mobile executes the VP encryption procedures and responds with the IS-95 Long Code Transition Response Order on the reverse traffic channel.

19. Privacy Mode Cmplt (SMEKey, PLCM—no key info) (A-Interface):

The BSC sends the Privacy Mode Complete message to the MSC, indicating the successful receipt of the encryption information in the Privacy Mode Command message. The Encryption Information IE contains the SME Key and PLC mask fields, including status, but no key are included.

The MSC stops timer T3280. If time T3280 expires before a Privacy Mode Complete message is received from the BSC, the MSC may initiate call clearing.

6.7.3   SME and VP Messages

This section contains detail descriptions of the A-Interface messages used to request SME and VP operations from a mobile station in traffic channel. Recall that if encryption information is available during call setup, the SME and VP operation can be activated through the CM Service Request, Assignment Request, and Assignment Complete A-Interface messages.

6.7.3.1   Privacy Mode Command

This message is sent from the MSC to the BSC to enable or disable SME or VP for a particular mobile station (Table 6-14).

The mandatory Encryption Information IE contains the required SME encryption keys (CMEA keys) and the CDMA PLC mask keys.

- BSAP Message Type: BSMAP
- SCCP Message Type: SCCP-Data Form1 (DT1)
- Direction: BSC ← MSC

Table 6-14   Privacy Mode Command Message (CDGIOS 6.1.4.18)

BitMap	Param IE	#Oct	Range	Type	IOS Ref
0000 0000 (00H) LLLL LLLL	BSMAP header	2	Msg Discrim. = 0 (BSMAP) L = BSMAP msg length	M	6.2.2.1 6.2.2.3

Table 6-14   Privacy Mode Command Message (CDGIOS 6.1.4.18) (Continued)

BitMap	Param IE	#Oct	Range	Type	IOS Ref
0101 0011 (53H)	Msg Type	1	Privacy Mode Command Msg	M	6.2.2.4
0000 1010 (0AH) LLLL LLLL xiii iisa llll llll kkkk kkkk kkkk kkkk kkkk kkkk kkkk kkkk kkkk kkkk kkkk kkkk kkkk kkkk kkkk kkkk *AND/ OR* xiii iisa llll llll uuuu uukk kkkk kkkk kkkk kkkk kkkk kkkk kkkk kkkk kkkk kkkk	Encryption Information	var-iable	L = 08H, 0AH, or 12H x = 1, k = key value i = 00001—SME s = 1,0—status (1=active) a = 1,0—algo avail (1=avail) l = 08H—key length Present when Voice Privacy is requested and MSC has keys available at time message is sent. x = 1, k = key value i = 00100—private longcode s = 1,0—status a = 1,0—algo avail l = 06H—key length u = 0—unused bits	M	6.2.2.12

6.7.3.2   Privacy Mode Complete

This message is sent from the BSC to the MSC to acknowledge the receipt of the Privacy Mode Command message and that VP and SME have been enabled (Table 6-15). This message can also be used to indicate that the mobile station has requested VP operation.

The optional Encryption Information IE contains the SME encryption (CMEA keys) and the CDMA PLC Mask fields, but does not contain the actual key values. This IE is used only by the BSC to indicate to the MSC the acceptance of VP and SME keys.

The optional Voice Privacy Request IE is used for indicating to the MSC that the mobile station has requested VP operation.

- BSAP Message Type: BSMAP
- SCCP Message Type: SCCP-Data Form 1 (DT1)
- Direction: BSC → MSC

Table 6-15 Privacy Mode Complete Message (CDGIOS 6.1.4.19)

BitMap	Param IE	#Oct	Range	Type	IOS Ref
0000 0000 (00H) LLLL LLLL	BSMAP header	2	Msg Discrim. = 0 (BSMAP) L = BSMAP msg length	M	6.2.2.1 6.2.2.3
0101 0101 (55H)	Msg Type	1	Privacy Mode Complete Msg	M	6.2.2.4
0000 1010 (0AH) LLLL LLLL xiii iisa llll llll *AND/ OR* xiii iisa llll llll	Encryption Information	Variable	L = 02H or 04H x = 1, i = 00001—SME s = 1,0—status (1 = active) a = 1,0—algo avail (1 = avail) l = 00H—key length i = 00100—private longcode l = 00H—key length	O,C	6.2.2.12
1010 0001 (A1H)	Voice Privacy Request	1		O,C	6.2.2.13

References

1. Wireless Week, *"Anti-Fraud Solutions Increase."* May 11 1998.
2. CDG-IOS version 3.1.1, *CDMA Development Group MSC to BS Interface Inter-Operability Specification*. June 1999.
3. CDG-IOS version 2.0, *CDMA Development Group MSC to BS Interface Inter-Operability Specification*. September 1998.
4. Telecommunications Industry Association, TIA/EIA/IS-634-A, *MSC–BS Interface (A-Interface) for Public 800 MHz*. July 1998.
5. Telecommunications Industry Association , TIA/EIA/TSB-80, *MSC–BS Interface (A-Interface) for Public 800 MHz*. October 1996.
6. Telecommunications Industry Association, TIA/EIA/IS-95-A, *Mobile Station–Base Station Compatibility Standard for Dual-Mode Wideband Spread Spectrum Cellular Systems*. May 1995.
7. American National Standards Institute, ANSI J-STD-008, *Personal Station–Base Station Compatibility Requirements for 1.8 to 2.0 GHz Code Devision Multiple Access (CDMA) Personal Communications Systems*. August 1995.
8. American National Standards Institute, ANSI TIA/EIA/IS-41-D, *Cellular Radio-Telecommunications Intersystem Operations*. December 1997.

CHAPTER 7

Radio Resource Management

When questioned about why they purchased a mobile phone, early mobile subscribers often replied that they bought the phone for emergency situations, such as an automobile breaking down on the highway or skidding off an icy country road. In fact, many wireless service providers targeted this market segment in their early advertising campaigns, touting the safety aspects of owning a wireless phone. However, as mobile phones became more commonplace, wireless service providers began reducing airtime rates and phone prices, enticing mobile subscribers to use their phones for much more than emergencies. This ingenious marketing strategy was a huge success, and today's mobile subscribers customarily use their phones throughout their daily routines, including the increasingly time-consuming daily work commute. Undoubtedly, one of the main reasons why wireless communication has been experiencing such high growth is because today's networks allow mobile subscribers to remain connected while moving throughout one or more networks.

Although some wireless networks, such as Wireless Local Loop systems, are deployed as alternates to wireline service, most networks are designed to support extensive mobility. As a mobile subscriber moves from the coverage area of one base station to that of another, it becomes necessary to "handoff" the mobile station from the original coverage cell to the target cell without dropping the call. The procedures used by wireless networks to accommodate the transfer of terrestrial and radio resources during handoffs affect network reliability, capacity, and voice quality. To facilitate handoffs, the *Mobile Switching Center* (MSC) and *Base Station Controller* (BSC) both contain Radio Resource Management functions that provide the ability to perform handoffs within a BSC, between BSCs, and across MSCs. Radio Resource Management is the function that manages network radio resources for voice, data, and overhead traffic. The BSC and MSC collectively work together to identify and allocate the necessary terrestrial and radio resources required to perform handoffs.

This chapter presents an overview of the Radio Resource Management functions at the BSC and MSC. Specifically, this chapter describes the following Radio Resource Management topics:

- Radio Channel Management
- Intra-BSC Soft Handoff
- Intra-MSC Inter-BSC Hard Handoff
- Inter-MSC Inter-BSC Hard Handoff
- Direct Inter-BSC Soft Handoff

The first functional area of Radio Resource Management described in this chapter is Radio Channel Management. In IS-95 CDMA systems, radio channel management mainly resides at the BSS, where both the BSC and associated cells, or *Base Transceiver Systems* (BTSs), are responsible for radio channel allocation, power control, and other CDMA radio-specific functions. Under certain conditions, such as in an Authentication-enabled network, the MSC may supply overhead radio channel information to be broadcast to mobile stations using paging channels.

Following Radio Channel Management, descriptions of the various CDMA handoff procedures are given in this chapter. Figure 7-1 illustrates some of the radio resource handoff scenarios that routinely occur in CDMA networks. Closely tied to handoffs is the concept of an anchor cell. CDMA systems use the idea of an anchor or designated cell to represent the mobile's location. When a mobile originates a call, the BSC and MSC receive a cell identifier that includes the cell and sector representing the mobile's location. This identifier is updated as a mobile station moves from one cell to another and drops the original cell.

The most common type of handoff shown in Figure 7-1 is the *Intra-BSC Soft Handoff*. An Intra-BSC Soft handoff is triggered when a mobile station moves from one cell to another cell (at the same frequency), both being controlled by the same BSC. In this scenario, the same BSC *Selection/Distribution Unit* (SDU) is used throughout the call, even after the handoff has occurred. Although an Intra-BSC Soft handoff is primarily a BSC function, the MSC is informed of any change in the anchor cell. A handoff from one BTS sector to another sector on the same BTS is known as a *softer handoff*. A second type of handoff illustrated in Figure 7-1 is the Inter-BSC Hard Handoff. An Inter-BSC Hard Handoff is triggered when a mobile moves from a cell belonging to one BSC to a neighboring cell belonging to the domain of a different BSC. Because processing related to the call is transferred to an SDU on the BSC controlling the target cell, this type of handoff is no longer considered a soft handoff. In the case of Inter-BSC Hard Handoffs, the MSC plays an integral role in Radio Resource Management by coordinating handoffs between BSCs. A successful hard handoff involves exchanging A-Interface messages between the source BSC, target BSC, and the MSC.

If both the source and target BSCs are under the domain of the same MSC, the hard handoff is known as an *Intra-MSC Inter-BSC Hard Handoff*. If a handoff involves only cells controlled by a single BSC, such as an inter-frequency or inter-frame-offset handoff, it is referred to as an *Intra-MSC Intra-BSC Hard Handoff*. As will be discussed later in this chapter, the Inter-BSC hard handoff procedures may also be used to accomplish an Intra-BSC hard handoff.

Also shown in Figure 7-1 is an Inter-BSC Hard Handoff involving two different MSCs. This handoff scenario is known as an *Inter-MSC Inter-BSC Hard Handoff*. In this case, IS-41 signaling takes place between the two MSCs in order to transfer handoff information from the source BSC/MSC to the target BSC/MSC.

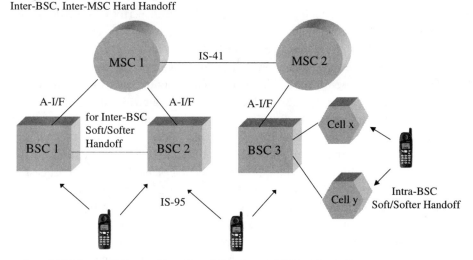

Figure 7-1 Types of Radio Resource Handoff Management

Direct Inter-BSC Soft Handoff occurs when a mobile station moves from a cell controlled by one BSC to a cell controlled by the another BSC, operating at the same frequency. In this handoff scenario, a direct signaling and traffic connection between the BSCs allows the SDU on the originating BSC to continue processing the call. The MSC has minimal participation, being notified only of any change in the anchor cell.

7.1 CDMA Overhead Radio Channel Management

7.1.1 Radio Channel Management Overview

In IS-95 CDMA systems, the BSC is primarily responsible for Radio Channel Management, which includes:

- Radio channel allocation/deallocation
- Radio channel encoding/decoding
- Radio traffic channel power control
- Overhead paging channel management

During setup of either a mobile origination or mobile termination call, the MSC is responsible for assigning terrestrial resources and the BSC is responsible for assigning radio resources. The BSC allocates radio channel resources, normally associated with a BTS, and BSC radio processing unit resources.

Radio channel encoding, decoding, and radio channel power control functions are all performed by the BSC, either at the SDU or the base station channel units. Specifically, the BSC executes CDMA channel encoding/decoding algorithms and performs open loop and traffic channel closed loop power management. Further details regarding radio channel coding schemes and power control algorithm are described in the IS-95 standard [5,6].

When a call is to be released, either the BSC or MSC initiates clearing of the radio channel, depending on the reason for the release. The MSC may initiate call clearing by sending a Clear Command message to the BSC, which indicates to the BSC that terrestrial and radio resource should be deallocated. The BSC may initiate terrestrial and radio channel deallocation when radio link failure occurs or when the mobile releases the call. Although both the MSC and BSC may initiate call clearing, the BSC is solely responsible for releasing radio resources.

CDMA networks utilize a technique known as *Overhead Paging* to broadcast network-specific information to all mobile stations using the network. These broadcast messages include network information such as SID, NID, CDMA frequency, registration types, handoff parameters, access parameters, and neighbor lists. Each idle mobile in the network monitors the paging channel for such broadcasts and stores relevant received information. Note that up to seven paging channels may be present on each CDMA channel. Overhead paging channel management is the responsibility of the BSC, which stores the network configuration, usually in a local database, and formats paging channel broadcast messages, such as the IS-95 System Parameters message. Under certain conditions, the MSC may also provide information to the BSC that is then included in overhead messages. Specifically, the MSC may send the BSC a RAND authentication parameter (see Section 6.1.1, "Authentication Parameters," on page 349) if network authentication is enabled and if the RAND parameter is generated at the MSC.

7.1.2   Set Control Channel Parameter Call Flow

The Set Control Channel Parameter message is an A-Interface message used by the MSC to notify the BSC of changes in the broadcast control channel information. CDGIOS specifies that the Set Control Channel Parameters message is used only when the MSC is required to send a broadcast RAND value. The call flow for MSC control channel changes is illustrated in Figure 7-2, followed by individual descriptions of each step.

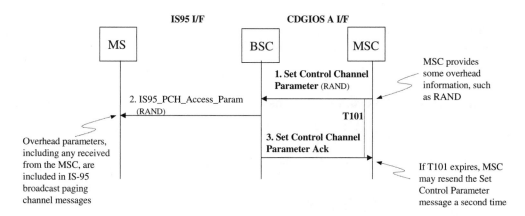

Figure 7-2   Set Control Channels Parameters call flow

1. Set Control Channel Parameters (A-Interface) :

The MSC sends a Set Control Channel Parameters message to the BSC, including any parameter that the MSC wants to broadcast over the paging channel to the mobile. As mentioned previously, CDGIOS indicates that this message be sent only by the MSC to change the RAND authentication parameter when both the MSC and BSC support MSC generated RAND. Note that if RAND is generated at the BSC, the MSC is not required to send this message.

The MSC may also include an optional Tag value that may later be used by the MSC to identify the acknowledgment received from the BSC. The same Tag value included in the Set Control Channel Parameters message is included by the BSC in the Set Control Channel Parameters Acknowledge message.

The MSC starts timer T101 to wait for an acknowledgment.

2. IS95_PCH_Access_Param (IS-95) :

The BSC packages the RAND value received from the MSC into an IS-95 Access Parameters message that is sent over the paging channel to mobile stations using the network. The IS-95 Access Parameters message is a broadcast message used by the BSC to define parameters used by the mobile stations when transmitting to the BSC over the access channel.

3. Set Control Channel Parameters Ack (A-Interface):

After the BSC updates the paging channel messages with the overhead information received from the MSC, it sends a Set Control Channel Parameters Acknowledgment message to the MSC. If a Tag value was included in the corresponding Set Control Channel

Parameters message received from the MSC, the same Tag value is included by the BSC in this message.

The MSC stops timer T101 upon receipt of the Set Control Channel Parameters Acknowledge message. If T101 expires before any receipt of the acknowledgment, the MSC may choose to resend the Set Control Channel Parameters message one more time.

7.1.3   Set Control Channel Parameters Messages

This section describes the individual A-Interface messages exchanged between the MSC and BSC during the MSC-initiated Set Control Channel Parameters procedure. The focus of this section is on the message structure and individual message parameters.

7.1.3.1   Set Control Channel Parameters

This *Base Station Management Application Part* (BSMAP) message is used by the MSC to change BSC overhead information being broadcast to the mobile station on the paging channel (Table 7-1). The MSC uses this message to transfer the RAND authentication parameter to the BSC when MSC-generated RAND is supported.

The Set Control Channel Parameters message contains an optional Tag IE that is used by the MSC to identify uniquely the Set Control Channel Parameters message that is sent to the BSC. If included by the MSC, the Tag value is stored by the BSC and returned in the Set Control Channel Parameters Acknowledgement message.

The Cell Identifier List parameter is a variable-length field that specifies a list of cells or a *Location Area Code* (LAC) to be paged by the BSC in the broadcast.

The Authentication Challenge Parameter (RAND) is a random number generated at the MSC that is used for Global Challenge authentication.

- BSAP Message Type: BSMAP
- SCCP Message Type: SCCP-Unit Data (UDT)
- Direction: BSC ← MSC

Table 7-1   Set Control Channel Parameters Message (CDGIOS 6.1.6.12)

BitMap	Param IE	#Oct	Range	Type	IOS Ref
0000 0000 (00H) LLLL LLLL	BSMAP header	2	Msg Discrim. = 0 (BSMAP) L = BSMAP msg length	M	6.2.2.1 6.2.2.3
0110 0010 (62H)	Msg Type	1	Set Control Channel Param Msg	M	6.2.2.4

Table 7-1   Set Control Channel Parameters Message (CDGIOS 6.1.6.12) (Continued)

BitMap	Param IE	#Oct	Range	Type	IOS Ref
0011 0011 (33H) tttt tttt tttt tttt tttt tttt tttt tttt	Tag	5	t = 00000000H–FFFFFFFFH	O,C	6.2.2.62
0001 1010 (1AH)	Cell Identi- fier List	Var- iable	Same as element in Table 3-5, Paging Request msg.	O,R	6.2.2.21
0100 0001 (41H) LLLL LLLL rrrr tttt nnnn nnnn nnnn nnnn nnnn nnnn nnnn nnnn	Authentica- tion Chal- lenge Parameter (RAND)	7	L = 05H, r = 0—reserved tttt = 0001—RAND n = RAND value	O,R	6.2.2.45

7.1.3.2   Set Control Channel Parameters Acknowledgment

This message is used by the BSC to acknowledge a previously received Set Control Channel Parameters message (Table 7-2).

The Set Control Channel Parameters message contains an optional Tag IE used to identify uniquely the Set Control Channel Parameters message that is being acknowledged. This optional parameter is included only if received in the Set Control Channel Parameters message being acknowledged.

- BSAP Message Type: BSMAP
- SCCP Message Type: SCCP-Unit Data (UDT)
- Direction: BSC → MSC

Table 7-2   Set Control Channel Parameters Ack Message (CDGIOS 6.1.6.13)

BitMap	Param IE	#Oct	Range	Type	IOS Ref
0000 0000 (00H) LLLL LLLL	BSMAP header	2	Msg Discrim. = 0 (BSMAP) L = BSMAP msg length	M	6.2.2.1 6.2.2.3

Table 7-2   Set Control Channel Parameters Ack Message (CDGIOS 6.1.6.13)
(Continued)

BitMap	Param IE	#Oct	Range	Type	IOS Ref
0110 0011 (63H)	Msg Type	1	Set Control Channel Param Ack	M	6.2.2.4
0011 0011 (33H)	Tag	5	Same as element in Table 7-1, Set Control Param msg.	O,C	6.2.2.62

7.2 IS-95 CDMA Intra-BSC Soft Handoff

In IS95 CDMA systems, an Intra-BSC Soft Handoff takes place when a mobile station is in the intersection of the coverage area of two (or more) BTSs, both of which are under the domain of the same BSC. The BSC is solely responsible for the execution of an Intra-BSC Soft Handoff. The MSC is not involved in the handoff, other than being notified by the BSC of any change in the designated cell, which is also referred to as the *anchor cell.*

7.2.1 Overview of Intra-BSC Soft Handoff

IS-95 CDMA systems utilize a pilot channel that is transmitted at all times on all active forward CDMA channels. Each BTS sector uses a time offset, specified in chips, of the Pilot PN sequence to identify a forward CDMA channel. Mobile stations continually search for pilots on the current CDMA frequency and measure their strengths. If the mobile station finds a pilot of sufficient strength not associated with any forward traffic channel it is currently using, it sends an IS-95 *Pilot Strength Measurement Message* (PSMM) to the BSC, indicating that the pilot should be added to the Active Set. The BSC may then assign a forward traffic channel with that pilot PN to the mobile station. The Active Set consists of pilots associated with forward traffic channels assigned to the mobile station. A pilot is dropped from the Active Set when it is determined that insufficient signal power is being received.

A soft/softer handoff add occurs when a mobile station determines that a pilot not currently in the Active Set should be added. As described above, the mobile notifies the BSC of the new pilot by sending an IS-95 PSMM, and the BSC then assigns a forward traffic channel, adding the pilot to the Active Set. The original pilot remains in the Active Set until it is determined that the received power is insufficient, at which time it is dropped. Note that the Active Set may contain one or more pilots at any given time. If the added pilot belongs to a different sector on the same BTS as the original pilot, the handoff is referred to as a *softer* handoff. If the pilot to be added belongs to a different BTS with the same frequency assignment, it is known as a *soft* handoff.

Intra-BSC handoffs involve the concept of a designated or anchor cell. During a mobile origination or termination call attempt, the BSC sends the MSC the initial anchor cell ID to the MSC in either a CM Service Request or Paging Response A-Interface message. The MSC may initially use the received Cell ID to verify that the cell is part of the network being served. When the designated Cell ID later changes due to a handoff, the MSC is informed by the BSC of the updated Cell ID, allowing it to validate the new cell. The MSC is notified that the designated cell has changed only after the previous anchor cell has been removed from the active pilot set. As long as the originating cell belongs to the active pilot set, it remains the designated cell.

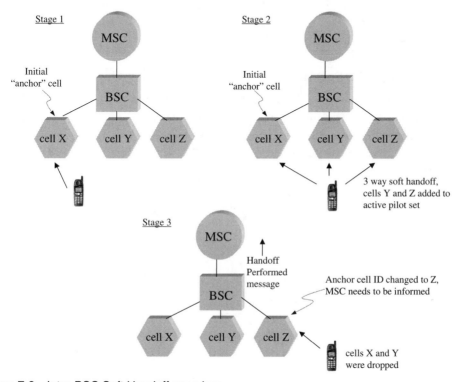

Figure 7-3 Intra-BSC Soft Handoff overview

Unlike an Inter-BSC Hard Handoff, all handoff messaging for Intra-BSC Soft Handoff occurs within the BSC, and the MSC has no knowledge of a soft handoff occurring as long as the initial designated cell remains in the active pilot set. The MSC is involved with an Intra-BSC handoff only when a previously designated cell is dropped from the active pilot set. When this happens, the BSC informs the MSC of the new designated cell by sending an A-Interface Hand-off Performed message. The assignment of a designated cell for a mobile in soft handoff is not specified in either IS-95 or CDGIOS and is, therefore, left to vendor implementation.

Figure 7-3 illustrates, from a network perspective, the stages of an Intra-BSC soft handoff. The mobile station shown in stage 1 of Figure 7-3 originates a call from cell X, which is then designated as the anchor cell. In stage 2, the mobile station moves into the coverage areas of cells Y and Z. Because the mobile station in stage 2 is in soft handoff with cells X, Y, and Z, the active pilot set contains all three associated pilots. Recall that when a mobile detects a pilot signal whose power level exceeds the soft handoff add threshold, the BSC may decide to add the pilot to the Active Set. At this point, cell X is still the anchor cell because the mobile remains in soft handoff with that cell. In stage 3, the mobile station moves out of the coverage area of cells X and Y, and cell Z becomes the new anchor cell after cell X is dropped from the active pilot set. An Intra-BSC Soft Handoff drop is initiated when a mobile detects that an active pilot strength decreases past its drop strength threshold for a period of time specified by the drop timer threshold. The BSC notifies the MSC of the change in the anchor cell by sending a Handoff Performed message over the A-Interface.

7.2.2   Intra-BSC Soft Handoff Call Flow

Figure 7-4 shows the call flow for an Intra-BSC Soft Handoff. The call flow illustrates both the IS-95 and A-Interface messaging involved when a mobile performs a soft handoff with a second cell. In Figure 7-4, the anchor cell is dropped after the soft handoff has been completed. The BSC informs the MSC of the change in anchor cell by sending an A-Interface Handoff Performed message.

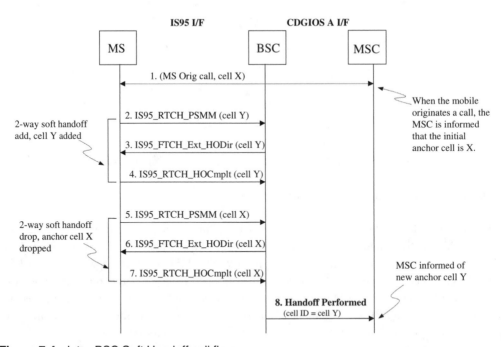

Figure 7-4   Intra-BSC Soft Handoff call flow

The call flow does not include the initial call setup, which involves the BSC specifying a designated cell ID in either a CM Service Request or a Paging Response message. Description of the individual steps involved in an Intra-BSC Soft Handoff follow Figure 7-4. Steps 2 through 4 illustrate soft handoff addition of cell Y, and steps 5 through 7 relate to dropping anchor cell X.

1. (MS Orig call, cell X) :

   A mobile-originated or -terminated call is set up between the BSC and MSC. During call setup, the BSC identifies the anchor cell as cell X by including its cell ID in either a CM Service Request or Paging Response message. The MSC validates the cell ID against its database containing valid network cell IDs.

2. IS95_RTCH_PSMM (cell Y) (IS-95):

   Upon detecting a pilot strength that exceeds its Soft Handoff Add Threshold (Tadd), the mobile station sends an IS-95 Pilot Strength Measurement Message over the reverse traffic channel. This message includes the PN phases and signal strengths (Ec/Io) of pilots in the active and candidate sets. The candidate set is a set of pilots that have been received with sufficient strength but have not yet been put into the Active Set. This message triggers the BSC to begin the soft handoff procedure to add cell Y.

3. IS95_FTCH_Ext_HODir (cell Y) (IS-95):

   The BSC sends an IS-95 Extended Handoff Direction message to the mobile station, directing the soft handoff addition.

4. IS95_RTCH_HOCmplt (cell Y) (IS-95):

   The mobile reports the success of the soft handoff by sending an IS-95 Handoff Completion message to the BSC.

5. IS95_RTCH_PSMM (cell X) (IS-95):

   Upon detecting a pilot signal that falls below its Soft Handoff Drop Threshold (Tdrop) for a period exceeding its Soft Handoff Drop Timer (TTdrop), an IS-95 Pilot Strength Measurement Message is sent by the mobile, including the Ec/Io strength measurement of the cell in question. In Figure 7-4, this message triggers the BSC to begin a soft handoff drop of the pilot associated with cell X.

6. IS95_FTCH_Ext_HODir (cell X) (IS-95):

   The BSC sends an IS-95 Extended Handoff Direction message to the mobile station, directing the soft handoff drop.

7. IS95_RTCH_HOCmplt (cell X) (IS-95):

   The mobile reports the success of the soft handoff drop by sending the IS-95 Handoff Completion message to the BSC.

8. Handoff Performed (Cell ID = cell Y) (A-Interface):

   The BSC sends an A-Interface Handoff Performed message to the MSC to indicate the success of the intra-BSC soft handoff. The MSC is informed of the change in the anchor cell ID from cell X to cell Y.

7.2.3   Intra-BSC Soft Handoff Messages

This section describes the individual A-Interface messages exchanged between the MSC and BSC for an Intra-BSC Soft Handoff. The focus of this section is the message structure and individual message parameters.

7.2.3.1   Handoff Performed

The Handoff Performed message is a BSMAP message sent as a class 2 connection-oriented *SCCP Data Form 1* (SCCP-DT1) message type. It is sent by the BSC to inform the MSC that an existing anchor or designated cell ID has been dropped and specifies the cell ID of the new anchor cell. Note that in CDGIOS, only a soft handoff drop triggers this message.

The mandatory Cause IE indicates the reason for sending the Handoff Performed message.

The required Cell Identifier List IE consists of the list of current active pilots involved in soft handoff with the mobile. The first cell in the list is the new anchor cell ID for this call (See Table 7-4 for the format of the Cell Identifier List IE).

- BSAP Message Type: BSMAP
- SCCP Message Type: SCCP-Data Form1 (DT1)
- Direction: BSC → MSC

Table 7-3   Handoff Performed (CDGIOS 6.1.5.12)

BitMap	Param IE	#Oct	Range	Type	IOS Ref
0000 0000 (00H) LLLL LLLL	BSMAP header	2	Msg Discrim. = 0 (BSMAP) L = BSMAP msg length	M	6.2.2.1 6.2.2.3
0001 0111 (17H)	Msg Type	1	Handoff Performed Msg	M	6.2.2.4
0000 0100 (04H) LLLL LLLL 0ccc cccc	Cause	3	L = 01H, c = cause 1BH—inter-BSC soft HO drop tgt 1DH—intra-BSC soft HO drop tgt	M	6.2.2.19
0001 1010 (1AH)	Cell Identifier List	Variable	Same as the element in Table 7-4, Handoff Required	O,R	6.2.2.21

7.2.4   Intra-BSC Soft Handoff Example Call Flow

Figure 7-5 shows a practical example of a summary message call flow for an Intra-BSC Soft Handoff. The purpose of Figure 7-5 is to present an overview of the messages exchanged between the BSC and MSC. Figure 7-6 contains an example Handoff Performed message.

In this example, a call is first set up on anchor cell X, which is associated with an initial reference pilot. After the call has been set up, the mobile then performs a soft handoff with a second pilot that is associated with cell Y. Recall that no A-Interface messaging occurs when the soft addition takes place.

After approximately 1 minute, the initial reference pilot associated with cell X is dropped from the mobile's active list, and the second pilot associated with cell Y becomes the reference pilot. The BSC informs the MSC of the change in the anchor cell by sending a Handoff Performed message across the A-Interface.

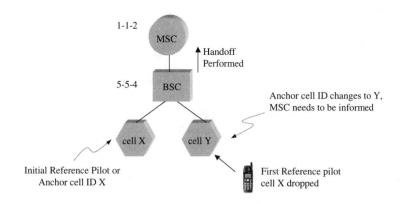

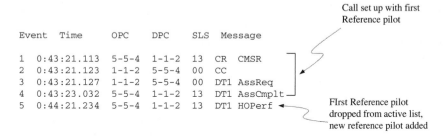

Figure 7-5   Intra-BSC Soft Handoff example call flow

```
**** MESSAGE NUMBER: 00005 ****
*** Start of CDGIOS MAP ***
                    Handoff Performed
0017 00001011 0b Data Length              11
0018 00000000 00 BSMAP Discriminator      00
0019 00001001 09 BSMAP Length             9
0020 00010111 17 Handoff Performed        23
0021 00000100 04 Cause                    4
0022 00000001 01 Length                   1
0023 00011101 1d Cause Value              Intra-BSC soft handoff drop
0024 00011010 1a Cell Identifier List     26
```

(Continued)

```
0025 00000011 03 Length                         3              New reference pilot
0026 00000010 02 Cell Identifier Discrim   CI Only             after first ref pilot
0027 00000100 04 CI Value                  04 11     ◄————————  dropped from active
0028 00010001 11                                                list
```

Figure 7-6   Handoff Performed message example

The new Cell Identity included in the Handoff Performed message example shown in Figure 7-6 contains the cell identifier assigned to cell Y. In this example, only one pilot remains in the Active Set after the pilot associated with cell X is dropped. Note that the cause value of the message indicates an *Intra-BSC Soft Handoff Drop*.

7.3   IS-95 to IS-95 Inter-BSC Hard Handoff

An Inter-BSC Hard Handoff occurs when a mobile station moves from the coverage area of a BTS that belongs to the domain of one BSC into coverage of another BTS that is under the domain of a different BSC. Assuming no direct A3/A7 connections (the A3/A7 interface is discussed later in this chapter), the SDU processing the call is switched from the source BSC to the target BSC.

If an Inter-BSC Hard Handoff involves a single MSC that controls both the target and source BSC, the handoff is referred to as an *Intra-MSC Inter-BSC Hard Handoff*. If the target and source are each controlled by a separate MSC, the handoff is known as an *Inter-MSC Inter-BSC Hard Handoff*. The A-Interface call flow and messaging is similar for both cases. However, the Inter-MSC Inter-BSC Hard Handoff requires IS-41 messaging between the source and target MSCs, which is used to communicate the hard handoff indication, hard handoff execution, relevant IS-95 parameters, and to set up any required inter-MSC terrestrial resources.

This section describes both Intra-MSC Inter-BSC and Inter-MSC Inter BSC Hard Handoff procedures.

7.3.1   Overview of Intra-MSC Inter-BSC Hard Handoff

When an Inter-BSC Hard Handoff occurs between two BSCs connected to a single MSC, the handoff is coordinated by the MSC. Figure 7-7 illustrates the four stages of an Intra-MSC Inter-BSC Hard Handoff. The first stage is known as the triggering and target determination stage and includes target pilot acquisition and a method of triggering the hard handoff. The second stage involves establishing target BSC resources and is followed by the third stage, which includes the actual execution of the hard handoff. The fourth and final stage involves releasing resources after the handoff has been completed. Each of the four stages is described in detail in the following sections.

Triggering and Target Determination Phase   One of the most interesting and technically challenging aspects of hard handoff is the handoff triggering method. As a mobile station moves from the domain of one BSC into the domain of another, a decision must be made regarding whether and when the hard handoff should occur. Two commonly used triggering techniques are round trip delay measurement and pilot beacon deployment.

During the Triggering phase, the mobile station detects a new pilot signal from the target BSC. This pilot signal may be in the form of a beacon signal to induce the hard handoff triggering on the same CDMA frequency of the existing cell and the same PN offset as the actual target pilot signal. In the round trip delay method, the BSC uses the measured round trip delay of the newly acquired border pilot to trigger the hard handoff. The triggering technique used is left to the discretion of equipment manufacturers and network service provider.

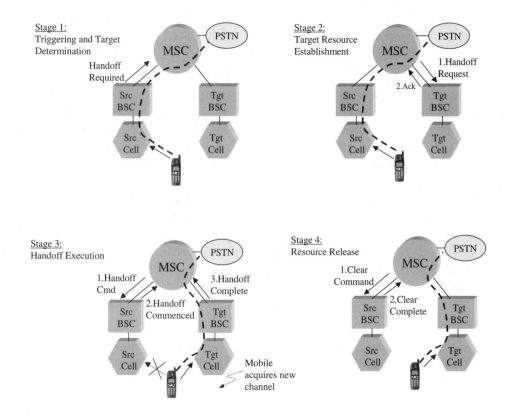

Figure 7-7   Intra-MSC Inter-BSC Hard Handoff overview

After being triggered for an Inter-BSC Hard Handoff by whatever technique has been implemented, the BSC initiates the Target Determination phase by sending a Handoff Required message to the MSC over the A-Interface. This message includes downlink pilot strength measurement information collected from the mobile, a requested service option, and a list of target candidate cells associated with the target BSC. Based on the information supplied by the source

BSC in the Handoff Required message or other implementation specific parameters, the MSC determines a candidate target list and proceeds with stage 2, Resource Establishment.

Resource Establishment at Target BSC Phase   During the Resource Establishment phase, the MSC requests the required terrestrial and radio resources from the target BSC. The MSC requests these resources by sending the target BSC an A-Interface Handoff Request message, which is packaged as an *SCCP Connection Request* (SCCP-CR). The target BSC acknowledges the Handoff Request message with a Handoff Request Acknowledge message, indicating that the resource allocation was successful. The BSC may piggyback the Handoff Request Acknowledge on an *SCCP Connection Confirm* (SCCP-CC) or it may send a separate SCCP-CC.

This Handoff Request Acknowledge message also includes IS-95 handoff parameters, such as Tadd and Tdrop, that are later used in the IS-95 Extended Handoff Direction message to initiate the mobile handoff. The target BSC starts transmitting forward traffic channel null frames to initiate communication with the mobile on the radio link.

Handoff Execution Phase   During the Handoff Execution phase, the MSC sends an A-Interface Handoff Command message to the source BSC, which includes handoff parameters that the MSC received from the target BSC in the Handoff Request Acknowledge message. The source BSC then sends an IS-95 Extended Handoff Direction message or IS-95 General Handoff Direction message to the mobile, directing the mobile to perform a hard handoff to the target BSC's CDMA frequency and frame offset. Upon receiving a mobile acknowledgment of the IS-95 Extended/General Handoff Direction message, the source BSC sends the MSC an A-Interface Handoff Commenced message, informing the MSC that the mobile has started executing the hard handoff.

After the mobile has successfully switched to the target BSC's radio channel, the target BSC acquires reverse traffic channel frames from the mobile. The mobile notifies the target BSC that the handoff has been completed by sending an IS-95 Handoff Completion message to the target BSC, which then informs the coordinating MSC by sending an A-Interface Handoff Complete message.

Resource Release at Source BSC Phase   The final phase of an Inter-BSC Hard Handoff involves clearing source BSC resources. After receiving notification that the handoff has been completed, the MSC proceeds to clear the previously allocated resources at the source BSC that are no longer needed. The MSC initiates call clearing by sending a Clear Command message to the source BSC, which prompts the BSC to clear all relevant radio and terrestrial resources. After clearing resources, the BSC sends a Clear Complete message to the MSC. Associated SCCP resources are also cleared.

7.3.2   Intra-MSC Inter-BSC Hard Handoff Call Flow

Figure 7-8 illustrates the call flow for an Intra-MSC Inter-BSC Hard Handoff. The call flow illustration groups the individual steps of the call flow into the four handoff phases previously discussed.

An Intra-MSC Inter-BSC Hard Handoff is initiated during the Triggering and Target Determination phase. In Figure 7-8, this phase includes only the first step in the call flow. The Resource Establishment Phase, which sets up radio and terrestrial resources at the target BSC, comprises steps 2 through 4. The hard handoff takes place in the Handoff Execution phase that includes steps 5 through 13. Finally, the Resource Release phase consists of steps 14 through 17. The scenario being described here assumes a successful hard handoff. Failure scenarios message handling is covered in Section 7.3.8, "IS-95 to IS-95 Inter-BSC Hard Handoff Failure Scenarios," on page 462.

The individual steps of the Intra-MSC Inter-BSC Hard Handoff call flow are described in detail following Figure 7-8.

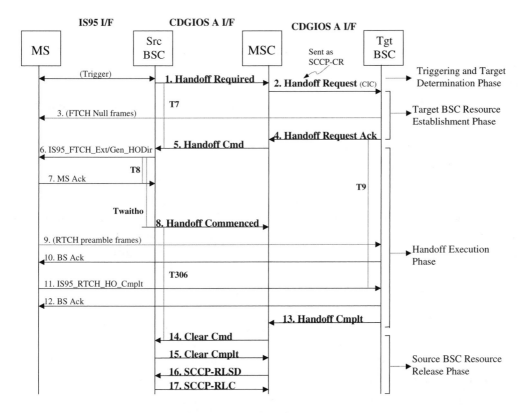

Figure 7-8 Intra-MSC Inter-BSC Hard Handoff call flow

Triggering and Target Determination Phase

1. Handoff Required (A-Interface):

In CDMA systems, either the mobile station or source BSC may trigger an Inter-BSC Hard Handoff. Typically, the mobile assists in the handoff triggering by first detecting then notifying the source BSC of a strong pilot received from a cell under the domain of a different BSC. If the target BSC is attached to a different MSC, an Inter-MSC Inter-BSC hard handoff will take place (see Section 7.3.3, "Overview of Inter-MSC Inter-BSC Hard Handoff," on page 428). The method used to trigger the hard handoff procedure is vendor implementation-specific. After triggering has occurred, the BSC initiates the inter-BSC handoff by sending an A-Interface Handoff Required message to the MSC.

The Handoff Required message contains information, including a list of candidate target cell IDs, that the MSC may use to determine the target cell or target cell list. In addition to a candidate target cell list, the BSC supplies the MSC with information regarding service option and pilot strength measurement that allows the MSC to determine the optimal target cell. The MSC makes the final decision as to which target cell(s) will be used, based on information it receives from the BSC, on its own internal information, or a combination of both.

The source BSC solicits an acknowledgment for the Handoff Required message by including the Response Request parameter in the message.

After sending the Handoff Required message, the source BSC starts timer T7. Upon receiving a Handoff Command message or a Handoff Required Reject message from the MSC, timer T7 is stopped.

Target BSC Resource Establishment Phase

2. Handoff Request (CIC) (A-Interface):

The MSC coordinates the Inter-BSC handoff by sending an A-Interface Handoff Request message to the selected target BSC. The Handoff Request message is sent as an SCCP-CR, soliciting that a new SCCP connection be established for subsequent handoff messaging. The Handoff Request messages is used to allocate terrestrial and radio resources at the target BSC. Much of the information contained in this message, such as the IS-95 radio link measurement parameters, is extracted by the MSC from the Handoff Required message previously received from the source BSC.

If the target BSC is unable to honor the handoff request, a Handoff Failure message is sent to the MSC, which will then terminate the inter-BSC handoff process and clear all associated handoff resources. The MSC may also indicate failure by sending a Handoff Required Reject message to the source BSC.

3. (FTCH null frames) (IS-95):

The target BSC, upon receipt of the Handoff Request message, allocates the necessary radio link and terrestrial circuit resources for the inter-BSC handoff, then prepares for the radio channel switchover by sending forward traffic null frames to the mobile station.

4. Handoff Request Ack (A-Interface):

Upon successful allocation of the radio and terrestrial resources needed to service the requested handoff, the target BSC sends a Handoff Request Acknowledge message to the MSC to inform it of the successful resource allocation. The Handoff Request Acknowledgment message may be sent as an SCCP-CC or *SCCP-Data Form 1* (SCCP-DT1) message depending on whether or not the target BSC has already confirmed the SCCP connection.

The target BSC starts timer T9 to wait for the mobile to acquire the target radio channel.

Handoff Execution Phase

5. Handoff Cmd (A-Interface):

The MSC, upon receipt of a Handoff Request Acknowledge message from the target BSC, begins the Handoff Execution phase by sending a Handoff Command message to the source BSC. This informs the source BSC that target resources were successfully allocated and that it should direct the mobile to switch to the new CDMA channel associated with the target cell.

The Handoff Command message contains information received earlier by the MSC in the Handoff Request Acknowledge message, which the source BSC includes in the IS-95 Extended Handoff Direction message. This information includes handoff parameters, such as Tadd, Tdrop, and Tcomp thresholds; TTdrop timer; neighborlist max-age; and other required CDMA parameters, such as frequency channel, *Private Long Code* (PLC) mask, and encryption indicators.

The source BSC stops timer T7 upon receipt of the Handoff Command or Handoff Required Reject message from the MSC. Upon timer T7 expiry, the source BSC may resend the Handoff Required message.

If a Handoff Required Reject message is received, the source BSC may resend the Handoff Required message once more. This call failure scenario is explained in more detail in Section 7.3.8.2, "Handoff Required Rejected—Handoff Failure at Target," on page 463.

6. IS95_FTCH_Ext/Gen_HODir (IS-95):

The source BSC directs the mobile to execute the hard handoff by sending it an IS-95 Extended Handoff Direction message or IS-95 General Handoff Direction message on the forward traffic channel. The IS-95 Extended/General Handoff Direction message is constructed by the source BSC with the associated target BSC handoff parameters received from MSC in the Handoff Command.

If the source BSC requires an acknowledgment from the mobile, it then starts timer T8 while waiting for the mobile to respond with an MS Acknowledgment Order. The source BSC may also use the quick repeats technique to send the IS-95 Extended/General Handoff Direction message to increase the probability of message reception at the mobile. In this case, the BSC will not solicit an acknowledgment from the mobile, and timer T8 is not used.

The source BSC may allow the mobile station to return to the old channel if the mobile is unable to acquire the target BSC. In this case, the IS-95 General Handoff Direction message is used and timer Twaitho is started. If the mobile indicates a target acquisition failure before timer Twaitho expires, the source BSC continues servicing the mobile on the old channel (see Failure scenario in Section 7.3.8.4, "Mobile Revert to Old Channel Before Twaitho Expires," on page 465). If timer Twaitho expires without any such failure indication, the BSC considers the hard handoff a success and sends a Handoff Commenced message to the MSC.

If the source BSC does not allow the mobile to return to the old channel and if quick repeats are used, the BSC will send the Handoff Commenced message to the MSC after sending the quick repeats.

The call flow in Figure 7-8 is for a source BSC that requires a mobile acknowledgment for the IS-95 Extended/General Handoff Direction message and which allows the mobile to revert to the old channel in case of failure, as well. Hence, both T8 and Twaitho timers are shown.

7. MS Ack (IS-95):

If the BSC requires an acknowledgment to the IS-95 Extended/General Handoff Direction message, it sets the ACK_REQ indicator to request an acknowledgement from the mobile. Upon receiving the IS-95 Extended/General Handoff Direction message, the mobile station sends an MS Ack Order to the source BSC. The source BSC then stops timer T8 upon receipt of the acknowledgment.

If timer T8 expires before the source BSC receives an acknowledgment from the mobile, and if the mobile still remains on the old channel, the source BSC will send a Handoff Failure message to the MSC with a cause value set to "reversion to old channel." If T8 expires while the radio link is lost with the mobile, the source BSC will initiate call clearing by sending a Clear Request to the MSC with cause value set to "radio interface failure." These call failure scenarios are further explained in Section 7.3.8.5, "T8 Expiry at Source BSC—Mobile Remains on Old Channel," on page 466 and Section 7.3.8.6, "T8 Expiry at Source BSC—RadioLink Failure," on page 467.

8. Handoff Commenced (A-Interface):

The Handoff Commenced message is sent from the source BSC to the MSC to indicate that the mobile has been directed to handoff to the target BSC and that the mobile is not expected to return to the source BSC. The timing of when the source BSC sends the Handoff Commenced messages depends on whether the source BSC allows the mobile to return and whether the IS-95 Extended/General Handoff Direction message was sent using the quick repeats method.

If the source BSC allows the mobile to revert to the old channel in case of target acquisition failure, it must wait for the Twaitho timer to expire before sending a Handoff Commenced message to the MSC. This scenario is illustrated in Figure 7-8. Notice that even though an IS-95 MS Acknowledgment Order is received from the mobile station, the source BSC waits for the timer to expire before sending the MSC a Handoff Commenced message.

If the source BSC does not allow the mobile to return in the event of target acquisition failure, the Handoff Commenced message is sent to the MSC immediately after the source BSC receives the IS-95 MS Acknowledgment Order from the mobile. In this case, timer Twaitho is not used.

If the IS-95 Extended/General Handoff Direction message is sent using quick repeats and if the mobile is not allowed to return to the source BSC, the BSC may not wait for an acknowledgment from the mobile. In this case, the source BSC may send the Handoff Commenced message to the MSC immediately after sending the quick repeats.

Upon sending the Handoff Commenced message, the source BSC starts timer T306 to wait for the completion of the hard handoff execution and the subsequent Clear Command from the MSC.

9. (RTCH preamble frames) (IS-95):

   As directed in the IS-95 Extended/General Handoff Direction message, the mobile switches to the new CDMA frequency channel and frame offset associated with the target BSC and begins sending reverse traffic channel preamble frames. The communication between the mobile station and the source BSC terminates.

10. BS Ack (IS-95):

   Once the target BSC acquires the reverse traffic frames from the mobile, it sends an IS-95 Base Station Acknowledgment Order to the mobile.

11. IS95_RTCH_HO_Cmplt (IS-95):

   The mobile sends an IS-95 Handoff Completion message to the target BSC to indicate to the target BSC that the handoff from the source BSC was successful. Timer T9 is stopped upon receipt of the IS-95 Handoff Completion message from the mobile.

12. BS Ack (IS-95):

   The target BSC acknowledges the IS-95 Handoff Completion message receipt by sending an IS-95 Base Station Acknowledgment Order to the mobile.

13. Handoff Cmplt (A-Interface):

   The A-Interface Handoff Complete message is sent from the target BSC to the MSC to indicate that the mobile station has successfully performed a handoff from the source BSC to the target BSC.

   If timer T9 expires before the target BSC receives an IS-95 Handoff Completion message or any reverse traffic channel frames from the mobile, the target BSC sends a Handoff Failure message to the MSC, indicating the failure of the hard handoff execution. For more details on the call flow for T9 timer expiry, please refer to Section 7.3.8.7, "T9 Expiry at Target BSC—Handoff Failure," on page 469.

Source BSC Resource Release Phase

The Resource Release phase comprises steps 14 through 17 in Figure 7-8. In this phase, the MSC initiates call clearing at the source BSC. The call flow used for releasing resources is identical to the MSC-initiated call clearing described in Section 3.5.1, "MSC-Initiated Call Clearing Call Flow," on page 203.

The source BSC stops timer T306 upon receipt of the Clear Command message from the MSC. If T306 expires and no Clear Command message is received, the source BSC initiates call clearing by sending a Clear Request message to the MSC. This call failure scenario is further explained in Section 7.3.8.8, "T306 Expiry at Source BSC," on page 470.

7.3.3   Overview of Inter-MSC Inter-BSC Hard Handoff

As discussed previously, an Inter-BSC Hard Handoff occurs when a mobile station moves from the coverage area of a BTS that belongs to the domain of one BSC into coverage of another BTS that is under the domain of a different BSC. If the source BSC and target BSC are controlled by different MSCs, the handoff is referred to as an Inter-MSC Inter BSC Hard Handoff. The MSC connected to the source BSC is known as the source MSC and the MSC connected to the target BSC is referred to as the *target MSC*. Figure 7-9 illustrates the four stages associated with an Inter-MSC Inter-BSC Hard Handoff.

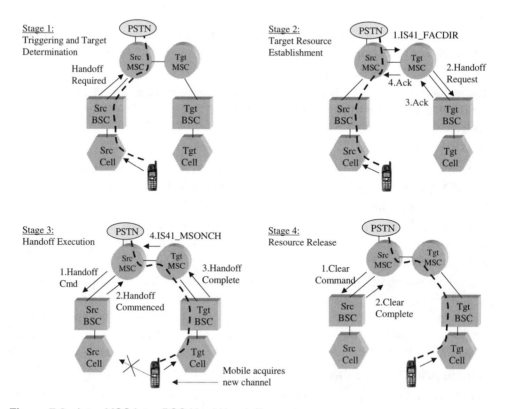

Figure 7-9   Inter-MSC Inter-BSC Hard Handoff overview

The process for the Inter-BSC Hard Handoff across two different MSCs is similar to an Intra-MSC Inter-BSC Hard Handoff, except that additional IS-41 messaging takes place between the source and target MSCs. The additional messaging is required to convey handoff-specific signaling and parameter information. Standardized IS-41 messaging between the two MSCs allows wireless service providers to implement hard handoffs between different vendor CDMA networks. IS-41 signaling requires a single dedicated timeslot, also referred to as a *DS0*, which may or may not be on the same trunk used for Inter-MSC voice. Inter-MSC voice trunks are also required for Inter-MSC Inter-BSC Hard Handoffs because digitized voice information must be sent from the source MSC to the target MSC. Depending on network configuration, it is possible to have one or more MSCs between the source and target MSCs. In such cases, multiple inter-MSC trunk circuits may be needed to execute Inter-MSC Inter-BSC Hard Handoffs.

The Triggering and Target Determination phase is the same as the Intra-MSC Inter-BSC Hard Handoff scenario. The Target Resource Establishment phase requires additional signaling not needed for Intra-MSC handoffs. In the case of Inter-MSC handoffs, the source MSC uses an IS41_FACDIR2 message to request a terrestrial resource from the target MSC and to send handoff parameters received from the source BSC in the Handoff Required message. The target MSC then proceeds with the handoff, notifying the target BSC of the request by sending a Handoff Request message over the A-Interface, as is done during an Intra-MSC Inter-BSC handoff.

Once the radio and terrestrial resources at the target BSC and the terrestrial resource at the target MSC have been established, the target MSC sends an IS41_facdir2 return result to the source MSC. In this type of hard handoff scenario, the land party remains connected to the source, or anchor, MSC.

The Handoff Execution phase for an Inter-MSC Inter-BSC Hard Handoff is similar to that of the Intra-MSC Inter-BS Handoff. Once the target MSC receives a a Handoff Complete message from the target BSC, it notifies the source MSC that the handoff was successful by sending an IS41_MSONCH message.

The Resource Release phase is identical to the Intra-MSC Inter-BSC Hard Handoff case.

7.3.4   Inter-MSC Inter-BSC Hard Handoff Call Flow

Figure 7-10 illustrates the call flow for an Inter-MSC Inter-BSC Hard Handoff. The call flow illustration groups the individual steps of the call flow into four handoff phases previously discussed.

An Inter-MSC Inter-BSC Hard Handoff begins with the Triggering and Target Determination phase. In Figure 7-10, this phase includes only the first step in the call flow.

The Resource Establishment Phase at the target BSC comprises stages 2 through 6, and involves setting up the terrestrial and radio resources at the target MSC and target BSC. These stages are similar to stages 2 through 4, described in Intra-MSC Inter-BSC Hard Handoff call flow. The only difference is the additional IS41_FACDIR2 TCAP invoke messaging that is required to set up inter-MSC terrestrial resources.

The Handoff Execution phase comprises stages 7–16. An IS41_MSONCH message is included for Inter-MSC handoff to indicate the successful arrival of the mobile station on the target BSC's radio channel. Finally, the Resource Release phase consists of steps 17–20.

Because the only difference between an Inter-MSC Inter-BSC and an Intra-MSC Inter-BSC Hard Handoff is the additional IS-41 messaging, only those call flow steps are described in the text following Figure 7-10.

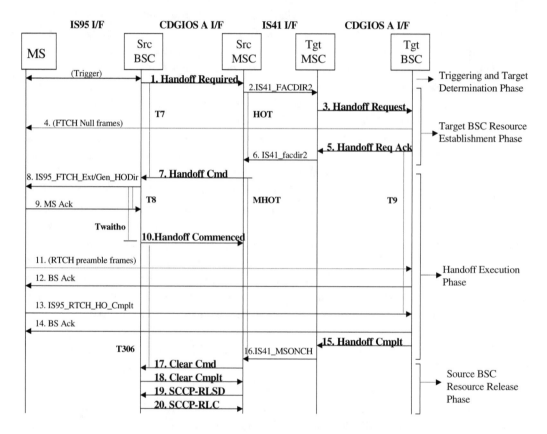

Figure 7-10 Inter-MSC Inter-BSC Hard Handoff call flow

Resource Establishment Phase

2. IS41_FACDIR2 (IS-41):

Upon receiving a Handoff Required message from the source BSC, the source MSC identifies the target BSC and its associated target MSC. The source MSC then allocates an inter-MSC trunk circuit between it and the target MSC to be used for call setup.

The source MSC then sends an IS41_FACDIR2 message to the target MSC, initiating the hard handoff process. This message includes the inter-MSC circuit ID, target cell ID, and other handoff-related parameters, such as CDMA pilot measurement reports. The source MSC then starts timer HOT (*Handoff Order Timer*) and waits for a return result for the IS41_FACDIR2 message [7]. If the HOT timer expires before a return result is received, the source MSC sends a Handoff Required Reject message to the source BSC. The default value for the HOT timer is 12 seconds.

6. IS41_facdir2 (IS-41):

Upon successful allocation of the radio and terrestrial resources needed to service the requested handoff, the target BSC sends a Handoff Request Acknowledge message to the target MSC. The target MSC then sends the source MSC an IS41_facdir2 return result message that contains handoff parameters received from the target BSC, which are to be included in the IS-95 Extended Handoff Direction sent to the mobile station. These parameters, such as the target CDMA frequency channel, frame offset, and long code mask, are necessary for the mobile to successfully perform a hard handoff. The source MSC stops timer HOT upon receipt of the IS41_facdir2 message.

The source MSC sends a Handoff Command message to source BSC, prompting it to direct the mobile to perform the hard handoff. The Handoff Command message contains parameters that the source MSC received in the previously received IS41_facdir2 message. It should be noted that parameters used in the IS-95 Extended Handoff Direction message that are not available over the IS-41 or A-Interfaces may be populated by the source BSC.

After sending the Handoff Command message, the source MSC starts timer MHOT (*Mobile Handoff Order Timer*) and waits for an IS41_MSONCH message from the target MSC, indicating the mobile arrival on the target radio channel. The default MHOT value is 7 seconds [7].

Handoff Execution Phase

16. IS41_MSONCH (IS-41):

Once the hard handoff is complete and the target BSC acquires the mobile on the reverse traffic radio channel, a Handoff Complete A-Interface message is sent to the target MSC by the target BSC. The target MSC then sends an IS41_MSONCH message to the source MSC, indicating the successful hard handoff. The source MSC stops timer MHOT and begins releasing source BSC resources by initiating the call clearing procedure.

7.3.5   Inter-BSC Hard Handoff Messages

This section describes the individual A-Interface messages exchanged between the MSC and BSC during Inter-BSC Hard Handoff. Because the A-Interface messaging is the same for both Inter-MSC and Intra-MSC Hard Handoffs, no distinction between those two scenarios is made here. The focus of this section is the message structure and individual message parameters.

7.3.5.1   Handoff Required

The Handoff Required A-Interface message (Table 7-4) is used by the source BSC to initiate a hard handoff. It is sent as an SCCP connection-oriented Data Form 1 message and utilizes the SCCP connection previously established during the original call setup between the source BSC and source MSC.

The mandatory Cause IE indicates the reason for sending the Handoff Required message.

The required target Cell Identifier List IE consists of the list of target candidate cells, in order of preference. A discriminator type 0, 2, 7, or 8 may be used to identify each target cell. Discriminator type 2 specifies only the cell ID, and type 7 specifies both the MSC_ID and cell ID. Discriminator types 0 and 8 are used to specify the entire global cell identity, including MCC, MNC, LAC, and cell ID. If the handoff is to a target cell contained in the source MSC's cell list, a discriminator type 2 is used; otherwise, cell discriminator type 0, 7, or 8 may be needed to identify a cell belonging to another MSC.

Following the Cell Identifier List IE is the Classmark Information Type 2 IE. This parameter contains information about the signaling modes that the mobile station supports. In the case of a Cellular (800-MHz) network, the information received by the BSC in the *Station Classmark* (SCM) Info field of the IS-95 Origination message is mapped into this IE. For PCS (1900-MHz) networks, the mapping is done using other origination message parameters because no SCM field is specified in the origination message described in J-STD-8. For example, in a PCS network, the parameters MOB_TERM and SLOTTED_MODE are mapped directly from J-STD-8 Origination message and the C = 1 (CDMA) parameter is mapped from the REQUEST_MODE field.

The required Response Request IE is used to solicit an acknowledgment from the MSC for the Handoff Required message. If the target BSC is successful in setting up the terrestrial resources for hard handoff, a Handoff Command message will be sent to the BSC. If the target BSC is unable to allocate resources for the hard handoff, a Handoff Required Reject message is expected from the MSC.

The required Encryption Information IE conveys the present Voice Privacy (VP) and Signaling Message Encryption (SME) mode of the mobile. If these features are not needed for the call, this IE is sent with an inactive status indication, and no keys are included.

The IS-95 Channel Identity IE is used for indicating a CDMA to CDMA hard handoff by setting the "Hard HO requested" bit to 1. The frame offset, Frequency Included bit (set to 1), and the CDMA channel number fields are set to the current active pilot's values. Some of the other fields within this IE, such as the power combined indicator bit, are needed for soft handoffs and are not specifically used for hard handoff.

The Mobile Identity ESN IE is needed by the target cell during hard handoff to generate the public long code mask used for forward and reverse traffic channels [5,6]. It is also useful for billing and call trace purposes.

The optional Downlink Radio Environment IE provides information regarding each cell contained in the Cell Identifier List IE. Specifically, it contains a list of target cell pilot strength and one-way delay measurements as reported by the mobile station in an IS-95 PSMM. Note that these strength measurements may be available to the source BSC only if the hard handoff triggering mechanism uses PSMM measurements, such as the pilot beacon triggering mechanism. The BSC may also explicitly request PSMM messages from the BTSs. The Downlink Radio Environment IE contains a cell identifier discriminator that applies to all cells present in this IE. Discriminator types of 0, 2, 7, or 8 are allowed. The pilot signal strength value has a range of 0 to 63 and is calculated by the following formula :

• *Pilot signal strength* $= -2 \times 10 \times \log_{10}(Ec/Io)$,

where (Ec/Io) is defined as the ratio of received pilot energy per chip to the total received spectral density, including noise and signals.

The CDMA target one-way delay is specified in units of 100 ns, and represents an estimation of the one-way delay from the mobile station to an individual target cell. This information is derived from the target PN phase measurements reported by the mobile in the IS-95 PSMM message [5,6]. The delay information and pilot strength measurement for each target cell may be used by the MSC to decide the final target BSC and cell to be used in the hard handoff. As mentioned earlier, how this information is used by the BSC and MSC during a hard handoff is vendor implementation-specific.

The required Service Option IE indicates the requested service option for the hard handoff.

The optional CDMA Serving One-Way Delay IE specifies the estimated one-way delay from the mobile to the current serving cell. The delay is computed by the BSC using the REF_PN parameter received from the mobile in the IS-95 PSMM message. The REF_PN parameter is the pilot used by the mobile to derive its time reference.

The target BSC may use this information to estimate the acquisition window used in the hard handoff reverse traffic channel acquisition.

The last element, the IS-95 MS Measured Channel Identity, specifies the CDMA band class and channel frequency number reported by the mobile in the IS-95 Candidate Frequency Search Report message. The IS-95 Candidate Frequency Search Report message contains information regarding the candidate frequency's received power and pilot Ec/Io. This IE is required if provided by the mobile station.

• BSAP Message Type:	BSMAP
• SCCP Message Type:	SCCP-Data Form1 (DT1)
• Direction:	Source BSC → MSC

Table 7-4 Handoff Required (CDGIOS 6.1.5.4)

BitMap	Param IE	#Oct	Range	Type	IOS Ref
0000 0000 (00H) LLLL LLLL	BSMAP header	2	Msg Discrim. = 0 (BSMAP) L = BSMAP msg length	M	6.2.2.1 6.2.2.3
0001 0001 (11H)	Msg Type	1	Handoff Required Msg	M	6.2.2.4
0000 0100 (04H) LLLL LLLL 0ccc cccc	Cause	3	L = 01H, c = cause 0EH—better cell 0FH—interference	M	6.2.2.19
0001 1010 (1AH) LLLL LLLL {dddd dddd (d=2) cccc cccc cccc ssss} *OR* {dddd dddd (d=7) iiii iiii iiii iiii iiii iiii cccc cccc cccc ssss} *OR* {dddd dddd (d=8) mmmm mmmm nnnn mmmm nnnn nnnn aaaa aaaa aaaa aaaa cccc cccc cccc ssss } *OR* {dddd dddd (d=0) tttt tttt tttt tttt tttt tttt tttt tttt tttt tttt cccc cccc cccc ssss}	Cell Identifier List (Target)	Variable	L = length of the list of Cell Identifiers d = cell discriminator 02H—Cellid 07H—MSCID, Cellid 08H—MCC,MNC,LAC,Cellid 00H—(MCC+MNC+LAC),Cellid Cell Identifiers: c = cell ID s = Sector Number, 0 for omni i = MSCID m = mobile country code (MCC) in BCD format n = mobile network code (MNC) in BCD format a = Location Area Code t = (MCC+MNC+LAC) vendor specific MSC ID using 5 octets	M	6.2.2.21

Table 7-4   Handoff Required (CDGIOS 6.1.5.4) (Continued)

BitMap	Param IE	#Oct	Range	Type	IOS Ref
0001 0010 (12H) LLLL LLLL	Classmark Information Type 2	5	Same as the element in Table 3-2, CM Service Request message	O,R	6.2.2.15
0001 1011 (1BH)	Response Request	1	In CDGIOS, MSC is required to respond to Handoff Required	O,R	6.2.2.35
0000 1010 (0AH) LLLL LLLL xiii iisa llll llll (08H) kkkk kkkk kkkk kkkk kkkk kkkk kkkk kkkk kkkk kkkk kkkk kkkk kkkk kkkk kkkk kkkk *AND/ OR* xiii iisa llll llll (06H) 0000 00kk kkkk kkkk kkkk kkkk kkkk kkkk kkkk kkkk kkkk kkkk	Encryption Information	Variable	L = 08H, 0AH, or 12H x = 1 i = 00001—SME s = 1,0—status (1 = active) a = 1,0—algo avail (1 = avail) l = 08H—key length k = key value Private Long Code present when Voice Privacy is requested x = 1 i = 00100—Private Long Code s = 1,0—status (1 = active) a = 1,0—algo avail (1 = avail) l = 06H—key length k = key value	O,R	6.2.2.12

Table 7-4   Handoff Required (CDGIOS 6.1.5.4) (Continued)

BitMap	Param IE	#Oct	Range	Type	IOS Ref
0010 0010 (22H) LLLL LLLL Hnnn ffff wwww wwww pppp pppp pPFr raaa aaaa aaaa	IS-95 Channel Identity (current channel)	Variable	L = length, r = 0—reserved H = hard HO requested = 1 n = number of chans to add = 1 f = frame offset P = power comb indicator = 0 F = frequency included = 1 a = ARFCN—CDMA ch # (Actual RF Channel Number) the following are not used for hard handoff and are ignored: w = walsh code chan index p = Pilot PN code	O,C	6.2.2.10
0000 1101 (0DH)	Mobile Identity (ESN)	7	Same as the element in Table 3-2, CM Service Request message	O,R	6.2.2.16
0010 1001 (29H) LLLL LLLL nnnn nnnn {Cell Identifier} rrSS SSSS DDDD DDDD DDDD DDDD	Downlink Radio Environment (Target)	Variable	L = length, r = 0—reserved n = number of cells in this IE Cell Identifier same as Cell identifier list entries S = downlink signal strength D = CDMA target one-way delay (in units of 100 ns)	O,C	6.2.2.25
0000 0011 (03H) ssss ssss ssss ssss	Service Option	3	Same as the element in Table 3-2, CM Service Request message	O,R	6.2.2.66

Table 7-4 Handoff Required (CDGIOS 6.1.5.4) (Continued)

BitMap	Param IE	#Oct	Range	Type	IOS Ref
0000 1100 (0CH) LLLL LLLL {Cell Identifier} DDDD DDDD DDDD DDDD	CDMA Serving One-Way Delay	Variable	L = length = 05H or 0AH Cell Identifier same as Cell identifier list entries types D = CDMA serving one-way delay (in units of 100 ns)	O,C	6.2.2.79
0110 0100 (64H) LLLL LLLL bbbb baaa aaaa aaaa	IS-95 MS Measured Channel Identity (Target)	4	L = length = 02H b = CDMA band class a = ARFCN (Actual Radio Freq Channel Number)	O,C	6.2.2.36

7.3.5.2   Handoff Request

The Handoff Request message is sent as an SCCP-CR, soliciting that a new SCCP connection be established for subsequent handoff messaging. This message is sent by the MSC to the target BSC to request the allocation of hard handoff resources (Table 7-5).

The parameters in the Handoff Request message are very similar to those found in Handoff Required message. In fact, many parameters contained in the Handoff Required message are directly mapped to the Handoff Request message by the MSC. During an Inter-MSC Inter-BSC Hard Handoff, these parameters are transferred from the source MSC to the target MSC using an IS41_FACDIR2 message.

The Encryption Information IE, Classmark Information Type 2 IE, target Cell Identifier List IE, IS-95 Channel Identity IE, Mobile Identity ESN IE, Downlink Radio Environment IE (Target), Service Option IE, CDMA Serving One-Way Delay IE, and IS-95 MS Measured Channel Identity (Target) are all directly mapped from the Handoff Required message to the Handoff Request message by the MSC.

The Cell Identifier List IE contains a list of target cell IDs, determined by the MSC and source BSC, to be used for the hard handoff.

The mandatory Channel Type IE has no impact on call processing and is not used by the BSC. The values are GSM A-Interface specific and are of no significance to IS-95 CDMA systems.

The required Circuit Identity Code Extension IE specifies the terrestrial circuit identity code to be used between the target MSC and the target BSC.

The required Mobile Identity IMSI IE is used by the target BSC and MSC to identify the mobile station uniquely.

- BSAP Message Type: BSMAP
- SCCP Message Type: SCCP-Connection Request (CR)
- Direction: Target BSC ← MSC

Table 7-5   Handoff Request (CDGIOS 6.1.5.5)

BitMap	Param IE	#Oct	Range	Type	IOS Ref
0000 0000 (00H) LLLL LLLL	BSMAP header	2	Msg Discrim. = 0 (BSMAP) L = BSMAP msg length	M	6.2.2.1 6.2.2.3
0001 0000 (10H)	Msg Type	1	Handoff Request Msg	M	6.2.2.4
0000 1011 (0BH)	Channel Type	5	Same as the element in Table 3-3, Assignment Request message	M	6.2.2.7
0000 1010 (0AH)	Encryption Information	Variable	Same as the element in Table 7-4, Handoff Required	M	6.2.2.12
0001 0010 (12H)	Classmark Information Type 2	5	Same as the element in Table 3-2, CM Service Request message	M	6.2.2.15
0001 1010 (1AH)	Cell Identifier List (Target)	Variable	Same as the element in Table 7-4, Handoff Required	M	6.2.2.21
0010 0100 (24H) LLLL LLLL mmmm mmmm mmmt tttt rrrr cccc	Circuit Identity Code Extension	5	L = 03H—length m = spanid, t = timeslot on span c = circuit mode = 0—full-rate r = reserved	O,R	6.2.2.23
0010 0010 (22H)	IS95 Channel Identity (current channel)	Variable	Same as the element in Table 7-4, Handoff Required	O,R	6.2.2.10
0000 1101 (0DH)	Mobile Identity (IMSI)	8–10	Same as the element in Table 3-2, CM Service Request message	O,R	6.2.2.16

Table 7-5 Handoff Request (CDGIOS 6.1.5.5) (Continued)

BitMap	Param IE	#Oct	Range	Type	IOS Ref
0000 1101 (0DH)	Mobile Identity (ESN)	7	Same as the element in Table 3-2, CM Service Request message	O,R	6.2.2.16
0010 1001 (29H)	Downlink Radio Environment (Target)	Variable	Same as the element in Table 7-4, Handoff Required	O,R	6.2.2.25
0000 0011 (03H) ssss ssss ssss ssss	Service Option	3	Same as the element in Table 3-2, CM Service Request message	O,R	6.2.2.66
0000 1100 (0CH)	CDMA Serving One Way Delay	Variable	Same as the element in Table 7-4, Handoff Required	O,R	6.2.2.79
0110 0100 (64H)	IS-95 MS Measured Channel Identity (Target)	4	Same as the element in Table 7-4, Handoff Required	O,C	6.2.2.36

7.3.5.3   Handoff Request Acknowledge

After allocating the resources needed for the hard handoff, the target BSC sends a Handoff Request Acknowledge message to the MSC, acknowledging the previously received Handoff Request message.

The Handoff Request Acknowledge message is a BSMAP message that can be sent as an SCCP-CC message or as an SCCP-DT1 message type, depending on implementation (Table 7-6). If an SCCP connection has not already been set up, this message is sent as an SCCP-CC message. Otherwise, the Handoff Request Acknowledge is sent as an SCCP-DT1 message.

This message contains target BSC handoff information that is eventually used by the source BSC to create the IS-95 Extended/General Handoff Direction message. The MSC transfers the parameters it receives in this message to the source BSC, using the Handoff Command message. The source BSC then uses the received information to construct the IS95 Extended/General Handoff Direction message that directs the mobile to handoff to the target cell.

The required IS-95 Channel Identity IE is used to specify the target radio channel parameters used in a CDMA to CDMA hard handoff. The Hard Hardoff and Frequency Included bit fields are set to 1 (assuming that the hard handoff involves a new CDMA frequency). The frame offset, CDMA channel number, walsh code index, and Pilot PN values are populated with the allocated target radio channel's parameters. This information is used in the IS-95 Extended Handoff Direction message to direct the mobile station to switch to the new radio channel.

The required target Cell Identifier List IE consists of the list of target candidate cells, in order of preference, that have been selected and allocated for the hard handoff by the target BSC. A discriminator type 0, 2, 7, or 8 may be used to identify each target cell. Discriminator type 2 specifies only the cell ID, and type 7 specifies both the MSC_ID and cell ID. Discriminator types 0 and 8 are used to specify the entire global cell identity, including MCC, MNC, LAC, and cell ID. If the handoff is to a target cell contained in the source MSC's cell list, a discriminator type 2 is used; otherwise, cell discriminator type 0, 7, or 8 is needed to identify a cell belonging to another MSC.

The required Extended Handoff Direction Parameters IE is used to communicate target BSC handoff parameters to the source BSC, which can then use the information to construct the IS-95 Extended Handoff Direction or IS-95 General Handoff Direction messages. Please see Table 7-6 for a complete list of the parameters included. For further information about how these parameters are used, refer to the IS-95 standards [5,6].

The required Hard Handoff Parameters IE is also used to provide the source BSC with information it needs to perform the hard handoff. This IE includes information such as the target CDMA frequency channel, number of reverse traffic channel preamble frames to be sent during hard handoff, reset layer 2 acknowledgment indicator (whether layer 2 acknowledgment sequence number is to be reset), reset forward traffic power control indicator, encryption mode, private long code mask indicator, and nominal transmit power offset (adjustment factor for open loop power estimation during mobile initial access).

Note that if encryption mode is enabled, the private long code mask and SME encryption keys will be used by the target BSC while communicating with the mobile. These encryption keys are sent to the target BSC earlier via the Handoff Required and Handoff Request messages.

- BSAP Message Type: BSMAP
- SCCP Message Type: SCCP-Connection Confirm (CC) or Data Form 1 (DT1)
- Direction: Target BSC → MSC

Table 7-6   Handoff Request Acknowledge (CDGIOS 6.1.5.6)

BitMap	Param IE	#Oct	Range	Type	IOS Ref
0000 0000 (00H) LLLL LLLL	BSMAP header	2	Msg Discrim. = 0 (BSMAP) L = BSMAP msg length	M	6.2.2.1 6.2.2.3
0001 0010 (12H)	Msg Type	1	Handoff Request Ack Msg	M	6.2.2.4

Table 7-6   Handoff Request Acknowledge (CDGIOS 6.1.5.6) (Continued)

BitMap	Param IE	#Oct	Range	Type	IOS Ref
0010 0010 (22H) LLLL LLLL Hnnn ffff wwww wwww pppp pppp pPFr raaa aaaa aaaa	IS-95 Channel Identity (Target)	Variable	L = length, r = 0—reserved H = hard HO requested = 1 n = number of chans to add f = frame offset, p = pilot PN code w = walsh code chan index P = power comb indicator F = frequency included = 1 a = ARFCN—CDMA ch. number	O,R	6.2.2.10
0001 1010 (1AH)	Cell Identifier List (Target)	Variable	Same as the element in Table 7-4, Handoff Required	O,R	6.2.2.21
0001 0000 (10H) LLLL LLLL aaaa nnnn rrrr AAAA AADD DDDD CCCC TTTT mmmm 0000 00ss ssss 00ii iiii 00dd dddd pppp pppp	Extended Handoff Direction Parameters	11	L = length, a = search window A size n = search window N size r = search window R size A = Tadd pilot threshold D = Tdrop pilot threshold T = TTdrop timer value C = Tcomp threshold m = neighbor max age s = soft slope, i = add intercept d = drop intercept p = target BS P_REV	O,R	6.2.2.73
0001 0110 (16H) rrrC CCCC pppR FEEM rrre NNNN	Hard Handoff Parameters	4	L = length, r = 0—reserved C = CDMA band class p = num. of RTCH preamble frames R = reset layer2 ack seq (1 = reset) F = reset forward TCH pwr ctrl E = encryption mode (1 = enabled) M = private long code mask e = nominal power extension (if e = 1, include N) N = norminal tx open loop power adjustment on mobile access	O,R	6.2.2.63

7.3.5.4   Handoff Command

The Handoff Command message is a BSMAP message sent as a connection-oriented SCCP-DT1 message type. This message is sent from the MSC with the purpose of instructing the source BSC to begin the handoff procedure. The Handoff Command message is also used by the MSC to acknowledge the Handoff Required received from the source BSC earlier .

The information in this message is primarily used by the source BSC to create the IS-95 Extended Handoff Direction message, which directs the mobile to handoff to the target cell's radio channel. The parameters in this message are transferred by the MSC from the corresponding Handoff Request Acknowledge message. In an Inter-MSC Inter-BSC hard handoff, these parameters are directly mapped from the IS41_facdir2 message. Note that not all of the parameters are supported by the IS41_facdir2, and therefore the source BSC may need to store some of the required information (Table 7-7).

The target Channel Identity IE, target Cell Identifier List IE, Extended Handoff Direction Parameters IE and Hard Handoff Parameters IE were all described for the Handoff Request Acknowledge message (see Section 7.3.5.3, "Handoff Request Acknowledge," on page 439).

- BSAP Message Type: BSMAP
- SCCP Message Type: SCCP-Data Form 1 (DT1)
- Direction: Source BSC ← MSC

Table 7-7   Handoff Command (CDGIOS 6.1.5.8)

BitMap	Param IE	#Oct	Range	Type	IOS Ref
0000 0000 (00H) LLLL LLLL	BSMAP header	2	Msg Discrim. = 0 (BSMAP) L = BSMAP msg length	M	6.2.2.1 6.2.2.3
0001 0011 (13H)	Msg Type	1	Handoff Command Msg	M	6.2.2.4
0010 0010 (22H)	IS-95 Channel Identity (Target)	Variable	Same as the element in Table 7-6, Handoff Request Ack	O,C	6.2.2.10
0001 1010 (1AH)	Cell Identifier List (Target)	Variable	Same as the element in Table 7-6, Handoff Request Ack	O,C	6.2.2.21
0001 0000 (10H)	Extended Handoff Direction Parameters	11	Same as the element in Table 7-6, Handoff Request Ack	O,C	6.2.2.73
0001 0110 (16H)	Hard Handoff Parameters	4	Same as the element in Table 7-6, Handoff Request Ack	O,R	6.2.2.63

7.3.5.5 Handoff Commenced

The Handoff Commenced message is a BSMAP message sent as a connection-oriented SCCP-DT1 message type. It is sent from the source BSC to the MSC to indicate that the mobile has acknowledged the IS-95 Extended/General Handoff Direction message and is in the process of hard handoff (Table 7-8). If the BSC sends the IS-95 Extended/General Handoff Direction message using quick repeats to increase the probability of message reception at the mobile, the source BSC does not wait for an acknowledgment from the mobile. The source BSC will, instead, send the Handoff Commenced message to the MSC immediately after sending the quick repeats. This message does not contain any specific handoff parameters.

- BSAP Message Type: BSMAP
- SCCP Message Type: SCCP-Data Form1 (DT1)
- Direction: Source BSC → MSC

Table 7-8   Handoff Commenced (CDGIOS 6.1.5.10)

BitMap	Param IE	#Oct	Range	Type	IOS Ref
0000 0000 (00H) LLLL LLLL	BSMAP header	2	Msg Discrim. = 0 (BSMAP) L = BSMAP msg length	M	6.2.2.1 6.2.2.3
0001 0101 (15H)	Msg Type	1	Handoff Commenced Msg	M	6.2.2.4

7.3.5.6 Handoff Complete

The target BSC sends the Handoff Complete message to the MSC after confirmation that the mobile has been acquired on the target cell's reverse traffic channel and the IS-95 Handoff Completion message has been received from the mobile (Table 7-9).

- BSAP Message Type: BSMAP
- SCCP Message Type: SCCP-Data Form1 (DT1)
- Direction: Target BSC → MSC

Table 7-9   Handoff Complete (CDGIOS 6.1.5.11)

BitMap	Param IE	#Oct	Range	Type	IOS Ref
0000 0000 (00H) LLLL LLLL	BSMAP header	2	Msg Discrim. = 0 (BSMAP) L = BSMAP msg length	M	6.2.2.1 6.2.2.3
0001 0100 (14H)	Msg Type	1	Handoff Complete Msg	M	6.2.2.4

7.3.6   Mapping of Handoff Parameters Between BSCs

The successful execution of hard handoffs requires both the BSC and MSC to map hand-off-related parameters across all three interfaces. In the hard handoff process, the BSC is responsible for mapping IS95 handoff parameters associated with the air interface with those exchanged over the A-Interface. The MSC, when involved with an Inter-MSC Hard Handoff, needs to map hard handoff-related A-Interface parameters with corresponding IS-41 message parameters that are exchanged between the source and target MSCs.

All CDMA hard handoff parameters that need to be conveyed between the target BSC and the source BSC are included in the messages and message parameters specified in CDGIOS. However, not all the required hard handoff information is present in the IS-41 message fields. The source BSC is, therefore, required to store handoff-related information in order to send the relevant information to the mobile station when directing a hard handoff.

The mapping of handoff-related parameters are described in two parts. First, the handoff parameter mappings associated with the initial hard handoff request, which are sent from the source BSC to the target BSC, are presented. Next, the mapping of handoff execution parameters sent from the target BSC to the source BSC is discussed.

7.3.6.1   Source BSC to Target BSC Handoff Parameter Mappings

The source BSC maps the initial IS-95-related hard handoff parameters, including pilot measurement information received from the mobile, to the A-Interface Handoff Required message. Upon receiving the Handoff Required message, the source MSC maps the handoff parameters to the IS41_FACDIR2 message, which it then sends to the target MSC. The target MSC maps the received IS-41 parameters to the A-Interface Handoff Request message that it then sends to the target BSC. Note that the IS-41 messaging is required only for an Inter-MSC Inter-BSC Hard Handoff.

Table 7-10 shows the mapping of handoff-related parameters that are transferred from the source BSC to the target BSC in the hard handoff process. In an Intra-MSC Inter-BSC Hard Handoff, these parameters can be mapped directly by the connecting MSC. However, for Inter-MSC Hard Handoffs, the Handoff Request parameters cannot all be mapped from the IS41_FACDIR2 message. In this case, the target MSC may need to format the message based on known information. In Table 7-10, these parameters are denoted with superscripts and are formatted as follows:

1. These IS-95 parameters are used to derive the A-Interface-mapped parameters.
2. Channel Type is formatted as full-rate speech and 13 kbps vocoder by MSC
3. Circuit ID is the terrestrial circuit allocated by the target MSC.
4. Hard handoff request bit is set to 1 to indicate a hard handoff request.
5. Number of channels to add is set to 1, for one target channel.
6. The Frequency Included bit is set to 1 to indicate that the CDMA frequency information of the serving cell is included in this message.

7. Service Option IE is mapped from the Handoff Required message in an Intra-MSC Inter-BSC Hard Handoff. In an Inter-MSC Inter-BSC Hard Handoff, a default service option is used, which may be changed later, using service negotiation procedures.

Table 7-10   Mapping of Handoff Request Parameters from Source to Target BSC

A-Interface Param IE	IS-95 Pilot Strength Measurement message -> (mobile to Source BSC)	A-Interface Handoff Required message -> (Source BSC to Source MSC)	IS-41 FACDIR2 message -> (Source MSC to Target MSC)	A-Interface Handoff Request Message (Target MSC to Target BSC)
Channel Type				Channel Type [2]
Encryption Info		SME Key	SME Key	SME Key
Encryption Info		Private Long Code key	CDMA Private Long Code Mask	Private Long Code key
Classmark Info		Classmark Info	CDMAStation-Classmark	Classmark Info
Cell ID List		Target Cell ID	TargetCellID	TargetCellID
Circuit ID Ext				Circuit ID [3]
IS95 Chan ID		Hard HO request		Hard HO request [4]
IS95 Chan ID		# of ch to add		# of ch to add [5]
IS95 Chan ID	REF_PN [1]	Frame offset	Frame offset	Frame offset
IS95 Chan ID		Freq included		Freq included [6]
IS95 Chan ID	REF_PN [1]	ARFCN	CDMA ch #	ARFCN

Table 7-10   Mapping of Handoff Request Parameters from Source to Target BSC
(Continued)

A-Interface Param IE	IS-95 Pilot Strength Measurement message -> (mobile to Source BSC)	A-Interface Handoff Required message -> (Source BSC to Source MSC)	IS-41 FACDIR2 message -> (Source MSC to Target MSC)	A-Interface Handoff Request Message (Target MSC to Target BSC)
Mobile ID			Mobile ID #	Mobile IMSI
Mobile ID		Mobile ESN	ESN	Mobile ESN
Downlink Radio		Target Cell ID	Target Cell ID	Target Cell ID
Downlink Radio	PILOT_STRE NGTH	Pilot strength	CDMAPilot-Strength	Pilot strength
Downlink Radio	PILOT_PN_P HASE [1]	Tgt 1-way delay	CDMATarget-OneWayDelay	Tgt 1-way delay
Service Option		Service Option		Service Option[7]
CDMA serving 1-way delay	REF_PN [1]	CDMA serving 1-way delay	CDMAServing-OneWayDelay	CDMA serving 1-way delay
IS-95 MS Measured ChanID		IS-95 MS Measured Channel ID		IS-95 MS Measured Channel ID

7.3.6.2   Target BSC to Source BSC Handoff Parameter Mappings

During the Handoff Execution phase, the target BSC sends handoff-related parameters to the target MSC in a Handoff Request Acknowledge message. The target MSC maps handoff-related parameters received over the A-Interface to parameters contained in the IS41_facdir2 message, which it then sends to the source MSC. The source MSC maps the received IS-41 parameters to the A-Interface Handoff Command message that it sends to the source BSC. Finally, the source BSC maps the received A-Interface parameters to the IS-95 Extended Handoff Direction message. The target BSC also sends system parameters to the mobile in the IS-95 In-Traffic System Parameters message after the IS-95 Handoff Completion message is received from the mobile.

Table 7-11 shows the mapping of handoff-related parameters that are being transferred from the target BSC to the source BSC. In an Intra-MSC Inter-BSC Hard Handoff, these parameters can be mapped directly by the connecting MSC. However, for Inter-MSC Hard Handoffs, the Handoff Request Acknowledgment parameters cannot all be mapped to the IS41_facdir2 message. In this case, the source MSC must format the Handoff Command message based on known information. In Table 7-11, these parameters are denoted with superscripts and are formatted as follows:

1. These handoff parameters: T_ADD, T_DROP, T_COMP, T_TDROP, RESET_L2, RESET_FPC, NOM_PWR_EXT, NOM_PWR, NUM_PREAMBLE, SOFT_SLOPE, ADD_INTERCEPT, DROP_INTERCEPT, and Target BS P_REV do not have any field entry in the IS41_facdir2 message. The source BSC needs to set these to prearranged values that are then included in the IS-95 Extended Handoff Direction message.
2. The HARD_INCLUDED field is set to 1 to indicate hard handoff parameters such as CDMA frequency and frame offset are included.
3. The ENCRYPT_MODE field is set to 0 or 1, depending on the mobile's encryption mode for this call. This parameter is not passed in the IS41_facdir2 message, but the source BSC will have this information because it has already been handling this call.
4. The PILOT_PN information is not being sent in the IS41_facdir2 message, at least for IS41D or any earlier version of IS-41. The source BSC, therefore, needs to store this information for every potential target cell ID and formats this field accordingly when sending the IS-95 Extended Handoff Direction message.
5. The PWR_COMB_IND bit is set to zero if the hard handoff involves only a single CDMA target radio channel.

Table 7-11   Mapping of Handoff Command Parameters from Target to Source BSC

A-Interface Param IE	IS-95 Ext Handoff Direction message (Source BSC to mobile) In-Traffic Sys Param message (Target BSC to mobile)	A-Interface Handoff Command message <- (Source MSC to Source BSC)	IS-41 facdir2 message <- (Target MSC to Source MSC)	A-Interface Handoff Request Ack message <- (Target BSC to Target MSC)
	IS95 Ext HO Dir:			
Ext HO Dir Param	SRCH_WIN_A	Search win A	Search win A	Search win A
Ext HO Dir Param	T_ADD [1]	Tadd thresh		Tadd thresh
Ext HO Dir Param	T_DROP [1]	Tdrop thresh		Tdrop thresh
Ext HO Dir Param	T_COMP [1]	Tcomp thresh		Tcomp thresh
Ext HO Dir Param	T_TDROP [1]	TTdrop thresh		TTdrop thresh
Ext HO Dir Param	SOFT_SLOPE [1]	SOFT_SLOPE		SOFT_SLOPE
Ext HO Dir Param	ADD_INTERCEPT[1]	ADD_ INTERCEPT		ADD_ INTERCEPT
Ext HO Dir Param	DROP_INTERCEPT[1]	DROP_ INTERCEPT		DROP_ INTERCEPT
Ext HO Dir Param	P_REV[1]	P_REV		P_REV
IS95 Chan ID	HARD_INCLUDED[2]	Hard HO request		Hard HO request
IS95 Chan ID	FRAME_OFFSET	Frame offset	Frame offset	Frame offset

Table 7-11   Mapping of Handoff Command Parameters from Target to Source BSC
(Continued)

A-Interface Param IE	IS-95 Ext Handoff Direction message (Source BSC to mobile) In-Traffic Sys Param message (Target BSC to mobile)	A-Interface Handoff Command message <- (Source MSC to Source BSC)	IS-41 facdir2 message <- (Target MSC to Source MSC)	A-Interface Handoff Request Ack message <- (Target BSC to Target MSC)
Hard HO Param	PRIVATE_LCM	Private long code mask indicator	Long code mask	Private long code mask
Hard HO Param	RESET_L2[1]	Reset layer2 ack		Reset layer2 ack
Hard HO Param	RESET_FPC[1]	Reset forward TCH pwr ctrl		Reset forward TCH pwr ctrl
Hard HO Param	ENCRYPT_MODE[3]	Encryption mode		Encryption mode
Hard HO Param	NOM_PWR_EXT [1]	Nom pwr ind		Nom pwr ind
Hard HO Param	NOM_PWR [1]	Mobile Nom tx pwr adjustment		Mobile Nom tx pwr adjustment
Hard HO Param	NUM_PREAMBLE[1]	Num of RTCH preamble frames		Num of RTCH pream frames
Hard HO Param	BAND_CLASS	Band class	Band class	Band class
IS95 Chan ID	CDMA_FREQ	ARFCN	CDMA ch #	ARFCN
IS95 Chan ID	PILOT_PN [4]	Pilot PN code		Pilot PN code
IS95 Chan ID	PWR_COMB_IND[5]	Pwr comb bit		Pwr comb bit

Table 7-11   Mapping of Handoff Command Parameters from Target to Source BSC
(Continued)

A-Interface Param IE	IS-95 Ext Handoff Direction message (Source BSC to mobile) / In-Traffic Sys Param message (Target BSC to mobile)	A-Interface Handoff Command message <- (Source MSC to Source BSC)	IS-41 facdir2 message <- (Target MSC to Source MSC)	A-Interface Handoff Request Ack message <- (Target BSC to Target MSC)
IS95 Chan ID	CODE_CHAN	Walsh code chan index	CDMA Code channel	Walsh code chan index
	IS95 In-Traffic Sys Param msg:			
Cell ID List	SID	Cell Identifier	TargetCellID	Cell Identifier
Cell ID List	NID	Cell Identifier	TargetCellID	Cell Identifier
Ext HO Dir Param	SRCH_WIN_A	Search win A	Search win A	Search win A
Ext HO Dir Param	SRCH_WIN_N	Search win N		Search win N
Ext HO Dir Param	SRCH_WIN_R	Search win R		Search win R
Ext HO Dir Param	T_ADD	Tadd thresh		Tadd thresh
Ext HO Dir Param	T_DROP	Tdrop thresh		Tdrop thresh
Ext HO Dir Param	T_COMP	Tcomp thresh		Tcomp thresh
Ext HO Dir Param	T_TDROP	TTdrop thresh		TTdrop thresh
Ext HO Dir Param	NGHBR_MAX_AGE	Neighbor max age		Neighbor max age

7.3.7   Intra-MSC Inter-BSC Hard Handoff Example Call Flow

Figure 7-11 shows a practical example of an Intra-MSC Inter-BSC Hard Handoff, including an overview of the network configuration and an A-Interface message summary flow. The
purpose of Figure 7-11 is to present an overview of the A-Interface messages exchanged
between the BSC and MSC. Subsequent figures illustrate the complete message contents,
including MTP3 and SCCP layers.

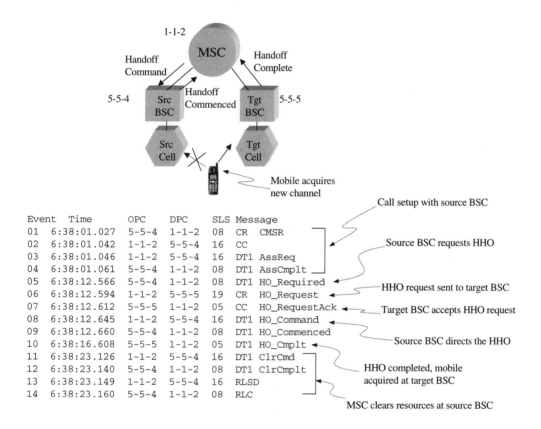

Figure 7-11   Intra-MSC Inter-BSC Hard Handoff example call flow

In this example, a call is first set up on the source BSC with point code 5-5-4. The SLS
selected by the source BSC is 8, and the *Signaling Link Selection* (SLS) chosen by the MSC is
16. After the call has been established, the mobile station transitions into a hard handoff with a
cell associated with the target BSC (point code 5-5-5), which is under the domain of the same
anchor MSC. The hard handoff-related A-Interface messaging begins when a Handoff Required
message is sent from the source BSC to the MSC. The MSC then sends a Handoff Request to the
target BSC. The target BSC, upon receipt of the Handoff Request, establishes an SCCP connec-

tion for the handoff. The SLS selected by the target BSC is 5, and the SLS chosen for this connection by the MSC is 19.

After allocating radio and terrestrial resources needed for the handoff, the target BSC sends a Handoff Request Acknowledgment message to the MSC, piggybacked on an SCCP-CC message.

Upon receiving the Handoff Request Acknowledgment message from the target BSC, the MSC constructs a Handoff Command message that is sent to the source BSC, which then directs the mobile to perform the hard handoff. In this example, the source BSC receives an acknowledgment from the mobile station, prompting it to send the MSC a Handoff Commenced message.

After acquiring the mobile station, the target BSC sends a Handoff Complete message to the MSC. The MSC then clears the resources associated with the source BSC by sending a Clear Command. At this point, the Inter-BSC Hard Handoff has been successfully completed.

The following decoded examples illustrate the individual A-Interface messages and message parameters associated with hard handoffs. These examples are similar to what may be seen on test equipment monitoring the two A-Interfaces during an Inter-BSC Hard Handoff.

```
**** MESSAGE NUMBER: 00005 ****
*** Start of MTP Level 3 ***
0003 10000011 83
     ----0011      Service Indicator          SCCP
     --00----      Network Priority           0
     10------      Network Indicator          National
0004 (3 Bytes)     Destination Point Code     1-1-2
0007 (3 Bytes)     Origination Point Code     5-5-4
0010 00001000 08 Signaling Link Selection     8
*** Start of SCCP ***
0011 00000110 06 Data Form 1                  06
0012 (3 Bytes)   Dest Local Reference         208086
0015 00000000 00 Segment/Reassembling         0
0016 00000001 01 Variable Pointer             01
*** Start of CDGIOS MAP ***
                 Handoff Required
0017 00111001 39 Data Length                  57
0018 00000000 00 BSMAP Discriminator          00
0019 00110111 37 BSMAP Length                 55
0020 00010001 11 Handoff Required             17
0021 00000100 04 Cause                        4
0022 00000001 01 Length                       1
0023 00001110 0e
     -0001110     Cause Value                  Better cell
0024 00011010 1a Cell Identifier List         26
0025 00000011 03 Length                       3
0026 00000010 02 Cell Identifier Discrim      CI Only         HHO Target Cell ID
0027 00011111 1f CI Value                     1f 53   ◄─────── requested by source
0028 01010011 53                                              BSC
0029 00010010 12 Classmark Info Type 2        18
0030 00000100 04 Length                       4
```

(Continued)

```
0031 00000000 00
     -----000    RF Power Capability      Class 1, vehicle and portable
     000-----    MOB_P_REV                0
0032 00000000 00
     -----000    Frequency Capability     band number 0
     00000---    Reserved                 0
0033 01110010 72
     -------0    Reserved                 0
     ------1-    Mobile Term              capable of rcving call
     -----0--    DTX                      incapable
     ----0---    Bandwidth                mobile limited to 20 MHz Band
     ---1----    Extended Protocol (EP)   Full reverse control channel
     --1-----    Slotted                  Slotted paging request allowed
     -1------    IS-95                    capable
     0-------    Reserved                 0
0034 00000000 00 Reserved                 0
0035 00011011 1b Response Request         27
0036 00001010 0a Encryption Information   10
0037 00000100 04 Length                   4
0038 10000100 84
     -------0    Algorithm Availability   Unavailable(Unsupported)
     ------0-    Algorithm Status         Inactive
     100001--    Algorithm Identifier     CMEA Algorithm
0039 00000000 00 Key Length               0
0040 10010000 90
     -------0    Algorithm Availability   Unavailable(Unsupported)
     ------0-    Algorithm Status         Inactive
     100100--    Algorithm Identifier     Private Longcode Algorithm
0041 00000000 00 Key Length               0
0042 00100010 22 IS-95 Channel Identity   34
0043 00000101 05 Length                   5
0044 10010111 97
     ----0111    Frame Offset             7
     -001----    Number of Channels to Add 1
     1-------    Hard Handoff             Hard handoff
0045 00001010 0a Walsh Code Channel Index 10
0046 00011000 18 Pilot PN Code (low part) 24
0047 10100001 a1
     -----001    ARFCN (high part)        1
     ---00---    Reserved
     --1-----    Frequency Included       in ARFCN
     -0------    Power Combined           No power combined
     1-------    Pilot PN Code (high part) 1
0048 11111001 f9 ARFCN (low part)         249
0049 00001101 0d Mobile Identity (ESN)    13
0050 00000101 05 Length                   5
0051 00000101 05
     -----101    Type of Identity         ESN
     ----0---    Odd/Even Indicator       even
     0000----    Fixed                    00
0052 (4 Bytes)   ESN Identity Digits      9f 4c 27 41
```

(Continued)

```
0056 00101001 29 Downlink Radio Environ't   41
0057 00000111 07 Length                     7
0058 00000001 01 Number of Cells            1
0059 00000010 02 Cell Identity Discrim      CI Only
0060 00011111 1f Cell Identification        1f 53 06 53 ...
0061 01010011 53
0062 00000110 06
0063 01010011 53
0064 00101110 2e
0065 00000011 03 Service Option             3
0066 10000000 80 Service Type               13K Speech
0067 00000000 00
0068 00001100 0c CDMA Serving 1-Way Delay   12
0069 00000101 05 Length                     5
0070 00000010 02 Cell ID                    Type 2
0071 10100011 a3 Cell & Sector Info         a3 d9
0072 11011001 d9
0073 11100110 e6 Delay                      e6 b7
0074 10110111 b7
```

Figure 7-12   Handoff Required message example

Figure 7-12 shows an example of a decoded Handoff Required message. Because the SCCP connection was previously established during the call setup, the DLR of 208086 included in this message references the current call connection between the source BSC and MSC.

In this example, the single cell contained in the target cell identifier list is identified by Cell ID only (discriminator type 2). Only Cell ID is provided because this is an Intra-MSC Hard Handoff within the domain of the same MSC. Recall that the Cell Identifier List (target) may contain multiple target cells, in order of preference. The inclusion of the Response Request IE indicates to the MSC that the MSC is required to respond to this Handoff Required message.

Encryption is not being used for this call, as indicated by the Encryption Information IE. The encryption availability bit specifies that encryption is not supported.

The Hard Handoff indication bit is set in the IS-95 Channel Identity IE, denoting that a hard handoff is requested by the source BSC. Also included in this IE is the Actual RF Channel Number, which specifies the frequency used for the current mobile connection.

Following the ESN IE is the Downlink Radio Environment IE. This IE contains downlink radio information regarding the cell (1f53) identified in the Cell Identifier List IE. It includes both downlink signal strength and round-trip delay values for the target cell.

The service option field is set to 13 k speech, and the CDMA Serving One-Way Delay parameter specifies the round-trip delay to the serving cell, which belongs to the source BSC.

```
**** MESSAGE NUMBER: 00006 ****
*** Start of MTP Level 3 ***
0003 10000011 83
     ----0011    Service Indicator          SCCP
     --00----    Network Priority           0
```

(Continued)
```
        10------    Network Indicator          National
0004 (3 Bytes)     Destination Point Code     5-5-5
0007 (3 Bytes)     Origination Point Code     1-1-2
0010 00010011 13   Signaling Link Selection   19
*** Start of SCCP ***
0011 00000001 01   Connection Request MT       01
0012 (3 Bytes)     Source Local References    160430
0015 00000010 02   Protocol Class             Class 2
0016 00000010 02   Mandatory Variable Ptr     Offset 0018
0017 00000100 04   Optional Pointer           Offset 0021
0018 00000010 02   Called Party Addr Length   2
0019 11000001 c1
        -------1   Subsys Number Indicator    Included
        ------0-   Point Code Indicator       Excluded
        --0000--   Global Title indicator     No GTT included
        -1------   Routing indicator          route by DPC/SSN
        1-------   Reserved for National use
0020 11111100 fc   Subsystem Number           252
0021 00001111 0f   Data PNC                   15
*** Start of CDGIOS MAP ***
                    Handoff Request
0022 01001001 49   Data Length                73
0023 00000000 00   BSMAP Discriminator        00
0024 01000111 47   BSMAP Length               71
0025 00010000 10   Handoff Request            16
0026 00001011 0b   Channel Type               11
0027 00000011 03   Length                     3
0028 00000001 01   Speech or Data Indicator   Speech
0029 00001000 08   Channel Rate and Type      Full rate TCH Channel Bm
0030 00000101 05   Speech Encoding Algorithm  13 Kb/s vocoder
0031 00001010 0a   Encryption Information      10
0032 00000100 04   Length                     4
0033 10000100 84
        -------0   Algorithm Availability     Unavailable(Unsupported)
        ------0-   Algorithm Status           Inactive
        100001--   Algorithm Identifier       CMEA Algorithm
0034 00000000 00   Key Length                 0
0035 10010000 90
        -------0   Algorithm Availability     Unavailable(Unsupported)
        ------0-   Algorithm Status           Inactive
        100100--   Algorithm Identifier       Private Longcode Algorithm
0036 00000000 00   Key Length                 0
0037 00010010 12   Classmark Info Type 2      18
0038 00000100 04   Length                     4
0039 (4 bytes)     Value                      00 00 72 00
0043 00011010 1a   Cell Identifier List (Target)
0044 00000011 03   Length                     3
0045 00000010 02   Cell Identifier Discrim    CI Only
0046 (2 bytes)     CI Value                   1f 53
0048 00100100 24   Circuit Identity Code Ext  36
0049 00000011 03   Length                     3
```

MSC sends HHO Target Cell ID to target BSC

(Continued)

```
0050 00000000 00 PCM MUX (high part)           0
0051 00110101 35
     ---10101    Time Slot                     15    ◄──  MSC assigns new CIC
     001-----    PCM MUX (low part)             1          resources for the
0052 00000000 00                                           HHO call with target
     ----0000    Circuit Mode                  Full-Rate   BSC
     0000----    Reserved                       0
0053 00100010 22 IS-95 Channel Identity        34
0054 00000101 05 Length                         5
0055 10010111 97
     ----0111    Frame Offset                   7
     -001----    Number of Channels to Add      1
     1-------    Hard Handoff                  Hard handoff
0056 00001010 0a Walsh Code Channel Index      10
0057 00011000 18 Pilot PN Code (low part)      24
0058 10100001 a1
     -----001    ARFCN (high part)              1
     ---00---    Reserved                       00
     --1-----    Frequency Included            in ARFCN
     -0------    Power Combined                No power combined
     1-------    Pilot PN Code (high part)      1
0059 11111001 f9 ARFCN (low part)             249
0060 00001101 0d Mobile Identity              13
0061 00001000 08 Length                        8
0062 00111110 3e
     -----110    Type of Identity              IMSI
     ----1---    Odd/Even Indicator            odd
     0011----    IMSI Identity Digits          310006192716377
0063 (7 Bytes)
0070 00001101 0d Mobile Identity              13
0071 00000101 05 Length                        5
0072 00000101 05
     -----101    Type of Identity              ESN
     ----0---    Odd/Even Indicator            even
0073 (4 Bytes)   ESN Identity Digits          9f 4c 27 41
0077 00101001 29 Downlink Radio Environ't     41
0078 00000111 07 Length                        7
0079 00000001 01 Number of Cells               1
0080 00000010 02 Cell Identity Discrim        CI Only
0081 00011111 1f Cell Identification          1f 53 06 53 ...
0082 01010011 53
0083 00000110 06
0084 01010011 53
0085 00101110 2e
0086 00000011 03 Service Option                3
0087 10000000 80 Service Type                 13K Speech
0088 00000000 00
0089 00001100 0c CDMA Serving 1-Way Delay     12
0090 00000101 05 Length                        5
0091 00000010 02 Cell ID                      Type 2
0092 10100011 a3 Value                        a3 d9
```

(Continued)

```
0093 11011001 d9
0094 11100110 e6 Delay                               e6 b7
0095 10110111 b7
0096 00000000 00 SCCP EOP
```

Figure 7-13   Handoff Request message example

Figure 7-13 shows an example of a decoded Handoff Request message. The application layer information is encompassed in an SCCP-CR message, which is sent from the MSC (1-1-2) to the target BSC (5-5-5) to establish a new SCCP connection. The SLR generated by the MSC to identify the SCCP connection is 160430.

Much of the information contained in the Handoff Request message is mapped directly from the Handoff Required message previously received by the MSC. One example is the target cell ID (1f53) that is included in the Cell Identifier List (Target) IE of this message.

A parameter not included in the Handoff Required is the Circuit Identity Code Extension IE. In this example, the MSC requests that timeslot 15 of PCM Mux 1 be used between the target BSC and MSC for voice.

```
**** MESSAGE NUMBER: 00007 ****
*** Start of MTP Level 3 ***
0003 10000011 83
     ----0011    Service Indicator           SCCP
     --00----    Network Priority            0
     10------    Network Indicator           National
0004 (3 Bytes)   Destination Point Code      1-1-2
0007 (3 Bytes)   Origination Point Code      5-5-5
0010 00000101 05 Signaling Link Selection    5
*** Start of SCCP ***                                    HO Request Ack sent
0011 00000010 02 Connection Confirm          02    ◄──── as SCCP-CC to estab-
0012 (3 Bytes)   Dest Local Reference        160430      lish SCCP connection
0015 (3 Bytes)   Source Local Reference      21437
0018 00000010 02 Protocol Class              Class 2
0019 00000001 01 Optional Pointer            01
0020 00001111 0f Data PNC                    15
*** Start of CDGIOS MAP ***
                 Handoff Request Acknowledge
0021 00011010 1a Data Length                 26
0022 00000000 00 BSMAP Discriminator         00
0023 00011000 18 BSMAP Length                24
0024 00010010 12 Handoff Request Ack         18
0025 00100010 22 IS-95 Channel Identity      34
0026 00000101 05 Length                      5
0027 10011110 9e
     ----1110    Frame Offset                14
     -001----    Number of Channels to Add   1
     1-------    Hard Handoff                Hard handoff
0028 11101100 ec Walsh Code Channel Index    236
0029 11010000 d0 Pilot PN Code (low part)    208
```

(Continued)

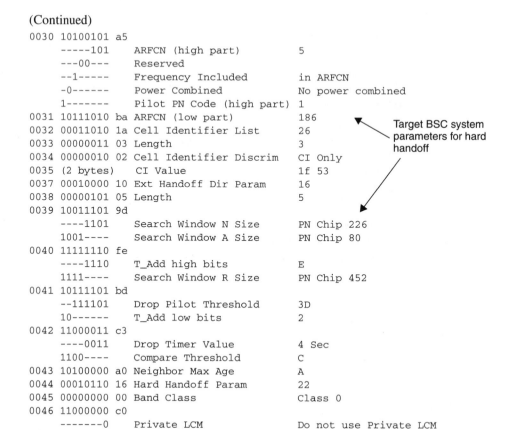

```
0030 10100101 a5
     -----101   ARFCN (high part)          5
     ---00---   Reserved
     --1-----   Frequency Included         in ARFCN
     -0------   Power Combined             No power combined
     1-------   Pilot PN Code (high part)  1
0031 10111010 ba ARFCN (low part)          186
0032 00011010 1a Cell Identifier List      26
0033 00000011 03 Length                    3
0034 00000010 02 Cell Identifier Discrim   CI Only
0035 (2 bytes)   CI Value                  1f 53
0037 00010000 10 Ext Handoff Dir Param     16
0038 00000101 05 Length                    5
0039 10011101 9d
     ----1101   Search Window N Size       PN Chip 226
     1001----   Search Window A Size       PN Chip 80
0040 11111110 fe
     ----1110   T_Add high bits            E
     1111----   Search Window R Size       PN Chip 452
0041 10111101 bd
     --111101   Drop Pilot Threshold       3D
     10------   T_Add low bits             2
0042 11000011 c3
     ----0011   Drop Timer Value           4 Sec
     1100----   Compare Threshold          C
0043 10100000 a0 Neighbor Max Age          A
0044 00010110 16 Hard Handoff Param        22
0045 00000000 00 Band Class                Class 0
0046 11000000 c0
     -------0   Private LCM                Do not use Private LCM
     -----00-   Encryption Mode            Encryption disabled
     ----0---   Reset FPC                  Do not reset Counter
     ---0----   Reset L2                   Do not reset L2 Ack
     110-----   Number of Preamble Frames  6
0047 00011100 1c
     ----1100   Nom Pwr                    C
     ---1----   Nom Pwr Ext1
0048 00000000 00 SCCP EOP
```

Target BSC system parameters for hard handoff

Figure 7-14   Handoff Request Acknowledge message example

Figure 7-14 shows an example of a decoded Handoff Request Acknowledge message. This message is piggybacked on an SCCP-CC message to the MSC to set up the new SCCP connection. A *Destination Local Reference* (DLR) value of 160430 references the MSC SCCP connection for this handoff call setup. Recall that by sending the Handoff Request Acknowledgment message, the target BSC (5-5-5) indicates that it has successfully allocated resources for the handoff request.

The target cell information packaged in this message is destined for the IS-95 Extended Handoff Direction message sent by the source BSC to the mobile station. The IS-95 Channel

Identity IE specifies the frame offset, Walsh code index, pilot PN offset, and CDMA frequency number of the channel allocated by the target BSC. The Cell Identifier List parameter includes the cell ID of the requested cell (1f53). The Extended Handoff Direction Parameters IE contains much of the information needed by the source BSC to construct the IS-95 Extended Handoff Direction message. Finally, the decoded Handoff Request Acknowledge message example illustrates the Hard Handoff Parameters IE. This IE contains hard handoff-specific parameters, such as the number of traffic channel preamble frames that the mobile station must send when performing a hard handoff.

```
**** MESSAGE NUMBER: 00008 ****
*** Start of MTP Level 3 ***
0003 10000011 83
     ----0011    Service Indicator           SCCP
     --00----    Network Priority            0
     10------    Network Indicator           National
0004 (3 Bytes)   Destination Point Code      5-5-4
0007 (3 Bytes)   Origination Point Code      1-1-2
0010 00010000 10 Signaling Link Selection    16
*** Start of SCCP ***
0011 00000110 06 Data Form 1                 06
0012 (3 Bytes)   Dest Local Reference        3
0015 00000000 00 Segment/Reassembling        0
0016 00000001 01 Variable Pointer            01
*** Start of CDGIOS MAP ***
                 Handoff Command
0017 00011010 1a Data Length                 26
0018 00000000 00 BSMAP Discriminator         00
0019 00011000 18 BSMAP Length                24
0020 00010011 13 Handoff Command             19
0021 00100010 22 IS-95 Channel Identity      34
0022 00000101 05 Length                      5
0023 10011110 9e
     ----1110    Frame Offset                14
     -001----    Number of Channels to Add   1
     1-------    Hard Handoff                Hard handoff
0024 11101100 ec Walsh Code Channel Index    236
0025 11010000 d0 Pilot PN Code (low part)    208
0026 10100101 a5
     -----101    ARFCN (high part)           5
     ---00---    Reserved                    00
     --1-----    Frequency Included          in ARFCN
     -0------    Power Combined              No power combined
     1-------    Pilot PN Code (high part)   1
0027 10111010 ba ARFCN (low part)            186
0028 00011010 1a Cell Identifier List        26
0029 00000011 03 Length                      3
0030 00000010 02 Cell Identifier Discrim     CI Only
0031 (2 bytes)   CI Value                    1f 53
0033 00010000 10 Ext Handoff Dir Param       16
0034 00000101 05 Length                      5
```

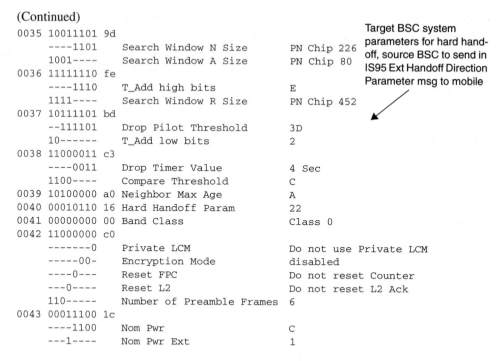

(Continued)
```
0035 10011101 9d
    ----1101    Search Window N Size        PN Chip 226
    1001----    Search Window A Size        PN Chip 80
0036 11111110 fe
    ----1110    T_Add high bits             E
    1111----    Search Window R Size        PN Chip 452
0037 10111101 bd
    --111101    Drop Pilot Threshold        3D
    10------    T_Add low bits              2
0038 11000011 c3
    ----0011    Drop Timer Value            4 Sec
    1100----    Compare Threshold           C
0039 10100000 a0 Neighbor Max Age           A
0040 00010110 16 Hard Handoff Param         22
0041 00000000 00 Band Class                 Class 0
0042 11000000 c0
    -------0    Private LCM                 Do not use Private LCM
    -----00-    Encryption Mode             disabled
    ----0---    Reset FPC                   Do not reset Counter
    ---0----    Reset L2                    Do not reset L2 Ack
    110-----    Number of Preamble Frames   6
0043 00011100 1c
    ----1100    Nom Pwr                     C
    ---1----    Nom Pwr Ext                 1
```

Figure 7-15   Handoff Command message example

Figure 7-15 shows an example of a decoded Handoff Command message. This message is an SCCP-DT1 message sent from the MSC (1-1-2) to the source BSC (5-5-4). The DLR value of three references the existing source BSC connection with the MSC.

The parameters within this message are mapped directly by the MSC from the previously received Handoff Request Acknowledge message. As described in the prior message example, the information contained in this A-Interface message is used by the source BSC to construct the corresponding IS-95 Extended Handoff Direction message.

```
**** MESSAGE NUMBER: 00009 ****
*** Start of MTP Level 3 ***
0003 10000011 83
    ----0011    Service Indicator           SCCP
    --00----    Network Priority            0
    10------    Network Indicator           National
0004 (3 Bytes)  Destination Point Code      1-1-2
0007 (3 Bytes)  Origination Point Code      5-5-4
0010 00001000 08 Signaling Link Selection   8
*** Start of SCCP ***
0011 00000110 06 Data Form 1                06
0012 (3 Bytes)  Dest Local Reference        208086
0015 00000000 00 Segment/Reassembling       0
0016 00000001 01 Variable Pointer           01
```

(Continued)
```
*** Start of CDGIOS MAP ***
                        Handoff Commenced
0017 00000011 03 Data Length              3
0018 00000000 00 BSMAP Discriminator      00
0019 00000001 01 BSMAP Length             1
0020 00010101 15 Handoff Commenced        21
```

Figure 7-16   Handoff Commenced message example

Figure 7-16 shows an example of a decoded Handoff Commenced message. This SCCP-DT1 message, which is sent from the source BSC (5-5-4) to the MSC (1-1-5), includes a DLR of 208086, which references the SCCP connection of the original call. This message is sent when the mobile acknowledges the handoff execution or when the source BSC informs the MSC that handoff execution is taking place. As shown in the decoded example, no call-specific parameters are included in this message.

```
**** MESSAGE NUMBER: 00010 ****
*** Start of MTP Level 3 ***
0003 10000011 83
     ----0011    Service Indicator          SCCP
     --00----    Network Priority           0
     10------    Network Indicator          National
0004 (3 Bytes)   Destination Point Code     1-1-2
0007 (3 Bytes)   Origination Point Code     5-5-5
0010 00000101 05 Signaling Link Selection   5
*** Start of SCCP ***
0011 00000110 06 Data Form 1                06
0012 (3 Bytes)   Dest Local Reference       160430
0015 00000000 00 Segment/Reassembling       0
0016 00000001 01 Variable Pointer           01
*** Start of CDGIOS MAP ***
                        Handoff Complete
0017 00000011 03 Data Length                3
0018 00000000 00 BSMAP Discriminator        00
0019 00000001 01 BSMAP Length               1
0020 00010100 14 Handoff Complete           20
```

Figure 7-17   Handoff Complete message example

Figure 7-17 shows an example of a decoded Handoff Complete message. Note that this message is an SCCP-DT1 message sent by the target BSC (5-5-5) to the MSC (1-1-2). The DLR value of 160430 references the MSC SCCP connection with the target BSC that has already been established. The sending of this message indicates that the target BSC has acquired the mobile in the reverse traffic channel and that the hard handoff was successful at the target BSC. As shown, no call-specific parameters are sent in this message.

7.3.8   IS-95 to IS-95 Inter-BSC Hard Handoff Failure Scenarios

The call flows and examples presented prior to this section described successful Inter-BSC Hard Handoff procedures. However, abnormal conditions sometimes exist, such as network call capacity limits being exceeded or radio signal loss, which result in hard handoff failures. It is important that the MSC and BSC properly handle any handoff failures so that both entities may reuse associated radio and terrestrial resources. This section describes the actions, as specified in CDGIOS, taken by both the MSC and BSC when hard handoff failures occur.

Figure 7-18 illustrates possible hard handoff call failure points for an Intra-MSC Inter-BSC Hard Handoff. A text box that summarizes the subsequent actions taken by the BSC or MSC denotes each failure point and includes a CDGIOS section reference.

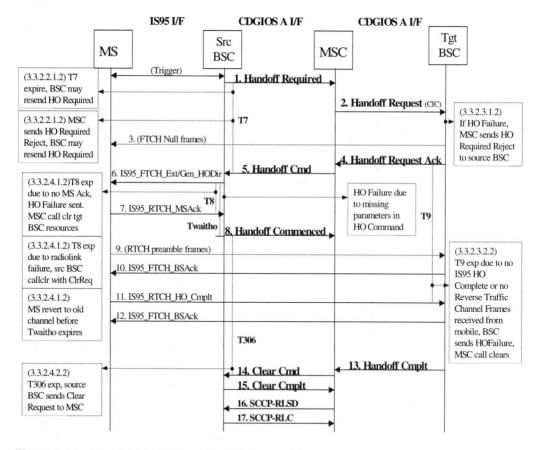

Figure 7-18   Inter-BSC Hard Handoff call failure points

The handling of Inter-MSC Inter-BSC Hard Handoff failures is very similar to the Intra-MSC Inter-BSC case described here. In fact, the A-Interface messaging is identical. The only difference is the additional IS-41 messaging needed to exchange handoff information between the target and source MSCs.

Following the summary Figure 7-18, each scenario is further described.

7.3.8.1   T7 Expiry at Source BSC

During the Target Determination and Target Resource Establishment Phase, the source BSC sends a Handoff Required message to initiate the handoff. Upon sending the Handoff Required message, the source BSC starts timer T7, which is used to wait for either a Handoff Command or Handoff Required Reject message from the MSC. Recall that the Handoff Command is sent from the MSC only after it has received confirmation that the target BSC was successfully able to allocate handoff resources. The Handoff Required Reject message may be sent by the MSC to refuse the handoff request.

As illustrated in Figure 7-19, if the timer T7 expires before either of these two messages is received, the source BSC may resend the Handoff Required message (stage 3). The decision to resend the Handoff Required message to the MSC is left to the BSC manufacturer.

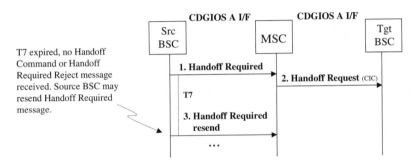

Figure 7-19   T7 Expiry at Source BSC Handoff call failure

7.3.8.2   Handoff Required Rejected—Handoff Failure at Target

When the source BSC initiates a Handoff Required message (Figure 7-20, stage 1), it starts timer T7 and waits for a Handoff Command message or a Handoff Required Reject message from the MSC. Upon receiving the Handoff Required message, the MSC sends a Handoff Request message to the selected target BSC (stage 2). If the target BSC is unable to process the requested handoff, it sends a Handoff Failure message to the MSC (stage 3) with the corresponding cause value. The Handoff Failure message is sent as an *SCCP-Connection Refused* (SCCP-CREF) and all associated SCCP references with the target BSC are then cleared.

Upon receiving the Handoff Failure message from the target BSC, the MSC sends a Handoff Required Reject message to the source BSC to indicate that the handoff request to the target BSC was unsuccessful (stage 4). If applicable, the Cause IE in the Handoff Required Reject message is set to reflect the reason specified in the Handoff Failure message. The source BSC may then choose to retry the Handoff Required message (stage 5). The decision of whether or not to retry is left to the BSC vendor. If an infrastructure manufacturer does implement a retry mechanism, it should be based on the cause value received in the Handoff Required Reject message and deemed reasonable for a hard handoff retry. For example, if the target BSC fails to allocate a terrestrial resource and includes the cause value "terrestrial CIC already allocated" in the Handoff Failure message, it is reasonable to retry. However, if the target BSC responds with a cause value of "BSC not equipped," the source BSC should not retry the Handoff Required message. Figure 7-20 shows the call flow for the Handoff Required Reject failure scenario, including a retry.

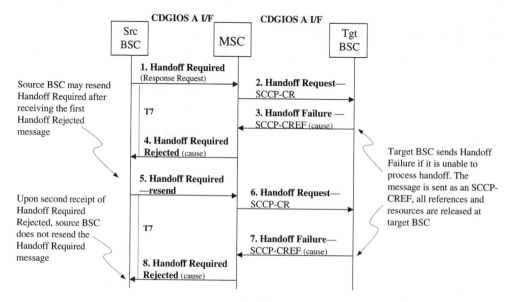

Figure 7-20 Handoff Required Rejected due to Handoff Failure at Target BSC

7.3.8.3   Handoff Command Missing Parameters at Source BSC

Missing parameters in the Handoff Command message also results in a failure. This handoff failure scenario, which occurs during the Handoff Execution stage, is shown in Figure 7-21.

When the source BSC sends the MSC a Handoff Required message (stage 1), it starts timer T7 and waits for a Handoff Command message or a Handoff Required Reject message from the MSC. After receiving the Handoff Required message, the MSC sends a Handoff Request message to the chosen target BSC, which responds with a Handoff Request Acknowledge message after allocating terrestrial and radio resources (stages 2–3). Upon receiving the Handoff Request Acknowledge message, the MSC sends a Handoff Command message to acknowledge the source BSC's Handoff Required message and to provide handoff-related parameters. The source BSC stops timer T7 upon receipt of the Handoff Command message (stage 4). If the Handoff Command message is rejected by the BSC, due to missing handoff parameters or because of a protocol error, it may send a Handoff Failure message to the MSC (stage 5) with the appropriate cause value. The MSC then clears the resources at the target BSC (stages 6–9).

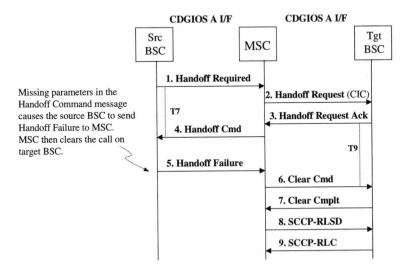

Figure 7-21   Handoff Command Missing Parameter at Source BSC call failure

7.3.8.4   Mobile Revert to Old Channel Before Twaitho Expires

Figure 7-22 shows the handoff failure scenario regarding a source BSC that allows a mobile station to revert back to the old radio channel and continue service after an unsuccessful acquisition of the target cell.

After receiving the Handoff Command message from the MSC, the source BSC constructs an IS-95 General Handoff Direction message that it then sends to the mobile station (stage 6). Recall that the IS-95 General Handoff Direction message is used to direct the mobile to the new target radio channel if mobile reversion to old channel is allowed. If an MS acknowledgment is needed, the source BSC starts timer T8 to wait for the mobile to send an MS Acknowledgment Order. The source BSC also starts timer Twaitho. In stage 7, the mobile sends an MS Acknowledge Order, acknowledging the receipt of the IS-95 General Handoff Direction message from the source BSC. Then, at stage 8, before timer Twaitho expires, the mobile sends an IS-95 Candidate Frequency Search Report to the source BSC, indicating that the mobile never acquired the target cell's frequency. The source BSC responds by sending a Handoff Failure message to the MSC with a cause value of "reversion to old channel" (stage 9). This typically happens if the mobile is unable to tune to the target CDMA frequency or if it is unable to acquire the forward traffic radio channel of the target cell.

The MSC then clears the resources at the target BSC (stages 10–13) by sending a Clear Command message to the target BSC. The mobile continues call processing with the source BSC.

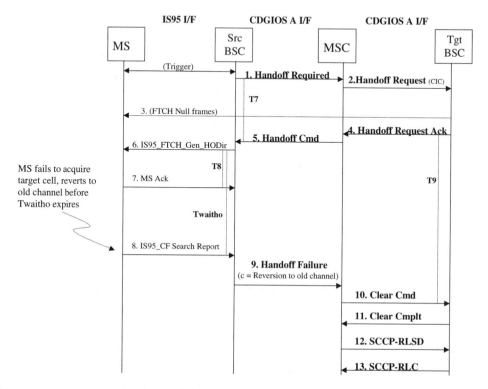

Figure 7-22 Mobile revert to old channel before Twaitho expires

Note that whenever handoff failure occurs and the resources at the target BSC need to be cleared, the call clearing procedure used depends on whether or not an SCCP connection has already been established with the target BSC. If an SCCP connection already exists, the MSC initiates call clearing by sending a Clear Command message. However, if the failure occurs after the Handoff Request message (sent as an SCCP-CR message) is received at the target BSC, the target BSC may send the Handoff Failure as an SCCP-CREF message to the MSC.

7.3.8.5   T8 Expiry at Source BSC—Mobile Remains on Old Channel

This handoff failure scenario, involving a mobile station that remains on the old radio channel after a hard handoff failure, is shown in Figure 7-23.

Stages 1 through 5 involving the initial handoff call setup are identical to those described in prior failure descriptions. At stage 6, the source BSC formats an IS-95 Extended/General Handoff Direction message and sends it to the mobile station, directing it to tune to the new target radio channel. The source BSC then starts timer T8 and waits for the mobile station to send an MS Acknowledgment Order. Note that if the quick repeats technique is used to deliver the IS-95 Extended/General Handoff Direction message, this scenario is not applicable. The source BSC also starts timer Twaitho if mobile reversion to the old channel is allowed.

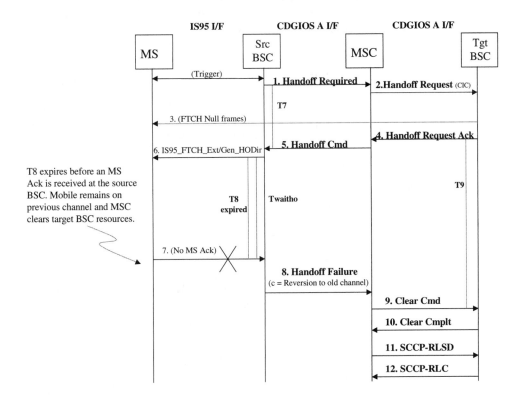

Figure 7-23 T8 Timer Expiry at Source BSC due to Mobile on old channel

Upon T8 expiry, the BSC sends a Handoff Failure message to the MSC with a cause value of "reversion to old channel" (stage 8). This normally occurs when the mobile station is unable to acquire the target cell.

The MSC then clears the resources at the target BSC (stages 9–12) by sending a Clear Command message to the target BSC. The mobile continues call processing with the source BSC.

7.3.8.6 T8 Expiry at Source BSC—RadioLink Failure

The handoff failure scenario shown in Figure 7-24 illustrates the procedures used when the radio link between the mobile station and source BSC is lost after the IS-95 Extended/General Handoff Direction message has been sent.

Stages 1 through 5 involving the initial handoff call setup are identical to those described in prior failure descriptions. At stage 6, the source BSC formats an IS-95 Extended/General Handoff Direction message and sends it to the mobile station, directing it to tune to the new target radio channel. The source BSC then starts timer T8 and waits for the mobile station to send an IS-95 MS Acknowledgment Order. Note that if the quick repeats technique is used to deliver the IS-95 Extended/General Handoff Direction message, this scenario is not applicable. The source BSC also starts timer Twaitho because mobile reversion to the old channel is allowed.

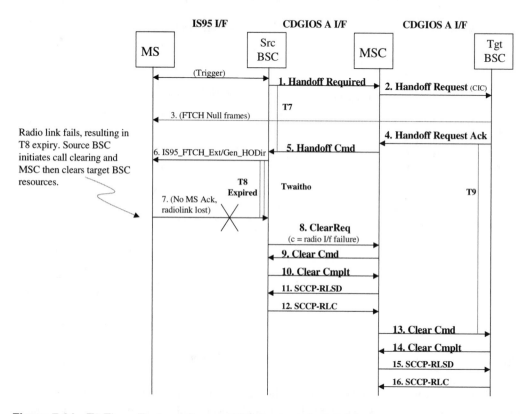

Figure 7-24 T8 Timer Expiry at Source BSC due to radio link failure

If T8 expires due to a lost radio link between the source BSC and the mobile station, the source BSC clears resources by sending a Clear Request to the MSC with cause value "radio interface failure" (stage 8). The MSC also initiates call clearing at the target BSC by sending a Clear Command message to the target BSC (stages 13–16). Note that this can occur concurrently with stages 9–12 after the indication of a handoff failure has been received by the MSC.

7.3.8.7 T9 Expiry at Target BSC—Handoff Failure

Figure 7-25 shows the procedure specified in CDGIOS to be followed when the target BSC fails to acquire the mobile station on the reverse traffic channel or when it does not receive an IS-95 Handoff Completion message.

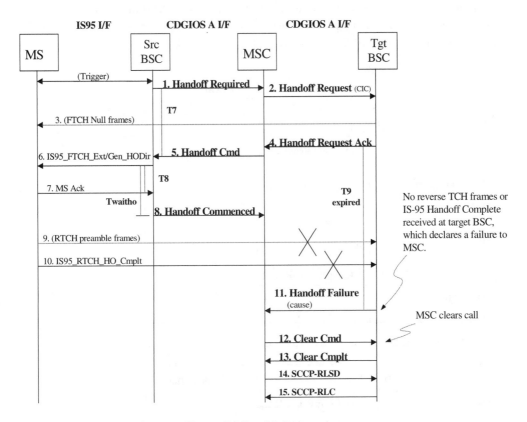

Figure 7-25 T9 Timer Expiry at Target BSC call failure

Stages 1 through 8 involving the initial handoff call setup are identical to those described in prior failure descriptions.

The target BSC, after allocating terrestrial and radio resources and sending a Handoff Request Acknowledge to the MSC, starts timer T9. The target BSC expects the mobile to be acquired on the reverse traffic channel at stage 9. If timer T9 expires before reverse traffic channel frames are acquired or an IS-95 Handoff Completion message is received, the target BSC declares a handoff failure by sending a Handoff Failure message to the MSC with a cause value of "radio interface failure."

Upon receipt of the Handoff Failure message, the MSC initiates call clearing by sending a Clear Command message to the target BSC. The target BSC clears all associated resources, and then responds with a Clear Complete message.

7.3.8.8   T306 Expiry at Source BSC

In this scenario, the Handoff Execution phase is successful, and the mobile arrives on the reverse traffic channel of the target cell. The failure occurs while waiting for the Clear Command message at the source BSC (see Figure 7-26).

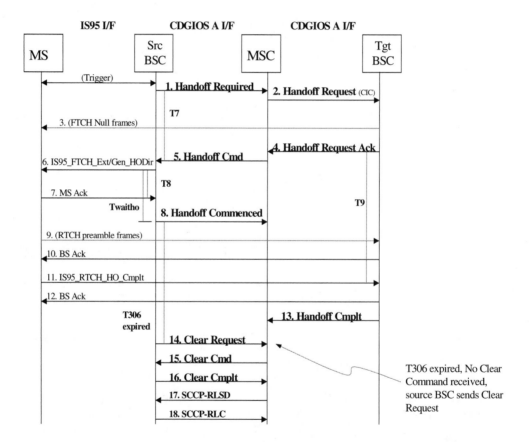

Figure 7-26 T306 Timer Expiry at Source BSC call failure

Stages 1 through 13 are similar to the description provided in Section 7.3.2, "Intra-MSC Inter-BSC Hard Handoff Call Flow," on page 422, for a successful Inter-BSC Hard Handoff. After the mobile successfully hands off to the target cell, the source BSC expects a Clear Command message from the MSC to initiate releasing resources. If timer T306 expires before a Clear Command message is received from the MSC, the source BSC initiates call clearing by sending a Clear Request message to the MSC. The MSC responds with a Clear Command message and resources at both the BSC and MSC are subsequently torn down (stages 14–18).

7.3.9   Handoff Failures Messages

The hard handoff failure scenarios previously described use two additional A-Interface messages not yet discussed. This section describes the message structure and message parameters of the Handoff Required Reject and Handoff Failure messages.

7.3.9.1   Handoff Required Reject

The Handoff Required Reject message is sent from the MSC to the source BSC to indicate that the handoff cannot be completed as requested by the source BSC in the Handoff Required message (Table 7-12). This BSMAP message is sent as a class 2 connection-oriented SCCP-DT1 message. The MSC may send this message if a Handoff Failure indication has been received from the target BSC during the hard handoff Resource Establishment phase.

The mandatory Cause IE specifies the reason why the MSC is rejecting the handoff. If this message is sent as a result of the receipt of a Handoff Failure message from the target BSC, the MSC may set this cause value to the cause value received in the Handoff Failure message.

- BSAP Message Type: BSMAP
- SCCP Message Type: SCCP-Data Form 1 (DT1)
- Direction: Source BSC ← MSC

Table 7-12   Handoff Required Reject (CDGIOS 6.1.5.9)

BitMap	Param IE	#Oct	Range	Type	IOS Ref
0000 0000 (00H) LLLL LLLL	BSMAP header	2	Msg Discrim. = 0 (BSMAP) L = BSMAP msg length	M	6.2.2.1 6.2.2.3
0001 1010 (1AH)	Msg Type	1	Handoff Required Reject	M	6.2.2.4
0000 0100 (04H) LLLL LLLL 0ccc cccc	Cause	3	L = 01H, c = cause 07H—operations & maint 20H—equipment failure 21H—no radio resources avail 22H—req terrestrial rsrc unavail 25H—BSC not equipped 2AH—handoff blocked 30H—requested transcoding/rate unavail 7FH—handoff procedure timeout	M	6.2.2.19

7.3.9.2   Handoff Failure

The Handoff Failure message is sent from either the source BSC or target BSC to indicate a failure resulting from handoff execution or resource allocation (Table 7-13). This message is sent an SCCP-DT1 or SCCP-CREF message type, depending on the state of the handoff when the failure occurs. If this message is sent by the target BSC in response to a Handoff Request message received from the MSC, it will be sent as an SCCP-CREF message in order to reject the SCCP connection setup. If an SCCP connection has already been established, as occurs when the Handoff Failure is sent by the source BSC during the Handoff Execution phase, this message is sent as an SCCP-DT1 message.

The Cause IE indicates the handoff failure reason at either the source BSC or target BSC.

At the source BSC, this message may be sent if the mobile fails to acknowledge the IS-95 Extended/General Handoff Direction message and reverts back to its old channel. A cause value of "reversion to old channel" will be included. Also, if the Handoff Command message is rejected at the source BSC, due to missing parameters or a protocol error, it sends a Handoff Failure message to the MSC. In this case, the cause value may be set to "BSC not equipped."

At the target BSC, the Handoff Failure message may be sent in response to an MSC Handoff Request message. If the target BSC fails to allocate terrestrial resources, a cause value of "requested terrestrial resource unavailable" will be included in the message. In the case where the BSC is unable to allocate a radio resource, a cause value of "no radio radio resource available" will be sent. The Handoff Failure message may also be sent from the target BSC if timer T9 expires before the target BSC acquires reverse traffic frames and an IS-95 Handoff Completion message is received from the mobile station. A cause value of "radio interface failure" may be sent for this failure condition.

- BSAP Message Type: BSMAP
- SCCP Message Type: SCCP-Data Form1 (DT1)/Connection Refused (CREF)
- Direction: BSC → MSC

Table 7-13   Handoff Failure (CDGIOS 6.1.5.7)

BitMap	Param IE	#Oct	Range	Type	IOS Ref
0000 0000 (00H)	BSMAP	2	Msg Discrim. = 0 (BSMAP)	M	6.2.2.1
LLLL LLLL	header		L = BSMAP msg length		6.2.2.3

Table 7-13   Handoff Failure (CDGIOS 6.1.5.7) (Continued)

BitMap	Param IE	#Oct	Range	Type	IOS Ref
0001 0110 (16H)	Msg Type	1	Handoff Failure	M	6.2.2.4
0000 0100 (04H) LLLL LLLL 0ccc cccc	Cause	3	L = 01H, c = cause 01H—radio interface failure 07H—operations and maint 0AH—reversion to old channel 20H—equipment failure 21H—no radio resources avail 22H—req terrestrial rsrc unavail 25H—BSC not equipped 26H—MS not equipped 30H—req transcoding/rate unavail 50H—terrestrial circ allocated 7FH—handoff procedure timeout	M	6.2.2.19

7.4 IS-95 to IS-95 Direct BSC-BSC Soft Handoff

In addition to the Intra-BSC Soft Handoff and Inter-BSC Hard Handoff scenarios discussed, CDGIOS allows for Inter-BSC Soft Handoffs. An IS-95 CDMA Inter-BSC Soft Handoff between two BSCs may occur when a mobile is in the intersection of the coverage area of two BTSs, each under the domain of different BSCs. In the case of Inter-BSC Soft Handoff, the two BSCs are directly connected by the A3 and A7 interfaces. These two interfaces allow the *Selection/Distribution Unit* (SDU) at the source BSC to continue processing calls, even if multiple connections to different cells, under the domain of different BSCs, is required. The exchange of user data between the two BSCs is based on packet technologies and is fundamentally different than the dedicated circuit approach used for the A2 interface.

Both the A3 and A7 interfaces play an important role in Inter-BSC Soft Handoff by providing a means for direct BSC-to-BSC communication. The A3 interface connects two BSCs, enabling an SDU at the source BSCs to communicate directly with a target BSC's radio traffic channel element, which is typically located at the BTS. This functionality allows a soft handoff to occur between the source BSC and the target BSC because the CDMA frame selection and distribution are done at a common SDU within the source BSC. The A3 interface is used for setting up the traffic connection between two BSCs during a direct Inter-BSC Soft Handoff, providing both signaling and user traffic capabilities. The function of the A3 signaling interface is to set up and subsequently release A3 user traffic connections, which may consists of user traffic channels over ATM virtual circuits (see Section 1.5.2, "ATM as Transport Layer," on page 14). For example, an A3 Connect signaling message sent from the target BSC to the source BSC will trigger an A3 traffic interface connection to be established from the SDU at the source BSC to the radio channel element at the target BSC.

The A7 interface is used to exchange signaling information between two BSCs. This interface is used to exchange handoff messages during a direct BSC-to-BSC soft handoff.

An Inter-BSC Soft Handoff Addition is said to occur if the SDU at the source BSC adds a cell belonging to a different BSC to the mobile's active pilot list. An Inter-BSC Soft Handoff Drop is said to occur if the SDU removes a cell belonging to a different BSC from the mobile's active list.

This section describes the A3, A7, and A1 (denoted as A-Interface in this book) messaging and call flow for direct BSC-to-BSC soft handoffs, including both direct Inter-BSC Soft Handoff Addition and Soft Handoff Drop procedures.

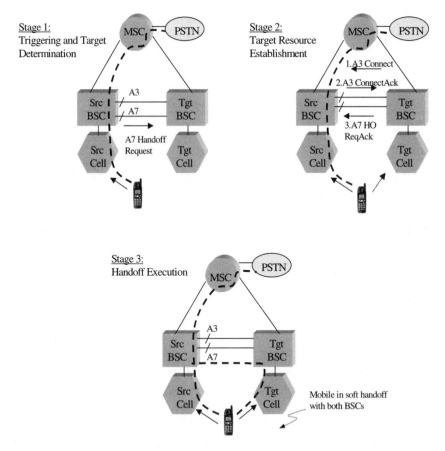

Figure 7-27   Direct BSC-to-BSC Soft and Softer Handoff Addition overview

7.4.1   Overview of a Direct BSC-to-BSC Soft Handoff

Figure 7-27 shows an overview of the stages involved in a direct BSC-to-BSC Soft Hand-off Addition. During the "Triggering and Target Determination Phase," the source BSC determines that a cell belonging to another BSC is to be added to the mobile's soft handoff active list. In this example, the two BSCs have a direct Inter-BSC connection. The Triggering Phase is vendor implementation-specific, but typically uses an IS-95 PSMM sent from the mobile that supplies a list of strong pilot signals. Upon detecting that a soft handoff should occur, the source BSC sends an A7-Handoff Request message to the target BSC to request that resources be established for the soft handoff.

During the "Resource Establishment" phase, the target BSC allocates a user traffic channel connection for the new cell to be added to the mobile's active pilot list. The resources are established using the A3-Connect and A3-Connect Ack messages. Once the A3 connection has been established, forward and reverse traffic channel frames are exchanged between the SDU at the source BSC and the traffic channel element at the target BSC's BTS, using the A3-CEData Forward and A3-CEData Reverse messages. These messages encapsulate traffic channel frames. After resources on the A3 interface have been successfully allocated, the target BSC sends an A7-Handoff Request Ack message to the source BSC.

The "Handoff Execution" phase starts with the source BSC, directing the mobile station to add the new target cell to the soft handoff active list. The source BSC does this by sending an IS-95 Extended Handoff Direction message to the mobile station. The mobile acknowledges this message by sending an IS-95 Handoff Completion message to the target BSC. The target BSC may then send an A-Interface Handoff Performed message to the MSC if the initial "anchor" or "designated" cell ID has been dropped (see Section 7.2.3.1, "Handoff Performed," on page 418, regarding Handoff Performed message).

After the Handoff Execution stage, the mobile is in an Inter-BSC Soft Handoff state and is making use of the A3 interface to communicate with cells from both the source and target BSCs. The main difference between the direct BSC-to-BSC Soft Handoff execution, and the Inter-BSC Hard Handoff execution is the establishment of the A3 user traffic that connects the source and target BSCs. This connection allows simultaneous communication between the source BSC's SDU and the target cell's traffic channel.

7.4.2   Direct BSC–BSC Soft Handoff Add Call Flow

Figure 7-28 shows the call flow for a direct BSC-to-BSC Soft Handoff Addition. The handoff is triggered when the source BSC determines that a cell belonging to a different BSC is to be added to the mobile's active list. The source BSC then notifies the target BSC by sending it an A7-Handoff Request message. Upon receiving the A7-Handoff Request message, the target BSC proceeds to set up the A3 connection. Once the SDU at the source BSC grants the connection, it begins verifying the forward link to the mobile by sending null traffic frames over the A3 connection. The source BSC then executes the handoff by sending the IS-95 Extended Handoff Direction message to the mobile station directing the soft handoff addition. The mobile acknowledges the handoff addition with an IS-95 Handoff Completion message and begins communicating with the newly added cell. At this point, the mobile has successfully performed the soft handoff addition.

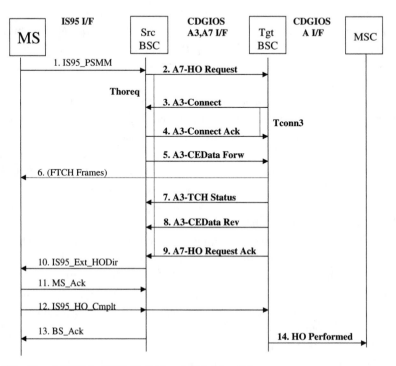

Figure 7-28   Direct BSC-to-BSC Soft Handoff Add call flow

1. IS95_PSMM (IS-95):

   The mobile sends an IS-95 PSMM to the BSC to request for a soft handoff addition.

2. A7-HO Request (A7-Interface):

   The source BSC requests a soft handoff addition of either one or more cells to the mobile's Active Set by sending an A7-Handoff Request to the target BSC. The source BSC starts timer Thoreq. The triggering mechanism is typically mobile-assisted through the use of an IS-95 PSMM message that provides the pilot signal strength of potential candidate cells to be added.

3. A3-Connect (A3-Interface):

   The target BSC, upon receipt of the A7-Handoff Request message, requests an A3 user traffic channel connection from the source BSC by sending an A3-Connect message. The target BSC then starts timer Tconn3 to wait for an A3-Connect Ack message from the source BSC.

If the A7-HO Request includes more than one cell in its request for soft handoff addition, the A3-Connect message may contain information regarding the multiple requested cells in its A3 Connect Information IE. The target BSC may also send a single A3-Connect message with multiple instances of the A3-Connect Information IE to create multiple A3 connections for the call. The target BSC also has the option of sending multiple A3-Connect messages, each containing information for one A3 connection to be set up. In this example call flow, only a single cell with a single A3 connection is set up.

4. A3-Connect Ack (A3-Interface):

The source BSC sends an A3-Connect Ack message to the target BSC to indicate the successful allocation of the user traffic channel on the A3 connection. The A3-Connect Ack may also be sent by the source BSC to acknowledge the addition of new cells to an existing A3 connection. The target BSC stops timer Tconn3 upon receipt of this message.

If Tconn3 expires before an A3-Connect Ack message is received, the target BSC will include these cells in the list of "uncommitted" cells in the A7-Handoff Request Ack.

5. A3-CEData Forw (A3-Interface):

The source BSC begins to transmit forward traffic channel frames to the target BSC's radio traffic channel. The packetized information is eventually sent to the mobile station on the IS-95 forward traffic channel.

6. (FTCH Frames) (IS-95):

The target radio channel sends out the forward traffic frames to the mobile station.

7. A3-TCH Status (A3-Interface):

The target BSC may send an A3-TCH Status message to the source BSC, indicating that the forward link has been established.

8. A3-CEData Rev (A3-Interface):

The target BSC begins transmitting the reverse traffic frames to the source BSC to synchronize the A3 traffic connection.

9. A7-HO Request Ack (A7-Interface):

Once the resources have been successfully established at the target cells, the target BSC sends an A7-Handoff Request Ack message to the source BSC to complete the handoff request. The source BSC then stops timer Thoreq.

If Thoreq expires before the receipt of an A7-Handoff Request Ack from the target BSC, the source BSC may resend the A7-Handoff Request message.

10. IS95_Ext_HODir (IS-95):

The source BSC directs the mobile to execute the soft handoff addition by sending an IS-95 Extended Handoff Direction message that includes information regarding the new cell's pilot.

11. MS_Ack (IS-95):

The mobile responds with an MS Ack Order.

12. IS95_HO_Cmplt (IS-95):

Upon successful soft handoff addition, the mobile sends an IS-95 Handoff Completion message.

13. BS_Ack (IS-95):

The BTS acknowledges the IS-95 Handoff Completion message with a BS Ack Order message. The mobile now is in soft handoff with both the source and target BSC's cells.

14. HO Performed (A-Interface):

If the "anchor" or "designated" cell ID has changed, the target BSC will send a Handoff Performed message to the controlling MSC so that it can update its reference cell ID information for the call.

7.4.3 Direct BSC–BSC Soft Handoff Add Messages

This section describes the A3 and A7 interface messages used in the Inter-BSC Soft Handoff Addition process. Unlike BSAP messages sent across the A1 interface, all A3 and A7 message parameters include the Information Element Identifier and the length of the IE. Recall that DTAP messages sent over the A1 interface omit the identifier if the information element is mandatory in the message structure (see Section 1.6.4, "BSAP Parameter Information Element (IE)," on page 19). The first octet in A3 and A7 messages is the Message Type II parameter, which is used to indicate the type of message. For example, a Message Type II value of 01H is used to identify an A3-Connect message.

Because the protocol used for the A3 and A7 interfaces is not necessarily SS7, SCCP connection-oriented features cannot be assumed to be available. The *Destination Local Reference* (DLR) and *Source Local Reference* (SLR) parameters, which are normally used by the SCCP layer to reference a specific call, are replaced by a Call Connection Reference IE. On the transport layer, ATM virtual circuit connections over AAL5 protocol are used.

7.4.3.1   A7-Handoff Request

The A7-Handoff Request message is sent from the source BSC to the target BSC to request soft and softer handoff resources (Table 7-14). Several of the parameters contained in this message are identical to those included in the A1 Handoff Request message. Therefore, only message parameters not previously described are discussed here. For a description of Cell Identifier List IE, Downlink Radio Environment IE, CDMA Serving One-Way Delay IE, and Mobile Identity (IMSI, ESN) IE, please refer to Section 7.3.5.2, "Handoff Request," on page 437.

The first unique parameter contained in the A7-Handoff Request message is the Call Connection Reference IE. This parameter specifies a unique connection reference that is used for the duration of the call.

The IS-95 Channel Identity IE is used for specifying the current channel of the mobile station being used at the source BSC. This parameter contains information needed by the target BSC, such as the current frame offset and CDMA frequency, to perform a soft handoff addition.

The Band Class IE specifies the CDMA band class of the call, such as an 800-MHz Cellular or a 1900-MHz PCS.

The information contained in the Service Configuration Record IE is used by the target BSC to format the IS-95 traffic channel frames, allowing it to communicate with the mobile station. The format of this record is as specified in IS-95.

The Privacy Information IE is similar to the voice privacy parameters contained in the Encryption Information IE described in Section 7.3.5.2, "Handoff Request," on page 437.

The optional A3 Signaling Address IE is used for identifying the entity that contains the SDU instance used for the call. If an A3 connection already exists, the target BSC uses the existing connection. If this element is not included, the target BSC uses the A7 signaling entity address for all A3 signaling messages related to the call.

The Correlation ID IE is used for correlating request and response messages. This parameter is similar to the Tag IE used in several A1 interface messages.

The optional SDU ID IE may be used by the target BSC to reference an SDU instance associated with the source BSC's SDU.

• Direction: Source BSC → Target BSC

Table 7-14   A7-Handoff Request (CDGIOS 6.1.12.1)

BitMap	Param IE	#Oct	Range	Type	IOS Ref
1000 0000 (80H)	Msg Type II	1	A7-Handoff Request Msg	M	6.2.2.5
0011 1111 (3FH) LLLL LLLL mmmm mmmm mmmm mmmm gggg gggg gggg gggg cccc cccc cccc cccc cccc cccc cccc cccc	Call Connection Reference	10	L = 08H m = market ID g = generating entity ID c = call connection ref value	O,R	6.2.2.98
0001 1010 (1AH) …….	Cell Identifier List (Target)	Variable	Same as the element in Table 7-4, Handoff Required	O,R	6.2.2.21

Table 7-14   A7-Handoff Request (CDGIOS 6.1.12.1) (Continued)

BitMap	Param IE	#Oct	Range	Type	IOS Ref
0010 0010 (22H) LLLL LLLL Hnnn ffff wwww wwww pppp pppp pPFr raaa aaaa aaaa	IS95 Channel Identity (current channel)	Variable	L = length, r = 0—reserved f = frame offset F = frequency included = 1 a = ARFCN -CDMA ch # the following are not used : H = hard handoff = 0 (soft) n = number of chans to add w = walsh code chan index p = Pilot PN code P = power comb bit indicator = 0	O,R	6.2.2.10
0101 1101 (5DH) LLLL LLLL 000b bbbb	Band Class	3	L = 01H, b = band class 00001—PCS band	O,R	6.2.2.106
0010 1001 (29H)	Downlink Radio Environment	Variable	Same as the element in Table 7-4, Handoff Required	O,R	6.2.2.25
0000 1100 (0CH)	CDMA Serving One Way Delay	Variable	Same as the element in Table 7-4, Handoff Required	O,R	6.2.2.79
0110 0001 (61H) LLLL LLLL ssss ssss	Service Config Record	Variable	L = length s = service config record	O,R	6.2.2.109
0001 1010 (1AH) LLLL LLLL riii iisa llll llll kkkk kkkk kkkk kkkk kkkk kkkk	Privacy Information	Variable	L = length, r = 0—reserved i = 00100—private longcode 00001—public longcode s = 1,0—status a = 1,0—algo avail l = key length k = privacy mask	O,R	6.2.2.143

Table 7-14 A7-Handoff Request (CDGIOS 6.1.12.1) (Continued)

BitMap	Param IE	#Oct	Range	Type	IOS Ref
0100 1001 (49H) LLLL LLLL tttt tttt pppp pppp pppp pppp aaaa aaaa aaaa aaaa aaaa aaaa aaaa aaaa	A3 Signaling Address	9	L = 07H—length t = address type = 01H—IPv4 p = TCP port a = A3 address	O,C	6.2.2.90
0001 0011 (13H) LLLL LLLL cccc cccc cccc cccc cccc cccc cccc cccc	Correlation ID	6	L = 04H—length c = correlation value	O,C	6.2.2.108
0100 1100 (4CH) LLLL LLLL ssss ssss	SDU ID	Variable	L = length s = SDU id	O,C	6.2.2.91
0000 1101 (0DH)	Mobile Identity (IMSI)	8–10	Same as the element in Table 3-2, CM Service Request message	O,R	6.2.2.16
0000 1101 (0DH)	Mobile Identity (ESN)	7	Same as the element in Table 3-2, CM Service Request message	O,R	6.2.2.16

7.4.3.2   A7-Handoff Request Ack

After allocating resources, this A7 message is sent from the target BSC to the source BSC in response to the previously received A7-Handoff Request (Table 7-15).

The Call Connection Reference IE specifies a unique connection reference value that is used to identify the connection for the duration of the call.

The required Cell Identifier List (committed) IE contains a list of cells allocated for the soft/softer handoff. If no cells are allocated, the length of this parameter is set to zero.

If included in the A7-Handoff Request message received from the source BSC, the Correlation ID IE is included in this message to assist in identifying which A7-Handoff Request message is being acknowledged.

The Neighbor List IE is a list of the committed target cell's neighbor list members. This parameter is used by the source BSC to update the mobile station's neighbor list.

The Cell Identifier List (uncommitted) IE is a list of cells that the target BSC was unable to allocate for the soft/softer handoff. This IE is mandatory if one of the cells that were requested by the source BSC has not been committed.

The Cause List IE contains a list of cause values specifying why each "uncommitted" cell was not allocated.

The A7 Control IE is used for controlling the A7 connection between the two BSCs. Currently, only the last bit (Send Source Transfer Report) of this IE is used. If the A7 Control IE is included in this message, the Send Source Transfer Report bit is always set to 1. Including this IE indicates to the source BSC that an A7 Source Transfer Performed message is to be sent in the event that a source transfer procedure is executed (see details in CDGIOSv3.0 [1]).

• Direction: Source BSC ← Target BSC

Table 7-15   A7-Handoff Request Ack (CDGIOS 6.1.12.2)

BitMap	Param IE	#Oct	Range	Type	IOS Ref
1000 0001 (81H)	Msg Type II	1	A7-Handoff Request Ack Msg	M	6.2.2.5
0011 1111 (3FH)	Call Connection Reference	10	Same as the element in Table 7-14, A7-Handoff Request	O,R	6.2.2.98
0001 1010 (1AH)	Cell Identifier List (Committed)	Variable	Same as the element in Table 7-4, Handoff Required	O,R	6.2.2.21
0001 0011 (13H)	Correlation ID	6	Same as the element in Table 7-14, A7-Handoff Request	O,C	6.2.2.108

Table 7-15   A7-Handoff Request Ack (CDGIOS 6.1.12.2) (Continued)

BitMap	Param IE	#Oct	Range	Type	IOS Ref
0100 1000 (48H) LLLL LLLL nnnn nnnn {(1st neighbor) pppp pppp pddd dddd Cell Identifier} {(2nd neighbor) ....}	Neighbor List	Variable	L = length, n = # of neighbors p = pilot PN d = least sig 7 bits of cell discrim 7—MSCID and CellID 8—MCC,MNC,LAC & cellID Cell Identifier is the same element as described in Table 7-4, Handoff Required.	O,C	6.2.2.83
0001 1010 (1AH) ……..	Cell Identifier List (Uncommitted)	Variable	Same as the element in Table 7-4, Handoff Required	O,C	6.2.2.21
0001 1001 (19H) LLLL LLLL {cccc cccc} {(2nd cause val)} …	Cause List	Variable	L = length, c = cause value 07H—OAM intervention 11H—servopt unavail 20H—equipment failure 21H—no radio resource avail 40H—ciphering algo not supp 41H—private long code unavail 42H—request mux option unavail 43H—privacy config unavail	O,C	6.2.2.142
0001 1111 (1FH) LLLL LLLL 0000 000s	A7 Control	3	L = 01H—length s = send source transfer report	O,C	6.2.2.97

7.4.3.3   A3-Connect

This message is used by the target BSC for setting up an A3 user traffic connection with the source BSC (Table 7-16).

The Call Connection Reference IE specifies a unique connection reference value that is used to identify the connection for the duration of the call.

The Correlation ID IE is used for correlating the A3-Connnect Ack response to this message. If this parameter is included, the source BSC echoes the value in the corresponding A3-Connect Ack message.

The SDU ID IE is used to reference the SDU instance at the source BSC associated with the soft/softer handoff. If this IE was included in the A7-Handoff Request message, it is also included in this message.

The A3 Connect Information IE contains a list of target cell information that is to be added to either a new or existing A3 connection and includes cell information such as pilot PN and code channel. Also included is the Traffic Circuit ID, which is simply an identifier for the A3 user traffic connection. The Extended Handoff Direction field specifies the handoff parameters for each target cell that is present or to be added to this A3 connection. Note that more than one A3 Connect Information IE instance can be included for an A3-Connect message.

- Direction: Source SDU ← Target channel element

Table 7-16   A3-Connect (CDGIOS 6.1.9.1)

BitMap	Param IE	#Oct	Range	Type	IOS Ref
0000 0001 (01H)	Msg Type II	1	A3-Connect Msg	M	6.2.2.5
0011 1111 (3FH) …….	Call Connection Reference	10	Same as the element in Table 7-14, A7-Handoff Request	O,R	6.2.2.98
0001 0011 (13H) ……..	Correlation ID	6	Same as the element in Table 7-14, A7-Handoff Request	O,C	6.2.2.108

Table 7-16   A3-Connect (CDGIOS 6.1.9.1) (Continued)

BitMap	Param IE	#Oct	Range	Type	IOS Ref
0100 1100 (4CH)	SDU ID	Var-iable	Same as the element in Table 7-14, A7-Handoff Request	O,C	6.2.2.91
0001 1011 (1BH) LLLL LLLL 0000 000I llll llll (Cell Info) [Cell Identifier 0000 0CPp pppp pppp hhhh hhhh] llll llll (05H)(TID) [llll llll (02H) tttt tttt tttt tttt llll llll (01H) rrrr rrrr] llll llll (09H)(EHO) [wwww nnnn rrrr aaaa aadd dddd cccc tttt mmmm 0000 00ss ssss 00ii iiii 00pp pppp vvvv vvvv] llll llll (CE) [cccc cccc cccc cccc ....]	A3 Connect Information	Var-iable	L = length I = new A3 indicator (1—new) l = length of Cell Info Record *Cell Info Record (Cell Info)*: {Cell Identifier same as element in Table 7-4 C = new cell indicator P = pwr comb indicator p = Pilot PN h = CDMA code channel } *Traffic Circuit Identity (TID)*: {t = traffic circuit ID r = traffic connection ID (AAL2 virtual circuit ID) } *Ext HO Dir params (EHO)*: {w = srch winA, n = srch winN r = srch winR a = Tadd, d = Tdrop, c = Tcomp t = Ttdrop, m = neigh max age s = IS-95B soft slope i = IS-95B add intercept p = IS-95B drop intercept v = target BSC P_REV} Channel Element ID (CE): {c = channel elem ID}	O,R	6.2.2.144

7.4.3.4   A3-Connect Ack

This message is sent by the source BSC to the target BSC and contains information about a new or existing A3 connection (Table 7-17).

The Call Connection Reference IE specifies a unique connection reference value that is used to identify the connection for the duration of the call.

The Correlation ID IE is used for correlating this response to the A3-Connect message and is to be included if the target BSC sends this IE in the A3-Connect message.

The A3 Connect Ack Information IE is the response to the A3 Connect Information IE received in the A3-Connect message. The soft handoff leg number is set by the source BSC and is referenced when the target cell sends an A3-CEData Reverse message to the source BSC's SDU. The send A3-TCH Status bit is used to indicate that a target cell should notify the source SDU when the target traffic channel has been transmitting to the mobile. The PMC (Packet Mode Channel) Cause field contains the reason for a failure to set up the A3 connection in the corresponding instance of the A3 Connect Information IE.

- Direction: Source SDU → Target channel element

Table 7-17   A3-Connect Ack (CDGIOS 6.1.9.2)

BitMap	Param IE	#Oct	Range	Type	IOS Ref
0000 0010 (02H)	Msg Type II	1	A3-Connect Ack Msg	M	6.2.2.5
0011 1111 (3FH) …….	Call Connection Reference	10	Same as the element in Table 7-14, A7-Handoff Request	O,R	6.2.2.98
0001 0011 (13H) ……..	Correlation ID	6	Same as the element in Table 7-14, A7-Handoff Request	O,C	6.2.2.108
0001 1100 (1CH) LLLL LLLL 00ss ssPT llll llll (05H)(TID) [llll llll (02H) tttt tttt tttt tttt llll llll (01H) rrrr rrrr] llll llll (CE) [cccc cccc cccc cccc …….] pppp pppp	A3 Connect Ack Information	Variable	L = length, l = length s = soft handoff leg# P = PMC cause present T = send A3-TCH status Traffic Circuit Identity (TID): {t = traffic circuit ID r = traffic connection ID (AAL2 virtual circuit ID)} Channel Element ID (CE): {c = channel elem ID} p = PMC cause value: 02H—already connected 03H—illegal A3 Connect 0AH—no resource avail	O,R	6.2.2.145

7.4.3.5   A3-CEData Forward

This A3 message is used for encapsulating the forward traffic channel frames from the source BSC's SDU to the target cell's channel element and may be sent every 20 ms, as specified in IS-95 (Table 7-18) [5,6].

The Forward Layer 3 Data IE includes the IS-95 forward traffic channel frames and power control information being sent from the source SDU to the target radio channel element.

The Message CRC is computed using the Message Type II IE and the Forward Layer 3 Data.

• Direction: Source SDU → Target channel element

Table 7-18   A3-CEData Forward (CDGIOS 6.1.9.7)

BitMap	Param IE	#Oct	Range	Type	IOS Ref
0000 0111 (07H)	Msg Type II	1	A3-CEData Forward Msg	M	6.2.2.5
0000 ssss gggg gggg eeee eeee rrrr ffff 0000 pppp cccc cccc cccc cccc …..	Forward Layer 3 Data	Var- iable	s = sequence number g = forw TCH gain e = rev TCH E_w/N_t r = rate set indicator f = forw TCH rate p = pwr ctrl subchan count c = forw TCH frames	M	6.2.2.120
cccc cccc cccc cccc	Message CRC	2		M	6.2.2.134

7.4.3.6   A3-CEData Reverse

This A3 message is used for encapsulating the reverse traffic channel frames from the target cell's channel element to the source BSC's SDU and may be sent every 20 ms as specified in IS-95 (Table 7-19) [5,6].

The Reverse Layer 3 Data IE contains IS-95 reverse traffic channel frames and control information sent from the target radio channel element to the source SDU. The soft handoff leg number contained in this message corresponds to the soft handoff leg number specified for this cell in the A3-Connect Ack.

The Message CRC is computed over the Message Type II IE and the Reverse Layer 3 Data.

• Direction: Source SDU ← Target channel element

Table 7-19   A3-CEData Reverse (CDGIOS 6.1.9.8)

BitMap	Param IE	#Oct	Range	Type	IOS Ref
0000 1000 (08H)	Msg Type II	1	A3-CEData Reverse Msg	M	6.2.2.5
llll ssss qqqq qqqq ggee eeee rrrr tttt 0000 000E cccc cccc cccc cccc	Reverse Layer 3 Data	Var-iable	l = soft handoff leg # s = sequence number q = rev TCH quality g = scaling e = pkt arrival time error r = rate set indicator t = rev TCH rate E = EIB c = rev TCH frames	M	6.2.2.121
cccc cccc cccc cccc	Message CRC	2		M	6.2.2.134

7.4.3.7   A3-Traffic Channel Status

The target BSC sends this message to inform the source SDU that the target traffic channel element (associated with a target cell) has started transmitting to the mobile (Table 7-20).

The Call Connection Reference IE specifies a unique connection reference value that is used to identify the connection for the duration of the call. The Cell Identifier List IE contains a list of cells to which the channel element status information refers.

The Channel Element Status IE provides the status of the channel elements at the target cell.

The SDU ID IE is used to reference the SDU instance at the source BSC associated with the soft/softer handoff. If this IE was included in the A7-Handoff Request message, it is also included in this message.

• Direction: Source SDU ← Target channel element

Table 7-20   A3-Traffic Channel Status (CDGIOS 6.1.9.15)

BitMap	Param IE	#Oct	Range	Type	IOS Ref
0000 1101 (0DH)	Msg Type II	1	A3-TCH channel status Msg	M	6.2.2.5
0011 1111 (3FH)	Call Connection Reference	10	Same as the element in Table 7-14, A7-Handoff Request	O,R	6.2.2.98
0001 1010 (1AH)	Cell Identifier List	Variable	Same as the element in Table 7-4, Handoff Required	O,R	6.2.2.21
0001 1000 (18H) LLLL LLLL 0000 000T	Channel Element Status	3	L = 01H—length T = transmitter on/off (1—on, 0—off)	O,R	6.2.2.141
0100 1100 (4CH)	SDU ID	Variable	Same as the element in Table 7-14, A7-Handoff Request	O,C	6.2.2.91

7.4.4   Direct BSC–BSC Soft Handoff Drop Call Flow

Figure 7-29 shows the call flow for removing one or more cells previously involved in a direct BSC-to-BSC soft or softer handoff. The cell removal is triggered when the source BSC determines that a cell belonging to another BSC is to be dropped from the mobile station's Active Set. The triggering is commonly based on mobile-assisted power measurement reports, but may also be caused by a BSC error or OA&M action. Once triggered, the controlling SDU at the source BSC sends an IS-95 Extended Handoff Direction message to the mobile, requesting that the pilot be dropped from its active list. The mobile acknowledges the request by sending an IS-95 Handoff Completion message, then stops communicating with the target cell. Next, the source BSC notifies the target BSC of the handoff drop request through an A7-Drop Target message. The target BSC then proceeds to tear down the associated A3 connection. The different stages of the call flow are as follows:

1. IS95_PSMM (IS-95):

   The mobile sends an IS-95 PSMM to the BSC to request for a soft handoff drop.

2. A3-CEData Forw (IS95_Ext_HODir-Drop) (A3-Interface):

   The source BSC requests a soft handoff drop of either one or multiple cells, due to a weakening in the target pilot's signal received at the mobile or action taken at the BSC. This handoff directive is also sent to the target BSC because it has an existing active pilot in the mobile's active pilot list. The IS-95 Extended Handoff Direction message is encapsulated in an A3-CEData Forward message that is sent across the A3 traffic connection.

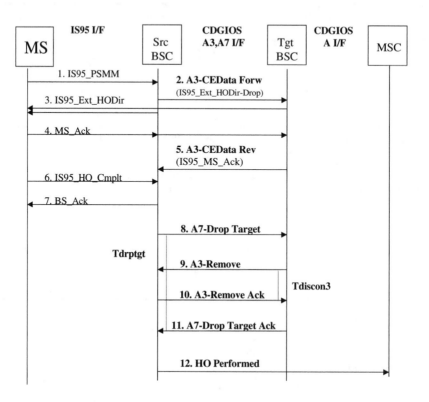

Figure 7-29   Direct BSC-to-BSC Soft Handoff Drop call flow

3. IS95_Ext_HODir (IS-95):

Both the target BSC and source BSC transmit the IS-95 Extended Handoff Direction.

4. MS_Ack (IS-95):

The mobile responds to the IS-95 Extended Handoff Direction message with an IS-95 MS Ack Order message.

5. A3-CEData Rev (IS95_MS_Ack) (A3-Interface):

The target channel element transfers the MS Ack Order reverse traffic frames to the source SDU.

6. IS95_HO_Cmplt (IS-95):

As soon as the target cell has been dropped from the mobile's active list, the mobile sends an IS-95 Handoff Completion message to the base stations. At this point, the target BSC no longer receives reverse traffic channel frames from the dropped cell.

7. BS_Ack (IS-95):

The source BSC acknowledges the IS-95 Handoff Completion message with an IS-95 BS Ack Order.

8. A7-Drop Target (A7-Interface):

The source BSC instructs the target BSC to drop the target cell's connection on the A3 interface by sending an A7-Drop Target message. The source BSC then starts timer Tdrptgt.

The target BSC may also remove the connection if it determines that it cannot support a soft handoff connection for the call. The target BSC removes the connection by sending the source BSC an A7-Target Removal Request message.

9. A3-Remove (A3-Interface):

The target BSC deallocates the resources associated with the specified cell or cells by sending an A3-Remove message to the source BSC's SDU. The target BSC starts timer Tdiscon3.

10. A3-Remove Ack (A3-Interface):

The source BSC acknowledges the resource deallocation by sending an A3-Remove Ack message. Upon receipt of this message, the target BSC stops timer Tdiscon3.

If Tdiscon3 expires before an A3-Remove Ack message is received, the target BSC may resend the A3-Remove message. If the received Call Connection Reference cannot be associated with any existing A3 traffic connection, the source BSC sends an A3-Remove Ack message with the appropriated cause value.

11. A7-Drop Target Ack (A7-Interface):

The target BSC acknowledges the A7-Drop Target request received from the source BSC by sending an A7-Drop Target Ack message. The source BSC stops timer Tdrptgt.

If Tdrptgt expires before an A7-Drop Target Ack is received, the source BSC may resend the A7-Drop message.

12. HO Performed (A-Interface):

The source BSC may send an A1-Interface Handoff Performed message to the connecting MSC if there is a change in the "reference" or "designated" cell ID.

7.4.5   Direct BSC-BSC Soft Handoff Drop Messages

The following section describes the A3 and A7 interface messages that are used in the Inter-BSC Soft Handoff Drop procedure.

7.4.5.1   A7-Drop Target

This message is sent from the source BSC to the target BSC to request a soft handoff drop of an active cell, including the deallocation of A3 connection resources (Table 7-21).

The Call Connection Reference IE and Cell Identifier List IE uniquely identify the cell or cells to be dropped.

The optional Correlation ID IE is used for correlating this message to a response. The target BSC echoes this value in the corresponding A7-Drop Target Ack message.

• Direction: Source BSC → Target BSC

Table 7-21   A7-Drop Target (CDGIOS 6.1.12.3)

BitMap	Param IE	#Oct	Range	Type	IOS Ref
1000 0010 (82H)	Msg Type II	1	A7-Drop Target Msg	M	6.2.2.5
0011 1111 (3FH)	Call Connection Reference	10	Same as the element in Table 7-14, A7-Handoff Request	O,R	6.2.2.98
0001 1010 (1AH)	Cell Identifier List	Variable	Same as the element in Table 7-4, Handoff Required	O,R	6.2.2.21
0001 0011 (13H)	Correlation ID	6	Same as the element in Table 7-14, A7-Handoff Request	O,C	6.2.2.108

7.4.5.2   A7-Drop Target Ack

This message is sent from the target BSC to the source BSC to acknowledge the request for a soft handoff drop of an active cell after deallocating A3 connection resources (Table 7-22).

The Call Connection Reference IE uniquely identifies the call connection.

The optional Correlation ID IE is used for correlating this response to the previously received A7-Drop Target message. The target BSC echoes the value previously received from the source BSC in the A7-Drop Target Ack message.

• Direction: Source BSC ← Target BSC

Table 7-22   A7-Drop Target Ack (CDGIOS 6.1.12.4)

BitMap	Param IE	#Oct	Range	Type	IOS Ref
1000 0011 (83H)	Msg Type II	1	A7-Drop Target Ack Msg	M	6.2.2.5

Table 7-22   A7-Drop Target Ack (CDGIOS 6.1.12.4) (Continued)

BitMap	Param IE	#Oct	Range	Type	IOS Ref
0011 1111 (3FH)	Call Connection Reference	10	Same as the element in Table 7-14, A7-Handoff Request	O,R	6.2.2.98
0001 0011 (13H)	Correlation ID	6	Same as the element in Table 7-14, A7-Handoff Request	O,C	6.2.2.108

7.4.5.3   A3-Remove

This message is sent from the target traffic channel element to the source SDU to request A3 connection resources be deallocated (Table 7-23).

The Call Connection Reference IE and A3 Remove Information IE uniquely identify the cell or cells to be removed.

The optional Correlation ID IE is used for correlating this message with a subsequent A3-Remove Ack message.

The optional SDU ID IE is sent only if it was previously included in the A7-Handoff Request message.

• Direction: Source SDU ← Target channel element

Table 7-23   A3-Remove (CDGIOS 6.1.9.3)

BitMap	Param IE	#Oct	Range	Type	IOS Ref
0000 0011 (03H)	Msg Type II	1	A3-Remove Msg	M	6.2.2.5
0011 1111 (3FH)	Call Connection Reference	10	Same as the element in Table 7-14, A7-Handoff Request	O,R	6.2.2.98
0001 0011 (13H)	Correlation ID	6	Same as the element in Table 7-14, A7-Handoff Request	O,C	6.2.2.108

Table 7-23   A3-Remove (CDGIOS 6.1.9.3) (Continued)

BitMap	Param IE	#Oct	Range	Type	IOS Ref
0100 1100 (4CH)	SDU ID	Variable	Same as the element in Table 7-14, A7-Handoff Request	O,C	6.2.2.91
0001 1110 (1EH) LLLL LLLL llll llll (05H) (TID) [llll llll (02H) tttt tttt tttt tttt llll llll (01H) rrrr rrrr] nnnn nnnn {Cell Identifier 1} {Cell Identifier 2}	A3 Remove Information	Variable	L = length Traffic Circuit Identity (TID): {t = traffic circuit ID r = traffic connection ID (AAL2 virtual circuit ID)} n = # of cells to be removed Cell Identifier List: {Cell Identifier same as element in Table 7-4}	O,R	6.2.2.146

7.4.5.4   A3-Remove Ack

This message is sent from the source SDU to the target traffic channel element after the deallocation of A3 connection resources (Table 7-24).

The Call Connection Reference IE uniquely identifies the call connection.

The optional Correlation ID IE is used for correlating this response to the corresponding A3-Remove message.

• Direction: Source SDU → Target channel element

Table 7-24   A3-Remove Ack (CDGIOS 6.1.9.4)

BitMap	Param IE	#Oct	Range	Type	IOS Ref
0000 0011 (04H)	Msg Type II	1	A3-Remove Ack Msg	M	6.2.2.5
0011 1111 (3FH)	Call Connection Reference	10	Same as the element in Table 7-14, A7-Handoff Request	O,R	6.2.2.98
0001 0011 (13H)	Correlation ID	6	Same as the element in Table 7-14, A7-Handoff Request	O,C	6.2.2.108

References

1. CDG-IOS version 3.1.1, *CDMA Development Group MSC to BS Interface Inter-Operability Specification*. June 1999.
2. CDG-IOS version 2.0, *CDMA Development Group MSC to BS Interface Inter-Operability Specification*. September 1998.
3. Telecommunications Industry Association, TIA/EIA/IS-634-A, *MSC–BS Interface (A-Interface) for Public 800 MHz*. July 1998.
4. Telecommunications Industry Association , TIA/EIA/TSB-80, *MSC–BS Interface (A-Interface) for Public 800 MHz*. October 1996.
5. Telecommunications Industry Association, TIA/EIA/IS-95-A, *Mobile Station–Base Station Compatibility Standard for Dual-Mode Wideband Spread Spectrum Cellular Systems*. May 1995.
6. American National Standards Institute, ANSI J-STD-008, *Personal Station–Base Station Compatibility Requirements for 1.8 to 2.0 GHz Code Devision Multiple Access (CDMA) Personal Communications Systems*. August 1995.
7. American National Standards Institute, ANSI TIA/EIA/IS-41-D, *Cellular Radio–Telecommunications Intersystem Operations*. December 1997.

CHAPTER   **8**

Terrestrial Circuit Management

In an open CDMA Network, the trunks connecting the *Base Station Controller* (BSC) and *Mobile Switching Center* (MSC) need to be managed and maintained by network operators to ensure that resources are used efficiently and reliably. In many cases, the MSC and BSC are physically separated and the terrestrial connections are established using leased T1 or E1 trunks. By effectively utilizing terrestrial resources, network operators can reduce operating expenses and improve system reliability. CDGIOS specifies the procedures and messaging, known as *Terrestrial Circuit Management* (TCM), to manage terrestrial resources effectively.

In addition to TCM, Terrestrial Facilities Management also includes the management of links, Link Sets, and Route Sets. Since these functions were already discussed in Chapter 2, "Signaling System 7 Basics," on page 29, this chapter focuses on the messages and procedures used to manage the states of terrestrial circuit resources shared between a BSC and MSC. Usually the term *terrestrial resource* refers to individual 64 kbps DS0 timeslots that are dedicated for *Pulse Code Modulation* (PCM) voice or data services traffic. This chapter also includes descriptions of the procedures and messages used to manage soft handoff resources between two BSCs, which may consist of packetized data and virtual circuits. The overall goal of TCM is to ensure that no hung resources exist and that all available circuits are utilized.

8.1 Terrestrial Circuit Management Overview

The TCM functions running on both the MSC and BSC utilize three procedures to manage the states of terrestrial circuits. Together, the three procedures provide the capability to reset the states of one or more circuits or to prevent the use of individual circuits. The procedures described in this section apply only to the circuits that compose the A2-Interface; the circuits

497

that are part of the A7-Interface are discussed separately in Section 8.5, "A7-Interface Global Reset," on page 528. The three TCM procedures are:

• Block and Unblock
• Reset Circuit
• Global Reset

The overall state of an individual terrestrial circuit is categorized by its usability state and traffic state. The usability state of a circuit indicates whether the circuit has been blocked by the BSC. The BSC sends a Block message to the MSC after identifying that a circuit (or group of circuits) is out of service, indicating to the MSC that it should not request the circuit (or circuits) for future call setups. The BSC may block circuits due to equipment failure or as a result of administrative procedures. The BSC unblocks a previously blocked circuit by sending an Unblock message to the MSC. In addition to the usability state, each terrestrial circuit has associated with it a traffic state. The traffic state specifies whether the circuit is Busy with a call or if it is Idle.

It is important to note that the usability state and traffic state of an individual circuit are independent of each other. For example, a circuit may be Blocked and Busy, if the Block message was sent by the BSC for a circuit already in use. A circuit is said to be available only when it is Unblocked and Idle. Both the MSC and BSC actively maintain the states of each individual terrestrial circuit.

Since usability and traffic state mismatches sometimes occur between the MSC and BSC, CDGIOS specifies two procedures for synchronizing the states. The Reset Circuit procedure is used to reset the state of an individual circuit and the Global Reset procedure is used to reset the states of all circuits shared between the MSC and BSC. Although Reset Circuit and Global Reset messages are sent by both the MSC and BSC, Block and Unblock messages are sent only by the BSC.

Each terrestrial circuit is assigned a logical identifier known as its *Circuit Identity Code* (CIC). Both the MSC and BSC use this logical identifier to reference a particular circuit. Section 8.1.5, "Spans and Circuits Identity Assignment," on page 502 describes how CIC values are coded in A-Interface messages.

8.1.1 Block and Unblock

The usability state of a CIC can be changed by the BSC through the use of the Block or Unblock procedures. Upon determining that a CIC should no longer be used, the BSC performs a local administrative procedure to designate the CIC as blocked, then sends an A-Interface Block messages to the MSC, informing the MSC of the unavailability of the circuit. The Block message may specify an individual CIC or a group of CICs to be blocked by the MSC. After receiving the Block message, the MSC designates the CIC as blocked and prevents it from being used in future call setups by removing it from its available CIC list. The MSC acknowledges each received Block message with a Block Acknowledge message.

The BSC typically blocks CICs when it determines that a previously configured range of CICs must be taken out of service for maintenance reasons or because of a failure. The MSC may also block CICs that it determines should no longer be used. Beause the MSC has control over which CICs are allocated for calls, no messaging is required to inform the BSC of MSC-blocked CICs. In the case of MSC blocked CIC's, the MSC simply does not allocate the locally blocked CICs when sending an Assignment Request message to the BSC.

Upon determining that a previously blocked CIC should be made available for use, the BSC sends an Unblock message to the MSC, specifying the CIC (or group of CICs) to be returned to service. The MSC acknowledges each received Unblock message with an Unblock Acknowledge message. As is discussed in Section 8.3, "Reset Circuits," on page 510 and Section 8.4, "Global System Reset," on page 516, the states of a CIC (or group of CICs) can also be changed to the Unblocked and Idle state through the use of the Reset Circuit or Global Reset messages.

To prevent inconsistencies in circuit states, the TCM functions at both the BSC and MSC wait for the remote end to acknowledge TCM messages before changing the state of a circuits. For example, if the BSC sends an Unblock message for a CIC and does not receive an acknowledgment from the MSC within a specified period of time, the CIC remains Blocked.

Since Block and Unblock messages are not associated with a *Signaling Connection Control Part* (SCCP) connection, the messages are sent as connectionless *SCCP Unit Data* (SCCP-UDT) class 0 messages. CDGIOS allows the BSC to send Block and Unblock messages for each CIC or to group of multiple CICs in a single message.

The Block and Unblock procedures and messages are discussed further in Section 8.2, "Blocks and Unblocks," on page 503.

8.1.2   Reset Circuit

The MSC or BSC performs the Reset Circuit procedure when a failure affecting part of the equipment occurs or when requested by network operators through *Operations and Mainenance* (OA&M) actions. A Reset Circuit message is also sent by the MSC or BSC whenever either entity detects that one or more CIC's have been idled, due to an abnormal SCCP release.

Reset Circuit is typically triggered when an SCCP connection associated with a call is lost unexpectedly. This is known as an *abnormal SCCP release* and occurs when one node unexpectedly sends an *SCCP Released* (SCCP-RLSD) message. The receiving node responds with the *SCCP Release Complete* (SCCP-RLC) and requests the remote end to idle the associated terrestrial circuit by sending a Reset Circuit message.

The Reset Circuit message is sent by the entity at the receiving end of an abnormal SCCP release to request the remote node to idle one or more CICs. Upon receiving a Reset Circuit, the remote end responds with a Reset Circuit Acknowledge message if it is able to idle the specified CIC (or group of CICs). If the Reset Circuit is initiated by the MSC and some of the specified circuits are blocked at the BSC, the BSC responds with a Block message in addition to the Reset Circuit Acknowledge message.

8.1.3   Global Reset

The Global Reset procedure is used by the BSC and MSC to bring the remote node into a known state after a global failure occurs, during initialization, and when requested by the network operator through the use of OA&M actions. Unlike the Block and Reset Circuit messages, which are sent for an individual CIC or group of CICs, the Reset message applies to all CICs. After receiving a Reset message, the remote node releases all affected calls and all affected call references. After placing its CICs in idle mode and upon expiry of a guard timer, a Reset Acknowledge message is sent to indicate the receipt of the Reset message.

8.1.4   Terrestrial Circuit States Transition

Figure 8-1 illustrates the states and state transitions associated with CICs at the BSC and MSC. Both the MSC and BSC maintain the current state of all configured CICs and utilize A-Interface messages to notify the remote end of state changes. Reset Circuit and Global Reset messages are used by both the MSC and BSC to reset CICs after an abnormal event has occurred or during initialization. The BSC may also use Block and Unblock messages to inform the MSC of changes in CIC availability at the BSC. Only CICs in the Unblocked and Idle state are available for use.

Global Reset   The MSC or BSC may send a Reset message to the remote end to synchronize the states of the configured CICs. Upon receiving a Reset message from the BSC, the MSC releases all existing call references and idles the CICs associated with the BSC. After idling the CICs, the MSC may locally block CICs that it determines should not be used or when it is directed to block them by the BSC.

The BSC, upon receiving a Reset message from the MSC, places all CICs in the Unblocked and Idle state. The BSC may then send block messages to prevent the MSC from allocating CICs that the BSC determines are out of service. For example, prior to receiving a Reset message from the MSC, the state of a CIC at the BSC may be Blocked and Busy. After receiving a Reset message, the BSC transitions the CIC to the Unblocked and Idle state, then executes the procedure to block the CIC (if conditions still exist that require the CIC to be blocked).

Assignment Request/ Assignment Complete   Although the BSC may request that a particular CIC be used for a call attempt, the MSC is responsible for specifying the terrestrial circuit used for a call. Upon sending an Assignment Request message to the BSC, the MSC transitions the state of the requested CIC from Unblocked and Idle to Unblocked and Busy. The BSC, after setting up the radio link and seizing the terrestrial circuit specified in the Assignment Request message, transitions the CIC state at the BSC to Unblocked and Busy, then sends an Assignment Complete.

Clear Command   As discussed earlier, either the BSC or MSC may initiate call clearing. BSC-initiated call clearing begins with the BSC sending a Clear Request message, which prompts the MSC to respond with a Clear Command message. Upon sending the Clear Command message to the BSC, the MSC releases call resources, then returns the previously allocated CIC to the Unblocked and Idle state. After receiving the Clear Command message, the BSC releases associated call resources, including Idling the CIC. As shown in Figure 8-1, it is also possible for a circuit to be blocked during a call, resulting in a Blocked and Busy state. The Blocked and Busy CIC is placed in the Blocked and Idle state after call clearing has occurred.

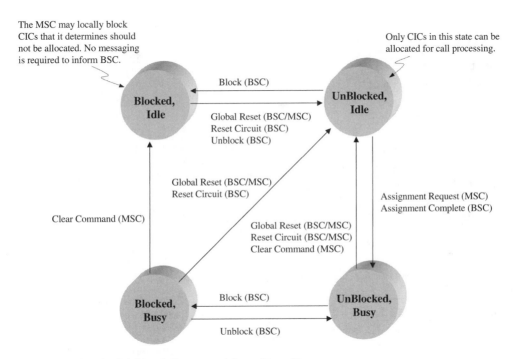

Figure 8-1   Terrestrial Circuit States and State Transitions

Reset Circuit   When the BSC or MSC performs a Reset Circuit action, the CIC (or group of CICs) is transitioned from its current state to the Unblocked and Idle state. If the CIC (or group of CICs) specified in the Reset Circuit initiated by the MSC is blocked at the BSC, the BSC responds with a Block message, and the circuit is transitioned to the Blocked and Idle state.

Block   When initiating the block procedure for a CIC, the BSC sends a Block message to the remote end and transitions the state of the circuit from Unblocked to Blocked, regardless of whether the circuit is Busy or Idle. The MSC, upon receiving the Block message, also places the CIC in the Blocked state.

Unblock   When the BSC determines that a CIC should be unblocked, it sends the MSC an Unblock message and places the CIC in the Unblocked state. The MSC, upon receiving the Unblock message, also places the circuit in the Unblock state.

A-Interface TCM messages such as Blocks, Unblocks, Reset Circuit, and Reset, are used to inform the remote end of local state change and to execute the required actions to make the remote and local states consistent. As was mentioned earlier, if A-Interface TCM messages are not acknowledged, the local end takes appropriate actions to ensure state consistency. For example, if the MSC does not acknowledge an Unblock message sent by the BSC, the CIC remains blocked at the BSC.

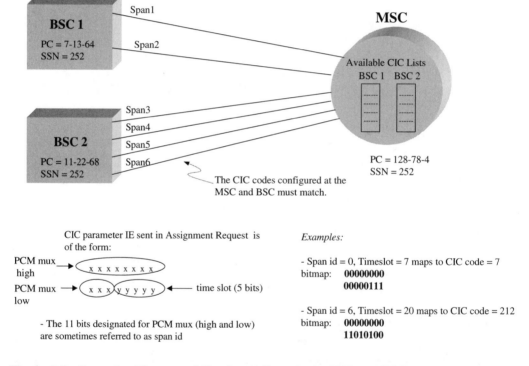

Figure 8-2   Example of Spans and Circuits configuration at BSC and MSC

8.1.5   Spans and Circuits Identity Assignment

Figure 8-2 illustrates voice trunks connecting the MSC and BSC. Recall that the A-Interface contains an A1-Interface used for signaling and an A2-Interface used to carry voice traffic between the MSC and BSC. The A2-Interface is comprised of CICs configured at both the MSC and BSC. Each CIC is associated with a particular timeslot on a trunk (sometimes referred to as *spans*) connecting the MSC and BSC. In order for the MSC and BSC to successfully coordinate the allocation of terrestrial resources for a call, logical CIC assignments at both the MSC and BSC must match. A mismatch in CIC assignments will result in a call without voice. For example, a CIC mismatch may cause the BSC to transmit PCM voice frames on a timeslot different than the MSC is expecting, and the MSC will be unable to connect the mobile subscriber to the intended land or mobile party.

A-Interface messages use a 16-bit field contained in the Circuit Identity Code or Circuit Identity Code Extension IE to identify CICs. The 16-bit CIC field contains an 11-bit field that identifies the PCM identity of the trunk (sometimes called the *Logical Span Id*) and a 5-bit field that specifies the timeslot. Figure 8-2 shows two examples of how CIC codes are computed from the logical span Id and timeslot.

To prevent invalid CIC assignments, any CICs configured at the MSC that are not configured at the BSC must be locally blocked at the MSC and removed from the MSC's available CIC list. If the MSC requests an invalid CIC from the BSC in the Assignment Request message, due to an error condition or invalid configuration, the BSC responds with an Assignment Failure message to the MSC.

8.2 Blocks and Unblocks

This section presents the call flow and messages for both the Block and Unblock procedures. Block and Unblock messages always originate from the BSC and are used to notify the MSC of changes in CIC states detected by the BSC. The MSC may also block circuits locally, however, because the MSC can prevent CICs from being used by simply removing the CICs from its available CIC list, no A-Interface messaging is required.

8.2.1 Block Call Flow

A Block message is sent from the BSC to the MSC after the BSC determines that a circuit or a group of circuits should not be used for call processing. Upon receiving the Block message, the MSC transitions the CIC state to Blocked and removes the CIC from its active CIC list. The blocked CICs remain out of service at the MSC until a Reset, Reset Circuit, or Unblock message is received from the BSC.

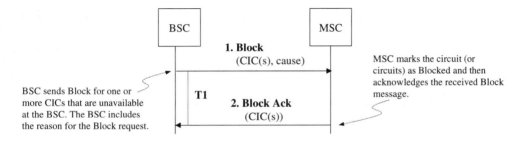

Figure 8-3   Block procedure at BSC call flow

Figure 8-3 shows the call flow for the Block procedure. The BSC initiates the blocking of one or more CICs by sending a Block message to the MSC. The Block message also contains a cause value that specifies the reason for the block request.

Upon receipt of the Block message, the MSC marks the circuit (or circuits) as blocked and acknowledges the BSC with a Block acknowledge message.

1. Block (A-Interface):

   Upon determining that a terrestrial circuit (or group of circuits) should be blocked, the BSC marks the CIC (or group of CICs) as blocked and sends a Block message to the MSC. The BSC starts timer T1 to wait for a Block Acknowledge message from the MSC.

   In addition to specifying the one or more CICs to be blocked, the Block message also contains the reason for issuing the block request. CDGIOS allowable cause values are OA&M intervention, no radio resource available, and equipment failure.

2. Block Ack (A-Interface):

   Upon receiving a Block message from the BSC, the MSC locally blocks the specified CICs and sends a Block Acknowledge message to the BSC, indicating to the BSC that the CICs have been blocked at the MSC. If the Block message received from the BSC specifies a group of circuits to be blocked and the MSC was unable to block all of the CICs, the MSC has the flexibility of specifying which circuits were successfully blocked in the Block Acknowledge message.

   CICs blocked by the MSC in response to a Block message from the BSC remain in the blocked state until the BSC sends an Unblock message or Reset Circuit message or if the MSC initiates a Global Reset.

   If a Block message is received by the MSC for a CIC that is already allocated to a call, the call is not dropped. In this case, the MSC sends a Block Acknowledge message immediately to the BSC and waits for normal call clearing before designating the CIC as blocked.

   The BSC stops timer T1 upon receipt of the Block Acknowledge message from the MSC. If T1 expires before a Block Acknowledge message is received, the BSC resends the Block message to the MSC once more and marks the circuit (or group of circuits) as blocked, regardless of whether it receives an acknowledgment from the MSC. If the MSC does not respond with a Block Acknowledge message, it is possible that a CIC state mismatch may exist and that the MSC will include the BSC blocked CIC in an Assignment Request message. If this occurs, the BSC responds to the Assignment Request with an Assignment Failure message with cause value "terrestrial resource unavailable." The BSC subsequently sends a Block message to the MSC with the cause value set to "no radio resource available."

8.2.2 Unblock Call Flow

Unblock messages are sent from the BSC to the MSC once the BSC determines that a previously blocked circuit (or a group of circuits) is available for service. Upon receiving an Unblock message, the MSC returns the specified CIC(s) to service and updates its available CIC list.

Figure 8-4 shows the call flow for the Unblock procedure. After determining that a CIC should be made available for service, the BSC sends an Unblock message to the MSC and starts timer T1.

Upon receipt of the Unblock message, the MSC marks the circuit as unblocked and sends the BSC an Unblock Acknowledge message. Detail descriptions of the individual call flow stages follow Figure 8-4.

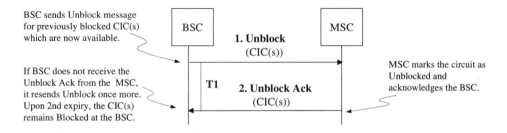

Figure 8-4 Unblock procedure at BSC call flow

1. Unblock (A-Interface):

   The BSC requests that the MSC unblocks one or more previously blocked terrestrial circuits by sending an Unblock message over the A-Interface. Upon sending the Unblock request, the BSC marks one or more CICs specified in the message as unblocked and starts timer T1 to wait for an Unblock Acknowledge.

2. Unblock Ack (A-Interface):

   Upon receipt of the Unblock message, the MSC marks the previously blocked CIC(s) as Unblocked and sends an Unblock Acknowledge message to the BSC. The Unblock Acknowledge message identifies the one or more CICs unblocked at the MSC. If a group of circuits is specified by the BSC in the Unblock message, the MSC may acknowledge individual circuits or the entire group in the Unblock Acknowledge message. This provides the MSC with the flexibility to indicate which of the requested CICs were successfully unblocked. The unblocked CIC(s) may then be allocated by the MSC for traffic services in future Assignment Request messages.

   The BSC stops timer T1 upon receipt of the Unblock Acknowledge message. If T1 expires before an Unblock Acknowledge message is received at the BSC, the BSC resends the

Unblock message a second and final time. If no acknowledgment is received for the second unblock attempt, the CIC remains blocked at the BSC.

8.2.3   Blocks and Unblocks Messages

The following sections contain descriptions of the A-Interface messages that are used in the Block and Unblock procedures.

8.2.3.1   Block

The Block message (Table 8-1) is sent by the BSC to request the MSC to block one or more terrestrial circuit or a group of terrestrial circuits. It is a BSMAP message that is sent as a connectionless *SCCP Unit Data* (SCCP-UDT) message type.

The first parameter following the message type *Information Element* (IE) is the mandatory Circuit Identity Code IE, which specifies the CIC to be blocked at the MSC.

The mandatory Cause IE contains the reason why the BSC is requesting the MSC to block the specified CIC. CDGIOS-allowable cause values are "operations and maintenance," "equipment failure," and "no radio resource available."

The optional Circuit Group IE provides a means of specifying a group of CICs to be blocked and avoids the need to send individual Block messages for each CIC. The BSC may use the Circuit Group IE in one of several ways.

The BSC may use the Circuit Group IE to specify an inclusive group of CICs to be blocked by setting the 1-bit "Inclusive" field to 1. In this case, the "Count" octet specifies the number of CICs to be blocked and is followed by the "First CIC" in the group. Upon receiving the Block message, the MSC blocks all CICs in the range [1st CIC, 1st CIC + count −1].

The second way that the BSC may use the Circuit Group IE is to specify a range of CICs, then selectively choose CICs within that range to be blocked. In this case, the 1-bit "Inclusive" field is set to zero and a Circuit Bitmap field that indicates which CICs in the group should be blocked is also included. For example, if the first two and the last four CICs of a 16-CIC group must be blocked, the Circuit Bitmap field is set to:

1111 0000

0000 0011

As with the inclusive method, the CIC group is specified using the Count and First CIC fields.

The final way that the BSC may use the Circuit Group IE to specify a range of CICs to be blocked is to set "All Circuits" field to 1. In this case, all CICs shared between the MSC and BSC are blocked.

It is possible to include multiple instances of the Circuit Group IE. However, the First CIC field in the first instance must match the mandatory Circuit Identity Code IE in the same message.

- BSAP Message Type: BSMAP
- SCCP Message Type: SCCP-Unit Data (UDT)
- Direction: BSC → MSC

Table 8-1   Block Message (CDGIOS 6.1.6.2)

BitMap	Param IE	#Oct	Range	Type	IOS Ref
0000 0000 (00H) LLLL LLLL	BSMAP header	2	Msg Discrim. = 0 (BSMAP) L = BSMAP msg length	M	6.2.2.1 6.2.2.3
0100 0000 (40H)	Msg Type	1	Block Msg	M	6.2.2.4
0000 0001 (01H) mmmm mmmm mmmt tttt	Circuit Identity Code	3	m = spanid t = timeslot	M	6.2.2.22
0000 0100 (04H) LLLL LLLL 0ccc cccc	Cause	3	L = 01H, c = cause 07H—OA&M intervention 20H—equipment failure 21H—no radio resource avail	M	6.2.2.19
0001 1001 (19H) LLLL LLLL 0000 00AI cccc cccc ffff ffff ffff ffff bbbb bbbb bbbb bbbb …… bbbb bbbB	Circuit Group	Variable	L = length A = All circuits indicator (1,0) I = Inclusive indicator (1,0) c = number of CICs included f = 1st CIC value (span,TS) b = bitmap of CICs included (1—this CIC included) B = bitmap of 1st CIC = 1	O,C	6.2.2.148

8.2.3.2   Block Acknowledge

The Block Acknowledge message is sent from the MSC to the BSC to acknowledge the blocking of a terrestrial circuit specified in a previously received Block message (Table 8-2). The Block Acknowledge message is a BSMAP message that is sent as a connectionless *SCCP Unit Data* (SCCP-UDT) message type.

The first parameter following the message type IE is the mandatory Circuit Identity Code IE, which specifies the CIC to be blocked at the MSC.

The optional Circuit Group IE provides a means of specifying a group of CICs blocked by the MSC and avoids the need to send individual Block Acknowledge messages for each CIC.

For more information about how this parameter is used please refer to the description provided for the Block message in Section 8.2.3.1, "Block," on page 506.

- BSAP Message Type: BSMAP
- SCCP Message Type: SCCP-Unit Data (UDT)
- Direction: BSC ← MSC

Table 8-2   Block Acknowledge Message (CDGIOS 6.1.6.3)

BitMap	Param IE	#Oct	Range	Type	IOS Ref
0000 0000 (00H) LLLL LLLL	BSMAP header	2	Msg Discrim. = 0 (BSMAP) L = BSMAP msg length	M	6.2.2.1 6.2.2.3
0100 0001 (41H)	Msg Type	1	Block Ack Msg	M	6.2.2.4
0000 0001 (01H)	Circuit Identity Code	3	Same as element in Table 8-1, Block message	M	6.2.2.22
0001 1001 (19H)	Circuit Group	Variable	Same as element in Table 8-1, Block message	O,C	6.2.2.148

8.2.3.3   Unblock

The Unblock message (Table 8-3) is sent from the BSC to the MSC to unblock one or more specified terrestrial circuits. This BSMAP message is sent as a connectionless SCCP-UDT message type.

The first parameter following the message type IE is the mandatory Circuit Identity Code IE, which specifies the CIC to be unblocked at the MSC.

The optional Circuit Group IE provides a means of specifying a group of CICs to be unblocked and avoids the need to send individual Unblock messages for each CIC. For more information about how this parameter is used please refer to the description provided for the Block message in Section 8.2.3.1, "Block," on page 506.

- BSAP Message Type: BSMAP
- SCCP Message Type: SCCP-Unit Data (UDT)
- Direction: BSC → MSC

Table 8-3 Unblock Message (CDGIOS 6.1.6.4)

BitMap	Param IE	#Oct	Range	Type	IOS Ref
0000 0000 (00H) LLLL LLLL	BSMAP header	2	Msg Discrim. = 0 (BSMAP) L = BSMAP msg length	M	6.2.2.1 6.2.2.3
0100 0010 (42H)	Msg Type	1	Unblock Msg	M	6.2.2.4
0000 0001 (01H)	Circuit Iden-tity Code	3	Same as element in Table 8-1, Block message	M	6.2.2.22
0001 1001 (19H)	Circuit Group	Var-iable	Same as element in Table 8-1, Block message	O,C	6.2.2.148

8.2.3.4   Unblock Acknowledge

The Unblock Acknowledge (Table 8-4) message is sent from the MSC to the BSC to acknowledge the unblocking of a terrestrial circuit specified in a previously specified Unblock message. This BSMAP message is sent as a connectionless SCCP-UDT message type.

The first parameter following the message type IE is the mandatory Circuit Identity Code IE, which specifies the CIC unblocked at the MSC.

The optional Circuit Group IE provides a means of specifying a group of CICs unblocked by the MSC and avoids the need to send individual Unblock Acknowledge messages for each CIC. For more information about how this parameter is used please refer to the description provided for the Block message in Section 8.2.3.1, "Block," on page 506.

- BSAP Message Type: BSMAP
- SCCP Message Type: SCCP-Unit Data (UDT)
- Direction: BSC ← MSC

Table 8-4 Unblock Acknowledge Message (CDGIOS 6.1.6.5)

BitMap	Param IE	#Oct	Range	Type	IOS Ref
0000 0000 (00H) LLLL LLLL	BSMAP header	2	Msg Discrim. = 0 (BSMAP) L = BSMAP msg length	M	6.2.2.1 6.2.2.3
0100 0011 (43H)	Msg Type	1	Unblock Ack Msg	M	6.2.2.4

Table 8-4   Unblock Acknowledge Message (CDGIOS 6.1.6.5) (Continued)

BitMap	Param IE	#Oct	Range	Type	IOS Ref
0000 0001 (01H)	Circuit Identity Code	3	Same as element in Table 8-1, Block message	M	6.2.2.22
0001 1001 (19H)	Circuit Group	Var-iable	Same as element in Table 8-1, Block message	O,C	6.2.2.148

8.3 Reset Circuits

The Reset Circuit procedure may be initiated by either the BSC or the MSC and is invoked when a failure affecting part of the equipment occurs or when requested by network operators through OA&M actions. The MSC or BSC sends a Reset Circuit message after either entity detects that a CIC has been idled, due to an abnormal SCCP release.

8.3.1 Reset Circuit at BSC Call Flow

Figure 8-5 illustrates the Reset Circuit message flow when the Reset Circuit action is initiated by the BSC. Upon determining that the state of one or more circuits needs to be reset, the BSC sends a Reset Circuit message to the MSC and starts timer T12. Upon receipt of the Reset Circuit message, the MSC idles the CIC(s) specified in the received message and sends the BSC a Reset Circuit Acknowledge.

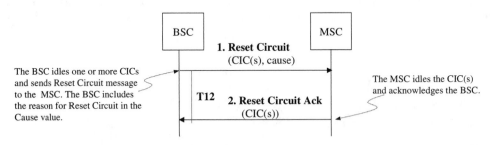

Figure 8-5   Reset Circuit at BSC call flow

1. Reset Circuit (A-Interface):

The BSC initiates a Reset Circuit action after determining that one or more circuits have been idled as a result of an abnormal SCCP release. The BSC sends a Reset Circuit message to the MSC, requesting that the circuit(s) be idled. The message includes a cause value that indicates the reason for the reset. After sending the Reset Circuit message, the BSC starts timer T12.

The MSC, upon receipt of the Reset Circuit message, clears any affected calls and idles the CIC(s).

2. Reset Circuit Ack (A-Interface):

The Reset Circuit Acknowledge message is sent from the MSC to the BSC after idling the CICs specified in the previously received Reset Circuit message. Any specified CICs that were in the blocked state prior to receiving the Reset Circuit message are transitioned to the unblocked state.

If an existing call is using a CIC specified in the Reset Circuit message received from the BSC, the call is cleared, and the CIC is returned to the Unblocked and Idle state.

The BSC stops timer T12 upon receipt of the Reset Circuit Acknowledge message from the MSC. If T12 expires before the Reset Circuit Acknowledge message is received, the BSC resends the Reset Circuit message. CDGIOS specifies that the Reset Circuit message be sent no more than three times.

8.3.2   Reset Circuit at MSC Call Flow

The MSC-initiated Reset Circuit message flow, which is very similar to the BSC-initiated scenario, is shown in Figure 8-6.

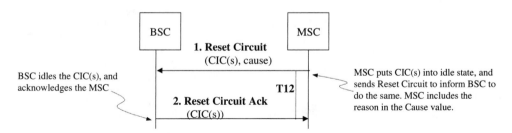

Figure 8-6   Reset Circuit at MSC call flow

8.3.3   Reset Circuit at MSC with Block Response Call Flow

The MSC may initiate a Reset Circuit for one or more CICs that are in the blocked state at the BSC. In such a scenario, the BSC responds to the Reset Circuit message received from the MSC with a Block message instead of a Reset Circuit Acknowledge. Any unblocked CICs are idled by the BSC, which then also sends a Reset Circuit Acknowledge message to the MSC. Figure 8-7 illustrates the call flow for a MSC-initiated Reset Circuit procedure when one or more of the specified CICs are blocked at the BSC.

1. Reset Circuit (A-Interface):

The MSC initiates the Reset Circuit procedure and sends a Reset Circuit message to the BSC to idle a group of circuits. The MSC starts timer T12.

2. Block (A-Interface):

The BSC determines that one or more CICs specified by the MSC in the Reset Circuit message are in the blocked state. The BSC then responds to the MSC with a Block message for the blocked CICs, indicating the reason for the blocking. The BSC starts Timer T1. The MSC stops timer T12 upon receipt of the Block message.

3. Reset Circuit Ack (A-Interface):

The BSC idles the remaining CICs specified in the Reset Circuit message, then informs the MSC of the action by sending a Reset Circuit Acknowledge message.

4. Block Ack (CICs) (A-Interface):

Upon receipt of the Block message, the MSC blocks the specified CICs and sends one or more Block Acknowledge messages to the BSC. The BSC stops timer T1 upon receipt of the Block Acknowledge message.

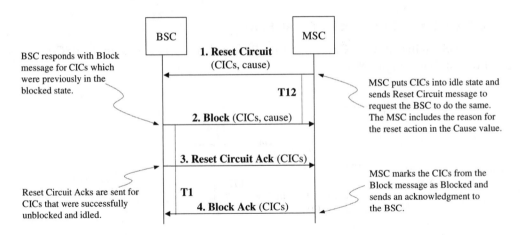

Figure 8-7   Reset Circuit at MSC with Block Response call flow

8.3.4   Reset Circuit Messages

The following sections provide detail descriptions of the A-Interface messages used in the Reset Circuit procedure.

8.3.4.1   Reset Circuit

The Reset Circuit message (Table 8-5) is a BSMAP message sent by either the BSC or MSC to idle one or more terrestrial circuits. The message is sent as a connectionless SCCP-UDT message type.

The mandatory Circuit Identity Code IE specifies the CIC to be reset (idled) by the remote node.

CDGIOS specifies that the mandatory Cause IE may be set to either "operations and maintenance" or "equipment failure," depending on the reason for initiating the Reset Circuit.

The optional Circuit Group IE provides a means of specifying a group of CICs to be reset and avoids the need to send individual Reset Circuit messages for each CIC. For more information about how this parameter is used, please refer to the description provided for the Block message in Section 8.2.3.1, "Block," on page 506.

- BSAP Message Type: BSMAP
- SCCP Message Type: SCCP-Unit Data (UDT)
- Direction: BSC ↔ MSC

Table 8-5   Reset Circuit Message (CDGIOS 6.1.6.8)

BitMap	Param IE	#Oct	Range	Type	IOS Ref
0000 0000 (00H) LLLL LLLL	BSMAP header	2	Msg Discrim. = 0 (BSMAP) L = BSMAP msg length	M	6.2.2.1 6.2.2.3
0011 0100 (34H)	Msg Type	1	Reset Circuit Msg	M	6.2.2.4
0000 0001 (01H) mmmm mmmm mmmt tttt	Circuit Identity Code	3	m = spanid t = timeslot	M	6.2.2.22
0000 0100 (04H) LLLL LLLL 0ccc cccc	Cause	3	L = 01H, c = cause 07H—OA&M intervention 20H—equipment failure	M	6.2.2.19
0001 1001 (19H)	Circuit Group	Variable	Same as element in Table 8-1, Block message	O,C	6.2.2.148

8.3.4.2   Reset Circuit Acknowledge

The Reset Circuit Acknowledge message (Table 8-6) is sent by either the BSC or MSC to acknowledge the idling of the terrestrial circuit associated with a previously received Reset message. This BSMAP message is sent as a connectionless SCCP-UDT type message.

The mandatory Circuit Identity Code IE specifies the CIC successfully reset (idled).

The optional Circuit Group IE provides a means of specifying a group of CICs that have been successfully reset (idled) and avoids the need to send individual Reset Circuit Acknowledge messages for each CIC. For more information about how this parameter is used, please refer to the description provided for the Block message in Section 8.2.3.1, "Block," on page 506.

- BSAP Message Type: BSMAP
- SCCP Message Type: SCCP-Unit Data (UDT)
- Direction: BSC ↔ MSC

Table 8-6   Reset Ciruit Acknowledge Message (CDGIOS 6.1.6.9)

BitMap	Param IE	#Oct	Range	Type	IOS Ref
0000 0000 (00H) LLLL LLLL	BSMAP header	2	Msg Discrim. = 0 (BSMAP) L = BSMAP msg length	M	6.2.2.1 6.2.2.3
0011 0101 (35H)	Msg Type	1	Reset Circuit Ack Msg	M	6.2.2.4
0000 0001 (01H)	Circuit Identity Code	3	Same as element in Table 8-1, Block message	M	6.2.2.22
0001 1001 (19H)	Circuit Group	Variable	Same as element in Table 8-1, Block message	O,C	6.2.2.148

8.3.5   Reset Circuit Example Call Flow

The example message summary shown in Figure 8-8 is similar to what would be seen on test equipment monitoring the A-Interface during an abnormal SCCP release. The purpose of the example is to illustrate the Reset Circuit procedure that is invoked after the abnormal release. The summary call flow is followed by the decoded example messages. The BSC's point code is 8-17-92, and the MSC's point code is 110-44-3.

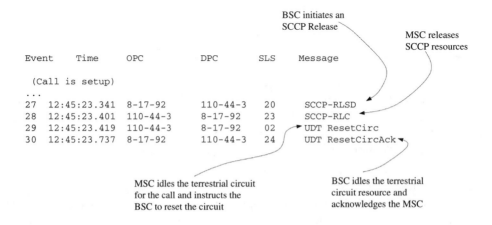

Figure 8-8   Reset Circuit after Abnormal SCCP Release example call flow

In the example shown in Figure 8-8, an established call is released abnormally by the BSC, and the MSC responds to the *SCCP Released* (SCCP-RLSD) message with *SCCP Release Complete* (SCCP-RLC). At this point the call was released at the SCCP layer but the associated CIC resource may not have been properly released. To ensure that the CIC has been idled at the BSC, the MSC sends a Reset Circuit message. Upon receiving the Reset Circuit message, the BSC idles the specified CIC and responds with a Reset Circuit Acknowledge.

```
**** MESSAGE NUMBER: 00029 ****
*** Start of MTP Level 3 ***
0003 10000011 83
     ----0011    Service Indicator         SCCP
     --00----    Network Priority          priority 0
     10------    Network Indicator         National
0004 (3 Bytes)   Destination Point Code    8-17-92          The MSC initi-
0007 (3 Bytes)   Origination Point Code    110-44-3    ◄─── ated a Reset Cir-
0010 00000010 02 Signaling Link Selection  2                cuit
*** Start of SCCP ***
0011 00001001 09 Message Type              UDT
0012 00000000 00
     ----0000    Protocol Class            Class 0
     0000----    Message Handling          no special options
0013 00000011 03 Called Party Address      Offset 0016
0014 00000101 05 Calling Party Address     Offset 0019
0015 00001010 0a Data Portion Pointer      Offset 0025
0016 00000010 02 Called Party Addr Length  2
0017 11000001 c1
     -------1    Subsys Number Indicator   Included
     ------0-    Point Code Indicator      Excluded
     --0000--    Global Title indicator    No global title included
     -1------    Routing indicator         route by DPC/SSN
     1-------    Reserved for National use
0018 11111100 fc Subsystem Number          252
0019 00000101 05 Calling Party Addr Length 5
0020 11000011 c3
     -------1    Subsys Number Indicator   Included
     ------1-    Point Code Indicator      Included
     --0000--    Global Title indicator    No global title included
     -1------    Routing indicator         route by DPC/SSN
     1-------    Reserved for National use
0021 11111100 fc Subsystem Number          252
0022 (3 Bytes)   Signaling Point Code      110-44-3
*** Start of CDGIOS MAP ***
                 Reset Circuit
0025 00001001 09 Data Length               9
0026 00000000 00 BSMAP Discriminator       00
0027 00000111 07 BSMAP Length              7
0028 00110100 34 Reset Circuit             52
0029 00000001 01 Circuit Identity Code Id  1
0030 00000000 00 PCM MUX (high part)       0                Circuit to be
0031 00000010 37                      ◄─────────────────── reset
     ---00111    Time Slot                 7
```

(Continued)
```
        011-----     PCM MUX (low part)        3
0032 00000100 04 Cause Id                      4
0033 00000001 01 Cause Length                  1
0034 00000111 07 Cause Value                   OA&M intervention
```

Figure 8-9   Reset Circuit message example

Figure 8-9 shows the message structure and content of a Reset Circuit message. In this example message, only one circuit is specified and is contained in the mandatory Circuit Identity Code IE. The Reset Circuit cause reason is set to OA&M intervention.

```
**** MESSAGE NUMBER: 00030 ****
*** Start of CDGIOS MAP ***
                   Reset Circuit Acknowledge
0028 00000110 06 Data Length               6
0029 00000000 00 BSMAP Discriminator       00
0030 00000100 04 BSMAP Length              4
0031 00110101 35 Reset Circuit Acknowledge 53
0032 00000001 01 Circuit Identity Code Id  1
0033 00000000 00 PCM MUX (high part)       0
0034 00000010 37                                    ◄─────────── Circuit which
        ---00111     Time Slot             7                     was reset
        011-----     PCM MUX (low part)    3
```

Figure 8-10   Reset Circuit Acknowledge message example

Figure 8-10 illustrates the message structure and content of the Reset Circuit Acknowledge message sent from the BSC to the MSC. The BSC informs the MSC that the specified circuit (PCM Mux 3 and timeslot 7) has been successfully idled.

8.4 Global System Reset

Either the BSC or MSC initiates the Global Reset procedure when a global failure occurs or as a result of initialization. The Global Reset procedure is always invoked when the first signaling link connecting a BSC and MSC is brought into service. Upon receiving a Global Reset message, the receiving node releases the affected calls and idles all associated circuits. In the case of the BSC, Block messages may also be sent for any unavailable CICs.

8.4.1   Global Reset at BSC Call Flow

Figure 8-11 shows the Global Reset procedure call flow when initiated by the BSC. The BSC starts the procedure by sending the Reset message to the MSC and starts timer T4. Upon receipt of the Reset message, the MSC starts timer T2, releases any affected calls, and marks all associated CICs as idle and unblocked. The MSC waits for guard timer T2 to expire before sending a Reset Acknowledge message to the BSC. In the meantime, the BSC may send Blocks to the MSC for CICs that it determines should be blocked. The call flow shown in Figure 8-11 is followed by descriptions of each individual step.

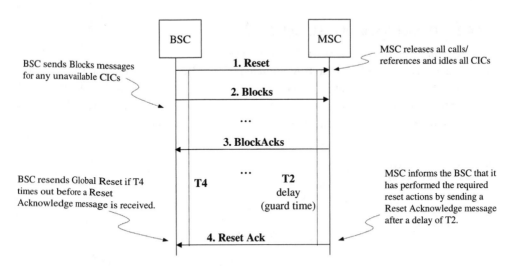

Figure 8-11   Global Reset at BSC call flow

1. Reset (A-Interface):

   Upon initialization or due to a global failure, the BSC initiates the Global Reset procedure by releasing affected calls, idling its CICs, and sending a Reset message to the MSC. The BSC then starts timer T4 to wait for a Reset Acknowledge message from the MSC.

   If the MSC receives a Reset message that indicates that the CDGIOS software version being used by the BSC is less than that being used at the MSC, the MSC may choose to ignore the Global Reset and take appropriate OA&M actions.

2. Blocks (A-Interface):

   While waiting for a Reset Acknowledge message, the BSC may send Block messages for any CICs that it determines should not be requested by the MSC.

3. Block Acks (A-Interface):

   Upon receiving a Block message from the BSC, the MSC locally blocks the specified CICs and sends one or more Block Acknowledge messages to the BSC.

4. Reset Ack (A-Interface):

   The MSC idles all associated CICs and releases affected calls upon receipt of the Global Reset indication from the BSC. After a guard timer delay of T2 seconds, the MSC sends a Reset Acknowledge message to the BSC, indicating that it has performed the necessary reset actions.

The BSC stops timer T4 upon receiving the Reset Acknowledge message from the MSC. If T4 expires before a Reset Acknowledge message is received, the BSC repeats the Global Reset procedure.

8.4.2   Global Reset at MSC Call Flow

As mentioned earlier, the MSC may also initiate a Global Reset. The message flow, illustrated in Figure 8-12, is similar to the BSC-initiated Global Reset scenario described in Section 8.4.1, "Global Reset at BSC Call Flow," on page 516. In the case of a MSC-initiated Global Reset, the MSC starts timer T16 upon sending the Reset message, and the BSC acknowledges the MSC with the Reset Acknowledge message after timer T13 expires.

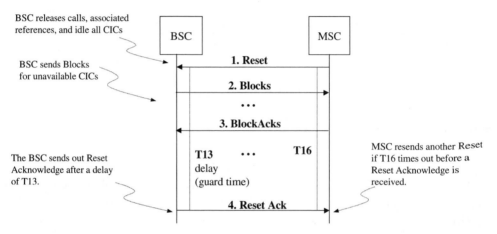

Figure 8-12   Global Reset at MSC call flow

8.4.3   Reset Glare Noted at BSC Call Flow

A Global Reset Glare may occur when both the BSC and MSC initiate the Global Reset procedure around the same time. A glare condition at the BSC occurs when the BSC-sent Reset message is lost or cannot be processed by the MSC. The call flow for Global Reset Glare at the BSC is shown in Figure 8-13. In the call flow shown, the BSC starts the Global Reset procedure and sends a Reset message to the MSC. Around the same time, the MSC also invokes the Global Reset procedure, sending a Reset message to the BSC. Upon receiving the Reset message from the MSC, the BSC determines that a Global Reset *glare* condition has occurred, assumes that its previously sent Reset message was lost, then processes the received Reset message. The BSC no longer proceeds with its own initiated Global Reset.

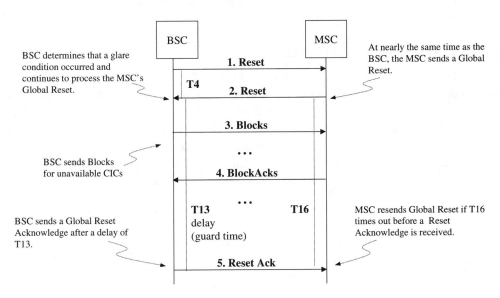

BSC determines that a glare condition occurred and continues to process the MSC's Global Reset.

At nearly the same time as the BSC, the MSC sends a Global Reset.

BSC sends Blocks for unavailable CICs

BSC sends a Global Reset Acknowledge after a delay of T13.

MSC resends Global Reset if T16 times out before a Reset Acknowledge is received.

Figure 8-13 Global Reset Glare noted at BSC call flow

1. Reset (A-Interface):

   A Reset is first sent by the BSC, and the BSC starts timer T4. The glare condition at the BSC occurs when this message is lost or cannot be processed by the MSC, and the MSC sends its own Reset message to the BSC.

2. Reset (A-Interface):

   The MSC starts the Global Reset procedure and sends out a Reset message to the BSC and starts timer T16.

   Upon receiving the Reset message, the BSC determines that a glare condition has occurred and continues to process the received Reset message. The BSC no longer proceeds with its own initiated Global Reset procedure and assumes that the Reset message it sent was lost. The BSC stops Timer T4 and starts delay timer T13.

3. Blocks (A-Interface):

   If required, Blocks messages are sent from the BSC for CICs not available at the BSC.

4. Block Acks (A-Interface):

   The MSC locally blocks the specified CICs and sends one or more Block Acknowledge messages to the BSC.

5. Reset Ack (A-Interface):

Upon expiry of timer T13, the BSC sends a Reset Acknowledge. The MSC stops timer T16 after receiving this message.

8.4.4   Reset Glare Noted at MSC Call Flow

Parallel Global Reset procedures at both the MSC and BSC may also result in a reset glare condition at the MSC. The message flow for such a condition is similar to the BSC glare scenario described in Section 8.4.3, "Reset Glare Noted at BSC Call Flow," on page 518. The main difference is that the MSC is the first node to send the Reset message. Upon receiving the Reset message from the BSC, the MSC determines that glare has occurred and proceeds to process the received Reset message. The MSC stops its own initiated Global Reset procedure. Figure 8-14 illustrates the message flow for Global Reset glare noted at the MSC.

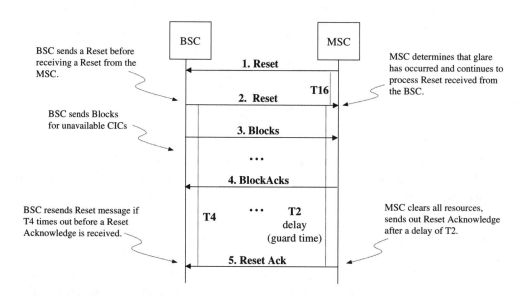

Figure 8-14   Global Reset Glare noted at MSC call flow

8.4.5   Reset Glare Noted at Both BSC and MSC

When both the MSC and BSC initiate Global Reset procedures at nearly the same time, it is possible for Reset Glare conditions to occur simultaneously at both nodes. Each node determines that Reset glare has occurred when a Reset message is received soon after the initial Reset message has been sent. When this occurs, both the MSC and BSC each assume that the Reset messages they previously sent were lost, act as though they are not performing a reset procedure, and process the received Reset message. The call flow for Reset glare noted at both the MSC and BSC is shown in Figure 8-15.

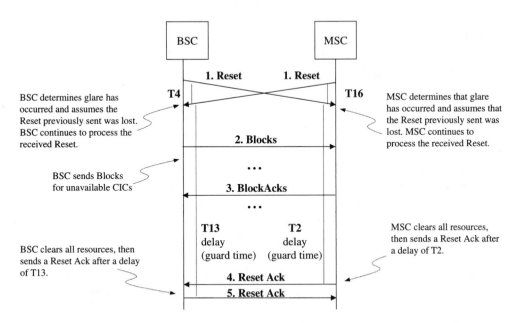

Figure 8-15   Global Reset Glare noted at both BSC and MSC call flow

1. Reset (A-Interface):

   Both the MSC and BSC send Reset messages at nearly the same time. The BSC starts timer T4 and the MSC starts timer T16.

   Upon receiving the Reset message from the MSC, the BSC notes that Reset glare has occurred, assumes that its previously sent Reset message has been lost, and continues to process the received Reset message. The BSC stops timer T4 and starts delay timer T13.

   Similarly, when the MSC receives the Reset message from the BSC, it notes that a Reset glare has occurred, assumes that its previously sent Reset message has been lost, and continues to process the received Reset message. The MSC stops timer T16 and starts delay timer T2.

2. Blocks (A-Interface):

   If required, Blocks messages are sent from the BSC for CICs not available at the BSC.

3. Block Acks (A-Interface):

   The MSC locally blocks the specified CICs and sends one or more Block Acknowledge messages to the BSC.

4. Global Reset Ack (A-Interface):

   The MSC sends a Reset Acknowledge message after delay timer T2 expires.

5. Global Reset Ack (A-Interface):

The BSC sends a Reset Acknowledge message after delay timer T13 expires.

8.4.6   Global Reset Messages

The following sections contain descriptions of the A-Interface messages used by both the MSC and BSC during a Global Reset.

8.4.6.1   Reset

The Reset message (Table 8-7) is a BSMAP message sent by either the BSC or MSC to initiate a Global Reset at the remote end. It is sent as a connectionless SCCP-UDT message type.

CDGIOS specifies that the mandatory Cause IE contained in the Reset message be set to "operations and maintenance" or "equipment failure." For an operator-induced Global Reset, the Reset message is sent with a Cause IE of "operations and maintenance."

The required Software Version IE is sent to the remote end to convey information regarding the CDGIOS software version being used. The CDGIOS version is specified using the $a.b.c$ format, where a is the major revision, b is the minor revision, and c is the point release. The Software Version IE also contains a load identity for each manufacturer software load and may be used by the wireless carrier to exchange information between network entities.

- BSAP Message Type: BSMAP
- SCCP Message Type: SCCP-Unit Data (UDT)
- Direction: BSC ↔ MSC

Table 8-7   Reset Message (CDGIOS 6.1.6.6)

BitMap	Param IE	#Oct	Range	Type	IOS Ref
0000 0000 (00H) LLLL LLLL	BSMAP header	2	Msg Discrim. = 0 (BSMAP) L = BSMAP msg length	M	6.2.2.1 6.2.2.3
0011 0000 (30H)	Msg Type	1	Global Reset Msg	M	6.2.2.4

Table 8-7   Reset Message (CDGIOS 6.1.6.6) (Continued)

BitMap	Param IE	#Oct	Range	Type	IOS Ref
0000 0100 (04H) LLLL LLLL 0ccc cccc	Cause	3	L = 01H, c = cause 07H—OA&M intervention 20H—equipment failure	M	6.2.2.19
0011 0001 (31H) LLLL LLLL aaaa aaaa bbbb bbbb cccc cccc mmmm mmmm	Software Version	Variable	L = length a = Major Revision b = Minor Revision c = Point Release m = manufacturer information	O,R	6.2.2.65

8.4.6.2   Reset Acknowledge

The Reset Acknowledge message is a BSMAP message sent by either the BSC or MSC to acknowledge a Global Reset (Table 8-8). It is sent after the local node has cleared all affected calls and associated SCCP connections. The Reset Acknowledge message is sent as a connectionless SCCP-UDT message type.

The required Software Version IE is sent by the BSC or MSC to the remote entity to convey CDGIOS software release information. For further details on the Software Version IE please see the description provided for the Reset message in Section 8.4.6.1, "Reset," on page 522.

- BSAP Message Type: BSMAP
- SCCP Message Type: SCCP-Unit Data (UDT)
- Direction: BSC ↔ MSC

Table 8-8   Reset Acknowledge Message (CDGIOS 6.1.6.7)

BitMap	Param IE	#Oct	Range	Type	IOS Ref
0000 0000 (00H) LLLL LLLL	BSMAP header	2	Msg Discrim. = 0 (BSMAP) L = BSMAP msg length	M	6.2.2.1 6.2.2.3
0011 0001 (31H)	Msg Type	1	Global Reset Ack Msg	M	6.2.2.4
0011 0001 (31H)	Software Version	Variable	Same as element in Table 8-7, Reset Message	O,R	6.2.2.65

8.4.7 Global Reset with Blocks Example Call Flow

Figure 8-16 contains a summary message call flow that is similar to what would be seen on test equipment monitoring the A-Interface when the first signaling link connecting a BSC and MSC is brought into service. The intent of this example is to illustrate the call flow associated with the Global Reset procedure, including the sending of Block messages by the BSC during system initialization. Subsequent figures illustrate the complete message's content, including MTP and SCCP layers. In this example, the BSC's point code is 1-1-1, and the MSC's point code is 1-2-4.

```
+----------------+-----------------+--------------------------+---
From   Time              OPC     DPC
+----------------+-----------------+--------------------------+---
  C    21:06:20,586,011                     MTP-L2    LSSU-SIOS
  D    21:06:20,589,772                     MTP-L2    LSSU-SIOS
  D    21:06:21,325,385                     MTP-L2    LSSU-SIO          MTP2 layer initial
  C    21:06:22,279,067                     MTP-L2    LSSU-SIO   ◄───   link alignment in
  D    21:06:22,283,210                     MTP-L2    LSSU-SIE          progress
  C    21:06:23,435,130                     MTP-L2    LSSU-SIE
  C    21:06:23,980,240  1-2-4   1-1-1      T+M       SLTM
  D    21:06:23,987,138  1-1-1   1-2-4      T+M       SLTM
  D    21:06:23,991,793  1-1-1   1-2-4      T+M       SLTA
  C    21:06:23,991,741  1-2-4   1-1-1      T+M       SLTA             MTP3 layer traffic
  D    21:06:24,005,011  1-1-1   1-2-4      MTP3      TRA        ◄───  started
  D    21:06:24,006,887  1-1-1   1-2-4      MTP3      TRA
  D    21:06:28,033,172  1-1-1   1-2-4      SCCP      UDT    SCMG  SST
  C    21:06:29,299,796  1-2-4   1-1-1      MTP3      TRA
  D    21:06:33,032,978  1-1-1   1-2-4      SCCP      UDT    SCMG  SST   ◄── SCCP layer
  C    21:06:33,040,961  1-2-4   1-1-1      SCCP      UDT    SCMG  SSA       brought into
  C    21:06:59,386,758  1-2-4   1-1-1      SCCP      UDT    SCMG  SST       service
  D    21:06:59,401,279  1-1-1   1-2-4      SCCP      UDT    SCMG  SSA
  C    21:07:21,499,754  1-2-4   1-1-1      SCCP      UDT    BSMAP  RST  ◄─ MSC sends
  D    21:07:21,649,647  1-1-1   1-2-4      SCCP      UDT    BSMAP  BLO     Reset message
  C    21:07:21,666,881  1-2-4   1-1-1      SCCP      UDT    BSMAP  BLA
  D    21:07:21,702,149  1-1-1   1-2-4      SCCP      UDT    BSMAP  BLO
  D    21:07:21,707,276  1-1-1   1-2-4      SCCP      UDT    BSMAP  BLO
  D    21:07:21,712,397  1-1-1   1-2-4      SCCP      UDT    BSMAP  BLO
  D    21:07:21,717,520  1-1-1   1-2-4      SCCP      UDT    BSMAP  BLO
  D    21:07:21,722,784  1-1-1   1-2-4      SCCP      UDT    BSMAP  BLO
  D    21:07:21,727,900  1-1-1   1-2-4      SCCP      UDT    BSMAP  BLO
  D    21:07:21,733,024  1-1-1   1-2-4      SCCP      UDT    BSMAP  BLO     BSC sends
  D    21:07:21,738,270  1-1-1   1-2-4      SCCP      UDT    BSMAP  BLO ◄── Blocks for
  D    21:07:21,743,400  1-1-1   1-2-4      SCCP      UDT    BSMAP  BLO     unavailable
  D    21:07:21,748,523  1-1-1   1-2-4      SCCP      UDT    BSMAP  BLO     CICs
  D    21:07:21,753,645  1-1-1   1-2-4      SCCP      UDT    BSMAP  BLO
  D    21:07:21,758,901  1-1-1   1-2-4      SCCP      UDT    BSMAP  BLO
  D    21:07:21,764,024  1-1-1   1-2-4      SCCP      UDT    BSMAP  BLO
  D    21:07:21,769,148  1-1-1   1-2-4      SCCP      UDT    BSMAP  BLO
  D    21:07:21,774,407  1-1-1   1-2-4      SCCP      UDT    BSMAP  BLO
  D    21:07:21,779,523  1-1-1   1-2-4      SCCP      UDT    BSMAP  BLO
```

(Continued)

```
C   21:07:21,906,386  1-2-4   1-1-1   SCCP   UDT   BSMAP   BLA
C   21:07:21,916,506  1-2-4   1-1-1   SCCP   UDT   BSMAP   BLA
C   21:07:21,926,762  1-2-4   1-1-1   SCCP   UDT   BSMAP   BLA
C   21:07:21,936,381  1-2-4   1-1-1   SCCP   UDT   BSMAP   BLA
C   21:07:21,946,758  1-2-4   1-1-1   SCCP   UDT   BSMAP   BLA
C   21:07:21,956,139  1-2-4   1-1-1   SCCP   UDT   BSMAP   BLA      <- MSC acknowl-
C   21:07:21,965,758  1-2-4   1-1-1   SCCP   UDT   BSMAP   BLA         edges Blocks
C   21:07:21,970,756  1-2-4   1-1-1   SCCP   UDT   BSMAP   BLA
C   21:07:21,975,635  1-2-4   1-1-1   SCCP   UDT   BSMAP   BLA
C   21:07:21,980,506  1-2-4   1-1-1   SCCP   UDT   BSMAP   BLA
C   21:07:21,985,505  1-2-4   1-1-1   SCCP   UDT   BSMAP   BLA
C   21:07:21,990,394  1-2-4   1-1-1   SCCP   UDT   BSMAP   BLA
C   21:07:21,995,382  1-2-4   1-1-1   SCCP   UDT   BSMAP   BLA
C   21:07:22,000,258  1-2-4   1-1-1   SCCP   UDT   BSMAP   BLA
C   21:07:22,005,131  1-2-4   1-1-1   SCCP   UDT   BSMAP   BLA
C   21:07:22,010,012  1-2-4   1-1-1   SCCP   UDT   BSMAP   BLA
D   21:07:23,923,049  1-1-1   1-2-4   T+M    SLTM
C   21:07:23,926,531  1-2-4   1-1-1   T+M    SLTA
C   21:07:24,305,785  1-2-4   1-1-1   T+M    SLTM
D   21:07:24,314,677  1-1-1   1-2-4   T+M    SLTA
D   21:08:16,534,568  1-1-1   1-2-4   SCCP   UDT   BSMAP   RSTA     <- BSC acknowl-
D   21:08:23,923,471  1-1-1   1-2-4   T+M    SLTM                     edges Reset
C   21:08:23,927,327  1-2-4   1-1-1   T+M    SLTA
C   21:08:25,312,844  1-2-4   1-1-1   T+M    SLTM
D   21:08:25,323,863  1-1-1   1-2-4   T+M    SLTA
```

Figure 8-16   Global Reset with Blocks after Initial Link Alignment example call flow

The initial messages in Figure 8-16 are associated with the alignment of the only *Signaling System 7* (SS7) signaling link connecting the MSC and BSC. MTP 2 alignment first takes place, followed by a traffic restart at MTP 3, then the exchange of signaling link test and maintenance messages. Next, the SCCP layers are brought into service at both nodes through the exchange of *Subsystem Test* (SST) and *Subsystem Allowed* (SSA) messages. Finally, the BSAP (application) layer *terrestrial circuit resource* function initiates a Global Reset to bring the associated CICs into service. In this example, the MSC initiates the Global Reset, and the BSC responds with multiple Block messages to inform the MSC of unavailable CICs. After completing its initialization and waiting for timer T13 to expire, the BSC responds to the previously received Reset message with a Reset Acknowledge message. At this point, both the link and terrestrial circuits are now available and in service.

```
1:C:  21:07:21,499,754  1-2-4   1-1-1   SCCP   UDT   BSMAP RST
----0011  Service Indicator           SCCP
--00----  Sub-Service: Priority        priority 0
10------  Sub-Service: Network Ind     National
***B3***  Destination Point Code       1-1-1
***B3***  Originating Point Code       1-2-4
00000011  Signaling Link Selection     3
00001001  SCCP Message Type            UDT
```

(Continued)

```
----0000   Protocol Class                    Class 0
0000----   Message Handling                  Discard message on error
00000011   Pointer to parameter              3
00001000   Pointer to parameter              8
00001101   Pointer to parameter              13
           Called address parameter
00000101   Parameter Length                  5
-------1   Subsystem No. Indicator           SSN present
------1-   Point Code Indicator              PC present
--0000--   Global Title Indicator            No global title included
-1------   Routing Indicator                 Route on DPC + SSN
1-------   For national use                  National address
11111100   Subsystem number                  252
***B3***   Called Party SPC                  1-1-1
           Calling address parameter
00000101   Parameter Length                  5
-------1   Subsystem No. Indicator           SSN present
------1-   Point Code Indicator              PC present
--0000--   Global Title Indicator            No global title included
-1------   Routing Indicator                 Route on DPC + SSN
1-------   For national use                  National address
11111100   Subsystem number                  252
***B3***   Called Party SPC                  1-2-4
           Data parameter
00001011   Parameter length                  11
CDGIOS (BSSMAP) (BSMAP)  RESET
-------0   Discrimination bit D              BSSMAP
0000000-   Filler                            0
00001001   Message Length                    9
00110000   Message Type                      48
00000100   IE Name                           Cause
00000001   IE Length                         1
-0100000   Cause Value                       Equipment failure
0-------   Extension bit                     No extension
00110001   IE Name                           Software Version
00000011   IE Length                         3
00000011   IOS version                       3.1.1
00000001
00000001
```

Figure 8-17 Global Reset message example

Figure 8-17 illustrates the message structure and content of a Reset message. The mandatory cause value is set to equipment failure because, in this example, the system was restarted, due to a system failure.

```
CDGIOS MSC - BSC (BSSMAP) (BSMAP)  BLO (= Block)
-------0   Discrimination bit D              BSSMAP
0000000-   Filler                            0
00000111   Message Length                    7
```

(Continued)

```
01000000   Message Type           64
00000001   IE Name                Circuit Identity Code
00000000   PCM Multiplex a-h      0
---00001   Timeslot in use        1
001-----   PCM Multiplex i-k      1
00000100   IE Name                Cause
00000001   IE Length              1
-0000111   Cause Value            OA&M intervention
0-------   Extension bit          No extension
```

Figure 8-18   Block message example

Figure 8-18 illustrates the message structure and content of a Block message. Because the SCCP and MTP layers are similar to those found in the Reset message example shown in Figure 8-17, they are not repeated here. In this example, the BSC sends individual Block messages for each CIC that it determines should be blocked. The Block message shown in Figure 8-18 requests that the MSC block the CIC associated with PCM mux 1 and timeslot 1. The reason specified for requesting the block is OA&M intervention.

```
CDGIOS MSC - BSC (BSSMAP) (BSMAP)   BLA (= Block Acknowledge)
-------0   Discrimination bit D     BSSMAP
0000000-   Filler                   0
00000100   Message Length           4
01000001   Message Type             65
00000001   IE Name                  Circuit Identity Code
00000000   PCM Multiplex a-h        0
---00001   Timeslot in use          1
001-----   PCM Multiplex i-k        1
```

Figure 8-19   Block Acknowledge message example

Figure 8-19 illustrates the message structure and content of a Block Acknowledge message. In this example message, the MSC acknowledges the blocking of a single CIC associated with PCM mux 1 and timeslot 1.

```
CDGIOS MSC - BSC (BSSMAP) (BSMAP)   RSTA (= Reset Acknowledge)
-------0   Discrimination bit D     BSSMAP
0000000-   Filler                   0
00000110   Message Length           6
00110001   Message Type             49
00110001   IE Name                  Software Version
00000011   IE Length                3
00000011   IOS version              3.1.1
00000001
00000001
```

Figure 8-20   Global Reset Acknowledge message example

Figure 8-20 illustrates the message structure and content of a Reset Acknowledge message sent by the BSC in response to the MSC-initiated Global Reset earlier. The software version IE specifies that CDGIOS 3.1.1 is being used.

8.5 A7-Interface Global Reset

In a CDMA network, direct connections between BSCs may exist to facilitate soft hand-offs between BSCs. Like the MSC–BSC interface, these BSC–BSC interfaces also require Terrestrial Facility Management procedures to maintain the integrity of the connections. Recall that the signaling portion of the BSC–BSC connection is referred to as the *A7-Interface* and that data is sent over the A3 traffic connection (See Section 1.3, "Open A-Interface Network Architecture," on page 6 and Section 7.4, "IS-95 to IS-95 Direct BSC-BSC Soft Handoff," on page 473). When a BSC experiences a failure that results in losing the A3/A7 connections, an A7 Global Reset procedure is performed to release all associated references and to reinitialize the connections.

8.5.1 A7 Global Reset at BSC Call Flow

During initialization or due to a failure that results in the BSC losing A7 transaction reference information, the BSC sends a A7-Reset message to one or more remote BSCs. The call flow for resetting the A7 connections is similar to that of a BSC-initiated Global Reset on the A1-Interface, described in Section 8.4.1, "Global Reset at BSC Call Flow," on page 516.

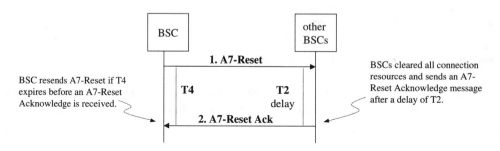

Figure 8-21 A7 Global Reset call flow

After releasing all affected resources, the BSC sends A7-Reset messages to other known BSCs and starts timer T4. Upon receipt of the A7-Reset message, the remote BSCs release all affected virtual calls and references, then wait for T2 seconds before sending an A7-Reset Acknowledge message to the initiating BSC. If timer T4 expires before an A7-Reset Acknowledge message is received, the initiating BSC repeats the reset procedure with the other BSC. Figure 8-21 shows the call flow when the A7 Reset procedure is initiated by a BSC.

8.5.2 A7 Global Reset Glare Noted at Initiating BSC

As with the A1-Interface, *Reset Glares* may also occur over the A7-Interface. If the initiating BSC receives a A7-Reset message after sending its own A7-Reset, it determines that A7-Reset glare has occurred and assumes that its previously sent A7-Reset message was lost. The initiating (original) BSC processes the received A7-Reset and sends a A7-Reset Acknowledge message after timer T2 expires. The call flow is illustrated in Figure 8-22.

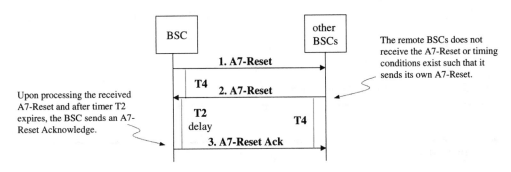

Figure 8-22   A7 Global Reset Glare noted at initiating BSC

8.5.3 A7 Global Reset Glare Noted at Two BSCs

It is possible that both the local and remote BSC encounter A7-Reset glare. Each node determines that Reset Glare has occurred when an A7-Reset message is received after the initial A7-Reset message has been sent. When this occurs, both the BSCs assume that the A7-Reset messages they previously sent were lost, stop timer T4, act as though they are not performing a reset procedure, and process the received A7-Reset message. Upon expiry of timer T2, each node sends a A7-Reset Acknowledge message to the remote end (Figure 8-23).

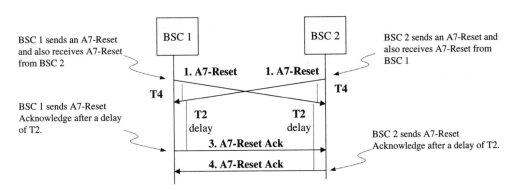

Figure 8-23   A7 Global Reset noted at two BSCs

8.5.4 A7 Global Reset Messages

The following sections describe the A7-Interface messages that are used in the A7 Global Reset procedure.

8.5.4.1 A7-Reset

The A7-Reset message is sent from one BSC to another BSC to initiate an A7 Global Reset (Table 8-9). All virtual connections, references, and associated transaction resources are released and reinitialized.

The required Cause IE and Software Version IE are identical to those described for the Reset message in Section 8.4.6.1, "Reset," on page 522.

- Direction: BSC ↔ BSC

Table 8-9   A7-Reset (CDGIOS 6.1.12.11)

BitMap	Param IE	#Oct	Range	Type	IOS Ref
1000 1010 (8AH)	Msg Type II	1	A7-Reset Msg	M	6.2.2.5
0000 0100 (04H) LLLL LLLL 0ccc cccc	Cause	3	L = 01H c = cause 07H—OA&M intervention 20H—equipment failure	O,R	6.2.2.19
0011 0001 (31H) …….	Software Version	Variable	Same element in Table 8-7, Reset Message	O,R	6.2.2.65

8.5.4.2 A7-Reset Ack

The A7-Reset Acknowledge message is sent from one BSC to another BSC to acknowledge the completion of an A7 Global Reset (Table 8-10).

The required Software Version IE is identical to that described for the Reset message in Section 8.4.6.1, "Reset," on page 522.

- Direction: BSC <-> BSC

Table 8-10 A7-Reset Ack (CDGIOS 6.1.12.12)

BitMap	Param IE	#Oct	Range	Type	IOS Ref
1000 1011 (8BH)	Msg Type II	1	A7-Reset Ack Msg	M	6.2.2.5
0011 0001 (31H)	Software Version	Variable	Same element in Table 8-7, Reset Message	O,R	6.2.2.65

References

1. CDG-IOS version 3.1.1, *CDMA Development Group MSC to BS Interface Inter-Operability Specification*. June 1999.
2. CDG-IOS version 2.0, *CDMA Development Group MSC to BS Interface Inter-Operability Specification*. September 1998.
3. Telecommunications Industry Association, TIA/EIA/IS-634-A, *MSC-BS Interface (A-Interface) for Public 800 MHz*. July 1998.
4. Telecommunications Industry Association , TIA/EIA/TSB-80, *MSC-BS Interface (A-Interface) for Public 800 MHz*. October 1996.
5. American National Standards Institute, ANSI T1.111, *Signaling System No. 7 (SS7)—Message Transfer Part (MTP)*. June 1992.
6. American National Standards Institute, ANSI T1.112, *Signaling System No. 7 (SS7)—Signaling Connection Control Part (SCCP)*. October 1992.

CHAPTER 9

A-Interface Integration

When a service provider decides to deploy an Open A-Interface CDMA network, an evaluation process normally takes place to select *Base Station Controller* (BSC) and *Mobile Switching Center* (MSC) vendors based on cost, schedule, and the features set supported by the manufacturers. This evaluation process often includes the review of previously run A-Interface compliance tests and sometimes involves independent laboratory testing at a service provider-selected testing location. Although the goal of A-Interface standard is to specify the interface in sufficient detail to ensure MSC–BSC interoperability, to reduce risk service providers almost always require that some level of MSC–BSC integration occur prior to deploying the network.

To integrate the BSC and MSC successfully, several project phases need to take place. These steps include initial requirements definition, software development, individual testing of both the BSC and MSC using simulators, and, finally, the integration of the BSC and MSC to verify A-Interface protocol compliance and overall internetworking.

This chapter provides an overview of the process of A-Interface integration, focusing on the tools and methodology used for the MSC–BSC integration.

9.1 MSC–BSC Integration Process

Figure 9-1 illustrates a process for integrating and testing an open A-Interface product. The process begins with discussions between the wireless service provider, the MSC vendor, and BSC vendors regarding system requirements. All three organizations must first decide on the specific version of the A-Interface protocol standard to be used, along with any additional customer specific requests. Also at this time, decisions may be made regarding areas of the A-Interface standard that are left to vendor implementation. For example, a decision may be made as to whether or not the MSC will retry an Assignment Request in the event that the MSC receives an Assignment Failure from the BSC. Once this information has been agreed upon, call flows are finalized and software development can begin. After individual software modules have been completed and tested at the subsystem level, the system is ready for integration testing.

The initial integration phase involves testing the MSC or BSC using a protocol simulator. This testing should focus on verifying that the node is fully compliant with the agreed-upon A-Interface specification. Simulator testing is an important technique for testing adversarial or error conditions because simulators can be easily programmed to emulate abnormal network conditions. Some adverse tests are extremely difficult to generate in a testing laboratory with the actual equipment, so simulation testing may be the only opportunity to test certain conditions before the equipment is deployed for *First Office Application* (FOA).

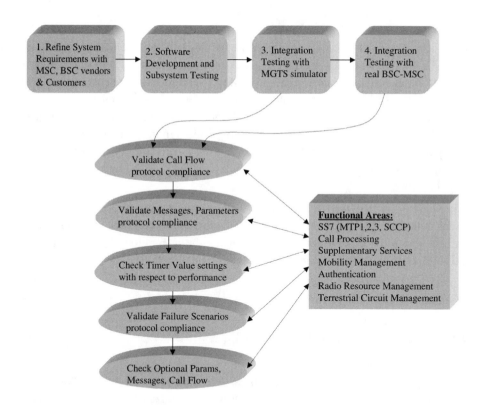

Figure 9-1   MSC–BSC A-Interface Integration process and tasks

After completing the simulated tests against a single node (MSC or BSC), a full set of tests should then be performed, using the connected pair.

The A-Interface integration normally includes verifying the following:

- Call flows are compliant with the agreed upon standard
- Parameters within the messages are compliant
- Timer values follow the recommended standard settings, unless agreed upon by all parties.
- Failure scenarios are compliant
- Optional parameters, messages, or call flow are acceptable

The first step to verifying interoperability and protocol compliance involves checking message flows. This type of testing ensures that the expected messages are transmitted and received at each call flow stage. Two examples of message flows typically tested are Call Delivery and *Signaling System 7* (SS7) link alignment.

Parameter checking includes making sure that mandatory A-Interface message parameters are present at all times. Parameter checking also includes verifying that optional parameters required for the specific conditional scenarios are present under those conditions.

Because the performance of a wireless network may be dependent on specified timer values, it is important to verify timer settings. Timer values should be set to the recommended default settings, unless otherwise agreed upon. Under certain conditions, changes to timer values may be justified. For example, in certain networks, increasing the T303 timer value to wait longer for an Assignment Request message from the MSC may improve performance under load.

For call failure scenarios, the equipment manufacturers for the both the BSC and MSC need to ensure that the failure call flows and procedures taken do not affect overall network performance. Recall that some failure scenarios are left to vendor implementation. One such example occurs when a Paging Request message is resent after T3113 expires. The technique used by the MSC to resend the Paging Request, such as to all BSCs, should not have an adverse affect on BSC load performance.

9.2 MSC/BSC Emulation using MGTS

A protocol simulator can be a powerful tool when used to verify A-Interface protocol compliance of the BSC or MSC. The simulator is typically programmed to emulate the remote end, providing a means of controlling A-Interface message flow and message content. An excellent tool commonly used by infrastructure manufacturers is the *Message Generator and Traffic Simulator* (MGTS) from Tekelec. The MGTS provides a full set of simulation features that greatly simplify protocol compliance integration testing. These features include:

- MSC/BSC SS7 Signaling Point Node Emulation
- State Machines Development
- Message Templates

The SS7 node emulator feature allows an MGTS card to emulate an MSC or BSC node, including emulation of SS7 protocol. An MGTS line card can be provisioned to emulate a T1 or E1 physical connection.

The heart of the MGTS simulation is the State Machine. The State Machine editor allows State Machines to be built for each call flow scenario, including failure conditions, such as timer expiry and unexpected messages reception. For a given call flow, the State Machine can transmit messages to the entity under test, as well as receive messages from the remote node. Transmitted and received messages can be easily analyzed using the MGTS message decoder feature.

The MGTS Message Editor feature allows individual message templates to be built for the A-Interface messages, as specified in the CDGIOS protocol standard. These messages are incorporated into the State Machines for transmission of A-Interface messages to the remote entity. To verify that the received messages are protocol-compliant, the messages received can be automatically checked against previously defined message templates.

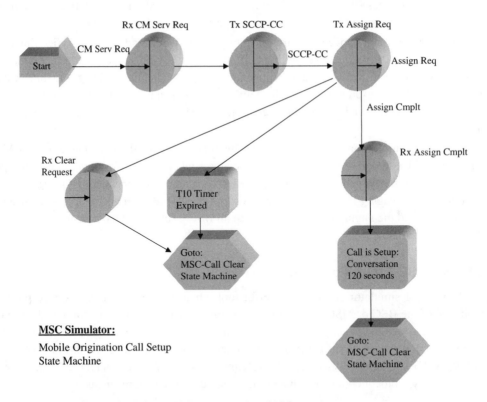

Figure 9-2   Example MGTS State Machine used as MSC emulator

Figure 9-2 shows a typical MGTS state machine. This example shows the mobile origination state machine of an MSC emulator. Each call flow state has a message template associated with it that traps the expected message and transfers control to the next stage in the state machine.

To perform integration protocol compliance tests, the infrastructure equipment under test is connected directly to the MGTS emulator, which acts as either a BSC or MSC. The relevant MGTS call flow scenarios represented by state machines are then individually run against the MSC or BSC to verify the responses. Figure 9-3 shows the typical setup for an MGTS connected to a BSC for protocol integration and testing.

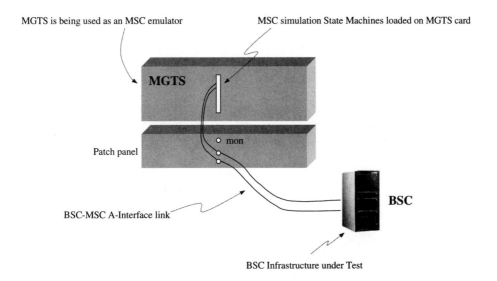

Figure 9-3 MGTS used as a MSC emulator for protocol compliance testing

9.3 MSC–BSC Integration Configuration

Figure 9-4 shows a typical configuration that may be used for MSC–BSC integration testing. It is important that both the MSC and BSC are configured with compatible settings. The following configuration parameters should be identified and agreed upon before the actual integration begins:

- MSC and BSC Point Codes
- Subsystem Number (252 for CDGIOS), MSC and BSC need to match
- Link Sets to each BSC
- Number of signaling links (usually at least two for redundancy)
- *Signaling Link Code* (SLC) of each signaling link
- Physical Span Id and timeslot of each signaling link
- Circuit Identity Code (Span ID, Timeslot) of the terrestrial circuits associated with

the spans connecting the BSC to the MSC
- Cell IDs, including which BSC they are controlled by
- Pilot PN offset of each cell and sectors
- Location Area Code (LAC)
- Mobile Country Code (MCC)
- *International Mobile Subscriber Identifier* (IMSI) of mobile stations
- *Electronic Serial Number* (ESN) of mobile stations
- A-Key of mobile stations

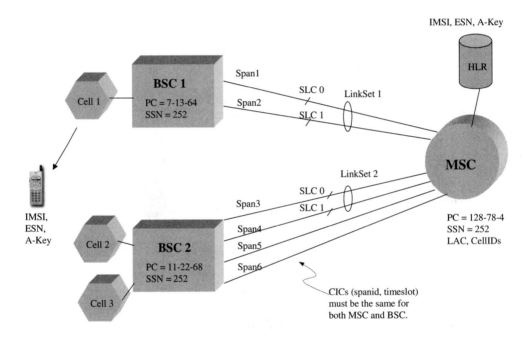

Figure 9-4   MSC–BSC Configuration

As discussed in Section 2.1, "The Signaling System 7 Network," on page 30, each BSC and MSC is an SS7 signaling point, and their point codes must be unique.

The Subsystem Number of both the MSC and BSC is specified in CDGIOS to be 252. This ensures that SS7 messages are routed to the proper subsystem entity within the node.

As shown in Figure 9-4, the BSC–MSC connection is comprised of one or more trunks. The number of trunks necessary is a function of the expected traffic load and network call model. The trunks consist of 64 kbps terrestrial circuit channels that may be used for either traffic or signaling.

The BSC–MSC interface is an SS7 point-to-point connection, and each BSC is connected to the MSC using a single Link Set, which consists of one or more signaling links. Usually at least two signaling links are used to provide redundancy in case of link failures. In addition to identifying the signaling links at both the BSC and MSC using trunk and timeslot designations, the links must also be assigned the same *Signaling Link Code* (SLC) at both entities. The SLC is a logical identifier used to specify a particular link within a Link Set. Although the SLC can be repeated for different Link Sets, it must be unique within a Link Set.

To ensure that the correct terrestrial traffic channels are allocated, both the BSC and MSC configurations have to agree on the *Circuit Identity Code* (CIC) assignments. The CIC is derived from the logical span (or trunk) ID and timeslot of each DS0 channel that is configured for carrying user traffic (see Section 8.1.5, "Spans and Circuits Identity Assignment," on page 502).

Aside from SS7 and terrestrial circuit parameters, the MSC and BSC need to define the identity of the cells controlled by each BSC. The Cell ID parameter and the Pilot PN code of each cell are stored in the database of the BSC and MSC and may be used for authorizing the access of subscribers.

Another configuration parameter often used in CDMA networks is the *Location Area Code* (LAC). The LAC consists of a logical grouping of cells, usually within the domain of a BSC. To efficiently page mobile subscribers during Call Delivery, the MSC may use the Location Area Code (LAC) parameter to page all cells within a LAC instead of flood-paging all network cells. When a mobile registers, the *Visitor Location Register* (VLR) stores the LAC information in its database.

The network stores the information regarding individual mobile subscribers in a *Home Location Register* (HLR). Because IMSI and ESN are used to identify each mobile uniquely, this information needs to be configured, whether the system is operating in a laboratory environment or is part of an operational network. In some laboratory environments, the HLR is simulated using test equipment or software stubs.

9.4 Protocol Analyzer Tools

A critical component to BSC–MSC integration is the use of an A-Interface monitoring tool. There are no definitive rules regarding which tool should be used; the decision should be based on personal preference and the environment in which the tool will be used. For example, if the monitor will be used for high-load tests, it may be best to choose a device that can be connected to a LAN, allowing various users to access information. Common SS7 monitoring tools used in the telecommunications industry are summarized in Table 9-1.

Table 9-1   Comparison of A-Interface Monitoring Equipment

Equipment	Features
Tekelec MGTS	Commonly used in telecommunication networks as a node emulator for application layer signaling, critical for A-Interface integration
Inet Spectra/Turbo 7	Easy to use, lightweight E1/T1 configurable Node emulation capability Excellent for SS7 troubleshooting Commonly used in telecommunication networks
Tektronix K1103	Easy to use, lightweight E1/T1 configurable Windows 3.11 based user interface Low price
Tektronix K1205	Easy to use, lightweight E1/T1 configurable Windows NT based Can be integrated into a LAN Has a useful automatic configuration feature

References

1. CDG-IOS version 3.1.1, *CDMA Development Group MSC to BS Interface Inter-Operability Specification*. June 1999.
2. Telecommunications Industry Association, TIA/EIA/IS-634-A, *MSC-BS Interface (A-Interface) for Public 800 MHz*. July 1998.

A-Interface for 3G

As wireless user demands for enhanced services and high bandwidth data connections grow, the drive for wireless infrastructure manufacturers to implement *third-generation* (3G) systems is accelerating. The increasing demand for high-bandwidth wireless data access has largely been fueled by the explosive growth of the Internet and the reduction in airtime costs that are being charged by wireless network service providers. The appeal of enhanced wireless services and high-bandwidth data connections is strong in both developed and developing countries. The mobility and flexibility provided with wireless high bandwidth data access appeals to many users in developed countries, and developing countries see high bandwidth wireless data as an opportunity to connect their populations to the Internet efficiently and quickly.

So far, the work to facilitate the evolution of CDMA networks from current second-generation systems to higher-quality, feature-rich 3G systems has taken place in the form of requirements definitions, design discussions, solution selections, and standardization process, covering all aspects of wireless network architecture. To implement these new changes in the most cost-effective and efficient manner, manufacturers must first agree on selected open interfaces and design solutions. These efforts are currently taking place in several standardization bodies, such as *International Telecommunications Union* (ITU), *Telecommunications Industry Association* (TIA), *European Telecommunications Standards Institute* (ETSI), and *Japan Association of Radio Industries and Businesses* (ARIB), and cover different technology areas, including the Radio Network, Access Network, and Core Network. Figure 10-1 shows the three main technology areas that are being enhanced for 3G capabilities.

The Radio Network area refers to the development of an efficient and superior air interface technology between mobile stations and base stations. It addresses standardization effort regarding the 3G air interface, which has been chosen to be wideband CDMA.

The Core Network area of responsibility is to implement enhanced and feature-rich network services such as Multimedia and high-speed data, using advanced technologies such as *Wireless Intelligent Network* (WIN), *Asynchronous Transfer Mode* (ATM), and *Mobile Internet Protocol* (MIP). The Core Network area also addresses inter-system interoperability regarding the support of 3G high-speed networks and advanced services, and is involved with improvements to the IS-41 North American Inter-System networking standard, the GSM MAP standard, and their network interoperability.

The Access Network is responsible for the access technology between the air interface and the network, including transport technology and application layer advances to support the 3G radio and Core Network capabilities. The Access Network area is the forum for MSC–BSC A-Interface standardization. This effort has been expanded to include the standardization of mobile high-speed packet data access interfaces to the packet data networks and the possible standardization of the interface between the BSC and base stations.

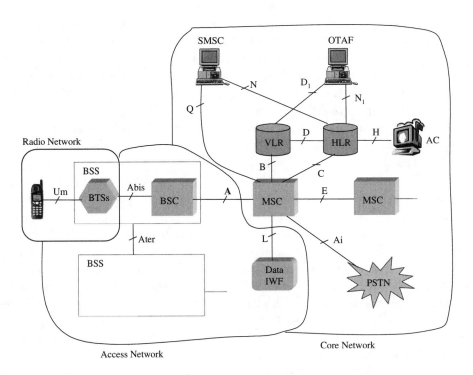

Figure 10-1 Technology areas for Third Generation development

As was discussed in Section 1.7.2, "The A-Interface Standard Evolution," on page 22, the *CDMA Development Group* (CDG) and TIA TR45.5 groups have both been taking on active roles in the A-Interface standardization effort. However, to further streamline and concentrate the A-Interface access network standardization process, the consortium *3rd Generation Partnership Project 2* (3GPP2) technical group TSG-A has taken on the responsibility of standardizing the interfaces between the Radio Access and Core Network. The first such A-Interface standard published that includes 3G capabilities is 3G-IOS version 4.0. This standard includes 3G phase 1 radio interface support for wideband CDMA (IS-2000), IS-95B extensions, 3G enhanced services support and 3G-high speed packet data interfaces. Following that, the next A-Interface IOS standard called *3G-IOS* version 5, will include 3G phase 2 radio access technology support.

The objective of this chapter is to present an overview of the development of the A-Interface for 3G wireless networks. The following topics are discussed:

- 3G Packet Data Access Network Architecture
- 3G Radio Access technology support
- Enhanced Services
- Forward and Backward Compatibility

The high speed *Packet Data* development is needed to support mobile data access to the internet or to private data networks and includes the design, development and implementation of the new interfaces and messaging required to support the access and mobility management to the packet data network.

The *3G Radio Access technology support* includes the enhancements to the A1, A3, and A7 interfaces to support new 3G radio frame types, channel structures, data rates, power control schemes, and other 3G CDMA radio technology improvements.

The *Enhanced Services* support on the A-Interface for 3G wireless networks includes changes in the messaging and parameters to support advanced services and features, such as:

- Tiered Services
- PACA Services
- Location Services
- Multimedia support
- Quality of Service support
- SMS Broadcast
- Multi-Language support
- User-Identification Module (UIM) support
- Vocoder Tandem Free Operation

Forward and Backward Compatibility support is critical for interoperability deployment between MSC and BSC vendors with different IOS versions and is an important issue when upgrading an existing live network to a more advanced IOS version.

10.1 3G Packet Data Architecture

Without a doubt, the key feature of 3G wireless networks is the capability to deliver high speed packet data services to mobile users. With the proliferation of the Internet, mobile users are increasingly demanding higher-speed data access.

To accommodate high-speed packet data services, the Access Network architecture includes open interfaces to an *Inter-Working Function* (IWF) that provides a gateway to the packet data network. This IWF serves as a terminating point for the packet data connection from the Internet/Intranet network and provides a direct *Point-to-Point Protocol* (PPP) link layer connection to the mobile station application. The support for packet data protocol includes different standards such as Internet Protocol (IPv4, IPv6, Mobile IP) and X.25.

For 3G networks, changes to existing A-Interface messaging is needed to allow mobile users to originate packet data calls and to allow the network to terminate packet data calls to a mobile station. Support is also needed for packet data IP mobility solutions, such as Mobile IP, because mobile users frequently move from one wireless network to another. Whereas mobility management is accomplished at the IP "macro" level, at the cellular network level, the packet data connection to the Internet/Intranet packet data network has to be maintained while the mobile user moves from one BSC or cell to another. Information such as Quality of Service indicators may also be solicited from the mobile.

An overview of the access network architecture that supports 3G packet data services is shown in Figure 10-2. The mobile data application typically resides in a *Terminal Equipment 2* (TE2), which is a data terminal device physically connected to a mobile station. The mobile station is known as a *Mobile Termination 2* (MT2) device, which has an interface such as RS-232 that can be linked to the TE2. This interface is referred to as the *Rm-Interface* and is specified in IS-707.5A [8].

On the infrastructure side, the BSC provides the Um air interface link to the mobile station and the associated radio resources for the packet data call. The MSC is involved only in the packet data call setup and does not participate in the packet data transfer.

Beyond the BSC, a packet data IWF provides the necessary functions to support packet data services for the mobile terminal. It establishes a reliable link layer to the mobile station using common link layer protocols such as PPP and provides the router gateway to the *Packet Data Network* (PDN), which can be either the Internet or private data networks. The L-Interface connects the BSC/MSC to the IWF function.

Work is proceeding on the 3G packet data access network architecture specification to split the functionality of the IWF further into two main entities:

• *Packet Control Function* (PCF)
• *Packet Data Serving Node* (PDSN)

The PCF is responsible for ensuring that the packet data services are delivered properly on the radio side. It also maintains the link layer status to the mobile station. The PCF interfaces directly with the PDSN to transfer user packet data through an interface known as the R–P (Radio-to-Packet data) interface. The ongoing work for 3G high-speed packet data includes the specification of this new interface, including the protocol used for the transfer of user packet data and the signaling necessary to set up the R–P connection for one or more mobile sessions.

The PDSN is the gateway to the packet data network and terminates the link layer to the mobile data application. It serves as a router for the packet data between the mobile data application and the packet data network. One of the main features of this split in functionality between the PCF and PDSN is mobility management. During a handoff that involves a change in the radio resource and PCF, the anchoring PDSN continues to provide the undisturbed network layer to the remote data application.

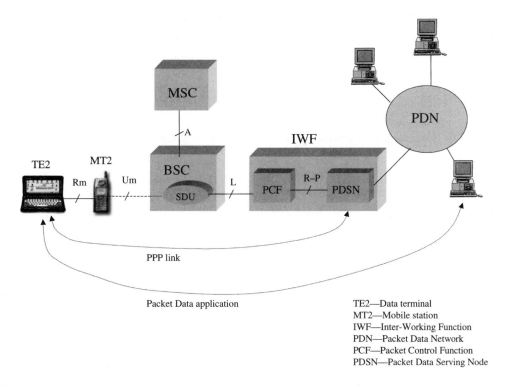

Figure 10-2 A-Interface network architecture with Packet Data support

At the packet data Application Layer, protocols such as TCP, UDP, Mobile IP, and higher layer protocols are exchanged between the mobile data terminal and the remote host over the packet data network. In 3G networks, work is ongoing to support IPv6, IP multicast and broadcast, optimal packet routing, and Mobile IP.

3G packet data services also provide extensive billing and accounting capabilities, whereby packet data users can be charged based on *Quality of Service* (QOS), location, air time, packets transferred, or bytes transferred. On the A-Interfaces, the billing, accounting, and QOS information needs to be supported and triggered.

10.2 3G Radio Support

As mentioned earlier, the main driver for 3G wireless network is the delivery high speed data services to and from a mobile user. Wideband CDMA has been chosen as the air interface to meet this requirement. Several standards bodies and technical groups have come together to define the new CDMA technology for wideband access and have developed the first phase of the standard known as *IS-2000*. The new CDMA technology comprises new logical/physical channel and frame structures, better power control schemes, and transmission techniques to enhance capacity and support high-speed access.

With regard to the access network, changes are required to support the new cdma2000 radio technology on the A1, A3, and A7 interfaces. These include new messaging and parameters to support:

- New cdma2000 radio channel structures
- New cdma2000 radio frame structures
- High-speed packet data burst transmission
- New cdma2000 service options and radio configurations
- Quality of Service indicators
- New cdma2000 link layer substates
- Enhanced power control schemes
- Soft handoff for high-speed data

The A3 and A7 interfaces are used during Inter-BSC Soft Handoff and, therefore, changes are needed to accommodate new CDMA radio interface technology.

The A1 interface needs to support the new service options and radio configurations associated with the new CDMA technology and must be able to distinguish them from the existing IS-95 CDMA technology.

10.3 Enhanced Services

In addition to high-speed packet data services and 3G radio access technology, enhanced subscriber services also contribute to the appeal of 3G wireless networks. This section discusses some of the enhanced services that may be provided in a 3G wireless network.

10.3.1 Tiered Services in User Zones

Tiered Services is a feature whereby individual subscribers or a group of user are provided customized services and special features within a User Zone. The definition of the User Zone may be geographical (e.g., a group of cells/sectors) or within a private network (e.g. a group of MSCs/BSCs/BTSs) (Figure 10-3). The customized services and features may include different billing tariffs, wireless PBX access, number hunting, and other private network services. Subscribers may be informed of the activation of tiered services through mobile terminal displays or audible alerts.

Regarding the A-Interface, the User Zone information must be included in A-Interface messaging to allow the network entity to trigger the tiered services when the mobile subscriber enters or leave a specific User Zone. The User Zone information may be sent from the BSC to the MSC when the mobile performs a registration (Location Updating Request) or when the mobile initiates a call setup (CM Service Request, Paging Response messages). Provisions to A-Interface messaging will be needed to support in-call User Zones changes when the mobile moves from one zone to another (Figure 10-3).

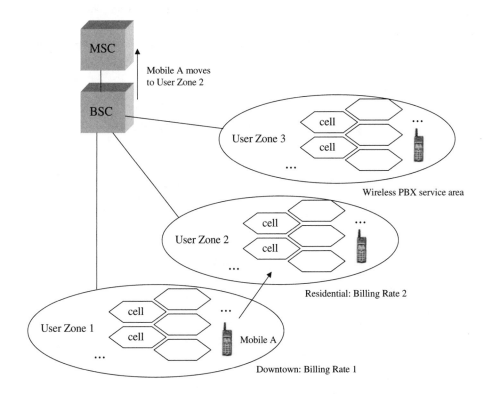

Figure 10-3 Tiered Services in User Zones

10.3.2 Priority Access Channel Assignment Service

Priority Access Channel Assignment (PACA) is a feature that provides a subscriber with priority access on call originations (Figure 10-4). The PACA service allows mobile originations to be queued when no traffic channel resources are immediately available within a cell coverage area. When radio resources do become available, the queued subscribers are served based on the first-come-first-served principle and according to priority assignments. Such a scenario can occur, for example, when an event with large crowds takes place and all available traffic channel elements are fully used, leading to originations being blocked. Depending on the priority of the mobile origination, its position in the queue may be higher or lower than other origination attempts. When radio resources become available, the call is set up automatically.

On the A-Interface, additional messaging may be required in the mobile origination call flow when the PACA service is triggered. If PACA is triggered, the MSC needs to inform the BSC of the subscriber's PACA service availability, including information such as the PACA priority and time stamp. The BSC then performs PACA queuing and resource allocation (Figure 10-4). The MSC updates the PACA queue information whenever the mobile places another PACA call or when the mobile cancels the PACA call.

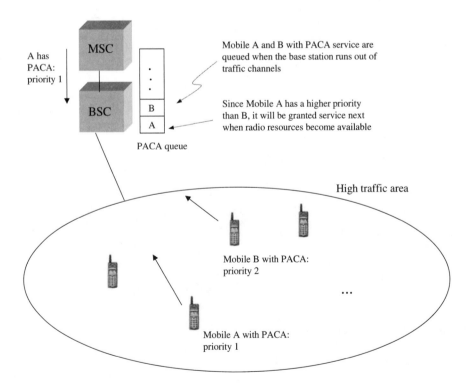

Figure 10-4 Priority Access services

10.3.3 Location Services

According to market analysts, revenue from location-based wireless services in the U.S. alone is projected to rise to $3.9 billion by the year 2004 [10]. If the location of a mobile station can be accurately determined, an assortment of location-based services can be offered by network service providers. By knowing the mobile's location, tailor-made information, such as directions to the nearest hotel or restaurant, can be delivered directly to the mobile. Enhanced 411 services, where an operator who knows exactly where the caller is can provide what is needed and enhanced roadside assistance, are two more promising examples of location-based services. In addition to market demands, the *Federal Communications Commission* (FCC) has mandated E911 compliance for U.S. wireless providers and much of the current location-based work centers on this near-term requirement (Figure 10-5).

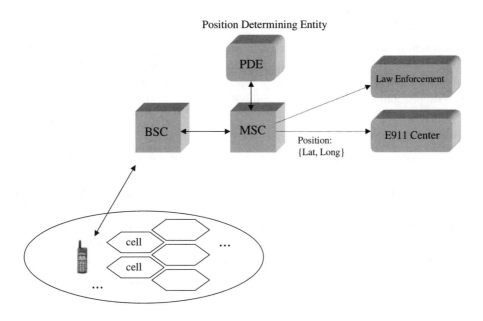

Figure 10-5 Location services

In 3G wireless systems, the BSC or network may implement position location functions in a *Position Determining Entity* (PDE), as shown in Figure 10-5. Several proposals have been made to implement the PDE in the MSC or BSC, and are all vendor-specific at this time. Support for advanced location services are also being specified for mobile units.

There is a number of different technology solutions for determining a mobile's location. Most of the solutions can be categorized as handset-based or network-based. The final solution will likely be a hybrid of these two approaches.

Handset-based location determination typically relies on the *Global Positioning System* (GPS) operated by the U.S. Department of Defense. GPS provides one of the most accurate methods of location determination, and many commercial applications already exist. The disadvantages of GPS are added mobile weight, battery drain, and the fact that its weak satellite signals cannot penetrate buildings.

Network-based location determination approaches have primarily focused on two tracking methods. The *Angle of Arrival* (AOA) method determines when a signal from a handset originates and its angle from several cell sites. The mobile's location is determined from the point of intersection of the projected lines. This technique requires a complex array of antennae and accuracy is reduced as the handset moves from the cell site. A second type of network-based location technology is the triangulation method, or *Time Difference of Arrival* (TDOA). Using this method, the location of a mobile station is determined by comparing the arrival times of the mobile station's signal at three different cell sites.

The current A-Interface support for location services is through the existing cell and sector information sent by the BSC when a mobile registers (Location Updating Request message) or performs a call setup (CM Service Request, Paging Response messages). For advanced position location applications, additional A-Interface messaging may be required to support the transfer of location application data between the mobile/BSC and the MSC/network.

10.3.4 Multimedia Support

Another interesting feature of proposed 3G networks is the support of simultaneous voice and data multimedia services. To support multimedia services, both the handset and network need to support multiple simultaneous calls from a single mobile station, including voice, circuit data, packet data, and video. As shown in Figure 10-6, these multiple sessions can be in the form of multiple circuit switched data calls or packet data call sessions. The independent and simultaneous control of the voice and packet data sessions includes the establishment and termination of each session/service independently, and mobility management during handovers.

On the A-Interface, there is a need to establish new call "instances" during the course of a call and to distinguish between the different services and sessions.

10.3.5 Quality of Service Support

A key element of multimedia and data services is the ability to support different *Quality of Services* (QOSs) for different individual mobile subscriber sessions. The QOS feature allows a mobile subscriber and the network to distinguish between different levels and qualities of network service classes in terms of the amount of bandwidth allocated, speed of access, throughput delay, billing tariffs, and frame error rates. QOS is most useful when it is being used for packet data and video services. QOS negotiation during a call setup or later while in a call allows the mobile station to establish a connection based on its capabilities, the radio resources available, and its desirable QOS and billing choices. For example, a subscriber may wish to access the network at a critical moment with high-quality data access, thus requesting high-QOS packet data services. The subscriber is then billed based on the high-QOS services received. The mobile station or network may negotiate the QOS at any time during the course of the call.

On the A-Interface, this QOS information is mainly supported via high-speed packet data interface messaging to the packet data network (Figure 10-6). Accounting, billing, and QOS information is sent when the QOS level is changed or negotiated.

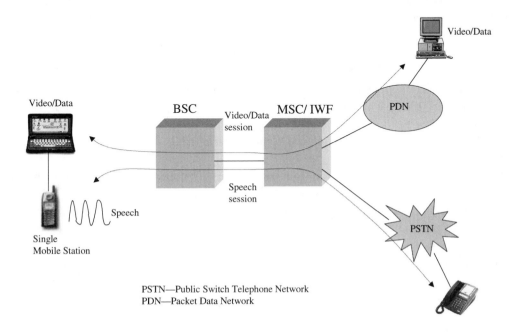

Figure 10-6   Multimedia services

10.3.6 Short Message Service Broadcast

In many mobile wireless applications, the network may find it useful to send broadcast messages to multiple mobile stations within a coverage area. Such applications include the sending of news subscriptions, stock quotes, greetings, or announcements from the network operator and application systems.

The support of such broadcast services can be provided through the *Short Message Service* (SMS) Broadcast Transport layer message type, which provides the necessary broadcast addressing. On the A-Interface, the SMS broadcast message can then be sent from the MSC to the BSC, using the *Application Data Delivery Service* (ADDS) messages and delivered to the mobiles over the air interface.

10.3.7 Multi-Language Support

In the modern wireless telecommunication world, the support for multiple languages is an added feature set that many international service providers' desire. This includes the display of multiple language characters in the calling party presentation, as well as in SMS messages.

On the A-Interface, messages that carries the calling party presentation need to support the corresponding language character sets. SMS messages that are sent in different languages are encoded within the SMS Teleservice and Transport Layer messages with a Preferred Language Indicator included.

10.3.8 User-Identification Module Support

The *User-Identification Module* (UIM) is an entity that contains information about a subscriber profile, such as mobile identity, preferred roaming list, and authentication keys. In CDMA networks, this UIM function has traditionally been integrated within the mobile station. In GSM networks, the UIM function resides in hardware that is removable from the subscriber station if required.

In 3G networks, the provisioning and administration of the subscriber profile in the UIM may be performed through *Over-the-Air Service Provisioning and Administration* (OTASPA). OTASPA allows the uploading and downloading of subscriber-specific parameters between the service provider and the mobile station, over the air interface. The present OTASP capability will be expanded to support mobile-initiated parameter update, such as the changing of preferred roaming list or network provider frequencies. Other useful capabilities include the uploading or downloading of subscriber-specific user data, such as SMS messages or stored phone book and address lists.

10.3.9 Vocoder Tandem-Free Operation

In current wireless networks, when a mobile-to-mobile call is connected, the speech path passes through two vocoders, once during the decoding of speech frames in the originating mobile direction and another time during the encoding of speech frames in the terminating mobile direction. This tandeming of vocoders in the speech path introduces unnecessary encoding/decoding actions because the same air interface technology is being used by both mobiles. The Vocoder Tandem-Free Operation is introduced to bypass this vocoder tandeming during a mobile-to-mobile call setup, with the goal of reducing throughput delay and improving voice quality.

To support Vocoder Tandem-Free Operation on the A-Interface, provisions have to be made to disable the encoding/decoding actions of speech frames at both vocoders during a mobile-to-mobile call.

10.4 Forward and Backward Compatibility

One of the most important issues for wireless network service providers regarding implementation of 3G wireless networks is backward compatibility with existing networks. A service provider that wants to add a new BSC to a live network will have to ensure that the new BSC can interoperate with the existing MSC, probably running a lower IOS revision level. Any new extensions to messages and parameters may have to be withheld from being sent to the remote end after being informed that the remote equipment is running a lower IOS standard version.

On the other hand, the existing infrastructure may also have to be forward compatible with a new IOS revision level, such that any new messaging or parameters can be accepted and ignored without causing any failures.

Another issue that arises for forward and backward compatibility is the support for intergeneration soft and hard handoffs in a network with mixed second generation and 3G systems. A handoff from an existing second generation cell to a 3G cell, and vice versa, should be supported by the both the BSCs and MSCs.

References

1. CDG-IOS version 3.1.1, *CDMA Development Group MSC to BS Interface Inter-Operability Specification*. June 1999.

2. CDG-IOS version 2.0, *CDMA Development Group MSC to BS Interface Inter-Operability Specification*. September 1998.

3. Telecommunications Industry Association, TIA/EIA/IS-634-A, *MSC–BS Interface (A-Interface) for Public 800 MHz*. July 1998.

4. Telecommunications Industry Association , TIA/EIA/TSB-80, *MSC–BS Interface (A-Interface) for Public 800 MHz*. October 1996.

5. Telecommunications Industry Association, TIA/EIA/IS-95-A, *Mobile Station–Base Station Compatibility Standard for Dual-Mode Wideband Spread Spectrum Cellular Systems*. May 1995.

6. American National Standards Institute, ANSI J-STD-008, *Personal Station–Base Station Compatibility Requirements for 1.8 to 2.0 GHz Code Devision Multiple Access (CDMA) Personal Communications Systems*. August 1995.

7. American National Standards Institute, ANSI TIA/EIA/IS-41-D, *Cellular Radio–Telecommunications Intersystem Operations*. December 1997.

8. Telecommunications Industry Association, TIA/EIA/IS-707A, *Data Service Options for Wideband Spread Spectrum Digital Cellular System*. March 1999.

9. James D. Solomon, *Mobile IP: The Internet Unplugged*, New York:Prentice Hall, 1998.

10. *CDMA World*, Dec 1999/ Jan 2000 Issue , Mobile Communications International.

A-Interface Messages

Table A-1   BSMAP Messages

Name	ID	Category	Direction	SCCP Type	IOS Ref
ADDS Page	65H	SS	BSC←MSC	UDT	6.1.7.1
ADDS Page Ack	66H	SS	BSC→MSC	UDT	6.1.7.4
ADDS Transfer	67H	SS	BSC→MSC	UDT	6.1.7.2
Assignment Complete	02H	CP	BSC→MSC	DT1	6.1.2.16
Assignment Failure	03H	CP	BSC→MSC	DT1	6.1.2.17
Assignment Request	01H	CP	BSC←MSC	DT1, CC	6.1.2.15
Authentication Request	45H	MM	BSC←MSC	UDT	6.1.4.1
Authentication Response	46H	MM	BSC→MSC	UDT	6.1.4.2
Base Station Challenge	48H	MM	BSC→MSC	DT1	6.1.4.5

Table A-1   BSMAP Messages (Continued)

Name	ID	Category	Direction	SCCP Type	IOS Ref
Base Station Challenge Response	49H	MM	BSC←MSC	DT1	6.1.4.6
Block	40H	FM	BSC→MSC	UDT	6.1.6.2
Block Acknowledge	41H	FM	BSC←MSC	UDT	6.1.6.3
Clear Command	20H	CP	BSC←MSC	DT1	6.1.2.21
Clear Complete	21H	CP	BSC→MSC	DT1	6.1.2.22
Clear Request	22H	CP	BSC→MSC	DT1	6.1.2.20
Complete Layer 3 Information	57H	CP	BSC→MSC	CR	6.1.2.1
Feature Notification	60H	SS	BSC←MSC	UDT	6.1.3.9
Feature Notification Ack	61H	SS	BSC→MSC	UDT	6.1.3.10
Handoff Command	13H	RR	BSC←MSC	DT1	6.1.5.8
Handoff Commenced	15H	RR	BSC→MSC	DT1	6.1.5.10
Handoff Complete	14H	RR	BSC→MSC	DT1	6.1.5.11
Handoff Failure	16H	RR	BSC→MSC	DT1,CREF	6.1.5.7
Handoff Performed	17H	RR	BSC→MSC	DT1	6.1.5.12
Handoff Request	10H	RR	BSC←MSC	CR	6.1.5.5
Handoff Request Acknowledge	12H	RR	BSC→MSC	CC, DT1	6.1.5.6
Handoff Required	11H	RR	BSC→MSC	DT1	6.1.5.4

Table A-1 BSMAP Messages (Continued)

Name	ID	Category	Direction	SCCP Type	IOS Ref
Handoff Required Reject	1AH	RR	BSC←MSC	DT1	6.1.5.9
Paging Request	52H	CP	BSC←MSC	UDT	6.1.2.3
Privacy Mode Command	53H	CP	BSC←MSC	DT1	6.1.4.18
Privacy Mode Complete	55H	CP	BSC→MSC	DT1	6.1.4.19
Rejection	56H	CP	BSC→MSC	UDT	6.1.8.1
Reset	30H	FM	BSC↔MSC	UDT	6.1.6.6
Reset Acknowledge	31H	FM	BSC↔MSC	UDT	6.1.6.7
Reset Circuit	34H	FM	BSC↔MSC	UDT	6.1.6.8
Reset Circuit Acknowledge	35H	FM	BSC↔MSC	UDT	6.1.6.9
Set Control Channel Parameters	62H	FM	BSC←MSC	UDT	6.1.6.12
Set Control Channel Parameters Acknowledge	63H	FM	BSC→MSC	UDT	6.1.6.13
SSD Update Request	47H	MM	BSC←MSC	DT1	6.1.4.4
SSD Update Response	4AH	MM	BSC→MSC	DT1	6.1.4.7
Unblock	42H	FM	BSC→MSC	UDT	6.1.6.4
Unblock Acknowledge	43H	FM	BSC←MSC	UDT	6.1.6.5

Table A-2   DTAP Messages

Name	Type	Category	Direction	SCCP Type	IOS Ref
ADDS Deliver	53H	SS	BSC↔MSC	DT1	6.1.7.3
ADDS Deliver Ack	54H	SS	BSC→MSC	DT1	6.1.7.5
Alert With Information	26H	CP	BSC←MSC	DT1	6.1.2.24
Authentication Request	45H	MM	BSC←MSC	DT1	6.1.4.1
Authentication Response	46H	MM	BSC→MSC	DT1	6.1.4.2
Base Station Challenge	48H	MM	BSC→MSC	DT1	6.1.4.5
Base Station Challenge Response	49H	MM	BSC←MSC	DT1	6.1.4.6
CM Service Request	24H	CP	BSC→MSC	CR	6.1.2.2
Connect	07H	CP	BSC→MSC	DT1	6.1.2.10
Flash With Information	10H	SS	BSC↔MSC	DT1	6.1.3.7
Flash With Information Ack	50H	SS	BSC→MSC	DT1	6.1.3.8
Location Updating Accept	02H	MM	BSC←MSC	CREF	6.1.4.9
Location Updating Reject	04H	MM	BSC←MSC	CREF	6.1.4.10
Location Updating Request	08H	MM	BSC→MSC	CR	6.1.4.8
Paging Response	27H	CP	BSC→MSC	CR	6.1.2.4
Progress	03H	CP	BSC←MSC	DT1	6.1.2.12

Table A-2 DTAP Messages (Continued)

Name	Type	Category	Direction	SCCP Type	IOS Ref
Rejection	56H	CP	BSC→MSC	DT1	6.1.8.1
SSD Update Request	47H	MM	BSC←MSC	DT1	6.1.4.4
SSD Update Response	4AH	MM	BSC→MSC	DT1	6.1.4.7

- CP—Call Processing
- MM—Mobility Management
- SS—Supplementary Services
- RR—Radio Resource Management
- FM—Terrestrial Facilities Management

A3/A7-Interface Messages

Table B-1   A3/A7-Interface Messages

Name	Msg Type II	Interface	Direction	IOS Ref
A3-Connect	01H	A3	Src SDU ←Tgt BTS	6.1.9.1
A3-Connect Ack	02H	A3	Src SDU →Tgt BTS	6.1.9.2
A3-Remove	03H	A3	Src SDU ←Tgt BTS	6.1.9.3
A3-Remove Ack	04H	A3	Src SDU →Tgt BTS	6.1.9.4
A3-Drop	05H	A3	Src SDU →Tgt BTS	6.1.9.5
A3-Propagation Delay Measurement Report	06H	A3	Src SDU ←Tgt BTS	6.1.9.6
A3-CEData Forward	07H	A3	Src SDU →Tgt BTS	6.1.9.7
A3-CEData Reverse	08H	A3	Src SDU ←Tgt BTS	6.1.9.8

Table B-1   A3/A7-Interface Messages (Continued)

Name	Msg Type II	Interface	Direction	IOS Ref
A3-CDMA Long Code Transition Directive	09H	A3	Src SDU →Tgt BTS	6.1.9.11
A3-CDMA Long Code Transition Directive Ack	0AH	A3	Src SDU ←Tgt BTS	6.1.9.12
A3-Traffic Channel Status	0DH	A3	Src SDU ←Tgt BTS	6.1.9.15
A7-Handoff Request	80H	A7	Src BS →Tgt BS	6.1.12.1
A7-Handoff Request Ack	81H	A7	Src BS ←Tgt BS	6.1.12.2
A7-Drop Target	82H	A7	Src BS →Tgt BS	6.1.12.3
A7-Drop Target Ack	83H	A7	Src BS ←Tgt BS	6.1.12.4
A7-Target Removal Request	84H	A7	Src BS ←Tgt BS	6.1.12.5
A7-Target Removal Response	85H	A7	Src BS →Tgt BS	6.1.12.6
A7-Source Transfer Performed	89H	A7	Src BS →Tgt BS	6.1.12.10
A7-Reset	8AH	A7	Src BS ↔ Tgt BS	6.1.12.11
A7-Reset Acknowledge	8BH	A7	Src BS ↔ Tgt BS	6.1.12.12
A7-Paging Channel Message Transfer	8CH	A7	Src BS →Tgt BS	6.1.12.13
A7-Paging Channel Message Transfer Ack	8DH	A7	Src BS ←Tgt BS	6.1.12.14

Table B-1 A3/A7-Interface Messages (Continued)

Name	Msg Type II	Interface	Direction	IOS Ref
A7-Access Channel Message Transfer	8EH	A7	Src BS ←Tgt BS	6.1.12.15
A7-Access Channel Message Transfer Ack	8FH	A7	Src BS →Tgt BS	6.1.12.16

A-Interface Parameters

Table C-1   A1-Interface Parameter Information Elements

Information Element Name	ID	IOS Ref
ADDS User Part	3DH	6.2.2.67
Authentication Challenge Parameter	41H	6.2.2.45
Authentication Confirmation Parameter - RANDC	28H	6.2.2.42
Authentication Data	59H	6.2.2.137
Authentication Event	4AH	6.2.2.114
Authentication Parameter COUNT	40H	6.2.2.47
Authentication Response Parameter	42H	6.2.2.46
Called Party ASCII Number	5BH	6.2.2.105
Called Party BCD Number	5EH	6.2.2.52

Table C-1   A1-Interface Parameter Information Elements (Continued)

Information Element Name	ID	IOS Ref
Calling Party ASCII Number	4BH	6.2.2.37
Cause	04H	6.2.2.19
Cause Layer 3	08H	6.2.2.55
CDMA Serving One Way Delay	0CH	6.2.2.79
Cell Identifier	05H	6.2.2.20
Cell Identifier List	1AH	6.2.2.21
Channel Number	23H	6.2.2.6
Channel Type	0BH	6.2.2.7
Circuit Group	19H	6.2.2.148
Circuit Identity Code	01H	6.2.2.22
Circuit Identity Code Extension	24H	6.2.2.23
Classmark Information Type 2	12H	6.2.2.15
CM Service Type	9xH[a]	6.2.2.51
Data Link Connection Identifier (DLCI)	none[c]	6.2.2.2
Downlink Radio Environment	29H	6.2.2.25
Encryption Information	0AH	6.2.2.12
Extended Handoff Direction Parameters	10H	6.2.2.73
Handoff Power Level	26H	6.2.2.31

Table C-1 A1-Interface Parameter Information Elements (Continued)

Information Element Name	ID	IOS Ref
Hard Handoff Parameters	16H	6.2.2.63
IS-95 Cause Value	62H	6.2.2.110
IS-95 Channel Identity	22H	6.2.2.10
IS-95 Information Records	15H	6.2.2.72
IS-95 MS Measured Channel Identity	64H	6.2.2.36
Layer 3 Information	17H	6.2.2.38
Location Area Identification	13H	6.2.2.43
Message Discrimination	none	6.2.2.1
Message Type	none	6.2.2.4
Message Waiting Indication	38H	6.2.2.48
Mobile Identity	0DH	6.2.2.16
Power Down Indicator	A2H	6.2.2.60
Protocol Discriminator	none[c]	6.2.2.39
Radio Environment and Resources	1DH	6.2.2.82
Registration Type	1FH	6.2.2.61
Reject Cause	44H	6.2.2.44
Reserved - Octet	none[c]	6.2.2.40
Response Request	1BH	6.2.2.35

Table C-1   A1-Interface Parameter Information Elements (Continued)

Information Element Name	ID	IOS Ref
RF Channel Identity	21H	6.2.2.8
Service Option	03H	6.2.2.66
SID	32H	6.2.2.9
Signal	34H	6.2.2.50
Slot Cycle Index	35H	6.2.2.17
Software Version	31H	6.2.2.65
Tag	33H	6.2.2.62
Voice Privacy Request	A1H[b]	6.2.2.13

a. This is a type 1 information element. The xxxx is 1/2 octet of data.

b. This is a type 2 information element, where there is 0 octet of data.

c. This is a type 3 information element that is contained as a mandatory element in a DTAP message.

A3/A7-Interface Parameters

Table D-1   A3/A7-Interface Parameter Information Elements

Name	ID	Interfaces	IOS Ref
A3 Connect Ack Information	1CH	A3	6.2.2.145
A3 Connect Information	1BH	A3	6.2.2.144
A3 Drop Information	1EH	A3	6.2.2.147
A3 Remove Information	20H	A3	6.2.2.146
A3 Signaling Address	49H	A7	6.2.2.90
A3 Traffic Circuit ID	03H	A3	6.2.2.96
A7 Control	1FH	A7	6.2.2.97
Air Interface Message	21H	A7	6.2.2.152
Band Class	5DH	A7	6.2.2.106

Table D-1   A3/A7-Interface Parameter Information Elements (Continued)

Name	ID	Interfaces	IOS Ref
BSC ID	04H	A7	6.2.2.125
Call Connection Reference	3FH	A3, A7	6.2.2.98
Cause List	19H	A3, A7	6.2.2.142
CDMA Long Code Transition Info	0EH	A3	6.2.2.128
CDMA Serving One Way Delay	0CH	A7	6.2.2.79
Cell Identifier List	1AH	A7	6.2.2.21
Cell Information Record	02H	A3	6.2.2.89
Channel Element ID	17H	A3	6.2.2.132
Channel Element Status	18H	A3	6.2.2.141
Correlation ID	13H	A3, A7	6.2.2.108
Downlink Radio Environment	29H	A7	6.2.2.25
IS-95 Channel Identity	22H	A7	6.2.2.10
Layer 2 Ack Request/Results	23H	A7	6.2.2.153
Mobile Identity	0DH	A7	6.2.2.16
Neighbor List	48H	A7	6.2.2.83
One Way Propagation Delay Record	09H	A3	6.2.2.119
PMC Cause	05H	A3	6.2.2.99
Privacy Info	1DH	A7	6.2.2.143

Table D-1   A3/A7-Interface Parameter Information Elements (Continued)

Name	ID	Interfaces	IOS Ref
SDU ID	4CH	A3, A7	6.2.2.91
Service Configuration Record	61H	A7	6.2.2.109

A-Interface Timers

Table E-1 A-Interface Timers

Timers	Recommend-ed Values	Range (sec)	Cate-gory	Trigger Entity	Description
T1	55 s	0–255	TFM	BSC	Block → BlockAck, UnBlock → UnBlockAck
T2	55 s	0–255	TFM	MSC	Delay in sending ResetAck after Reset is received
T4	60 s	0–255	TFM	BSC	Reset → ResetAck
T7	10 s	0–255	RR	Src BSC	Handoff Required → Handoff Cmd
T8	10 s	0–255	RR	Src BSC	IS95 Ext Handoff Dir → MSAck Order
T9	10 s	0–255	RR	Tgt BSC	Handoff Request Ack → Handoff Cmplt
T10	5 s	0–99	CP	MSC	AssignReq → AssignCmplt

Table E-1   A-Interface Timers (Continued)

Timers	Recommend-ed Values	Range (sec)	Cate-gory	Trigger Entity	Description
T12	60 s	0–255	TFM	both	Reset Circuit → Reset Circuit Ack
T13	55 s	0–255	TFM	BSC	Delay in sending ResetAck after Reset is received
T16	60 s	0–255	TFM	MSC	Reset → ResetAck
T20	5 s	0–99	CP	BSC	AssignFailure → ClrCmd AssignFailure → AssignReq (Retry)
T62	5 s	0–99	SS	MSC	Flash With Info → Flash With Info Ack
T63	(see description)	0–99	SS	MSC	FeatureNotification → FeatureNotification Ack. Recommended: $T63 = 4.72 + (1.28 \times 2^{\text{slot cycle index}})$
T101	10 s	0–99	RR	MSC	Set Ctrl Chan Param → Set Ctrl Chan Param Ack
T300	5 s	0–99	CP	BSC	ClrReq → ClrCmd
T301	30 s	0–99	CP	MSC	AssignCmplt → Connect
T303	12 s	0–99	CP	BSC	CMServReq/ PageRsp → AssignReq, or CMServReq/ PageRsp → ClrCmd CMServReq/ PageRsp → SCCP-RLSD CMServReq/ PageRsp → SCCP-Cref
T306	5 s	0–99	RR	BSC	Handoff Commenced → ClrCmd
T315	5 s	0–99	CP	MSC	ClrCmd → ClrCmplt

Table E-1   A-Interface Timers (Continued)

Timers	Recommended Values	Range (sec)	Category	Trigger Entity	Description
T3113	(see description)	0–99	CP	MSC	PageRequest → PageResponse ADDS Page → ADDS Page Ack Recommended: $T3113 = 4.72 + (1.28 \times 2^{\text{slot cycle index}})$
T3210	30 s	0–99	MM	BSC	LocUpdateReq → LocUpdate Accept LocUpdateReq → LocUpdate Reject
T3230	5 s	0–99	CP	BSC	CMServReq/PageRsp → SCCP-CC CMServReq/PageRsp → SCCP-CREF
T3260	30 s	0–99	MM	MSC	Auth Request → Auth Response
T3270	5 s	0–99	MM	MSC	SSD Update Req → BS Challenge
T3271	15 s	0–99	MM	MSC	BS Challenge Rsp → SSD Update Rsp
T3280	15 s	0–99	CP	MSC	Privacy Mode Cmd → Privacy Mode Cmplt
Twaitho	-	-	RR (IS95)	Tgt BSC	IS-95 Ext HO Direction Msg → IS-95 Candidate Freq Search Report Msg/ A1 Clear Command

- CP—Call Processing
- MM—Mobility Management
- SS—Supplementary Services
- RR—Radio Resource Management
- FM—Terrestrial Facilities Management

A3/A7 Timers

Table F-1   A3/A7-Interface Timers

Timers	Recommend-ed Values	Range (sec)	Cate-gory	Trigger Entity	Description
Tacm	0.5 s	0–1.0	A7	BSC	A7-Access Channel Msg Transfer → A7-Access Channel Msg Transfer Ack
Tdrptgt	5 s	1–10	A7	Src BSC	A7-Drop Target → A7-Drop Target Ack
Thoreq	1 s	0–5	A7	Src BSC	A7-HO Request → A7-HO Request Ack
Ttgtrmv	5 s	1–10	A7	Tgt BSC	A7-Tgt Removal → A7-Tgt Removal Response
Tchanstat	0.5 s	0–1.0	A3	Src BSC	A3-Connect Ack → A3-TCH Status
Tconn3	0.5 s	0–1.0	A3	Tgt BSC	A3-Connect → A3-Connect Ack

Table F-1   A3/A7-Interface Timers (Continued)

Timers	Recommend-ed Values	Range (sec)	Cate-gory	Trigger Entity	Description
Tdiscon3	0.5 s	0–1.0	A3	Tgt BSC	A3-Remove → A3-Remove Ack
Tlongcode	1 s	0–10	A3	Src BSC	A3-LongCode Transition Directive → A3-LongCode Transition Directive Ack
Tpcm	1 s	0–2.0	A7	BSC	A7-Paging Channel Msg Transfer → A7-Paging Channel Msg Transfer Ack

Glossary

3G   Third Generation. This is the general term used for third generation mobile networks deploying wideband CDMA radio technology and broadband switching networks.

3GPP2   Third Generation Partnership Project 2. An independent consortium of standard bodies that was formed to address the ANSI/TIA/EIA-41 network evolution to 3G technologies.

A-Interface   The interface between a Base Station Controller and a Mobile Switching Center. This comprises the A1, A2, and A5 interfaces. The descriptions of A-Interface messages throughout the book are referenced in the Index section.

Abis-Interface   The interface between a Base Station Controller and a Base Transceiver System.

Ai-Interface   MSC–PSTN Interface.

Ater-Interface   The interface between two Base Station Subsystems. This comprises the A3 and A7 interfaces. The descriptions of Ater-Interface messages throughout the book are referenced in the Index section.

A1-Interface   The interface between the MSC and BSC that carries signaling information.

A2-Interface   The interface between the MSC and BSC that carries user data traffic, typically in the form of 56 kbps or 64 kbps PCM timeslots.

A3-Interface   SThe interface between the SDU of a BSS and the channel element of another BSS. It is used for Inter-BSS Soft and Softer Handoffs. It comprises both signaling and user traffic channels.

A5-Interface   The interface between the SDU at a BSC and the IWF at the MSC that is used for carrying byte stream data in circuit mode data calls.

A7-Interface   The interface between two BSSs that carries signaling information during Inter-BSS Soft and Softer Handoffs.

A-Key   A unique secret 64-bit key used in Authentication procedures.

AAL   ATM Adaptation Layer. The ATM Adaptation Layer is used for converting higher-layer user data into the ATM layer.

AAL2   ATM Adaptation Layer 2. This AAL is used for connection-oriented, variable-bit-rate traffic that has precise timing requirements, such as voice and video.

AAL5   ATM Adaptation Layer 5. This AAL is used for delay-tolerant, variable bit rate traffic requiring minimal sequencing or error detection support, such as signaling and control data.

AC   Authentication Center. A network entity responsible for authentication procedures to validate mobile user network access.

ADDS   Application Data Delivery Service. A data delivery service between a network entity and a mobile station. Examples include SMS and OTASP.

ADT   Authentication Directive Timer. This IS-41 timer is triggered when the IS41_AUTHDIR message is sent and is stopped when the IS-41_authdir is received. Default = 6 seconds.

AERM   Alignment Error Rate Monitor. The SS7 MTP2 signal unit error monitor used during alignment procedures.

ANSI   American National Standards Institute. The official U.S. standards-setting body that includes members from industry, government, and professional institutions.

ART   Authentication Request Timer. This IS-41 timer is triggered when the IS41_AUTHREQ message is sent and is stopped when the IS-41_authreq is received. Default = 6 seconds.

ASRRT   Authentication Status Report Response Timer. The IS-41 timer ASRRT is started whenever an authentication operation that requires an authentication status report is initiated. Default = 6 seconds.

ASRT   Authentication Status Report Timer. This IS-41 timer is triggered when the IS41_ASREPORT message is sent and is stopped when the IS-41_asreport return result is received. Default = 6 seconds.

ATM   Asynchronous Transfer Mode. A high bandwidth transmission technology using connection-oriented, packet-like switching and multiplexing techniques.

AUTHBS   The authentication result computed during a Base Station Challenge.

AUTHR   The authentication result computed during the Global Challenge process.

AUTHU   The authentication result computed during a Unique Challenge.

ARFCN   Actual Radio Frequency Channel Number. This refers to CDMA channel frequency.

B8ZS   Binary 8 Zero Substitution. A coding technique to introduce ones density requirements for digital transmission links in North America.

B-Interface   The MSC–VLR Interface in an IS-41 network.

BCD   Binary Coded Decimal. A method of representing decimal numbers using 4 binary bits.

BIB   Backward Indicator Bit. The status bit in an SS7 signal unit used by MTP 2 for both positive and negative message acknowledgment.

BSAP   Base Station Application Part. The application layer protocol for the A-Interface.

BSC   Base Station Controller. A network entity responsible for the interface between radio base stations and the MSC, which provides call control, radio resource, and mobility functions.

BSCT   Base Station Challenge Timer. This IS-41 timer is triggered when the IS41_BSCHALL message is sent and stopped when the IS-41_bschall is received. Default = 3 seconds.

BSMAP   Base Station Management Application Part. The application layer at both the BSC and MSC that is responsible for direct BSC-to-MSC functions. BSMAP information is not passed to the mobile station.

BSN   Backward Sequence Number. The sequence number of the SS7 signal unit that is to be acknowledged.

BSS   Base Station Subsystem. The network entity that interfaces the mobile station and the switching network, typically comprising the BSC and BTSs.

BTS   Base Transceiver System. The radio equipment that is responsible for communicating with the mobile station and interfacing with the BSC.

C-Interface   The MSC-HLR Interface in an IS-41 network.

CAS   Channel Associated Signaling. A method of signaling whereby call control information is transferred over the same circuits used for voice or data using in-band signaling techniques.

CAVE   Cellular Authentication and Voice Encryption. The authentication algorithm used in CDMA networks by both the Authentication Center and the mobile station.

CBA   Changeback Acknowledgment. The acknowledgment to a Changeback Declaration.

CBD   Changeback Declaration. The SS7 network management message used for indicating that traffic is to be diverted back to a signaling link that was previously unavailable.

CCS   Common Channel Signaling. A method of signaling whereby the call control information for a group of circuits is transferred over one or more channels separate from the traffic-carrying circuits.

CDG   CDMA Development Group. An worldwide industry consortium of network operators, equipment manufacturers, and industry partners that focuses on CDMA development and deployment.

CDGIOS   CDG Inter-Operability Specification. The open interface standard specification for interoperability between a BSC and MSC in a CDMA network.

CDMA   Code Division Multiple Access. A multiple access technology that utilizes spread spectrum techniques to accommodate multiple users sharing the same spectrum, each user is identified by a unique spreading code.

cdma2000 A term for the third generation wideband CDMA technology. IS-2000 is the first such standard describing this broadband air interface technology.

CFU Call Forwarding Unconditional. A Call Forwarding service whereby all calls are forwarded unconditionally to a specified number.

CFB Call Forwarding Busy. A Call Forwarding service whereby calls to a mobile that is busy are forwarded to a specified number.

CFNA Call Forwarding No Answer. A Call Forwarding service whereby calls to a mobile that does not answer are forwarded to a specified number.

CIC Circuit Identity Code. In the A-Interface context, this is a 2-octet number that uniquely identifies a specific circuit in the connection between the BSC and the MSC.

CMEA Cellular Message Encryption Algorithm. The encryption algorithm used in CDMA system that is described in "Common Cryptographic Algorithms," governed under the *US International Traffic and Arms Regulations* (ITAR) and the Export Administration Regulations.

CMT Cellular Messaging Teleservice. An SMS teleservice type for CDMA networks, comprising short message transfer to a mobile station.

CNIP Calling Number ID Presentation. A subscriber feature whereby the Calling Party Number can be displayed for an incoming call.

CNIR Calling Number ID Restriction. A subscriber feature whereby the subscriber's number can be restricted from being display at the called party's terminal/mobile station.

COA Changeover Acknowledgment. The acknowledgment to a Changeover Order.

COO Changeover Order. The SS7 network management message used for indicating that traffic is to be diverted to another redundant signaling link within the same linkset when that signaling link becomes unavailable.

COUNT An authentication parameter that keeps track of the number of calls made by a mobile station. It provides an added level of security to help identify clone mobile stations.

CPT Cellular Paging Teleservice. An SMS teleservice type for CDMA networks comprising paging-like data transfer to a mobile station.

D-Interface The HLR–VLR Interface in an IS-41 network.

D_1-Interface The VLR–OTAF Interface in an IS-41 network.

DCE Data Circuit-Terminating Equipment. A device that communicates with a DTE to establish a connection. In the A-Interface circuit data context, it comprises an MT2 and the modem at the IWF, and is responsible for the digital-to-analog modem interface to the PSTN.

DLCI Data Link Connection Identifier. In the A-Interface context, this DTAP parameter can be used to indicate different *Signaling Access Point Identifiers* (SAPI) on the radio interface.

DLR Destination Local Reference. A unique number generated by a remote signaling node and is used by the local signaling node in referencing an SCCP connection.

DN Directory Number. A number that can be dialed from the PSTN network to the mobile subscriber or a telecommunication terminal.

DPC Destination Point Code. An SS7 network address used for identifying the destination address of an SS7 network entity.

DS0 Digital Signal Level 0. A single 64 kbps PCM channel. A T1 or E1 digital carrier is made up of DS0s.

DTAP Direct Transfer Application Part. The application layer at the BSC, MSC, and mobile station that is responsible for call control and mobility management. DTAP information is exchanged between the MSC and mobile. The BSC mainly acts as a pipe for data transfer.

DTE Data Terminal Equipment. A terminal that interfaces to a DCE to transfer data. In the case of wireless data, this is normally a laptop or PC that is connected via RS-232 to a modem (DCE).

DTMF Dual Tone Multi-Frequncy. A signaling technique for representing digits on a push button pad by the combination of two in-band tones.

E1 The digital transmission standard by ITU-T, comprising 32 64-kbps PCM channels that provides a data rate of 2.048 Mbps.

E-Interface The MSC–MSC Interface in an IS-41 network.

Ec/Io The ratio of received pilot energy per chip to the total received spectral density, including noise and signals.

EIA Electronics Industry Alliance. An industry standards body concerned with the development of industry standards in electronics, electronic information, and telecommunications.

ESF Extended Superframe Format. A framing format for T1 carriers that provides frame synchronization and error detection.

ESN Electronic Serial Number. A unique 32-bit serial number for each mobile phone.

EVRC Enhanced Variable Rate Codec. An enhanced vocoding technique to increase radio link capacity by maintaining a low data rate with improved voice quality.

FIB Forward Indicator Bit. The status bit used for indicating acknowledgment in an SS7 signal unit.

FOA First Office Application. A term frequently used for referring to the first official customer field deployment of infrastructure equipment.

FISU Fill-In Signal Unit. An SS7 signal unit that does not contain any user data, used for keeping alive an SS7 link when no other signal units are being transmitted.

FSN Forward Sequence Number. The sequence number of a transmitted SS7 signal unit, used for acknowledgment purposes by the received node.

GPS Global Positioning System. A satellite-based positioning system.

GSM Global Systems for Mobile. A mobile communications technology standard that originated in Europe and includes specifications for a TDMA-based air interface, an A-Interface, and GSM MAP interfaces between networks.

GT   Global Title. An SS7 SCCP layer addressing scheme whereby a string of digits is used instead of the point code.

GTT   Global Title Translation. A form of SS7 SCCP layer routing scheme by translating a global title address into a destination point code and subsystem number.

H-Interface   The HLR–AC Interface in an IS-41 network.

HLR   Home Location Register. A centralized database of a mobile network operator that is used to store subscriber profiles.

HOT   Handoff Order Timer. This IS-41 timer is triggered when the IS41_FACDIR2 message is sent and is stopped when the IS-41_facdir2 is received. Default = 12 seconds.

IE   Information Element. In the A-Interface and Ater-Interface context, this refers to the parameters within the A-Interface and Ater-Interface messages.

IETF   Internet Engineering Task Force. A technical working group that develops Internet standards.

IMSI   International Mobile Subscriber Identifier. A number used for identifying a mobile subscriber station. The IMSI and ESN uniquely identify a mobile station.

IMSI_11_12   The 11th and 12th digits of an IMSI, usually set to the *Mobile Network Code* (MNC), which identifies the service provider's region.

IMSI_S   The 10 least significant digits of the mobile station's IMSI.

IMSI_S1   The least significant 7 bits of IMSI_S

IMSI_S2   The 3 most significant bits of IMSI_S.

IN   Intelligent Network. A network utilizing separate nodes to provide advanced call capabilities and enhanced subscriber services.

IP   Internet Protocol. A connectionless network layer protocol that became a commonly used standard for the Internet and other networks.

IPCP   The PPP Internet Protocol Control Protocol. The PPP link protocol that is used for setting up IP services, such as temporary IP addresses and TCP/IP header compression.

IPv4   Internet Protocol Version 4. The current version of IP protocol that forms the basis of the Internet. The address field is limited to 32 bits.

IPv6   Internet Protocol Version 6. The new enhanced IP protocol to IPv4. The address field is expanded to 128 bits.

IS   Interim Standard. A standard that has been approved by TIA but not yet approved by ANSI as an official national standard.

IS41_AUTHDIR   Authentication Directive. This IS-41 message is used when the AC or HLR invokes an authentication directive such as an SSD Update or Unique Challenge.

IS41_authdir   Authentication Directive return result or error.

IS41_AUTHREQ   Authentication Request. This IS-41 message is used for requesting an authentication procedure to be performed at the Authentication Center, such as during a Global Challenge.

IS41_authreq   Authentication Request return result or error.

IS41_ASREPORT   Authentication Status Report. This IS-41 message is to report to the AC the result of an authentication comparison or an SSD Update.

IS41_asreport   Authentication Status Report return result or error.

IS41_BSCHALL   Base Station Challenge. This IS-41 message is used for requesting a Base Station Challenge at the AC, used during an SSD Update procedure.

IS41_bschall   Base Station Challenge return result or error.

IS41_FACDIR2   Facility Directive 2. This IS-41 message is for requesting a terrestrial circuit to be allocated between two CDMA network nodes.

IS41_facdir2   Facility Directive 2 return result or error.

IS41_MSONCH   Mobile on Channel. This IS-41 message is used during an Inter-MSC Hard Handoff to indicate to the source MSC that the mobile has been acquired at the target MSC.

IS41_msonch   Mobile on Channel return result or error.

IS41_REGNOT   Registration Notification. This IS-41 message is sent when a mobile registers in a network to allow the network to register mobility and subscriber information.

IS41_regnot   Registration Notification return result or error.

IS41_SMDPP   SMS Delivery Point-to-Point. This IS-41 message is used by the SMSC or other network entities for delivering SMS or other application data messages to the network.

IS41_smdpp   SMS Delivery Point-to-Point return result or error.

IS41_SMSREQ   SMS Request. This IS-41 message is used for requesting an address to deliver the SMS to a mobile station.

IS41_smsreq   SMS Request return result or error.

ISLP   Intersystem Link Protocol. The adaptation layer protocol used for the A5-Interface to adapt data rates between the RLP frames and terrestrial circuit frames for circuit data services.

ISO   International Organization for Standardization. A voluntary, nongovernment United Nations organization whose role is to define international standards in all fields.

ISUP   ISDN User Part. A commonly used SS7 user part for call control.

ITU   International Telecommunications Union. A treaty organization of the United Nations that is responsible for recommending telecommunication standards for equipment and network operation internationally and provides spectrum frequency regulations.

IWF   Inter-Working Function. In the A-Interface context, this is the network entity that interfaces and converts between CDMA digital user data and fixed network modulated data.

L-Interface   The IWF–Serving MSC/BSC Interface in an IS-41 network.

LAC   Location Area Code. A logical grouping of cells in a cellular network.

LCP   The PPP Link Control Protocol. The protocol used for setting up and configuring a PPP link, such as maximum unit size, link quality, and compression.

LFU   Link Force Uninhibit. An SS7 SNM message used for forcing an uninhibition of a link at the remote node.

LIA   Link Inhibit Acknowledge message. The acknowledgment to a Link Inhibit message.

LID   Link Inhibit Denied. This SS7 SNM message is sent to indicate a denial to a link inhibit request.

LIN   Link Inhibit message. An SS7 SNM message used for indicating a link inhibition.

LLI   Link Local Inhibit test message. An SS7 SNM link maintenance message sent periodically by a node that locally inhibited a link.

LRI   Link Remote Inhibit test message. An SS7 SNM link maintenance message sent periodically by a node that has a link that is remotely inhibited.

LSSU   Link Status Signal Unit. An SS7 signal unit type used for indicating the status of an SS7 link.

LUA   Link Uninhibit Acknowledge message. The acknowledgment to a Link Uninhibit message.

LUN   Link Uninhibit message. An SS7 SNM message used for indicating a link uninhibition.

MAP   Mobile Application Part. A term used for referring to the application layer in a mobile network.

MCC   Mobile Country Code. A code that specifies a county or region of mobile operation.

MFR1   Multi-Frequency R1 Signaling. A North American digital signaling protocol that uses in-band signaling tones for call control.

MFR2   Multi-Frequency R2 Signaling. A European interexchange signaling protocol that uses compelled in-band signaling for call control.

MHOT   Mobile Handoff Order Timer. This IS-41 timer is started during an Inter-MSC Hard Handoff when the source MSC sends a Handoff Command message to the source BSC. This timer is stopped when an IS41_MSONCH message is received from the target MSC, indicating the mobile arrival on the target radio channel. Default = 7 seconds.

MIN   Mobile Identification Number. A 10-digit number that identifies the mobile, such as a directory number.

MIP   Mobile Internet Protocol. An IP protocol that allows mobile Internet Protocol users to roam to a different network seamlessly.

MNC   Mobile Network Code. Identifies a mobile service provider's region.

MSC   Mobile Switching Center. A switching center with mobility functions, capable of interfacing a mobile radio network with the wireline network.

MSU   Message Signal Unit. An SS7 data-carrying signal unit that is neither an FISU or LISU.

MT2   Mobile Termination 2. An MT2 has a non-ISDN Rm interface, such as RS-232, that can be linked to a TE2.

MTP   Message Transfer Part. The SS7 layers that are responsible for the transfer of application messages at the user part.

MTP1   Message Transfer Part 1. The SS7 physical layer.

MTP2   Message Transfer Part 2. The SS7 datalink layer responsible for synchronization, error detection, and correction.

MTP3   Message Transfer Part 3. The SS7 network layer at level 3 whose role is link, route, and traffic management.

MWI   Message Waiting Indication. A supplementary service that notifies users of pending messages at a network application entity such as a voice mail center.

N-Interface   The HLR–SMSC Interface in an IS-41 network.

N_1-Interface   The HLR–OTAF Interface in an IS-41 network.

NAM   Number Assignment Module. The memory module whereby a mobile subscriber's specific parameters are located, such as mobile identity and frequency list.

NID   Network Identity. The number given to identify different sub-networks within a network provider's system.

OC-3   Optical Carrier level 3. A SONET optical signal that supports data rates of up to 155.52 Mbps.

OPC   Origination Point Code. An SS7 network address used for identifying the message-originating address of an SS7 network entity.

ORDQ   Rejection Order Qualification Code. This field in the IS-95 Reject Order message is used to indicate the reason that the mobile rejected a forward link message.

OTAF   Over-the-Air Function. A network entity that provides OTASP functions.

OTASP   Over-the-Air Service Provisioning. A features that allows mobile subscriber to subscribe to a network service provider through information exchange and parameter downloads over the air-interface, without interfacing with a third party vendor.

OTASPA   Over-the-Air Service Provisioning and Administration. An entity that allows the over-the-air uploading and downloading of subscriber-specific parameters between the service provider and the mobile station.

PACA   Priority Access Channel Assignment. A feature that provides a subscriber with priority access on call originations.

PCF   Packet Control Function. A network entity that is responsible for ensuring that packet data services are delivered properly on the radio network by interfacing with a PDSN.

PCM   Pulse Code Modulation. A commonly used sampling technique for converting an analog voice signal to a digital representation.

PDE   Position Determining Entity. A network entity with position location functionalities.

PDN   Packet Data Network. A network implementing packet data protocols, such as IP.

PDSN   Packet Data Serving Node. A gateway router for the packet data between the mobile data application and the packet data network.

PPP   Point-to-Point Protocol. A connection-oriented datalink protocol for communication between two terminals. Network layer protocols such as IP can encapsulate packets into PPP frames on an established link.

PSMM   IS-95 Pilot Strength Measurement Message. This message is sent by the mobile to report pilot measurement strengths when triggered.

PSTN   Public Switched Telephone Network. A common term for public voice telephone networks.

PVC   Permanent Virtual Circuit. A virtual circuit between two nodes in a packet network that provides a circuit-like connection requiring no setup and teardown of connections for data transfers.

Q-Interface   The MSC–SMSC Interface in an IS-41 network.

QOS   Quality of Service. A measure of the quality of subscriber network services in terms of error rates, delay, bandwidth and other metrics.

R–P Interface   The PCF (Radio)-to-PDSN (Packet data) Interface in a 3G access network architecture.

RAND   A 32-bit random number that is broadcast over the paging channel in the IS-95 Access Parameters message and is used as a CAVE algorithm input during Global Challenges.

RANDBS   A 32-bit random number generated by the mobile station that is used as an input to the CAVE algorithm during a Base Station Challenge.

RANDC   Authentication Confirmation Parameter. This is the 8 most significant bits of the broadcast RAND value.

RANDSSD   A 56-bit random number generated by the Authentication Center used during the SSD Update procedure.

RANDU   A 24-bit random number that is generated by either the Authentication Center or MSC used during Unique Challenges.

RLP   Radio Link Protocol. The protocol layer above IS-95 traffic frames that provides the required increased radio transmission reliability necessary for data transmissions, primarily through retransmission schemes.

Rm-Interface   The interface between an TE2 and MT2.

RNT   Registration Notification Timer. This IS-41 timer is triggered when the IS41_REGNOT message is sent and is stopped when the IS-41_regnot is received. Default = 12 seconds.

RS-232   A commonly used standard that specifies the synchronous and asynchronous data transmission characteristics between two data communication devices.

SADT Short Message Air Delivery Timer. This IS-41 timer is triggered by the MSC when an ADDS Deliver/Page message is sent and is stopped when an ADDS transport layer acknowledgment is received. Default = 18 seconds.

SAPI Signaling Access Point Identifier. In the A-Interface context, the SAPI identifies a logical service connection between the mobile and the network entity, provided by the lower datalink layer.

SCCP Signaling Connection Control Part. The SS7 network layer above MTP3 that provides connectionless and connection-oriented functions, and advanced routing schemes.

SCCP-CR Connection Request. An SS7 SCCP message used for setting up a connection-oriented session.

SCCP-CC Connection Confirm. An SS7 SCCP message used for confirming the establishment of an SCCP connection.

SCCP-CREF Connection Refused. An SS7 SCCP message used for refusing the request of an SCCP connection setup.

SCCP-DT1 Data Form 1. An SS7 SCCP message used for data transfer after an SCCP connection has been established.

SCCP-IT Inactivity Test. An SS7 SCCP message used for keeping alive an SCCP connection.

SCCP-RLC Release Complete. An SS7 SCCP message used for indicating the completion of an SCCP connnection release.

SCCP-RLSD Released. An SS7 SCCP message used for releasing an SCCP connection.

SCCP-UDT Unit Data. An SS7 SCCP message used for connectionless data transfer.

SCM Station Classmark. An IS-95 parameter that specifies the capabilities of a mobile station to the network during network registration and access.

SCMG SCCP Management. The SCCP entity that is responsible for the management and maintenenance of SCCP functions, such as subsystem states.

SCP Service Control Point. An SS7 centralized database that contains information pertaining to an SSP.

SDH Synchronous Digital Hierarchy. An ITU standard for optical transmission.

SDL Signaling Data Link. A term for the SS7 datalink.

SDU Selection/ Distribution Unit. An entity within the BSC that is responsible for CDMA digital frame conversion and adaptation from PCM frames, delivering signaling and traffic frames to the mobile, and performing power control.

SIB Busy. An LSSU that is sent to indicate the congested status of a signaling node.

SID System Identity. The number given to identify a network provider's system.

SIE Emergency Alignment. An LSSU that is sent to indicate the emergency alignment status of a link.

SIN Normal Alignment. An LSSU that is sent to indicate the normal alignment status of a link.

SIO Out-of-Alignment. An LSSU that is sent to indicate the out-of-alignment status of a link.

SIOS Out-of-Service. An LSSU that is sent to indicate the out-of-service status of a link.

SIPO Processor Outage. An LSSU that is sent to indicate that a node is experiencing processor outage.

SLC Signaling Link Code. The 4-bit number that is used to identify uniquely a signaling link within a link set.

SLR Source Local Reference. A unique number generated by a local node that is used by the remote node for referencing an SCCP connection.

SLS Signaling Link Selection. A 5- or 8-bit number used for the selection of an outgoing signaling link to a destination point code, used for load-sharing purposes.

SLTA Signaling Link Test Acknowledge. The acknowledgment to a Signaling Link Test Mesage.

SLTM Signaling Link Test Message. An SS7 link maintenance test message that is sent to ensure the integrity of the signaling link under test.

SME Signaling Message Encryption. An encryption technique used in CDMA networks to increase the security of signaling frames exchanged between the BSC and mobile stations.

SMS Short Message Service. A supplementary network service that allows short messages to be sent to and from a mobile station.

SMSC Short Message Service Center. A network entity that is capable of SMS functions.

SMT Short Message Delivery Timer. This IS-41 timer is triggered when the IS41_SMDPP message is sent and is stopped when the IS-41_smdpp is received. Default = 45 seconds.

SNM Signaling Network Management. The SS7 function that is responsible for SS7 link, route, and traffic management.

SONET Synchronous Optical Network. An optical fiber transmission standard that provides optical carrier signals in multiples of 51.84 Mbps, known as *Optical Carrier level-1* (OC-1).

SPC Service Programming Code. A secret code assigned to a mobile station that is used by the Service Programming Lock feature.

SPL Service Programming Lock. A feature used during OTASP sessions to prevent fraudulent access of OTASP parameters.

SS7 Signaling System 7. A commonly used Common Channel Signaling standard for Internetwork operations.

SSA Subsystem Allowed. An SCCP management message sent to indicate that a local subsystem number is allowed to be communicated to.

SSD Shared Secret Data. A 128-bit second-level security key derived from the A-Key.

SSD_A The 64 most significant bits of the SSD parameter used as an input to the CAVE Algorithm.

SSD_B The 64 least significant bits of the SSD parameter used for Voice Privacy (VP) and Signal Message Encryption (SME).

SSN Subsystem Number. A unique number at an SS7 node to identify a logical entity associated with a specific function or software. For example, an A-Interface entity has an SSN of 252 and an IS-41 MSC entity has a recommended SSN of 8.

SSP Service Switching Point. An SS7 signaling end point that originates and terminates SS7 messages.

SSP Subsystem Prohibited. An SCCP management message sent to indicate that a local subsystem number is prohibited and should not to be communicated to.

SSPR System Selection for Preferred Roaming. A feature that allows a mobile to access a list of preferred service providers' networks.

SST Subsystem Status Test. An SCCP management message sent to solicit the subsystem status of a remote signaling point.

STP Signaling Transfer Point. A signaling node that relays or routes SS7 messages to another signaling node.

SUERM Signal Unit Error Rate Monitor. The SS7 MTP2 signal unit error monitor.

T1 A digital transmission link comprising 24 64 kbps PCM channels that provides a data rate of 1.544 Mbps. A commonly used digital transmission standard in North America.

Tadd Soft Handoff Add Threshold. The IS-95 Ec/Io threshold for adding pilots to an active soft handoff list.

TCAP Transaction Capabilities Application Part. An application layer above the SCCP layer that allows the higher MAP applications to have transaction capabilities.

Tcomp Soft Handoff Comprison Threshold. The IS-95 Ec/Io threshold for sending PSMM when the Candidate Set pilot exceeds the Active Set pilot by this amount (x0.5db).

TCP Transmission Control Protocol. A connection-oriented, end-to-end transport layer protocol that provides sequenced and reliable delivery between network nodes.

Tdrop Soft Handoff Drop Threshold. The IS-95 Ec/Io threshold for dropping pilots from an active soft handoff list.

TE2 Terminal Equipment 2. A data terminal device with a non-ISDN Rm interface, usually physically connected to an MT2.

TCM Terrestrial Circuit Management. The management function in the MSC and BSC that manages the terrestrial circuits between the two entities.

TFM Terrestrial Facility Management. The management function in the MSC and BSC that manages the connections between the two entities, including the signaling links and terrestrial circuits of the spans.

TIA Telecommunications Industry Association. A standards group made up of individuals from telecommunication manufacturers, service providers and the government, which develops and publishes ANSI accredited standards.

Tias   Send Inactivity Timer. An SCCP timer, which when expires, triggers the local node to send an Inactivity Test message to the remote end to keep an SCCP connection alive.

Tiar   Receive Inactivity Timer. An SCCP timer, which when expires, triggers the local node to release an SCCP connection due to inactive traffic.

TRA   Traffic Restart Allowed. An SS7 SNM message that is sent to indicate that MTP3 traffic is allowed to be exchanged.

TRW   Traffic Restart Waiting. An SS7 SNM message that is sent to indicate that a local node is waiting for MTP3 traffic to be allowed.

TSB   Telecommunications Systems Bulletin. These bulletins are not formal standards, but instead contain technical information deemed valuable and timely to the industry.

TSG   Technical Specification Group. The technical working groups within 3GPP2.

TSG-A   TSG task group for the A-Interface, responsible for developing the 3G A-Interface standard between the radio access network (BSC) and the core network (MSC).

TTdrop   Soft Handoff Drop Timer. The IS-95 timer threshold for dropping pilots from an active soft handoff list.

UDP   User Datagram Protocol. A connectionless transport layer protocol that provides unreliable delivery between network nodes.

UIM   User-Identification Module. An entity that contains information about a subscriber profile such as mobile identity, preferred roaming list, and authentication keys.

Um-Interface   The interface between the mobile station and the BSS. In the CDMA A-Interface context, this is the CDMA air interface.

VLR   Visitor Location Register. A centralized database of a mobile network operator that is used to store subscriber profiles for quick and easy reference. A mobile's profile is added to the VLR upon registration or during an origination attempt.

VMN   Voice Mail Notification. An SMS teleservice type for CDMA networks, comprising voice mail notification data transfer to a mobile station.

VMS   Voice Mail Service. A supplementary service that stores and delivers voice mail messages to mobile subscribers.

VP   Voice Privacy. An encryption technique using a CDMA Private Long Code mask for spreading in the reverse traffic channel and for data scrambling in the forward traffic channel.

WIN   Wireless Intelligent Network. The Intelligent Network services for mobile networks.

WLL   Wireless Local Loop. A technology for wireless access at the local loop.

X.25   A packet switching protocol standard.

Index

X

Z